FROM BEHAVIOR THEORY
TO BEHAVIOR THERAPY

Edited by

Joseph J. Plaud
Judge Rotenberg Educational Center
Canton, Massachusetts

Georg H. Eifert
West Virginia University

Foreword by Cyril Franks

Allyn and Bacon
Boston • London • Toronto • Sydney • Tokyo • Singapore

To Brianna, my source of strength
J.J.P.
To Daniel
G.H.E.

Senior Editor: Carla F. Daves
Series Editorial Assistant: Susan Hutchinson
Manufacturing Buyer: Suzanne Lareau

Copyright © 1998 by Allyn & Bacon
A Viacom Company
Needham Heights, MA 02194

Internet: www.abacon.com
America Online: keyword: College Online

Library of Congress Cataloging-in-Publication Data

From behavior theory to behavior therapy / edited by Joseph J. Plaud
   and Georg H. Eifert.
       p.   cm.
    Includes bibliographical references and index.
    ISBN 0-205-17477-9
    1. Behavior therapy.   I. Plaud, Joseph J. (date)   II. Eifert, Georg H. (date)
RC489.B4F76   1998
616.89' 142—dc21   97-23806
                                                         CIP

Printed in the United States of America
10 9 8 7 6 5 4 3 2 1   02 01 00 99 98

CONTENTS

PART III: *Perspectives on the Relation between Behavior Theory and Behavior Therapy*

FOREWORD: THE IMPORTANCE OF BEING THEORETICAL

No wind makes for him that hath no intended port to sail into.
Essays, Michael Eyquem de Montaigne (1533–1592)

Exactly one hundred years ago, *The Importance of Being Earnest* opened in London to much acclaim. It has remained a yardstick for aspiring playwrights to this day. But while exquisitely aware of the need to be earnest, being theoretical was of understandably little concern. While appropriately aware of the importance of being earnest, the author, Oscar Wilde, had little concern with theoretical issues. Regrettably, many contemporary behavior therapists express similar sentiments. Even seasoned practitioners seem to disregard the fact that a theoretical framework, which is what behavior therapy is all about, could make them more effective behavioral clinicians. Technique-oriented manuals are plentiful and much in demand while, at least as far as most clinicians are concerned, the relatively few texts that deal predominantly with theory are rarely consulted. Conceptual innovations that translate into clinical procedures are few and far between, and even those of recent promise, such as Shapiro's (1989, 1995) work on eye movement desensitization and reprocessing, await solid verification. Ironically, one of the few nonedited books, possibly the only one to deal substantively with theoretical and conceptual issues in behavior therapy across the board rather than with one model, was written by a philosopher rather than a psychiatrist or psychologist (Erwin, 1978).

The Association for Advancement of Behavior Therapy (AABT) began in 1966 as an informed interest group for those who believed that theory and practice were intertwined and of equal importance. Unfortunately, over the years theory and practice grew apart and it is now clinical techniques, professional concerns, and private practice that receive the most attention. This is not what the founders of the AABT had in mind. Recent years have seen some sporadic attempts to counteract this theoretical trend. For example, the theme for the 1994 AABT convention was "Bridging the Gap from Science to Clinical Practice" and, a few years earlier, an AABT Special Interest Group was developed with the explicit purpose of encouraging and supporting clinically relevant theoretical and philosophic interests (Franks, 1987). Sadly but predictably, response from the membership at large was less than enthusiastic. Lip service was paid to the notion that behavior therapy is a conceptual approach rather than a collection of techniques per se, but this is about as far as it went.

All contributors to the present volume share a common respect for theory and data and the invitation to write this Foreword gives me the opportunity to elaborate on those matters and place the short but dynamic history of behavior therapy in context. In this respect, the scholarly and thorough nature of the chapters that follow facilitates this process, leaving me free to paint a broad canvas rather than fill in the details.

The name *behavior therapy* was introduced independently in three continents: in the U.S.A., Lindsley, Skinner, and Solomon (1953) were the first to use this term in print to refer to their therapeutic use of an operant conditioning model with hospitalized psychotic patients. In the U.K., Eysenck (1959) used it to refer to his largely Pavlovian-based application of "modern learning theory" to therapy. In South Africa, Lazarus (1958) applied the term to the addition to objective laboratory procedures to traditional psychotherapy. Which of these three developments took precedence and how independent they were of each other is of little relevance. Many similar labels abound, usually with somewhat different origins and connotations: "behavior modification," "behavioral analysis," "conditioning therapy," and "multimodal therapy," to name but a few. All share a similar methodology and, with the possible exception of certain interpretations of applied behavioral analysis, all share a common allegiance to theory.

Most forms of psychotherapy, and medicine itself for that matter, operate at one or more of three conceptual levels: the rational, the empirical, and the notional. The rational, the ideal to which we all strived when the AABT began, is theory-driven: a carefully selected theory is used to generate and test laboratory-derived predictions geared toward eventual clinical intervention. Culled mainly from the Maudsley tradition that led in part to the formation of the AABT, Eysenck (1960, 1964) assembled two noteworthy collections of studies that exemplify this approach. Franks's (1964) edited text and the journal *Behaviour Research and Therapy*, launched in 1963, served similar purposes.

The development of systemic desensitization by Wolpe (1958), the first verbal alternative to psychodynamically based procedures for coping with neurotic problems, is an outstanding illustration of the rational approach. Prior to 1958, conditioning was largely a procedure for modifying simple behaviors of animals or severely retarded human beings. Based on the relevant literature, in particular Hull and Pavlov, Wolpe induced neurotic states in cats by the administration of punishing but nondamaging shocks. These untoward reactions were subsequently removed by getting the animals to eat in the presence of small, and in later sessions progressively larger, anxiety-evoking stimuli. From these beginnings, Wolpe was led to believe that human neurotic anxieties might be alleviated in a similar fashion. Subsequent controlled studies provided empirical confirmation. It was no longer necessary to think in terms of effective verbal therapy as something confined to the psychoanalytic couch.

The fact that alternative theoretical explanations for Wolpe's findings have been proposed, some tenable and others less so, does not detract from the importance of his accomplishment. A good theory is no more than the best available approximation until a better one comes along. Most theories are tactical oversimplifications. If any theory were as complex as the actual facts, it could probably not be effectively studied in terms of the methodology of the time.

Theory-based clinical procedures are hard to come by and empiricism, more cost-effective and more easily achieved, is more often than not the investigative strategy of choice. Medical practice rests increasingly upon validated clinical procedure rather than tested theory. Empirical validation comes first and then, if at all, attention is given to theory. The use of electroshock therapy for the treatment of depression and CO_2 to alleviate anxiety are cases in point. Although well-controlled evaluations continue to demonstrate the efficacy of these procedures in specific situations, neither has any generally accepted theoretical rational.

It is essential to rely upon empirical evaluation rather than clinical impression alone. Facile appeal to the idea of empiricism without substantiation can sometimes lead to questionable clinical procedures. For example, technical eclecticism, a term coined by Lazarus in 1967, refers to the use of "whatever seems to work" in the clinical situation regardless of theoretical origin. To be fair, Lazarus has thought through his position in a commendably rigorous fashion and insists that it is desirable, if not invariably essential, for all procedures subsumed under the rubric of technical eclecticism to rest upon systematic validation. But this caveat notwithstanding, a small number of his followers use clinical procedures that have little or no empirical basis. Wittingly or otherwise, like many other mental health practices, the clinically seductive notion of technical eclecticism can lead to opportunism if not rigorously monitored.

At least to my way of thinking, Ellis's rational-therapy is another example of conceptual misuse. Rational-emotive therapy began life in 1955 as Rational Therapy. It was then changed by Ellis to Rational-Emotive Therapy (RET)—the name by which it is generally known—to broaden the concept; and in 1993 Ellis changed the name yet again, to Rational-Emotive Behavior Therapy (REBT), on the grounds that it "omits the highly behavioral aspect that rational-emotive therapy has favored right from the start." But regardless of its name, RET disregards both the empirical foundations of behavior therapy and the desirable cornerstone of the rational. This becomes even more crucial when the name is changed to Rational-Emotive *Behavior* Therapy. Much of RET, and now REBT, is predicated upon neither adequate empirical validation nor theory and, to this day, research remains mostly in the realm of recommendations for future priorities. RET arose and still arises largely out of intuition, clinical impression, and the gifted mind of Ellis, with a nod to the philosophers Epictetus and Marcus Aurelius (Franks, 1995).

The notional is another matter, for the most part an appeal to whim and fancy bereft of evidence—a perverse way of thinking endorsed by many anti-intellectual clinicians. Saying so makes it so, and most of the fleeting fad therapies of the day operate at this level. This, of course, is not to advocate total rejection of the notional. The hunch or gut feeling as a starting point for investigation at either the empirical or rational level can be strategically advantageous. People are more than machines, no matter how exquisite, and behavior therapy can gracefully accommodate a dash of art in addition to its main ingredients. Without serendipity and the notional, many advances in the natural sciences might have been delayed. For example, it is said, perhaps apocryphally, that the elusive structure of the benzene molecule was literally dreamed up when the chemist concerned fell asleep on a London bus. An intuitive element, sometimes unrecognized, may be present in many otherwise rational strategies. From this perspective, the informed practice of behavior therapy becomes a dynamic blend of the rational, the empirical, and the notional, an interacting mosaic of intuition, clinical observation, empiricism, and, possibly above all, theory and rationality.

According to Krasner (1971), in the 1950s and 1960s fifteen streams within psychology coalesced into the belief that the data of behavioral science could be usefully extrapolated to the field of clinical psychology. These include the impact of behaviorism as a concept in experimental psychology, instrumental conditioning research, systemic desensitization, Dollard and Miller's (1950) pioneering interpretation of psychoanalysis in terms of learning theory (while tacitly assuming that a psychodynamic model is fundamental and their bridging mechanism little more than a translation of truth as they saw it into a form more palatable to learning theorists), Pavlovian conditioning and its offshoots, and more. High on Krasner's list was the experimental and clinical program of Eysenck and his group at the Maudsley Hospital. I was a member of this team and, for me, this is where behavior therapy began.

Although the war had been over for six years, Britain was still struggling to recoup from a devastating assault: nerves were frayed, food rationing was in effect, everyday necessities such as fuel for heating were often unavailable, and, due to intensive bombing, housing remained in short supply. The need for mental health services was great and resources were limited. Only psychodynamic therapy by a trained physician was sanctioned and psychologists were permitted to treat patients only under the direct supervision of a physician, if at all. Psychopharmacology had relatively little to offer, and social workers served mainly as community assistants to members of the medical profession.

Psychologists seemed to have little to contribute in an era in which the disease model of mental illness prevailed. Understandably, newly graduated psychologists began to question the utility of spending undergraduate years studying behavioral science only to find that the practice of clinical psychology had little to do with this aspect of their training. Despite strong resistance from the psychiatric community, this led to the search for a meaningful alternative that would be acceptable to behavioral scientists. From the start, open-minded inquiry took precedence over ideology. Many learning theory models were considered, found wanting for one reason or another, and discarded. Hull's vision of a quantitative, data-based psychology influenced us strongly at first but it soon became apparent that his formulae were rarely capable of predicting what a laboratory animal might do, let along a human being. It seemed at that time that the work of Pavlov offered the most promise. Yet while Pavlov made precise quantitative measurements, his predictions were primarily qualitative and this was an unfortunate limitation. Nevertheless, it was our hope that by leaning heavily on learning theory and empirical validation a testable model would lead eventually to effective clinical intervention.

In 1957, I emigrated to the United States with the firm intention of staying for five years at the most. It was my naive belief that what the Maudsley group had to offer would be more acceptable in the New World. Disillusionment soon set in and it became painfully clear that, if anything meaningful were to be accomplished, behavioral clinicians—the few that could be assembled—would have to take matters into their own hands. In the United Kingdom I had been closely involved with the British Association for Advancement of Science and their public-spirited dedication to the advancement of knowledge rather than personal or professional aggrandizement. It was with such factors in mind that the AABT was named and formed. The initial membership, a mix of psychologists and psychiatrists, was less than two score. Today, there are almost five thousand members, but numbers alone do not guarantee a return to our theory-based foundations. The charter name of the organization was the Association for Advancement of Behavior Therapies. Then it was pointed out that, regardless of specific variations, most behavior therapists shared similar learning-theory orientations and methodologies—a paradigmatic shift in clinical psychology, it could be argued by some, even if most nonbehavioral clinicians resisted recognition of this change at the time. It became increasingly clear, and this is no semantic quibble, that the use of the plural "therapies" was inconsistent with this perspective, and the name was changed to what it is today. As an aside, it is disquieting to note that a recent motion to change the name of the AABT to include "cognitive therapies" in its masthead was only very narrowly defeated.

The flexibility of behavior therapy and the de-emphasis of dogma are mixed blessings, presenting hazards as well as advantages. Unresolved issues are numerous, procedures and models are diverse, and different opinions vie for recognition. Things are not as cut and dried as we had believed in the formative years.

At risk of oversimplification, psychology in the late twentieth century has been characterized by Craighead, Craighead, Kazdin, and Mahoney (1994) as a multifaceted, dynamic tension between three power forces: thinking, feeling, and doing. Cognition, affect, and behavior compete with each other for theoretical primacy. A similar three-way contrast of emphasis characterizes the evolution of behavior therapy. The 1960s was the era of ideology and polemics, an era in which insecure and unaccepted behavior therapists strove to present a united front against the common psychodynamic "foe." This was the decade of oversimplification, grandiose claims, and intolerance. In the 1970s, as behavior therapists became more secure and more accepted, missionary zeal was abandoned in favor of a search for new frontiers—it was the era of biofeedback, behavioral psychopharmacology, behavioral medicine, and much more. Sophisticated methods of treatment, improved methodology, and better outcome procedures were developed. Behavior therapy, in the words of London (1984), "grew a belly" and behavior therapists began to take a critical yet constructive look at themselves rather than the perceived failings of other schools of therapy. In 1983, a significant event occurred with the publication of an edited text dealing exclusively with *failures* in behavior therapy (Foa & Emmelkamp, 1983).

Early behavior therapists were forced to rely upon simplistic, direct S-R conditioning techniques on two accounts: first, the belief that only behavior mattered and that this was all that was necessary to bring about behavior change, and second, the inescapable fact that such techniques were all that were available to behavior therapists at that time. As cognition and affect came increasingly into the picture, more sophisticated assessment and intervention procedures were developed and more appropriate models constructed. In the 1980s, new ways of looking at data and new ways of obtaining data, borrowed from experimental and social psychology and from nonpsychological disciplines, were incorporated into this expanding framework. Nonlinear cause-and-effect approaches that took into account a broad array of historic, socioeconomic, and biological events were considered. Integrative models requiring alternative ways of thinking and new ways of providing clinical services, such as the overlooked and still neglected interbehaviorism of Kantor, were explored (see Delprato, 1995, for an update on Kantor's interbehaviorism). Unfortunately, then as now, such considerations remained the concern of the few. For the majority of behavior therapists, increasingly involved with clinical practice and professional issues, theory assumed a lesser role.

At the present time, the mid-1990s, Krasner's fifteen streams seem to have coalesced into some half a dozen distinct, sometimes overlapping, domains: radical behaviorism and applied behavioral analysis; methodological behaviorism; neobehavioral (S-R) theory; cognitive behavior therapy; social learning theory; and paradigmatic behaviorism. The major assumption of applied behavioral analysts and most radical behaviorists is that behavior is exclusively a function of its consequences. The methodology of choice is the experimental analysis of behavior and the manipulation of environmental variables through the direct application of laboratory-based conditioning principles. There are no intervening variables and mentalistic inferences, if acknowledged at all, are not taken into consideration. While not unequivocally rejected (Kitchener, in press), theory is regarded by most Skinnerians as less important than data. Since behavior is idiopathic, the emphasis is on single-subject methodology (see Kohlenberg & Tsai, 1991, for an articulate presentation of a currently relevant radical behaviorist psychotherapy).

Methodological behaviorism is more behavioral than behavioristic: it adopts the methodology of behavioral science but not the total rejection of intervening variables. Private events exist but can be studied only indirectly through the observation of behavior. Group designs and statistical inference are favored. There is significant overlap between methodological behavioral and neobehavioral (S-R) theory. The neobehavioral model is mediational and relies primarily on the principles of classical conditioning and the work of Pavlov, Hull, Tolman, Guthrie, Spence, Mowrer, Wolpe, and others. Watson features in both radical behaviorism and neobehavioral (S-R) theory.

Cognitive behavior therapy, to be discussed in greater detail shortly, is increasingly equated with behavior therapy by contemporary practitioners. Cognitive behavior therapists emphasize cognitive processes, and thoughts become the primary mediators of behavior change. Based on limited theory and sparse data, some cognitive behavior therapists describe this approach as a new paradigm within behavior therapy. Emotion and affect, it is asserted, cannot be subsumed under the traditional laws that govern behavior. Unfortunately, with the notable exception of Bandura's (1977, 1986) social learning theory, neither the new laws and their theoretical substrate nor a rigorous methodology for their investigation have as yet been delineated.

Finally, there is Staats's paradigmatic behaviorism, originally called social behaviorism, an ambitious and thoughtful attempt to establish a unifying philosophy of science and theory that emphasizes the integration of conditioning with more traditional concepts in personality, clinical, and social psychology (Staats, 1990). Psychology at large, argues Staats, is disunified and lacks a consistent approach. By contrast, multilevel and hierarchical paradigmatic behaviorism attempts to bridge such diverse fields as biological mechanisms, learning theory, child development, personality, social and clinical psychology, and more. Given limited recognition for many years, paradigmatic behaviorism is gaining increasing acceptance in behavior therapy and beyond (Eifert & Evans, 1990).

Contemporary behavior therapy tends to emphasize overt change, behavioral specificity, and current rather than historical determinants. Diverse disciplines and methodologies are incorporated into an overarching model that takes into account behavioral, cognitive, and affective parameters. When behavior therapy was unencumbered by such refinements, it was relatively easy for Eysenck (1959) to define behavior therapy in terms of something vaguely called "modern learning theory" and leave it at that. Since that time, definitions of behavior therapy have evolved and proliferated. In their attempt to avoid the reification of behavior therapy, O'Donohue and Krasner (1995) speciously avoid the issue altogether, resting content to define behavior therapy as "the behavior of behavior therapists and their clients." Be this as it may, most definitions fall into one of two classes: doctrinal or epistemological. Doctrinal definitions attempt to link behavior therapy to specific theories or principles of learning, whereas epistemological definitions are more inclined to characterize behavior therapy in terms of what behavior therapists actually do (Erwin, 1978). Doctrinal definitions tend to be exclusive and narrow, whereas the more comprehensive epistemological definitions tend to be so accommodating that virtually any measurable procedure can be classified as behavior therapy. By excluding little, such definitions lose discriminatory sensitivity.

Behavior therapists still cannot agree about either the nature or the role of conditioning. Some behavior therapists, fortunately few, strive to integrate behavior therapy and psychodynamic therapies, a position that I find totally unacceptable for reasons detailed elsewhere (Franks, 1984). Another theoretical parting of the ways pertains to the relative roles of heredity and environment. Sometimes the debate extends beyond the realm of the scientific, where it clearly belongs, into the arena of socioeconomic and political thought. For example, Wilson's (1975) sociobiology implies that the trends across cultures, if such trends exist, toward tribal aggression, territoriality, and some specific division of labor between the sexes are largely genetic or evolutionary rather than learned. Critics sometimes object not so much on evidential grounds as from the belief that acceptance of this idea would somehow challenge free will and the prospects for social progress.

Other behavior therapists accept trait theories unconditionally, and then there are those who take a diametrically opposite point of view, stressing behavioral specificity. Yet others believe that self-control cannot possibly exist since there is no such thing as the "self." Ultimately, the notion of the "self" and the closely related matters of free will and determinism are probably personal issues that are unlikely to be resolved by evidence. Empiricists and philosophers move along parallel as well as independent tracks and there is no single, agreed way to negate or conceptualize the notion of self-control (Karoly, 1995). There have been a number of attempts to develop a behavioral theory of the self, none very successful to date. Perhaps the most pressing issue confronting behavior therapists at this time, however, is the phenomenal rise of cognitive behavior therapy.

Many behavior therapists now identify themselves as cognitive behavior therapists and claim that they practice both behavior therapy *and* cognitive therapy. The implicit and sometimes explicit assumption is that these are two different realms, rather than points of emphasis on a single spectrum. The perceived explanatory and clinical limitations of conditioning and modeling led many cognitive behavior therapists to postulate a paradigm shift within behavior therapy that mirrored the changes that were taking place in mainstream psychology.

When Kuhn (1970) launched his somewhat vague and inconsistently formulated ideas about paradigms, he probably had little awareness of the way in which this concept would be misused. Kuhn meant it to apply to the natural sciences, but psychologists later extended this concept, equally uncritically, to a different arena. If early behavior therapists overreacted to the "stigma" of mentalism, cognitive behavior therapists are now overreacting in the opposite direction. Depending on the meaning attached to the word "paradigm," it can be argued that, in any field, paradigms are rare and paradigm shifts even rarer. On this basis, the presence and impact of paradigms in behavior therapy, clinical psychology, and even psychology at large become matters of definition and debate. Disregarding this caveat, many cognitive behavior therapists insist that a paradigm shift within behavior therapy has occurred. The lack of consensus about the nature of a paradigm and a lack of meaningful data seem to present little impediment to this contention. For most cognitive behavior therapists, cognitive behavior therapy is, without question, a revolutionary new way of thinking. The fact that all behavior therapy utilizes cognition to a greater or lesser extent is overlooked, as is the more tempered argument that both mainstream behavior therapy techniques and more directly cognitive procedures operate through similar CNS mechanisms but probably involve different access routes. Despite different points of emphasis, the two represent different facets of a common behavioral entity (Zinbarg, 1993). From this perspective, cognitive behavior therapists might do better to concentrate on the development of a testable theory and the use of a more rigorous methodology rather than the making of grandiose claims. For the present, the Scottish legal verdict "not proven" is probably the best that can be said about this putative new paradigm.

When all is said, if not always done, behavior therapists can justifiably feel pleased with their professional accomplishments, but this does not necessarily mean that they are, as yet, living in the best of all possible worlds. Behavioral clinicians do not always practice what they preach, and the gap between research and clinical practice remains great. The rise of a guild mentality, the de-emphasis of theory, and the numerous unresolved or unresolvable issues outlined above present escalating problems. On the positive side, a small but growing number of potentially influential behavior therapists are beginning to think in terms of multidisciplinary, nonlinear interactions rather than one-to-one stimulus–response models and in terms of the need for a return to theory and concept.

The flexibility of behavior therapy—some would call it a lack of unity and cohesiveness—is both an advantage and a disadvantage. As I wrote a decade and a half ago, "In the year 2081 will there be behaviour therapy at all, either as we know it today or in some highly evolved form? Will it have fragmented into a dozen or more disparate fields or will some common underlying behavioural theme be found to encompass them all? And if so, will this umbrella term be so inclusive and indiscriminate that it excludes nothing?" (Franks, 1981).

This observation is as relevant now as it was when first written. The move toward unification is as tenuous in behavior therapy as it is in psychology at large. We are still struggling with specifics and mini-theories rather than generality. While unquestionably to be studied, thought about, and worked toward, unification may lie in the distant future or perhaps in the never-never land of unrealized dreams. As the twentieth century draws to a close, psychologists remain in a position to make few valid predictions about behavior. At best, it is only possible to make a limited number of predictions about certain circumscribed behavioral interactions with any expectations of accuracy. In this respect, psychology resembles medicine and physics in the sixteenth and seventeenth centuries, when not even the circulation of the blood was known and when it was as much as physicists could do to unravel the simple relationship between pressure and volume in gasses. Even Newton achieved only moderate generality and it was left to Einstein, several hundred years later, to produce a more universal but still incomplete theory of gravitation. At that time, many physicists, including Einstein, had a gut belief in the rhetoric of the grand unified theory (GUT). Maxwell's electrodynamics had begun to unify electricity and light, phenomena previously treated separately, and Eddington believed that his theory of electrons and quantum mechanics meant that a GUT was just around the corner. In the 1980s, string theory emerged—a mathematically powerful but experimentally untestable attempt at unification in the natural sciences. But with all of this, unification in physics remains elusive to this day (Feynman, cited by Gleick, 1992, pp. 430 ff.). And so it is with behavior therapy, Staats's (1995) persuasive argument to the contrary notwithstanding.

Whether behavior therapy achieves some form of unification or whether it fragments into disparate fields is a matter that only the future can decide. Whatever the outcome, there is no doubt that theory is of importance. The few who are concerned about these matters must do everything they can to stem the neglect of theory by the behavior therapy majority. As yet there is a spectrum of theories within behavior therapy and unification seems more a hope for the distant future than a foreseeable accomplishment. Borrowing Wittgenstein's (1958, p. 32) felicitous phrase, O'Donohue and Krasner (1995) see the major theories within contemporary behavior therapy as little more than a "complicated network of similarities overlapping and crisscrossing: sometimes overall similarities, sometimes similarities of detail." Once again, I concur.

Finally, it needs to be noted that should the term *behavior therapy* vanish from the face of the earth, which I think unlikely in the foreseeable future, this need not necessarily be a disaster if the goals and aspirations toward which we strive, theorists and clinicians alike, are achieved. As theorists, our primary concern is with the advancement of knowledge. As mental health professionals, our primary concern is with the alleviation of human suffering—including our own as we struggle painfully to achieve our goals. It is as important to travel hopefully and bravely as to arrive and, if we cannot make all clinicians behavior therapists, as we travel this road the least that we can do is to encourage and facilitate an awareness of theory and a sense of scholarly integrity.

Cyril M. Franks
Distinguished Professor Emeritus
Graduate School of Applied and Professional Psychology
Rutgers University
Princeton, New Jersey

References

Bandura, A. (1977). Self-efficacy: Towards a unifying theory of behavioral change. *Psychological Review, 84*, 199–215.

Bandura, A. (1986). *Social foundations of thought and action: A social cognitive theory.* Englewood Cliffs, NJ: Prentice-Hall.

Craighead, L. W., Craighead, W. E., Kazdin, A. E., & Mahoney, M. J. (Eds.). (1994). *Cognitive and behavioral interventions: An empirical approach to mental health problems.* Boston: Allyn & Bacon.

Delprato, D. J. (1995). Interbehavioral psychology: Critical, systematic, and integrative approach to clinical services. In W. O'Donohue & L. Krasner (Eds.), *Theories of behavior therapy: Exploring change* (pp. 609–636). Washington, DC: American Psychological Association.

Dollard, J., & Miller, N. E. (1950). *Personality and psychotherapy.* New York: McGraw-Hill.

Eifert, G. H., & Evans, I. M. (Eds.). (1990). *Unifying behavior therapy: Contributions of paradigmatic behaviorism.* New York: Springer.

Ellis, A. (1993). Changing Rational-Emotive Therapy (RET) to Rational Emotive Behavior Therapy. *The Behavior Therapist, 16*, 257–258.

Erwin, E. (1978). *Behavior therapy: Scientific, philosophical and moral foundations.* New York: Cambridge University Press.

Eysenck, H. J. (1959). Learning theory and behaviour therapy. *Journal of Mental Science, 195,* 61–75.

Eysenck, H. J. (Ed.). (1960). *Behaviour therapy and the neuroses.* London: Pergamon.

Eysenck, H. J. (Ed.). (1964). *Experiments in behaviour therapy.* London: Pergamon.

Foa, E. G., & Emmelkamp, P. M. G. (Eds.). (1983). *Failures in behaviour therapy.* New York: Wiley.

Franks, C. M. (Ed.). (1964). *Conditioning techniques in clinical practice and research.* New York: Springer.

Franks, C. M. (1981). 2081: Will we be many or one—or none? *Behavioural Psychotherapy, 9,* 287–290.

Franks, C. M. (1984). On conceptual and technical integrity in psychoanalysis and behavior therapy: Two fundamentally incompatible systems. In H. Arkowitz & S. B. Messer (Eds.), *Psychoanalytic and behavior therapy* (pp. 223–247). New York: Plenum.

Franks, C. M. (1987). Behavior therapy and the AABT: Personal recollections, conceptions, and misconceptions. *The Behavior Therapist, 10,* 171–174.

Franks, C. M. (1995). RET, REBT and Albert Ellis. *Journal of Rational-Emotive and Cognitive-Behavior Therapy, 13,* 91–97.

Gleick, J. (1992). *Genius: The life and science of Richard Feynman.* New York: Pantheon.

Karoly, P. (1995). Self-control theory. In W. O'Donohue & L. Krasner (Eds.), *Theories of behavior therapy: Exploring behavior change* (pp. 259–285). Washington, DC: American Psychological Association.

Kohlenberg, R. J., & Tsai, M. (1991). *Functional analytic psychotherapy.* New York: Plenum.

Kitchener, R. (In press). Skinner's theories of theories. In W. O'Donohue & S. R. Kitchener (Eds.), *Psychology and philosophy: Interdisciplinary problems responses.* Boston: Allyn & Bacon.

Krasner, L. (1971). Behavior therapy. In P. H. Mussen (Ed.), *Annual Review of Psychology (Vol. 22).* Palo Alto, CA: Annual Reviews.

Kuhn, T. S. (1970). *The structure of scientific revolutions* (2nd ed). Chicago: University of Chicago Press.

Lazarus, A. A. (1958). New methods in psychotherapy: A case study. *South African Medical Journal, 33,* 660–664.

Lazarus, A. A. (1967). In support of technical eclecticism. *Psychological Reports, 21,* 415–416.

Lindsley, O. R., Skinner, B. F., & Solomon, H. C. (1953). *Studies in behavior therapy (Status Report 1).* Waltham, MA: Metropolitan State Hospital.

London, P. (1984). Review of G. T. Wilson & C. M. Franks, *Contemporary Behavior Therapy: Conceptual and Empirical Foundations. Contemporary Psychology, 29,* 376–378.

O'Donohue, W., & Krasner, L. (1995). Introduction. In W. O'Donohue & L. Krasner (Eds.), *Theories of behavior therapy: Exploring behavior change* (pp. xi–xix), Washington, DC: American Psychological Association.

Shapiro, F. (1989). Eye movement desensitization: A new treatment for post-traumatic stress disorder. *Journal of Behavior Therapy and Experimental Psychiatry, 20,* 211–217.

Shapiro, F. (1995). *Eye movement desensitization and reprocessing: Basic principles, protocols, and procedures.* New York: Guilford.

Staats, A. W. (1990). Paradigmatic behavior therapy: A unified framework for theory, research, and practice. In G. H. Eifert & I. M. Evans (Eds.), *Unifying behavior therapy: Contributions of paradigmatic behaviorism* (pp. 14–54). New York: Springer.

Staats, A. W. (1995). Paradigmatic behaviorism and paradigmatic behavior therapy. In W. O'Donohue & L. Krasner (Eds.), *Theories of behavior therapy: Exploring behavior change* (pp. 659–693). Washington, DC: American Psychological Association.

Wilson, E. O. (1975). *Sociobiology: The new synthesis.* Cambridge, MA: Harvard University Press.

Wittgenstein, L. (1958). *Philosophical investigations* (G. E. M. Anscombe, Trans.). New York: Macmillan.

Wolpe, J. (1958). *Psychotherapy by reciprocal inhibition.* Stanford, CA: Stanford University Press.

Zinbarg, R. E. (1993). Information processing and classical conditioning: Implications for exposure therapy and the integration of cognitive therapy and behavior therapy. *Journal of Behavior Therapy and Experimental Psychiatry, 24,* 129–139.

PREFACE

Editing *From Behavior Theory to Behavior Therapy* has been a labor of joy. Our intent in publishing this handbook is to meet a basic need in both the academic and professional communities: integration of basic learning theories with applied clinical psychology and behavior therapy. A book with this mission has not been published since 1970, when Kanfer and Phillips published *Learning Foundations of Behavior Therapy*. A number of edited volumes have appeared in the last two decades on either the theoretical bases *or* the practice of behavior therapy, but the two fields have not been integrated in a single volume. This volume presents a forceful argument for behavior therapy integration. Contributors examine the latest findings in basic and experimental behavioral research, and indicate their relevance for both the understanding, assessment, and treatment of the major psychological disorders. In other words, contributors present clinically relevant contributions from the major areas of modern behavior theory—radical behaviorism (classical and operant conditioning approaches), cognitive behaviorism, paradigmatic behaviorism, and social learning theory—and show their potential or demonstrated relevance for improving behavior therapy practice. Even though individual contributors may place greater emphasis on one or more of these theoretical approaches, an attempt is made in each chapter to argue for integration of the different behavior theories. Integration of behavior theories and behavior therapy are also illustrated in the different chapters by clinical examples, thereby presenting a balance of theory and the implications of theory for clinical behavior therapy.

As this handbook presents both theoretical analyses and clinical applications, we believe that this different approach will ensure that *From Behavior Theory to Behavior Therapy* will serve to advance the field of behavior therapy. The academician will find comprehensive treatments of theoretical and philosophical issues in contemporary behavior theory. The clinician will find examples of the latest behavior therapy approaches to major psychological disorders as they can be derived from our current knowledge of behavior theory. Both the academician and clinician will also find balanced arguments and analyses concerning the potential integration of behavior therapy. Authors in this handbook demonstrate how contemporary knowledge of behavior principles can be applied to the behavioral treatment of the major psychological dysfunctions. We hope that all who read the scholarly contributions in a variety of clinical areas will come to a new appreciation of the relevance of behavior theory for the continuous improvement of behavioral applications.

There have been many individuals who have contributed to this project. Beyond the many scholars who shared their expertise in a variety of areas of behavior therapy as represented in the chapters of this handbook, the editorial staff of Allyn and Bacon have been both inspirational and appreciated. We thank Mylan Jaixen, Carla Daves, and Susan Hutchinson for keeping us on target and assisting us in all the ways that matter in terms of publishing a major handbook of behavior therapy. We also thank our intellectual mentors, who prepared us to be behavioral theoreticians as well as behavior therapists. For J.J.P.: Joseph Wolpe of Pepperdine University; Leo Reyna of Nova Southeastern University; Cyril Franks of Rutgers University; Gordon Kulberg, Geoffrey Thorpe, and Jeffrey Hecker of the University of Maine; Ronald Drabman, Patricia Dubbert, Thomas Payne, and Thomas Mosley of the University of Mississippi; and Jackson Department of Veterans Affairs Medical Centers. For G.H.E.: Ian Evans of the University of Waikato, New Zealand (formerly at the University of Hawaii and SUNY Binghamton); Wolf Lauterbach of the Goethe Universität Frankfurt, Germany; Dietmar Schulte of the Ruhr Universität Bochum, Germany; and Arthur Staats of the University of Hawaii. We would also like to thank the expert reviewers of the draft of our manuscript for this book, including Geary Alford of the University of Mississippi Medical Center and Patrick Friman of the Father Flanagan's Boys Home and Creighton University.

No major handbook on any topic can be published without the support of family. J.J.P. derives the energy to complete this project from his daughter, Brianna. It is she to whom the first coeditor dedicates the contents of this handbook. She continues to teach me, in the words of William James, that "the greatest use of life is to spend it for something that will outlast it." In the spirit of that very statement by William James, G.H.E. dedicates this book to his son, Daniel, who is a seemingly endless source of joy and love, and who makes it all worthwhile.

ABOUT THE EDITORS

Joseph J. Plaud   Joseph J. Plaud is a clinical psychologist whose graduate training was primarily focused on behavioral assessment and treatment. He received his B.A. from Clark University in 1987 and his Ph.D. from the University of Maine in 1993. He is currently Director of Clinical Services for the New Beginnings program at the Judge Rotenberg Center (JRC, formerly Behavior Research Institute) in Canton, Massachusetts. The New Beginnings program is a behaviorally based assessment and treatment program for adolescents and young adults with a history of sexually offending behaviors. Prior to joining JRC he was a member of the clinical psychology faculty at the University of North Dakota, and Director of Clinical Services for the Specialized Treatment of Offenders Program (STOP) at the North Dakota Developmental Center in Grafton, North Dakota. He has clinical and research interests in the application of behavior principles to everyday life as well as abnormal behavior. Research areas include the study of behavioral allocation and choice, behavioral momentum, quantitative analyses of human behavior, and stimulus equivalence. Other clinical and research areas include sexual disorders and sexual dysfunctions, the conditioning and habituation of human sexual arousal, anxiety disorders, mood disorders, the study of how mental health professionals make and justify treatment decisions, and behavioral gerontology (especially Alzheimer's disease). Plaud is interested in the philosophical and historical foundations of psychology, with particular interests in the theoretical underpinnings of behaviorism and behavior therapy. He is a Clinical Fellow of the Behavior Therapy and Research Society.

Georg H. Eifert   Georg H. Eifert (Johann Wolfgang Goethe Universität Frankfurt, Germany) is Eberly Distinguished Professor of Clinical Psychology in the Department of Psychology at West Virginia University in Morgantown. He also is an Adjunct Professor of Behavioral Medicine and Psychiatry at West Virginia University's School of Medicine. He was previously Chief of the Psychology Division at the University of Mississippi Medical Center where he also directed the Anxiety Research and Therapy Clinic. Before moving to the United States he was an Associate Professor in Clinical Psychology and Foundation Head of the Division of Psychology in the School of Behavioral Sciences at James Cook University of North Queensland, Australia. Prior to moving to Australia, he had a faculty position in his native Germany at the Goethe Universität in Frankfurt where he completed his doctoral dissertation on the acquisition and extinction of phobias. He also obtained a Graduate Diploma in Psychology at the Ruhr Universität in Bochum. A clinical board member of the Australian Psychological Society, he served several terms on the National Council of the Australian Psychological Society. He also serves on several editorial boards, including the *Journal of Behavior Therapy and Experimental Psychiatry, Behaviour Change, Clinical Psychology and Psychotherapy,* and the *Journal of Cognitive Psychotherapy.* Apart from over 70 research articles and book chapters, he coedited a book entitled *Unifying Behavior Therapy: Contributions from Paradigmatic Behaviorism.* He has a strong interest in the theoretical foundations and the conceptual advancement and integrative development of behavior therapy. His research has mainly focused on the origin, assessment, and treatment of phobic fear, panic, and illness-related fears, including the assessment and treatment of heart-focused anxiety and pain. He has been particularly interested in how the knowledge derived from studying basic psychological processes can be used to develop more comprehensive and integrative theories and treatments of anxiety-related disorders.

ABOUT THE CONTRIBUTORS

Anne Marie Albano   Anne Marie Albano is an Assistant Professor of Psychology and Codirector of the Anxiety Research and Treatment Center at the University of Louisville. Dr. Albano received her degree in clinical psychology from the University of Mississippi in 1991. She completed her predoctoral internship at the Tufts University–Boston Veteran's Affairs Internship Consortium, and a postdoctoral fellowship in anxiety disorders at the Center for Stress and Anxiety Disorders at the State University of New York at Albany. Dr. Albano's primary research interests are in the development of valid assessment methods and effective cognitive behavioral treatment protocols for anxiety disorders in children and adolescents. In addition, her work is focused on examining maintenance variables in anxiety, particularly within the family. Dr. Albano is the coauthor with Wendy Silverman, Ph.D. of *The Anxiety Disorders Interview Schedule for DSM-IV, Child Version.* She is currently the Associate Editor of *Cognitive and Behavioral Practice,* and is actively involved in developing continuing education programs for the Association for Advancement of Behavior Therapy (AABT).

Beverley Kim Beach   Beverley Kim Beach is a Zimbabwean by birth and nationality. She received her B.A. in Psychology from Smith College in Massachusetts, and her M.A. and Ph.D. in Clinical Psychology from West Virginia University. She now works in private practice in Harare, Zimbabwe.

Shawn Cahill   Shawn Cahill is a doctoral candidate in clinical psychology at Binghamton University, State University of New York. He is completing his predoctoral internship at the Medical University of South Carolina and VAMC Consortium, Charleston, South Carolina, and will continue as a postdoctoral fellow through the National Crime Victims Research and Treatment Center.

Maureen H. Carrigan   Maureen H. Carrigan is a doctoral candidate in clinical psychology at Binghamton University (SUNY). She began a predoctoral internship in clinical psychology at the Charleston Consortium (Medical University of South Carolina and Veterans Affairs Medical Center) in the fall of 1997.

Ian M. Evans   Ian M. Evans completed his Ph.D. at the Institute of Psychiatry (Maudsley Hospital), London University, and is currently Professor of Psychology and Director of Clinical Training at the University of Waikato in New Zealand. Prior to this appointment he was director of the clinical program at Binghamton University (SUNY), and before then on the faculty at the University of Hawaii. His research focuses on the organization of behavioral repertoires, and he has an interest in the conceptual foundations of behavior therapy and behavioral assessment. He is a Fellow of the American Psychological Association.

John P. Forsyth   John P. Forsyth is Assistant Professor of Psychology at the University of Albany–State University of New York. He received his B.A. in psychology from Providence College, his M.A. and Ph.D. in clinical psychology at West Virginia University, and completed his clinical internship as Chief Psychology Resident at the University of Mississippi Medical Center. He has received several junior scholar awards including the Don Hake Award for Outstanding Graduate Student Career, and the Outstanding Dissertation Award by the Association for Advancement of Behavior Therapy. He has written numerous scholarly articles, and recently finished guest editing a special volume of the journal *Behavior Therapy* titled *Thirty Years of Behavior Therapy: Promises Kept, Promises Unfulfilled.*

Cyril M. Franks   Cyril M. Franks received his doctorate from the University of London Institute of Psychiatry, and is Distinguished Professor Emeritus at Rutgers University. He is the cofounder and first president of the Association for Advancement of Behavior Therapy (AABT), and the first editor of the journal *Behavior Therapy*. Professor Franks also has a B.Sc. from the University of Wales and an M.A. from the University of Minnesota. Professor Franks is the author of over 300 journal articles and book chapters, and has edited many books in behavior therapy. His interests are in the conceptual and theoretical foundations of behavior therapy.

Alice G. Friedman   Alice G. Friedman is an Associate Professor of Psychology at Binghamton University (SUNY). She completed her doctoral training at Virginia Tech, an internship at West Virginia University Medical Center, and post-doctoral training at University of Oklahoma Health Sciences Center. She was on the staff of St. Jude Children's Research Hospital before joining the faculty at Binghamton University. Her research and clinical interests focus on psychological aspects of acute and chronic illness, particularly with children.

George A. Gaither   George A. Gaither received his B.A. degree from the University of South Florida in 1994. He is currently a doctoral student in the clinical psychology program at the University of North Dakota, where he received his M.A. in 1996. His research interests include behavioral treatments for sexual offending behaviors, penile plethysmography, behavioral momentum, and stimulus equivalence.

Jill S. Goldberg   Jill S. Goldberg, a senior-level graduate student in clinical psychology at Binghamton University, is currently completing an internship at the District of Columbia Commission of Mental Health. Her research and clinical interests focus on assessment and intervention with children with disabilities and their families.

Robert P. Hawkins   Robert P. Hawkins is Professor Emeritus of Psychology at West Virginia University, earned his doctorate at the University of Pittsburgh, then taught at University of Washington and Western Michigan University. He has been a clinical child behavior analyst for over thirty years. He is a Fellow of the American Psychological Association, American Psychological Society, and American Association of Applied and Preventative Psychology. He has authored and co-edited numerous articles, chapters, and books, including a forthcoming book on measurement of behavioral outcomes.

Jeff Holm   Jeff Holm is an associate professor of psychology at the University of North Dakota, and Director of Clinical Training. He received his A.B. from Hope College in 1981 and his Ph.D. in clinical psychology from Ohio University in 1987. His research interests focus on assessment and measurement as well as treatment of headache and other psychophysiological disorders, and the development and expression of sexual aggressive behaviors and other factors involved in sexually coercive incidents.

Arthur C. Houts   Arthur C. Houts is Professor and Director of Clinical Training at the University of Memphis. He has an interest in the theoretical and philosophical foundations of behavior therapy. He is proud to have maintained a most enriching collaboration and friendship with his teacher, Len Krasner, for over 20 years.

Leonard Krasner   Leonard Krasner is Clinical Professor, Department of Psychiatry and Behavioral Sciences at Stanford University. He received his Ph.D. from Columbia University. He has authored, co-authored, edited, and co-edited numerous books and articles on behavior therapy. The continuing collaboration with Art Houts for many years has been fruitful and exciting.

C. W. Lejuez   C. W. Lejuez is a clinical psychology graduate student at West Virginia University. He is interested in the experimental analysis of behavior and laboratory models of psychopathology. His current research focuses on conditioned fear and the use of carbon dioxide in studies of aversive conditioning.

Marcia L. Moberg   Marcia L. Moberg holds an M.A. in psychology from the University of North Dakota and is currently a Ph.D. candidate in experimental psychology at the same institution. Ms. Moberg's research interests include the areas of aging and age-related diseases and psychology and the law, specifically jury decision making and child witness testimony.

Tracy L. Morris   Tracy L. Morris is an Assistant Professor of Psychology at West Virginia University. Dr. Morris' primary research interests are in the developmental psychopathology of social anxiety.

Thomas H. Mosley, Jr.   Thomas H. Mosley, Jr. is an Assistant Professor of Medicine (Geriatrics) and Psychiatry (Psychology) at the University of Mississippi Medical Center, where he is the director of the Geriatric Memory Assessment Clinic. His research is primarily in the areas of dementia and neuropsychological correlates of cerebral abnormalities observed on MRI.

Kimberly B. Mullen   Kimberly B. Mullen is a doctoral candidate in child clinical psychology at West Virginia University. Her research and clinical interests are in the functional assessment and intervention of excess behaviors in children and persons with developmental disabilities, and in the assessment and treatment of children exposed to traumatic life events. She is co-author of several book chapters.

Jennifer O'Donnell   Jennifer O'Donnell recently obtained her Ph.D. in psychology from West Virginia University, where she conducted experiments on stimulus control and aversive conditioning with humans. She currently works as a postdoctoral research assistant at Parsons State Hospital, a research center affiliated with the University of Kansas.

Akiko Okifuji   Akiko Okifuji is currently a Research Assistant Professor in the Department of Anesthesiology at Washington University Medical School in Seattle, Washington. She obtained her doctoral degree in clinical psychology at Binghamton University and completed an internship and postdoctoral training at Western Psychiatric Institute. She conducts research on assessment and treatment of individuals with chronic pain with the goal of developing more complete models for understanding the phenomenon of chronic pain.

Richard R. Rosenkranz   Richard R. Rosenkranz received his B.A. degree from the University of Kansas in 1993 and his M.A. in Psychology from the University of North Dakota in 1996. His research interests include behavioral treatments for sexual dysfunctions, marital and family therapy, and factors involved in condom use.

Kurt Salzinger   Kurt Salzinger is Professor of Psychology and Director of the Graduate Program in Clinical and School Psychology at Hofstra University. A past president of the New York Academy of Sciences, he is currently president of the American Association of Applied and Preventive Psychology and winner of the American Psychopathological Association Award for his research in schizophrenia.

David W. Schaal   David W. Schaal received his Ph.D. from the University of Florida in 1988. An Associate Professor of Psychology, he performs behavioral pharmacology research with rats and pigeons. His current research involves the study of interactions of abused drugs with food deprivation and drugs as discriminative stimuli. Dr. Schaal also studies the effects on operant behavior of signaled and unsignaled delayed reinforcement.

Joseph R. Scotti   Joseph R. Scotti is Associate Professor of Psychology at West Virginia University and earned his doctorate in clinical psychology at the State University of New York at Binghamton. He has been active in the field of developmental disabilities for twenty years, has authored several reviews on intervention effectiveness and standards of practice, and is coeditor of a forthcoming volume on principles, programs, and practices in behavioral intervention.

Sandra T. Sigmon   Sandra T. Sigmon is Associate Professor in the Clinical Psychology program at the University of Maine, Orono, Maine. Her current research interests include women's health issues, predisposing factors in depression, and seasonal affective disorder. Recent publications are on coping styles associated with depression and psychological factors in seasonality.

Kristin S. Vickers   Kristin S. Vickers is a doctoral student in the Clinical Psychology program at the University of North Dakota. Her research and clinical interests include understanding the determinants and correlates of depression and the treatment of mood, anxiety, and eating disorders.

Nancy D. Vogeltanz   Nancy D. Vogeltanz is an Associate Professor of Psychology and Neuroscience at the University of North Dakota, Departments of Psychology and Neuroscience, Grand Forks, North Dakota. Dr. Vogeltanz's clinical and research interests are in behavior therapy, anxiety disorders, and women's health issues, including women's alcohol abuse, depression, and childhood sexual abuse.

Joseph Wolpe   Joseph Wolpe has a long and distinguished career as a psychiatrist and behavior therapist, and is one of the founders of behavior therapy. His 1958 book *Psychotherapy by Reciprocal Inhibition* is one of the most significant texts in psychiatry and psychology. The therapeutic technique that he pioneered, systematic desensitization, was one of the first empirically validated techniques in behavior therapy. Dr. Wolpe has also directly participated in the training of hundreds of psychiatrists and psychologists over the past 40 years. He co-founded the largest association dedicated to behavior therapy, the Association for Advancement of Behavior Therapy (AABT), and served as its second president. The interdisciplinary nature of his work has helped psychiatrists work closely with psychologists, sociologists, social workers, and a variety of other behavioral scientists. He also founded one of the most important journals in our field, the *Journal of Behavior Therapy and Experimental Psychiatry*, which he still edits. He maintains an active clinical practice and academic position at Pepperdine University, continues to be a major researcher, and is involved in the training of behavioral scientists.

1

FROM BEHAVIOR THEORY TO BEHAVIOR THERAPY: AN OVERVIEW

GEORG H. EIFERT
Department of Psychology
West Virginia University

JOSEPH J. PLAUD
Department of Psychology
Judge Rotenberg Educational Center

Behavior Theory in Behavior Therapy

Much of mainstream behavior therapy has lost its link with basic research and behavior theory. Instead, many behavior therapists have adopted vague notions about the so-called cognitive control of emotions and behavior (Eifert & Evans, 1990; Plaud & Vogeltanz, 1993) and now identify themselves as cognitive-behavior therapists claiming that they practice both behavior and cognitive therapy. A related development has been the recent renaming of most professional *behavior* therapy associations in Europe and Australasia to *cognitive-behavior* therapy associations. This pseudointegration is the result of divisive debates and confusion within behavior therapy about its conceptual base, and it is meant to prevent further divisions and appease professional separatists. However, these changes have led only to more confusion and serve to solidify the unnecessary cognitive-behavioral dichotomy.

We will attempt to provide a brief answer as to why this shift from behaviorist to cognitive theories has occurred and argue that we need a different type of behaviorist theory—one that is focused on human functioning and that is clinically relevant—rather than a replacement of behaviorism with some type of cognitivism. We also need to reestablish the link between basic behaviorist theory and research and behavior therapy. Behavior therapy is arguably the only treatment approach derived from the empirical science of psychology, that is, the uniqueness, rapid expansion, and proliferation of behavior therapy has been fueled largely by its reciprocal relation to psychological principles and theories. Accordingly, the unique strength of behavioral approaches to therapy rests, at least in part, on their continuing linkage and dynamic reciprocal relationship with the basic empirical science of psychology. This book makes a strong case for reestablishing this lost link to prevent further separatist divisions in behavior therapy and to enhance the overall effectiveness of therapists employing the behavioral approach.

The Link between Behavior Theory and Behavior Therapy

Early behavior therapists did not question that experimentally based behavioral theories were the foundation of behavior therapy. The connection was succinctly expressed in the statement of aims and scope that appeared in the first issue of the first behavior therapy journal, *Behaviour Research and Therapy,* and is reproduced below:

> *In recent years there has been an ever-growing interest in applying modern learning theories to the improvement of learning efficacy. . . . The application of learning theory and the experimental method to clinical psychology also promises to carry this discipline beyond mere psychometry and close the gap between the laboratory and the clinic. . . . The main conception unifying all these different approaches has been the belief that behavioral disorders of the most divergent type are essentially learned responses, and that modern learning theory has much to teach us regarding the acquisition and extinction of such responses. This conception, cutting across many existing boundary lines which separate psychiatry, education, clinical psychology, remedial teaching, psychotherapy, social work and psychoanalysis, forms the basis for the appearance of this Journal.*

In ensuing years a number of factors have weakened the link between basic behavioral research and applied behavioral practice. It may have been somewhat naive to assume that merely applying these theories, without much development and extension, to all sorts of clinical problems would automatically result in a comprehensive range of powerful interventions. An increasing number of studies revealed some limitations of the early *simple* conditioning models (cf. Meichenbaum, 1977; Rachman, 1977) that were based largely on animal research. These models would have required systematic theory extensions to account for the emotion-eliciting, reinforcing, and behavior-directive functions of language and other symbolic stimuli, which are characteristic of complex human behavior (Staats, 1972).

Unfortunately, the development of such theory extensions was neglected, and theoretical-conceptual advances, in general, have lagged behind advances in the development and fine-tuning of behavioral treatments (Ross, 1985). Moreover, research studies in the field of experimental analysis of behavior focused on narrow, frequently idiosyncratic aspects of behavior. Again, many of these studies were conducted with infrahumans and, consequently, did not consider the important role of language in controlling maladaptive responses in humans. As a result, many behavior therapists began to perceive behavioral models as too mechanistic, inflexible, removed from clinical reality, and ultimately as irrelevant (Evans, Eifert, & Corrigan, 1990). Hence, a growing number of behavior therapists turned to cognitive explanations of behavior and treatments, because such explanations *appeared* to be more flexible and, most importantly, because cognitive explanations and techniques address areas of *human* experience, such as language, thought, and imagery, that were frequently given only token attention in early behavior theory and research.

As a result of these developments, and also because the field began to expand into many other areas and disciplines (e.g., behavioral medicine), behavior therapy came to mean different things to different people (Peterson, 1993). Yet it seems beyond question that the impressive success of behavior therapy and its subsequent expansion are attributable to the application of the experimental-empirical approach to understanding and treating abnormal behavior. Not all behavior therapists, however, recognized this link. For instance, as noted by Plaud and Vogeltanz (1993), behavioral scholars such as Isaac Marks have disputed that behavior therapy has grown from basic experimental psychology, arguing that behavior therapists do not read experimental journals (Marks, 1981). The history of the development of behavior therapy (e.g., Kazdin, 1978) decisively contradicts Marks's argument. But the fact that he puts it forward is indicative of a more general problem: clinicians frequently fail to recognize that their clinical practice is dependent on behavioral theory and research. In order to remedy this situation, researchers should constantly draw attention to the ways in which their findings are relevant to and continue to shape the practice of behavior therapy.

The Challenge of the "Cognitive Revolution"

Over the last twenty years the field has been inundated with descriptions, analyses, and evaluations of cognitive-behavioral concepts and technologies in specialist journals (e.g., *Cognitive Therapy and Research*), edited books (e.g., Kendall, 1991), and monographs (e.g., Beck & Emery, 1985). Yet where in all these writings have the conceptual foundations of the various cognitive-behavioral theories and treatments been adequately defined and elaborated on? And where is the evidence that the "cognitive revolution" has deposed the role of environmental influences and consequences in favor of hypothesized inner processes (Krasner, 1988)? We are concerned that the increased preoccupation with hypothesized inner processes will weaken the behavior therapy movement unless theories about private events are appropriately related to and integrated with basic behavioral concepts and research findings as, for instance, has been done in paradigmatic behavioral theory (Staats & Eifert, 1990) or contextual behavioral accounts of rule-governed behavior (Hayes & Hayes, 1992); we believe that such integrative accounts will actually strengthen the field.

The field's emphasis on cognitive-behavioral theorizing has obscured many of the advances made in basic research and their potential relevance for behavior therapy. In other words, progress in such areas as experimental and applied behavior analysis, paradigmatic behaviorism, and new developments in classical conditioning theories have been overlooked or not properly understood; in the place of such theories, cognitive models have emerged as explanations of behavior. Yet these cognitive approaches have not been uniformly embraced by the field (cf. Eysenck, 1987; Wolpe, 1990). For instance, Plaud and Vogeltanz (1991) pointed out major theoretical and methodological errors in the study of classical conditioning as a cognitive phenomenon. Moreover, Eifert (1990) has shown how the neglect of advances in understanding the verbal-symbolic control of emotional behavior has impeded the development and inclusion of verbal-symbolic techniques (derived from basic conditioning principles) in more comprehensive theory-based behavioral interventions.

In 1972, Hans Eysenck rejected the investigation of cognitive phenomena, arguing that this would lead to a reduction in scientific rigor and that cognitive events cannot be studied objectively. Today, more than twenty years later, this criticism no longer holds. Behavior therapy could benefit a great deal from both the research methodology and the findings of experimental cognitive psychology. For instance, experimental cognitive studies employ basic cognitive science research methods and use objective, quantifiable, and observable measures such as reaction time, response latencies, and recall scores as their main source of data. These are objective measures of behavior that are not only useful to study dysfunctional cognitive processes, but they are also potentially useful as treatment outcome measures (Watts, McKenna, Sharrock, & Trezise, 1986). It is not the methods used that differentiate behavioral from cognitive research. The point of contention is cognitive researchers' reliance on various internal structures to explain their data using a variety of concepts borrowed from information and computer sciences, such as networks, nodes, schema, and so forth. These concepts are supposedly explanatory, but they are more often descriptive and circular by definition. They are neither derived from, nor are they based on, basic psychological research. In other words, no attempts are made to link and relate the findings from the cognitive literature with other relevant findings and fields of study such as conditioning or physiology.

What we need is a conceptual bridge between experimental cognitive findings and other behavioral research. We believe that the translation of structural interpretations into a functional framework—a functional analysis of cognitive behavior—may provide the necessary bridge to integrate the two fields of study. For instance, the observation that panic patients are hypervigilant to changes in bodily functioning does not explain how this attentional bias comes about in the first place. We need to ask questions such as, Is there an adaptive value for becoming hypervigilant to heart rate and other bodily changes? What are the contingencies that have given these stimuli discriminative properties? And what function do these behaviors serve within a given context? Answers to these questions may emerge if we employ knowledge from contemporary behaviorist theory, which recognizes the complexities and subtleties that transcend any simple classical conditioning or reinforcement mechanism. We need to examine how the principles of semantic conditioning produce differences in information processing, and how such differences are related to changes in verbal-emotional behavioral repertoires and in the functional contingencies of rule-governed behavior. Such linking of new and relevant findings and theories across different fields of study has not been given enough attention in behavior therapy, and this book is meant to be a step in that direction.

We are eager to avoid any polemic and divisive arguments such as "since there is really nothing new about cognitive concepts and techniques, we should therefore not give them any special status or even discard them." Wolpe (1990) rightly cautioned that cognitive-behavioral procedures are easily acceptable if it is realized that cognition is a category of behavior. In other words, just because the conceptual foundations of language and imagery-based interventions are currently still unsatisfactory does not necessarily make those interventions ineffective or mean that we should not engage in them. Likewise, it may be short-sighted to say that the principles underlying cognitive-behavioral interventions can simply be adequately (re)formulated with existing concepts from any of the behaviorisms in their current state of development. The huge integrative task ahead of us can only be accomplished if more attention and effort is devoted to relating concepts and research findings from different behavioral fields such as radical behaviorism, paradigmatic behaviorism, and contextualism (Eifert & Evans, 1990; see also Plaud, 1993).

An Example of the Application of Behavior Theory to Behavior Therapy

One cutting edge area of basic behavioral theorizing that may have significant implications for future developments in behavior therapy concerns behavioral momentum. Behavioral momentum utilizes a theoretical framework tying behavior theory to physics. Isaac Newton's second law of physical motion to explain behavioral dynamics (Nevin, 1992; Nevin, Mandell, & Atak, 1983; Plaud & Gaither, 1996). Newton's second law states that, assuming a body is traveling through space under constant conditions, when an external force is imposed, the change in velocity is directly proportional to the force that is imposed, and inversely proportional to the mass of the body (Nevin, 1992):

$$\triangle V = f/m$$

For example, the rate at which a person on in-line skates traveling at a constant speed will slow down is directly proportional to the force that the skater applies his or her foot to the ground (i.e., the brakes) and inversely proportional to the size and weight of the skater. Nevin has transferred this law of physical motion to behavioral dynamics (Plaud & Gaither, 1996). In this way, velocity (V) stands for operant response rate, and mass (m) stands for the response strength, and force (f) refers to the change in the contingencies for the behavior.

The use of these techniques in clinical behavioral contexts was first reported by Mace, Hock, Lalli, West, Belfiore, Pinter, and Brown (1988) in a series of experiments. In each phase of the intervention with persons with developmental disabilities living in a group home environment, a group of requests with which each subject had a high probability of complying (high-p requests) were paired with a second group of requests with which each subject had a low probability of complying (low-p requests). For example, the behavioral theoreticians/researchers found that one subject had a high probability of complying with requests such as "Give me a hug" or "Give me five," and a low probability of complying with requests such as "Put your lunch box away." During the behavioral intervention, the researcher first issued a series of high-p requests and then issued a low-p request. In this way, Mace et al. were able to increase the occurrence of compliant behavior, decrease the latency in initiating tasks, and decrease the duration of tasks. Mace et al. showed that the positive changes in compliance to low-p requests were not merely a result of increased attention by the researcher, and that compliance to the low-p requests was affected by the amount of time that had elapsed between the issuance of the last high-p request and the issuance of the low-p request, with greater compliance occurring when the time was shorter.

Behavioral momentum, a theoretical paradigm, may have significant implications for behavior therapy: adapting Newton's second law of physical motion as a metaphor to understand and predict which behaviors may persist in the face of altered environmental contingencies (Plaud & Gaither, 1996). Relapse prevention strategies and effective behavior therapy regimens rely upon the persistence of adaptive behaviors (usually shaped in a clinic) to novel or changed situations. Behavioral momentum is a model for how to shape strong behavior that will have a greater probability of persisting in new life situations: maximize behavioral velocity (through operant contingencies) as well as behavioral mass (through densely reinforcing environments). The combination of these two factors will produce behavior that is more resistant to extinction in the long run. Therefore, an important implication of this behavioral model for behavior therapy is that a highly reinforcing environment not only increases the frequency of a behavior (cf. Skinner, 1938) but also establishes as well as maintains over the long run the behavior's resistance to changing contingencies, one of the most fundamental goals of behavior therapy (Plaud, Gaither, & Lawrence, in press).

Reestablishing the Link between Behavior Theory and Behavior Therapy

The general purpose of this book is to present a forceful argument for the integration of behavior theory and behavior therapy. To achieve this goal, chapters in this book critically analyze the contributions of the behaviorisms to the behavior therapy movement and to encourage the development of a more integrative and unified approach in behavior therapy. In doing so, contributors focus on some of the more recent advances that clinicians and clinical researchers may be unfamiliar with. Several of the chapters address recent attempts within behavioral conceptions to account for the types of learning processes that are more unique and central to human functioning (such as language, thought, and imagery). For instance, Forsyth and Eifert discuss how a new behavior analytic approach to verbal (rule-governed) behavior has led to a new behavioral treatment called Acceptance and Commitment Therapy (ACT) (Hayes, 1987; Hayes & Hayes, 1992; Hayes, Jacobson, Follette, & Dougher, 1994). Several chapters examine the role of language and other symbolic stimuli in understanding and treating maladaptive emotional behavior and the potential for improving behavior therapy by drawing on behavioral methods and research findings from *Experimental Cognitive Psychology.*

Apart from the general significance of these conceptual developments and empirical data for behavior therapy, there is another very important and specific reason why these developments are presented in this book. Therapists have been frustrated with radical behaviorists' failure to account for language and thought processes in terms that are clinically useful for them. A further source of frustration has been the radical behaviorist dictum that emotions are consequences, or at best epiphenomena, of behavior rather than stimuli that may control behavior (Skinner, 1974). This dictum contradicts the clinical day-to-day experience of therapists and, indeed, other prominent behavioral research that has focused on assessing and changing maladaptive emotional responses (e.g., Eysenck, 1987; Levey & Martin, 1987; Wolpe, 1958, 1990). In any case, the reluctance by early radical behavioral researchers to deal with covert processes and private events in a manner understood by, and useful to, clinicians has been one of the main reasons for the declining importance of *all* basic experimental behavioral research in behavior therapy and why ever-increasing numbers of clinical behavior therapists have turned their back on all basic behavioral research in favor of cognitive concepts, explanations, and techniques.

This book is an attempt to remedy this situation by narrowing the enlarging gap between basic behavioral research and behavior therapy. One of the major conclusions is that behavior therapists should not divorce themselves from ongoing research in basic and applied behavior analysis as well as other basic behavioral research. The question then is how behavior therapists, or clinical psychologists in general for that matter, can benefit from new developments in behavioral theories and research. We concur with Hayes (1987) who suggested that the *mutual cooperation model* between experimental and clinical psychologists is a weak model of integration between the two disciplines. According to this model, the duty of clinical psychologists is to pass along research questions and hypotheses to experimental psychologists, who are responsible for testing the ideas proposed by clinical psychologists, and therefore both will share in the knowledge gained from this experimental and clinical connection.

Hayes (1987) outlines an alternative model, the *mutual interest model*, in which experimental psychologists and clinical psychologists can productively work together, integrating experimental and clinical phenomena, as long as they share a mutual interest in a specific area of psychology. As an example, Hayes discusses behavior analytic research that focuses on the role of verbal behavior in human functioning. These researchers want to know such things as "What happens when you talk to someone?" and "Can you talk to people in such a way that they become more or less sensitive to changes in the environment?" These questions are very similar to those asked by clinical researchers interested in semantic therapies. It is quite possible that answers to these kinds of questions in either subdisciplines will be of significant interest to researchers asking similar questions in the other subdiscipline. Based on this conception of a mutual interest model of basic science and clinical science integration, contributors to this book analyze the potential of recent advances in behavioral theory and research for advancing behavior therapy and discuss how behavior therapy would be served by continued integration of clinical phenomena with basic and applied behavior research.

The behavioral movement has been one of the most successful in the history of psychological science, but our job is not finished—it has barely begun. Likewise, the behaviorisms have clearly made important contributions to the growing success of behavior therapy. We believe that the field could be more successful if it tapped the resources created by recent advances in basic behavioral theory and research. To utilize these resources, however, we need to build conceptual, methodological, and practical bridges that help behavior therapists recognize the utility and potential of these new developments. To make advances relevant for behavior therapy, new theoretical concepts and findings need to be related to existing knowledge and clinical practice. Advances in basic behavioral theories and research, as impressive as they may be, will have little impact on the field of behavior therapy unless they are made relevant *and* unless behavior therapists recognize them as relevant. Our book is an attempt to show that relevance for all behavior therapists. We also hope that the chapters in this book, when taken as a whole, will allow behavior therapists to ponder and predict how past and recent developments will affect the future of behavior therapy as we proceed into the twenty-first century.

Organization of the Book

One of the major themes of this book is that behavior therapy techniques do not exist in a theoretical vacuum, but that they are derived from behavioral theories and research, and, at least to some extent, also from other psychological research and principles. As any other science, however, behavior therapy is conducted within a social network. Despite a considerable degree of conceptual diversity characteristic of the field in general, the chapters that follow are composed by individuals who share the vision and commitment that behavior therapy is foremost an application and extension of behavioral principles for the solution of human problems.

In the preface to this book, written by one of the founders and first president of the *Association for Advancement of Behavior Therapy* (AABT), Cyril Franks presents an overview of the rich and varied behavior theories of the past several decades that led to the discovery and implementation of various behavior therapy technique. Further, Franks argues that it is important to understand the behavior theory behind behavior therapy interventions, and he provides several examples to support the argument.

Part I: Behavior Theory as the Basis of Behavior Therapy

Following our brief introductory chapter, the second chapter in Part I is by Art Houts and Len Krasner on behavior theory on the theoretical foundation of behavior therapy. Both authors are eminent behavior therapists and veterans in the art of applying and extending behavioral principles to clinical practice across a variety of clinical settings and populations (Ullmann and Krasner's 1969 classic volume on a psychological approach to abnormal behavior is exemplary of this approach, and even twenty-five years after its first publication, it is still very relevant and difficult to surpass). Houts and Krasner trace the origins of behavior theory in our psychology, physiology, and philosophy of the past, and relate advances in neobehavioral and behavioral systems of psychology to the development and advancement of behavior therapy from the 1950s to the present. The authors argue that to properly understand what behavior therapy was and is, as well as to apply behavior principles, it is important to understand behavior theory and how it relates to clinical practice.

Part II: Applications of Behavior Theory in Behavior Therapy

Based on the rich theoretical foundations of behavior therapy outlined in Part I, Part II focuses on applications of behavior theory for the treatment of specific DSM–IV disorders in order to (a) illustrate the need to integrate theory and therapy, (b) provide specific clinical situations in which integration has been done or could be done, and (c) provide for both the clinician and researcher an update on state-of-the-art behavioral interventions for a number of major disorders based on recent advances in our general understanding of behavior theory and how it specifically relates to common psychological dysfunctions.

Behavior therapy has made a unique, successful, and lasting contribution to the understanding, assessment, and treatment of anxiety disorders—in fact, behavior therapy's most impressive results have been achieved with persons suffering from anxiety disorders (cf. Giles, 1993). Chapter 3, written by John Forsyth and Georg Eifert, analyzes behavior theory and therapy approaches to the assessment and treatment of anxiety disorders, carefully relating advances in the behavioral conceptualization of anxiety to treatment approaches. Rather than discussing the various types of DSM-IV anxiety disorders, which has been skillfully done in several other books (e.g., Barlow, 1993), this chapter focuses on aspects of anxiety that have been relatively neglected in the past, but where recent advances and direct extensions from behavior theory can be applied with great promise. Some of these areas involve overcoming the problem of avoidance of emotional discomfort, balancing acceptance and change, and innovative classical conditioning interventions for the modification of negative affect (e.g., disgust) frequently associated with feared objects, situations, or events. This chapter will also discuss how concepts and principles derived from paradigmatic behaviorism can be utilized to conceptualize anxiety disorders and how paradigmatic behaviorism may serve to provide unique innovative avenues for treatment.

It was in reference to the phenomenon of depression that the recognition of the importance of verbal mediation gave the strangely oxymoronic phrase "cognitive-behavior therapy" its immense popularity. As a consequence, depression has become one of the most disunified and fragmented areas of study within clinical psychology. Research on the biological, operant, social, and cognitive determinants of depression, as well as treatment approaches derived from these models, are largely unrelated and take little notice of each other. Chapter 4 scrutinizes recent basic science contributions for their potential to contribute to a more integrative understanding of depression that is not only clinically useful for the treatment of depression but also for the prevention of relapse. Eifert, Beach, and Wilson's analysis of depression from a comprehensive and integrative behavioral perspective is a particularly good challenge to the increasing tendency within behavior therapy to neglect its early behavior theory roots and their contribution to psychopathology in favor of accepting the validity and professional dominance of medical model categories.

To emphasize that behavior therapy has not only relevance for the treatment of the most common "neurotic" problems (i.e., anxiety and depression; cf. Barlow, 1993), Kurt Salzinger relates advances in behavioral theories of the etiology and maintaining factors of schizophrenia to behavioral intervention techniques for persons suffering from this very debilitating disturbance (Chapter 5). Salzinger discusses the theoretical and clinical formulations of others as well as his own cutting edge research in this area. Some of the earliest behavioral interventions were actually directed at persons suffering from psychotic disorders, and despite some success, behavior therapists subsequently moved away from this population (Scotti et al., 1993). Yet interest in this area has noticeably increased over the past decade and new advances have been made (Scotti et al., 1993). It is particularly heartening to read that so much of behaviorism's rich set of principles and techniques has relevance for and can be applied to alleviate the suffering of individuals diagnosed with schizophrenia. The relevance of theoretically comprehensive models of substance use and abuse are articulated by Carl Lejuez, Dave Schaal, and Jennifer O'Donnell in Chapter 6. The authors point out that in order to understand the phenomenon, the behavior therapist must understand the importance of conditioning principles as in any other behavior, as well as the internal stimuli that enter into contingencies, particularly in the development of substance use.

Chapter 7, written by Joe Plaud and Jeff Holm, presents a detailed theoretical behavioral analysis of male and female sexual dysfunctions as another area where behavior therapists have made a remarkable difference in both treatment effectiveness and efficiency. Sexual dysfunctions is also a field of study where behavior therapists have from the very beginning attempted a direct translation and extension of behavioral principles to interventions techniques. Based on an evaluation of these early efforts, Plaud and Holm provide a detailed bridging between contemporary behavior theory and therapy in the assessment and treatment of sexual dysfunctions in the general population as well as in chronic medical illness populations.

Although many theories of sexual behavior claim that both normal and abnormal sexual behavior in humans is "learned," the data have been mixed on the behavioral parameters of sexual arousal and function (O'Donohue & Plaud, 1994). Although problems exist with the empirical data in support of a conditioning-based model of sexual behavior, behavioral theories of the etiology and modification of various paraphilic and dysfunctional sexual behavior claim that abnormal sexual behavior is learned and can be counterconditioned. Chapter 8, written by George Gaither, Richard Rosenkranz, and Joe Plaud, reviews recent behavioral research in this area that addresses whether habituation, sensitization, classical conditioning, and operant conditioning parameters are involved in human sexual behavior, sharing data from their sexual behavior laboratory, and relate their empirical findings to a more general discussion of behavior theory and therapy for sexual disorders.

Behavior therapy has been encouragingly effective for the treatment of many problems of adulthood (cf. Barlow, 1993; Giles, 1993), but behavior theory and therapy have also made a remarkable contribution to the understanding, assessment, and treatment of children and older adults. Chapters 9 through 11 review those contributions, current developments, and future potential for specific problems and populations. Together, these chapters on problems of children and older adults discuss the role of behavior theory and other theoretical and clinical considerations relevant for children, examine specific treatment implications for children and older adults, and point out the close connection between advances in behavior theory and improvements in behavior therapy for these special populations.

As was the case with behavioral interventions for adults, particularly in the United States, early interventions for childhood disorders focused on the most severe problems that frequently had a reputation for being refractory to treatment: autism, developmental disabilities, and conduct disorders. Early interventions for those problems often attempted a direct and literal translation of behavioral principles to behavioral interventions (cf. Meyer & Evans, 1989). Scotti, Mullen, and Hawkins discuss, elaborate, and analyze the current status of behavioral theories and therapy relating to these pervasive and severe disorders of childhood (Chapter 9). These authors elaborate on the rich tradition of behavior theory in understanding and treating disorders of childhood and demonstrate that tactics such as depriving patients of basic rights or using punitive and aversive techniques are neither essential nor typical parts of the behavioral approach, but frequently no more than superficial elements of crude practice. Scotti and his colleagues provide many examples of how behavioral principles can be translated into nonaversive interventions to change the self-defeating and frequently destructive behavior of persons with severe disabilities.

Although research in behavioral explanations and treatments of adult anxiety disorders has been one of the most prolific and successful chapters of behavior therapy, our understanding and treatments of childhood anxiety disorders are lagging behind advances in other areas. We believe Chapter 10, written by Anne Marie Albano and Tracy Morris, makes a contribution to closing this gap. These experts in childhood anxiety disorders discuss the applicability of behavioral theories to the genesis of anxiety as applied to children, and based upon such theoretical analyses they present specific treatment recommendations. This chapter also provides compelling examples of how research into behavioral principles can be complemented by advances from other areas of psychological science, in this case from developmental psychopathology. It appears that a successful integration of these two research areas has great relevance and potential for improving our understanding and treatment of anxiety problems in children.

Chapter 11, written by Joe Plaud, Tom Mosley, and Marcia Moberg, focuses on the other end of the developmental continuum and examines behavioral processes in older adults. The authors elaborate on the use of behavior principles, including stimulus control and reinforcement strategies to maximize behavioral allocation and choice, in general geriatric populations including individuals suffering from dementia. Specific behavioral theories will be tied into behavior therapy techniques, and a strong case is made for the integration of behavior theory with behavior therapy.

Few areas have witnessed such a rapid acceptance, proliferation, and profusion of behavioral interventions as the field of behavioral medicine in general, and behavioral pediatrics in particular—the topic of Chapter 12 by Alice Friedman. Behavioral medicine, with its focus on empiricism and accountability, has historically relied heavily upon behavioral techniques in the development and evaluation of treatment approaches. The field has some shining examples of the direct application of experimental findings to clinical settings. For instance, behavioral feeding programs designed to eliminate failure to thrive in infants were based directly on operant principles. While initially tied to state-of-the-art experimental findings, behavioral strategies tend to lose this connection in actual practice. Scientific findings have led to the development of techniques for application, but rarely has this relationship been reciprocal so that strategies in practice are sometimes based on obsolete experimental findings. Further, as behavioral medicine tends to be oriented around disease entities rather than behavioral constructs, research tends to be fragmented with little communication between areas. The lack of an integrative behavioral framework has further hindered the development of behavioral medicine as a psychological science rather than a collection of techniques. Friedman discusses these major impediments to linking behavioral theory and practice within behavioral medicine followed by suggestions for bridging the gap. Included is a critique of areas that exemplify these difficulties along with a discussion of some areas within behavioral medicine that have more successfully linked practice to basic behavioral principles, integrated findings from other areas of psychology, and have brought clinical findings back to the lab for further exploration.

Nancy Vogeltanz, Sandra Sigmon, and Kristen Vickers provide an analysis of the application of behavioral principles to women's health issues (Chapter 13), which is an area of growing concern in the bio-social sciences. The authors show how principles derived from behavior theory can be applied to resolve a number of clinical issues concerning women, including problem drinking behavior patterns.

Part III: Perspectives on the Relation between Behavior Theory and Behavior Therapy

The chapters in Parts I and II provide an overview of theoretical paradigms in behavior therapy and examples of how behavior theory and therapy can be integrated in the context of DSM-IV. The final chapters (Part III) appraise the future of this relationship beyond DSM-IV. Chapter 14 synthesizes some of the major issues surrounding the relation between behavioral theories and therapy and examines the future of behavior therapy as a clinical science. Evans, Cahill, and Carrigan wrote that chapter with the purpose of developing a visionary perspective of the future relation between theory and therapy in an era of rapidly changing behavior classification systems.

The book began with an analysis on the relation between behavior theory and therapy by one of the founders of the behavior therapy movement, Cyril Franks. The final chapter will contain observations and analyses from three generations of behavior therapists: Joe Wolpe, another founder of behavior therapy; Georg Eifert, a professor of clinical psychology who has developed and practiced behavior therapy principles on three continents during the past fifteen years; and Joe Plaud, a newer scholar and contributor to this debate who has had several publications addressing the relation of behavior theory to behavior therapy. We relate our analyses to the specific diagnostic categories discussed, examine future trends emerging from the preceding chapters, and elaborate upon the continuing relation of behavior theory to behavior therapy. The book concludes with an appeal to all scientist–practitioners to continue with the critical evaluation and application of the principles of behavior to the alleviation of human suffering in all age groups.

An Invitation

As we approach the final years of the twentieth century, a century that witnessed the birth of the behavior therapy movement, it becomes increasingly important to reexamine the forces that shaped the development, advancement, and success of behavior therapy. The limitations of early conditioning models and treatments have led many behavior therapists to abandon behaviorist principles and replace them with loosely defined cognitive theories and treatments. Systematic theory extensions to human behavior, using new concepts and processes derived from and built upon the basic principles, can help prevent further divisive debates over whether psychological dysfunctions are the result of conditioning *or* cognition and whether they should be treated with conditioning *or* cognitive techniques.

The chapters in this book analyze how major behavioral theories and research have contributed to the advancement of behavior therapy. In view of the fact that many behavior therapists have lost touch with the relation between behavior theory and behavior therapy, and faced with the challenges of the "cognitive revolution," the field stands to benefit conceptually and practically from integrating and utilizing the resources provided by recent advances in basic behavioral theory and research. The chapters in this book attempt to build conceptual, methodological, and practical bridges to help behavior therapists (a) gain a better understanding of the dysfunctional processes involved in different adult and childhood disorders and (b) recognize and use basic behavioral research and concepts for assessment as well as planning and implementation of treatment. We invite the reader to consider at all points the richness that an understanding of behavior theory can give to the creative design and implementation of behavior therapy techniques. If this book helps readers to make their therapies more science-based and more effective, it will have served its purpose.

References

Barlow, D. H. (Ed.). (1993). *Clinical handbook of psychological disorders* (2nd ed.). New York: Guilford.

Beck, A. T., & Emery, G., with Greenberg, R. L. (1985). *Anxiety disorders and phobias: A cognitive perspective.* New York: Basic Books.

Eifert, G. H. (1990). The acquisition and treatment of phobic anxiety: A paradigmatic behavioral perspective. In G. H. Eifert & I. M. Evans (Eds.), *Unifying behavior therapy: Contributions of paradigmatic behaviorism* (pp. 173–200). New York: Springer.

Eifert, G. H., & Evans, I. M. (Eds.). (1990). *Unifying behavior therapy: Contributions of paradigmatic behaviorism.* New York: Springer.

Evans, I. M., Eifert, G. H., & Corrigan, S. A. (1990). A critical appraisal of paradigmatic behaviorism's contribution to behavior therapy. In G. H. Eifert & I. M. Evans (Eds.), *Unifying behavior therapy: Con-tributions of paradigmatic behaviorism* (pp. 293–317). New York: Springer.

Eysenck, H. J. (1972). Behaviour therapy is behaviouristic. *Behavior Therapy, 3,* 609–613.

Eysenck, H. J. (1987). Behavior therapy. In H. J. Eysenck & I. M. Martin (Eds.), *Theoretical foundations of behavior therapy* (pp. 3–35). New York: Plenum.

Giles, T. R. (Ed.). (1993). *Handbook of effective psychotherapy.* New York: Plenum.

Hayes, S. C. (1987). A contextual approach to therapeutic behavior change. In N. Jacobson (Ed.), *Psychotherapists in clinical practice: Cognitive and behavioral approaches.* New York: Guilford.

Hayes, S. C., & Hayes, L. (1992). Some clinical implications of contextual behaviorism: The example of cognition. *Behavior Therapy, 23,* 225–249.

Hayes, S. C., Jacobson, N. S., Follette, V. M., & Dougher, M. J. (1994). *Acceptance and change: Content and context in psychotherapy.* Reno: Context Press.

Kazdin, A. E. (1978). *History of behavior modification: Experimental foundations of contemporary research.* Baltimore: University Press.

Kendall, P. C. (Ed.). (1991). *Child and adolescent therapy: Cognitive-behavioral approaches.* New York: Guilford.

Krasner, L. (1988). Paradigm lost: On a historical/sociological/economic perspective. In D. Fishman, F. Rotgers, & C. Franks (Eds.), *Paradigms in behavior therapy* (pp. 23–44). New York: Springer.

Levey, A. B., & Martin, I. M. (1987). Evaluative conditioning: A case for hedonic transfer. In H. J. Eysenck & I. M. Martin (Eds.), *Theoretical foundations of behavior therapy* (pp. 113–132). New York: Plenum.

Mace, F. C., Hock, M. L., Lalli, J. S., West, B. J., Belfiore, P., Pinter, E., & Brown, D. K. (1988). Behavioral momentum in the treatment of noncompliance. *Journal of Applied Behavior Analysis, 21,* 123–141.

Meichenbaum, D. (1977). *Cognitive-behavior modification: An integrative approach.* New York: Plenum.

Meyer, L. H., & Evans, I. M. (1989). *Non-aversive intervention for behavior problems: A manual for home and community.* Baltimore: Paul H. Brookes.

Marks, I. (1981). Behavioral concepts in the treatment of neuroses. *Behavioural Psychotherapy, 9,* 137–154.

Nevin, J. A. (1992). An integrative model for the study of behavioral momentum. *Journal of the Experimental Analysis of Behavior, 57,* 301–316.

Nevin, J. A., Mandell, C., & Atak, J. R. (1983). The analysis of behavioral momentum. *Journal of the Experimental Analysis of Behavior, 39,* 49–59.

O'Donohue, W., & Plaud, J. J. (1994). The conditioning of human sexual arousal. *Archives of Sexual Behavior, 23,* 321–344.

Peterson, L. (1993). Behavior therapy: The long and winding road. *Behavior Therapy, 24,* 1–5.

Plaud, J. J. (1993). Paradigmatic behaviorism, pragmatic philosophy and unified science. *The Behavior Therapist, 16,* 101–103.

Plaud, J. J., & Gaither, G. A. (1996). Behavioral momentum: Implications and development from reinforcement theories. *Behavior Modification, 20,* 183–201 (in press).

Plaud, J. J., Gaither, G. A., & Lawrence, J. B. (In press). Operant schedule transformations and human behavioral momentum. *Journal of Behavior Therapy and Experimental Psychiatry.*

Plaud, J. J., & Vogeltanz, N. (1991). Behavior therapy: Lost ties to animal research? *The Behavior Therapist, 14,* 89–93, 115.

Plaud, J. J., & Vogeltanz, N. D. (1993). Behavior therapy and the experimental analysis of behavior: Contributions of the science of human behavior and radical behavioral philosophy. *Journal of Behavior Therapy and Experimental Psychiatry, 24,* 119–127.

Rachman, S. (1977). The conditioning theory of fear acquisition. *Behaviour Research and Therapy, 15,* 375–387.

Ross, A. O. (1985). To form a more perfect union: It is time to stop standing still. *Behavior Therapy, 16,* 195–204.

Scotti, J. R., McMorrow, M. J., & Trawitzki, A. L. (1993). Behavioral treatment of chronic psychiatric disorders: Publication trends and future directions. *Behavior Therapy, 24,* 527–550.

Skinner, B. F. (1974). *About behaviorism.* London: Jonathan Cape.

Skinner, B. F. *The Behavior of Organisms.* New York: Appleton-Century-Crofts.

Staats, A. W. (1972). Language behavior therapy: A derivative of social behaviorism. *Behavior Therapy, 3,* 165–192.

Staats, A. W., & Eifert, G. H. (1990). A paradigmatic behaviorism theory of emotion: Basis for unification. *Clinical Psychology Review, 10,* 539–566.

Ullmann, L., & Krasner, L. (1969). *A psychological approach to abnormal behavior.* New York: Prentice-Hall.

Wolpe, J. (1958). *Psychotherapy by reciprocal inhibition.* Palo Alto, CA: Stanford University Press.

Wolpe, J. (1990). *The practice of behavior therapy* (4th ed.). New York: Pergamon.

Watts, F. N., McKenna, F. P., Sharrock, R., & Trezise, L. (1986). Colour naming of phobia-related words. *British Journal of Clinical Psychology, 77,* 97–108.

2

PHILOSOPHICAL AND THEORETICAL FOUNDATIONS OF BEHAVIOR THERAPY

ARTHUR C. HOUTS
Department of Psychology
University of Memphis

LEONARD KRASNER
Stanford University
School of Medicine

Since its inception during the post–World War II emergence of American and British clinical psychology and psychiatry, behavior therapy has comprised a diverse confederation of behavioral scientists who viewed their work as marking a break with certain traditional assumptions about human behavior. In this sense, behavior therapy was a protest movement held together by a common understanding that the then-dominant view of inner dynamic causes of human behavior needed to be replaced with a more objective analysis that featured outer, environmental causes (Krasner, 1971). In addition to embracing a more behavioristic theory of psychology, behavior therapists were also united by a general endorsement of certain philosophical assumptions about how to build reliable knowledge, a science of behavior, that would be the basis for better interventions to reduce human suffering in the mental health field.

Standing as we do at the close of the second half of the twentieth century, it is useful to reflect on this diverse array of investigators who launched a new approach to mental health problems at the close of the first half of the century. As an identifiable and cohesive community of behavioral scientists, behavior therapy is approaching the age of fifty years. What has become of this distinctive set of ideas over the course of nearly fifty years? How have the core ideas of behavior therapy changed over this period? Would a profile of the beliefs and values of the first generation of behavior therapists be endorsed or even recognized by a subsequent generation?

These questions are the focus of this chapter, but before we address them using our own approach, it is important to note that others have also begun to reflect on what has developed as behavior therapy over the past half century. Two prominent participant–observers of the behavior-therapy movement, Skinner and Wolpe, addressed these questions and arrived at rather pessimistic evaluations about the continuity of ideas as well as prospects for the future.

Skinner's relevance to the behavior-therapy movement was always central as one of the founders, having coined the term "behavior therapy" to describe early work that extended animal laboratory findings to human patients in the Metropolitan State Hospital in Waltham, Massachusetts (Lindsley, Skinner, & Solomon, 1953). The title of Skinner's paper in the August, 1987 issue of the *American Psychologist*, "Whatever Happened to Psychology as the Science of Behavior?", expressed his disenchantment with the current scene in behavior therapy and psychology more generally. His chief complaint was how the entire field had been swept away with enthusiasm for cognitive psychology.

> *A curve showing the appearance of the word* cognitive *in the psychological literature would be interesting. A first rise could probably be seen around 1960; the subsequent acceleration would be exponential. Is there any field of psychology today in which something does not seem to be gained by adding that charming adjective to the occasional noun? The popularity may not be hard to explain. When we became psychologists, we learned new ways of talking about human behavior. If they were "behavioristic," they were not very much like the old ways. The old terms were taboo, and eyebrows were raised when we used them. But when certain developments seemed to show that the old ways might be right after all, everyone could relax. Mind was back. Cognitive psychologists like to say that "the mind is what the brain does," but surely the rest of the body plays a part. The mind is what the* body *does. It is what the* person *does. In other words, it is behavior, and that is what behaviorists have been saying for more than half a century (pp. 783–784).*

In looking back over his half century of developing the experimental analysis of behavior, Skinner was not sanguine about how the field of psychology had developed, and he placed blame on cognitive psychology and the helping professions that offered psychotherapy.

As major contributor to and founder of the behavior-therapy movement, Wolpe expressed his disenchantment in a 1986 paper in *Comprehensive Psychiatry* entitled "Misrepresentation and Underemployment of Behavior Therapy." This was also a bitter paper in which Wolpe reviewed current psychiatry, psychology, and psychotherapy literature to demonstrate his contention that "Despite its well-documented record of success in the treatment of the neuroses, behavior therapy is little taught in departments of psychiatry because of an inaccurate image based on misinformation" (p. 192). He documented and illustrated with research reports and literature reviews the claim that "Misinformation about behavior therapy has a long history. The earliest reports elicited a great deal of scorn from the psychiatric establishment" (p. 192). For example, Wolpe referred to a review of his 1958 book *Psychotherapy by Reciprocal Inhibition* that had many factual errors, and he noted that "Misreporting, often with pejorative overtones, has been the rule ever since" (p. 192). Similar to Skinner's lament about the rise of cognitive ideas, Wolpe noted that:

More harmful of late have been allegations by the cognitivists that revive in a new way the idea of behavior therapy being simple and mechanistic. In promoting a number of idiosyncratic cognitive techniques that they claim (without justification) to have improved the results of behavior therapy, they also assert that standard behavior therapy overlooks thoughts and feelings (p. 193).

In effect, according to Wolpe, the theoretical and practical roots of behavior therapy were deviated from, misunderstood, and misrepresented.

These two rather bleak assessments of "whatever happened to behavior therapy" have also been counterbalanced with more hopeful assessments. For example, two more recent presidential addresses to the Association for the Advancement of Behavior Therapy welcomed the inclusion of cognitive ideas and projected a bright future for the field (Craighead, 1990; Kendall, 1992).

Our own approach to "whatever happened to behavior therapy" has been different in that we have been engaged in an ongoing study of the "value systems" of the scientists who started behavior therapy and continue to expand the field (Krasner & Houts, 1984). Our approach is intended to be more descriptive than evaluative. Yet our own framework for studying the philosophical and theoretical assumptions of behavioral scientists impels us to recognize that we, too, endorse implicit and perhaps unacknowledged values in our choice of methods and questions. In this respect, we can be rather explicit about the assumptions we endorse regarding the question of values in science.

The Question of "Values" in Science

In our earlier work we noted that the question about the role of values in science had been framed around the issue of whether or not scientific claims and procedures were either value-free or value-laden (Krasner & Houts, 1984). In the past decade this has been a continuing theme in the interdisciplinary field known as science studies. Although one can find instances where commentators on the field have upheld the value-free position (Gross & Levitt, 1994; Weinberg, 1992; Wolpert, 1992), the overwhelming majority of the literature on this question has served to strengthen and elaborate the position that science is value-laden. In our ongoing investigation of the value systems of behavioral scientists, we have continued to rely on the work of science studies scholars who have elaborated the proposition that science is fundamentally value-laden, rather than value-free.

Contributions from the History of Science

As we noted over a decade ago, studies in the history of science beginning with Kuhn's (1962) seminal work, *The Structure of Scientific Revolutions,* have dislodged the picture of scientific change as being characterized by ever more progressive knowledge that is objective and detached from human influence. Due to Kuhn's influence on the field, the very concepts of history of science have changed. Even those who opposed the more radical interpretations of Kuhn, such as Lakatos (1978) and Laudan (1977), ended up with conceptual bases for investigations into the history of science that included the role of assumptions and influences that went far beyond the antiseptic, rational reconstruction of orthodox logical empiricism (see reviews by Gholson & Barker, 1985; O'Donohue & Krasner, 1995). The pristine picture of theory change and theory development being driven solely by the objective discovery of new facts and the rigorous application of formal logic became muddied even in the eyes of those anti-Kuhnians who tried to salvage the traditional picture of scientific progress. An irony of these developments was that as professional historians of science began to investigate the "facts" of history across a wide array of disciplines, the "facts" did not fit with the tidy rationalist picture of the history of science championed by traditional historians and philosophers of science.

In rethinking some fundamental concepts for doing historical investigation, it became increasingly clear that the very ideas of objectivity and value neutrality were themselves ideas that arose in a certain historical context and were retained because they served a valuable rhetorical function in the scientific community. Historical and philosophical analyses similar to those of Gadamer (1974) have contributed to a rethinking of some of the fundamental concepts of history. Gadamer noted that the concept of prejudice arose in the context of eighteenth-century debates regarding theological matters. The claim that one side was biased functioned rhetorically to persuade listeners to take up the opposing side, which was by implication more objective. This connotation of bias with prejudice has been a fundamental strategy of those who have argued for the value-free position with respect to science. The claim takes the form that science and knowledge obtained by scientific methods is better than other approaches because it is free of bias, prejudice, and values. What is important in this context is that the idea of objectivity is itself not objective and value-free. As Gadamer noted, this contradiction then raises serious questions about concepts such as "*the* historical truth." The concept of "truth" itself has a history, and therefore it makes little sense to speak of "truth" with singularity in historical investigation.

For Gadamer (1974), the very idea of a bias or a prejudice in knowledge claims took on a different, largely positive meaning within his philosophical hermeneutics. Instead of trying to deny bias and prejudice in the understanding of history, Gadamer tried to elevate these concepts to a status of being taken for granted as inevitable. That is, bias and prejudice are inevitable, so why pretend otherwise? In this way, the whole point of studying history could then become highly relevant for understanding the present. The temporal distance between ourselves and ancient texts could then be turned to our advantage and made an asset rather than a liability. By confronting the differences between ancient cultures and our own contemporary culture, we could see our own biases and prejudices in operation. In this manner the problem of historical knowledge was made open-ended, and to understand the present became a major reason to study history.

Proctor (1991) has conducted a major historical analysis of the claim that science is value-free, and his analysis has placed this claim in relative historical context. In other words, the claim that science is value-free itself has a history as a claim, and to understand this history enables those on the current scene to appreciate how the claim of value neutrality is used today and what may be mistaken in such usage. Proctor has noted that the claim of value neutrality for science functioned as a shield at the turn of the century to protect the autonomy of science from political influence. In Germany, especially with Weber as a founder of value neutrality, this coincided with attempts to elevate the social sciences above various political and religious influences. "Value neutrality armed sociologists against movements to politicize or moralize the sciences" (Proctor, 1991, p. 265). In promoting the value neutrality of science, it was also necessary to locate values somewhere, and these were consigned to subjectivity and the private whims of individuals. "The complementary principles of neutral science and subjective value together provided the key elements in the liberal conception of science and society. Science was rendered impervious to moral critique, morals and religion were left unmarked by advances in scientific knowledge" (p. 266). In effect, Proctor has argued that the idea of science as a value-neutral enterprise was an idea created to serve certain purposes, mostly political ones, where issues of values were to be avoided so that disciplines could be established and protected as self-sustaining with the aid of public funds.

By historicizing the claim to value neutrality and thereby taking the claim down from its lofty philosophical pedestal, historians opened the door further toward scholars of science who pointed out the many ways in which science is value-laden. One important recent analysis was offered by Longino (1990), a philosopher of science who was influenced by recent historical and sociological analyses of science. In Longino's analysis, science is a type of social knowledge where values play a pervasive role. She has noted five ways in which values shape scientific knowledge.

1. *Practices.* Contextual values can affect practices that bear on the epistemic integrity of science.
2. *Questions.* Contextual values can determine which questions are asked and which ignored about a given phenomenon.
3. *Data.* Contextual values can affect the description of data, that is, value-laden terms may be employed in the description of experimental or observational data, and values may influence the selection of data or of kinds of phenomena to be investigated.
4. *Specific assumptions.* Contextual values can be expressed in or motivate the background assumptions facilitating inferences in specific areas of inquiry.
5. *Global assumptions.* Contextual values can be expressed in or motivate the acceptance of global, frameworklike assumptions that determine the character of research in an entire field (Longino, 1990, p. 86).

Longino's analysis is very close to the one we offered in our previous work, and we think that she has made a significant advance toward detailing the many ways in which science is value-laden. It is worth noting that Longino does not go as far as some recent radical sociologists in denying a significant role to the "natural world" in constraining the kinds of knowledge claims that are made. In this respect, her analysis is more moderate, while still embracing a value-laden view of science.

Contributions from Sociology of Science

Among the four core disciplines that compose the field of science studies (history, philosophy, psychology, and sociology of science), sociology of science has undergone the most radical and sweeping changes in the past decade (Jasanoff et al., 1994; Pickering, 1992). Although considerable efforts have been made to establish and expand psychology of science (Gholson et al., 1989; Giere, 1992; Gorman, 1992; Shadish & Fuller, 1994), most of this work has focused on cognitive psychology or cognitive science and has not directly addressed the issue of values in science to the extent that sociologists have continued to address this important issue. Some understanding of these developments in the sociology of science is useful to place in critical context the approach that we have pursued in our ongoing study of the value systems of behavioral scientists.

The question of values in science has always been of major concern to sociologists of science. In his early formulations of sociology of science, Merton (1938) attributed the rise of modern science to the influence of surrounding cultural values, especially Puritanism in seventeenth-century England. This fundamental idea that the development and progress of science was somehow significantly influenced by development and changes in the larger culture surrounding the scientific community was always a controversial assertion. Although a number of investigators may have granted that modern science arose out of particular cultural traditions, they were also quick to close the door on the possibility that further developments in science could be significantly influenced by cultural traditions. This was, after all, the point of asserting that scientific knowledge and scientific procedures ensure a high degree of value neutrality. The structural-functional school of sociology of science, founded by Merton, developed as the "objective" study of scientific communities. Studies of the reward system in science and social stratification were the hallmark of this approach (e.g., Cole & Cole, 1973; Merton, 1973; Zuckerman & Merton, 1971). Within this approach to the sociology of science, basic epistemological assumptions regarding the validity of scientific procedures were not questioned. Indeed, the scientific community was largely valorized by this approach.

Maintaining science in its traditional and culturally privileged place with respect to other approaches to knowledge did not last in the sociology of science (Mulkay, 1980). The sociology of interests and values asserted that the notion that scientific procedures guaranteed some form of objective knowledge was false (Barnes, 1974, 1982). Instead, these investigators pointed to such societal influences as military and industrial funding of science. This macrosociological critique focused on the larger social and cultural contexts in which scientific research proceeded. The idea of the lone scientist assiduously following scientific procedures and arriving at an objective view of the world was rejected. Also, the Mertonian view of the scientific community as being guided by certain noble norms was discredited by empirical investigations of the behavior of scientists. In the sociology of science, based on the analysis of interests and values, the scientific community as an object of study lost its innocence.

The sociology of interests and values formed much of the background of our own study of value systems of the behavioral scientists who made up the behavior therapy movement in the decade following World War II. Using survey methods that are described below, we assessed the values that behavior therapists held about science, about psychology, and about major cultural, religious, and political concepts. We have continued that approach by extending the survey methods to the second generation of behavioral scientists and comparing them with the second generation of a sample of psychologists who were not affiliated with the behavior-therapy movement. Before turning to a description of the methods and a report of our findings, it is important to note that the sociology of science has changed considerably in recent years since our approach was first developed.

Constructivist Sociology of Science and "Relativism"

Whereas previous sociologists of science found values and interests at work in the relationship between the scientific community and the larger community that funded and supported scientific work, the most recent sociologists of science have found "values and interests" at work in the day-to-day operations of the scientific laboratory. Known under various banners such as social constructivists, radical relativists, and "actor network theorists," this loosely knit group of investigators pioneered the intensive case study of working scientific laboratories (Collins, 1985; Collins & Pinch, 1982; Gilbert & Mulkay, 1984; Knorr-Cetina, 1981; Knorr-Cetina & Mulkay, 1983; Latour, 1987; Latour & Woolgar, 1986; Pickering, 1984; Woolgar, 1988). For present purposes of placing our own investigation into the larger context of science and technology studies, the most important difference between these sociologists of science and their immediate predecessors concerned their challenge to traditional epistemology (see reviews by Fuller, 1988, 1989). These investigators took the sociological analysis of knowledge to its logical but rather extreme conclusion in noting that the object of knowledge in scientific inquiries, "nature," is itself constructed or manufactured from the activities of the scientific investigators. This radical claim challenged one of the major conclusions of older sociology of knowledge (e.g., Mannheim, 1936; Stark, 1958), which had arrived at the traditional conclusion that knowledge obtained from scientific methods was somehow special precisely because it was not manufactured from whole cloth by human imagination and activity. In the more recent and radical analysis of the sociology of knowledge, scientific knowledge was said to be on an equal footing with other claims to knowledge throughout various cultures. According to this analysis, the Archimedean point of universal objective knowledge was lost, and the point of view ushered in a kind of relativism. Various investigators have disagreed over how far to take the point about cultural relativism. However, almost all agree that the traditional notion of universally applicable laws of nature must be abandoned as a figment of the imagination of modern scientific culture.

A brief digression about the issue of relativism is important because the charge of relativism, typically functioning as an epithet, has often been leveled against those who have claimed that science is value-laden rather than value-free, and the constructivist sociologists have received their share of scorn in this regard (e.g., Bunge, 1992; Slezak, 1989). A first thing to note is that the very concept of relativism as the absence of any universally accepted standard invokes the concept of "universally accepted standard." In the relativism vs. objectivism game of binary logic, there are only two ways out. The rhetorical moves of this game have been explicated most eloquently by Smith (1988), who has provided an extensive analysis of the verbal exhanges that have taken place over this issue in the context of aesthetics. The moves are the same as those played out in the repetitive debates regarding the relativism charge about science being value-laden. For example, to assert that science is value-laden has often been taken by opponents of the position as necessarily implying that one scientific theory is as good (or bad) as any other, because standards of appraisal are also value-laden. Smith (1988) has called this the "egalitarian fallacy":

> *We may take note here of the recurrent anxiety/charge/claim—I shall refer to it as the Egalitarian Fallacy—that, unless one judgment can be said or shown to be more "valid" than another, then all judgments must be "equal" or "equally valid." Although the radical contingency of all value certainly does imply that no value judgment can be more "valid" than another* in the sense *of an objectively truer statement of the objective value of an object (for these latter concepts are then seen as vacuous), it does not follow that all value judgments are equally valid. On the contrary, what does follow is that the concept of "validity"* in that sense *is unavailable as a parameter by which to measure or compare judgments (or anything else) (p. 98).*

In making a claim that science is value-laden rather than value-free, what is asserted is that the very idea of value neutrality is mistaken. Just as nothing whatsoever is claimed regarding the value of some set of ideas and assumptions relative to a mythical objective standard, so nothing is precluded regarding the comparative value of some set of ideas and assumptions relative to another set of ideas and assumptions. Scientists and those who study scientists can and do make relative value judgments in many aspects of their work. In asserting that science and science studies are both value-laden, nothing is lost *relative* to some universal foundation or absolute standard, because such a universal foundation or absolute standard is precisely what is being rejected.

Interestingly, a number of social constructivist sociologists have embraced, almost always implicitly rather than explicitly, a kind of psychological behaviorism. Like behaviorists, they eschew any form of mentalism, cognitive representationalism, and the centrality of the human as agent (Woolgar, 1989). Like behaviorist psychologists, they also base their claims about the scientific enterprise on intensive, local, direct observation of scientists at work in addition to the verbal reports of scientists about their work. It should be noted, however, that with the exception of Bloor (1983) who acknowledged Skinner's epistemological points in the analysis of verbal behavior, most of these constructivist sociologists do not refer directly to nor give credit for influence from behaviorial psychologists. The similarities between behavior analysis, operational analysis, and various social constructivist analyses of scientific laboratories have been elaborated in more detail in two previous papers (Houts, 1994; Houts & Haddock, 1992).

One important reading of the constructivist sociologist's work is that just as the object of study in natural science investigation, "nature," is very much a product of human invention by way of interacting with the object, so too are the objects of social science investigation. In this regard, values and interests are to a significant degree objects manufactured by the investigator as he or she interacts with the subjects (scientists) under investigation. In this regard, our previous investigation and the follow-up investigation reported below should be seen as the results of our efforts to arrange circumstances for our research subjects to produce responses that we could then label as expressions about values and assumptions. We are not claiming to have accomplished anything more, and we are satisfied with an analysis of our own work based on a behavioral analysis of verbal behavior. In fact, we would encourage readers to avoid the all-too-easy inference that we have somehow revealed the "minds" and "cognitive biases" of behavioral scientists.

A Psychological Approach to "Values" in Science

What our approach contributes to the study of values in science is a psychological perspective on the question of how groups of scientists cohere and maintain their identity over time. Our approach is decidedly psychological because we suppose that individuals come to endorse certain distinctive beliefs that are widely held by other members of their group. We refer to these beliefs and assumptions as "values" because we suppose that they are determined more by where one goes to school, what the social contingencies for a successful career are, and who one associates with, rather than by some rational weighing of "the evidence." To put it rather simply, we suppose that the fundamental beliefs and assumptions of scientists are mostly a matter of "I like it" or "I don't like it." Further in agreement with some sociological analyses, we are inclined to view most of the "good reasons" and rational arguments for particular beliefs and assumptions as coming after the fact of their acquisition rather than before, as in traditional rational reconstructions of scientific reasoning.

In our approach to studying the values of behavioral scientists, we have used a combination of survey methodology and psychometric techniques for summarizing responses to questionnaires. We have recognized the reflexive nature of this investigation. That is, we have employed some rather traditional psychological methods to study the psychology of psychologists (and psychiatrists). We made such assumptions as: (1) a subject's verbal response (assent or dissent) to a verbal stimulus can tell us something useful about what the subject believes, (2) a subject's verbal response to a questionnaire item is at least correlated with the subject's practices when he or she evaluates knowledge claims in the far richer social context of actual scientific work, and (3) the summarization of subjects' responses provide us with at least a partial picture of the shared values of the community of scientists to which the subject belongs. We also assumed that the fruitfulness of our approach should be judged according to the outcomes achieved. We have become increasingly aware, as the foregoing review attests, that much work can and needs to be done to further our understanding of the psychological community by taking rather different approaches, such as the analysis of citation patterns, phenomenological value analysis of the texts produced by major psychologists, experimental studies of the review process, and historical and sociological case studies of influential laboratories and graduate programs.

From this perspective, we turn to the methods we employed to study the value systems of behavioral scientists in the second generation of the behavior-therapy movement. Following the presentation of methods, we report the results we obtained. In the final section of the chapter we discuss the implications of our results for the behavior-therapy movement and for the future of studies of scientists as subjects.

Groups and Methods

Five groups of scientists have been included in our investigations: (1) Behavior Therapy Founders, 1945–1955; (2) Comparison Psychologists, 1945–1955; (3) Students of Behavior Therapy Founders, 1956–1975; (4) Students of Comparison Psychologists, 1956–1975; and (5) Second-Generation Behavior Therapy Contributors to Journals, 1956–1975. Results for the first two groups were reported in Krasner and Houts (1984) and represented the first generation of behavioral scientists along with a comparison group of nonbehavioral psychologists who were active in the same period from 1945 to 1955. We then collected responses from three second-generation groups. Two of these groups, the behavioral students and the comparison students, were individuals nominated by our first-generation groups in response to the request to list their outstanding students. These two student groups represented the direct decendents of our first-generation samples. A third group from the second generation comprised scientists who were active in the behavior therapy movement by way of publications but who were not direct decendents of the original founders of behavior therapy.

Our first pool of subjects, the first generation, was recruited by letters of invitation and contained 230 psychologists who were active in the period 1945 to 1955. The group comprising the innovators of behavior therapy consisted of 130 behavioral scientists who met the following criteria: (a) self-identification of their work as behavior therapy during the period 1946 to 1976, (b) citation of the subject's work in publications on behavior therapy in the thirty-year period, (c) at least one publication or presentation prior to 1956 (dissertations included), and (d) professional contact with at least one other member of this group. Of this sample, 87 subjects provided usable responses to our measures for an overall response rate of 67 percent. Our original comparison sample consisted of 100 psychologists who were randomly selected from first authors of all articles published in APA journals (there were only six journals) from 1945 to 1956. These individuals did not identify their work as behavior therapy and were not conducting research around a common theme. Complete information was returned by 37 percent of this sample. Responses from these two groups were collected over a two-year period from 1979 to 1981, and the results of this study were reported in Krasner and Houts (1984).

In the three-year period of 1984 to 1987, similar data were collected from three additional samples of behavioral scientists who formed the second generation. All three groups met the criteria of obtaining their doctoral degrees after 1955 and before 1976. The first of these three pools of subjects contained 174 students named by our original behavioral subjects as their outstanding students. From this group, 62 completed all aspects of the study for a response rate of 36 percent. The second subject pool consisted of the 69 students nominated by our original comparison group, and complete information was obtained for 17 subjects for a response rate of 25 percent. The third subject pool contained 209 behavioral scientists whose names appeared on two or more publications in one of six behavioral journals (*Behaviorism, Behavior Therapy, Behaviour Research and Therapy, Journal of Applied Behavior Analysis, Journal of Behavior Therapy and Experimental Psychiatry, Journal of the Experimental Analysis of Behavior*) from their inception to 1975. Complete information was obtained for 57 subjects for a response rate of 27 percent.

With the exception of the rather high return rate for the original behavioral group, our return rates for the other four groups were comparable to the typical response rates obtained in other surveys of professional groups. We were able to assess the representativeness of our samples by collecting data from nonresponders and by comparing the results obtained for those who responded on the first as opposed to the second wave of recruitment via mail (Rossi, Wright, & Anderson, 1983). In these analyses of nonresponders and late responders (considered hypothetically as nonresponders), we found the same pattern of results as in our analyses of those who responded to the first wave of recruitment. It is likely that our findings are representative of the groups from which we sampled.

Measures

In the extension of our original investigation to the second generation of behavioral scientists, we collected all of the demographic information and questionnaire data that we had collected from the first generation (Krasner & Houts, 1984). What is presented in this chapter is what we previously referred to as the discipline specific values that were assessed using two questionnaires, both of which asked respondents to indicate their agreement or disagreement (on a 5-point Likert scale) with statements about the best way to gain knowledge and with propositions of theoretical significance in psychology.

Epistemological Style Questionnaire (ESQ).   This twenty-four item set of questions was developed by Krasner and Houts (1984). The ESQ was desgined to measure agreement and disagreement with general epistemological propositions regarding how scientists should proceed to gain or advance knowledge. In our previous study we identified four clusters of items that proved interpretable and showed acceptable levels of internal consistency to be treated as separate subscales of the ESQ (Krasner & Houts, 1984). We replicated the factor structure of the ESQ using the second-generation sample and identified the same four internally consistent subscales: (1) Metaphorism, (2) Rationalism, (3) Reductionism, and (4) Antiempiricism.

The *Metaphorism* subscale of the ESQ contained eight items that yield a bipolar score indicating subjects' endorsement of or opposition to some basic assumptions about determinism and the relationship between psychology and the physical sciences. The basic concept behind higher scores on this subscale is agreement that determinism is an incorrect assumption and that psychology should avoid use of traditional methods such as those used in the physical sciences. Items scored in the positive direction and contributing to higher scores on the overall subscale indicate endorsement of an intuitive approach to knowledge along the lines advocated by humanistic psychologists (e.g., Maslow, 1968). Items scored in the negative direction and lowering the overall subscale score indicate rejection of the intuitive mode of knowing and endorsement of traditional rational and empirical science such as that found in traditional interpretations of the natural sciences (e.g., Hempel, 1965; Nagel, 1961).

The *Rationalism* subscale of the ESQ contained seven items. The basic idea of this subscale is endorsement of the belief that logical deduction and theoretical constructs are to be preferred as opposed to empirical observations and inductive inferences as alternative approaches to attaining knowledge. Higher scores on this scale indicate agreement with the general idea that rationally (logically) derived theory is superior to strict operationism and inductive inference from empirical observations. Individuals who scored higher on this subscale tended to agree with statements such as "Hypothetico-deductive method is superior to inductive method," and they disagreed with statements such as "Observation of raw data is both prior to and independent of theory."

The *Reductionism* subscale of the ESQ comprised three items. The basic idea of this subscale is that psychologists should follow theoretical and empirical reduction as a prescriptive practice to advance knowledge, and a higher score indicates endorsement of reductionism as an epistemological prescription.

The *Antiempiricism* subscale of the ESQ comprised six items scored for agreement or disagreement. Higher scores on this subscale indicated opposition to the view that data are "given" in some uncomplicated and objective manner to the scientific observer. Further, individuals who scored higher on this factor tended to doubt the traditional view that scientific disputes will be setttled if we just collect enough "raw data" and let the preponderance of evidence arbitrate our disagreements.

Theoretical Orientation Survey (TOS).   We used Coan's (1979) short version of the TOS which contains thirty-two items scored for agreement or disagreement. Coan demonstrated that the TOS can be reliably factored into eight subscales and provided reliable and valid data in his study of a national probability sample of psychologists. Krasner and Houts (1984) replicated Coan's subscale structure of the TOS, and the current sample of second-generation behavior scientists once again replicated the eight subscales.

With the exception of two subscales tapping endorsement of either *biological determinism* or *environmental determinism* and one other assessing agreement with *physicalism,* the remaining five subscales address agreement along bipolar theoretical beliefs relevant to psychology. Higher scores on the three aforementioned subscales indicate agreement with the respective concepts. The five bipolar subscales of the TOS include the following sets of beliefs: (1) Factual vs. theoretical orientation, (2) Impersonal causality vs. personal will, (3) Behavioral vs. experiential content emphasis, (4) Elementarism vs. holism in units of analysis, and (5) Quantitative vs. qualitative methods of analysis. Higher scores on the five bipolar subscales of the TOS indicate positive endorsement of the first and capitalized pole of the scale. For example, higher scores on (1) are typical of individuals or groups that agree to put a premium on data collection as opposed to building a theory.

Results

In what follows, we have presented our results in graphic rather than numerical form in order to show overall patterns in our data. Results from each of these questionnaires were factor analyzed to identify subscales that were then submitted to reliability analysis for internal consistency. Between group differences on subscales were established by multivariate analysis of variance, followed by one-way analysis of variance with follow-up tests according to the Tukey HSD method (.05 level of significance). Throughout the graphic presentations, we followed the convention of identifying statistically significant differences between group means on various subscales by labeling them with different superscripts. For example, for two data points along the same line in a given figure, if both have been labled "a," the means did *not* differ reliably. Likewise, if both were labeled "b," the means did not differ reliably. However, for data points along the same line in a figure, all those labeled "a" differed reliably from all those labeled "b," p < .05. If a data point along a line in a given figure has no superscript label, then that particular mean did not differ reliably from any of the others represented on the same line.

Figure 2-1 shows the results for all five groups on the Rationalism and Metaphorism subscales of the ESQ. As indicated by average scores on the Rationalism subscale, the three behavior-therapy groups were more likely to favor empiricism and inductive inference as opposed to theoretical speculation and logical deduction as the epistemological heuristic for advancing knowledge. A similar pattern was evident on the Metaphorism subscale of the ESQ. With the exception of the second-generation behavior-therapy group that entered via the journals (labeled Beh Journals), the same pattern held for the contrast between behavior therapists and their respective non-behavior-therapy contemporaries. That is, the behavior-therapy groups tended to endorse determinism as a working assumption, and they were also more sympathetic to the idea that psychology can advance by imitating the methods of the physical sciences. In contrast, the two comparison groups favored intuitive approaches to know-

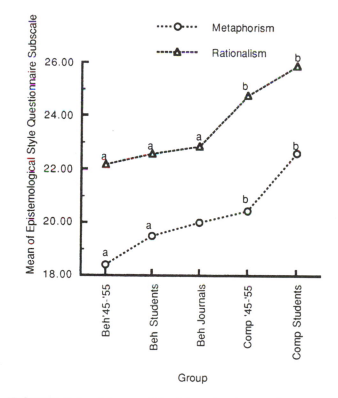

FIGURE 2-1. Means of the Metaphorism and Rationalism subscales of the Epistemological Style Questionnaire for three behavior therapy groups and two comparison groups. Means along the same line with a different superscript differ significantly, $p < .05$.

ledge and tended to reject the idea that social science methods should be the same as physical science methods.

Figure 2-2 shows the results for the five groups on the Reductionism and Antiempiricism subscales of the ESQ. On the Reductionism subscale, the three behavior-therapy groups differed significantly from the two comparison groups by favoring the belief that psychology can and should attempt to reduce its concepts to those consistent with the physical sciences. However, on the Antiempiricism subscale, the typical pattern differentiating the behavior-therapy groups from the comparison groups no longer held. There was a break within the behavior-therapy groups from first to second generation. Whereas the originators of the behavior-therapy movement endorsed the belief that data will prevail, both second-generation groups are more like the nonbehavioral comparison groups in doubting the primacy of data.

To summarize the findings on basic assumptions about how knowledge is best attained, we found a clear difference between members of the behavior-therapy move-

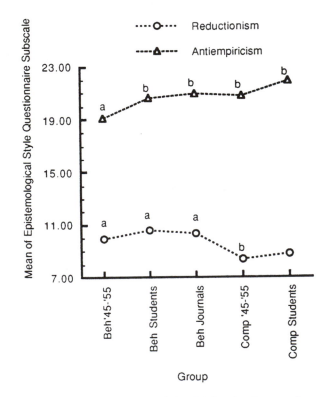

FIGURE 2-2.   Means of the Reductionism and Antiempiricism subscales of the Epistemological Style Questionnaire for three behavior therapy groups and two comparison groups. Means along the same line with a different superscript differ significantly, p < .05.

ment and comparison samples that was maintained across two generations. The one exception to this general trend of continuity was the discontinuity observed between the first-generation behavioral group and the second-generation behavioral groups with respect to the objectivity and primacy of data. Another way of saying this is that what is to be counted as a "fact of the matter" appears to have become problematic for the behavior-therapy movement in the second generation. Further, there seems to be considerable doubt as to whether "facts of the matter," even if they could be established, are believed to be the final arbiters of what theories get the upper hand in psychology. Yet another way of saying this is that the second-generation behavioral groups abandoned the article of faith that stated that data may be taken to be objective and the bottom line in decisions to accept or reject a theory.

For the most part, the overall pattern of our findings on the TOS subscales was similar to that observed on the ESQ subscales. Figure 2-3 shows results for four of the eight

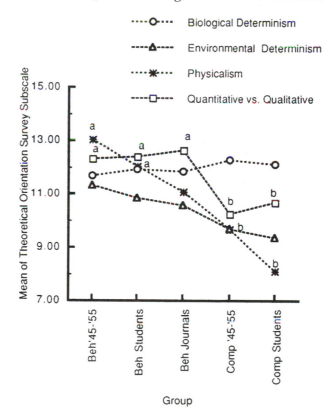

FIGURE 2-3.   Means of the Biological Determinism, Environmental Determinism, Physicalism, and Quantitative vs. Qualitative subscales of the Theoretical Orientation Survey for three behavior therapy groups and two comparison groups. Means along the same line with a different superscript differ significantly, p < .05.

TOS scales. Interestingly, the five groups did not differ significantly on their endorsements of Biological and Environmental determinism as assumptions about human behavior. With respect to Physicalism, the first-generation behavior-therapy group and their second-generation students were more sympathetic to this belief than the two comparison groups. The second-generation behavior-therapy group that entered the movement via journal contributions was not reliably different from any of the other four groups on this dimension. With respect to quantitative as opposed to qualitative methods, the familiar pattern was observed with the three behavior-therapy groups differing reliably from the comparison groups by favoring quantitative as opposed to qualitative methods of analysis and research synthesis.

Figure 2-4 shows group differences for the other four subscales of the TOS. Once again, the familiar pattern was present with the three behavioral groups differing from

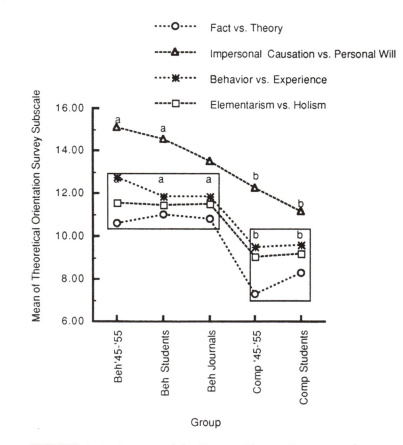

FIGURE 2-4. Means of the Fact vs. Theory, Impersonal Causation vs. Personal Will, Behavior vs. Experience, and Elementarism vs. Holism subscales of the Theoretical Orientation Survey for three behavior therapy groups and two comparison groups. Means along the same line with a different superscript differ significantly, $p < .05$.

the two comparison groups. In contrast to the comparison samples across both genera-tions, the behavior-therapy groups across both generations endorsed the primacy of fact and observation over theory and speculation, the primacy of observable behavior over personal subjective experience, and the greater emphasis on analysis of constituent parts over holistic types of analysis. The only exception to the familar pattern of differ-ences between the five groups on these four subscales of the TOS occurred with the second-generation behavior-therapy group that entered the movement via the journals. This group failed to differ reliably from the other four groups in terms of endorsing the belief of impersonal causation as opposed to personal will as a controlling factor in hu-man behavior.

As another means of summarizing these findings on the ESQ and TOS, we conducted a second-order factor analysis of the four ESQ and eight TOS subscales.

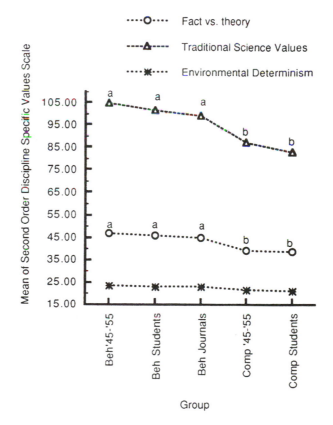

FIGURE 2-5.   Means of Second Order Disci-pline Specific factors (Fact vs. Theory, Traditional Science Values, and Environmental Determinism) for three behavior therapy groups and two com-parison groups. Means along the same line with a different superscript differ significantly, $p < .05$.

This analysis resulted in reducing the twelve subscales to three interpretable and highly reliable second-order scales. We referred to these three second-order scales as Second Order Discipline Specific values to distinguish them from our more general measures of values concerning matters like social and political philosophy, which are not reported in this chapter. The three Second Order Discipline Specific scales are: Fact vs. Theory, Traditional Scientific Values, and Environmental Determinism. The Fact vs. Theory scale refers to subjects' endorsement of empiricism and observation as opposed to abstract and theoretical speculation. The Traditional Scientific Values scale represents endorsement of rather standard empirical social science values, such as that theoretical and empirical reductionism is to be preferred, terms should be operationally defined, and quantitative methods are superior to qualitative analysis. The Environmental Determinism scale simply refers to subjects' endorsement of environmental as opposed to biological determinism as a fundamental belief about human behavior.

Figure 2-5 shows the results for all five groups on these three Second Order Discipline Specific scales. Here we can see the clear overall pattern where the three behavioral groups do not differ from each other, but they clearly differ from the two comparison groups on the Fact vs. Theory and the Traditional Scientific Values dimensions. As you would expect from the earlier presentation of TOS factors, the five groups failed to differ reliably from each other in terms of their endorsement of environmental as opposed to biological determinism.

Continuity and Discontinuity of Values and the Future of Behavior Therapy

Our investigation of the philosophical and theoretical assumptions of individuals identified with the behavior-therapy movement over two generations has shown that there is considerable continuity in basic values that distinguished the behavior-therapy movement from other contemporary psychologists. However, there is also some indication from our findings that there is discontinuity among behavioral scientists between the first and second generations. These discontinuities are of interest in making speculative guesses about the future of the behavior-therapy movement.

Continuity of the Values of Behavioral Scientists

We found a repeated overall pattern across the different subscales of the ESQ and TOS such that the individuals identified with the behavior-therapy movement were, for the most part, consistently different from their respective contemporaries who were not identified with the behavior-therapy movement. This overall pattern in our findings is consistent with Kuhn's (1970) observations that communities of scientists share a disciplinary matrix and set of practices otherwise known as a paradigm. When one looks at the behavior-therapy movement against a backdrop of contemporary social scientists not identified with the behavior-therapy movement, the behavior-therapy movement stands out as being clearly different in terms of the endorsement of certain philosophical and theoretical assumptions. For the most part, these differences between behavior therapists and their contemporaries remained as significant differences across two generations of scientists spanning the period of 1945 to 1975.

When we aggregated our individual subscales to form second-order factors, we obtained a more global assessment of the differences between members of the behavior-therapy movement and their contemporaries. Behavior therapists in both generations were clearly distinguished from their respective nonbehavioral cohorts by endorsing the primacy of basic observation and empiricism over philosophical speculation and theory-building. In this regard, the behavior-therapy movement has represented a point in the continuing historical stream of modern psychology's movement away from speculative philosophy and abstract theorizing toward a more empirical and observational foundation (Boring, 1950; Kantor, 1963). However much behavior therapists may argue among themselves about the purity of one or another subset of values held commonly among behavior therapists, it is worth pointing out and emphasizing that behavior therapy continues to be an identifiably distinct community when contrasted against the background of alternative views in psychology.

In our aggregated analyses, we also found that behavior therapists were distinguished from their respective contemporaries in their strong endorsement of what we termed *Traditional Science Values.* This label reflected the strong preference of behavior therapists for such features of their discipline as: quantitative as opposed to qualitative analyses; operational definition of terms; experimental and empirical methods of investigation; a more rational and empirical, as opposed to intuitive, epistemology; and the endorsement of some version of the unity of science thesis wherein the social sciences are viewed as sharing common methods of investigation with the physical sciences if not reducibility from one to the other. Interestingly, our analyses also showed that at the more global level, behavior therapists across both generations were not distinguished from their respective cohorts with respect to environmental determinism and biological determinism. Contrary to the caricature of behavior therapists as rejecting physiological and genetic influences on behavior, this finding should clarify that the behavior therapy movement is not so simplistic as to place all causal emphasis on environmental factors to the exclusion of physiological and genetic ones.

Discontinuity of Values between Generations of Behavior Therapists

Although we found rather striking continuity of basic values from one generation to the next among behavior therapists, we also noted several points where one or another of the second-generation behavior-therapy groups either differed from the first-generation behavior-therapy group or failed to be distinguished from the two comparison groups. We found instances where there were changes in both second-generation behavior-therapy groups as compared to the first generation of founders of behavior therapy, and we also found instances where the direct decendants of the first-generation group remained more like their mentors than did their contemporaries who entered the behavior-therapy movement via journal contributions as opposed to being a direct decendant of the first-generation group.

Both second-generation groups of behavior therapists broke away from the first-generation behavior therapists in rejecting the primacy of raw data over theory and rejecting the idea that observation can be theory neutral. On the Antiempiricism subscale of the ESQ, both second-generation behavior-therapy groups were indistinguishable from their respective comparison groups and clearly different from the first generation of behavior therapists. Unlike the founders of the movement, the second generation of behavior therapists viewed the relationship between "data" and "the world" as more problematic and recognized that more than appeals to "*the* data" were involved the settlement of scientific debates. By the time the behavior-therapy movement entered the second generation, the value-laden nature of observation became more prominent than the former view favoring the relative objectivity of simple observation. Across all of the twelve subscales that we obtained responses to, only this one showed a clear break from the first-generation behavior therapists by both second-generation behavior-therapy groups.

On two of the TOS subscales, Physicalism and Impersonal Causation vs. Personal Will, the second-generation behavior-therapy group that entered the movement via journal contributions failed to be distinguished from the comparison groups even though the first-generation behavior therapists and their direct descendants were so distinguished. The Physicalism subscale of the TOS refers specifically to the fundamental ideas of stimulus response theories wherein terms should be confined to those that refer to physically real, observable events. For example, subjects who score higher on this scale agree with such statements as: "All concepts used in psychological theory should be explicitly definable in terms of observed physical events" and "Any meaningful statement about mental events can be translated into a statement about behavior with no serious loss of meaning." It is quite likely that this movement away from basic S-R theories reflects the entry of cognitive ideas into the behavior-therapy movement through individuals who made contributions to the journals.

Such a trend would also be consistent with the other instance where the second-generation behavior therapists that entered via journal contributions failed to maintain the difference observed in both the first generation and their direct descendants: Impersonal Causation vs. Personal Will. This subscale of the TOS reflects the relative endorsement by respondents of the ideas that human behavior is determined and can therefore be predicted, as opposed to the ideas that human behavior is subject to free will and therefore cannot be predicted in principle. Part of the influence of the cognitive trend in behavior therapy was an emphasis on self-control and the self as an agent that controls behavior, as distinct from assumptions about environmental determinism (Mahoney, 1977).

Whether such ideas entered the behavior-therapy movement more from those who contributed to the journals than from those who were direct descendants cannot be answered by these data alone. This speculative hypothesis could be supported, however, by a further analysis of the literature in terms of the introduction of cognitive ideas of self-control and the rejection of S-R physicalistic concepts. It may well be that these concepts were in fact introduced by a few direct descendants of the first generation of behavior therapists, and their introduction then attracted others to the behavior-therapy movement who were to comprise the sample we collected from journal contributors.

Conclusions and Outlook: The Future of Behavior Therapy

We have not yet completed data collection on the third generation of behavior therapists. In our framework, this includes those who completed degrees in the period from 1976 to 1995. What has been rather remarkable about the first two generations has been the relative consistency of the values of behavior therapists as compared to their nonbehavior therapist contemporaries. Behavior therapy was and remains a movement unified by some philosophical and theoretical foundations. In this sense, behavior therapy has not lost its identity even though one can readily identify controversies and disagreements that have occurred within the behavior-therapy movement.

One such controversey between first- and second-generation behavior therapists was about whether or not to include the word "cognitive" as a description of what was done by behavior therapists. Although opinions on this matter differed sharply in the 1970s and 1980s, our investigations suggest that most of what made behavior therapy unique remained intact. Even though the oxymoron "cognitive-behavior therapy" was introduced into the literature, the fear that this would lead to the abandonment of basic scientific assumptions did not materialize. Behavior therapists, even "cognitive" behavior therapists, did not turn to mysticism, and they did not denounce empiricism.

We are optimistic about behavior therapy and the future, not only because we can forsee the continuation of the influence of the behavior therapy movement on the mental health field, but also because being hopeful about the future has always been a major feature of behavior therapy as a distinct community of behavioral scientists. The optimism of behavior therapy was given classic expression in *Walden Two,* and the utopian stream of influence has been a part of the basic outlook of behavior therapy ever since the end of World War II. As we approach the year 2001, it is fitting not only to identify and recall the philosophical and theoretical foundations that have made behavior therapy unique, but also to look forward to the continuation of that founding vision. We can make and have a better world.

References

Barnes, B. (1974). *Scientific knowledge and sociological theory.* London: Routledge & Kegan Paul.

Barnes, B. (1982). *T.S. Kuhn and social science.* New York: Columbia University Press.

Bloor, D. (1983). *Wittgenstein: A social theory of knowledge.* New York: Columbia University Press.

Boring, E. G. (1950). *A history of experimental psychology.* Englewood Cliffs, NJ: Prentice-Hall.

Bunge, M. (1992). A critical examination of the new sociology of science: Part 2. *Philosophy of the Social Sciences, 22,* 46–76.

Coan, R. W. (1979). *Psychologists: Personal and theoretical pathways.* New York: Irvington.

Cole, J., & Cole, S. (1973). *Social stratification in science.* Chicago: University of Chicago Press.

Collins, H. M. (1985). *Changing order: Replication and induction in scientific practice.* London and Beverly Hills: Sage.

Collins, H. M., & Pinch, T. J. (1982). *Frames of meaning: The social construction of extraordinary science.* London: Routledge & Kegan Paul.

Craighead, W. E. (1990). There's a place for us: All of us. *Behavior Therapy, 21,* 3–23.

Fuller, S. (1988). *Social epistemology.* Bloomington: Indiana University Press.

Fuller, S. (1989). *Philosophy of science and its discontents.* New York: Westview.

Gadamer, H. G. (1974). *Truth and method.* New York: Continuum.

Gholson, B., & Barker, P. (1985). Kuhn, Lakatos, and Laudan: Applications in the history of physics and psychology. *American Psychologist, 40,* 755–769.

Gholson, B., Shadish, W. R., Neimeyer, R. A., & Houts, A. C (Eds.). (1989). *Psychology of science: Contributions to metascience.* Cambridge: Cambridge University Press.

Giere, R. N. (Ed.). (1992). *Cognitive models of science: Minnesota studies in the philosophy of science, Vol. 15.* Minneapolis: University of Minnesota Press.

Gilbert, G. N., & Mulkay, M. (1984). *Opening Pandora's box: A sociological analysis of scientists' discourse.* Cambridge: Cambridge University Press.

Gorman, M. E. (1992). *Simulating science: Heuristics, mental models, and technoscientific thinking.* Bloomington: Indiana University Press.

Gross, P. R., & Levitt, N. (1994). *Higher superstition: The academic left and its quarrel with science.* Baltimore: Johns Hopkins University Press.

Hempel, C. G. (1965). *Aspects of scientific explanation.* New York: The Free Press.

Houts, A. C. (1994). Operational analysis, behavior analysis, and epistemology in science and technology studies. *Mexican Journal of Behavior Analysis, 20,* 101–143.

Houts, A. C., & Haddock, C. K. (1992). Answers to philosophical and sociological uses of psychologism in science studies: A behavioral psychology of science. In R. N. Giere (Ed.), *Cognitive models of science: Minnesota studies in the philosophy of science, Vol. 15* (pp. 367–400). Minneapolis: University of Minnesota Press.

Jasanoff, S., Markle, G. E., Petersen, J. C., & Pinch, T. (1994). *Handbook of science and technology studies.* London and Beverly Hills: Sage.

Kantor, J. R. (1963). *The scientific evolution of psychology.* Chicago: Principia.

Kendall, P. C. (1992). Healthy thinking. *Behavior Therapy, 23,* 1–11.

Knorr-Cetina, K. D. (1981). *The manufacture of knowledge: An essay on the constructivist and contextual nature of science.* Oxford: Pergamon.

Knorr-Cetina, K. D., & Mulkay, M. J. (Eds.). (1983). *Science observed: Perspectives on the social study of science.* London: Sage.

Krasner, L. (1971). Behavior therapy. In P. H. Mussen (Ed.), *Annual Review of Psychology* (Vol. 22). Palo Alto, CA: Annual Reviews.

Krasner, L., & Houts, A. C. (1984). A study of the "value" systems of behavioral scientists. *American Psychologist, 39,* 840–850.

Kuhn, T. S. (1962). *The structure of scientific revolutions.* Chicago: University of Chicago Press.

Kuhn, T. S. (1970). *The structure of scientific revolutions* (2nd ed.). Chicago: University of Chicago Press.

Lakatos, I. (1978). *The methodology of scientific research programmes.* Cambridge: Cambridge University Press.

Latour, B. (1987). *Science in action.* Cambridge, MA: Harvard University Press.

Latour, B., & Woolgar, S. (1986). *Laboratory life: The construction of scientific facts.* Princeton: Princeton University Press.

Laudan, L. (1977). *Progress and its problems: Towards a theory of scientific growth.* Berkeley: University of California Press.

Lindsley, O. R., Skinner, B. F., & Solomon, H. C. (1953). *Studies in behavior therapy* (Status Report I). Waltham, MA: Metropolitan State Hospital.

Longino, H. E. (1990). *Science as social knowledge: Values and objectivity in scientific inquiry.* Princeton, NJ: Princeton University Press.

Mahoney, M. J. (1977). Reflections on the cognitive learning trend in psychotherapy. *American Psychologist, 32,* 5–13.

Mannheim, K. (1936). *Ideology and utopia.* London: Routledge & Kegan Paul.

Maslow, A. H. (1968). *Toward a psychology of being.* (2nd ed.). New York: Van Nostrand.

Merton, R. K. (1938). *Science, technology, and society in seventeenth-century England.* Bruges, Belgium: St. Catherine Press.

Merton, R. K. (Ed.). (1973). *The sociology of science: Theoretical and empirical investigations.* Chicago: University of Chicago Press.

Mulkay, M. (1980). Sociology of science in the West. *Current Sociology, 28,* 1–184.

Nagel, E. (1961). *The structure of science: Problems in the logic of scientific explanation.* New York: Harcourt, Brace, & World.

O'Donohue, W., & Krasner, L. (1995). Theories in behavior therapy: Philosophical and historical contexts. In W. O'Donohue & L. Krasner (Eds.),

Theories of behavior therapy: Exploring behavior change (pp. 1–22). Washington, DC: American Psychological Association.

Pickering, A. (1984). *Constructing quarks: A sociological history of particle physics.* Chicago: University of Chicago Press.

Pickering, A. (Ed.). (1992). *Science as practice and culture.* Chicago: University of Chicago Press.

Proctor, R. N. (1991). *Value-free science? Purity and power in modern knowledge.* Cambridge, MA: Harvard University Press.

Rossi, P. H., Wright, J. D., & Anderson, A. B. (Eds.). (1983). *Handbook of survey research.* New York: Academic Press.

Shadish, W. R., & Fuller, S. (Eds.). (1994). *The social psychology of science.* New York: Guilford.

Skinner, B. F. (1987). Whatever happened to psychology as the science of behavior? *American Psychologist, 42,* 780–786.

Slezak, P. (1989). Scientific discovery by computer as empirical refutation of the strong programme. *Social Studies of Science, 4,* 563–600.

Smith, B. H. (1988). *Contingencies of value: Alternative perspectives for critical theory.* Cambridge, MA: Harvard University Press.

Smith, L. D. (1986). *Behaviorism and logical positivism: A reassessment of the alliance.* Stanford, CA: Stanford University Press.

Stark, W. (1958). *The sociology of knowledge.* London: Routledge & Kegan Paul.

Weinberg, S. (1992). *Dreams of a final theory: The search for the fundamental laws of nature.* New York: Pantheon.

Wolpe, J. (1958). *Psychotherapy by reciprocal inhibition.* Stanford, CA: Stanford University Press.

Wolpe, J. (1986). Misrepresentation and underemployment of behavior therapy. *Comprehensive Psychiatry, 27,* 192–200.

Wolpert, L. (1992). *The unnatural nature of science: Why science does (not) make common sense.* London: Faber & Faber.

Woolgar, S. (Ed.). (1988). *Knowledge and reflexivity: New frontiers in the sociology of knowledge.* London: Sage.

Woolgar, S. (1989). Representation, cognition and self: What hope for an integration of psychology and sociology? In S. Fuller, M. De Mey, T. Shinn, and S. Woolgar (Eds.), *The cognitive turn: Sociological and psychological perspectives on science* (pp. 201–224). Dordrecht, Netherlands: Kluwer.

Zuckerman, H., & Merton, R. K. (1971). Patterns of evaluation in science: Institutionalization, structure, and functions of the referee system. *Minerva, 9,* 66–100.

3

PHOBIC ANXIETY AND PANIC: AN INTEGRATIVE BEHAVIORAL ACCOUNT OF THEIR ORIGIN AND TREATMENT

JOHN P. FORSYTH
Department of Psychology
SUNY Albany

GEORG H. EIFERT
Department of Psychology
West Virginia University

Despite behavior therapy's significant contributions toward treating anxiety-related disorders, conceptual accounts of anxiety remain controversial. Early behavior therapists approached the problem of anxiety acquisition and treatment as one of simple Pavlovian (respondent) conditioning and extinction, respectively. Several efficacious therapeutic techniques were derived from the respondent conditioning model, such as systematic desensitization and in-vivo exposure (Wolpe, 1958; Eysenck, 1987). These techniques, rooted in the conditioning theories of Hull (1943), Pavlov (1927), Skinner (1938), and Watson (1930), focused on the role of observable behavior while minimizing the role of cognitive mediation. It was not long, however, before evidence mounted questioning the adequacy of respondent conditioning theory as a comprehensive account for fear onset. Perhaps most damaging were findings that fears could be learned in the absence of direct conditioning experiences (Eifert, 1987, 1990; Forsyth & Eifert, 1996a; Rachman, 1977). Although several researchers (e.g., Eifert, 1990; Eysenck, 1987; Seligman, 1971) responded to these challenges by extending and modifying the basic respondent conditioning position, the more popular response was to abandon conditioning notions and behavior theory in favor of cognitive concepts and treatments (e.g., Bandura, 1977, 1995; Mahoney, 1977; Meichenbaum, 1977). This abandonment, as we will describe in the first section of this chapter, was fueled by a narrow view of respondent conditioning requiring an identifiable conditioned stimulus (CS) or unconditioned stimulus (UCS). We present a revised view emphasizing the unconditioned response or UCR (i.e., a negatively evaluated abrupt and aversive systemic "alarm" response) as the critical conditioning event in human fear acquisition. Using examples of specific phobias and illness fears, we illustrate how alarms can account for fear acquisition without a readily identifiable aversive environmental event. Although we will emphasize the importance of the UCR in fear conditioning, we will also analyze the role of language to account for how an individual comes to learn that the UCR means fear or anxiety.

Since the 1970s, increased recognition has been given to the role of language and verbal-symbolic processes in relation to emotional phenomena. Such a recognition should have led to an extension of behavior theory and basic behavioral principles to account for language-emotion relations, but it did not. Neither respondent nor operant theory were sufficiently developed during this critical period to account for language-emotion relations in a manner useful for clinicians. Moreover, Skinner's (1938, 1974) statement that emotions are simply collateral by-products or epiphenomena of other behavior sealed the door on any interesting contributions from behavior analysis to the problem of language-emotion relations. In this vacuum, cognitive and cognitive behavior theorists have developed elaborate theoretical accounts of anxiety and fear by introducing new concepts and principles borrowed from information and computer science (e.g., Barlow, 1988; Beck & Emery, 1985; Lang, 1984, 1985; Lazarus, 1991). Recognizing the importance of language and verbal-symbolic processes in human behavior was a move in the right direction for behavior therapy, but as we will indicate in the second part of this chapter, abandoning basic behavioral principles and behavior theory in favor of cognitive concepts and theory was not. We will specifically describe and relate recent advances from two behavioral theories that extensively address the function of language-symbolic behavior and its role in the origin, maintenance, and change of anxiety-related phenomena: Paradigmatic or Psychological Behaviorism (PB) (Staats, 1972, 1995; Staats & Eifert, 1990) and clinical behavior analytic formulations derived from Radical Behaviorism (RB) (Hayes, 1987; Hayes & Hayes, 1992; Hayes & Wilson, 1994). Both approaches avoid unproductive attempts to define what anxiety is or is not, but emphasize the relation between language and what we call anxiety or fear as an inseparable unit. They also discuss how this relation is established, how it functions once learned, and how it can be modified or changed in therapy.

Texts covering the major psychological disorders often include at least one chapter on anxiety disorders, describing etiological and treatment differences, consistent with the *Diagnostic and Statistical Manual of Mental Disorders-IV* (DSM-IV) (American Psychiatric Association, 1994). In this chapter, we adopt a radically different approach. Many behavior therapists and clinical behavior analysts (e.g., Hayes, Wilson, Gifford, Follete, & Strosahl, 1996) are uneasy about the current nosological diagnostic system, and for good reason. Foremost, this system classifies disorders and anxiety subtypes based on symptoms defined topographically and structurally rather than functionally. Emphasis on the topography of symptom clusters has created the false impression that subtypes of anxiety-related problems are truly different and discrete entities. Clearly, there is considerable overlap between the various anxiety disorders in terms of similar learning processes, but this has been obscured by arbitrary delineations based on symptom differences. Throughout this chapter, but particularly in the third part, we suggest a different method to classify, assess, and treat anxiety problems using dimensional and functional criteria based on common behavioral processes.

Before proceeding with our arguments, we challenge the reader to put aside for a moment some of the following commonly held assumptions about anxiety: (a) anxiety is some*thing* to be discovered rather than what a person does; and (b) our task as behavior therapists is to help clients "get rid of," "control," or "eliminate" faulty feelings or thoughts associated with anxiety that are typically viewed as "the problem" from both the client's and therapist's perspective. In the place of these assumptions, we offer a different view of anxiety and fear and its treatment, and hence psychological health.

Conditioning in Phobic Anxiety and Panic: The Moribund Patient Is Alive and Well

As indicated, a major source of dissatisfaction with behavioral accounts of anxiety emerged from clinical observations suggesting that traumatic environmental conditioning events could not be identified for a number of clinical fears. Part of the dissatisfaction can be traced to disagreements over what constitutes a direct conditioning event and what is it that is being conditioned in fear acquisition.

What Is Being Conditioned?: Reemphasizing the UCR, Not the UCS

Critics and proponents of respondent accounts of human fear acquisition often equate direct conditioning with methodological arrangements and procedures that typify respondent preparations in the laboratory. Evidence for direct traumatic conditioning is usually based on being able to manipulate or identify the occurrence of some traumatic or painful UCS and its relation to some object or event in the environment (Eysenck, 1987). Yet such a view has created difficulties for the theory. For instance, Menzies and Clarke (1995) suggest that many clinical fears cannot be construed in terms of CS–UCS pairings and that identifying a UCS to account for fear onset is the exception rather than the rule (see also Lazarus, 1971; Rachman, 1977). Failure to document a traumatic event has been taken to indicate that the fear must have been acquired indirectly via another pathway (Menzies & Clarke, 1995; Lazarus, 1971; Rachman, 1977, 1991). We do not dispute that fears can be acquired in other ways than by direct traumatic conditioning experiences. What is at issue is the emphasis on identifying a precipitating environmental UCS that later becomes associated with a previously neutral stimulus as the *only* evidence for direct conditioning. As Eysenck (1987) argued, such a relation is evidence for direct conditioning from the experimenter's or therapist's vantage point but not necessarily from the subject's or client's viewpoint. From the client's perspective, direct conditioning involves aversive bodily events that can be evoked by either an environmental or a bodily UCS (e.g., low blood sugar levels). Indeed, the core concern that brings many clients into therapy is not a fear of an environmental UCS per se, but a fear of unpleasant aversive bodily responses (UCR/CR) that they label as "fear" or "anxiety."

Thus, one might ask, what is it that is being conditioned: is it the UCS or the UCR? What seems critical for respondent conditioning is not a particular UCS, but a UCR of sufficient intensity to become associated with objects or situations with a high probability of acquiring fear-evoking functions, which also includes evaluative labels of those objects or events (Eysenck, 1987; Eifert, 1987; Martin & Levey, 1987). In other words, respondent processes, or what accounts for fear acquisition, depends on the UCR, not some identifiable UCS capable of evoking it. If the UCR occurs by chance, as in a panic attack, then fear conditioning may occur. Alternatively, if a UCS occurs without a UCR, for whatever reason, then there will be no conditioning. Unfortunately, treating respondent preparations and respondent processes as monotypic has led many to conclude that the theory is too simplistic to account for the majority of fears. However, when we broaden our view of direct conditioning to emphasize the *processes* and not simply the *preparations* involved, then statements such as "direct conditioning of any kind accounts for relatively few phobias" seem premature (Lazarus, 1971; Rachman, 1977, 1978). For instance, Barlow (1988) suggested that many conditioning experiences consist mainly of panic attacks (i.e., false alarms) in contexts that prevent escape rather than actual direct experience with painful environmental traumatic events (i.e., UCSs). Arguably, such events are more obscure when the UCS is bodily (interoceptive), which may account for the failure of clinicians to document a UCS in the onset of many phobic fears. Yet, expanding our view of direct conditioning to include and emphasize the aversive response functions that predominate in clinical phobias seems warranted. It is to a discussion of this view that we now turn.

Panic and Alarms in Direct Conditioning

According to Barlow (1988), fear is a biologically derived central nervous system (CNS) response that can be characterized in terms of true, false, and learned alarms. True alarms are defined as a "fight or flight" response or a "predisposition to act" when confronted with real danger or threat of harm. Such responses are associated with intense and often abrupt neurobiological reactions (e.g., increased blood flow and oxygen intake, heart rate acceleration). They are also frequently associated with verbal evaluations of threat or harm (e.g., "I've got to get out of here") to events that the social–verbal community teaches us are threatening or dangerous (Forsyth & Eifert, 1996b). As such, true alarms are generally considered adaptive responses.

In contrast to true alarms, false alarms occur in the absence of real threat or harm (cf. Carter & Barlow, 1995). Panic attacks with their characteristic sudden and intense autonomic surges are one common clinical example of false alarms. As another example, an unforeseen physiological response (e.g., increased heart rate or sweating) to a drug such as caffeine may evoke a false alarm. Although false alarms may be inherently unpleasant (Carter & Barlow, 1995), considerable learning is likely to be involved in how one comes to view false alarms as something dangerous that needs to be controlled or eliminated. To some persons, a fast or irregular heartbeat is just that: a felt beating heart that does its job and corrects itself. In other individuals, the same bodily sensations may elicit a different acquired and verbally mediated formulation of what they think it *means* to have a fast or irregular heartbeat (e.g., "I'm having a heart attack," or "I'm going to die"). The concept of learned alarms specifically addresses how this kind of learning may occur.

Considerable evidence now exists supporting the view that the repeated occurrence of false alarms can result in learned alarms through their association with some internal or external cue (cf. Barlow, 1988). In respondent preparations, false alarms represent both the UCS and UCR, whereas learned alarms indicate CRs that develop from exposure to verbal and nonverbal objects or events that have a high probability of eliciting fear responses. In terms of respondent processes, the false alarm functions as the direct conditioning event and does not necessarily require an environmental UCS. When learned alarms are associated with an exteroceptive (i.e., external or environmental) cue that does not represent any real threat of harm, we usually refer to such problems as specific phobias, whereas alarms associated with otherwise benign interoceptive (i.e., internal or bodily) cues fit under the rubric of panic disorder or illness phobias (Eifert, 1992).

Learned Alarms to External Stimuli: Specific Phobias

In contrast to the etiological accounts put forth by Öst and Hugdahl (1983) and the criticisms of direct traumatic conditioning (Menzies & Clarke, 1995), many phobic fears are not learned primarily through direct traumatic experiences with environmental events (cf. Barlow, 1988). Rather, most persons with specific phobias, social phobias, illness phobias, and agoraphobia report experiencing an intense, overwhelming false alarm in situations or contexts that are subsequently feared. In fact, the experience of false alarms or panic attacks in phobic disorders is now a central defining diagnostic feature. According to DSM-IV, "exposure to the phobic stimulus almost invariably provokes an immediate anxiety response, which may take the form of a situationally bound or situationally predisposed panic attack" (APA, 1994, p. 410).

Empirical support for a conditioning interpretation of most phobias points to the experience of panic attacks (false alarms) as the common denominator in fear onset. For instance, in a retrospective study of a large sample of clinical phobics, Merckelbach and associates (1989) found evidence suggesting that all conditioning experiences involved frightening internal or bodily sensations. Similarly, McNally and Steketee (1985) reported that in a group of animal phobics the most frequently cited feared consequence of encountering a phobic animal was not the animal, but rather the consequences that the animal had come to represent, namely aversive bodily sensations and panic. It appears that panic frequency and the response to specific internal or external cues do not appear to differentiate persons with specific phobias from panic patients or from individuals with specific illness fears (Bass, 1990; Craske, 1991; Eifert, 1992). Indeed, this type of learning also seems to occur in persons with illness phobias in response to bodily symptoms; that is, autonomic cues signal alarm, which subsequently becomes conditioned to a bodily system or the functioning of an organ (Barlow, 1988; van den Hout, van der Molen, Griez, & Lousberg, 1987). One intriguing example of this type of learning is a specific fear relating to the heart and its functioning that we refer to as heart-focused anxiety or cardiophobia (Eifert, 1992; Eifert et al., 1996; Eifert & Forsyth, 1996).

Learned Alarms to Internal Stimuli: Panic and Illness Phobias

According to the continuity assumption, which suggests similar learning processes between internal and environmental events, learned alarms may also become associated with bodily or interoceptive cues through a process of interoceptive conditioning. The term "intero-interoceptive" conditioning applies to a learned relation between internal somatic cues and other bodily sensations associated with the alarm response, whereas "extero-exteroceptive" conditioning involves learning a relation between exteroceptive or environmental cues and alarms (Razran, 1961). Indeed, the conditioning theory of panic holds that detectable somatic sensations become interoceptive conditioned stimuli for fear, making the panic attack a self-enhancing process (Carter & Barlow, 1995; Griez & van den Hout, 1983a; Wolpe & Rowan, 1988). As an example, the traumatic nature of an initial panic attack or heightened autonomic arousal may serve as an aversive UCS/UCR complex that becomes conditioned with otherwise harmless cardioceptive cues (CS). Later, false alarms may become strongly associated with specific heart–related cues that set the occasion for subsequent learned alarms. Once learned, internal cues may function similarly in panic disorder and illness phobias such as cardiophobia (Eifert, 1992), as do external cues for persons with specific phobias in that they signal the possibility of danger or another false alarm (e.g., Chambless, Caputo, Bright, & Gallager, 1984; Clark et al., 1988; Ehlers & Margraf, 1989; Foa, 1988; van den Hout et al., 1987). With panic disorder, however, persons often fear multiple diffuse bodily sensations, whereas cardiophobic fears are focused on the heart and primarily elicited by cues that are associated with cardiac functioning such as chest pain or tachycardia (Eifert et al., 1996). Although traditional descriptions of panic attacks (e.g., Ley, 1985) typically consider the symptoms such as difficulty breathing, heart palpitations, and chest pain consequences of panic attacks rather than their cause, the evidence now suggests just the opposite. Bodily cues can serve as antecedents or triggers for panic and function to evoke learned alarms (e.g., Barlow, 1988; Craske, 1991; Eifert, 1992; Carr, Lehrer, Hochron, & Jackson, 1996; Wolpe & Rowan, 1988).

Some theorists (e.g., McNally, 1990) have argued that panic disorder is difficult to account for in terms of interoceptive conditioning. He asks that if certain physiological sensations are considered the CS, then what constitutes the CR? Because panic and illness phobias are indexed by the occurrence of physiological sensations, it becomes unclear how to identify and separate the CS from the CR. As Eysenck (1987) argues, however, "the phrase *CS-only presentation* is only meaningful for the experimenter who controls the UCS, but not for the subject who experiences the CR as identical to the UCR" (p. 18). When the CS is part of the UCR/CR complex, the occurrence of the UCR/CR will often amplify the original value of the CS, which is not the case for exteroceptive stimuli. For instance, pairing a picture of a snake with shock does not lead to the snake growing in size or moving closer to the viewer. In contrast, a fear response to internal cues may be intensified, in part, because individuals cannot truly escape from or avoid these cues. As Barlow (1988) pointed out, "situations that prevent, even partially, the powerful action tendency to escape during a false alarm [the UCR] most likely intensify the alarm further, resulting in strong emotional learning" (p. 225).

Eysenck (1987) raised a similar point noting that what seems to account for the persistence of most phobic fears, and their relative strength, is the similarity between the

UCS and the UCR in Pavlovian Type B conditioning. In this type of respondent conditioning, the CS (heart palpitations) is part of the UCS (increased arousal or alarm) that elicits a complete UCR that may intensify the original CS. For instance, Campbell, Sanderson, and Laverty (1964) were able to produce an intense conditioned fear response in human subjects to neutral tones in just one trial. Such rapid acquisition is unusual in laboratory respondent fear conditioning preparations. However, these authors used succinylcholine as the UCS, which produces immediate respiratory paralysis in a matter of seconds. Once injected, subjects could not breathe, nor could they control the interoceptive effects produced by the drug. The result was that subjects believed they were suffocating and dying. The consequences of naturally occurring and laboratory-induced conditioned alarms are seldom as powerful as succinylcholine. Yet common examples of this kind of learning are well documented in chemotherapy patients who develop moderate to severe conditioned nausea to many neutral stimuli associated with the administration of chemotherapy (e.g., Burish & Carey, 1986; Redd & Andrykowski, 1982). One principal factor that seems to account for conditionability in these patients is the strength and similarity between the nausea-induced properties of the drug (UCS) and the intensity of the initial nausea response (UCR).

Overall, the evidence and arguments regarding the direct traumatic conditioning of phobic fear seem to share one common etiological thread: the occurrence of false alarms capable of evoking a complete UCR. These false alarms are the principle traumatic event *and* what is being conditioned in phobic fear acquisition (Barlow, 1988; Eysenck, 1987; Martin & Levey, 1985; Wolpe & Rowan, 1988). In fact, Barlow (1988) suggested that false alarms may be one of the "missing links" in the traumatic conditioning etiology of some phobias. This missing link has served as the rationale for most exposure-based treatments and laboratory fear induction procedures such as carbon dioxide (CO_2) inhalation, lactate infusion, and hyperventilation provocation. These induction procedures produce abrupt and escalating bodily or systemic responses that many researchers now believe mirror the bodily sensations that serve as the direct conditioning event for learned alarms across the anxiety disorders (cf. Rapee, Brown, Antony, & Barlow, 1992). In particular, the effects of repeated inhalations of high concentrations of CO_2 rapidly and reliably produce an intense urge to ventilate and a wide range of short-lived physical symptoms (e.g., hyperventilation, heart pounding, dizziness, blurred vision, tachycardia, breathlessness, and paresthesia) in both anxious and nonanxious populations (e.g., Barlow, 1988; Barlow, Brown, & Craske, 1994; Gorman et al., 1984; Griez & van den Hout, 1982, 1983a, 1983b). The rapid and strong panicogenic effects of CO_2 inhalation, and our ability to control its parameters carefully in the laboratory, suggested to us that it might act as a powerful systemic UCS to study the etiological role of alarms in the acquisition of phobic fears.

Conditioned Alarms in the Laboratory: Using CO_2 Inhalation as a UCS

Until recently, virtually all laboratory conditioning paradigms have emulated the typical traumatic conditioning view of fear acquisition by pairing environmental stimuli differing in phobic qualities (e.g., snakes, spiders, flowers) with environmental pain or trauma (e.g., shock, noise). This research has been limited by (a) the intensity of the UCS employed, which is often set at mild levels by the research participant; (b) the effects of shock, noise, or tactile stimulation that do not produce the commonly reported features of the alarm response observed clinically; and (c) the omission of research examining how bodily or interoceptive cues may become associated with UCRs to elicit fear responses. Responding to these and other limitations, we developed a laboratory differential fear conditioning methodology that employed an interoceptive UCS in the form of repeated twenty-second inhalations of 20 percent CO_2-enriched air paired with both internal (human heart beating arhythmically or sperm swimming) and external (snake moving or flowers swaying in the wind) animated video stimuli (Forsyth, Eifert, & Thompson, 1996; Forsyth & Eifert, in press). The results from these extero-interoceptive conditioning preparations were promising. We found that CO_2 inhalation reliably induced abrupt systemic autonomic responses in normal subjects (e.g., heart rate increased on average fifteen beats per minute in conjunction with the CO_2). We also observed self-reported distress and conditioning across a variety of autonomic response domains, including skin conductance and frontalis muscle tension (see also van den Bergh et al., 1995, for a related CO_2 conditioning study using odors). The strongest conditioning effects were obtained with the moving snake and the arhythmically beating heart. Although our findings lend much-needed experimental support for the etiological role of alarms in human fear acquisition, the question remains as to why one learns to respond to such events with fear or anxiety. It is to a discussion of how such learning takes place that we will now turn.

The Importance of Language and Private Events for Understanding and Treating Anxiety

Growing dissatisfaction with nonmediational behavioral accounts that eschewed acknowledging the relation between language and emotional meaning in a manner useful for clinicians created a void within behavior therapy that was filled by cognitive theories and therapies. Recognizing the importance of language and emotion in human affairs, cognitive theorists emphasize how language-symbolic processes convey emotional meaning and how emotions depend on such processes. The principal objection behaviorists have to the cognitive view of emotions is not related to the phenomena they refer to, but to the explanations offered for the phenomena. Typically, cognitive explanations start with legitimate observations of language-behavior relations, but propose other unobservable, hypothetical, or mediational processes to account for them. For example, self-efficacy theory (Bandura, 1977, 1995), bioinformational theory (Drobes & Lang, 1995; Lang, 1977, 1985, 1993) and cognitive models of anxiety (Beck & Emery, 1985) all place heavy emphasis on cognitive-mediational constructs (e.g., networks, nodes, expectancies, appraisals, and schemata) borrowed from information and computer science. Cognitive theorists are not typically interested in accounting for observed language-emotion relations as a function of the conditions that produce them. As a result, cognitive behavior therapists are placed in a weakened position because they are left to rely on unobservable, hypothetical, and nonmanipulable constructs as targets for change. Still, cognitive theories have great appeal and were quickly absorbed by the behavior therapy movement—a move that is also reflected in recent name changes of many professional behavior therapy organizations.

One could argue that cognitive theory has identified an important problem and deficit within traditional behavior theory by focusing thinking, language, and their presumed relation in a manner that is potentially useful for clinicians. Yet the question remains whether behavior theory is really inept in accounting for the origins of language and emotional behavior. In other words, introducing cognitive theory to account for language and emotional behavior was one solution; developing behavior theory to account for language-emotion relations is another. Behavior theorists have begun to meet this challenge with an analysis of language that has led them to develop a psychology of cognition and emotion, while still avoiding a cognitive psychology.

Language and the Meaning of Anxiety

The availability and pervasiveness of language is one significant difference between animal and human behavior (Eifert, Forsyth, & Schauss, 1993). Language serves important symbolic functions by providing humans with emotional experiences without exposure to the actual physical stimuli or events that ordinarily elicit those responses (Staats & Eifert, 1990). For instance, both "knowing what to do" and "knowing what to feel" (Scruton, 1980) involve verbal understanding, some activity, and the relation between them. To account for how such relations are learned and function, we must address the meaning of verbal events in the psychological sense and not in the literal sense. Many nonbehavioral theorists and therapists erroneously treat what clients say literally as equivalent to what is going on psychologically (e.g., "I can't fly in a plane *because* I am anxious," or "I can't speak in front of a group *because* I will panic"). A behavioral approach to the psychological meaning of verbal-symbolic events entails different assumptions and strategies. Most notably, verbal relations are contextually sensitive and functionally defined (Hayes & Wilson, 1993). Thus, the meaning of anxiety in a psychological sense represents a complex act of relating largely arbitrary verbal-symbolic events with other events and psychological functions in and within a context.

This brings us to one of the unique and important features of the language of feeling (i.e., emotion words), which is its referential or relational quality. For instance, words such as anxiety and fear either implicitly or explicitly establish relations with other events such as "I am anxious or afraid of . . . something, some event, or someone (including the self)." Simply to say, "anxious," "afraid," "love," or "depressed" without some relational referent would strip these words of their meaning (i.e., their functions). The relational quality of terms denoting emotions, in turn, can only be identified by certain descriptions. These descriptions are often tied to occurrences of behavior and events with a variety of stimulus functions (e.g., eliciting, evocative, reinforcing, punishing) and meanings (e.g., good, bad, pleasant, unpleasant, painful). In turn, people often describe their emotional experiences metaphorically in ways that others can understand (e.g., "When I feel anxious it's like a knife going through my chest," or "When I'm depressed, I feel empty"). These metaphorical extensions have no real counterpart inside the person. Instead, they function to communicate the meaning of emotional experience by identifying and relating events with known stimulus functions.

Although this is a complex topic, the central point is that one cannot know what it *means* to feel X without first *understanding* what it is to feel X. To do this, however, requires verbal specification of "what is felt" (either privately or overtly) in order for it to be labeled as such. Second, the concept of anxiety is related to meaning and function. Nothing about the form of central nervous system responses (e.g., increased heart rate, electrodermal activity) requires them to stand for a particular emotional description (e.g., anxiety). Similarly, nothing inherent in the formal properties of words denoting emotional experience (e.g., anxiety, fear, anguish, terror, joy) requires them to stand in relation to a particular bodily or environmental referent. Depending on the cultural context, a variety of emotions may arise from the same biological system; conversely, elements from several different systems may be incorporated into a single emotion. For the most part, however, biology only contributes to, and sets limits upon, the social construction of emotional behavior (Averill, 1980). Accordingly, the stimuli and events placed in a relation and the nature of that relation are determined by the social verbal community without regard for the formal properties of the stimuli involved (Hayes & Hayes, 1989). As such, relations between the "language of anxiety" and the "feeling of anxiety" are arbitrary in the sense that we learn to use certain words, and not others, to convey emotion (cf. Forsyth & Eifert, 1996b). Thus, when we see an emotion on someone's face, we are establishing a relation based on a history of learning such relations (e.g., a grimace *means* fear). We will now describe and relate two behavioral traditions (respondent and operant) that have specifically and extensively addressed how these arbitrary relations are learned and function.

The Respondent Tradition and Language Behavior Therapy: Paradigmatic Behaviorism

Overview and Basic Tenets

Paradigmatic behavioral theory (e.g., Staats, 1972, 1996; Staats & Eifert, 1990) states that the acquisition and maintenance of fear and anxiety do not require direct experience with painful or aversive events. Rather, the association of inappropriate or negative-emotion eliciting verbal-symbolic stimuli with certain stimulus events (e.g., situations, objects, images, or words) is sufficient for those objects or situations to acquire aversive functions. Central to the discussion of anxiety are two major tenets of PB. The first is that biologically derived central nervous system responses (or alarms) are at the core of anxiety problems (cf. Eifert, 1990; Staats & Eifert, 1990). However, this CNS response is not sufficient for anxiety to occur. For instance, a person may show comparable patterns of CNS activation while being chased in a game of tag and being chased in the city by a mugger, but it is more likely that the latter case will be described as fear. The second tenet states that the experience of anxiety or fear requires an association between CNS response functions and some negative verbal or symbolic evaluation. This association can be acquired directly through aversive respondent conditioning or indirectly through semantic conditioning (Staats & Eifert, 1990).

Semantic Conditioning and Emotional Meaning

The term *semantic conditioning*, first coined by Razran (1939), refers to the application of respondent conditioning principles to language, and specifically, the acquisition of meaning and language functions (see also Mowrer, 1954; Osgood, 1969). Thus, a word stimulus paired with an unconditioned stimulus (UCS) that elicits an emotional response will also come to elicit the emotional response. For example, the word *snake* (CS) may elicit some sensory visual response (r_{sm}) of snakes after having been associated with a picture of a snake. Thereafter, if the snake picture is associated with a strong CNS response (e.g., pain or alarm), then the word *snake* would likely come to elicit part or all of this response (r_{sm}). According to PB, it is through this process of primary semantic conditioning, involving verbal and nonverbal conditioned and unconditioned stimuli, that words come to elicit a conditioned evaluative response and therefore become meaningful (e.g., liked/disliked, good/bad) (cf. Martin & Levey, 1978, 1987; see also Maltzman, Raskin, Gould, & Johnson, 1965; Staats & Eifert, 1990; Staats & Staats, 1957, 1958; Staats, Staats, & Crawford, 1962; Staats, Staats, & Heard, 1959). In turn, directly established stimulus functions to words can also transfer to other words, symbols, and events indirectly via higher-order conditioning.

Higher-Order Conditioning and the Transfer
of Emotion-Eliciting Functions

The principle of higher-order conditioning states that when a stimulus, previously neutral with respect to a particular response, has acquired CS functions to elicit that response (r_{sm}), the stimulus can now transfer the response to another neutral stimulus. This is possible, in part, because the CS functions as a higher-order UCS in new learning situations. For instance, suppose a child has learned an association between the word *hurt* and sensations produced directly upon touching a hot stove, but has no experience with the word *bite*. The word *bite* at this point is a meaningless nonsense syllable. Thereafter, the child hears the word *bite* in relation to dogs. The child then asks a teacher, "What does *bite* mean?" and the teacher responds *"Bite means hurt."* As a result, the child may not only respond to *bite* as equivalent to *hurt*, but may also learn that *dogs bite*, meaning that they *hurt*, and may subsequently avoid dogs. Over the last thirty years, many studies have shown higher-order conditioning and transfer of functions to new stimuli by means of language (e.g., Eifert, 1984, 1987; Hekmat, 1977; Maltzman, 1968; Osgood, 1969; Razran, 1961; Staats, 1963, 1975, 1996; Staats & Staats, 1957, 1958).

Affective, Reinforcing, and Directive Functions
of Verbal-Symbolic Stimuli

The principles reviewed thus far have primarily emphasized the acquisition and transfer of emotional meaning responses based on respondent preparations. In discussing the stimulus functions of language, however, both respondent and operant functions are mutually related. According to PB, once stimuli acquire *affect*-eliciting respondent functions (*A*-function), they will also function as *reinforcers* and punishers (*R*-function), and evoke either approach or escape and avoidance behavior (Directive or discriminative function) (Staats, 1975). Similarly, stimuli that have acquired punishing or reinforcing functions through operant operations will transfer those functions to other stimuli present that may then also function as emotion elicitors in respondent conditioning situations. Whereas the reinforcement value of any stimulus is defined by its emotion-eliciting functions that can occur either naturally or through previous conditioning, the directive functions of emotional stimuli are primarily shaped through experience (for summaries, see Staats, 1990, 1995, 1996). This research on the acquisition and transfer of emotive functions via language has served as a basis for PB's concept of the verbal-emotional repertoire.

The Verbal-Emotional Repertoire

A history of emotional learning over one's lifetime helps to establish the language-emotional repertoire consisting of many verbal-symbolic stimuli that elicit both positive and negative emotional responses which also have reinforcer and directive stimulus functions. Persons who suffer from anxiety disorders will have likely developed complex repertoires of a variety of verbal and other symbolic events capable of eliciting negative affective responses that also function as punishers and direct escape and avoidance behavior (Staats, 1972, 1996; Staats & Eifert, 1990). For example, for some persons who are otherwise healthy, the sensations of a beating heart or chest pain may lead to a sequence of verbal and autonomic events that result in the belief that they are having a heart attack (Eifert, 1992). In this instance, a fast or irregular heartbeat is not just a felt beating heart. Instead, it is an acquired and verbally mediated formulation of what it *means* to have a fast or irregular heartbeat or chest pain (e.g., "I have heart disease," or "I am suffering from a heart attack"). Not only may the person respond to such sensations by rushing to an emergency room, but any other public or private stimulus events associated with this response may now acquire similar negative functions (e.g., exercise, smoking, working hard). Persons can also condition and recondition themselves in ways not explicitly taught by relating a variety of language-symbolic events capable of evoking affective-reinforcing-directive functions (Eifert, 1984, 1987). By doing so, persons establish various stimulus functions to otherwise neutral stimulus events. Clinically, anxiety-related problems are viewed as resulting from deficit and inappropriate verbal-emotional learning, which serves as a basis for subsequent problems. Therefore, language-based therapeutic strategies explicitly target the emotive functions of language.

Language-Based Behavior Therapy

Altering Emotion-Eliciting Functions of Language.   Central to many behavior therapies are attempts to change emotional responses to stimuli or events by somehow getting clients to confront the feared objects or aversive bodily events in a safe context. This procedure facilitates corrective emotional learning and fear reduction (e.g., Eysenck, 1987; Rachman, 1977; Wolpe, 1958). This is often achieved, or at least initiated, in therapy either directly or indirectly using language, which is one of the most powerful methods by which to influence human behavior (Eifert, 1987; Staats, 1972). If this is the case, then therapeutic strategies that systematically alter the emotion-eliciting functions of verbal behavior may also produce changes in the reinforcing and directive functions of other verbal-symbolic events in the client's repertoire. Likewise, altering the reinforcing or directive functions of events may foster changes in their emotion-eliciting functions. For instance, many clients enter therapy with elaborate rules, reasons, and justifications for what they have done, why they do what they do, and what they believe needs to be done to overcome their problems (e.g., "I can't keep myself from getting anxious about speaking in front of people," or "I must not exert myself in order to avoid having a heart attack"). On the surface, these verbal utterances of the "problem" cannot cause any harm (e.g., being afraid that one might have a heart attack is not the same as having a heart attack). As clients struggle with their problems verbally, however, previously unrelated events can acquire negative emotional functions indirectly (e.g., "To control my anxiety, I must keep from going outside"). The thought of going outside may bring about the thought or image of having a panic attack and elicit avoidance behavior. Thus, the goal of language-based therapies is to identify and alter the A-R-D functions of language. This general strategy is based on the premise that language exerts control over behavior and altering the functions of language can produce changes in behavior. Language processes are therefore considered as both targets (dependent variable) and mediators (independent variable) for generalized therapeutic effects (cf. Lohr & Hamberger, 1990).

Emotional Modification and the Process of Change: Semantic Counterconditioning. Semantic conditioning procedures have been suggested as useful techniques to modify inappropriate verbal-emotive functions (Hekmat, 1977, 1990; Staats, 1972, 1996). The process can be summarized as follows: stimuli that elicit a negative emotional response can be altered directly by pairing the negative-eliciting stimulus with a stimulus known to elicit a positive emotional response. Such language-based interventions work through the verbal-emotional repertoire by using words to elicit an emotional response in the client; as a result, changes also occur in the A-R-D functions of words in relation to the events they refer to. Such collateral changes in stimulus functions may account, in part, for generalization of treatment gains beyond the therapeutic context. Several experimental and clinical studies have shown the effectiveness of this intervention strategy for accelerating or inhibiting the process of extinction (Eifert, 1984; Eifert & Schermelleh, 1985; Staats, 1972). Semantic conditioning is also operative in many well-established behavioral treatments for anxiety-related problems (e.g., systematic desensitization, cue-controlled relaxation and imagery, imaginal flooding, and covert desensitization).

The Operant Tradition and Recent Contributions from Clinical Behavior Analysis

Skinner's Treatment of Emotion and Its Social-Verbal Basis
Critics of radical behaviorism often wrongly state that Skinner denied the reality of private events such as feelings or emotions. Skinner's difficulty has never been with the reality of feelings, but rather with their assumed deterministic nature or causal role. Throughout Skinner's writings, he makes the *strategic* and methodological assumption that emotions are not causes or determinants of behavior (Skinner, 1938). For instance, it does not help in the solution to a practical problem to be told that some feature of an in-

dividual's behavior is due to anxiety or fear; we also need to know how fear and anxiety have been induced and how they may be altered. Skinner (1974) points out that "any therapeutic attempt to reduce the 'effects of anxiety' must operate upon the circumstances, not upon the intervening state," but his statement that "the middle term is of no functional significance, either in a theoretical analysis or in the practical control of behavior" is dubious (pp. 180–181). In our view, this statement has seriously impeded an effective behavioral analysis of an important aspect of human behavior. Although Skinner gradually moved toward acknowledging that emotional events can have stimulus properties, his most important contribution was the recognition that emotional events are social-verbal constructions that require an analysis of the social contingencies that give rise to respondent and operant functions and verbal behavior (Skinner, 1957, 1984).

Overview and Basic Tenets: Verbal Labeling and Tacting
One of the fundamental functional units identified by Skinner (1957) is the tact. Tacts are distinguished from other verbal behavior, in part, because a response of a given form is more likely in the presence of some nonverbal stimulus event as a result of a history of generalized reinforcement provided by the verbal community, beginning with simple examples. For instance, if a child says "ball" because of a history of generalized reinforcement (e.g., "good," "that's right," "yes") for saying "ball" in the presence of such objects, the statement is a tact. Principles used to explain public tacts also apply to private events occurring within the skin. For example, suppose a parent sees a child smiling, giggling, and laughing and asks, "You're anxious, aren't you?" After many such occasions, the child's overt behavior that we would otherwise call happiness may come to mean "anxious." Thereafter, when the parent asks the child how he or she feels given similar overt accompaniments, the child may respond, "I'm anxious." This example of tacting is unlikely in our verbal community. Yet it illustrates the point that tacting private events is arbitrary in the same manner as tacting public events. Unlike public tacts, however, private tacts are necessarily inexact because the verbal community is unable to provide differential reinforcement for specific unseen private events in the same way as for observable events (Skinner, 1957). This is one reason why many different emotion words can be associated with similar bodily events, and different bodily events may be associated with similar emotional descriptions. Emotional meaning, therefore, is derived from a history of relating language with either public or private events with known psychological functions. However, an adequate functional account of verbal behavior requires knowledge of the person's history and the sources of control over present behavior (Hayes & Hayes, 1989). For instance, saying "I feel anxious" without a history of generalized reinforcement would not constitute private tacting according to Skinner's definition. The observation that people name objects or events without a history of prior conditioning or generalized reinforcement (e.g., saying "dog" in the presence of a real dog after only seeing the word or a picture of a dog, or saying "I feel anxious" when seeing the word *snake* or a picture of a snake) presented difficulties for Skinner's account of verbal behavior. More recently, behavior analysts have addressed these difficulties by referring to the principle of *stimulus equivalence*, which can account for the learning of relations not explicitly taught.

Stimulus Equivalence

In general terms, stimulus equivalence involves teaching subjects to match comparison stimuli to sample stimuli (cf. Hayes & Hayes, 1989; Sidman, 1992, 1994). The stimuli are said to be equivalent if the relation between the samples and comparisons can be shown to have the properties of reflexivity, symmetry, and transitivity (Sidman & Tailby, 1983). For a relation to be reflexive, each stimulus must be matched to itself (e.g., given the word *speech* as a sample; the subject matches it to a comparison stimulus *speech* from another array and vice versa). To show symmetry, the trained relation between two stimuli must be functionally reversible: when "given *speech*, pick *embarrassment*" is trained; "given *embarrassment*, pick *speech*" is likely to emerge without direct reinforcement (*speech = embarrassment*). Similarly, when "given *speech*, pick *anxiety*" is trained, "pick *anxiety*, given *speech*" emerges without reinforcement. Finally, for a relation to be transitive, a subject must be taught to match *speech* to *embarrassment*, and then *embarrassment* to *anxiety*, and, without further training and a history of reinforcement for doing so, the subject will likely match *speech* to *anxiety* and *anxiety* to *speech*. Thus, with equivalence, training two relations directly yields four new derived bidirectional relations not explicitly taught. Although there is no logical requirement that equivalence relations must be derived (Vaughan,1989), the major interest in stimulus equivalence is precisely because these relations are derived and seem to correspond with language phenomena. The importance of stimulus equivalence for language resides in the fact that humans not only learn to respond to one event in terms of another, but also respond to stimulus events because of the stimulus functions of other events (cf. Sidman, 1994).

Transfer of Psychological Functions through Equivalence Classes

Relations among stimuli are important because other functions can be moderated by those relations. With language, we are interested in words not as objects, but as events that have psychological functions (i.e., meaning) because they are placed in relations with other events. Sidman and Tailby (1983) assert that, by definition, the existence of a class of equivalent stimuli permits any variable that affects one member of the class to affect all members. If the function is acquired by other members of the class from which the stimulus was selected, but not by members of other classes, the function is said to have transferred through the equivalence class (cf. Dougher & Markham, 1994). This process, in turn, is relevant for emotional learning. For example, studies have shown that when shock is paired with one member of a class, electrodermal and avoidance responses transfer to other members of the class that were never previously reinforced with shock (e.g., Dougher et al., 1994). A variety of other stimulus functions have also been reported to transfer through equivalence classes such as discriminative stimulus control (e.g., Lazar & Kotlarchyk, 1986), conditioned reinforcement and punishment (Greenway, Dougher, & Wulfurt, 1992), contextual control (Gatch & Osborne, 1989; Kohlenberg, Hayes, & Hayes, 1991), and consequential functions (Hayes, Kohlenberg, & Hayes, 1991; Kohlenberg et al., 1991). This research addresses how persons may develop strong emotional responses to events simply through language relations and how contextual cues can set constraints on what functions will transfer from one stimulus to the next. For example, suppose the word *snake* is paired with shock in the presence of a red light, but in the presence of a green light the shock is not forthcoming. As a result, the word *snake* and other stimuli in a class associated with this word may elicit respondents only in the presence of the red light and not in the presence of the green light. Thus, humans learn to respond to relations among events and that such relational responding is dependent upon contextual or environmental circumstances.

Contextual Control Over Verbal-Emotional Relations

Hayes (1994a) argued that the context will select any given relational response between events and stimulus functions associated with those events. These relations can be arbitrary and are established and influenced by contextual cues, which may include other words, their sequence, the nonverbal context, and other events. For instance, an otherwise healthy person may learn a relation between chest pain and heart attack such that in the context of being alone, labeling sensations emanating from the chest as "pain" may lead to a sequence of events by which the person believes that having chest pain equals having a heart attack. Yet similar cardiac sensations produced during an exercise stress test in the safe context of a cardiology clinic may establish different stimulus relations with very different functions. This example shows how verbal meaning can be understood as relations between events with a variety of psychological functions (e.g., reinforcing, eliciting, establishing, discriminating, and evoking) that depend on the contextual contingencies that establish and modify them (Hayes & Hayes, 1989, 1992). Thus, labeling one's bodily sensations as "anxiety" in one instance and "excitement" in another does not necessarily depend on the formal properties of what is felt (they may feel the same). It does depend, however, on the application of a particular relational response between what is felt and what is said. It is precisely because humans are capable of contextually controlled relational responding that words can be flexibly applied, modified, and combined in new ways. Often such relational responding takes the form of rules that can establish and maintain such relations.

Rules, Rule-Following, and Verbal-Emotional Relations

In the traditional behavior analytic account, most psychologically significant behavior is contingency shaped. An important subset of this behavior, however, is rule-governed. Behavior analysts have emphasized rules in the sense of governing events. According to Reese (1989), most rules can be formally identified by the specification of a relation between two or more events, or in Skinner's (1966, 1969) terms, they represent contingency specifying stimuli. Hayes and his associates, however, have defined rules simply as verbal antecedents that derive their functions from their participation in relational frames (e.g., Hayes & Wilson, 1994; Zettle & Hayes, 1982). Simply put, an antecedent verbal stimulus relation or rule is something that tells us what to do, when to do it, and what will happen when we do it. Thus, to understand a rule requires established relations between words as specified in the rule, their environmental referents, and stimulus functions that can be thought of as a culmination of complex sets of relational responding (e.g., stimulus equivalence, transfer of functions, and framing relationally). Rules are effective, in part, because they establish verbal relations with other aspects of the nonverbal world (e.g., objects or events). As a result, rule following is possible in entirely different contexts from that in which the rule was established. Rules also functionally establish previously unrelated stimulus functions (e.g., physiological respondent and operant avoidance and escape functions) with events specified in the rule (Hayes & Hayes, 1989).

One immediate and beneficial consequence of rule following is that it may bring us into contact with contingencies that would not have been contacted, or would have been otherwise contacted with deleterious effects (e.g., "If you have chest pain, go to the emergency room," or "Don't touch the stove when it is hot"). Alternatively, rule following may have deleterious effects when it results in an *insensitivity* to contingencies that might suggest otherwise. Such insensitivity is often seen in clients with anxiety or fear-related difficulties (e.g., "I can't speak in front of a group *because* I will have an anxiety attack," or "I can't fly in planes *because* I am too scared"). Clinically, many persons who come into therapy have established elaborate rules and stimulus relations that are largely ineffective. In fact, many behavior problems occur when ineffective *verbal* behavior gets in the way of effective action. If this is the case, what can be done about it?

New Clinical Behavior Analytic Interventions
Changing the Social-Verbal Context.   Clinical behavior analysts seek to understand how the talking that goes on during therapy sessions impacts the client's problems that occur outside the sessions. Functional Analytic Psychotherapy (FAP) (Kohlenberg & Tsai, 1991) is derived from behavior analytic principles and based on four assumptions: (1) problematic behavior can be directly observed in session, (2) the occurrence of problematic behavior in session is functionally similar to problematic behavior as it occurs outside of therapy in daily life, (3) the client–therapist relationship is a social environment where instances of problematic behavior can be evoked and changed using basic behavior analytic principles, and (4) many behavior problems are related to verbal behavior. Although clinical behavior analysts adopt a noncausal view of feelings, private events are not ignored in the therapeutic process. Rather, it is assumed that the salience of what the client thinks, feels, and does can be potentiated or depotentiated in the therapeutic context by influencing the environmental variables controlling such actions.

Kohlenberg, Tsai, and Dougher (1993) describe both operant and respondent behaviors relevant to expressing feelings and show how avoidance of negative emotions (e.g., anxiety, dysphoria) can lead to diminished contact with the environment. In particular, clients have developed rigid verbal repertoires leaving them with inflexible and ineffective ways of interacting with the world. The FAP approach is generally designed to create a therapeutic environment that evokes, shapes, and reinforces feeling and its expression and acceptance. Thus, a primary clinical strategy is to alter the emotive functions of language (i.e., behavior–behavior relations), rather than the feelings themselves, by establishing a new verbal context in therapy that changes the functions of these relations. This approach, referred to as emotional acceptance, is at the core of clinical behavior analytic strategies.

Balancing Acceptance and Change.   Experiential avoidance refers to an unwillingness to experience unpleasant thoughts, feelings, and other private events that are believed to be the primary problem for the client (Hayes, Wilson, Gifford, Follete, & Strosahl, 1996). Acceptance-based strategies adopt a different view of private events and psychological health. Acceptance allows anxiety-provoking thoughts and feelings to occur without making attempts to control them, that is, acceptance entails giving up or letting go of the struggle to change or control anxiety (cf. Dougher, 1994; Hayes, 1994b; Jacobson, 1992). This process involves experiencing events fully and without defense for what they are (e.g., unpleasant bodily sensations) and not as what we say they are (e.g., panic, signs of imminent death). In a technical sense, acceptance involves contacting automatic or direct stimulus functions of events, such as bodily sensations, without acting to reduce or manipulate those functions. Accordingly, private events are neither viewed as the causes of suffering nor as obstacles to change.

In contrast, most mainstream cognitive-behavioral approaches view psychological problems differently, that is, negative or unpleasant thoughts and feelings are the problem, and therefore, must be either eliminated, controlled, modified, or reduced. For instance, one of the primary goals of cognitive therapists is to target hypothesized dysfunctional cognitions or other entities (e.g., low self-efficacy) presumed to underlie or causally influence the observable behaviors for which the client is receiving treatment (Forsyth, Lejuez, Hawkins, & Eifert, 1996). Clients typically share this view regarding the causes of their behavior (e.g., "I can't go on a plane because I'm anxious, and I'm anxious because my plane might crash"). Thus, cognitive therapists attempt to change or replace dysfunctional thoughts and appraisals with more adaptive ones. Using the above example, they will help the patient make an accurate realistic assessment of the probability of dying in a plane crash. The general strategy of modifying or controlling maladaptive thoughts and self-statements is based on the assumption that if the therapist can get patients to think or feel differently, they will act differently.

Likewise, the PB approach accepts the notion that private responses can have stimulus properties and evoke behavior (e.g., Staats & Eifert, 1990). As discussed, these principles have been applied in traditional language-based behavior therapies and led to the systematic use of emotionally relevant and behavior-directive self-statements (cf. Eifert, 1987; Hekmat, 1990; Staats, 1972). These interventions are aimed at changing the client's overt behavior indirectly by altering the affective (eliciting), reinforcing, and directive (S^D) functions of verbal events in the client's repertoire. Such treatments have been moderately successful in reducing or eliminating anxiety responses that involve unpleasant bodily sensations (Eifert, 1990; Hekmat, 1990). The adoption of this general strategy could, however, account for some treatment failures with semantic and cognitive therapies. By explicitly targeting "unhealthy" private events in therapy, both paradigmatic and cognitive-behavioral interventions play into the very social-verbal system that clinical behavior analytic approaches consider the source of the problem (cf. Hayes & Wilson, 1994). In other words, the problem is not that individuals experience unpleasant thoughts or feelings but that individuals make every effort to avoid or reduce experiencing these private events. As a result of this "discomfort anxiety" (Ellis, 1980; Ellis & Robb, 1994), individuals never contact the natural contingencies to find out that they can act effectively *despite* unpleasant emotions and thoughts.

Behavior analytic psychotherapies offer some intriguing alternative treatment strategies and targets (e.g., Hayes & Wilson, 1994; Koerner, Jacobson, & Christensen, 1994; Kohlenberg & Tsai, 1991; Linehan, 1994; Marlatt, 1994). The labeling of bodily arousal as unpleasant is an example of verbal learning and subject to the same principles that describe how other behavior is controlled. For instance, phobic clients will do everything they can to escape or avoid confrontation with, or even thinking about, the feared stimulus. In the process, they will also produce the very feelings that they want to avoid and may inadvertently establish functional relations between unpleasant bodily sensations and other stimuli. Instead of helping clients in their struggle to control or eliminate distressing thoughts or feelings, behavior analytic treatments attempt to alter the struggle itself, often verbally, with the goal of getting clients to behave *despite* what they think or feel. The struggle for control and emotional avoidance is the "context" or "system" in which the client operates; a system that, by the time the client seeks help in therapy, is largely ineffective. A new social-verbal context is established in therapy that does not fit with the client's existing verbal-emotional or verbal-motor repertoires. Therefore, influencing these repertoires is a primary goal of new behavior analytic intervention strategies. This is accomplished, in large part, by undermining, weakening, and altering the functions of verbal relations. Paradoxical techniques are particularly useful for this purpose, but other techniques (e.g., metaphors) are also used (cf. Hayes & Wilson, 1994).

At a conceptual level, paradoxical techniques place both the "symptoms" and explanations in a different context, one in which symptoms lose their original function and meaning. For persons with anxiety disorders, anxiety or fear often cease to be mere words, but represent a series of other involuntary events (the symptoms) and stimulus functions of what it means to have anxiety. Paradoxical techniques undermine this preexisting system of verbal constructions and reactions regarding reality by breaking the cycle of repetitive behavior that forms the *attempted solution:* "Clinical experience has shown that, ironically, it is often the patient's very attempts to solve the problem that maintain [the problem]. The attempted solution becomes the true problem" (Nardone & Watzlawick, 1993, p. 51). The therapist can deliberately create a paradox such that previously avoided and unwanted symptoms become voluntary.

Clinically, paradoxical techniques commonly take the form of verbal injunctions (e.g., "If you don't want it, you've got it") and symptom prescriptions (e.g., "I want you to make yourself panic each time you leave your house"). If taken literally, such injunctions are nonsensical and contrary to what the social-verbal community dictates. Paradoxical techniques are used in therapy explicitly to break relational or functional equivalence classes. Such changes frequently have the unexpected effect of altering the maintaining functions of these patterns without necessarily changing their form or content. Such techniques create a therapeutic double bind by implying that the only way to change is to remain unchanged (cf. Hayes & Wilson, 1994). Therapists who carefully use reframing or paradoxical verbal interventions may also rapidly and simultaneously alter the affective, reinforcing, and directive functions of both verbal and other stimuli in the client's natural environment. Indeed, it is likely that paradoxical and semantic counterconditioning interventions may involve similar learning processes (Forsyth & Eifert, 1996b).

Although outcome data on the clinical efficacy of acceptance-based interventions is scant, such techniques are at the core of many effective behavioral (e.g., FAP—Kohlenberg & Tsai, 1991; and ACT—Hayes & Wilson, 1994) and some nonbehavioral approaches (e.g., Bateson, Jackson, Haley, & Weakland, 1963; Nardone & Watzlawick,

1993; Selvini, Boscolo, Cecchin, & Prata, 1978). We need to explore systematically the possibility of combining treatments that attempt to balance acceptance and change (cf. Wilson, 1996). Traditional behavioral interventions have focused almost exclusively on change. Acceptance-based interventions, on the other hand, have a different focus and treatment goal. The goal of treatment is no longer to be in control of anxiety but to give up wanting to control anxiety with a concomitant commitment to behavior change. In this way, individuals can learn to do all the things that they previously said they could not do because of uncontrollable anxiety. By giving up the desperate desire for change, fundamental change will actually become more likely. Within such a context, behavioral techniques that require action from the client (e.g., breathing retraining and confronting feared situations) do not become obsolete but are employed in a new context. For instance, rather than using exposure as a method to eliminate anxiety, it could be explicitly used as a means of experiencing anxiety and learning to act effectively regardless of how one feels. Indeed, there is evidence to suggest that panic control treatments work in part because they undermine experiential avoidance (Hayes et al., 1996).

Manualized cognitive-behavioral interventions that aim to control specific phobias and panic disorder have received considerable empirical support. For example, Brown and Barlow (1995) report that 75 percent of patients treated with a panic control protocol were panic-free at two-year follow-up. Remarkable as these success rates are, they also imply that a significant portion of patients does not respond well to traditional control-oriented protocols. Failure rates could even be higher when manualized protocols are applied in nonresearch clinical settings with more heterogeneous patients. We suspect that at least some of these treatments fail not because the techniques are ineffective, but because they attempt to control something that is essentially uncontrollable: learned alarms. If a preoccupation with control is indeed responsible for at least some treatment failures, a useful strategy could be to use the same interventions in a context that balances change with an acceptance that panic episodes *may* continue to occur. Unfortunately, systematic outcome data on acceptance-based interventions are still lacking. Given that manualized cognitive-behavioral protocols are empirically supported and efficacious for many individuals with anxiety problems (Brown & Barlow, 1995), acceptance-based interventions should be used with caution. We should, however, begin to explore how empirically supported cognitive-behavioral interventions could be integrated with acceptance-based behavior analytic treatments, and these possibilities should be vigorously examined at both the basic experimental and clinical applied level (cf. Zvolensky & Eifert, 1997).

A Theory-Driven Approach to Assessing and Treating Anxiety

In this chapter, we have eschewed a discussion of different anxiety disorder "subtypes" and focused instead on key behavioral processes that cut across different anxiety phenomena. Although the DSM-IV classificatory system is a useful heuristic, it tells us little about what behavioral processes account for the origin, maintenance, and change of different clinical manifestations of anxiety-related problems. As Wolpe (1989) argued, "while response similarity in maladaptive habits provides a convenient basis for placing [persons] in diagnostic pigeonholes (e.g., anorexia, claustrophobia, or stuttering), common pigeonholes do not necessarily imply common treatment, because the stimulus antecedents vary" (p. 7). Although shifting the emphasis from differences to commonalities is difficult, such a shift is necessary for a careful functional assessment and idiographic treatment approach that emphasizes behavioral processes.

Dimensional Classification Emphasizing Common Behavioral Processes

Essentially, anxiety disorders currently recognized in DSM-IV can be placed along three continuous functional dimensions: (1) *origin of the feared or anxiety arousing stimulus* (internal or bodily versus external and environmental), (2) *stimulus specificity* (general versus specific), and (3) *the nature of the psychophysiological response* (abrupt versus sustained). According to this functional-dimensional classification as illustrated in Table 3-1, panic disorder can be understood as an abrupt psychophysiological response to a general class of internal stimulus events, whereas specific phobias and posttraumatic stress disorder (PTSD) represent abrupt psychophysiological responses to specific external stimulus events. Illness phobias can be represented along the internal-specific-abrupt dimension, whereas hypochondriasis would represent an internal-general-sustained concern over disease.

This dimensional classification scheme is based on stimulus-response relations, rather than the form or topography of behavior, and may lead to similar intervention strategies for ostensibly different disorders as long as their etiology and maintenance involve similar behavioral principles and processes. Further, it directs attention toward the contextual variables maintaining such problems that serve as the basis for any intervention. For example, we may conceptualize the acquisition of specific phobias, illness

TABLE 3-1.   Dimensional and Functional Similarities across the DSM-IV Anxiety and Related Disorders

	Origins of Anxiety-Provoking Stimulus		Stimulus Specificity		Nature of Systemic Response	
	Internal	External	Specific	General	Abrupt	Sustained
Specific phobia		X	X		X	
PTSD		X	X		X	
Social phobia (specific)		X	X		X	
Agoraphobia		X		X		X
Social phobia (general)		X		X		X
GAD		X		X		X
Panic disorder	X			X	X	
Illness phobia	X		X		X	
Hypochondriasis	X			X		X
OCD	X			X		X

phobias, social phobia (specific), and PTSD similarly in terms of common behavioral processes (e.g., an abrupt systemic conditioned response acquired to a specific event). Furthermore, generalized anxiety disorder, panic disorder, and social phobia (general) may be understood as a function of similar learning processes (e.g., sustained fear response acquired to a general class of stimulus events). This type of process and theory-driven approach, where treatments are matched to classes of behavior defined functionally, would be beneficial for the advancement of behavior therapy, because it relates basic behavioral principles and theory to the practice of behavior therapy (Eifert, 1996; Eifert, Evans, & McKendrick, 1990).

Functional Assessment and Treatment

Behavioral assessment is similarly affected by diagnostic categorizations and inadequate theoretical models. The widespread use of the triple-response mode concept (verbal-cognitive, physiological, and overt motor-behavioral), with its arbitrary distinctions between "modes," is fundamentally at odds with a behavioral approach to assessment (Forsyth & Eifert,1996c). Few would argue with the contention that people exhibit thinking behavior, physiological behavior, and overt motor behavior all the time and that these responses are often interrelated in some way. Yet from an assessment and treatment approach we must ask, why (if at all) are they related? This question redirects our attention away from the response components per se to an examination of the environmental circumstances that control these responses. The observation that two people with panic disorder show similar response patterns does not address how the two patterns came to be similar in the first place.

A number of manualized comprehensive treatment packages for phobic anxiety and panic disorder have been developed. These standardized protocols are useful for research purposes and helpful to practitioners by keeping them on track and pushing for behavior change. Although the empirical data favoring the use of manualized treatments are encouraging, there remains some concern about the uncritical and rigid use of standardized treatment manuals in the absence of individual case formulations guided by conceptual models and behavior theory (Evans, 1996). Manual-based treatment has been accused of emphasizing technique at the expense of individual problem analysis and tailoring of treatment (e.g., Wolpe, 1989). Treatments are typically described and conceptualized at the level of procedure (a specific technique such as exposure) rather than at the level of principle (e.g., extinction) and process (e.g., learning). A review of studies examining the issue (Eifert, Schulte, Zvolensky, Lejuez, & Lau, 1997), however, revealed that tailoring treatment to target an individual's particular problem beyond the level of clinical diagnosis does not seem to improve overall treatment outcome for individuals with phobic anxiety and panic disorder (Schulte, Künzel, Pepping, & Schulte-Bahrenberg, 1992) or for individuals with obsessive-compulsive disorder (Emmelkamp, Bouman, & Blaauw, 1994).

We believe manualized and idiographic theory-driven interventions are not mutually exclusive approaches in behavior therapy but can be combined in a complementary fashion (cf. Eifert et al., 1997). Treatments can become more flexible through individualized combinations of modules based on a functional theory-driven analysis of the individual patient's needs. For instance, some treatment manuals contain modules that target dysfunctional processes and behaviors that may occur in different disorders. As an example, persons with panic disorder and hypochondriasis often experience thoracic breathing and hyperventilation problems (McNally, 1990). A module for teaching diaphragmatic breathing may therefore benefit patients with either one or both of these diagnoses (Eifert, 1996). On the other hand, since not all individuals with panic disorder or hypochondriasis hyperventilate, those who do not hyperventilate may not require use of that module. In this way, a treatment manual could be supplemented by a functional analysis to reveal which modules need to be implemented for a given patient, which modules are not necessary, and what (if any) additional treatment should be applied. Studies will need to determine whether and how much of such treatment individualization is necessary and desirable (cf. Eifert et al., 1997). At any rate, an idiographic and functional approach to treating anxiety both benefits from and makes a contribution to behavior theory by elucidating common behavioral processes that cut across diagnostic subtypes.

Conclusions

The nature of anxiety-related phenomena and their role in human behavior are not well understood by much of psychology, including behavior therapy. A central reason for this is that researchers and clinicians alike have assumed that anxiety exists awaiting our discovery rather than viewing it as what people do. This has resulted in a preoccupation with the many response dimensions of anxiety (e.g., cognitive, physiological, and overt behavioral) in an attempt to address "what anxiety is or is not."

This chapter took a different approach by asking two different and perhaps fundamental questions about anxiety and fear: (1) what are the critical learning processes that account for fear acquisition?, and (2) how is it that people learn to be anxious and afraid as a function of such processes? To answer the first question, we attempted to address some common misconceptions regarding respondent conditioning accounts of fear acquisition. Most notably, we argued that the critical variable to consider is the UCR and not the identification of an environmental UCS capable of evoking it. Clinically, the response is important because many clients report experiencing an intense UCR that later becomes associated with objects or situations and do not, in most cases, report having experience with direct pain or harm caused by the feared object or situation. Further, the UCR is also critical from an intervention standpoint, in part because it often represents the reason why clients come into therapy. Simply put, clients with anxiety or fear-related difficulties do not like feeling the way they do. Behavior theorists, however, have largely overlooked how it is that persons come to learn to label learned alarms as fear that they need to control, eliminate, or reduce. Thus, we need to address how it is that persons associate some psychophysiological events with fear and anxiety and why it is that they seek help from behavior therapists for this problem. In our view, answering this question requires a systematic analysis of language and how verbal-symbolic behavior is functionally related to motor behavior.

Both PB and RB take the perspective that language is at the core of how we come to know our feelings. The corollary of this perspective is that feelings in humans are closely related to language. Thus, when we speak of feelings such as anxiety or fear, and whether they are good or bad, we are using language and other symbolic processes. Such functional relations are taught, modified, and changed by experience within a particular social-verbal community that ultimately establishes and maintains them. The treatment implications for anxiety and fear-related problems that derive from both approaches are different from the mainstream behavior therapy approach. Rather than trying to help the client eliminate, control, or reduce the unwanted feeling or bodily state, semantic interventions seek to undermine the client's struggle for control by getting clients to experience what is there to be felt for what it is and not for what a client says it is. Thus, the context for anxiety and fear-related problems are unsuccessful attempts to avoid and control feelings, and the therapeutic solution is to get clients to behave despite what they think and feel. To accomplish this goal, we need to address the types of verbal relations that are largely ineffective in a given client and how they function to maintain their problems.

Behavioral formulations of anxiety were among the first and most influential fields of study where knowledge and findings from the science of psychology in general, and behavior theory in particular, were applied to improve our understanding and treatment of this common clinical problem (e.g., Wolpe, 1958). More recently, empirically supported treatment protocols have been developed that employ a structured technique-oriented approach to controlling phobic anxiety and panic. When applied in a flexible theory-driven way, the use of such manuals need not be antithetical to the original values of behavior therapy that emphasize idiographic individualized assessment and treatment. In addition, the treatment of anxiety could also be an area where we see a merger between control-oriented protocols and idiographic approaches that seek to balance acceptance and change in the individual patient. The fact that acceptance-based procedures are rooted in behavioral principles that are still very much the subject of empirical investigation in the basic science (e.g., Hayes et al., 1991; Sidman, 1994) makes this approach even more appealing. A step back to the lab and basic science could be one of the most exciting steps forward for our field because such a step seeks to reestablish the link between basic science and clinical interventions—a hallmark of good behavior therapy, past and present.

References

American Psychiatric Association. (1994). *Diagnostic and statistical manual of mental disorders* (4th ed.). Washington, DC: Author.

Averill, J. R. (1980). Emotion and anxiety: Sociocultural, biological, and psychological determinants. In A. O. Rorty (Ed.), *Explaining emotions* (pp. 37–72). Berkeley: University of California Press.

Bandura, A. (1977). Self-efficacy: Toward a unifying theory of behavior change. *Psychological Review, 84*, 191–215.

Bandura, A. (1995). Comments on the crusade against the causal efficacy of human thought. *Journal of Behavior Therapy and Experimental Psychiatry, 26*, 179–190.

Barlow, D. H. (1988). *Anxiety and its disorders: The nature and treatment of anxiety and panic.* New York: Guilford.

Barlow, D. H., Brown, T. A., & Craske, M. G. (1994). Definitions of panic attacks and panic disorder in the DSM–IV: Implications for research. *Journal of Abnormal Psychology, 103*, 553–564.

Bass, C. M. (1990). Functional and cardiorespiratory symptoms. In C. M. Bass (Ed.), *Somatization: Physiological and psychological illness* (pp. 171–206). London: Blackwell.

Bateson, G., Jackson, D. D., Haley, J., & Weakland, J. H. (1963). A note on the double-bind. *Family Processes, 2,* 154–161.

Beck, A. T., & Emery, G. (1985). *Anxiety disorders and phobias: A cognitive perspective.* New York: Basic Books.

Brown, T. A., & Barlow, D. H. (1995) Long-term outcome in cognitive-behavioral treatment of panic disorder: Clinical predictors and alternative strategies for assessment. *Journal of Consulting and Clinical Psychology, 63,* 754–765.

Burish, T. G., & Carey, M. P. (1986). Conditioned aversive responses in cancer chemotherapy patients: Theoretical and developmental analysis. *Journal of Consulting and Clinical Psychology, 54,* 593–600.

Campbell, D., Sanderson, R., & Laverty, S. G. (1964). Characteristics of conditioned response in human subjects during extinction trials following a single traumatic conditioning trial. *Journal of Abnormal and Social Psychology, 66,* 627–639.

Carr, R. E., Lehrer, P. M., Hochron, S. M., & Jackson, A. (1996). Effect of psychological stress on airway impedance in individuals with asthma and panic disorder. *Journal of Abnormal Psychology, 105,* 137–141.

Carter, M. M., & Barlow, D. H. (1995). Learned alarms: The origins of panic. In W. O'Donohue & L. Krasner (Eds.), *Theories of behavior therapy: Exploring behavior change* (pp. 209–228). New York: Guilford.

Chambless, D. L., Caputo, G. C., Bright, P., & Gallagher, R. (1984). Assessment of fear of fear in agoraphobics: The Body Sensations Questionnaire and the Agoraphobic Cognitions Questionnaire. *Journal of Consulting and Clinical Psychology, 6,* 1090–1097.

Clark, D. M., Salkovskis, P. M., Gelder, M., Koehler, C., Martin, M., Anastasiades, P., Hackman, A., Middleton, H., & Jeavons, A. (1988). Tests of a cognitive theory of panic. In I. Hand & H. U. Wittchen (Eds.), *Panic and phobias 2* (pp. 149–158). Berlin: Springer–Verlag.

Craske, M. G. (1991). Phobic fear and panic attacks: The same emotional states triggered by different cues? *Clinical Psychology Review, 11,* 599–620.

Dougher, M. J. (1994). The act of acceptance. In S. C. Hayes, N. S. Jacobson, V. M. Follette, & M. J. Dougher (Eds.), *Acceptance and change: Content and context in psychotherapy* (pp. 37–45). Reno: Context Press.

Dougher, M. J., & Markham, M. R. (1994). Stimulus equivalence, functional equivalence, and the transfer of function. In S. C. Hayes, L. J. Hayes, M. Sato, & K. Ono (Eds.), *Behavior analysis of language and cognition* (pp. 71–90). Reno: Context Press.

Dougher, M. J., Augustson, E., Markham, M. R., Greenway, D. E., & Wulfert, E. (1994). The transfer of respondent eliciting and extinction functions through stimulus equivalence classes. *Journal of the Experimental Analysis of Behavior, 62,* 331–352.

Drobes, D. J., & Lang, P. J. (1995). Bioinformational theory and behavior therapy. In W. O'Donohue & L. Krasner (Eds.), *Theories of behavior therapy: Exploring behavior change* (pp. 229–257). Washington, DC: American Psychological Association.

Ehlers, A., & Margraf, J. (1989). The psychophysiological model of panic attacks. In P. M. G. Emmelkamp (Ed.), *Anxiety disorders: Annual series of european research in behavior therapy* (pp. 2–26). Amsterdam: Swets.

Eifert, G. H. (1984). The effects of language conditioning on various aspects of anxiety. *Behavior Research and Therapy, 22,* 13–21.

Eifert, G. H. (1987). Language conditioning: Clinical issues and applications in behavior therapy. In H. J. Eysenck & I. M. Martin (Eds.), *Theoretical foundations of behavior therapy* (pp. 167–193). New York: Plenum.

Eifert, G. H. (1990). The acquisition and treatment of phobic anxiety: A paradigmatic behavioral perspective. In G. H. Eifert & I. M. Evans (Eds.), *Unifying behavior therapy: Contributions of paradigmatic behaviorism* (pp. 173–200). New York: Springer.

Eifert, G. H. (1992). Cardiophobia: A paradigmatic behavioral model of heart-focused anxiety and nonanginal chest pain. *Behaviour Research and Therapy, 30,* 329–345.

Eifert, G. H. (1996). More theory-driven and less diagnosis-based behavior therapy. *Journal of Behavior Therapy and Experimental Psychiatry, 27,* 75–86.

Eifert, G. H., Evans, I. M., & McKendrick, V. (1990). Matching treatments to client problems not diagnostic labels: A case for paradigmatic behavior therapy. *Journal of Behavior Therapy and Experimental Psychiatry, 21,* 163–172.

Eifert, G. H., & Forsyth, J. F. (1996). Heart-focused and general illness fears in relation to parental medical history and separation experiences. *Behaviour Research and Therapy, 34,* 735–739.

Eifert, G. H., Forsyth, J. P., & Schauss, S. L. (1993). Unifying the field: Developing an integrative paradigm for behavior therapy. *Journal of Behavior Therapy and Experimental Psychiatry, 24,* 107–118.

Eifert, G. H., Hodson, S. E., Tracey, D. R., Seville, J. L., & Gunawardane, K. (1996). Heart-focused anxiety, illness beliefs, and behavioral impairment: Comparing healthy heart-anxious patients with cardiac and surgical inpatients. *Journal of Behavioral Medicine, 19,* 385–399.

Eifert, G. H. & Schermelleh, K. (1985). Language conditioning, emotional instructions, and cognitions in conditioned responses to fear-relevant and fear-irrelevant stimuli. *Journal of Behavior Therapy and Experimental Psychiatry, 16,* 101–110.

Eifert, G. H., Schulte, D., Zvolensky, M. J., Lejuez, C. W., & Lau, A. W. (1997). Manualizing behavior therapy: Merits and challenges. *Behavior Therapy, 28,* 499–509.

Ellis, A. (1980). Rational-emotive therapy and cognitive behavior therapy: Similarities and differences. *Cognitive Therapy and Research, 4,* 325–340.

Ellis, A., & Robb, H. (1994). Acceptance in rational-emotive therapy. In S. C. Hayes, N. S. Jacobson, V. M. Follette, & M. J. Dougher (Eds.), *Acceptance and change: Content and context in psychotherapy* (pp. 91–102). Reno: Context Press.

Emmelkamp, P. M. G., Bouman, T. K., & Blaauw, E. (1994). Individualized versus standardized therapy: A comparative evaluation with obsessive-compulsive patients. *Clinical Psychology and Psychotherapy, 1,* 95–100.

Evans, I. M. (1996). Individualizing therapy, customizing clinical science. *Journal of Behavior Therapy and Experimental Psychiatry, 27,* 99–105.

Eysenck, H. J. (1987). The role of heredity, environment, and "preparedness" in the genesis of neurosis. In H. J. Eysenck & I. M. Martin (Eds.), *Theoretical foundations of behavior therapy* (pp. 379–402). New York: Plenum.

Foa, E. B. (1988). What cognitions differentiate panic disorder from other anxiety disorders? In I. Hand and H. U. Wittchen (Eds.), *Panic and phobias 2* (pp. 159–166). Berlin: Springer-Verlag.

Forsyth, J. P., & Eifert, G. H. (1996a). Systemic alarms in fear conditioning—I: A reappraisal of what is being conditioned. *Behavior Therapy, 27,* 441–462.

Forsyth, J. P., & Eifert, G. H. (1996b). The language of feeling and the feeling of anxiety: Contributions of the behaviorisms toward understanding the function-altering effects of language. *Psychological Record, 46,* 607–649.

Forsyth, J. P., & Eifert, G. H. (1996c). Cleaning up "cognition" in triple-response fear assessment. *Journal of Behavior Therapy and Experimental Psychiatry, 27,* 87–98.

Forsyth, J. P., & Eifert, G. H. (1997). Response intensity in content-specific fear conditioning comparing 20% vs. 13% CO_2-enriched air as unconditioned stimuli. *Journal of Abnormal Psychology* (in press).

Forsyth, J. P., Eifert, G. H, & Thompson, R. N. (1996). Systemic alarms in fear conditioning—II: An experimental methodology using 20% CO_2 inhalation as a UCS. *Behavior Therapy, 27,* 391–415.

Forsyth, J. P., Lejuez, C., Hawkins, R. P., & Eifert, G. H. (1996). A critical evaluation of cognitions as causes of behavior. *Journal of Behavior Therapy and Experimental Psychiatry, 27,* 369–376.

Gatch, M. B., & Osborne, J. G. (1989). Transfer of contextual stimulus function via equivalence class development. *Journal of the Experimental Analysis of Behavior, 51,* 369–378.

Gorman, J. M., Askanazi, J., Liebowitz, M. R., Fyer, A. J., Stein, J., Kinney, J. M., & Klein, D. F. (1984). Response to hyperventilation in a group of patients with panic disorder. *American Journal of Psychiatry, 141,* 857–861.

Greenway, D. E., Dougher, M. J., & Wulfurt, E. (1992). *Transfer of consequential functions via stimulus equivalence: The role of generalization.* Paper presented at the 18th Annual Meeting of the Association for Behavior Analysis, San Francisco, May 1992.

Griez, E., & van den Hout, M. A. (1982). Effects of carbon dioxide–oxygen inhalations on subjective anxiety and some neurovegetative parameters. *Journal of Behavior Therapy and Experimental Psychiatry, 13,* 27–32.

Griez, E., & van den Hout, M. A. (1983a). Carbon dioxide and anxiety: Cardiovascular effects of a single inhalation. *Journal of Behavior Therapy and Experimental Psychiatry, 14,* 297–304.

Griez, E., & van den Hout, M. A. (1983b). Treatment of phobophobia by exposure to CO_2–induced anxiety symptoms. *Journal of Nervous and Mental Disease, 171,* 506–508.

Hayes, S. C. (1987). A contextual approach to therapeutic change. In N. S. Jacobson (Ed.), *Psychotherapists in clinical practice: Cognitive and behavioral perspectives* (pp. 327–387). New York: Guilford.

Hayes, S. C. (1994a). Relational frame theory: A functional approach to verbal events. In S. C. Hayes, L. J. Hayes, M. Sato, & K. Ono (Eds.), *Behavior analysis of language and cognition* (pp. 9–30). Reno: Context Press.

Hayes, S. C. (1994b). Content, context, and the types of psychological acceptance. In S. C. Hayes, N. S. Jacobson, V. M. Follette, & M. J. Dougher (Eds.), *Acceptance and change: Content and context in psychotherapy* (pp. 13–32). Reno: Context Press.

Hayes, S. C. (1995). In M. K. Lassen (Moderator), *Update on case conceptualization and the process of change: Emerging controversies or consensus?* Clinical roundtable presented at the Annual Meeting of the Association for Advancement of Behavior Therapy, Washington, DC, November 1995.

Hayes, S. C., & Hayes, L. J. (1989). The verbal action of the listener as a basis for rule-governance. In S. C. Hayes (Ed.), *Rule-governed behavior* (pp. 153–190). New York: Plenum.

Hayes, S. C., & Hayes, L. J. (1992). Some clinical implications of contextualistic behaviorism: The example of cognition. *Behavior Therapy, 23,* 225–249.

Hayes, S. C., Kohlenberg, B. S., & Hayes, L. J. (1991). The transfer of specific and general consequential functions through simple and conditional equivalence classes. *Journal of the Experimental Analysis of Behavior, 56,* 119–137.

Hayes, S. C., & Wilson, K. G. (1993). Some applied implications of a contemporary behavior-analytic account of verbal events. *The Behavior Analyst, 16,* 283–301.

Hayes, S. C., & Wilson, K. G. (1994). Acceptance and commitment therapy: Altering the verbal support for experiential avoidance. *The Behavior Analyst, 17,* 289–303.

Hayes, S. C., Wilson, K. G., Gifford, E. V., Follette, V., & Strosahl, K. (1996). Experiential avoidance and behavioral disorders: A functional dimensional approach to diagnosis and treatment. *Journal of Consulting and Clinical Psychology, 64,* 1–16.

Heckmat, H. (1977). Semantic behavior therapy: Unidimensional or multidimensional? *Behavior Therapy, 8,* 805–809.

Heckmat, H. (1990). Semantic behavior therapy of anxiety disorders: An integrative approach. In G. H. Eifert & I. M. Evans (Eds.), *Unifying behavior therapy: Contributions of paradigmatic behaviorism* (pp. 201–219). New York: Springer.

Hull, C. L. (1943). *Principles of behavior.* New York: Appleton-Century-Crofts.

Jacobson, N. S. (1992). Behavioral couple therapy: A new beginning. *Behavior Therapy, 23,* 493–506.

Koerner, K., Jacobson, N. S., & Christensen, A. (1994). Emotional acceptance in integrative behavioral couple therapy. In S. C. Hayes, N. S. Jacobson, V. M. Follette, & M. J. Dougher (Eds.), *Acceptance and change: Content and context in psychotherapy* (pp. 109–118). Reno: Context Press.

Kohlenberg, B. S., Hayes, S. C., & Hayes, L. J. (1991). The transfer of contextual control over equivalence classes through equivalence classes: A possible model of social stereotyping. *Journal of the Experimental Analysis of Behavior, 56,* 505–518.

Kohlenberg, B. S., & Tsai, M. (1991). *Functional analytic psychotherapy.* New York: Plenum.

Kohlenberg, B. S., Tsai, M., & Dougher, M. J. (1993). The dimensions of clinical behavior analysis. *The Behavior Analyst, 16,* 271–282.

Lang, P. J. (1977). Physiological assessment of anxiety and fear. In J. D. Cone & R. P. Hawkins (Eds.), *Behavioral assessment: New directions in clinical psychology* (pp. 178–195). New York: Brunner/Mazel.

Lang, P. J. (1984). Cognition and emotion: Concept and action. In C. Izard, J. Kagan, & R. Zajonc (Eds.), *Emotion, cognition, and behavior* (pp. 193–226). New York: Cambridge University Press.

Lang, P. J. (1985). The cognitive psychophysiology of emotion: Fear and anxiety. In A. H. Tuma & J. D. Maser (Eds.), *Anxiety and the anxiety disorders* (pp. 131–170). Hillsdale, NJ: Erlbaum.

Lang, P. J. (1993). The network model of emotion: Motivational connections. In R. S. Wyer & T. K. Srull (Eds.), *Perspectives on anger and emotion: Advances in social cognition, Vol. 6* (pp. 109–133). Hillsdale, NJ: Erlbaum.

Lazar, R. M., & Kotlarchyk, B. J. (1986). Second-order control of sequence-class equivalences in children. *Behavioral Processes, 13,* 205–215.

Lazarus, A. A. (1971). *Behavior therapy and beyond.* New York: McGraw–Hill.

Lazarus, R. S. (1991). Cognition and motivation in emotion. *American Psychologist, 46,* 352–367.

Ley, R. (1985). Agoraphobia, the panic attack and the hyperventilation syndrome. *Behaviour Research and Therapy, 23,* 79–81.

Linehan, M. M. (1994). Acceptance and change: The central dialectic in psychotherapy. In S. C. Hayes, N. S. Jacobson, V. M. Follette, & M. J. Dougher (Eds.), *Acceptance and change: Content and context in psychotherapy* (pp. 73–86). Reno: Context Press.

Lohr, J. M., & Hamberger, L. K. (1990). Verbal, emotional, and imagery repertoires in the regulation of dysfunctional behavior: An integrative conceptual framework for cognitive-behavioral disorders and interventions. In G. H. Eifert & I. M. Evans (Eds.), *Unifying behavior therapy: Contributions of paradigmatic behaviorism* (pp. 153–172). New York: Springer.

McNally, R. J. (1990). Psychological approaches to panic disorder: A review. *Psychological Bulletin, 108,* 403–419.

McNally, R. J., & Steketee, G. S. (1985). The etiology and maintenance of severe animal phobias. *Behaviour Research and Therapy, 23,* 431–435.

Mahoney, M. J. (1977). Reflections on the cognitive learning trend in psychotherapy. *American Psychologist, 32,* 5–13.

Maltzman, I. (1968). Theoretical conceptions of semantic conditioning and generalization. In T. R. Dixon & D. L. Horton (Eds.), *Verbal behavior and general behavior theory* (pp. 291–339). Englewood Cliffs, NJ: Prentice-Hall.

Maltzman, I., Raskin, D. C., Gould, J., & Johnson, O. (1965). *Individual differences in the orienting reflex and semantic conditioning and generalization under different UCS intensities.* Paper presented at the Annual Meeting of the Western Psychological Association, Honolulu, June 1965.

Marlatt, G. A. (1994). Addiction, mindfulness, and acceptance. In S. C. Hayes, N. S. Jacobson, V. M. Follette, & M. J. Dougher (Eds.), *Acceptance and change: Content and context in psychotherapy* (pp. 175–197). Reno: Context Press.

Martin, I. M., & Levy, A. B. (1978). Evaluative conditioning. *Advances in Behavior Research and Therapy, 1,* 57–102.

Martin, I. M., & Levy, A. B. (1985). Conditioning, evaluations and cognitions: An axis for integration. *Behavior Research and Therapy, 23,* 167–175.

Martin, I. M., & Levy, A. B. (1987). Knowledge, action, and control. In H. J. Eysenck & I. M. Martin (Eds.), *Theoretical foundations of behavior therapy* (pp. 133–152). New York: Plenum.

Meichenbaum, D. (1977). *Cognitive-behavior modification: An integrative approach.* New York: Plenum.

Menzies, R. G., & Clarke, J. C. (1995). The etiology of phobias: A nonassociative account. *Clinical Psychology Review, 15,* 23–48.

Merckelbach, H., Ruiter, C. D., van den Hout, M. A., & Hoekstra, R. (1989). Conditioning experiences and phobias. *Behaviour Research and Therapy, 6,* 657–662.

Mowrer, O. H. (1954). The psychologist looks at language. *American Psychologist, 9,* 660–694.

Nardone, G., & Watzlawick, P. (1993). Clinical practice, processes, and procedures. In G. Nardone & P. Watzlawick (Eds.), *The art of change* (pp. 45–72). San Francisco: Jossey-Bass.

Osgood, C. E. (1969). The nature and measurement of meaning. In J. G. Snider & C. E. Osgood (Eds.), *Semantic differential technique: A sourcebook* (pp. 3–41). New York: Aldine-Atherton.

Öst, L. G., & Hugdahl, K. (1983). Acquisition of agoraphobia, mode of onset and anxiety response patterns. *Behaviour Research and Therapy, 21,* 623–631.

Pavlov, I. P. (1927). *Conditioned reflexes: An investigation of the activity of the cerebral cortex.* New York: Dover.

Rachman, S. (1977). The conditioning theory of fear acquisition. *Behavior Research and Therapy, 15,* 375–387.

Rachman, S. (1978). *Fear and courage.* San Francisco: Freeman.

Rachman, S. (1991). Neo-conditioning and the classical theory of fear acquisition. *Clinical Psychology Review, 11,* 155–173.

Rapee, R., Brown, T. A., Antony, M. M., & Barlow, D. H. (1992). Response to hyperventilation and inhalation of 5.5% carbon dioxide–enriched air across the DSM-III-R anxiety disorders. *Journal of Abnormal Psychology, 101,* 538–552.

Razran, G. H. S. (1939). A quantitative study of meaning by a conditioned salivary technique (semantic conditioning). *Science, 90,* 89–90.

Razran, G. H. S. (1961). The observable unconscious and the inferable conscious in current Soviet psychophysiology: Interoceptive conditioning, semantic conditioning, and the orienting reflex. *Psychological Review, 68,* 81–150.

Redd, W. H., & Andrykowski, M. A. (1982). Behavioral interventions in cancer treatment: Controlling aversion reactions in chemotherapy. *Journal of Consulting and Clinical Psychology, 50,* 1018–1029.

Reese, H. W. (1989). Rules and rule-governance: Cognitive and behavioristic views. In S. C. Hayes (Ed.), *Rule-governed behavior* (pp. 3–84). New York: Plenum.

Schulte, D., Künzel, R., Pepping, G., & Schulte-Bahrenberg, T. (1992). Tailor-made versus standardized therapy of phobic patients. *Advances in Behaviour Research and Therapy, 14,* 67–92.

Scruton, R. (1980). Emotion, practical knowledge and common culture. In A. O. Rorty (Ed.), *Explaining emotions* (pp. 519–536). Berkeley: University of California Press.

Seligman, M. E. P. (1971). Phobias and preparedness. *Behavior Therapy, 2,* 307–320.

Selvini, P. M., Boscolo, L., Cecchin, G., & Prata, G. (1978). *Paradox and counterparadox: A new model in the therapy of the family in schizophrenic transaction.* New York: Aronson.

Sidman, M. (1992). Equivalence relations: Some basic considerations. In S. C. Hayes & L. J. Hayes (Eds.), *Understanding verbal relations* (pp. 15–27). Reno: Context Press.

Sidman, M. (1994). *Equivalence relations and behavior: A research story.* Boston: Authors Cooperative.

Sidman, M., & Tailby, W. (1983). Conditional discrimination vs. matching to sample: An extension of the testing paradigm. *Journal of the Experimental Analysis of Behavior, 37,* 23–44.

Skinner, B. F. (1938). *The behavior of organisms.* New York: Appleton.

Skinner, B. F. (1957). *Verbal behavior.* New York: Appleton-Century-Crofts.

Skinner. B. F. (1966). An operant analysis of problem solving. In B. Kleinmuntz (Ed.), *Problem solving: Research, method, and theory* (pp. 225–257). New York: Wiley.

Skinner, B. F. (1969). *Contingencies of reinforcement: A theoretical analysis.* Englewood Cliffs, NJ: Prentice-Hall.

Skinner, B. F. (1974). *About behaviorism.* New York: Knopf.

Skinner, B. F. (1984). The operational analysis of psychological terms. *Behavioral and Brain Sciences, 7,* 547–581.

Staats, A. W. (1963). *Complex human behavior* (with contributions by C. K. Staats). New York: Holt, Rinehart, & Winston.

Staats, A. W. (1972). Language behavior therapy: A derivative of social behaviorism. *Behavior Therapy, 3,* 165–192.

Staats, A. W. (1975). *Social behaviorism.* London: Erwin-Dorsey.

Staats, A. W. (1990). Paradigmatic behavior therapy: A unified framework for theory, research, and practice. In G. H. Eifert & I. M. Evans (Eds.), *Unifying behavior therapy: Contributions of paradigmatic behaviorism* (pp. 14–54). New York: Springer.

Staats, A. W. (1995). Paradigmatic behaviorism and paradigmatic behavior therapy. In W. O'Donohue & L. Krasner (Eds.), *Theories of behavior therapy: Exploring behavior change* (pp. 659–692). Washington, DC: American Psychological Association.

Staats, A. W. (1996). *Behavior and personality.* New York: Springer.

Staats, A. W., & Eifert, G. H. (1990). The paradigmatic behaviorism theory of emotions: Basis for unification. *Clinical Psychology Review, 10,* 539–566.

Staats, C. K., & Staats, A. W. (1957). Meaning established by classical conditioning. *Journal of Experimental Psychology, 54,* 74–80.

Staats, A. W., & Staats, C. K. (1958). Attitudes established by classical conditioning. *Journal of Abnormal and Social Psychology, 57,* 37–40.

Staats, A. W., Staats, C. K., & Crawford, H. L. (1962). First-order conditioning of a GSR and the parallel conditioning of meaning. *Journal of General Psychology, 67,* 159–167.

Staats, A. W., Staats, C. K., & Heard, W. G. (1959). Language conditioning of meaning to meaning using a semantic generalization paradigm. *Journal of Experimental Psychology, 57,* 187–192.

van den Bergh, O., Kempynck, P. J., van de Woestijne, K. P., Baeyens, F., & Eelen, P. (1995). Respiratory learning and somatic complaints: A conditioning approach using CO_2-enriched air inhalation. *Behaviour Research and Therapy, 5,* 517–527.

van den Hout, M. A., van der Molen, M., Griez, E., & Lousberg, H. (1987). Specificity of interoceptive fears to panic disorder. *Journal of Psychopathology and Behavioral Assessment, 9,* 99–106.

Vaughan, M. E. (1989). Rule-governed behavior in behavior analysis: A theoretical and experimental history. In S. C. Hayes (Ed.), *Rule-governed behavior* (pp. 97–118). New York: Plenum.

Watson, J. B. (1930). *Behaviorism.* New York: Norton.

Wilson, G. T. (1996). Acceptance and change in the treatment of eating disorders and obesity. *Behavior Therapy, 27,* 417–439.

Wolpe, J. (1958). *Psychotherapy by reciprocal inhibition.* Stanford, CA: Stanford University Press.

Wolpe, J. (1989). The derailment of behavior therapy: A tale of conceptual misdirection. *Journal of Behavior Therapy and Experimental Psychiatry, 20,* 3–15.

Wolpe, J., & Rowan, V. C. (1988). Panic disorder: A product of classical conditioning. *Behaviour Research and Therapy, 26,* 441–450.

Zettle, R. D., & Hayes, S. C. (1982). Rule-governed behavior: A potential theoretical framework for cognitive-behavior therapy. In P. C. Kendall (Ed.), *Advances in cognitive-behavioral research and therapy, Vol. 1* (pp. 73–118). New York: Academic Press.

Zvolensky, M. J., & Eifert, G. H. (1997). *Acceptance and commitment therapy (ACT): A viable behavior therapy for anxiety disorders?* Manuscript submitted for publication.

4

DEPRESSION: BEHAVIORAL PRINCIPLES AND IMPLICATIONS FOR TREATMENT AND RELAPSE PREVENTION

GEORG H. EIFERT
Department of Psychology
West Virginia University

BEVERLEY K. BEACH
Department of Psychology
West Virginia University

PETER H. WILSON
School of Psychology
Flinders University of South Australia

Major depression is the most common single psychiatric disorder with a total of 17.1 percent of the population experiencing a major depressive episode during their life and 10.3 percent reporting a depressive episode in the last twelve-month period (Kessler et al., 1994). In the United States alone, this disorder affects about 8 million people at any one time. Depression has a debilitating impact on various affective, cognitive, and motoric areas of functioning and is associated strongly with suicidal risk and untimely deaths (Weinsten, Kaiser, & Saturno, 1989). Moreover, depression claims considerable financial loss due to reduced productivity and treatment costs that exceed $10 billion per year (Teuting, Koslow, & Hirschfeld, 1982).

Given these high prevalence rates and human and financial costs, it is not surprising that depression is a widely studied disorder and that several behavioral and

Acknowledgments: We wish to acknowledge Arthur Staats and Elaine Heiby for their original development of the paradigmatic behavioral theory of depression discussed and expanded in this chapter; the first author is particularly grateful for several years of stimulating discussion and collaboration with Arthur Staats. We also thank Judy Mathews for her suggestions and comments.

cognitive models of depression models have been proposed (e.g., Beck, 1967, 1976; Lewinsohn, 1974; Rehm, 1977, 1990; Seligman, 1975). With few notable exceptions (e.g., Lewinsohn, Hoberman, Teri, & Hautzinger 1985), however, the relatively independent development of each theory has resulted in separate and univariate models with competing concepts, research, and treatment strategies (Heiby, 1992).

Following a brief overview of the most prominent current psychological account of unipolar depression, the cognitive model, we will attempt to integrate major concepts and research relating to unipolar depression by specifying and expanding the paradigmatic behavioral (PB) model of depression originally developed by Staats and Heiby (1985; Heiby & Staats, 1990). The goal of this model is to integrate a large number of variables and processes that have been proposed in other largely univariate theories of depression. The areas covered include the inherited and acquired biological risk factors, historical antecedent events, psychological vulnerability in the form of deficient and inappropriate basic behavioral repertoires, current antecedent or precipitating events, and the stimulus properties and consequences of depressive symptoms. The PB model relates these variables in a manner that is useful for clinicians to understand depression in a more comprehensive way and for guiding the idiographic assessment and treatment of persons suffering from a major depressive episode. Although our focus will be on behavioral research, other research with relevance for the PB model will also be examined. Finally, we will delineate implications of the model for the treatment and prevention of relapse of depression.

Current Psychological Accounts of Depression

Overview of Cognitive Model of Depression

There is at this time no completely satisfactory single theory of the etiology of depression, and most researchers and clinicians seem to agree that depression occurs as a result of complex relations between biochemical and psychological factors. Any explanation of depression must account for a number of important features: the heterogeneity of symptoms, the episodic nature or more chronic appearance of depression, and the presence or absence of adverse environmental events prior to the episode. During the past ten to twelve years, most interest has centered on the presence of dysfunctional cognitions in depression (Clark & Steer, 1996).

Beck (1967, 1976) suggests that depressed people engage in negative and irrational distortions in their perceptions of life events or daily situations. Similarly, Seligman (1975) argues that people who become depressed are prone to making certain types of attributions about events. In the case of adverse events, these attributions are internal, stable, and global, resulting in a "pessimistic explanatory style." Both Beck's and Seligman's theories represent an interaction between the occurrence of an acute or chronic life stressor and the presence of maladaptive cognitive strategies to deal with these events; this interaction ultimately leads to the emergence of a depressive episode. Research on life events (Brown & Harris, 1978) has revealed that depressed people do encounter a higher number of adverse events in the period prior to the onset of an episode in comparison to nondepressed controls. However, the higher rate of events does not in itself account for depression because (a) some people also experience similar numbers and types of events as depressed subjects without becoming depressed, (b) some people become depressed without any apparent environmental precipitant, and (c) adverse life events are not uniquely precipitant of depression, but may also occur prior to other disorders such as schizophrenia or agoraphobia. Thus, cognitive theorists have argued that the *appraisal* of events plays a mediating role between the occurrence of a life event and the onset of depression, and that a particular type of cognitive appraisal of events will specifically lead to depression rather than to another disorder.

Cognitive accounts of depression are frequently couched in terms of human information processing (e.g., Williams, Watts, MacLeod, & Matthews, 1988). It is argued that negative automatic thoughts in depression arise from the operation of negative cognitive schemata. These schemata are hypothesized networks of associations through which information is organized and stored, and which influence the perception and retrieval of information following exposure to relevant situations or moods. The best evidence for the existence of such schemata comes from studies with the Modified Stroop Color-Naming Test in which people are asked to identify the color of negative and neutral (or other control) words (cf. MacLeod & Mathews, 1991). Depressed subjects show longer latencies to name the colors of negative words. The longer response latencies are interpreted as indicating that depression-related memories and associations triggered during access to the particular network interfere with the color-naming task. The most important support for the existence of a schema would come from studies of depression-prone people during periods of remission. These type of data are somewhat scarce, however, and the results to date have been inconsistent (e.g., Hedlund & Rude, 1995). There is good support for the view that the thinking of depressed people is characterized by negative appraisals of their own performance, negative predictions about the future, and internal attributions about failure events (Haaga, Dyck, & Ernst, 1991). What is less clear is precisely what role these cognitive aspects play in relation to the onset of an episode. Beck (1967, 1976) suggests that negative distorted thinking is simply "involved" in depression, but one must ask: is dysfunctional thinking a cause or a consequence of depressed mood, or both a cause and a consequence? We will return to this issue when we discuss the PB model of depression.

Disunified Knowledge: Need for Integrative Behavioral Approach

Typically, univariate models view factors such as neurochemical dysregulation, language and cognition, self-control, conditioning, and deficient reinforcement as independent or even in opposition to each other. As a result, these models do not adequately address interactions between variables and the heterogeneity of depressive phenomenology (Eifert, Forsyth, & Schauss, 1993; Staats, 1996; Staats & Heiby, 1985). Some authors (e.g., Ferster, 1973; Nezu, 1987; Willner, 1985) have recognized the need to develop more comprehensive and interactional frameworks that can organize and integrate the diverse facets of depression. Lewinsohn, Hoberman, Teri, and Hautzinger (1985) advanced one of the most integrative comprehensive behavioral-cognitive models of depression, which was derived from Lewinsohn's (1974) behavioral theory of depression.

This model focuses on a decrease in response-contingent reinforcement (a decrease in pleasant events or an increase in unpleasant events) as a primary cause of depression.

The model of Lewinsohn and colleagues (1985) proposes that the occurrence of antecedents (e.g., adverse life events) initiates the depressogenic process by disrupting substantial, important, and relatively automatic behavior patterns of an individual. Such disruptions, and the emotional upset they typically engender, are related to the occurrence of depression to the extent that they lead to a reduction of positive reinforcement or to an elevated rate of aversive experience. As a consequence, the balance of the quality of life of a person's interactions with the environment is shifted in a negative direction. The real or perceived inability to reverse the impact of this stress leads to a heightened state of self-awareness and self-focused attention that engenders a state of self-denigration, behavioral withdrawal, and dysphoria—the core symptoms of depression. These processes are moderated by individual differences and environmental variables that systematically increase (vulnerabilities) or decrease (immunities) the probability for the occurrence of depression.

The model proposed by Lewinsohn and associates is largely congruent with the behavioral model described in this chapter in that it encompasses important environmental and personal factors involved in the development and maintenance of depression. Although it also alludes to various vulnerabilities and immunities, it does not relate these factors in the same organized fashion as the PB model of depression is able to do with its roots in a behavioral framework that encompasses basic and advanced learning principles as well as personality and biological processes (psychological and biological vulnerabilities).

The Paradigmatic Behavioral Model of Depression

Paradigmatic behaviorism (PB) is an integrative multilevel theory originally developed by Arthur Staats (1968, 1975, 1996) that provides a bridge between basic levels and principles of behavior (i.e., the physiological and conditioning bases of behavior) and the more advanced and specifically human levels of functioning (i.e., learning through language, thinking, and other symbolic processes). Rather than competing with basic physiological and conditioning principles, this human learning level of theory builds upon these principles. Staats (1972, 1990, 1995, 1996) developed a general framework model of abnormal behavior and extended it to explain several specific disorders including depression and anxiety. These models relate specific biological, emotional, conditioning, and personality processes in the etiology and maintenance of psychological dysfunctions and integrate previously unrelated and competing concepts into one psychobiological framework. For example, in the past, language and other symbolic processes have been difficult to conceptualize in a behavioral framework, but by including and emphasizing higher-order classical conditioning principles, PB theory can account for the important role of language in depression and anxiety disorders (Eifert, 1987, 1990; Staats & Eifert, 1990).

In 1985, Staats and Heiby developed the backbone of an integrative, interactional, multivariate model of depression to accommodate the heterogeneity of major depression. According to this theory, deficient or inappropriate fundamental skills, or basic behavioral repertoires (BBRs) in the emotional-motivational, language-cognitive, and sensory-motor response domains, constitute a psychological vulnerability for a person to develop depression. Repertoires evolve continuously in a cumulative and hierarchical manner as a result of inappropriate and deficient learning conditions. Environmental events interact with these repertoires to produce the state of dysphoria, which, in turn, engenders other depressive symptoms by reducing the affective-reinforcing-directive (A-R-D) function of environmental stimuli. That is, if a stimulus fails to evoke a positive or negative affective response, it will not be reinforcing and will not evoke a motoric response. Heiby and Staats (1990) revised the original PB theory of depression by adding biological factors to the model. Staats (1996) also included a feedback loop (vicious cycle) to explain how the stimulus properties and consequences of the depressive symptoms (particularly the state of dysphoria) affect the individual's behavior in undesirable ways, which, in turn, affect the individual's social environment in negative ways.

Our expanded model, summarized in Figure 4-1, is designed to continue the development of the PB approach to depression. This model builds on and incorporates the original PB model of depression as well as subsequent theory developments proposed by Staats (e.g., 1996). Our model can be summarized as follows: psychological *and* biological vulnerabilities (BBRs, 0_1 and 0_2) are incurred via genetic and environmental influences (S_1). These endogenous variables continuously evolve and interact with environmental factors (S_2) to produce depressive symptoms in the emotional-motivational, language-cognitive, and sensory-motor domains. These symptoms have stimulus properties (s) that may evoke positive and negative environmental consequences (C). In turn, as depicted in the feedback loops in Figure 4-1, these consequences and the protracted state of dysphoria affect the individual's current life situation, behavioral repertoires, and biological vulnerabilities in a vicious cycle fashion.

The model shown in Figure 4-1 specifies five general domains that interact to produce depressive symptoms. For each of these domains, we list several key variables proposed by Staats and Heiby that have received empirical support. Congruent with recent changes to the PB model (Staats, 1993, 1995, 1996), the expanded depression model (a) separates inherited and acquired biological vulnerabilities; (b) introduces relevant organismic and environmental factors (e.g., parental unavailability, deficient problem-solving skills) not included in the earlier model; (c) delineates all the core symptoms of unipolar depression as listed in DSM-IV (1994); and (d) documents relations between symptoms, behavioral repertoires, and biological factors.

The PB model of depression is not so much a *new* theory of depression but a metatheory or a framework that serves to organize a variety of concepts and empirical findings that are relevant for understanding and treating depression. This heuristic framework may guide both researchers and clinicians in their activities. At a science level, the model encourages interdisciplinary research to obtain a more comprehensive understanding of depression. At a practical level, the model helps clinicians organize and relate individual client problems to design treatments and help prevent relapse of depression. As previously noted (Eifert, 1992; Staats & Heiby, 1985), paradigmatic frameworks of abnormal behavior are framework models. They contain a summary of relevant factors and their interrelations, whose pertinence remains to be determined in

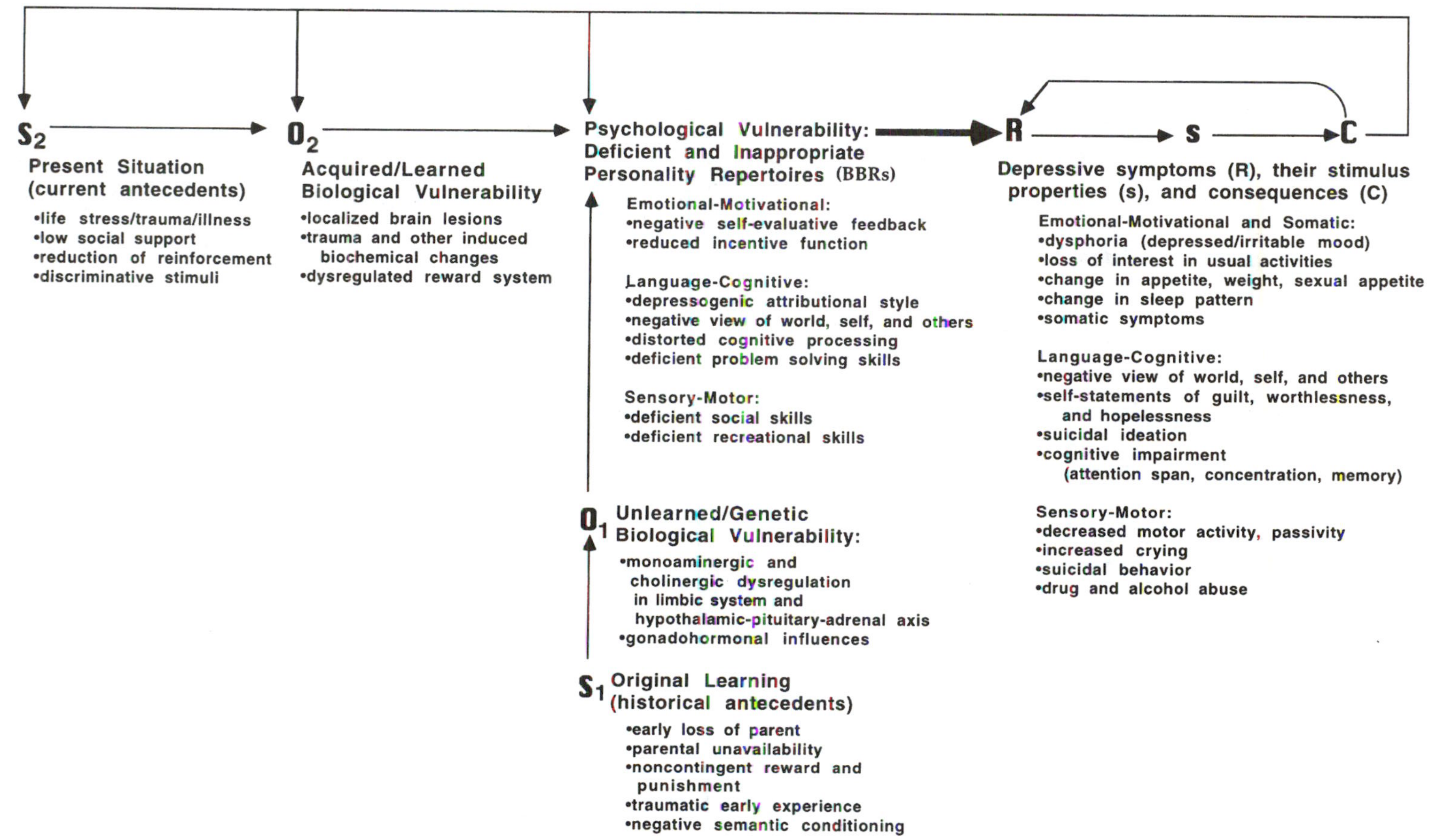

FIGURE 4-1. An integrative paradigmatic behavioral model of depression (derived and expanded from Staats & Heiby, 1985; Heiby & Staats, 1990; cf. Staats, 1996).

the individual case. In other words, not all factors are relevant for all cases, but all factors are *potentially* relevant. It should also be noted that, while the various paradigmatic domains are reviewed below sequentially, this separation is artificial and does not reflect the interactional and evolutional nature of depressive phenomena.

Historical Antecedents/Previous Learning (S_1)

Staats and Heiby (1985; Staats, 1996) stressed the need to investigate how each personality deficit (or maladaptive response pattern) is acquired. We will therefore now review current etiological knowledge that could assist in the prevention and treatment of these maladaptive repertoires.

Early Loss and Trauma

Childhood loss of a parent, particularly of a mother and before age eleven (Brown & Harris, 1978), is associated with a two to three times greater risk for developing depression (Bifulco, Brown, & Harris, 1987). Such loss appears to have more impact on girls than boys (Cadoret, O'Gorman, Heywood, & Troughton, 1985) and is related to reactive depression (Parker, Kiloh, & Hayward, 1987) and a higher rate of suicidal gestures (Willner, 1985). Depressive risk may be compounded by multiple exit events (e.g., death, separation, migration) incrementally reducing a person's ability to cope with future life stress (Goodyer & Altham, 1991).

Two explanations for the depressogenic effects of early loss have been proposed. First, parental loss may constitute a loss of social reinforcement, particularly if alternate sources are limited (Ferster, 1973; Staats & Heiby, 1985). Behavioral responding is similar in primates experiencing early parental loss and laboratory animals placed on an extinction schedule (Willner, 1985). An initial protest stage characterized by agitation, crying, and stereotyped behavior is followed by a behavioral extinction or despair stage characterized by changes in brain-wave activity, and decreased social contact, play, locomotion, appetite, and environmental responsiveness (Teuting et al., 1982). Biochemical diatheses, such as norepinephrine and dopamine deficits, seem to accentuate the effects of early loss (Teuting et al., 1982).

The second mechanism proposed to account for the depressogenic effects of early loss involves the lack of a parental model and the subsequent development of deficient behavioral repertoires involving interpersonal and mastery skills (Brown & Harris, 1978; Willner, 1985). In support of this theory, two-thirds of women raised in institutions fail to develop appropriate interpersonal and parenting skills (Quinton, Rutter, & Liddle, 1984). Unfortunately, many of the studies investigating the effects of early parental loss (and parental unavailability) rely upon retrospective accounts, and thus may be subject to recall biases.

An increased incidence of reactive depression (Bifulco et al., 1987; Parker & Hadzi-Pavlovic, 1992) and two cognitive diatheses, namely dysfunctional attitudes and depressogenic attributions (Whisman & Kwon, 1992), have been associated with parental unavailability and a lack of parental care (e.g., indifference and low responsiveness and control). It is possible that this emotional and caretaking unavailability is the critical factor in the relation between maternal loss and increased risk for depression (Roy, 1983).

Parental unavailability may also increase the salience of interpersonal stimuli, rendering the child sensitive to rejection and thus susceptible to "interpersonal depression" (Staats & Heiby, 1985).

Parental depression is associated with parental unavailability (Reid & Morrison, 1983); maternal protectiveness and hostility (Weissman, 1983); poor command-giving (Forehand, Lautenschlager, Faust, & Graziano, 1986); inconsistent, lax, and ineffective parenting; unrealistically high expectations; and a lack of emotional regulation (Cummings & Davies, 1994). Poor communication and deficient affective involvement have been found in over 75 percent of depressed patients' families of origin (Miller, Kabacoff, Keitner, & Epstein, 1986). As cautioned by Forehand, McCombs-Thomas, Wierson, Brody, and Fauber (1990), differences in the specificity and breadth of the parenting definitions used may affect findings in this research area.

Although the precise transmission mechanisms are unclear, maternal depression has been associated with (a) infant developmental delays and insecure attachment and depressive reactions (Anthony, 1983); (b) child and adolescent somatic, behavioral, and emotional problems, academic and peer difficulties, substance use, and depressive and suicidal symptomatology (Billings & Moos, 1985; Cohler, Gallant, Grunebaum, & Kaufman, 1983); and (c) withdrawal and sadness, as well as school, legal, and peer-relation problems (Weissman, 1983).

In both animals and humans, the experience of uncontrollable reward and punishment has led to depressed affect and behavior, passivity, and neurochemical changes characteristic of depression (Lamb, Davis, Tramill, & Kleinhammer-Tramill, 1987; Teuting et al., 1982). Beach (1993) found that passivity, hopelessness, personal helplessness (the attribution of positive events to external, specific, and/or unstable sources) is related to children's perceptions of unwarranted maternal punishment and to the absence of merited maternal reward. Fortunately, these deficits may be rectified by subsequent exposure to controllable outcomes (Maier & Seligman, 1976).

Apart from early parental loss, the other major childhood risk factors for depression are the presence of physical and/or sexual abuse, and the witnessing of abuse between parents. For both child and adult survivors, strong associations have been found between these early traumata and a number of psychological vulnerabilities and depressive symptoms. Vulnerabilities and symptoms include deficient conflict resolution and coping skills, deficient self-regulation, poor interpersonal skills, low self-esteem, hopelessness, passivity, emotional constriction, depressed affect, irritability, anxiety, guilt, suicidal behavior, alcohol abuse, social withdrawal, somatic complaints, and sleep problems (Herman, 1992; Hibbard, Spence, Tzeng, Zollinger, & Orr, 1992; Malinowsky-Rummel & Hansen, 1993; Wolfe, Gentile, & Wolfe, 1989). Symptoms are severe enough to warrant a depression diagnosis in 58 percent of sexually abused children (McLeer, Deblinger, Atkins, Foa, & Ralphe, 1988). Conclusions from these studies, however, are hampered by a number of methodological problems, including the use of retrospective reports and different definitions of abuse.

Negative Semantic Conditioning Regarding the World and the Self
Although depressogenic affective responses and evaluations may be classically conditioned to verbal and tangible stimuli by parents, teachers, and other emotionally rele-

vant persons, individuals may also condition themselves (Staats & Eifert, 1990). For instance, depressed individuals learn to pair the self with negatively valenced and self-recriminatory labels and to pair the world and their outcomes with depressogenic evaluations, thereby fostering the negative cognitive triad that is central in Beck's (1976) theory of depression. Such an extensive conditioned verbal-emotional repertoire is likely to engender low self-esteem, pessimistic expectations, and helplessness (Staats & Heiby, 1985). Semantic conditioning may also be involved in the transmission of attributional styles and could explain the high correlation between maternal and child depressogenic attributions (Seligman et al., 1984).

Unlearned Biological Vulnerability (O_1)

The biological basis of depression is not fully understood, although various regulatory disturbances involving the limbic system and faulty neurochemical transmission appear to constitute a biological vulnerability (Thase, Frank, & Kupfer, 1985). Of course, the susceptibility to develop a depressive disorder may itself be a result of genetic predisposition, specific neurotransmitter disturbances, learning history during early development, or some combination of these factors.

Genetic Predisposition

Genetic theories posit the existence of a depressive biological predisposition. No single mechanism of genetic transmission has yet been established, and support for this theory is derived from family and twin studies. For instance, morbidity for depression is eight times higher in the biological than in the adoptive parents of persons with unipolar depression (Wender, Kety, Rosenthal, & Schulsinger, 1986). Concordance rates for monozygotic twins reared apart range between 40 and 76 percent, whereas those of dizygotic twins and siblings are only about 10 percent (Kandel, 1991; Tsuang, 1978). Thus, there is some support for a genetic vulnerability to depression.

Biochemical Dysregulation

Biochemical theories of depression postulate that some depressions may result from innate (O_1) or traumatically acquired (O_2) deficient neurotransmission at important sites in the central nervous system. Dysregulation of sleep, appetite, mood and pleasure, and the increased anxiety evidenced in depressive episodes have been related to reduced innervation of noradrenergic neurons from the locus ceruleus and serotonergic neurons from various nuclei of the brainstem, innervating the limbic forebrain, hypothalamus, hippocampus, and other regions of the cerebral cortex (Kandel, 1991; Thase et al., 1985). In addition, serotonergic and dopaminergic deficits may exist in subsets of depressed individuals (Golden & Janowsky, 1990). It is currently postulated that depleted norepinephrine function impacts the hypothalamic release of corticotrophic-releasing hormone (CRH), which subsequently influences the release of adrenocorticotropic hormone (ACTH) by the pituitary gland (Harte & Eifert, 1995; Harte, Eifert, & Smith, 1995). In turn, ACTH partially controls the adrenal gland's release of cortisol (Teuting et al., 1982). Nonsuppression of cortisol, as assessed by the dexamethasone suppression test (DST), has been demonstrated in fifty to sixty percent of depressed individuals compared to 0 percent of nondepressed subjects (Appelboom-Fondu, Kirkhofs, & Mendlewicz, 1988).

There are other indications of a biological involvement in depression. For example, individuals with endogenous depression, on average experience Rapid Eye Movement (REM) sleep onset forty-five minutes earlier and a greater proportion of REM sleep than nondepressed and nonendogenously depressed individuals (Kupfer, 1976; Kupfer & Thase, 1983; Vogel, Neill, Hagler, & Kors, 1990). These sleep disturbances suggest a sub-type-specific physiological disturbance that may be related to a cholinergic agent, physostigmine, and to an increase of ACTH relative to NE (Golden & Janowsky, 1990). Interestingly, tricyclics with anticholinergic properties (e.g., amitryptaline) prolong REM sleep onset and reduce the amount of time spent in REM sleep (Golden & Janowsky, 1990). Attempts to use REM latency as a predictor of response to cognitive therapy, however, have not been successful (e.g., Simons & Thase, 1992).

A finding of special importance for psychological theories of depression is that environmental stress (S_2), such as inescapable shock, has been found to result in neurotransmitter dysfunctions (Siever & Davis, 1985; Teuting et al., 1982). Not all evidence is supportive of a biochemical basis for depression, and research in this area has faced numerous methodological difficulties. For example, evidence for the neurochemical theories is partially derived from correlations between depressive symptoms and plasma and urinary levels of specific neurotransmitters, including the monoamines (norepinephrine [NE] and dopamine [DA]), an indoleamine (serotonin), and their metabolites. Urinary tests are not conclusive, however, because diet, drugs, and activity levels influence urinary neurotransmitters and metabolite levels (Harte & Eifert, 1995; Thase et al., 1985).

The impaired ability to experience pleasure in depressed individuals may be related to dysregulation of the telencephalic-diencephalic reward center (Willner, 1985). Functional deficits of DA, rather than NE as previously assumed, in the mesolimbic system may impede the transmission of action potentials from the emotional/motivational system (including the amygdala) to the motor system, thereby reducing motoric efforts to elicit pleasurable stimuli and to avoid painful ones. Although speculative, this relation may provide a physiological basis for the A-R-D function of salient stimuli—a central tenet of paradigmatic behavioral theory.

Psychological Vulnerability

As with biological factors, psychological vulnerabilities vary between individuals (Heiby, 1989). Although the relation of depressogenic behavioral repertoires to biological and environmental risk factors has not been investigated, some psychological-biological relations have been reported. We hope that further delineation of these "psychological units" will provide a guiding framework for future interdisciplinary research called for by Willner (1985).

Emotional-Motivational Repertoire

This response domain consists of affective responses to stimuli, some of which are verbal (Staats & Eifert, 1990), that may constitute an important depressogenic repertoire.

Reduced incentive function.   According to the PB theory of emotion (Staats & Eifert, 1990), motoric responding depends upon the A-R-D function of a stimulus. If, due to a depressive inability to experience pleasure (Rehm, 1990), stimuli do not elicit affective responses in a depressed individual, these stimuli will not be able to function as a reinforcer for this individual nor will the person approach or avoid them. In this way, dysphoria may result in generalized behavioral suppression. Three mechanisms may account for reduced A-R-D function: (1) neurochemical reward system dysregulations may reduce an individual's positive affective experience and ability to enjoy reinforcers; (2) the sadder-but-wiser effect (Alloy & Abramson, 1979), or labeling the self, world, and future in negatively valenced terms, may induce a negative outcome expectancy that reduces motivation and thus behavior (Staats & Heiby, 1985); and (3) setting events, such as pain, fatigue, aversive stimulation, and lack of predictability, may reduce the relative value of stimuli that are typically preferred (Horner & Vaughan, 1993).

Depressogenic self-evaluative feedback and self-reinforcement.   Depressed individuals have been shown to engage in verbal behavior that reduces motivation. They have been found to rate their own performance less favorably than equivalent performances by others (Rehm, 1990), to reinforce their own performance infrequently (Heiby, 1981), to expect negative feedback from others (Willner, 1985), and to underestimate the amount of positive feedback actually given to them (Curtis, 1990). In some cases, this self-evaluative style is related to the tendency of depressive persons to selectively apply perfectionist standards of performance to themselves, whereas in other cases it indicates that their *perceived* abilities and performance do not meet their perfectly normal standards (Hewitt & Flett, 1991). In any case, such self-critical evaluations may engender the provision of insufficient self-reward and excessive self-punishment (Curtis 1990), both of which reduce the A-R-D function of their own accomplishments. Moreover, the tendency to withhold self-reinforcement, found in a subset of depressed individuals, renders them more susceptible to reductions in environmental reinforcement (Heiby, 1983a, 1983b).

Sensory-Motor Repertoire

This response domain describes motoric responses to, and actions upon, the environment. Specific skill deficiencies pertinent to depression include social and recreational skill deficits.

Deficient social skills.   Depression has been associated with deficient communication and interaction skills, including decision-making, problem-solving (McLean, 1976), assertiveness (Curtis, 1990), ambiguous expressive communication (Prkachin, Craig, Papagorgis, & Reith, 1977), shorter communications, slowed social responding, and decreased ability to reinforce others (Teuting et al., 1982). Additional skill deficits, which may be partially explained by psychomotor retardation (Staats & Heiby, 1985), include a relatively high rate of active listening, short speech durations, few hand movements (Bouhuys, Jansen, & van den Hoofdaaker, 1991), a low voice, constricted posture, and reduced eye movements and facial expression (Ulrich & Harms, 1985). Additional depressive nonverbal behaviors include downcast eyes and increased frowning and sighing (Biglan et al., 1985).

Although these depressive behaviors may initially evoke sympathy and support from other persons, their persistence tends to become burdensome and aversive to others, who may then withdraw (Biglan et al., 1985). Such social consequences appear more typical of depressed males than depressed females (Joiner, Alfano, & Metalsky, 1992). In response to this type of interpersonal loss, some depressed persons engage in hostile behavior or escalate their depressive behavior to regain support (Coyne, 1976; Joiner et al., 1992; Hirschfeld, Klerman, Clayton, Keller, & Andreasen, 1984). Either response may further tax the patience and coping ability of others and lead them to withdraw (Teichman & Teichman, 1990).

Depressive behavior may also impede the formation of new friendships. It has been found to evoke negative responses in the first three minutes of interaction with strangers (Gotlib & Robinson, 1982). Typical responses to depressed persons include negative affective reactions; and verbal and nonverbal rejection signals, including less frequent smiles, less aroused and pleasant facial expressions, fewer supportive comments, and a higher proportion of negative conversational content (Gotlib & Robinson, 1982; Teichman & Teichman, 1990). Thus, marked sensitivity of depressed individuals to social criticism may, at least in part, reflect their increased exposure to interpersonal rejection (Coyne, 1976).

Deficient recreational skills/pursuits.   Depressed mood is correlated with a reduced number of activities, fewer group interactions, and smaller social networks (Teuting et al., 1982). This reduced engagement in recreational activities may result from reduced incentive function (Staats & Heiby, 1985), learned passivity, and/or inadequate learning of recreational repertoires (Lewinsohn, Hoberman, Teri, & Hautzinger, 1985). Cohler and associates (1983) demonstrated that children of mothers reporting deficient leisure skills had significantly fewer hobbies and interests, and that children of mothers reporting fewer interpersonal contacts and less interpersonal satisfaction had poorer peer relations and fewer friends. Observational reports by significant others are necessary to support these findings, which are based solely on self-report and thus subject to a depressive person's tendency to underestimate self-performance.

Language-Cognitive Repertoire

This response domain describes overt verbalizations or covert processes that are believed to play a major role in the initiation and maintenance of depressive mood and behavior. It should be noted that, as with all covert phenomena, self-report biases may have confounded the findings described below.

Depressogenic attributional style.   Depressed persons exhibiting this cognitive vulnerability tend to attribute negative events to internal, stable, and/or global factors (Seligman et al., 1984) and desirable events to external, unstable, and specific causes (Barthe & Hammen, 1981; Persons & Rao, 1985). Thus, the individual assumes responsibility for failure but takes no credit for success (Abramson, Metalsky, & Alloy, 1989).

This cognitive vulnerability may be restricted to semantically conditioned events or those that are perceived as controllable (Staats & Heiby, 1985).

Inappropriate view of the self, world, and future.   According to Beck's (1967, 1976) cognitive distortion model, depressed persons perceive (a) the self as deficient and worthless, (b) the world as demanding and defeating, and (c) the future as an extension of the current misery. Although this "negative cognitive triad" has received some clinical and other empirical support (Biglan et al., 1985; Rehm, 1990), its etiology remains unclear. Beck posits that these distortions are derived from negative life experiences. However, not all individuals who have suffered negative life events exhibit these distortions. Thus, an alternate etiological explanation involving negative semantic conditioning (Staats & Heiby, 1985) might be more appropriate. According to this theory, individuals may develop a negative cognitive triad if they are exposed to (and later engage in) the repeated pairing of themselves, the world, and the future with negatively valenced descriptors. Empirical validation of this theory is required.

Distorted cognitive processing.   Beck (1967, 1976) and his associates (Beck, Rush, Shaw, & Emery, 1979) propose that the negative cognitive triad may be maintained by a number of depressive cognitive-processing errors such as (a) arbitrary inference: drawing self-defeating conclusions without sufficient evidence; (b) overgeneralization: drawing conclusions based upon a single incident; (c) magnification or enhancement of the significance of one aspect of a situation or one specific event; (d) all-or-nothing thinking; and (e) mental filtering: selective focusing on negative information while excluding any positive evidence.

Empirical findings support the presence of these negative biases in depression. Depressed individuals tend to focus their conversation upon negative personal events (Biglan et al., 1985), be highly self-critical (Franche & Dobson, 1992), focus selectively on and overestimate their own negative behavior, recall more unpleasant than pleasant self-descriptors, and overestimate negative feedback and underestimate positive feedback from others (Clark & Steer, 1996; Willner, 1985). This selective processing appears to be especially pertinent for personally salient events, often involving relationship or achievement issues (Hammen, Ellicott, & Gitlin, 1989; Hammen, Marks, Mayol, & de-Mayo, 1985). Thus, for a dependent depressed person whose self-worth is related to interpersonal relations, depressive episodes may be associated with, and predicted by, negative interpersonal events (Segal et al., 1992). Conversely, for a self-critical group of depressed individuals, depression may be related to achievement issues (Hammen et al., 1989, 1985).

Deficient problem-solving/coping skills.   Depressed individuals demonstrate significantly more problem avoidance and less support-seeking (Veiel, Kuhner, Brill, & Ihle, 1992), generate fewer and less-effective solutions, conceptualize fewer obstacles and subsequent alternative solutions, demonstrate a pessimistic orientation towards problems, and make less-effective decisions (Marx, Williams, & Claridge, 1992; Nezu & Ronan, 1987). Further, depressive deficits in interpersonal problem solving appear to be a skills deficit rather than a performance deficit (Marx et al., 1992).

Stable Repertoires or Concomitants of Depressed Mood?

The question of whether depressogenic repertoires are stable vulnerabilities, activated by depressogenic events, or simply concomitants of depressed mood, is critical to a PB model of depression (cf. Staats, 1996). Resolution of this question is impeded, however, by an over-reliance on cross-sectional and correlational studies. Longitudinal investigations of repertoire stability have produced mixed results (Persons & Miranda, 1992). For instance, although depressogenic attributions have been found to be relatively stable (Seligman et al., 1984), persist despite symptomatic remission (Eaves & Rush, 1984), and precede and predict depression (Seligman et al., 1984), a number of studies have found this cognitive style to covary with depressive symptoms (Persons & Miranda, 1992). The debate about the stability of psychological repertoires has also been heavily influenced by a wealth of studies supporting mood-congruent information processing in depressed persons (cf. MacLeod & Mathews, 1991). Strong evidence has accumulated that, during a depressed state, information stored during previous depressed states as well as perceptual cues, thoughts, and expectations associated with sadness are more readily retrieved and generated than positively valenced information (Greenberg & Safran, 1984; MacLeod & Mathews, 1991; Weingarter & Murphy, 1977). According to this expansion of state-dependent learning theory, stable latent repertoires may only be accessible during depressed mood states. Persons and Miranda (1992) suggested that the assessment and modification of these repertoires may therefore depend upon depressed mood induction.

Current Antecedents/Present Situation (S₂)

The depressogenic impact of current life events depends on an individual's learning history (S_1) and their current biological and psychological vulnerabilities. Although the full range of diathesis-stress interactions have not yet been determined, a number of antecedent and setting events have been identified.

Life Stress

Risk of depression, particularly nonchronic reactive depression, is increased in the six-month period following undesirable life events (Billings & Moos, 1984; Lloyd, 1980; Roy, Breire, Doran, & Pichar, 1985), particularly exit events such as separations and death. Chronic mild stress, including work-related stress, unemployment, marital problems, and homemaking and child-care demands, have also been related to increased depressive risk (Brown & Harris, 1978; Willner, 1985).

Personality variables, such as an individual's appraisal and coping repertoires, have been shown to mediate the depressogenic impact of negative life events. For instance, 20 percent of sexually assaulted women were found to develop major depression within one year after the assault (Burnam, Stein, Golding, & Siegel, 1988), but attributions of future helplessness and self-blame accounted for as much as 67 percent of the variance in post-rape depression scores (Frazier, 1990). Similarly, over 50 percent of chronic pain patients and up to 33 percent of hospitalized medical patients experience clinical depression, but the meaning ascribed to illness, the perception of physician supportiveness, and perceived competence and availability of cognitive and behavioral coping strategies to deal with adverse life events have been shown to mediate the experience of pain and illness-related depression (Barkwell, 1991; Rosenberg, Peterson, Hayes, & Hatcher, 1988; Schermelleh-Engel, Eifert, Moosbrugger, & Frank, 1997).

Low Social Support
During periods of high stress, lack of social support increases fourfold the likelihood of depression (Billings & Moos, 1984) and impedes recovery (Veiel et al., 1992). The importance of social support is potentiated for women who suffered a childhood maternal loss (Brown & Harris, 1978). The presence of an affectionate supportive partner and good living conditions may moderate and attenuate this depressive risk (Parker & Hadzi-Pavlovic, 1984; Quinton et al., 1984). However, due to the association between a history of negative parenting and unsupportive adult partnerships (Hickie et al., 1990), adult depressive risk is frequently perpetuated. Again, reliance on retrospective and subjective reports and varying definitions of social support make it difficult to draw any firm conclusions from this research area.

Reduction of Current Reinforcement
Inadequate social reinforcement has been associated with a depressive subtype characterized by functional serotonergic deficits, irritability, guilt, and serious suicide attempts (Willner, 1985). Reinforcement loss may result from marital separation, bereavement, restricted activity due to neonate care, loss of a job, and geographic relocation (Gaylord & Symons, 1986; Lloyd, 1980; Phillips, 1986; Rehm, 1990; Staats & Heiby, 1985), and may be exacerbated by concomitant financial hardship (Rodgers, 1991). These stressors may induce depression through reduced response-contingent interpersonal reinforcement (Lewinsohn, 1974) and/or via an overgeneralized extinction effect in that all activities formerly associated with the lost object may become unavailable or unrewarding (Ferster, 1973). The depressive behavior that ensues may result in further loss of interpersonal reinforcement, thereby setting up a vicious cycle and perpetuating the depression (Joiner et al., 1992).

Discriminative Stimuli for Depressive Behavior
Certain people, activities, and/or situations may serve as discriminative stimuli for depressive behavior. For instance, the presence of an empathic, supportive person may evoke helpless and depressive behavior. If assistance or sympathy is delivered, such behavior will be reinforced. Depressive behavior evoked by threatening interpersonal stimuli (e.g., aggression) may be maintained through negative reinforcement, that is, the response-contingent termination of the angry or aggressive behavior (Biglan et al., 1985). Finally, negatively valenced physical or verbal stimuli associated with a former loss or social rejection may trigger depressive mood and behavior.

Acquired Biological Vulnerability (O₂)

Human physiology and neurochemistry are continuously evolving to accommodate environmental changes, including acute physiological trauma and drug action. While DSM-IV (APA, 1994) separates organically induced depressions from other depressive disorders, this separation seems artificial and is not adhered to in the PB model of depression; depressogenic biological changes are incorporated in the diathesis-stress model as acquired biological vulnerabilities (O_2) (Staats, 1993, 1996).

Localized Brain Lesions

Stroke-induced unilateral brain damage has been associated with impaired affect regulation and reduced comprehension and expression of the emotional aspects of speech (Schwartz, Davidson, & Maer, 1975). Endogenous depression has been associated with damage to the left frontal lobe, whereas reactive symptoms appear to be linked to right parietal and temporal lobe damage. The resultant difficulties in emotional perception and expression may affect social interactional skills (Willner, 1985).

Trauma-Induced Biochemical Changes

Exposure to mild stress sensitizes NE cells so that they respond more rapidly to subsequent stressors (Post, 1992). Uncontrollable and unpredictable stress induces other biochemical vulnerabilities including NE and DA depletions, an increase in ACTH relative to NE, enhanced neurotransmitter re-uptake, and reduced receptor number and sensitivity (Teuting et al., 1982).

Other Acquired Precipitants of Biochemical Change

Pharmacological agents (e.g., oral contraceptives, reserpine, and beta blockers), biological conditions (such as hypothyroidism, cortisol-secreting tumors, and postpartum hormonal changes), and chronic alcohol and phencyclidine consumption may evoke depressive reactions via monoaminergic and serotoninergic dysregulations, respectively (Aneshensel & Huba, 1983; Caracci, Migone, & Mukherjee, 1983; Pietraszek et al., 1991). Other precipitants include methyldopa, steroids, psychostimulants, and west-to-east travel across two or more time zones (Patten & Lamarre, 1992).

Behavioral Deficits and Excesses: Depressive Symptoms

Evidence for the cluster of behavioral deficits and excesses which constitute the DSM-IV criterion symptoms will now be presented and related, where possible, to biological and psychological vulnerabilities.

Emotional-Motivational and Somatic Symptoms

Depressed/irritable mood (dysphoria).   This symptom is recognized as the defining feature of major depression in DSM-IV (APA, 1994). Dysphoria also has a central place in the PB model and is considered a cause (or may exacerbate) many of the other symptoms of depression (Staats & Heiby, 1985; Staats, 1996). Dysphoria is a conglomeration of stimulus circumstances that in their complexity produce a deep, pervasive, lasting negative emotional state (Rose & Staats, 1988; Staats & Eifert, 1990). This negative emotional state occurs as a consequence of the unique interaction between an individual's current environmental situation, personality repertoires, and biological vulnerabilities. Staats and Eifert (1990) pointed out that an important reason why emotional conditioning principles have not been seen as basic in depression is that dysphoria does not have the specific, immediate, ephemeral characteristics of a discrete emotional response. For example, the emotional response experienced by a phobic person is intense but short-lived and occurs only when the individual is confronted with the feared stimulus, whereas depressed individuals experience a continuing pervasive emotional state of dysphoria. In any case, differentiating discrete emotional responses from persisting emotional states should not imply separate and independent processes. For instance, Staats (1996) points out that the emotional state may function as a background condition that can be made more positive or negative by more ephemeral emotional responding.

Loss of interest in usual activities.   Depressed individuals exhibit diminished interest or pleasure in most activities of the day (Nelson & Charney, 1981). Diminished interest and pleasure can be explained by (a) changes in the A-R-D value of salient stimuli, (b) the redirection of attention through avoidance of unpleasant events (Ferster, 1973; Grosscup & Lewinsohn, 1980), (c) a low level of response-contingent reinforcement received from self and others (Youngren & Lewinsohn, 1980; Nelson & Craighead, 1977), and (d) decreased activation of the mesolimbic DA system due to stress-induced dysregulation of the ACh and NE systems (Carson & Adams, 1980).

Somatic symptoms.   Somatic complaints such as pain, respiratory, gastrointestinal, cardiac, and sleep problems are frequently presented to physicians and occasionally result in hospitalizations (Lombardi, 1990; Wilson, Widmer, Cadoret, & Judiesch, 1983). It is estimated that 12 to 35 percent of medical patients are significantly depressed and that in a majority of these cases, depression remains undiagnosed (Lombardi, 1990). Given the risk of suicide in depressed persons, physicians should consider a diagnosis of depression when patients present with the above constellation of somatic symptoms (Wilson, Widmer, Cadoret, & Judiesch, 1983).

Change in sleep, appetite, weight, and sexual appetite.   Dysregulated sleep patterns as well as early onset and a larger proportion of REM sleep have been linked to cholinergic stimulation of the pontine reticular formation (Golden & Janowsky, 1990). These symptoms exist in about two-thirds of endogenously depressed adults, but are rare in adolescence, suggesting a delayed onset of REM dysregulation (Appelboom-Fondu et al., 1988; Kerkhofs, Hoffman, De Martelaere, Linkowski, & Mendlewicz, 1985). Atypical depression is characterized by hypersomnia and shortened REM latency without the frequent awakenings typical of endogenous depression, accompanied by increased appetite, weight gain, agitation, and headaches (Garvey, Mungas, & Tolletson, 1984; Quitkin et al., 1985). Increased appetite and weight gain was specifically associated with serotonin depletion, whereas reduced appetite and weight loss was associated with enhanced serotonin function (Willner, 1985).

Motor Symptoms
Decreased motor activity, passivity, and withdrawal.   Psychomotor retardation, including reduced initiation and maintenance of speech and task performance, has been

found to be more prevalent among females, older individuals, and persons evidencing late onset depression (Avery & Silverman, 1984). Dopaminergic deficits are thought to contribute to this symptomatology and DA-enhancing drugs, such as amphetamines, have been found to alleviate retarded depression (Willner, 1985).

Suicidal behavior.   Childhood and adolescent unipolar depression is the most prominent risk factor for adult suicidality (Rao, Weissman, Martin, & Hammond, 1993), and 37 percent of depressed children attempt suicide during their life (Kovacs, Golston, & Gatsonia, 1993). The coexistence of conduct and/or substance abuse has been found to triple the suicide risk (Kovacs et al., 1993; Whitters, Cadoret, Troughton, & Reuben, 1987). Given that childhood depression typically persists into adulthood (Rao et al., 1993), the above statistics probably underestimate the lifetime prevalence of suicidality in depressed individuals.

Drug and/or alcohol use.   A subset of depressed persons, particularly those with a family history of alcoholism or sociopathy, abuse drugs and alcohol (Cadoret et al., 1985; Smith & North, 1988). Chronic alcohol use may compound the depressive experience through reduced social functioning and increased depressive symptoms (Aneshensel & Huba, 1983). A dysregulated HPA axis and beta-endorphin/ACTH ratio may be a biochemical risk factor for both alcoholism and depression (Blum, Wallace, & Hall, 1986).

Language-Cognitive Symptoms

Cognitive impairment.   Although some studies suggest that depressed persons exhibit memory deficits, including impaired free and delayed recall (Curtis, 1990), it is still controversial whether depression actually has a negative impact on memory or merely increases self-critical appraisal of memory (see MacLeod & Mathews, 1991). Two explanations for potential memory defects have been proposed: (1) reduced performance may result from decreased motivation and task persistence, perhaps reflecting negative outcome expectations (Willner, 1985); and (2) the amount of information processed and stored may be reduced during depressive episodes because of ruminative thinking when the exclusive processing of a particular concern may divert attention and disturb encoding (Nelson & Mazure, 1985). Ruminative thinking occurs in 53 percent of persons with endogenous depression and coincides with pathological guilt, motor retardation, and morning mood worsening (Nelson & Mazure, 1985).

Guilt, worthlessness, hopelessness, and suicidal ideation.   Persons with reactive depression tend to (a) hold inappropriate notions of sinfulness, guilt, and unworthiness; (b) perceive themselves to be of inferior self-worth, intelligence, attractiveness, romantic appeal, and social status; (c) recall a greater number of experiences reflecting negatively on the self, and (d) predict negative personal outcomes (Curtis, 1990; King, Naylor, Segal, Evans, & Shain, 1993). Hopelessness is a central feature of depression and is often displayed during, and may be activated by, stressful situations (Miranda, 1992; Rosenbaum, Carlson, & Guthrie, 1987). Its depressogenic effects have been found to account for 25 percent of the variance in adult depression beyond the 10 percent of variance accounted for by life stress (Dixon, Heppner, Burnett, & Lips, 1993). Approximately 85 percent of depressed individuals who express hopelessness have suicidal thoughts (Kovacs et al., 1993). Not surprisingly, hopelessness is a critical predictor of suicidality in depressed individuals (Beck, Steer, Kovacs, & Garrison, 1985).

Implications of PB Model for Treatment and Relapse Prevention

In this section, we will outline some practical clinical implications of the PB model and propose an idiographic model-driven approach to the assessment and treatment of depression. We will then briefly review the status of treatment outcome research for depression using conventional group design studies and delineate risk factors for the recurrence of depression and its prevention.

Idiographic Assessment and Treatment of Depression

The PB model is a comprehensive resource for diagnosticians and other clinicians because it accords biological, conditioning, language-cognitive, and personality processes their proper place in the etiology and treatment of depression. Therapists may use the wealth of information from the different domains of the model to guide therapeutic questioning and functional analyses. The PB model encourages and requires a comprehensive assessment that is likely to include historical antecedents, biological risk factors, deficient and inappropriate behavioral repertoires, current environmental antecedents and consequences of the problematic behavior, and idiographic symptom patterns. Idiographic client models and treatment plans may then be generated by eliminating any irrelevant model components and targeting only the critical areas in treatment. We have termed this approach to treatment Paradigmatic Behavior Therapy (Eifert, 1996; Eifert, Evans, & McKendrick, 1990; Staats, 1990, 1995), because interventions are guided by integrative models of psychological dysfunctions and individualized case formulations.

Environmental and personal resources should be assessed, developed, and utilized to change depressogenic repertoires and prevent relapse following treatment (Staats & Heiby, 1985). Thus, unlike the current diagnostic system, the PB model provides sufficiently specific and detailed information to allow for a better matching of treatment to individual needs. This information can be used to design individualized treatment programs where only those model components are targeted that have been identified in the functional analysis as contributing to that particular client's problem (Eifert, 1996; Eifert et al., 1990). This individualized approach could improve treatment efficiency and also reduce client frustration by omitting irrelevant treatment components from standardized treatment manuals. For example, if a client's primary deficit is in the language-cognitive domain (e.g., negative self-talk), cognitive restructuring is indicated. However, if a client demonstrates deficient sensory-motor skills (e.g., lacks assertive behavior), then assertiveness training should be provided. The efficiency and efficacy of this specific deficit-treatment matching does not always lead to superior outcomes (cf. Eifert, Schulte, Zvolensky, Lejuez, & Lau, 1997). There are, however, several studies with depressed individuals suggesting that matching treatment (behavioral or cognitive) to the predominant type of deficits (social skills deficit or dysfunctional attributional styles) produces better outcomes than a nonmatching of depression type and treatment (Gavino, Godoy, Rodriguez-Naranjo, & Eifert, 1996; Heiby, 1986; McNight, Nelson, Hayes, & Jarrett, 1984).

Treatment Outcome and Relapse Prevention

Response to Treatment

There is now a large body of group-based research on the efficacy of cognitive-behavioral treatments (CBT) for depression (Hollon et al., 1992; Persons, 1993). Studies in this area have been subjected to meta-analyses in at least four different research reports (Dobson, 1989; Nietzel, Russell, Hemmings, & Gretter, 1987; Robinson, Berman, & Neimeyer, 1990; Steinbrueck, Maxwell, & Howard, 1983). A number of studies of CBT for depression have indicated a success rate of about 60 to 70 percent for recovery from a given episode (Blackburn, Bishop, Glen, Whalley, & Christie, 1981; Elkin et al., 1989; Murphy, Simons, Wetzel, & Lustman, 1984; Hollon et al., 1992; Rush, Beck, Kovacs, & Hollon, 1977). CBT has been found to be as efficacious as antidepressant medication during initial treatment of the depressive episode. However, the importance of selecting treatments that are most appropriate for a given individual is reinforced by the findings of a recent study by Stewart, McGrath, Quitkin, and Rabkin (1993). These authors found that patients who failed to respond to CBT eventually had a good outcome after treatment with imipramine. This is a small study, but an important one which warrants replication. Whether the reverse result holds, with imipramine failures responding to CBT, is an interesting question awaiting empirical examination. Thus, there is some suggestion that differential responsiveness may still underlie the overall similarity in outcomes in large samples.

The large NIMH study (Elkin et al., 1989) indicates that interpersonal psychotherapy is at least as effective as CBT, and, indeed, showed better outcomes on some measures. The growing body of literature on interpersonal aspects of depression (e.g., Hops et al., 1987), including the work on expressed emotion (Hooley, Orley, & Teasdale, 1986) and studies reviewed earlier on social antecedents, suggest that altering the social environment may produce significant treatment benefits.

Predicting Treatment Outcome and Relapse

It is well established that unipolar depression is characterized by a highly recurrent course in which episodes of depression alternate with periods that vary from complete remission to partial symptomatic expression. Estimates of the overall rate of relapse or recurrence are as high as 50 percent by the end of two years (Wilson, 1996). Despite this high rate of recurrence, and in view of the large volume of research on causal processes in depression reviewed in this chapter, it is somewhat surprising how few studies have examined factors that provoke either relapse or promote maintenance following recovery from an episode. Researchers tend to make the general assumption that similar processes are at work in the initiation of each episode. For instance, there is evidence (e.g., Paykel & Tanner, 1976) that adverse life events precede not only the onset of the disorder, but that they also precede subsequent episodes. In a comprehensive review of available data, Wilson (1996) identified a number of factors that predict patient response to treatment: (1) pretreatment variables, such as the number and type of previous life events, duration of the disorder, number of episodes of the disorder, coexistence of other disorders, age, gender, and socioeconomic status; (2) the person's status at pretreatment itself, such as severity of problem, types of symptomatology, cognitive style, and sub-classification of type of disorder if relevant (e.g., dysthymia vs. major depressive episode); (3) compliance with treatment, speed of recovery, course of disorder during treatment, and quality of therapy; (4) the person's status at post-treatment, degree of improvement, level of severity on post-test measures, and degree of change on theory-related dependent variables; and (5) occurrence and reaction to life events, social support, and adherence to continued use of procedures.

Based on these variables that predict response to treatment, the following specific risk factors are associated with relapse: (a) post-treatment residual depressive symptomatology (e.g., Beck Depression Inventory score > 9); (b) post-treatment dysfunctional cognitions, such as those measured by the Automatic Thoughts Questionnaire or the Dysfunctional Attitude Scale; (c) low perceived competence to control or cope with negative thoughts; (d) chronicity of problem (e.g., history of dysthymia, multiple prior episodes); (e) high "expressed emotion" environment (i.e., patients who live in environments where they are exposed to high levels of expression of critical comments or overprotective behavior towards them); (f) marital disturbance and poor social support; (g) dissatisfaction with major life areas; and (h) coexisting medical problems (e.g., chronic pain). These factors and their interactions are represented at various points in the PB model, which may help draw a therapist's attention to their assessment in order to evaluate and posssibly reduce risk of relapse.

Implications of Outcome Prediction for
Relapse Prevention Programs

Wilson (1996) suggests that clients who meet any of the above criteria should be identified as cases requiring closer monitoring during a two-year follow-up period. If the first two criteria are met, further treatment might be considered prior to termination. If the other criteria are met, steps might be implemented to deal specifically with these issues before termination. Clients who are at high risk for relapse might receive several pre-termination sessions aimed at providing relapse-prevention strategies, such as preparation for predictable adverse life events. The concluding sessions might be gradually spread out over several months. Moreover, Wilson points out that behavioral treatments for depression should not be viewed as necessarily short-term (i.e., three months or so). Instead, relapse risk should be assessed systematically and routinely, and high-risk patients should be provided with specific relapse-prevention strategies to enhance maintenance of gains made during therapy.

Finally, the conceptual model proposed by Marlatt and Gordon (1985) in the addictive disorders may be instructive in our efforts to deal with the prevention of relapse in depression. Wilson (1992) suggests that the most effective long-term outcomes are likely to be achieved if the initial treatment enhances an individual's perception of control over their reactions to important adverse events. As a result, individuals learn to recognize and respond to high-risk situations with less negative and more positive outcome expectancies about the use of coping responses in these situations. As individuals come to use such coping strategies in future situations, these strategies become important parts of their behavioral repertoire, increasing their sense of mastery and facilitating the maintenance of effective coping strategies. We have pointed out elsewhere (Schermelleh et al., 1997) that increased confidence to deal with aversive events and emotions results from the knowledge of having acquired a behavioral repertoire of adequate coping strategies—a repertoire that Rosenbaum (1990) aptly termed "learned resourcefulness." Confidence is further increased by positive experiences made with these strategies and when individuals attribute these experiences to themselves. Wilson (1992) emphasized the importance of developing interventions aimed specifically at the maintenance of coping strategies for depression. These strategies should target those deficits outlined in the PB model that render persons vulnerable to the recurrence of depression.

Conclusions

The PB model of depression is an integrative, interactional, multivariate framework theory that aims to accommodate the complexity and heterogeneity of major depression. It organizes and relates a large number of psychological and biological variables and processes and displays them in a heuristic framework-type model. Yet the model requires further development in a number of areas. Most importantly, the type of interrelations between biological, environmental, and psychological processes, as well as processes and principles regulating these interrelations, require further specification and investigation (Heiby, 1989).

More of the research on treatment outcome and treatment outcome prediction in depression needs to be driven by theoretical developments in the area: models such as the one presented in this chapter are an excellent basis for such efforts. A combination of theory-driven and empirically derived methods for assessing depression can be used to predict outcome and ought to become a routine part of our assessment strategies both prior to treatment and when considering termination.

Group studies suggest that several major treatments for depression exist supported by good evidence for short-term efficacy but with relapse rates of at least 30 percent over two years. To date, few predictors of differential response to treatment have been identified, and both CBT and tricyclic drugs seem to produce changes on psychological and biological variables that are related to the hypothesized mechanisms thought to underlie the two separate treatments. Poor short-term outcome is predicted by severity of depression and other variables not specifically related to theories of depression. On the other hand, poor long-term outcome seems to be related to several variables of more theoretical interest that could be identified and conceptualized within a PB framework. These variables include post-treatment dysfunctional thinking, occurrence of further adverse life events, and quality of the interpersonal environment. This knowledge can be utilized to identify persons at high risk for relapse and implement relapse prevention interventions for those people. A new line of depression research would involve the development of model-driven programs aimed at assessing risk for relapse and prevention of relapse.

Much of current (group) treatment outcome research typically ignores the heterogeneity among depressed individuals (Wolpe & Michaels, 1986) and randomly assigns subjects to treatment conditions independent of any individual problem analysis. Such traditional research designs (cross-sectional group studies) and statistical analyses (analyses of variance and multiple regressions) have provided important results regarding general trends in treatment outcome. More sophisticated research designs (e.g., single subject, time-series, and longitudinal designs) and statistical analyses (e.g., structural equation modeling) could be utilized to assess the adequacy and efficacy of model-derived treatments for individual depressed patients (Heiby, 1992; Minuchin, 1985; Wilkinson, 1993). Such methodological refinements would allow for more conclusive statements regarding treatment efficacy. We also need empirical studies investigating the effects of model-based treatments on the recurrence and relapse prevention of depression.

In sum, one of the major merits of the PB model is that it provides a comprehensive framework that incorporates and relates all major aspects of depression in a systematic fashion. As a result, therapists who use such frameworks are less likely to adopt an atheoretical eclectic, and frequently overinclusive, approach. At the same time, they are less likely to adopt an "exclusionary approach" where they focus on one set of variables (overt behavior *or* cognitive processes *or* physiological imbalances) at the expense of excluding important others. We recognize that assessment and treatment based on a PB model of depression may not necessarily lead to better outcomes than would be expected to result from a comprehensive functional analysis—one that carefully assesses and relates all relevant factors involved in a clinical problem (Wolpe, 1986). The fact is, however, that only a small fraction of therapists actually conduct such analyses (Scotti, Evans, Meyer, & Walker, 1991). One reason could be that clinicians lack comprehensive, convenient, and heuristic conceptual integrative frameworks to guide their assessments and organize their findings and clinical decision-making in a time-efficient manner. In this regard, the PB model might help researchers and therapists organize and relate the multitude of variables involved in major depression so that they can design more incisive studies, more comprehensive assessments, and more effective treatments for this common and very debilitating problem.

References

Abramson, L. Y., Metalsky, G. I., & Alloy, L. B. (1989). Hopelessness depression: A theory-based subtype of depression. *Psychological Review, 96,* 358–372.

Alloy, L. B., & Abramson, L. Y. (1979). Judgment of contingency in depressed and nondepressed students: Sadder but wiser? *Journal of Experimental Psychology: General, 108,* 441–485.

American Psychiatric Association. (1994). *Diagnostic and statistical manual of mental disorders* (4th ed.).

Washington. DC: American Psychiatric Association.

Aneshensel, C. S., & Huba, G. J. (1983). Depression, alcohol use and smoking over one year: A four-wave longitudinal causal model. *Journal of Abnormal Psychology, 92,* 134–150.

Anthony, E. J. (1983). An overview of the effects of maternal depression on the infant and child. In H. L. Morrison (Ed.), *Children of depressed parents: Risk,* identification, and intervention (pp. 1–16). New York: Grune & Stratton.

Appelboom-Fondu, J., Kirkhofs, M., & Mendlewicz, J. (1988). Depression in adolescents and young adults: Polysomnographic and neuroendocrine aspects. *Journal of Affective Disorders, 14,* 35–40.

Avery, D., & Silverman, J. (1984). Psychomotor retardation and agitation in depression: Relationship to age, sex and response to treatment. *Journal of Affective Disorders, 7,* 67–76.

Barkwell, D. P. (1991). Ascribed meaning: A critical factor in coping and pain attenuation in patients with cancer-related pain. *Journal of Palliative Care, 7,* 5–14.

Barthe, D. G., & Hammen, C. L. (1981). The attributional model of depression: A naturalistic extension. *Personality and Social Psychology Bulletin, 7,* 53–58.

Beach, B. K. (1993). *The origins of depressogenic attributional style: An analysis of maternal and child correlates of attributional style, parenting style and depression.* Unpublished master's thesis. West Virginia University, Morgantown, WV.

Beck, A. T. (1967). *Depression: Clinical, experimental, and theoretical aspects.* New York: Harper & Row.

Beck, A. T. (1976). *Cognitive therapy and the emotional disorders.* New York: International University Press.

Beck, A. T., Rush, A. J., Shaw, B. F., & Emery, G. (1979). *Cognitive therapy of depression.* New York: Guilford.

Beck, A. T., Steer, R. A., Kovacs, M., & Garrison, B. (1985). Hopelessness and eventual suicide: A 10-year prospective study of patients hospitalized with suicidal ideation. *American Journal of Psychiatry, 142,* 559–563.

Bifulco, A. T., Brown, G. W., & Harris, T. O. (1987). Childhood loss of a parent, lack of adequate parental care and adult depression: A replication. *Journal of Affective Disorders, 13,* 129–139.

Biglan, A., Hops, H., Sherman, L., Friedman, L. S., Anther, J., & Osteen, V. (1985). Problem-solving interactions of depressed women and their husbands. *Behavior Therapy, 16,* 431–451.

Billings, A. G., & Moos, R. H. (1984). Chronic and nonchronic unipolar depression: The differential role of environmental stressors and resources. *The Journal of Nervous and Mental Disease, 172,* 65–75.

Billings, A. G., & Moos, R. H. (1985). Children of parents with unipolar depression: A controlled 1-year follow-up. *Journal of Abnormal Child Psychology, 14,* 149–166.

Blackburn, I. M., Bishop, S., Glen, A. I. M., Whalley, L. J., & Christie, J. E. (1981). The efficacy of cognitive therapy in depression: A treatment trial using cognitive therapy and pharmacotherapy, each alone and in combination. *British Journal of Psychiatry, 139,* 181–189.

Blum, K., Wallace, J. E., & Hall, W. C. (1986). A commentary on the pathogenesis and biochemical profile of alcohol-induced depression. *Journal of Psychoactive Drugs, 18,* 161–162.

Boyhuys, C., Jansen, C. J., & van der Hostdakker, R. H. (1991). Analysis of observed behaviors displayed by depressed patients during a clinical interview. *Journal of Affective Disorders, 21,* 79–88.

Brown, G. W., & Harris, T. (1978). *Social origins of depression: A study of psychiatric disorder in women.* New York: The Free Press.

Burnam, M. A., Stein, J. A., Golding, J. M., & Siegel, J. M. (1988). Sexual assault and mental disorders in a community population. *Journal of Consulting and Clinical Psychology, 56,* 843–850.

Cadoret, R. J., O'Gorman, W. O., Heywood, E., & Troughton, E. (1985). Genetic and environmental factors in major depression. *Journal of Affective Disorders, 9,* 155–164.

Caracci, G., Migone, P., & Mukherjee, S. (1983). Phencyclidine abuse and depression. *Psychosomatics, 24,* 932–933.

Carson, T. C., & Adams, H. E. (1980). Activity valence as a function of mood change. *Journal of Abnormal Psychology, 89,* 368–377.

Clark, D. A., & Steer, R. A. (1996). Empirical status of the cognitive model of anxiety and derepression. In P. M. Salkovskis (Ed.), *Frontiers of cognitive therapy* (pp. 75–96). New York: Guilford.

Cohler, B. J., Gallant, D. H., Grunebaum, H. U., & Kaufman, C. (1983). Social adjustment among schizophrenic, depressed, and well mothers and their school-aged children. In H. L. Morrison (Ed.), *Children of depressed parents: Risk, identification, and intervention* (pp. 65–97). New York: Grune & Stratton.

Coyne, J. (1976). Depression and the response of others. *Journal of Abnormal Psychology, 85,* 186–193.

Cummings, E. M., & Davies, P. T. (1994). Maternal depression and child development. *Journal of Child Psychology and Psychiatry, 35,* 73–112.

Curtis, R. (1990). Mood disorders and self-defeating behavior. In B. B. Wolman & G. Stricker (Eds.), *De-*

pressive disorders: Facts, theories and treatment methods (pp. 162–188). New York: John Wiley.

Dixon, W. A., Heppner, P., Burnett, J. W., & Lips, B. J. (1993). Hopelessness and stress: Evidence for an interactive model of depression. *Cognitive Therapy and Research, 17,* 39–52.

Dobson, K. S. (1989). A meta-analysis of the efficacy of cognitive therapy for depression. *Journal of Consulting and Clinical Psychology, 57,* 414–419.

Eaves, G., & Rush, A. J. (1984). Cognitive patterns in symptomatic and remitted unipolar major depression. *Journal of Abnormal Psychology, 93,* 31–40.

Eifert, G. H. (1987). Language conditioning: Clinical issues and applications in behavior therapy. In H. J. Eysenck & I. M. Martin (Eds.), *Theoretical foundations of behavior therapy* (pp. 167–193). New York: Plenum.

Eifert, G. H. (1990). The acquisition and cognitive-behavioral therapy of phobic anxiety. In G. H. Eifert & I. M. Evans (Eds.), *Unifying behavior therapy: Contributions of paradigmatic behaviorism* (pp. 173–200). New York: Springer.

Eifert, G. H. (1992). Cardiophobia: A paradigmatic behavioral model of heart-focused anxiety and non-anginal chest pain. *Behaviour Research and Therapy, 30,* 329–345.

Eifert, G. H. (1996). More theory-driven and less diagnosis-based behavior therapy. *Journal of Behavior Therapy and Experimental Psychiatry, 27,* 75–86.

Eifert, G. H., Evans, I. M., & McKendrick, V. (1990). Matching treatments to client problems not diagnostic labels: A case for paradigmatic behavior therapy. *Journal of Behavior Therapy and Experimental Psychiatry, 21,* 163–172.

Eifert, G. H., Forsyth, J. P., & Schauss, S. L. (1993). Unifying the field: Developing an integrative paradigm in behavior therapy. *Journal of Behavior Therapy and Experimental Psychiatry, 24,* 107–118.

Eifert, G. H., Schulte, D., Zvolensky, M. J., Lejuez, C. W., & Lau, A. W. (1997). Manualizing behavior therapy: Merits and challenges. *Behavior Therapy, 28,* 499–509.

Elkin, I., Shea, T., Watkins, J. T., Imber, S. D., Sotsky, S. M., Collins, J. F., Glass, D. R., Pilkonis, P. A., Leber, W. R., Docherty, J. P., Feister, S. J., & Parloff, M. B. (1989). National Institute of Mental Health treatment of depression collaborative research program: General effectiveness of treatments. *Archives of General Psychiatry, 46,* 971–982.

Ferster, C. B. (1973). A functional analysis of depression. *American Psychologist, 28,* 857–870.

Forehand, R., Lautenschlager, G. J., Faust, J., & Graziano, W. G. (1986). Parent perceptions and parent-child interactions in clinic-referred children: A preliminary investigation of the effects of maternal depressive moods. *Behaviour Research and Therapy, 24,* 73–75.

Forehand, R., McCombs-Thomas, A., Wierson, M., Brody, G., & Fauber, R. (1990). Role of maternal functioning and parenting skills in adolescent functioning following parental divorce. *Journal of Abnormal Psychology, 99,* 278–283.

Franche, R. L., & Dobson, K. (1992). Self-criticism and interpersonal dependency as vulnerability factors to depression. *Cognitive Theory and Research, 16,* 419–435.

Frazier, P. A. (1990). Victim attributions and post-rape trauma. *Journal of Personality and Social Psychology, 59,* 298–304.

Garvey, M. J., Mungas, D., & Tolletson, G. D. (1984). Hypersomnia in major depression disorders. *Journal of Affective Disorders, 6,* 283–286.

Gavino, A., Godoy, A., Rodriguez, C., & Eifert, G. H. (1996). How can behavior therapy treat the same disorder with different techniques and different disorders with the same technique? *Journal of Behavior Therapy and Experimental Psychiatry, 27,* 107–117.

Gaylord, M., & Symons, E. (1986). Relocation stress: A definition and need for services. *Employee Assistance Quarterly, 2,* 31–36.

Golden, R. N., & Janowsky, D. S. (1990). Biological theories of depression. In B. B. Wolman & G. Stricker (Eds.) *Depressive disorders: Facts, theories and treatment methods* (pp. 3–21). New York: Wiley.

Goodyer, I. M., & Altham, P. M. E. (1991). Life exit events and recent social and family adversities in anxious and depressed school-age children and adolescents—I. *Journal of Affective Disorders, 21,* 219–228.

Gotlib, I. H., & Robinson, A. (1982). Responses to depressed individuals: Discrepancies between self-report and observer-rated behavior. *Journal of Abnormal Psychology, 91,* 231–240.

Greenberg, L. S., & Safran, J. D. (1984). Hot cognition—emotion coming in from the cold: A reply to Rachman and Mahoney. *Cognitive Therapy and Research, 8,* 591–598.

Grosscup, S. J., & Lewinsohn, P. M. (1980). Unpleasant and pleasant events and mood. *Journal of Clinical and Consulting Psychology, 36,* 252–259.

Haaga, D. A., Dyck, M. J., & Ernst, D. (1991). Empirical status of cognitive theory of depression. *Psychological Bulletin, 110,* 215–236.

Hammen, C., Ellicott, A., & Gitlin, M. (1989). Vulnerability to specific life events and prediction of course of disorder in unipolar depressed patients. *Canadian Journal of Behavioral Science, 21,* 377–388.

Hammen, C., Marks, T., Mayol, A., & deMayo, R. (1985). Depressive self-schemas, life stress and vulnerability in depression. *Journal of Abnormal Psychology, 94,* 308–319.

Harte, J. L., & Eifert, G. H. (1995). The effects of running, setting and attentional focus on athletes' catecholamine and cortisol excretion, and mood. *Psychophysiology, 32,* 49–54.

Harte, J. L., Eifert, G. H., & Smith, R. (1995). The effects of running and meditation on beta-endorphin, corticotrophin releasing hormone and cortisol in plasma, and on mood. *Biological Psychology, 40,* 251–265.

Hedlund, S., & Rude, S. (1995). Evidence of latent depressive schemas in formerly depressed individuals. *Journal of Abnormal Psychology, 104,* 517–525.

Heiby, E. M. (1981). Depression and frequency of reinforcement. *Behavior Therapy, 12,* 549–555.

Heiby, E. M. (1983a). Depression as a function of self- and environmentally controlled reinforcement. *Behavior Therapy, 14,* 430–433.

Heiby, E. M. (1983b). Toward the prediction of mood change. *Behavior Therapy, 14,* 110–115.

Heiby, E. M. (1986). Social versus self-control skills deficits in four cases of depression. *Behavior Therapy, 17,* 158–169.

Heiby, E. M. (1989). Multiple skills deficits in depression. *Behaviour Change, 6,* 76–84.

Heiby, E. M. (1992). Some implications of chaos and multivariate theories for the assessment of depression. *European Journal of Psychological Assessment, 8,* 70–73.

Heiby, E. M., & Staats, A. W. (1990). Depression: Classification, explanation, and treatment. In G. H. Eifert & I. M. Evans (Eds.), *Unifying behavior therapy: Contributions of paradigmatic behaviorism* (pp. 220–246). New York: Springer.

Herman, J. L. (1992). Complex PTSD: A syndrome in survivors of prolonged and repeated trauma. *Journal of Traumatic Stress, 5,* 377–391.

Hibbard, R. A., Spence, C., Tzeng, O. C. S., Zollinger, T., & Orr, D. P. (1992). Child abuse and mental health among adolescents in dependent care. *Journal of Adolescent Health, 13,* 121–127.

Hickie, I., Wilhelm, K., Parker, G., Boyce, P., Hadzi-Pavlovic, D., Brodaty, H., & Mitchell, P. (1990). Perceived dysfunctional intimate relationships: A specific association with the non-melancholic depressive subtype. *Journal of Affective Disorders, 19,* 99–107.

Hirschfeld, R. M. A., Klerman, G. L., Clayton, P. J., Keller, M. B., & Andreasen, N. C. (1984). Personality and gender-related differences in depression. *Journal of Affective Disorders, 7,* 211–221.

Hollon, S. D., DeRubeis, R. J., Evans, M. D., Wiemer, M. J., Garvey, M. J., Grove, W. M., & Tuason, V. B. (1992). Cognitive therapy and pharmacotherapy for depression: Singly and in combination. *Archives of General Psychiatry, 49,* 774–781.

Hooley, J. M., Orley, J., & Teasdale, J. D. (1986). Levels of expressed emotion and relapse in depressed patients. *British Journal of Psychiatry, 148,* 642–647.

Hops, H., Biglan, A., Sherman, L., Arthur, J., Friedman, L., & Osteen, V. (1987). Home observations of family interactions of depressed women. *Journal of Consulting and Clinical Psychology, 55,* 341–346.

Horner, R., & Vaughan, B. (1993). The effects of setting events on problem behavior. In R. Horner (Chair), *Contextual analysis of behavior: Empirical Analysis.* Symposium conducted at the 16th Meeting of the Association for Behavior Analysis, Chicago, IL.

Joiner, T. E., Alfano, M. S., & Metalsky, G. I. (1992). When depression breeds contempt: Reassurance seeking, self-esteem and rejection of depressed college students by their roommates. *Journal of Abnormal Psychology, 101,* 165–173.

Kandel, E. R. (1991). Disorders of mood: Depression, mania, and anxiety disorders. In E. R. Kandel, J. H. Schwartz, & T. M. Jessell (Eds.), *Principles of neural science* (3rd ed.) (pp. 869–883). East Norwalk, CT.: Appleton & Lange.

Kerkhofs, M., Hoffman, G., De Martelaere, V., Linkowski, P., & Mendlewicz, J. (1985). Sleep EEG recordings in depressive disorders. *Journal of Affective Disorders, 9,* 47–53.

Kessler, R. C., McGonagle, K. A., Zhao, S., Nelson, C. B., Hughes, M., Eshleman, S., Wittchen, H. U., & Kendler, K. S. (1994). Lifetime and 12-month prevalence of DSM-III-R psychiatric disorders in the United States. *Archives of General Psychiatry, 51,* 8–19.

King, C. A., Naylor, M. W., Segal, H. G., Evans, T., & Shain, B. N. (1993). Global self-worth, specific self-perceptions of competence, and depression in adolescents. *Journal of the American Academy of Child and Adolescent Psychiatry, 32,* 745–752.

Kovacs, M., Golston, D., & Gatsonia, C. (1993). Suicidal behaviors and childhood-onset depressive disorders: A longitudinal investigation. *Journal of the American Academy of Child and Adolescent Psychiatry, 32,* 8–20.

Kupfer, D. J. (1976). REM latency: A psychobiological marker for primary depressive disorder. *Biological Psychiatry, 11,* 159–174.

Kupfer, D. J., & Thase, M. E. (1983). The use of the sleep laboratory in the diagnosis of affective disorders. *Psychiatric Clinics of North America, 6,* 3–25.

Lamb, D. G., Davis, S. F., Tramill, J. L., & Kleinhammer-Tramill, P. J. (1987). Noncontingent reward-induced learned helplessness in humans. *Psychological Reports, 61,* 559–564.

Lewinsohn, P. M. (1974). Clinical and theoretical aspects of depression. In K. S. Calhoun, H. E. Adams, & K. M. Mitchell (Eds.), *Innovative treatment methods of psychopathology* (pp. 63–120). New York: Wiley.

Lewinsohn, P. M., Hoberman, H., Teri, L., & Hautzinger, M. (1985). In S. Reiss & R. R. Bootzin (Eds.), *Theoretical issues in behavior therapy* (pp. 331–359). New York: Academic Press.

Lloyd, C. (1980). Life events and depressive disorders reviewed. II. Events as precipitating factor. *Archives of General Psychiatry, 37,* 541–548.

Lombardi, K. L. (1990). Depressive states and somatic symptoms. In B. B. Wolman & G. Stricker (Eds.), *Depressive disorders: Facts, theories and treatment methods,* (pp. 149–161). New York: Wiley.

McLean, P. (1976). Therapeutic decision-making in the behavioral treatment of depression. In P. O. Davidson (Ed.), *Behavioral management of anxiety, depression and pain* (pp. 54–89). New York: Brunner/Mazel.

McLeer, S. V., Deblinger, E., Atkins, M. S., Foa, E. B., & Ralphe, D. L. (1988). Post-traumatic stress disorder in sexually abused children. *Journal of the American Academy of Child and Adolescent Psychiatry, 28,* 650–654.

MacLeod, C., & Mathews, A. M. (1991). Cognitive-experimental approaches to the emotional disorders. In P. R. Martin (Ed.), *Handbook of behavior therapy and psychological science* (pp. 116–150). New York: Pergamon.

McKnight, D. L., Nelson, R. O., Hayes, S. O., & Jarrett, R. B. (1984). Importance of treating individually assessed response classes in the amelioration of depression. *Behavior Therapy, 15,* 315–335.

Maier, S. F., & Seligman, M. E. P. (1976). Learned helplessness: Theory and evidence. *Journal of Experimental Psychology, General, 105,* 3–46.

Malinowsky-Rummell, R., & Hansen, D. (1993). Long-term consequences of childhood physical abuse. *Psychological Bulletin, 114,* 68–79.

Marlatt, G. A., & Gordon, J. R. (1985). *Relapse prevention: Maintenance strategies in the treatment of addictive behaviors.* New York: Guilford.

Marx, E. M., Williams, J. M. G., & Claridge, G. C. (1992). Depression and social problem solving. *Journal of Abnormal Psychology, 101,* 78–86.

Miller, I. W., Kabacoff, R. I., Keitner, G. I., & Epstein, N. B. (1986). Family functioning in the families of psychiatric patients. *Comprehensive Psychiatry, 279,* 302–312.

Minuchin, P. (1985). Families and individual development: Provocations from the field of family therapy. *Child Development, 56,* 289–302.

Miranda, J. (1992). Dysfunctional thinking is activated by stressful life events. *Cognitive Theory and Research, 16,* 473–483.

Murphy, G. E., Simons, A. D., Wetzel, R. D., & Lustman, P. J. (1984). Cognitive therapy and pharmacotherapy: Singly and together in the treatment of depression. *Archives of General Psychiatry, 41,* 33–41.

Nelson, J. C., & Charney, D. S. (1981). They symptoms of major depression. *American Journal of Psychiatry, 138,* 1–13.

Nelson, J. C., & Mazure, C. (1985). Ruminative thinking: A distinctive sign of melancholia. *Journal of Affective Disorders, 9,* 41–46.

Nelson, R. E., & Craighead, W. E. (1977). Selective recall of positive and negative feedback, self-control behaviors, and depression. *Journal of Abnormal Psychology, 86,* 379–388.

Nezu, A. M. (1987). A problem–solving formulation of depression: Literature review and proposal of a pluralistic model. *Clinical Psychology Review, 7,* 121-144.

Nezu, A. M., & Ronan, G. F. (1987). Social problem solving and depression: Deficits in generating alternatives and decision-making. *Southern Psychologist, 3,* 29–34.

Nietzel, M. T., Russell, R. L., Hemmings, K. A., & Gretter, M. (1987). Clinical significance of psychotherapy for unipolar depression: A meta-analytic approach to social comparison. *Journal of Consulting and Clinical Psychology, 55,* 156–161.

Parker, G., & Hadzi-Pavlovic, D. (1984). Modification of levels of depression in mother-bereaved women by parental and marital relationships. *Psychological Medicine, 14,* 125–135.

Parker, G., & Hadzi-Pavlovic, D. (1992). Parental representations of melancholic and nonmelancholic depressives: Examining for specificity to depressive type and for evidence of additive effects. *Psychological Medicine, 22,* 657–665.

Parker, G., Kiloh, L. G., & Hayward, L. (1987). Parental representations of neurotic and endogenous depressives. *Journal of Affective Disorders, 13,* 75–82.

Patten, S. B., & Lamarre, C. J. (1992). Can drug-induced depressions be identified by their clinical features? *Canadian Journal of Psychiatry, 37,* 213–215.

Paykel, E. S., & Tanner, J. (1976). Life events, depressive relapse and maintenance treatment. *Psychological Medicine, 6,* 481–485.

Persons, J. B. (1993). Outcome of psychotherapy for unipolar depression. In T. R. Giles (Ed.), *Handbook of effective psychotherapy* (pp. 305–323). New York: Plenum.

Persons, J. B., & Miranda, J. (1992). Cognitive theories of vulnerability to depression: Reconciling negative evidence. *Cognitive Theory and Research, 16,* 485–502.

Persons, J. B., & Rao, P. A. (1985). Longitudinal study of cognitions, life events, and depression in psychiatric patients. *Journal of Abnormal Psychology, 94,* 51–63.

Phillips, L. W. (1986). Behavior analysis in a case of post-partum depression. *Journal of Behavior Therapy and Experimental Psychiatry, 17,* 101–104.

Pietraszek, M. H., Urano, T., Sumioshi, K., Serizawa, K., Takahashi, S., Takada, Y., & Takada, A. (1991). Alcohol-induced depression: Involvement of serotonin. *Alcohol and Alcoholism, 26,* 155–159.

Post, R. M. (1992). Transduction of psychosocial stress into the neurobiology of recurrent affective disorder. *American Journal of Psychiatry, 149,* 999–1010.

Prkachin, K. M., Craig, K. D., Papagorgis, D., & Reith, G. (1977). Nonverbal communication deficits and response to performance feedback in depression. *Journal of Abnormal Psychology, 86,* 224–234.

Quinton, D., Rutter, M., & Liddle, C. (1984). Institutional rearing, parenting difficulties and marital relationships. *Psychological Medicine, 14,* 107–124.

Quitkin, F. M., Rabkin, J. G., Stewart, J. W., McGrath, P. J., Harrison, W., Davies, M., Goetz, R., Puig-Antich, J. (1985). Sleep of atypical depressives. *Journal of Affective Disorders, 8,* 61–67.

Rao, U., Weissman, M.M., Martin, J.A., & Hammond, R. W. (1993). Childhood depression and risk of suicide: A preliminary report of a longitudinal study. *Journal of the American Academy of Child and Adolescent Psychiatry, 32,* 21–27.

Rehm, L. (1977). A self-control model of depression. *Behavior Therapy, 8,* 787–804.

Rehm, L. (1990). Cognitive and behavioral theories. In B. B. Wolman & G. Stricker (Eds.), *Depressive disorders: Facts, theories and treatment methods* (pp. 64–91). New York: Wiley.

Reid, W. H. & Morrison, H. L. (1983). Risk factors in children of depressed parents. In H. L. Morrison (Ed.), *Children of depressed parents: Risk, identification, and intervention* (pp. 33–46). New York: Grune & Stratton.

Robinson, L. A., Berman, J. S., & Neimeyer, R. A. (1990). Psychotherapy for the treatment of depression: A comparative review of controlled outcome research. *Psychological Bulletin, 108,* 30–49.

Rodgers, B. (1991). Models of stress, vulnerability and affective disorder. *Journal of Affective Disorders, 21,* 1–13.

Rose, G. D., & Staats, A. W. (1988). Depression and the frequency and strength of pleasant events: Exploration of the Staats-Heiby theory. *Behaviour Research and Therapy, 26,* 489–494.

Rosenbaum, A. J., Carlson, G. A., & Guthrie, D. (1987). Coping strategies, self-perceptions, hopelessness and perceived family environments in depressed and suicidal children. *Journal of Consulting and Counseling Psychology, 55,* 361–366.

Rosenbaum, M. (1990). A model for research on self-regulation: Reducing the schism between behaviorism and general psychology. In G. H. Eifert & I.

M. Evans (Eds.), *Unifying behavior therapy: Contributions of paradigmatic behaviorism* (pp. 126–149). New York: Springer.

Rosenberg, S. J., Peterson, R. A., Hayes, J. R., & Hatcher, J. (1988). Depression in medical inpatients. *British Journal of Medical Psychology, 61*, 245–254.

Roy, A. (1983). Early parental loss and depression. In F. Flach (Ed.), *Affective disorders*, (pp. 19–28). New York: Norton.

Roy, A., Breier, A., Doran, A. R., & Pichar, D. (1985). Life events in depression: Relationship to subtypes. *Journal of Affective Disorders, 9*, 143–148.

Rush, A. J., Beck, A. T., Kovacs, M., & Hollon, S. (1977). Comparative efficacy of cognitive therapy and pharmacotherapy in the treatment of depressed outpatients. *Cognitive Therapy and Research, 1*, 17–37.

Schermelleh-Engel, K., Eifert, G. H., Moosbrugger, H., & Frank, D. (1997). Perceived competence and anxiety as determinants of maladaptive and adaptive coping strategies of chronic pain patients. *Personality and Individual Differences, 22*, 1–10.

Schwartz, G. E., Davidson, R. J., & Maer, F. (1975). Right hemisphere specialization for emotion in the human brain: Interactions with cognition. *Science, 190*, 286–288.

Scotti, J. R., Evans, I. M., Meyer, L. H., & Walker, P. (1991). A meta-analysis of intervention research with problem behavior: Treatment validity and standards of practice. *American Journal of Mental Retardation, 96*, 233–256.

Segal, Z. V., Vella, D. D., Shaw, B. F., & Katz, R. (1992). Cognitive and life stress predictors of relapse in remitted unipolar depressed patients: Test of the congruency hypothesis. *Journal of Abnormal Psychology, 101*, 26–36.

Seligman, M. E. P. (1975). *Learned helplessness: On depression, development, and death.* San Francisco: Freeman.

Seligman, M. E. P., Peterson, C., Kaslow, N. J., Tanenbaum, R., Alloy, L.B., & Abramson, L. Y. (1984). Attributional style and depressive symptoms among children. *Journal of Abnormal Psychology, 93*, 235–238.

Siever, L. J., & Davis, K. L. (1985). Overview: Toward a dysregulation hypothesis of depression. *American Journal of Psychiatry, 142*, 1017–1031.

Simons, A. D., & Thase, M. E. (1992). Biological markers, treatment outcome, and 1-year follow-up in endogenous depression: Electroencephalographic sleep studies and response to cognitive therapy. *Journal of Consulting and Clinical Psychology, 60*, 392–401.

Smith, E. M., & North, C. S. (1988). Familial subtypes of depression: A longitudinal perspective. *Journal of Affective Disorders, 14*, 145–154.

Staats, A. W. (1968). *Learning, language and cognition.* New York: Holt, Rinehart, & Winston.

Staats, A. W. (1972). Language behavior therapy: A derivative of social behaviorism. *Behavior Therapy, 3*, 165–192.

Staats, A. W. (1975). *Social behaviorism.* Homewood, IL.: Dorsey.

Staats, A. W. (1990). Paradigmatic behavior therapy: A unified framework for theory, research, and practice. In G. H. Eifert & I. M. Evans (Eds.), *Unifying behavior therapy: Contributions from paradigmatic behaviorism* (pp. 14–54). New York: Springer.

Staats, A. W. (1993). Personality theory, abnormal psychology, and psychological measurement: A psychological behaviorism. *Behavior Modification, 17*, 8–42.

Staats, A. W. (1995). Paradigmatic behaviorisim and paradigmatic behavior therapy. In W. O'Donohue & I. Krasner (Eds.), *Theories of behavior therapy* (pp. 659–692). Washington, DC: American Psychological Association.

Staats, A. W. (1996). *Behavior and personality.* New York: Springer.

Staats, A. W., & Eifert, G. H. (1990). A paradigmatic behaviorism theory of emotion: Basis for unification. *Clinical Psychology Review, 10*, 539–566.

Staats, A. W., & Heiby, E. M. (1985). Paradigmatic Behaviorism's theory of depression: Unified, explanatory, and heuristic. In S. Reiss & R. R. Bootzin (Eds.), *Theoretical issues in behavior therapy* (pp. 279–330). New York: Academic Press.

Steinbrueck, S. M., Maxwell, S. E., & Howard, G. S. (1983). A meta-analysis of psychotherapy and drug therapy in the treatment of unipolar depression with adults. *Journal of Consulting and Clinical Psychology, 51*, 856–863.

Stewart, J. W., McGrath, P. J., Quitkin, F. M. & Rabkin, J. G. (1993). Chronic depression: Response to placebo, imipramine, and phenelzine. *Journal of Clinical Psychopharmacology, 13*, 391–396.

Teichman, Y., & Teichman, M. (1990). Interpersonal view of depression: Research and integration. *Journal of Family Psychology, 3*, 349–367.

Teuting, P., Koslow, S. H., & Hirschfeld, R. M. A. (1982). *Science Reports: Special report on depression research.* Washington, DC: U.S. Government Printing Office.

Thase, M. E., Frank, E., & Kupfer, D. J. (1985). Biochemical processes in major depression. In E. E. Beckham & W. R. Lebel (Eds.), *Handbook of depression: Treatment, assessment and research* (pp. 816–913). Homewood, IL: Dorsey.

Tsuang, M. T. (1978). Genetic counseling for psychiatric patients and their families. *American Journal of Psychiatry, 135*, 1465–1475.

Ulrich, G., & Harms, K. (1985). A videoanalysis of the non-verbal behavior of depressed patients before and after treatment. *Journal of Affective Disorders, 9*, 63–67.

Veiel, H. O. F., Kuhner, C., Brill, G., & Ihle, W. (1992). Psychosocial correlates of clinical depression after psychiatric in-patient treatment: Methodological issues and baseline differences between recovered and non-recovered patients. *Psychological Medicine, 22*, 415–427.

Vogel, G. W., Neill, D., Hagler, M., & Kors, D. (1990). A new animal model of endogenous depression: A summary of present findings. *Neuroscience and Biobehavioral Reviews, 14*, 85–91.

Weingarter, H., & Murphy, D. L. (1977). Mood-state-dependent retrieval of verbal associations. *Journal of Abnormal Psychology, 86*, 276–284.

Weinsten, M. C., Kaiser, H. H., and Saturno, P. J. (1989). Economic impact of youth suicides and suicide attempts. In *Report of the Secretary's Task Force of Youth Suicide: Vol IV: Strategies for the Prevention of Youth Suicide* (pp. 4-82–4-93) (DHSS Publication No. ADM 89-1624). Washington, DC: U.S. Government Printing Office.

Weissman, M. M. (1983). The depressed mother and her rebellious adolescent. In H. L. Morrison (Ed.), *Children of depressed parents: Risk, identification, and intervention* (pp. 99–113). New York: Grune & Stratton.

Wender, P. H., Kety, S. S., Rosenthal, D., & Schulsinger, F. (1986). Psychiatric disorders in the biological and adoptive studies of adopted individuals with affective disorders. *Archives of General Psychiatry, 43*, 923–929.

Whisman, M. A., & Kwon, P. (1992). Parental representations, cognitive distortions, and mild depression. *Cognitive Theory and Research, 16*, 557–568.

Whitters, A. C., Cadoret, R. J., Troughton, E., & Reuben, B. (1987). Suicide attempts in antisocial alcoholics. *Journal of Nervous and Mental Disease, 75*, 624–626.

Wilkinson, R. B. (1993). The Staats-Heiby theory of depression: The role of event frequency and affect reevaluated. *Behaviour Research and Therapy, 31*, 97–104.

Williams, J. M. G., Watts, F. N., MacLeod, C., & Matthews, A. (1988). *Cognitive psychology and emotional disorders.* New York: Wiley.

Willner, P. (1985). *Depression: A psychobiological synthesis.* New York: Wiley.

Wilson, D. R., Widmer, R. B., Cadoret, R. J., & Judiesch, K. (1983). Somatic symptoms: A major feature of depression in a family practice. *Journal of Affective Disorders, 5*, 199–207.

Wilson, P. H. (1992). Depression. In P. H. Wilson (Ed.), *Principles and practice of relapse prevention* (pp. 128–156). New York: Guilford.

Wilson, P. H. (1996). Relapse prevention: Overview of research findings in the treatment of problem drinking, smoking, obesity and depression. *Clinical Psychology and Psychotherapy, 3*, 231–248.

Wolfe, V. V., Gentile, C., & Wolfe, D. A. (1989). The impact of sexual abuse on children: A PTSD formulation. *Behavior Therapy, 20*, 215–228.

Wolpe, J. (1986). Individualization: The categorical imperative of behavior therapy practice. *Journal of Behavior Therapy and Experimental Psychiatry, 17*, 145–153.

Wolpe, J., & Michaels, E. (1986). The subcategorization of nonpsychotic depression in behavioral and nonbehavioral research. *Journal of Behavior Therapy and Experimental Psychiatry, 17*, 91–93.

Youngren, M. A., & Lewinsohn, P. M. (1980). The functional relation between depression and problematic interpersonal behavior. *Journal of Abnormal Psychology, 89*, 333–341.

5

SCHIZOPHRENIA: FROM BEHAVIOR THEORY TO BEHAVIOR THERAPY

KURT SALZINGER
Department of Psychology
Hofstra University

Given the resistance of schizophrenia to any form of therapy for many years (particularly before the era of drugs began), it is not surprising that early on behavior analysts were given the opportunity to experiment with such patients. Indeed, any tracing of the history of behavior therapy would show that application of behavior-analytic principles was made possible whenever those in charge of the patients (typically psychiatrists, who in those days wanted only those patients that they could talk to by engaging in psychoanalysis or some modification of that technique) were otherwise unable to deal with the disorder. Autism and mental retardation in children and schizophrenia among adults are good examples of disorders that made possible the transfer from behavior theory to behavior therapy. The later shift from theory to application with minor disorders did not take place in a serious way (although Wolpe [1958] being himself a psychiatrist was able to use new techniques on patients with such minor disorders such as phobias and other anxiety disorders and thus able to pioneer behavioral procedures) until psychologists became interested in independent practice. As a result of all this, schizophrenia provides us with a good example of the early and perhaps less sophisticated application of the principles of behavior theory.

What is schizophrenia? If we wanted to reinforce the public's stereotype of abnormal behavior, we would trot out the chronic schizophrenic patient in the back ward of some state hospital. The number of such chronic patients with florid symptoms, however, has been drastically reduced, and more and more we view schizophrenia in its acute or controlled stages. It is, nevertheless, interesting to note that some of the early operant work with patients (Lindsley, 1956) took place with exactly such chronic long-stay patients in large part, as already mentioned, because nobody else was interested in working with them or thought that they could do anything for them.

How It All Began

The wonder of it all is how long it took to move from behavior theory, or what we used to call learning theory, to behavior therapy. For decades we had evidence for the power of our techniques to change the behavior of organisms up and down the phylogenetic scale. At some point, I am sure that a historian will provide an account and an explanation for the advent of behavior therapy, examining the question of what it takes before a theory and its findings are applied in actual practice.

Perhaps an even more surprising instance of a lack of transfer of theory to application is to be found in education, where students are supposed to "learn," a subject that psychologists had studied for many years. Skinner (1954) encapsulated that lack of transfer in the title of one of his papers, "The Science of learning and the art of teaching." He could as easily have written an article for clinical psychology, using the title, "The Science of learning and the art of psychotherapy." Indeed, even today I sometimes hear one of my colleagues say to a student, "There are no hard and fast rules of how to help people; therapy is not a science; you just do the best you can to apply some principles to the art of helping people, and sometimes it all actually works." One of the important issues then in tracing the path from theory to practice is to make that path so obvious that people take it. The extent to which people do that is a topic I am not in a position to comment on. It is, however, sufficiently important for someone to undertake such an investigation. In this chapter, I will make an attempt to trace some of the pathways from behavior theory to behavior therapy, particularly with respect to its application to schizophrenia.

With respect to operant methods, the first pathway consisted of an almost literal transfer of the techniques of the animal laboratory to a human enclosure (e.g., Lindsley, 1956). The second pathway was paved with questions about particular classes of behavior, being aware that, at least in human behavior, one cannot as easily represent all behavior by one class of responses. (We have more recently discovered that animal behavior is also complex and animals' classes of behavior also differ from one another.) This approach adapted the concepts from the animal laboratory, by way of Greenspoon's (1955) and Verplanck's experiments (1955) to verbal behavior in general, and through Salzinger and Pisoni's experiments (1958) more specifically to schizophrenic verbal behavior. The third pathway led to the application of learning paradigms to determine if they might explain, or at least simulate, the acquisition of various forms of abnormal behaviors and thus suggest ways of eliminating them. The fourth route started from the peculiar characteristics of schizophrenia and arrived at behavior-analytic explanations. The final and fifth trail led behavior analysts to a high-speed highway (as yet hardly ever taken) from the theories of schizophrenia to the typical responses emitted by schizophrenic patients, a route that I firmly believe is the best way to effective behavior therapy.

The First Pathway: The Completely Empirical Approach

In behavior analysis, as opposed to Wolpe's application of classical conditioning based on a theoretical derivation, operant conditioning was applied in an empirically derived, defiant manner. Behavior analysts said essentially, "If I can condition a rat, a bird, or a fish, why can't I change the behavior of a person?" Then several rather literal applications of behavior theory took place. After Dunlap (1932) and Watson and Rayner (1920), and in the more recent past, conditioning of a very retarded individual (Fuller, 1949), came Lindsley's (1956) construction of what was essentially a rather large Skinner box for chronic schizophrenic patients. Patients had a knob to manipulate and Lindsley tried out a group of potential reinforcers, including food items and pictures of nudes to determine what control he could produce. He found that some schedules of reinforcement would crowd out such aberrant behaviors as hallucinations and self-destructive behaviors because they strengthened incompatible behaviors.

Essentially, what we had in the early days were attempts to see if we could condition arbitrary behaviors such as knob pulling. A similar approach was taken with both normal and abnormal children. For instance, Gewirtz and Baer (1958) used as a response the dropping of marbles into one of two holes, and Ferster and DeMyers (1961), working with autistic children, had their subjects pull plungers. Then came the token economies (Ayllon & Azrin, 1968; Atthowe & Krasner, 1968) in which the response classes were still not very inventive; they consisted of such behaviors as making beds, toilet care, and dressing. The important variables included conditioned reinforcers, tokens that could be delivered immediately on the emission of desirable behaviors. Response classes reinforced eventually included discussions in groups (therapy?), and reinforcers eventually included appointments with social workers to obtain home visits.

In large measure, the early approach to behavior modification (and that was the term used in those days) consisted of searching out problem behaviors and asking such questions as, Is the behavior excessive or inadequate? Then appropriate conditioning techniques were applied. Sometimes the choice of the response classes to be conditioned was determined by a polemical point that the investigators wanted to make. In an example of the latter, Haughton and Ayllon (1965) decided to condition a fifty-four-year-old female patient, who had been hospitalized for twenty-three years, to hold a broom while standing up. They used cigarettes and tokens exchangeable for cigarettes as reinforcers. When reinforcement was contingent on broom holding, that response increased in frequency; when extinction was imposed, the broom holding response permanently decreased to 0, as evidenced by a two-year follow-up. The reason for this experiment was twofold: First they wanted to show that one can condition and extinguish practically any behavior with the proper reinforcement contingency. Secondly, they used the conditioning essentially to set a trap for two unsuspecting board-certified psychiatrists by asking them to observe the behavior and to evaluate it. This is what they got from the psychiatrists (p. 97):

Her constant and compulsive pacing holding a broom in the manner she does could be seen as a ritualistic procedure, a magical action. When regression conquers the associa-

tive process, primitive and archaic forms of thinking control the behavior. . . . By magic, she controls others, cosmic powers are at her disposal and inanimate objects become living creatures. Her broom could be then: (1) a child that gives her love and she gives him in return her devotion; (2) a phallic symbol; (3) the scepter of an omnipotent queen. Her rhythmic and prearranged pacing in a certain space are not similar to the compulsion of a neurotic; but because this is a far more irrational, far more controlled behavior from a primitive thinking, this is a magical procedure in which the patient carries out her wishes . . .

Although, the reader was no doubt uncomfortable discovering how a patient was seemingly arbitrarily handled (I suspect that a human subjects committee today would not have permitted such a procedure), we must look at this experiment with the eyes of someone three decades ago. Most important for our point here is that this displays the confidence of that time that we could condition any behavior. This shows that at first, the choice of response classes to be altered, as in the case of Lindsley (1956), was as arbitrary as our choice for other animals. The fact that the psychiatrists did not have the foggiest notion of how the patient came to emit this bizarre behavior in a sense constituted added reassurance that the psychiatrists were probably equally wrong about behaviors whose history we are not privy to, and that behavioral interpretations of psychotic behavior must be right for other psychotic behavior, such as delusional speech and hallucinatory behavior (cf. Layng & Andronis, 1984, below).

In this empirical foray into schizophrenia by means of behavior theory, investigators concentrated on showing how basic principles of behavior theory could be applied to the behavior of schizophrenic patients. Thus Salzinger and Pisoni (1958) showed that one could increase or decrease different verbal response classes by presenting or omitting reinforcing events. We also showed that only that particular response class would change on which the reinforcer was contingent (Salzinger, Portnoy, & Feldman, 1964) and that the number of extinction responses following reconditioning was greater than that following the original conditioning (Salzinger & Pisoni, 1958). Another basic-behavior theory principle is the establishment of conditioned reinforcers. In 1965, Salzinger, Feldman, Cowan, and Salzinger established a conditioned reinforcer in a four-year-old boy variously diagnosed as autistic, schizophrenic, and retarded by pairing candy with verbal reinforcement. When we first began to work with him, he essentially failed to speak; after we conditioned him to speak, we were able to demonstrate that the experimenter's speech constructed to be as long as the child's speech increased the length and frequency of the child's utterances. Theobold and Paul (1976) used the arbitrary response of marble dropping with schizophrenic patients participating in a larger token-economy study. Comparing two groups of schizophrenic patients, one with a four-year history of contingent pairing of praise with tangible reinforcers and the other with noncontingent pairing, they found that the contingent-history group continued to respond at a higher rate, with application of praise, than the noncontingent-history group, whose response rate after first increasing steadily declined. Clearly we have another instance of the transfer of behavior-theory principles to the schizophrenic behavior world.

The Second Route: Particular Response Classes

In the second stage, behavior analysts started to look at the problems as specified in the clinical literature, such as hallucinations, delusions, thought disorder, and shallowness of affect. Critical questions were whether these classes of response characterized schizophrenic patients, and if they did, whether they actually constituted response classes. As already mentioned, Salzinger and Pisoni (1958, 1960, 1961; Salzinger, Portnoy, & Feldman, 1964) quite early did a series of studies that were initially methodologically motivated but eventually focused on discovering the nature of schizophrenia, that is, the distinguishing features of schizophrenia.

The methodological question addressed by our studies was the validity of the information obtained through the interview. Since shallowness of affect was considered to be a significant diagnostic criterion for schizophrenia, we tried to determine the extent to which the interviewer might influence how shallow in affect the patient appeared to the interviewer. The procedure was quite straightforward. We chose a class of responses consisting of statements, such as "I am sad, happy, angry; I feel awful, wonderful, terrific." The reason for choosing statements that began with either "I" or "we" was to provide the interviewer with a warning stimulus for noticing an affective statement to reinforce. In brief, we found that verbal reinforcers such as "Yeah," "yes," "I see," "mmm hm," and "I can understand that" increased the frequency of the response class of affect from baseline and caused, when withdrawn, a decrease in such statements. We also found that we could make the reinforcement contingent on speech in general, thus getting the patient to speak more in general by such a contingency.

These studies showed that behavior modification could take place in the course of relatively brief interviews. Because the typical interviewer makes no attempt to program his or her reinforcement with respect to what the patient says, such an effect could occur without the interviewer's intent to modify anything. This showed that the typical disagreement between interviewers in arriving at a diagnosis of schizophrenia could be attributed to the varying reinforcement contingencies that different interviewers apply. From a behavior therapy point of view, this shows that one can modify a patient's verbal behavior without too much difficulty, including a verbal response deemed to be a diagnostic characteristic of schizophrenia. I should mention in this regard that we also found that the rate of conditioning related to outcome of illness: those patients who showed changes due to a change in reinforcement contingency within a period as short as ten minutes were more likely to have left the hospital after six months than those who showed little or no change in affect statements due to changes in reinforcement contingency (Salzinger & Portnoy, 1964).

I wrote about the place of operant conditioning of verbal behavior in psychotherapy some time ago (Salzinger, 1969) and made the point that we should use the conditioning paradigm to change the verbal behavior that most interests us in the direction we believe to be most helpful to patients. Clarity of speech in schizophrenic patients, who are proverbially incomprehensible, would certainly be a worthwhile goal, as would be the shaping of social verbal skills. Simple observation makes clear that schizophrenic patients lack social skills and thus behavior analysts have conditioned social skills of schizophrenic patients.

In practice, social-skills programs have had limited success. Thus, to cite but one recent example, Hayes, Halford, and Varghese (1995) were able to demonstrate that social-skills training led to more improvements than engaging in discussion groups. Nevertheless, this improvement did not translate itself to better community living. Liberman, Kopelwicz, and Young (1994) maintained that one must take what they call a biobehavioral approach, including psychopharmacological treatment together with behavioral treatment administered continuously with ongoing assessments and including behavioral family management and community cooperation. The results are so limited these days because so much of schizophrenic behavior must be modified from the problems of inadequate reinforcement histories—never having learned social skills, for example, to having such symptoms that they interfere with the acquisition of any skills. I believe we need to return to the application of our techniques to small samples of patients who are followed up in great detail and worked on with the same intensity, that is, the kind of conditioning that we used to administer to animals in controlled environments.

The Third Route: From Behavior Analytic Paradigms to the Acquisition of Aberrant Behavior

One approach to discovering how to help people with problems is to examine the various learning and conditioning paradigms extant in behavior theory that could be involved in the production of such problems. This is a variant of the completely empirical approach. It asks whether particular learning paradigms could generate various patterns of aberrant behavior. Then, if the paradigms can do so at least theoretically, we can investigate and eliminate the aberrant behavior by employing the elimination procedures appropriate to the paradigms of acquisition. I summarized some of the major paradigms and related various forms of aberrant behavior to them (Salzinger, 1975).

The first paradigm that I examined was what has come to be called superstition (Herrnstein, 1966). A reinforcer is made available at random, or at least independent of behavior, as far as the dispenser of the reinforcement is concerned, and yet a response class becomes ensnared in the contingency. In the pigeon, you get bobbing and weaving behavior and among human beings you get such behaviors as baseball batters hiking up their pants just before they step into the batter's box. For the batter, those responses could easily become part of the chain of responses that culminates in hitting the ball far out of the park, or at least some desirable distance, without actually having any effect on the distance the ball travels. In psychopathology, and particularly in schizophrenia, you might get some of the rituals that are found in that disorder by a similar mechanism. Questions to be asked here include: Under what conditions are such superstitions more likely to be acquired? Is deprivation or some other establishing operation particularly important here? Are we all more vulnerable to such conditioning when under stress or suffering from schizophrenia?

Another superstition paradigm consists of repeatedly introducing a stimulus when an animal happens, for other reasons, to respond in a particular way (e.g., particularly quickly). Eventually, the animal starts to respond more quickly when the experimenter introduces that particular stimulus at a time that the animal would ordinarily be responding slowly. In other words, the happenstance contiguity of stimulus and response confers on that stimulus the power of a discriminative stimulus, a stimulus in the presence of which a certain class of behavior is likely to be reinforced. It is not difficult to conjure up a situation in which schizophrenics respond in the presence of stimuli as if they had discriminative power that we know they do not have. The possibility arises for schizophrenic patients to be more sensitive to such contingencies than normal individuals. To get to the next stage with this paradigm, it is then useful to ask, If we find greater sensitivity to superstitious conditioning, what can we do to extinguish such behavior? And perhaps even more important, Should we concentrate on schizophrenic patients in remission or at risk to prevent such superstitious conditioning from taking place, by training them to discriminate between superstitious and real-contingency relations?

Let us next look at the extinction paradigm (what could be more basic except for conditioning?). Conditioning is faster than extinction—a fact that makes intermittent reinforcement so powerful a technique and behavior in general not so easily eliminated. One fact we know about extinction is that response rate at first tends to be quite variable, indeed often to occur in higher bursts than during conditioning, that it eventually diminishes, and that accompanying all of that is some emotional behavior that we can observe in animals by monitoring the effects of the autonomic nervous system. We can observe such emotional behavior in human beings when they are disconnected during a telephone conversation.

The stressful life event that, as we will see later, is thought to be critical by some as a trigger for schizophrenia, essentially results in extinction (Salzinger, 1980). Look at the list of stressful life events (Dohrenwend, Krasnoff, Askenasy, & Dohrenwend, 1978). The losses that the list promotes as stressful life events very often result in the loss of positive reinforcement, such as loss of a job, retirement, and loss of a spouse. All these events result in a reduction of many different positive reinforcers. Even more interesting is the case of an event such as a promotion, graduation from school, or birth of a child; all of these supposedly happy events result very often in loss of reinforcement, such as being unable to kid around as much with fellow workers as one used to, after one has been promoted to supervise them; or consider the loss of reinforcement incurred by graduation when one has to go out to new places to work and lose the reinforcement of the friends at school. Or examine the case of the third instance, where the birth of a child has produced the loss of the ability to go out every time one wants to because one has to get a babysitter, and one has to forego doing more desirable things to change the baby's diaper or feed it. As we will see later, the degree to which a schizophrenic episode is evoked by stressful life events would then be describable by a conditioning paradigm, namely extinction. It also implies that the appropriate therapy then would provide such patients with a repertory that would make access to reinforcement again available.

I have reviewed only a few learning paradigms; the point of this section is to show that there are a great many learning paradigms (Salzinger, 1975) that one could investigate to shed light on the nature of schizophrenia and thus derive treatment techniques that might well be more effective than the more empirical ones presently employed.

The Fourth and Fifth Roads: Characteristics of, and Theories about, Schizophrenia

I will consider these two roads together because once one leaves a superficial description of schizophrenia, theory (at some level) must be invoked in discussing the "characteristics" of a disorder. When we speak of the characteristics of schizophrenia, we are talking about diagnosis and its problems (Salzinger, 1978), which have by no means been solved. In other words, we still find varying degrees of disagreement between various diagnosticians. When I wrote my book on schizophrenia more than twenty years ago (Salzinger, 1973), I suggested that the disorder was like a unicorn—a mythological beast whose very basic characteristics were still being debated, such as whether it actually had one or two horns. Nevertheless, many pictures of unicorns, indeed many beautiful pictures and tapestries, adorn the walls of many museums. At this time, I will contend that schizophrenia has changed to be more like a camel, that is, a horse built by too many schizophrenia experts. The category of schizophrenia has changed in its breadth from time to time. It was made narrow in DSM-III and then emancipated in DSM-IIIR and DSM-IV, that is, allowed to become more heterogeneous. In addition, the onslaught of genetic research, using adoption studies in which children of known schizophrenic mothers were placed in normal homes, championed a still broader category, that is, spectrum disorders (schizophrenialike personality disorders). With this relaxed criterion for finding genetic effects in children of schizophrenic mothers raised in normal adopting families, the genetic effects manifested themselves much more boldly, of course. The point here is that changes in the breadth of the category of schizophrenia are not unknown, nor are those changes unmotivated.

One solution to the problem of heterogeneity of the category has recently been "discovered" in the new concept of comorbidity. Now, when there is disagreement, we have the "you are right, too" argument. This reminds me of a story of two men who were unable to come to an agreement about an issue and who therefore went to a rabbi. The rabbi listened to the first person and immediately replied, "You are right." The other person of course objected, "Rabbi, you have not heard my side." And the rabbi agreed, "Let's hear your side." After the other man had finished, the rabbi said unhesitatingly, "You're right." A third person who overheard the proceedings, shouted, "Rabbi, how can they both be right?" The rabbi's answer came through clear as a bell, " You're right, too."

A recent review of diagnosis in general, and of schizophrenia in particular, by Clark, Watson, and Reynolds (1995) reported, using lifetime diagnoses, that 91 percent of schizophrenic patients had at least one comorbid condition. To cite one example, 47 percent of patients diagnosed as schizophrenic also suffered from substance abuse disorder. In other cases, the problem was one of the DSM allowing two different diagnoses for what might well be one disorder. The example given by Clark et al. is schizotypal personality disorder and schizophrenia. The authors also stated that "schizophrenia is a category that is well-known for its within-group variability and may represent a set of etiologically distinct disorders rather than a single diagnosis" (p. 133).

Now, if you are not yet convinced that the diagnosis of schizophrenia has problems, consider the fact that many investigators have, in response to the heterogeneity of the category, devised a dimensional analysis in terms of severity of the disorder, in terms of whether the patient was paranoid or not, and in terms of the prominence and frequency of symptoms. Clark and colleagues listed additional ways of categorizing schizophrenic patients into manageable categories, such as positive (or acute or reactive) vs. negative (or chronic or process) symptoms. They also mention other ways of subdividing the category of schizophrenia. We might just point to one other problem, namely that of the related category "schizoaffective." In the old days, we used the appellation "schizoaffective" to cover cases of schizophrenia that did not seem as severe as the usual cases of schizophrenia and that showed more emotional lability than schizophrenics usually do. It was recognized as a subtype of schizophrenia by DSM-II, as an independent category in DSM-III, and by some investigators, according to Clark et al., this compromise category has been viewed as two different categories, one more schizophrenic and one more affective.

Despite this profusion of categories, subcategories with and without revisions, an increasing amount of evidence has accrued showing schizophrenia to "run" in certain families (Gottesman, 1991); evidence coming from adoption studies as well as from twin studies has implicated some common genes in schizophrenia. Furthermore, the degree of bizarre behavior and the resistance to treatment associated with this diagnosis have led to a large number of theories about what could possibly account for such behavior. An interesting exercise in this regard is to trace how a basic difference (I prefer this term to "deficit" because it is neutral about its relative contribution to the problem behavior that constitutes schizophrenia) in schizophrenia might interact with how the person is affected by the environment. To a behavior analyst, of course, it is most important to play out such gene-environment interaction and to make use of behavior analysis to see how it works.

Before we do this, however, let us examine the diathesis-stressor model (Gottesman, 1991), that is, how nonbehavior analysts view this interaction. This model states essentially that some people have a predisposition to schizophrenia, the diathesis consisting of genetic factors that interact with stressors provided by the environment. In accordance with this model, genetic factors are essential, but not sufficient, to produce schizophrenia. It is clear, of course, that normal behavior is also dependent on a diathesis, that is, genetic factors need to interact with the environment, including stressors but in the main consisting of continuous interactions with the environment. Such environmental interactions must take place in a manner rather well specified by behavior theory, that is, by occasions for responses, by responses (classes of responses to be accurate), and by consequences of those responses. Thus, heredity is definitely not in opposition to environment; both are essential for behavior to occur. Interestingly enough, the usual specification of interaction of genetics and environment for disorders such as schizophrenia is by way of stressors from the environment. Common sense tells us that when you stress a vulnerable person you put him or her at greater risk of getting a disorder. The data, however, are not so clear on this subject. Dohrenwend, Shrout, Link, and Skodol (1987) investigated the effect of stressful life events on episodes of schizophrenia both in first episode and later-onset patients. They took the precaution of comparing schizophrenic patients, not just to normal controls, but also to depressed patients, finding as a result that although the latter would have episodes of depression after stressful life events of a fateful sort, the former failed to react in that fashion. More specifically, episodes of schizophrenia did not necessarily follow stressful life events. Episodes, in other words, could not be ascribed to fateful life events, such as loss of a child, physical disease, or injury. What did relate to such episodes were events likely to result in a loss of social networks. This is, of course, very interesting to a behavior theorist because it suggests that what is at fault in such cases is the loss of occasions to behave in particular ways and therefore the possibility of having such behaviors reinforced.

As mentioned above, I suggested that the manner in which stressful life events produce depression is by reducing the number of positive reinforcers available to people suffering the event or by increasing the punishers that they must endure (Salzinger, 1980). Examples given were cases in which a person suffering the loss of a child would suffer a reduction in positive reinforcement. This suggests that the lack of relationship between stressful life events and episodes in schizophrenic patients found by Dohrenwend et al. was due to the fact that schizophrenic patients do not, under such circumstances, bear a loss of reinforcers. Because schizophrenic persons have, to begin with, few reinforcers in their lives except for a very few stemming from their limited social interaction, they may well not have the many reinforcers to lose which depressed (or potentially depressed) individuals start with. Dohrenwend et al. found that an episode is likely only when an event diminishes the few social reinforcers that schizophrenic persons have (reduction in social networks). Furthermore, in the case of depression, a reduction in reinforcers may well be due to their protracted mourning or other emotional response to stressful life events, which emotional behavior by itself might reduce the number of positive, primarily social reinforcers.

Now what we do not know from the findings of various genetic effects differentiating classes of patients from one another as well as from normal controls is anything about the pathway from gene to behavior. It is that which needs to be specified (Salzinger, 1992), that is, how we get from gene, or for that matter from a difference in dopamine uptake at synapses, to the kind of behavior we characterize as schizophrenic. At this point, we must therefore examine some behavioral theories of schizophrenia.

First, let us talk about the basic nature of this disorder. Schizophrenia used to be viewed as a deteriorating disorder, and as already indicated, some continue to view it that way. On the other hand, others have presented a different model for it altogether (Zubin & Spring,1977). According to this model, the disorder has its ups and downs and may get better or worse. This view, of course, leaves much room for triggering events for the so-called episodes.

Zubin and Steinhauer (1981), in an article written to "break the logjam of schizophrenia" as they put it, surveyed various etiological models to explain the onset of schizophrenia. They listed six models containing potential causal variables:

- ecology: this includes socioeconomic status, physical and social characteristics of the environment in which the patient lives, social networks, and ethnic status;
- development: this includes prenatal complications, such as inadequate nutrition, and the patterning of various classes of behavior in complexity of cognition the child is capable of;

- genetics: this set of variables has been firmly established and is based on studies following up twins and adopted children of schizophrenic mothers raised in conventional families;
- learning theory: this includes the reinforcement history of the patient, acquisition of "faulty" behavior resulting in ineffectual social relations, and inadequate coping responses;
- the internal environment: this refers primarily to the biochemistry of the body, including following the neurotransmitter as it crosses the synaptic clefts in the nervous system and including specific substances such as dopamine in excess; and
- neurophysiology: this includes the measurement of neurological function of the brain through such measures as event-related potentials.

Zubin and Steinhauer (1981) speak of two kinds of vulnerability, one that is inborn and one that is acquired. The inborn vulnerability includes genetic, neurophysiological, and internal variables, whereas the acquired vulnerability includes the ecological, developmental, and learning theory variables. Of course, we must add to this that learning is not completely determined by environmental variables. What constitutes a discriminative stimulus or a reinforcer may well be partially determined by inborn factors (e.g., some forms of mental retardation). Similarly, the genetic variable cannot express itself in the absence of the environment that evokes particular behaviors. These models must, in other words, interact. Taking the diathesis-stressor model seriously, these authors view schizophrenia as an episodic disorder in which there is an interaction between a basic vulnerability and so-called triggering events. "[T]he triggering event necessary to elicit an episode is not to be confused with etiological life events giving rise to the various etiotypes (ecological, developmental, learning). These are long term influences that induce vulnerability. Triggering events, in comparison, are short term recent inducers of sufficient stress to produce a crisis" (p. 482). And as Dohrenwend and colleagues already showed us, the triggering events appear to be reductions of social networks that are basically weak in the first place. Disruption of the social supports were very much involved in differentiating schizophrenic patients from both normal and depressed patients.

Here we have a very important finding for behavior therapists: whether social networks of schizophrenic patients (Hammer, Makiesky-Barrow, & Gutwirth, 1978) are viewed as part of vulnerability or as part of triggering event, as behavior analysts we have a model of social behavior that allows us to characterize the state of the particular patient's interaction and, therefore, the therapeutic intervention to be employed (Bellack, Morrison, & Mueser, 1992; Salzinger, 1981). The importance of social networks and social behavior in general makes the conditioning of such responses a very logical class to be manipulated. The inadequacy of schizophrenic social behavior, beginning with their earlier inability to make friends as adolescents (Kreisman, 1970), along with the importance of "negative expressed emotion" (EE) (Leff & Vaughn, 1985) in their interactions with other family members, makes behavior therapy directed at both family members and patients a highly effective route to travel in the remediation of schizophrenic difficulties.

It is interesting to note that although Bellack et al. (1992) reviewed various methods of behavioral intervention with schizophrenic patients, their view of schizophrenia is rather pessimistic compared with that of Zubin and Steinhauer (1981). The former call schizophrenia "a pernicious, debilitating disorder that has profound consequences for the patient, the family, and the social environment in which the patient lives" (p. 135). They go on to say that only a small fraction of patients recover substantially. By way of contrast, Zubin and Steinhauer (1981) reject what they call the myth of the schizophrenic as a person condemned to a permanent affliction accompanied by slow degeneration. Instead, they assume the vulnerability model, the importance of which is that behavior therapy must be directed not only at the disorder and its manifestations but at its ups and downs. Moreover, special attention needs to be given to the patients not only when they are suffering from an episode, but also when they seem free of it, so that the next episode can be prevented.

It is possible to view the vulnerability model from a different point of view than the stressor-diathesis perspective. The behavior-theory model of conditioning lends itself readily to interpretation of how people get along in life. Snyder (1977) compared reinforcement patterns in problem and nonproblem families. He found that problem families tended to reinforce prosocial behavior less often and deviant behavior more often than did nonproblem families. In addition, problem families were less likely to repeat responses positively reinforced and more likely to repeat punished responses than the nonproblem families. This kind of approach seems much more likely to give us insight into how the environment interacts with the vulnerability of a schizophrenic patient than the more vague global kinds of ratings of emotional expression of a family. The point is that, as already mentioned, schizophrenic episodes arise in many cases for which no precipitating incident occurs. We must, therefore, look for some other factors in the environment of the patient. Here we can go from behavior theory to behavior therapy through a behavioral analysis of what specifically takes place in the family environment that results in high or low emotional expression. What is more, if one is to help such families, this would provide us with the information for specific advice to give to families, or the patients for that matter.

The handling of brain-injured children may serve as a model for dealing with schizophrenic patients. When we trained mothers of brain-injured children, the most universal change that we found consisted of an increased use of positive reinforcers by the mothers in guiding their children's behavior (Salzinger, Feldman, & Portnoy, 1970). Instructions to the family not to aggravate the schizophrenic patient who lives among them is not specific enough. The reduction of aversive stimuli and the increase of positive reinforcers is easier to explain and is effective, in part, because positive reinforcement evokes positive reinforcement from its recipient.

No matter what the basic conception of schizophrenia, most investigators agree that coping ability—including social skills, self management, and thus ability to handle expressed emotion—are critical. Bellack et al. (1992) present a useful review of these two areas of behavior therapy and add compliance with medical regimes (taking antipsychotic drugs) as another critical area in which to apply behavior therapy. How do these techniques stem from behavior theory? They are derived from behavior theory in the most basic way, that is, by using reinforcement contingency in the token economy, as already mentioned, and as modified and developed by other investigators (e.g., Paul & Lentz, 1977; Paul & Menditto, 1992). Paul and Menditto describe what they have come to call the social-learning approach:

> *Organized group and unit-wide modalities are used extensively for skills training; focus includes self-care, interpersonal skills, problem-solving, communication, stress management, and prevocational, vocational, and housekeeping skills as well as reduction, elimination, or control of bizarre and inappropriate behavior. Both group and unit-wide modalities use concrete instruction and education, modeling, prompting, shaping, direct cognitive and associative training, differential reinforcement and contingency management, graduated exposure, response costs, time out, and extinction procedures (p. 48).*

Such programs include procedures that eventually wean patients from tokens and provide generalization training so that social reinforcement from the community and family takes over as soon as possible. Paul has for some years now shown the clear superiority of social learning (token economies) over other kinds of treatment, whether milieu or the classical individual treatment of chronic schizophrenic patients. In any case, the various kinds of intervention listed are obviously very familiar to anyone knowledgeable in behavior theory and the responses chosen for modification are clearly those that have been ascribed to the schizophrenic diagnostic category. These responses include positive symptoms, such as peculiar movements, inappropriate affect, delusions, hallucinations, and dangerous behaviors; negative symptoms, such as deficits in social and communication skills and in self-care; as well as vocational and prevocational skills. We need to add here that Paul has been advocating systematic observation of the behavior of the staff–patient interaction to make certain that the conditioning procedures have been carried out as required and of the patients to observe the outcome.

Scotti, McMorrow, and Trawitzki (1993) examined publication trends with respect to the behavioral treatment of chronic psychiatric patients. Following in the footsteps of Bellack (1986), who in his presidential address lamented behavior therapy's neglect of chronic patients, they surveyed a number of journals and found that the neglect was not only in number but also in quality of studies, as indicated by the dearth of functional analysis and follow-up data (a point also made by Paul and Menditto, 1992). The target behaviors of the 256 articles surveyed were most frequently social behavior along with activities of daily living, hallucinations, delusions, idiosyncratic repetitive body movements, or infrequently occurring speech. The reason for the reduction in behavioral research with schizophrenic patients must be, in part, attributed to the fact that behavioral clinical students of today more often wish to become independent practitioners than they used to. Because of their interest in becoming private practitioners, students have eschewed placement in state hospitals where they are likely to be exposed to psychotic patients. Finally, early work with psychotic patients was done by experimental psychologists with a background in animal work. These researchers were not particularly interested in becoming independent practitioners and, therefore, continued to work with such patients. They have not been replaced as they retired or went on to study other phenomena. Another point made by Scotti and colleagues is the dearth of behavioral theories of psychosis.

I will present an approach that is expressly behavioral, the Immediacy Theory (Salzinger, 1984). The Immediacy Theory says essentially that the behavior of schizophrenic patients is primarily controlled by stimuli immediate in their environment. This hypothesis came from data we collected in our laboratory and seemed to summarize a great deal of other data as well. Furthermore, such a formulation seemed bolstered by the dopamine hypothesis of schizophrenia, which says that such behavior stems from an excess of this neurotransmitter at the synapses between neurons. In other words, the biochemical hypothesis would predict faster responding to stimuli because impulses would more quickly course across synapses, which is exactly what would be predicted by the immediacy hypothesis. What this implies behaviorally is that schizophrenic individuals are exposed to what is only a subset of stimuli surrounding them and therefore a subset of stimuli surrounding normal individuals. Thus, a set of instructions that has to last for say up to an hour in controlling behavior is much less likely to do so in schizophrenic than in normal individuals, as I found in a study conducted in 1957.

In that experiment, subjects had to judge the heaviness of weights using a series of responses consisting of "very light," "light," "medium," "heavy," and "very heavy." First they judged a series of 200, 250, 300, 350, and 400 g weights presented in random order. Then they had to judge the same series after lifting a so-called anchor weight (900 g) before lifting the weight to be judged. Finally, they were instructed to correct their judgment for the effect of the anchor weight. The results showed that schizophrenic patients were less able to correct for the immediate effect they felt when making judgments than a comparable group of normal subjects. In another experiment, Salzinger and Pisoni (1960) demonstrated that extinction of a verbal response class was more rapid in schizophrenic patients than in normal physically ill patients, again showing that when the immediate stimulus, in this case the reinforcer, was absent, the effect of the recent stimulus diminished, that is, the response rate very rapidly abated. A third experiment showed that schizophrenic patients produced speech in which the spans of connected words were shorter than those of normal subjects (Salzinger, Portnoy, & Feldman, 1966; Salzinger, Portnoy, Pisoni, & Feldman, 1970). These results demonstrated, once again, that schizophrenic subjects tended to be controlled by stimuli close in time. Here, the stimuli in question were response-produced as in one word uttered by a speaker controlling the next one but not necessarily those that follow even seconds later. Many experiments supplying evidence for this formulation are to be found in Salzinger (1984).

The question here is, if the immediacy hypothesis is correct, how would this influence behavior? What it means in terms of behavior analysis is that only some occasions would serve as discriminative stimuli for such individuals, and only some consequences would serve as effective reinforcers. Moreover, rules would be expected to influence such people only close to the time that they were expressed, and only very recent reinforcement history would be expected to be effective in controlling their behavior. The kinds of behavior conditioned would also be less predictable in schizophrenic patients, since in our society a great deal of behavior is reinforced by events occurring over a series of responses, rather than after each and every response. Thus, the combination of the tendency to respond predominantly to immediate stimuli with conditioning and other forms of behavioral control would then give rise to what I have called Immediacy Theory.

Such a theory can explain how typically schizophrenic symptoms can be produced in people predominantly responding to immediate stimuli. Thus, delusions are primarily responses to stimuli in isolation. A person joking "I'll kill you if you do that again" might well be taken literally by a schizophrenic patient because the words are responded to in isolation (not taking into account that the group had been joking or that the person uttering the words is smiling). Hallucinations also are amenable to explanation by the Immediacy Theory. The effect of conditioning is such that all of us think from time to time that we can see somebody who is not there. This might be occasioned most often when a number of other discriminative stimuli beside that of the person him- or herself produce the operant response of "seeing." Thus, if you have made a date to meet someone at a particular place and that person is never late and someone of a similar height and weight and dress just came in, you might well think, "There he is!" Of course, when this happens to normal people, the incorrect response is checked because responding to additional stimuli (the differences between the person who came in and the one you have been waiting for) become important in controlling your "seeing." The point of exploring this hypothesis is that whatever difference one posits about what makes schizophrenic patients different from normal individuals and people suffering from other kinds of disorders is that one must investigate both theoretically and then empirically how the basic difference—the one that the genetic difference suggests (and which I formulated as the Immediacy Theory)—interacts with the environmental variables. It is here that behavior theory becomes important, because it serves to provide a behavioral mechanism intervening between the basic difference and the ultimate behavior that manifests itself as symptoms. Once we have that, we can begin to talk about how we might intervene to reduce the typically schizophrenic behavior.

We have recently begun to explore this area with respect to hallucinations and delusions (Leibman, 1995; Leibman & Salzinger, 1995). Basically, as I suggested in Salzinger (1984), the task at hand is to transfer the behavior that is so often controlled by immediate stimuli to more remote ones. Using treatment derived from the assumptions of Immediacy Theory, six patients received treatment for a period of some six weeks. Treatment consisted essentially of transferring responses from immediate stimuli to more remote ones. This was accomplished by preventing some responses such as hallucinations and delusions from occurring and thus allowing the patient to respond to more remote stimuli, which was also promoted by the treatment procedures. Although the results of this short-term therapy with relatively little compliance with respect to homework (that is, with no possibility of reminding patients of the procedures to be followed when the therapist was not around) were moderate and short-lived, they exceeded supportive treatment given subjects on the same ward.

Conclusions

I reviewed the progress of behavior analytic treatment of schizophrenia from theory to therapy. I found what I believed to be five stages:

1. A completely empirical approach of simply applying the techniques of conditioning to arbitrary behaviors of schizophrenic patients to determine the nature of the contingencies acting on them.
2. Application of procedures to particular response classes, that is, the aberrant behaviors but primarily obvious ones.
3. Investigation of the conditioning paradigms to determine which might simulate the behaviors found in schizophrenic behavior.
4. and 5. were combined. The fourth approach started from the characteristic responses of schizophrenia (such as delusions and hallucinations or shallow affect) and applied conditioning techniques to ameliorate these characteristics of schizophrenic patients. The fifth approach, which has not yet come to be much applied in this field, but which I believe should be applied, starts from a theory concerning the basic difference inherent in schizophrenia and then tries to change schizophrenic behavior by concentrating on that basic difference.

References

Atthowe, J. M., Jr., & Krasner, L. (1968). Preliminary report on the application of contingent reinforcement procedures (token economy) on a "chronic" psychiatric ward. *Journal of Abnormal Psychology, 73*, 37–43.

Ayllon, T., & Azrin, N. (1968). *The token economy.* New York: Appleton-Century-Crofts.

Bellack, A. S. (1986). Schizophrenia: Behavior therapy's forgotten child. *Behavior Therapy, 17*, 199–214.

Bellack, A. S., Morrison, R. L., & Mueser, K. T. (1992). Behavioral interventions in schizophrenia. In S. M. Turner, K. S. Calhoun, & H. E. Adams (Eds.), *Handbook of clinical behavior therapy.* pp. 135–154 New York: Wiley.

Clark, L. A., Watson, D., & Reynolds, S. (1995). Diagnosis and classification of psychopathology: Challenges to the current system and future directions. *Annual Review of Psychology, 46*, 121–153.

Dohrenwend, B. S., Krasnoff, L., Askenasy, A. R., & Dohrenwend, B. P. (1978). Exemplification of a method for scaling life events: The PERI Life Events Scale. *Journal of Health Social Behavior, 19*, 205–229.

Dohrenwend, B. P., Shrout, P. E., Link, B. G., & Skodol, A. E. (1987). Social and psychological risk factors for episodes of schizophrenia. In H. Haefner, W. F. Gattaz, & W. Janzarik (Eds.), *Search for the causes of schizophrenia* (pp. 275–296). Berlin: Springer-Verlag.

Dunlap, K. (1932). *Habits: Their making and unmaking.* New York: Liveright.

Ferster, C. B., & DeMyers, M. K. (1961). The development of performances in autistic children in an automatically controlled environment. *Journal of Chronic Diseases, 13*, 312–345.

Fuller, P. R. (1949). Operant conditioning of a vegetative human organism. *American Journal of Psychology, 62*, 587–590.

Gewirtz, J. L., & Baer, D. M. (1958). Deprivation and satiation of social reinforcers as drive conditions. *Journal of Abnormal and Social Psychology, 57*, 165–172.

Gottesman, I. I. (1991). *Schizophrenia genesis.* New York: Freeman.

Greenspoon, J. (1955). The reinforcing effect of two spoken sounds on the frequency of two responses. *American Journal of Psychology, 68*, 409–416.

Hammer, M., Makiesky-Barrow, S., & Gutwirth, L. (1978). Social networks and schizophrenia. *Schizophrenia Bulletin, 4*, 522–545.

Haughton, E., & Ayllon, T. (1965). Production and elimination of symptomatic behavior. In L. P. Ullmann & L. Krasner (Eds.), *Case studies in behavior modification* (pp. 94–98). New York: Holt, Rinehart, & Winston.

Hayes, R. L., Halford, W. K., & Varghese, F. T. (1995). Social skills training with chronic schizophrenic patients: Effects on negative symptoms and community functioning. *Behavior Therapy, 26,* 433–449.

Herrnstein, R. J. (1966). Superstition: A corollary of the principles of operant conditioning. In W. K. Honig (Ed.), *Operant behavior: Areas of research and application* (pp. 33–51). New York: Appleton.

Kreisman, D. (1970). Social interaction and intimacy in preschizophrenic adolescence. In J. Zubin & A. M. Freedman (Eds.), *The psychopathology of adolescence.* New York: Grune & Stratton.

Layng, T. V. J., & Andronis, P. T. (1984). Toward a functional analysis of delusional speech and hallucinatory behavior. *The Behavior Analyst, 7,* 139–156.

Leff, J., & Vaughn, C. (1985). *Expressed emotion in families.* New York: Guilford.

Leibman, M. (1995). *Modifying hallucinatory-delusional behavior in schizophrenic patients through control transfer to remote stimuli.* Unpublished doctoral dissertation, Hofstra University, Hempstead, NY.

Leibman, M., & Salzinger, K. (1995). *Treating schizophrenic patients' hallucinations and delusions through control transfer to remote stimuli.* Poster session presented at the Annual Meeting of the Association for Advancement of Behavior Therapy, Washington, DC, November 1995.

Liberman, R. P., Kopelwicz, A., & Young, A. S. (1994). Biobehavioral treatment and rehabilitation of schizophrenia. *Behavior Therapy, 25,* 89–107.

Lindsley, O. R. (1956). Operant conditioning methods applied to research in chronic schizophrenia. *Psychiatric Research Reports, 5,* American Psychiatric Association.

Paul G. L., & Lentz, R. J. (1977). *Psychosocial treatment of chronic mental patients: Milieu versus social-learning programs.* Cambridge, MA: Harvard University Press.

Paul, G. L., & Menditto, A. A. (1992). Effectiveness of inpatient treatment programs for mentally ill adults in public psychiatric facilities. *Applied & Preventive Psychology, 1,* 41–63.

Salzinger, K. (1969). The place of operant conditioning of verbal behavior in psychotherapy. In C. M. Frank (Ed.), *Behavior therapy: Appraisal and status* (pp. 375–395). New York: McGraw-Hill.

Salzinger, K. (1973). *Schizophrenia: Behavioral aspects.* New York: Wiley.

Salzinger, K. (1975). Behavior theory models of abnormal behavior. In M. Kietzman, S. Sutton, & J. Zu-

bin (Eds.), *Experimental approaches to psychopathology* (pp. 213–244). New York: Academic Press.

Salzinger, K. (1978). A behavioral analysis of diagnosis. In R. L. Spitzer and D. F. Klein (Eds.), *Critical issues in psychiatric diagnosis.* New York: Raven Press.

Salzinger, K. (1980). The behavioral mechanism to explain abnormal behavior. *Annals of the New York Academy of Sciences, 340,* 66–87.

Salzinger, K. (1981). Remedying schizophrenic behavior. In S. M. Turner, K. S. Calhoun, & H. E. Adams (Eds.), *Handbook of clinical behavior therapy* (pp. 162–190). New York: Wiley.

Salzinger, K. (1984). The immediacy hypothesis in a theory of schizophrenia. In W. D. Spaulding & J. K. Cole (Eds.), *Theories of schizophrenia and psychosis* (pp. 231–282). Lincoln: University of Nebraska Press.

Salzinger, K. (1992). Connections: A search for bridges between behavior and the nervous system. *Annals of the New York Academy of Sciences, 658,* 276–286.

Salzinger, K., Feldman, R. S., Cowan, J. E., & Salzinger, S. (1965). Operant conditioning of verbal behavior of two young speech-deficient boys. In L. Krasner and L. P. Ullmann (Eds.), *Research in behavior modification* (pp. 82–105). New York: Holt, Rinehart, & Winston.

Salzinger, K., Feldman, R. S., & Portnoy, S. (1970). Training parents of brain-injured children in the use of operant conditioning procedures. *Behavior Therapy, 1,* 4–32.

Salzinger, K., & Pisoni, S. (1958). Reinforcement of affect responses of schizophrenics during the clinical interview. *Journal of Abnormal and Social Psychology, 57,* 84–90.

Salzinger, K., & Pisoni, S. (1960). Reinforcement of verbal affect responses of normal subjects during the interview. *Journal of Abnormal and Social Psychology, 60,* 127–130.

Salzinger, K., & Pisoni, S. (1961). Some parameters of the conditioning of verbal affect responses of schizophrenic subjects. *Journal of Abnormal and Social Psychology, 63,* 511–516.

Salzinger, K., & Portnoy, S. (1964). Verbal conditioning in interviews: Application to chronic schizophrenics and relationship to prognosis for acute schizophrenics. *Journal of Psychiatric Research, 2,* 1–9.

Salzinger, K., Portnoy, S., & Feldman, R. S. (1964). Experimental manipulation of continuous speech in schizophrenic patients. *Journal of Abnormal and Social Psychology, 68,* 508–516.

Salzinger, K., Portnoy, S. & Feldman, R.S. (1966). Verbal behavior in schizophrenics and some comments toward a theory of schizophrenia. In P. Hoch & J. Zubin (Eds.), *Psychopathology of schizophrenia* (pp. 98–128). New York: Grune & Stratton.

Salzinger, K., Portnoy, S., Pisoni, D., & Feldman, R. S. (1970). The immediacy hypothesis and response-produced stimuli in schizophrenic speech. *Journal of Abnormal Psychology, 76,* 258–264.

Scotti, J. R., McMorrow, M . J., & Trawitzki, A. L. (1993). Behavioral treatment of chronic psychiatric disorders: Publication trends and future directions. *Behavior Therapy, 24,* 527—550.

Skinner, B. F. (1954). The science of learning and the art of teaching. *Harvard Educational Review, 24,* 86–97.

Snyder, J. J. (1977). Reinforcement analysis of interaction in problem and nonproblem families. *Journal of Abnormal Psychology, 86,* 528–535.

Theobold, D. E., & Paul (1976). Reinforcing value of praise for chronic mental patients as a function of historical pairing with tangible reinforcers. *Behavior Therapy, 7,* 192–197.

Verplanck, W. S. (1955). The control of the content of conversation: Reinforcement of statements of opinion. *Journal of Abnormal and Social Psychology, 51,* 668–676.

Watson, J. B., & Rayner, R. (1920). Conditioned emotional reactions. *Journal of Experimental Psychology, 3,* 1 –14.

Wolpe, J. (1958). *Psychotherapy by reciprocal inhibition.* Stanford, CA: Stanford University Press.

Zubin, J., & Spring, B. (1977). Vulnerability—A new view of schizophrenia. *Journal of Abnormal Psychology, 86,* 103–126.

Zubin, J., & Steinhauer, S. (1981). How to break the logjam in schizophrenia: A look beyond genetics. *The Journal of Nervous and Mental Disease, 169,* 477–492.

6

BEHAVIORAL PHARMACOLOGY AND THE TREATMENT OF SUBSTANCE ABUSE

C. W. LEJUEZ
Department of Psychology
West Virginia University

DAVID W. SCHAAL
Department of Psychology
West Virginia University

JENNIFER O'DONNELL
Department of Psychology
West Virginia University

It may be argued, at least among scientists, that the moral implications of drug use and abuse have long since given way to the quest to understand it as a biopsychological phenomenon. Even in the culture at large, education and treatment are as frequently cited as approaches to problems of drug abuse as are societal censure and incarceration. It is equally true, however, that current approaches to education and treatment are as driven by traditional, nonscientific concepts, such as personal responsibility and spirituality, as they are by biopsychological concepts. Whether these are fortunate or unfortunate circumstances is not a matter addressed by the present chapter. Rather, we hope to show that basic biobehavioral research has resulted in important improvements in drug-abuse treatment, and is likely to continue to do so. In this paper we will review research in behavioral pharmacology that has helped shape several current approaches to drug-abuse treatment. We also will describe some of those treatments. Our goal is to show that basic behavioral pharmacology has helped, and will continue to help, shape, and refine drug-abuse treatment.

Behavioral pharmacology, at least the part that has made the most significant advances in the understanding of drug abuse over the past few years, has been conceptualized as the union of two scientific disciplines: the experimental analysis of behavior and pharmacology (Branch & Schaal, 1990). A major characteristic of behavioral phar-

Acknowledgments: The preparation of this chapter was supported, in part, by Grant R29 DA08053 to D. W. Schaal from the National Institute on Drug Abuse.

macology is that research findings in the experimental analysis of behavior are useful and relevant whether or not drugs are part of the experimental manipulation. Throughout this chapter, we will refer to research both within and outside of behavioral pharmacology, provided that it has contributed in some way to the understanding of drug abuse and drug-abuse treatment.

Stimulus Functions of Drugs

Behavioral pharmacology has become a very diverse science, both methodologically and conceptually. At its root, however, behavioral pharmacology involves the controlled observation of behavior in whole animals exposed to drugs. In many cases, effects of drugs are tested by simply administering them to animals, observing alterations in learned or unlearned behavior, and comparing that altered behavior to behavior in the absence of drugs. For example, activity levels of rats typically are increased following administration of moderate doses of *d*-amphetamine (Campbell & Fibiger, 1971), and cocaine may increase or decrease rates of food-reinforced responding depending on response rate prior to cocaine injection (Schaal, Miller, & Odum, 1995). In general, differential behavioral effects of drugs reflect both their different pharmacological mechanisms of action *and* the current and historical behavioral conditions under which the drugs are tested (Barrett, 1987).

Effects such as those described above help establish a broad understanding of the behavioral pharmacology of drugs, and also are relevant to a complete understanding of drug abuse. Research in behavioral pharmacology that has the clearest relevance to understanding drug abuse, however, involves procedures in which the drugs serve a specific functional stimulus role. Drugs of abuse most clearly function as such when they are used as reinforcers, discriminative stimuli, and unconditioned or conditioned stimuli. This review will deal exclusively with studies of such stimulus functions and their relevance to treating drug abuse.

Drugs as Reinforcers

In an early study by Spragg (1940), a chimpanzee that had been made dependent on morphine learned to open a box with a wooden stick to retrieve a syringe loaded with morphine, which the experimenter then injected intramuscularly. The likelihood of opening the box increased with time since the last injection, suggesting that the behavior of opening the box was negatively reinforced by reductions in early signs of morphine withdrawal symptoms. Years later, Headlee, Coppock, and Nichols (1955) showed that restrained rats would move their heads to one side if it resulted in administration of morphine or codeine. When the development of reliable and long-lasting intravenous cannulae allowed the study of drug self-administration in monkeys (Thompson & Schuster, 1964) and rats (Weeks, 1962), the study of drugs of abuse as reinforcers began to flourish.

Subsequently it was shown that rats and monkeys would self-administer most of the drugs commonly administered by humans, including opiates (Thompson & Schuster, 1964), stimulants (Pickens & Thompson, 1968), barbiturates (Meisch & Lemaire, 1988) and other anxiolytic drugs (Ator & Griffiths, 1993), phencyclidine (Carroll, 1985), and alcohol (Meisch & Thompson, 1973). Furthermore, it has been shown that physical dependence on the drug is not necessary for drugs to serve as reinforcers. These were important developments in the understanding of drug abuse for several reasons. First, self-administration of drugs by animals causes one to question the notion that human drug abuse reflects weak morals or a lack of will; the morality of a rat has little place in understanding a rat's drug self-administration. Second, the conceptual contribution of "reinforcement" to an understanding of drug abuse hardly can be overestimated. Drugs of abuse exploit behavioral processes that have evolved in animals for other reasons; therefore, understanding those behavioral processes *in general* aids in our understanding of drug abuse. Third, starting with relatively simple drug-reinforcement procedures, researchers have studied many factors involved in drug abuse, including behavioral, pharmacological, and physiological factors. Such research has often suggested straightforward approaches to treating drug abuse in humans.

The literature on drug self-administration is so vast that we can provide only a very selective consideration of it. The goals of the present chapter may best be served by addressing (1) the utility of self-administration procedures for determining the reinforcing efficacy of drugs, (2) the behavioral economics of drug self-administration, and (3) alterations in self-administration by the administration of other drugs.

Reinforcing Efficacy of Abused Drugs

If levels of responding that produce access to an active drug are higher than responding that produces access to the drug vehicle (i.e., saline), the drug may be called a reinforcer. The development of self-administration techniques allowed investigators to determine whether both common drugs of abuse as well as new or not commonly abused drugs could be viewed as reinforcers. Techniques that have been employed in such assessments include "substitution" procedures in which the reinforcing efficacy of one drug is assessed by substituting it for another drug that has been established as a reinforcer for a given subject (e.g., Young & Woods, 1981), choice procedures in which two doses of drug are available concurrently (e.g., Iglauer & Woods, 1974), and procedures in which the number of responses per infusion is increased systematically until the subject stops responding or responds much less (i.e., the progressive ratio, or PR, schedule; Griffiths, Findley, Brady, Dolan-Gutcher, & Robinson, 1975). In general, some drugs are more reinforcing than others, larger doses are preferred to smaller ones, and animals will work harder to receive drugs that are more potent, delivered in higher doses, and delivered more immediately. Such methodologies are irreplaceable in the preclinical investigation of potential therapeutic compounds because they allow valid assessments of a drug's abuse potential. Drugs with high abuse potential (i.e., those which are highly reinforcing) may be kept off the market, or physicians may limit prescription of such agents to patients without histories of drug abuse.

Behavioral Economics of Drug Self-Administration

The reinforcing efficacy of any drug is determined by the interaction of multiple variables operating on the subject, including the drug itself, the dose consumed, and the work required for each unit dose. These factors were studied in research with rats

(Meisch & Thompson, 1971, 1973), which showed that rates of ethanol-reinforced lever-pressing depended on the dose per infusion and the number of presses required for a drug infusion. Frequently, response rates maintained by drug are a bitonic function of dose, with intermediate doses producing the highest rates, and high doses, low doses, and saline (i.e., the drug vehicle) producing low rates (e.g., Downs & Woods, 1974). Such results have been observed under many conditions with several drugs (see review by Meisch & Lemaire, 1993).

More recently, researchers in the experimental analysis of behavior have demonstrated the utility of applying relatively simple economic principles to the understanding of reinforced behavior in general (e.g., Hursh, 1984). By this view, reinforced responses are seen as the unit of exchange for reinforcing commodities. Increases in the number of responses required for the same amount of reinforcement (e.g., dose), *or* decreases in the amount of reinforcement for the same number of responses, are understood as manipulations of the same basic quantity (i.e., *unit price,* which is equal to the number of responses per infusion or dose per infusion). This suggests that alterations in responses per drug infusion *or* the dose per infusion are functionally identical, because both are ways to alter unit price.

Studies of drug self-administration in which dose per infusion and responses per infusion have been altered were conducted many years prior to the application of economic concepts to drug self-administration. In a theoretical review of such studies, Bickel, De-Grandpre, Higgins, and Hughes (1990) attempted to determine whether manipulations of these two independent variables were, in fact, functionally identical. Plotting the amount of drug consumed as a function of unit price revealed monotonically decreasing functions of shallow slope resembling those found in the study of economics. That is, the amount of drug consumed decreased as unit price increased. Unit price, then, provides a way to compare drug reinforcers using these two independent variables.

Practically speaking, a behavioral economics of drug self-administration suggests several modes of behavioral treatment of drug abuse that focus on the conditions of access to alternative activities, as well as on conditions of access to the abused drug. These suggestions have been supported by several basic research findings (see review by Carroll, 1996). For example, Marilyn Carroll has shown that access to a nondrug reinforcer can reduce drug-reinforced behavior of experienced animals (Carroll, Carmona, & May, 1991) and can delay or prevent the acquisition of drug-reinforced behavior (Carroll & Lac, 1993). The ability of alternative reinforcers to reduce drug-reinforced behavior has been shown to depend both on the unit price of the drug reinforcer (Carroll et al., 1991) and on the unit price of the alternative reinforcer (Nader & Woolverton, 1991). Thus, under conditions in which the price of the drug is very high and the price of valued alternative commodities is relatively low, alternatives compete with the drug reinforcers and reduce rates of drug taking. The obvious suggestion is that drug-abuse treatment may be improved if alternatives to drugs are made available. How this suggestion has been put into practice is discussed below.

Pharmacological Treatment of Drug Self-Administration
Pharmacological treatment of drug abuse probably exploits several known behavioral processes, although the certainty with which a therapeutic effect can be attributed to a *specific* behavioral mechanism of a drug treatment is debatable. Perhaps the clearest case

in which drug treatment for substance abuse exploits behavioral processes is the use of disulfiram (Antabuse) for treatment of chronic alcohol abuse. Disulfiram has few effects when used alone, but when used in concert with alcohol, it interrupts the metabolism of alcohol so that levels of acetaldehyde quickly increase, causing a variety of unpleasant symptoms, including severe headache, nausea, vomiting, breathing difficulties, and chest pain (Kitson, 1977). In addition to the threat of punishment or the experience of punishment for drinking, disulfiram treatment takes advantage of the fact that the probability of drinking in chronic drinkers is not always very high. Taking disulfiram when the probability of drinking is low (e.g., first thing in the morning) may function similarly to "commitment responses" studied in basic research on self-control with animals (Rachlin & Green, 1972). That is, taking disulfiram in the morning commits the individual to not drink later in the day because drinking will be punished. This commitment response prevents the individual from having to choose later between drinking and not drinking, which probably would lead to drinking.

Another common pharmacological treatment of drug abuse that exploits behavioral mechanisms is replacement therapy with methadone and nicotine. Methadone maintenance programs have been in place for decades now, and recent evidence suggests that methadone is an effective component of treatment of opiate abuse (Payte & Zweben, 1991). Nicotine replacement therapy, primarily in the form of gum or the transdermal patch, is a more recent development (Cepeda-Benito, 1993). Both therapies have multiple functions. In addition to lessening the serious risks of drug consumption through more established methods (e.g., intravenous administration of heroin, and the consumption of nicotine by smoking tobacco), these therapies reduce cravings for the abused drugs presumably by acting on the same neurons in much the same way as the abused drugs. Thus, behaviorally speaking, taking replacement drugs may be considered analogous to feeding a hungry animal prior to the opportunity to self-administer food. The probability of consuming the illicit drug decreases when the safer substitute is taken first.

A few current pharmacological treatments of drug abuse are less clearly tied to behavioral mechanisms, although they do have support from basic research. For example, buprenorphine, a mixed opiate agonist-antagonist, has been shown to decrease heroin, morphine, and cocaine self-administration in monkeys and humans (Mello & Mendelson, 1995) and is being increasingly employed in treatments for abuse of these drugs and for polydrug abuse. Although the behavioral data suggesting the utility of buprenorphine are clear, the precise behavioral mechanisms by which the drug reduces abuse, particularly nonopioid and polydrug abuse, remain unknown. In some respects, naltrexone, an opioid antagonist that blocks many of the effects of heroin and morphine, is similar to buprenorphine. It has been shown to reduce heroin self-administration in humans (Mello, Mendelson, Kuehnle, & Sellers, 1981), which is not surprising for an opioid antagonist, but it is also being used to treat cocaine and alcohol addiction.

Finally, treatments for drug abuse include pharmacotherapies commonly used to treat psychological disorders in general. Many people treated for drug abuse also can be diagnosed as having depression, and so treatment with antidepressant drugs is increasingly popular (McGrath, Nunes, Stewart, Goldman, Agosti, Ocepek-Welikson, & Quitkin, 1996; Tutton & Crayton, 1993). Some investigators have suggested that antidepressants (e.g., imipramine and fluoxetine) have more direct effects on drug abuse. That is, they may not only work indirectly by alleviating depressive symptoms, but also may alter central nervous system responses to drugs in ways that reduce their reinforcing value. Benzodiazepines (i.e., anxiolytics) have become a standard part of treatment during alcohol detoxification, and may be prescribed to alleviate anxiety associated with abstinence from the abused drug (Miller, 1995). It should be noted that in every case of pharmacological treatment mentioned here, responsible clinicians prescribe the drugs as part of a more comprehensive treatment plan.

Summary

Drug self-administration has been studied in many ways, and in the present review we have given only a small sample of this research. We have excluded, for example, discussions of factors such as genotype (Files, Andrews, Lewis, & Samson, 1993), stress (Piazza, Deminiere, le Moal, & Simon, 1990), prior drug exposure (Horger, Shelton, & Schenk, 1990), nutritional circumstances (Carroll & Meisch, 1984), and the periodic presentation of important events (Falk, 1971) that predispose experimental animals, and perhaps humans, to drug taking. Even without the details of these studies, however, one easily can guess at their implications. Studies such as these and the others reviewed here support the contention that the conception and study of drugs as reinforcers has been the most significant contribution of behavioral pharmacology for understanding and treating substance abuse.

Drugs as Discriminative Stimuli

Drugs have been known to serve as "signals," or discriminative stimuli, for environmental events for decades (Girden & Culler, 1937). Since then, many procedures have been used to examine the discriminative stimulus effects of drugs. State-dependent learning procedures, for example, have been conceived of by some (Overton, 1988; Schaal, McDonald, Miller, & Reilly, 1996) as instances of discriminative stimulus control by drugs. Modern investigations of drug discrimination typically employ two-response procedures, in which one response (e.g., pressing one lever) is reinforced with food when a drug is administered prior to the session, and another response (e.g., pressing a different lever) is reinforced in the drug's absence. In such procedures, drugs assume the role served by more traditional discriminative stimuli such as colors and tones. That is, which lever the animal presses in a given session depends on whether or not the drug had been administered prior to that session. Many drugs, not limited to drugs of abuse, have been shown to control differential lever-pressing after such training (see Colpaert & Balster, 1988).

A somewhat surprising, but very reliable, finding is that discriminative control by drugs usually is pharmacologically specific. That is, the discriminative control of a drug will transfer to other drugs in the same pharmacological class, but not to drugs in other classes. For example, methadone will function as morphine in animals trained to discriminate morphine, because both drugs are opiate agonists (Colpaert, 1978), but it will not function as *d*-amphetamine. This general finding has allowed drug-discrimination procedures to be employed in sophisticated studies of pharmacological mechanisms of drug effects (e.g., Picker, Craft, Negus, Powell, Mattox, Jones, Hargrove, & Dykstra, 1992). Thus, drug discrimination has facilitated the investigation of the pharmacological mechanisms of abused drugs (Colpaert & Balster, 1988), which may suggest rational pharmacological treatments of drug abuse. For example, naltrexone blocks the discriminative stimulus effects of morphine, and hence may be useful in the treatment of morphine abuse.

There may be more direct relations, however, between discriminative functions of drugs and their implications for treating drug abuse. In screening drugs for abuse potential, for example, those that substitute for known reinforcing drugs (i.e., drugs that replace others as discriminative stimuli), such as cocaine, may be suspected of being reinforcers themselves. One must view such assertions skeptically. In a dramatic demonstration of the power of behavioral variables to alter the effects of abused drugs, Ator and Griffiths (1993) showed that the discriminative stimulus effects of midazolam in rhesus monkeys were enhanced (i.e., lower doses were sufficient to produce the same behavioral effects as higher doses) when monkeys were allowed to self-administer the drug. When the same amount and distribution of injections were administered response-independently, however, midazolam was less effective as a discriminative stimulus because larger doses were required for responding to occur at former levels. Thus, sensitivity to the discriminative stimulus effects of midazolam were increased or decreased depending on whether subjects self-administered it or received it response-independently. Continued investigations of the relation between discriminative and reinforcing functions (or abuse potential) of drugs are required before firm conclusions regarding this issue can be reached.

Drugs as Stimuli in Pavlovian Conditioning Procedures

In studies by Goldberg and associates (Goldberg & Schuster, 1967; Goldberg, Woods, & Schuster, 1969), the power of stimuli associated with drugs was assessed in morphine-dependent monkeys. In one study (Goldberg et al., 1969), a baseline of morphine-reinforced behavior was employed. Rates of this behavior were moderate and steady as long as occasional morphine administrations were continued. Rates increased significantly, however, when a stimulus that had previously been paired with opiate withdrawal induced by the opiate antagonist nalorphine was presented, thus indicating that withdrawal-associated stimulus had acquired some of the behavioral properties of morphine withdrawal itself. In another study (Goldberg & Schuster, 1967), responding on a schedule of food reinforcement was occasionally interrupted by the presentation of a tone, which was followed five minutes later by administration of nalorphine. After several such pairings of tone with nalorphine, monkeys' response rates were suppressed in the presence of the tone prior to the administration of nalorphine. Indeed, eventually the tone elicited a full-blown withdrawal syndrome, complete with vomiting, *by itself,* that is, before or in the absence of the nalorphine infusion. These studies show that environmental events associated with drugs can become powerful determinants of drug-related behavior.

Regarding drugs as unconditioned stimuli (US) has resulted in several important advances in understanding the behavioral mechanisms of drug abuse. Tolerance to the effects of drugs often is conceptualized as the development of physiological and behavioral responses elicited by drug-correlated stimuli (i.e., conditioned stimuli, or CS), which compensate for the initial effects of the drug (see review by Siegel, 1990). Recent research suggests strongly that drugs also can serve as CSs (Bormann & Overton, 1993) and as conditioned facilitators of Pavlovian CS–US relations (Parker, Schaal, & Miller, 1994). These multiple and often powerful behavioral functions of drugs have suggested interpretations of the behavioral mechanisms of drug craving, and have resulted in important additions to successful drug-abuse treatment programs (O'Brien, McLellan, Alterman, & Childress, 1992).

Summary

Drugs can serve as reinforcers, discriminative stimuli, and as unconditioned and conditioned stimuli. Drugs that serve as reinforcers for humans usually also are reinforcers for other animals. The reinforcing value of a drug as well as its ability to acquire other stimulus functions depend in part on the drug's pharmacological mechanisms of action, but also are determined by the behavioral conditions under which it is administered or made available. Thus, behavioral pharmacology and the experimental analysis of behavior are intimately connected. Research in behavioral pharmacology has implications for treatment of human drug abuse because it deals with both the behavioral and the pharmacological mechanisms by which drugs exert their effects. In the remainder of this chapter, we will clarify some of these implications by considering basic and applied research on and treatment for human drug abuse. Throughout, we will consider the stimulus functions of drugs for the using and abusing individual.

Molar Determinants of Substance Abuse

According to many current theories of substance abuse, substance use functions to improve an individual's internal state through means such as reducing tension or increasing feelings of personal control. As a result, the likelihood of future substance use, and eventual abuse, is increased. This mediational view of substance abuse (Vuchinich & Tucker, 1996), and reinforcement in general (Rachlin, Battalio, Kagel, & Green, 1981), has been challenged on the grounds that the relation between behavior and its consequences can be established without the need for internal mediating states. The alternative view places control over substance use and abuse in the environment and not within the individual.

According to an environment-based account, substance use and abuse is considered in terms of a choice situation in which the individual chooses between substance use and all other available activities in the environment (Vuchinich, 1995). For example, substance relapse has been shown to be a function of negative life events (Tucker, Vuchinich, & Pukish, 1995), such that when there is little reinforcement available for activities other than substance use, substance use (and in this case relapse) is more likely to occur. Specifically, it has been suggested that characteristics of reinforcers, such as rate, delay, response cost or effort, and magnitude determine the value of alternative behaviors and thus determine choices that are made. The assumption is that alternatives

that have the highest rate or probability of large, immediate reinforcement and that require minimal response effort will be preferred over other alternatives. For individuals
who use drugs or alcohol, substance use provides large reinforcers (e.g., a "high") that
are reliable, frequent, and fairly immediate. Also, drugs and alcohol usually are readily
available so there may be little response effort involved.

The adequacy of the choice paradigm to account for substance use has been studied
experimentally with humans. For example, Vuchinich, Tucker, and Rudd (1987) examined choice between immediate consumption of alcoholic beverages or money when the
probability of earning money and the delay to money delivery were varied. Subjects
were assigned to a condition in which they received either a high or low probability of
earning money, and money was received either the same day, after two weeks, or after
eight weeks. Preference for alcohol varied indirectly with probability of earning money
and directly with delay. That is, subjects preferred alcohol to money more when the
probability of earning money was lower and as payment delay decreased.

The basis of the choice account of substance use is the matching law (Herrnstein,
1961), a quantitative description of choice behavior. Although the matching law typically is used to describe basic aspects of human and animal behavior, it also has been
applied to areas such as the maintenance of "pain" behavior of chronic pain patients
(Fernandez & McDowell, 1995), self-injurious behavior and social interaction maintained by attention (McDowell, 1981; Conger & Killeen, 1974), and disruptive behavior
of a girl with mental retardation (Martens & Houk, 1989). In its simplest form, the
matching law is:

$$B_1/[B_1 + B_2] = R_1/[R_1 + R_2]$$

where B_1 is the rate of behavior allocated to one alternative (i.e., consuming alcoholic
beverages), B_2 is the rate behavior allocated to a second alternative (i.e., interacting with
family), R_1 is the rate of reinforcement obtained on the first alternative, and R_2 is the rate
of reinforcement obtained on the second alternative. The matching law puts all behavior in a larger context in the sense that the reinforcing value of a particular activity is a
relative matter, determined in part by what other activities are available and the reinforcing value of those activities. This relative value, then, determines how frequently an
individual will engage in an activity, or how much time or resources will be devoted to
the activity. In this equation, the relative rate of obtained reinforcement is the key variable determining the relative rate of behavior allocated to either alternative, and thus
which alternative will be preferred. Although reinforcement rate is the most common
variable used with the matching law, the equation also may use magnitude and delay of
reinforcement to predict how frequently an individual will choose an alternative.

The value of applying the matching law to substance use is that it can help a therapist estimate, for a particular individual, the reinforcing value of nondrug alternatives,
depending on particular features of those alternatives (e.g., rate, delay, or magnitude of
reinforcement). Using this information, the individual's environment can be manipulated (e.g., by decreasing delay to and increasing magnitude of other reinforcers) so that
other alternatives become more desired than drugs and alcohol. As a result of this

change in reinforcement, other activities will increase and by necessity substance use will decrease or possibly be eliminated.

Substance Abuse Treatment and Research with Humans

Treatment Based on Pavlovian Conditioning Procedures

Although treatment for substance abuse often has initial success, relapse is a common problem (Heather, 1990). Possibly the most astounding and disheartening feature of relapse is that although individuals successfully achieve drug and alcohol abstinence during treatment, they often may relapse only a few days or weeks following the termination of treatment (Childress, Hole, Ehrman, Robbins, McLellan, & O'Brien, 1993). Laboratory studies have shown that Pavlovian conditioning principles reduce the reinforcing effects of drugs. As a result, these principles have been incorporated into the treatment of substance abuse to reduce the occurrence of relapse in the natural environment (Heather, 1990; O'Brien et al., 1992). Pavlovian conditioning-based treatments address the problem of relapse by targeting craving. When the drug abuser discontinues drug use and is taken out of the context that was associated with drug use (i.e., placed into inpatient treatment), these individuals often report both a strong conviction towards remaining abstinent and a weakened craving for drugs. Once they are reexposed to individuals and situations that previously were paired with drug use, however, cravings for previously abused drugs return and relapse typically occurs (O'Brien et al., 1992).

Operationally defined from a Pavlovian conditioning perspective, cravings are either drug-compensatory or drug-same conditioned responses that occur only when the individual is exposed to drug-related contexts (Childress et al., 1993; Siegel, 1990). In the case of drug-compensatory conditioned responses, regulatory bodily changes occur in the presence of conditioned stimuli (e.g., drug paraphernalia, fellow drug users) to counteract the anticipated effects of drugs or alcohol. If the individual does not engage in substance use following these compensatory bodily changes, he or she feels considerable pain and discomfort (i.e., withdrawal). As a result, the individual may engage in substance use as a form of escape or avoidance from withdrawal symptoms.

In the case of drug-same conditioned responses, external stimuli that have been paired with drug use produce some of the same bodily sensations that previously have been caused by the drug itself (i.e., the conditioned and unconditioned responses are similar). According to Childress et al. (1993), "certain cues that previously had signaled the arrival of a drug (the sight of a certain neighborhood or a car) seem to set off a whole host of feelings and reactions" (p. 74). Consequently, future drug use may be triggered. Research has suggested that the development of drug-compensatory or drug-same conditioned responses may be a function of the nature and mechanisms of a particular drug (Paletta & Wagner, 1986; Siegel, 1989). Although the function of drug-compensatory and drug-same conditioned responses are different, both types of responses considerably increase the probability of relapse (Childress et al., 1993).

Most of the support for a Pavlovian conditioning-based theory of relapse has come from animal studies (see Siegel, 1990, for a review). Recent laboratory work with cocaine and opiate abusers, however, has found similar results with humans (Childress et al., 1993; O'Brien et al., 1992). Specifically, decreased skin temperature and galvanic skin responses, and increased subjective ratings of cravings were found in detoxified cocaine and opiate abusers in response to drug-related stimuli. Interestingly, cocaine abusers exhibited drug-same conditioned responses to cocaine-related stimuli, but not to opiate-related stimuli. Similarly, opiate abusers exhibited drug-same conditioned responses to opiate-related stimuli, but not to cocaine-related stimuli. These studies show that conditioned responses are specific to certain stimuli.

In some treatments for substance abuse, individuals may be instructed to avoid stimuli that are related to past drug use (e.g., fellow drug users, drug paraphernalia; Heather, 1990). Support for this strategy comes from studies of returning Vietnam veterans who were addicted to heroin while in Vietnam and treated before returning home (O'Brien, Nace, Mintz, Meyers, & Ream, 1980; Robins, Davis, & Goodwin, 1974). In these studies, it was found that the rate of relapse for these soldiers was significantly less than for other comparable groups of civilians. As a result, it was suggested that relapse was less likely in the veterans because, unlike the civilians, they were removed from the context in which heroin use occurred. Despite the repeated finding that avoidance of drug-related stimuli will prevent the occurrence of cravings and subsequent relapse, several researchers are skeptical of the applicability of these studies to typical drug abusers. For example, Childress et al. (1993) have questioned the efficacy of the avoidance approach, suggesting that long-term avoidance of all drug cues is virtually impossible for most individuals. Furthermore, by avoiding drug-related stimuli, individuals never learn more adaptive behavior that is incompatible with taking drugs. As alternatives to the avoidance approach, both aversive counterconditioning and extinction procedures, based on basic laboratory research, have been proposed for treatment.

Aversive Counterconditioning

In an aversive counterconditioning procedure, stimulus properties of an abused substance (e.g., presentation of a powder substance or a drug-related odor) are paired with unpleasant bodily sensations (e.g., chemical-induced nausea or shock-induced pain). Using this procedure, it is hoped that future exposure to those stimulus properties will elicit unpleasant bodily sensations, and thus decrease or terminate craving of the actual substance in the future. Although aversive counterconditioning has been shown to have considerable effects in the laboratory (e.g., Garcia, Ervin, & Koelling, 1966), support for this procedure in the natural environment is equivocal (see Heather, 1990, and Marlatt, 1994, for reviews).

The lack of success of aversive counterconditioning procedures could be explained by Pavlovian conditioning principles. One main reason is the similarity between unpleasant bodily sensations produced by aversive counterconditioning and drug-compensatory conditioned responses (e.g., nausea or sickness). Because substance abusers may learn that substance use temporarily counteracts unpleasant bodily sensations that are part of a drug-compensatory conditioned response, it should not be surprising that drug use may be attempted to similarly counteract the unpleasant bodily sensations produced by aversive counterconditioning. In both cases, drug use is reinforced by the temporary removal of these unpleasant bodily sensations, and, thus, the likelihood of future drug use is increased.

The main problem with aversive counterconditioning, then, may be that external drug-related stimuli, rather than the administration and ingestion of the drug itself, are conditioned to become aversive. One way to overcome this problem would be to pair shock- or nausea-inducing chemicals with the self-administration of a particular drug in addition to drug-related stimuli. As a result, both drug-related stimuli and drug self-administration may become associated with immediate unpleasant bodily sensations, limiting both craving and the negatively reinforcing effects of drug administration. Unfortunately, ethical issues concerning the advocation of drug use as a component of treatment may preclude the use of such a technique outside of controlled laboratory studies using animals.

Extinction

In an extinction procedure (often referred to as cue exposure), conditioned stimuli are presented repeatedly in a safe environment where substance use cannot occur (e.g., in-patient clinic). As a result of repeated presentations of the conditioned stimuli in the absence of drugs or alcohol, the intensity of conditioned responses weaken over time and eventually extinguish completely (Siegel, 1990). When successful, this procedure increases the likelihood that recovering patients who are exposed to drug-related cues in the natural environment will abstain from using drugs and alcohol following the termination of treatment. O'Brien et al. (1992) found that groups of recovering cocaine addicts who received extinction training with either supportive-expressive psychotherapy or standard drug counseling had significantly lower treatment-dropout rates and significantly higher rates of negative urine samples compared to groups who did not receive extinction training. Although still somewhat new, the extinction procedure has generated considerable attention, and many researchers consider it to be the key to understanding and treating substance abuse (Heather, 1990).

Applying Behavioral Principles to Treatment: Cocaine Dependence

Higgins and Budney (1993) have outlined a six-month outpatient treatment for cocaine dependence that is based on behavioral principles. The focus of the treatment is to "re-arrange the drug user's environment so that (1) drug use and abstinence are readily detected, (2) drug abstinence is positively reinforced, (3) drug use results in an immediate loss of reinforcement, and (4) the density of reinforcement derived from nondrug sources is increased to compete with the reinforcing effects of drugs" (pp. 98). Specifically, participants frequently supply urine samples (e.g., every other day) that are analyzed for cocaine content. Results of these samples immediately are supplied to the participant, therapists, and significant others who previously have agreed to provide support throughout treatment. During the first three months of treatment, the participant earns $2.50 for the first negative sample. As long as the patient does not provide a positive sample, the value of each consecutive negative sample increases by $1.25. If the patient provides a positive sample, however, the value for the following negative sample is reduced back to $2.50. Consecutive negative samples following a positive sample increase in value as above, and after five consecutive negative samples following a positive sample, the value of the next negative sample is reset to the value prior to the last positive sample. After several months, lottery tickets replace money as the reinforcer.

The program also includes the community reinforcement approach to increase the density of reinforcement available for nondrug alternatives (Sisson & Azrin, 1989). The community reinforcement approach has been shown to improve problematic relationships between individuals (Azrin, Naster, & Jones, 1973), and substance abuse treatment outcome data have shown its efficacy as a component of substance abuse treatment (Azrin, 1976). First, willing significant others and the participant determine activities that are of interest to the participant. Following each negative sample, significant others engage in those activities with the participant, whereas following each positive sample, the activity is postponed and significant others may provide only abstinence-related support to the participant. This approach also focuses on providing skills and opportunities to participants such as training him or her to avoid situations and individuals that are antecedents to drug use, employment and educational counseling, assertiveness training, and the encouragement of participation in new or former recreational activities.

One basis for this behavioral treatment is laboratory research showing that the efficacy of reinforcement and punishment are inversely related to the delay that separates the behavior and its consequences. A second basis is studies on choice and behavioral economics showing that the value of drugs and alcohol are determined, in part, by the ease with which other reinforcers can be obtained and the relative value of those reinforcers (Carroll et al., 1991). Incorporating these principles, it is hoped that abstinence can be achieved through reinforcement of abstinence, punishment of drug use, increasing the value of available nondrug reinforcers (e.g., more structured time with significant others), and providing opportunities to obtain presently unavailable reinforcers to the patient (e.g., new recreational activities).

Several studies (e.g., Budney, Higgins, Delaney, Kent, & Bickel, 1991; Higgins, Delaney, Budney, Bickel, Hughes, Foerg, & Fenwick, 1993) have found Higgins and Budney's treatment to be very effective in establishing and maintaining cocaine abstinence. These studies have shown that over six months, participants in this program achieved significantly greater overall and consecutive periods of abstinence than subjects receiving standard outpatient drug and alcohol counseling based on the disease-model of treatment (to match the financial benefits of the behavioral treatment, patients in the standard condition were paid $5 per week regardless of urine sample results). Furthermore, in a single-case analysis of the efficacy of this behavioral treatment (Budney et al., 1991), two cocaine-dependent individuals not only remained abstinent from cocaine during the eighteen-week treatment, but also at 1- and 5-month follow-ups. One possible concern with implementing this treatment is the financial cost. As pointed out by Higgins and Budney (1993), however, this program has been shown to be very effective and is considerably less expensive (costs are $11–$12 per day across three months) than the cost of a typical twenty-eight-day inpatient hospitalization (Holder & Blose, 1991).

Experiential Avoidance and Acceptance

According to Hayes, Wilson, Gifford, Follette, and Strosahl (1996) "many forms of psychopathology can be conceptualized as unhealthy efforts to escape and avoid emotions, thoughts, memories, and other private experiences" (pp. 1152). These efforts to escape or avoid negative feelings often are counterproductive, because they increase the intensity, frequency, and duration of these negative feelings. Hayes et al. (1996) have suggested that this unhealthy pattern of behavior, referred to as experiential avoidance, may be a primary component of substance abuse. Specifically, substance abuse becomes a strategy for avoiding negative feelings or moods such as depression, trauma, or anxiety (Hayes et al., 1996; Marlatt, 1994). For example, Childress, McLellan, Natale, & O'Brien (1986) found that craving and withdrawal often were correlated with emotions such as anger, anxiety, and depression. Furthermore, in a study by Sanchez-Craig (1984) it was found that over 80 percent of the drinking episodes reported by subjects were aimed at altering subjective experiences such as increasing pleasure or decreasing depression. Although substance use may temporarily postpone negative feelings or create positive feelings, the negative feelings often reappear in more extreme forms shortly following substance use. Thus, a vicious cycle develops in which the individual must use drugs more frequently and at greater quantities to regain temporary relief (Marlatt, 1985).

Basic experimental support for the concept of experiential avoidance may be found in the aversive control literature with animals. For example, animals can easily be trained to avoid predictable (Sidman, 1953) and unpredictable (Herrnstein & Hineline, 1966) shocks, and in some circumstances even schedules of positive reinforcement can serve as aversive conditions from which animals will escape (Azrin, 1961). In behavioral pharmacology, it has long been known that anxiolytics drugs, such as benzodiazepines and barbiturates, and alcohol can increase low response rates occurring under conditions in which each response is punished by electric shock (Cook & Davidson, 1973; Geller & Seifter, 1960). Opiate agonists can reduce response rates under a procedure in which each response reduces the intensity of a continuously presented shock (i.e., a shock-titration procedure; Weiss & Laties, 1958). The effects of other abused drugs that do not clearly reduce the aversive function of events nevertheless may be modified by stressful circumstances. For example, food deprivation increases self-administration of a variety of drugs (see Carroll & Meisch, 1984, for a review) and exposure to other stressful procedures can predispose animals to acquiring amphetamine-reinforced behavior (Piazza et al., 1990). The point is that, although empirical bases for the concept of experiential avoidance may be somewhat diffuse, life is filled with events that cause negative feelings and drugs may interact with those events in ways that increase the probability that drug abuse will result.

As a treatment for substance abuse resulting from experiential avoidance, clients are taught to accept their negative feelings (Hayes et al., 1996; Marlatt, 1994). For many substance abusers, attempts to control negative feelings through various means, including substance use, have failed. It is believed that the often desperate attempts to control or alleviate the negative feelings are part of the problem that maintains the negative feelings (Nardone & Waltzlawick, 1993). Therefore, the individual is encouraged to let go of the struggle to control these feelings, while making a commitment to positive behavior change (Hayes, 1994; Hayes & Melancon, 1989).

Although intuitively appealing, there are several potential problems with acceptance-based treatments for substance abuse. First, there has been no research showing that acceptance-based treatments are more effective for substance abuse treatment than are more traditional behavioral treatments that have been shown to be effective (Hayes et al., 1996). Second, although much of the basis for experiential avoidance can be conceptualized from a tight behavior-analytic framework, a behavior-analytic explanation for acceptance strategies is presently unavailable. Evidence for the use of acceptance-based treatments is still only loosely tied to, and extrapolated from, experimental work on stimulus equivalence and rule-governed behavior (cf. Hayes & Wilson, 1994).

Pitfalls of Substance-Abuse Treatment

Generalizing Treatment Effects from the Laboratory to the Natural Environment

One issue that typically has been the Achilles heel of treatment for substance abuse, as well as for many other disorders, is that treatment effects often do not generalize to settings outside of treatment. As a result, many patients who achieve abstinence while undergoing treatment may relapse soon after treatment termination. To address this problem, generalization issues should be considered when designing and implementing substance-abuse treatments. Specifically, we suggest that therapists be sensitive to differences between the treatment setting and the post-treatment environment. Furthermore, treatments should include a component for easing the patient's transition back into their everyday environment. For example, if the community reinforcement approach is used, therapists should consider whether the social support available during treatment will be available following treatment. Additionally, when using aversive counterconditioning, extinction, or other treatments that attempt to change the function of drug-related stimuli, it is essential to change the functions of as many drug-related stimuli in the natural environment as possible. Some of these stimuli may not be as obvious as are fellow drug users and drug paraphernalia (e.g., coffee in the morning, certain music). Generalization of effects is an important issue in the treatment of behavioral disorders, and, unfortunately, often is overlooked. Because the goal of treatment is permanent behavior change, therapists must take steps to ensure that this behavior change is supported by the individual's natural environment.

Replacing Substance Abuse with Other Behavior

A second issue that often is overlooked in the treatment of substance abuse is the need to replace substance abuse with more healthy and adaptive behavior. Based on Vuchinich's (1995) molar theory of substance abuse, the likelihood of remaining abstinent is positively affected by the relative reinforcement available for engaging in other types of behavior (e.g., spending time with family). That is, relapse is likely for someone has few friends, recreational activities, or career goals. To minimize the probability of relapse, substance-abuse treatments could include various types of skills training (e.g., social, employment, and coping skills), as suggested by the community reinforcement approach (Sisson & Azrin, 1989). It is hoped that once patients acquire interests unrelated to substance use, these interests will fill the functional needs (e.g., recreation or stress reduction) once filled by substance use.

Conclusion

Although basic operant, respondent, and behavioral pharmacology research has uncovered many important principles related to substance abuse, it has been suggested that these principles are absent from most current treatments for substance abuse (Heather, 1990). The lack of clear application of basic research findings to treatment, however, is not a result of incompatibility. The present chapter provides findings from basic research and highlights the role played by behavioral principles in the development and maintenance of substance abuse. As mentioned above, there are only a few treatments that directly apply behavioral principles (e.g., community reinforcement approach, aversive counterconditioning). Many of the active ingredients in nonbehavioral treatments for substance abuse, however, can be translated into a behavioral framework (e.g., Marlatt, 1985). One example is Alcoholics Anonymous (AA), which includes behavioral principles such as praise for abstinence, response (drinking) prevention through the implementation of a social-support network, and the provision of non-drinking alternatives (e.g., regular meetings) that decrease the relative reinforcement for drinking. In addition to technical similarities between behavioral principles and AA, there also may be more broad theoretical similarities. In both AA and behavior-analytic theory, there is a deemphasis of the individual and a focus on external control. In AA, the individual must realize that drinking is a disease that they cannot overcome on their own; to achieve abstinence, the individual must give control over to God. In behavior-analytic theory, control also is removed from the individual. Unlike AA, however, environmental contingencies are the locus of control over substance use and abuse.

In conclusion, an experimental analysis of substance abuse is alive and well, and has contributed to the understanding and treatment of substance abuse in the natural environment. We encourage basic researchers and therapists to continue to collaborate in the development and implementation of substance-abuse treatment.

References

Ator, N. A., & Griffiths, R. R. (1993). Differential sensitivity to midazolam discriminative-stimulus effects following self-administered versus response-independent midazolam. *Psychopharmacology, 110,* 1–4.

Azrin, N. H. (1961). Time-out from positive reinforcement. *Science, 133,* 382–383.

Azrin, N. H. (1976). Improvements in the community reinforcement approach to alcoholism. *Behavior Research and Therapy, 14,* 339–348.

Azrin, N. H., Naster, B. J., & Jones, R. (1973). Reciprocity counseling: A rapid-learning based procedure for marital counseling. *Behavior Research and Therapy, 11,* 364–382.

Barrett, J. E.(1987). Nonpharmacological factors determining the behavioral effects of drugs. In H. Y. Meltzer (Ed.), *Psychopharmacology: The Third Generation of Progress* (pp. 1493–1501). New York: Raven Press.

Bickel, W. K., DeGrandpre, R. J., Higgins, S. T., & Hughes, J. R. (1990). Behavioral economics of drug self-administration. I. Functional equivalence of response requirement and unit dose. *Life Science, 47*, 1501–1510.

Bormann, N. M., & Overton, D. A. (1993). Morphine as a conditioned stimulus in a conditioned emotional response paradigm. *Psychopharmacology, 112*, 277–284.

Branch, M. N., & Schaal, D. W. (1990). The role of theory in behavioral pharmacology. In T. Thompson, P. B. Dew, & J. E. Barrett, (Eds.), *Advances in Behavioral Pharmacology, Vol. 6.* Orlando: Academic Press.

Budney, A. J., Higgins, S. T., Delaney, D. D., Kent, L., & Bickel, W. K. (1991). Contingent reinforcement of abstinence with individuals abusing cocaine and marijuana. *Journal of Applied Behavior Analysis, 24*, 657–665.

Campbell, B. A., & Fibiger, H. C. (1971). Potentiation of amphetamine-induced arousal by starvation. *Nature, 233*, 424–425.

Carroll, M. E. (1985). Concurrent phencyclidine and saccharin access: Presentation of an alternative reinforcer reduces drug intake. *Journal of the Experimental Analysis of Behavior, 43*, 131–144.

Carroll, M. E. (1996). Reducing drug abuse by enriching the environment with alternative reinforcers. In L. Green & J. H. Kagel (Eds.), *Advances in behavioral economics, Vol. 3: Substance use and abuse*, pp. 37–68. Norwood, NJ: Ablex.

Carroll, M. E., Carmona, G. N., & May, S. A. (1991). Modifying drug-reinforced behavior by altering the economic conditions of the drug and a nondrug reinforcer. *Journal of the Experimental Analysis of Behavior, 56*, 361–376.

Carroll, M. E., & Lac, S. T. (1993). Autoshaping I.V. cocaine self-administration in rats: Effects of non-drug alternative reinforcers on acquisition. *Psychopharmacology, 110*, 5–12.

Carroll, M. E., & Meisch, R. A. (1984). Enhanced drug-reinforced behavior due to food deprivation. In T. Thompson, P. B. Dews, & J. E. Barrett (Eds.), *Ad-*

vances in Behavioral Pharmacology (pp. 47–88). Orlando: Academic Press.

Cepeda-Benito, A. (1993). Meta-analytic review of the efficacy of nicotine chewing gum in smoking treatment programs. *Journal of Consulting and Clinical Psychology, 61*, 822–830.

Childress, A. R., Hole, A. V., Ehrman, R. N., Robbins, S. J., McLellan, A. J., & O'Brien, C. P. (1993). Cue reactivity and cue reactivity interventions in drug dependence. *Behavioral treatments for drug abuse and dependence* (National Institute of Drug Abuse Monograph Series No. 137, pp. 73–95). Washington, DC: U.S. Government Printing Office.

Childress, A. R., McLellan, A. T., Natale, M., & O'Brien, C. P. (1986). Mood states can elicit conditioned withdrawal and cravings in opiate abuse patients. In L. Harris (Ed.), *Problems of drug dependence* (National Institute of Drug Abuse Monograph Series No. 76, pp. 137–144). Washington, DC: U.S. Government Printing Office.

Colpaert, F. C. (1978). Discriminative stimulus properties of narcotic analgesic drugs. *Pharmacology, Biochemistry, and Behavior, 9*, 863–887.

Colpaert, F. C., & Balster, R. L. (1988). *Psychopharmacology Series 4: Transduction Mechanisms of Drug Stimuli.* Berlin: Springer-Verlag.

Conger, R., & Killeen, P. (1974). Use of concurrent operants in small group research: A demonstration. *Pacific Sociological Review, 17*, 399–414.

Cook, L., & Davidson, A. B. (1973). Effects of behaviorally active drugs in a conflict-punishment procedure in rats. In S. Garatini, E. Mussini, & L. O. Randall (Eds.), *The benzodidiazepines.* New York: Raven Press, pp. 327–345.

Downs, D. A., & Woods, J. H. (1974). Codeine- and cocaine-reinforced responding in rhesus monkeys: Effects of dose on response rates under a fixed-ratio schedule. *Journal of Pharmacology and Experimental Therapeutics, 191*, 179–188.

Falk, J. L. (1971). The nature and determinants of adjunctive behavior. *Physiology & Behavior, 6*, 577–588.

Fernandez, E., & McDowell, J. J. (1995). Response-reinforcement relationships in chronic pain syndrome: Applicability of Herrnstein's law. *Behaviour Research and Therapy, 33*, 855–863.

Files, F. J., Andrews, C. M., Lewis, R. S., & Samson, H. H. (1993). Effects of ethanol concentration and fixed-ratio requirement on ethanol self-administration by P rats in a continuous access situation. *Experimental Alcohol Clinical and Research, 17,* 61–68.

Garcia, J., Ervin, F. R., & Koelling, R. A. (1966). Learning with prolonged delay of reinforcement. *Psychonomic Science, 5,* 121–122.

Geller, I., & Seifter, J. (1960). The effects of meprobamate, barbiturates, *d*-amphetamine, and promazine on experimentally-induced conflict in the rat. *Psychopharmacology, 1,* 482–492.

Girden, E., & Culler, E. (1937). Conditioned responses in curarized striate muscle in dogs. *Journal of Comparative Psychology, 23,* 261–264.

Goldberg, S. R., & Schuster, C. R. (1967). Conditioned suppression by a stimulus associated with nalorphine in morphine-dependent monkeys. *Journal of the Experimental Analysis of Behavior, 10,* 235–242.

Goldberg, S. R., Woods, J. H., & Schuster, C. R. (1969). Morphine: Conditioned increases in self-administration in rhesus monkeys. *Science, 166,* 1306–1307.

Griffiths, R. R., Findley, J. D., Brady, J. V., Dolan-Gutcher, K., & Robinson, W. W. (1975). Comparison of progressive ratio performance maintained by cocaine, methylphenidate, and secobarbital. *Psychopharmacologia, 43,* 81–83.

Hayes, S. C. (1994). Content, context, and the types of psychological acceptance. In S. C. Hayes, N. S. Jacobson, V. M. Follette, & M. J. Dougher (Eds.), *Acceptance and change: Content and context in psychotherapy* (pp. 13–32). Reno: Context Press.

Hayes, S. C., & Melancon, S. M. (1989). Comprehensive distancing, paradox, and the treatment of emotional disorders. In L. M. Ascher (Ed.), *Therapeutic paradox,* pp. 184–218. New York: Guilford.

Hayes, S. C., & Wilson, K. G. (1994). Acceptance and commitment therapy: Altering the verbal support for experimental avoidance. *The Behavior Analyst, 17,* 289–303.

Hayes, S. C., Wilson, K. G., Gifford, E. V., Follette, V. M., & Strosahl, K. (1996). Experiential avoidance and behavioral disorders: A functional dimensional approach to diagnosis and treatment. *Journal of Consulting and Clinical Psychology, 64,* 1152–1168.

Headlee, C. P., Coppock, H. W., & Nichols, J. R. (1955). Apparatus and techniques involved in a laboratory method of detecting the addictiveness of drugs. *Journal of the American Pharmaceutical Association: Scientific Edition, 44,* 229–231.

Heather, N. (1990). Treatment of alcohol problems: With special reference to the behavioral approach. In D. J. K. Balfour (Ed.), *Psychotropic drugs of abuse: International encyclopedia of pharmacology and therapeutics, Section 130* (pp. 283–312). Elmsford, NY: Pergamon.

Herrnstein, R. J. (1961). Relative and absolute strength of a response as a function of frequency of reinforcement. *Journal of the Experimental Analysis of Behavior, 4,* 267–272.

Herrnstein, R. J., & Hineline, P. N. (1966). Negative reinforcement as shock-frequency reduction. *Journal of the Experimental Analysis of Behavior, 9,* 421–430.

Higgins, S. T., & Budney, A. J. (1993). Treatment of cocaine dependence through the principles of behavior analysis and behavioral pharmacology. *Behavioral treatments for drug abuse and dependence* (National Institute of Drug Abuse Monograph Series No. 137, pp. 97–121). Washington, DC: U.S. Government Printing Office.

Higgins, S. T., Delaney, D. D., Budney, A. J., Bickel, W. K., Hughes, J. R., Foerg, F., & Fenwick, J. W. (1991). A behavioral approach to achieving initial cocaine abstinence. *American Journal of Psychiatry, 148,* 1218–1224.

Holder, H. D., & Blose, J. O. (1991). Typical patterns and cost of alcoholism treatment across a variety of populations and providers. *Alcoholism, 15,* 190–195.

Horger, B. A., Shelton, K., & Schenk, S. (1990). Preexposure sensitizes rats to the rewarding effects of cocaine. *Pharmacology, Biochemistry, and Behavior, 37,* 707–711.

Hursh, S. R. (1984). Behavioral economics. *Journal of the Experimental Analysis of Behavior, 42,* 435–452.

Iglauer, C., & Woods, J. H. (1974). Concurrent performances: Reinforcement by different doses of intravenous cocaine in rhesus monkeys. *Journal of the Experimental Analysis of Behavior, 22,* 179–196.

Kitson, T. M. (1977). The disulfiram-ethanol reaction. *Journal of Studies in Alcohol, 38,* 96–113.

McDowell, J. J. (1981). On the validity and utility of Herrnstein's hyperbola in applied behavior analysis. In C. M. Bradshaw, E. Szabadi, & C. F. Lowe (Eds.), *Quantification of steady-state operant behaviour* (pp. 311–324). Amsterdam: Elsevier/North-Holland.

McGrath, P. J., Nunes, E. V., Stewart, J. W., Goldman, D. Agosti, V. Ocepek-Welikson, K., & Quitkin, F. M. (1996). Imipramine treatment of alcoholics with primary depression: A placebo-controlled clinical trial. *Archives of General Psychiatry, 53,* 232–240.

Marlatt, G. A. (1985). Relapse prevention: Theoretical rationale and overview of the model. In G. A. Marlatt & J. R. Gordon (Eds.), *Relapse prevention: Maintenance strategies in the treatment of addictive behaviors* (pp. 3–70). New York: Brunner/Mazel.

Marlatt, G. A. (1994). Addiction and acceptance. In S. C. Hayes, N. S. Jacobson, V. M. Follette, & M. J. Dougher (Eds.), *Acceptance and change: Content and context in psychotherapy* (pp. 175–197). Reno: Context Press.

Martens, B. K., & Houk, J. L. (1989). The application of Herrnstein's law of effect to disruptive and on-task behavior of a retarded adolescent girl. *Journal of the Experimental Analysis of Behavior, 51,* 17–27.

Meisch, R. A., & Lemaire, G. A. (1988). Oral self-administration of pentobarbital by rhesus monkeys: Relative reinforcing effects under concurrent fixed-ratio schedules. *Journal of the Experimental Analysis of Behavior, 50,* 75–86.

Meisch, R. A., & Lemaire, G. A. (1993). Drug self-administration. In J. P. Huston (Series Ed.) & F. van Haaren (Vol. Ed.), *Techniques in the behavioral and neural sciences: Vol. 10, Methods in behavioral pharmacology* (pp. 257–300). Amsterdam: Elsevier.

Meisch, R. A., & Thompson, T. (1971). Ethanol intake in the absence of concurrent food reinforcement. *Psychopharmacologia, 22,* 72–79.

Meisch, R. A., & Thompson, T. (1973). Ethanol as a reinforcer: Effects of fixed-ratio size and food deprivation. *Psychopharmacologia, 28,* 171–183.

Mello, N. K., & Mendelson, J. H. (1995). Buprenorphine treatment of cocaine and heroin abuse. In A. Cowan & J. W. Lewis (Eds.), *Buprenorphine: Combatting drug abuse with a unique opioid,* pp. 241–287. New York: Wiley-Liss.

Mello, N. K., Mendelson, J. H., Kuehnle, J. C., & Sellers, M. L. (1981). Operant analysis of human heroin self-administration and the effects of naltrexone. *Journal of Pharmacology and Experimental Therapeutics, 216,* 30–39.

Miller, N. S. (1995). Pharmacotherapy in alcoholism. *Journal of Addiction Research, 14,* 23–46.

Nader, M. A., & Woolverton, W. L. (1991). Effects of increasing the magnitude of an alternative reinforcer on drug choice in a discrete-trials choice procedure. *Psychopharmacology, 105,* 169–174.

Nardone, G., & Waltzlawick, P. (1993). The art of change. San Francisco: Jossey-Bass.

O'Brien, C. P., McLellan, A. T., Alterman, A., & Childress, A. R. (1992). Psychotherapy for cocaine dependence. In *Cocaine: Scientific and social dimensions. Ciba Foundation Symposium, 166* (pp. 207–216). Chichester, England: Wiley.

O'Brien, C. P., Nace, E. P., Mintz, J., Meyers, A. L., & Ream, N. (1980). Follow-up of Vietnam veterans. 1. Relapse to drug use after Vietnam service. *Drug and Alcohol Dependency, 5,* 333–340.

Overton, D. A. (1988). Similarities and differences between behavioral control by drug-produced stimuli and by sensory stimuli. In F. Colpaert & R. Balster (Eds.), *Transduction mechanisms of drug stimuli* (pp. 176–198). Berlin: Springer-Verlag.

Paletta, M. S., & Wagner, A. R. (1986). Development of context-specific tolerance to morphine: Support for a dual-process interpretation. *Behavioral Neuroscience, 100,* 611–623.

Parker, B. K., Schaal, D. W., & Miller, M. (1994). Drug discrimination using a Pavlovian conditional discrimination paradigm in pigeons. *Pharmacology, Biochemistry and Behavior, 49,* 955–960.

Payte, J. P., & Zweben, J. E. (1991). Methadone maintenance treatment: A primer for physicians. *Journal of Psychoactive Drugs, 23,* 165–176.

Piazza, P. V., Deminiere, J. M., le Moal, M., Simon, H. (1990). Stress- and pharmacologically-induced behavioral sensitization increases vulnerability to acquisition of amphetamine self-administration. *Brain Research, 514,* 22–26.

Pickens, R., & Thompson, T. (1968). Cocaine-reinforced behavior in rats: Effects of reinforcement magnitude and fixed-ratio size. *Journal of Pharmacological Experimental Therapy, 161,* 122–129.

Picker, M. J., Craft, R. M., Negus, S. S., Powell, K. R., Mattox, S. R., Jones, S. R., Hargrove, B. K., & Dykstra, L. A. (1992). Intermediate efficacy mu opioids: Examination of their morphine-like stimulus effects and response rate-decreasing effects in morphine-tolerant rats. *Journal of Pharmacology and Experimental Therapeutics, 263,* 668–681.

Rachlin, H., Battalio, R., Kagel, J., & Green, L. (1981). Maximization theory in behavioral psychology. *The Behavioral and Brain Sciences, 4,* 371–417.

Rachlin, H., & Green, L. (1972). Commitment, choice, and self-control. *Journal of the Experimental Analysis of Behavior, 17*, 15–22.

Robins, L. N., Davis, D. H., & Goodwin, D. W. (1974). Drug use by U. S. Army enlisted men in Vietnam: A follow-up on their return home. *American Journal of Epidemiology, 101*, 690–700.

Sanchez-Craig, M. (1984). *A therapist's manual for secondary prevention of alcohol problems: Procedures for teaching moderate drinking and abstinence.* Toronto: Addiction Research Foundation.

Schaal, D. W., McDonald, M. P., Miller, M. A., & Reilly, M. P. (1996). Discrimination of methadone and cocaine by pigeons without explicit discrimination training. *Journal of the Experimental Analysis of Behavior , 66*, 193–203.

Schaal, D. W., Miller, M. A., & Odum, A. L. (1995). Cocaine's effects on food-reinforced pecking in pigeons depends on food-deprivation level. *Journal of the Experimental Analysis of Behavior, 64*, 61–73.

Sidman, M. (1953). Two temporal parameters of the maintenance of avoidance behavior by the white rat. *Journal of Comparative and Physiological Psychology, 46*, 253–261.

Siegel, S. (1989). Pharmacological conditioning and drug effects. In A. J. Goudie & M. W. Emmett-Oglesby (Eds.), *Psychoactive drugs: Tolerance and sensitization* (pp. 115–180). Clifton, NJ: Humana Press.

Siegel, S. (1990). Classical conditioning and opiate tolerance and withdrawal. In D. J. K. Balfour (Ed.), *Psychotropic drugs of abuse: International encyclopedia of pharmacology and therapeutics, Section 130* (pp. 59–85). Elmsford, NY: Pergamon.

Sisson, R. W., & Azrin, N. H. (1989). The community reinforcement approach. In R. K. Hester & W. R. Miller (Eds.), *Handbook of alcoholism treatment approaches: Effective alternatives* (pp. 242–258). New York: Pergamon.

Spragg, S. D. (1940). Morphine addiction in chimpanzees. *Comparative Psychological Monographs, 15,* 132.

Thompson, T., & Schuster, C. R. (1964). Morphine self-administration, food-reinforced and avoidance behaviors in rhesus monkeys. *Psychopharmacologia, 5,* 87–94.

Tucker, J. A., Vuchinich, R. E., & Pukish, M. (1995). Molar environmental context surrounding recovery from alcohol problems by treated and untreated problem drinkers. *Experimental and Clinical Psychopharmacology, 3,* 195–204.

Tutton, C. S., & Crayton, J. W. (1993). Current pharmacotherapies for cocaine abuse: A review. *Journal of Addiction Research, 12,* 109–127.

Vuchinich, R. E. (1995). Alcohol abuse as a molar choice: An update of a 1982 proposal. *Psychology of Addictive Behaviors, 9,* 223–235.

Vuchinich, R. E., & Tucker, J. A. (1996). The molar contexts of alcohol abuse. In L. Green & J. H. Kagel (Eds.), *Advances in behavioral economics,* pp. 133–162. Norwood, NJ: Ablex.

Weeks, J. R. (1962). Experimental morphine addiction: Method for automatic intravenous injections in unrestrained rats. *Science, 138,* 143–144.

Weiss, B., & Laties, V. G. (1958). Fractional escape and avoidance on a titration schedule. *Science, 128,* 1575–1576.

Young, A. M., & Woods, J. H. (1981). Maintenance of behavior byketamine and related compounds in rhesus monkeys with different self-administration histories. *Journal of Pharmacology and Experimental Therapeutics, 218,* 720–727.

7

SEXUAL DYSFUNCTIONS

JOSEPH J. PLAUD
Department of Psychology
Judge Rotenberg Educational Center

JEFFREY E. HOLM
Department of Psychology
University of North Dakota

Behavioral researchers have studied the relationship of behaviorally based conditioning models of sexual arousal to sexual dysfunctions as well as sexual disorders (Alford, Plaud, & McNair, 1995; Barbaree & Marshall, 1991; O'Donohue & Plaud, 1994; Plaud et al., 1997). As further elaborated in the following chapter on sexual disorders, one of the central functions of basic behavioral research in the area of human sexuality is to scientifically study the parameters of sexual arousal in relation to habituation, classical, and operant conditioning. Behavioral models of sexual arousal in humans rely upon conditioning models as a theoretical foundation for the explanation of sexual dysfunctions in males and females (Alford, Plaud, & McNair, 1995; O'Donohue & Plaud, 1994).

Although it is not surprising that behavioral accounts of sexual behavior focus on the significance of conditioning and habituation, there are differences in the extent to which different behavioral theories emphasize the role of conditioning-related factors (Alford, Plaud, & McNair, 1995; O'Donohue & Plaud, 1994; Skinner, 1969; Watson, 1925). Theories of sexual functioning that are not explicitly conditioning-based accounts also rely on the principle that, at least to some extent, sexual behavior and arousal are learned. For example, theories derived from anthropology and sociology have also claimed that males and females learn patterns of sexual behavior through a variety of societal and cultural mechanisms (Davenport, 1987; DeLamater, 1987).

Learning theories have been widely applied in clinical contexts (e.g., Masters & Johnson, 1970) to explain the shaping, maintenance, and modification of sexual dysfunctions. It is, therefore, important to evaluate the empirical validity of the relation of conditioning and habituation processes to sexual arousal and behavior. Such an attempt was undertaken by O'Donohue and Plaud (1994) and Alford, Plaud, and McNair (1995) in their comprehensive reviews of the literature on the conditioning of human sexual arousal. What follows is a brief overview of the conditioning of human sexual arousal.

Habituation and Sensitization

Habituation and sensitization are two of the most basic principles of learning and behavior (Domjan & Burkhard, 1986; O'Donohue & Plaud, 1994). There are five possible patterns of responding that can result from repeated presentations of a constant eliciting stimulus (O'Donohue & Plaud, 1991): (1) response magnitude can systematically decrease; (2) response magnitude can systematically increase; (3) response magnitude can remain constant; (4) response magnitude can be unsystematic; and (5) response magnitude can vary between these in any complex variation. When (1) is not due to physiological fatigue or response adaptation, then habituation is said to occur. When (2) is shown, sensitization is evident.

O'Donohue and Geer (1985) reported a study which demonstrated short-term habituation of male sexual arousal. They found that both physiological and subjective arousal decreased significantly more in a condition of constant stimulation in comparison with a varied stimulus condition.

O'Donohue and Plaud (1991) and Plaud et al. (1997) found evidence for the long-term habituation of male sexual arousal. Long-term habituation occurs when short-term (intra-session) habituation occurs, habituated arousal spontaneously recovers, across habituation sessions the magnitude of spontaneous remission decreases, or the number of trials to habituation decreases across sessions. These studies show that habituation processes may influence sexual responsivity both in the short term, and over time. In behavior therapy, strategies that include dishabituation procedures may increase sexual arousal (e.g., varying sexual stimuli, sexual positions, and environmental stimuli).

Classical Conditioning

O'Donohue and Plaud (1994) reviewed studies of the classical conditioning of human sexual arousal, concentrating on the following criteria: (1) Was the CS presented alone in order to test for familiarity with the CS? (2) Were any novel CSs used in order to test for the unconditioned effects of the CS? (3) Was the US presented alone to test for any prior sensitization or habituation to the US? (4) Was backward conditioning investigated (i.e., was the US presented prior to the CS?) in order to test for any effects of temporal order? (5) Was a truly random control procedure utilized (i.e., presentation of CS, US, each programmed entirely independently) in order to test for all nonassociative effects? and (6) Could other factors such as subject awareness of the experimental procedures account for the findings as plausibly as a conditioning explanation?

A classic experiment designed to test classical conditioning of sexual arousal was conducted by Langevin and Martin (1975). These researchers performed two classical conditioning experiments designed to control for prior methodological flaws. In the first experiment, sexually explicit slides served as the unconditioned stimuli. In addition, slides taken from other nonerotic material and pretested for sexual arousal were included as neutral stimuli. They found that penile tumescence occurred to the conditioned stimuli, and the conditioned response extinguished when the CS was presented alone for ten trials. They also found that penile tumescence was not affected by the "intensity" of the US. In a second experiment designed to overcome the possibility that slides served as weak USs, Langevin and Martin used movies depicting unclothed females as the USs. They found that the mean amplitude of nonzero CRs decreased compared to the first experiment. The researchers concluded that classical conditioning of sexual arousal may not be demonstrable with USs that elicit mild arousal. They also concluded that CRs did not have a relationship to US intensity under the conditions of their experiment. At best this study provides equivocal evidence for classical conditioning of sexual arousal.

Although there has been noted progress in the methodological sophistication of the research investigating the classical conditioning of sexual arousal (O'Donohue & Plaud, 1994), more research in this area is needed, especially with regard to patterns of female sexual arousal. At present, however, there is evidence that sexual arousal can be classically conditioned. In terms of behavior therapy, particular attention should be paid by the therapist to the stimuli that elicit sexual responding, either as unconditioned stimuli (i.e., sexually explicit stimuli), or those stimuli that come to elicit sexual arousal by contingent pairings with sexually explicit materials. The setting in which sexual behavior is emitted, therefore, may have much to do with the elicitation of male and female sexual responding.

Operant Conditioning

Skinner (1969, 1988) has convincingly argued that past and present contingencies of survival (i.e., natural selection) and past and present contingencies of reinforcement (i.e., operant principles) shape much sexual behavior. In an operant analysis, sexual contact has come to function as a powerful primary reinforcer through the contingencies of survival.

According to Skinner, the contingencies of survival have played a role in shaping global behavioral patterns exhibited by different organisms. However, natural selection is also complemented in the lifetime of the organism through selection of behaviors by its consequences. Operant conditionability represents an adaptive response in evolution because organisms responsive to immediate environmental consequences survived temporally unstable shifts in prevailing environmental features. This selection of behavior Skinner termed "operant conditioning" and the behaviors selected through consequences are called "operants."

O'Donohue and Plaud (1994) used the following criteria developed by Millenson and Leslie (1979) in their evaluation of studies claiming to demonstrate the operant conditionability of sexual behavior. These criteria include the following: (1) breaking of the contingency produces a short-term increase in responding (an "extinction burst") in operant but not classical conditioning; (2) intermittent reinforcement produces greater resistance to extinction in operant conditioning, but this effect is not seen in classical conditioning; (3) complex skeletal behavior (striated muscle) is readily conditioned in operant but not classical conditioning; (4) autonomic behavior is readily conditioned in classical but not operant conditioning; (5) the conditioned response is not usually a component of behavior elicited by the reinforcer in operant conditioning, in contrast to classical conditioning; and (6) in operant but not classical conditioning the experimenter usually specifies the nature of the conditioned response (within the often broad constraints of biological preparedness).

An example of a study that provides some support for the operant conditionability of sexual arousal was undertaken by Rosen, Shapiro, and Schwartz (1975). The researchers found that subjects demonstrated increased penile tumescence to a discriminative stimulus when monetarily reinforced for such responding, in contrast to a yoked control group that received noncontingent reinforcement in the presence of the same discriminative stimulus.

Cliffe and Parry (1980) used sexual stimuli to test the matching law, a mathematical statement of behavioral allocation and choice (Plaud, 1992). Originally formulated by Herrnstein (1970), the matching law states that when concurrent variable-interval schedules of reinforcement are in effect, there exists a matching relation between relative overall number of responses and the overall relative number of reinforcement presentations. A variable-interval schedule of reinforcement is one in which a reinforcer is presented for the first response that occurs after a variable amount of time has passed since the previous reinforcer presentation. Concurrent schedules exist when two (or more) schedules are in effect at the same time. Cliffe and Parry studied the sexual behavior of a male pedophile, who was on three concurrent variable-interval schedules: the first concurrent choice involved choosing (by pressing keys) to view either slides of women or men; the second condition, between slides of men or children; and the third, between slides of women or children. Results showed that the matching law accurately described the subject's behavior in the first two conditions, and also accurately predicted performance in the third condition.

As with studies of habituation and classical conditioning, there exists empirical support for the operant conditioning of sexual arousal, but like classical conditioning, the data base at present is limited by the constraints of the methodologies employed, and there is a paucity of studies of female sexual arousal. In terms of behavior therapy, operant contingencies involving reinforcers and discriminative stimuli set the occasion for increasing the range and repertoire of sexual responses. The conclusion that emerges from a review of basic and applied conditioning studies is that conditioning and habituation processes may be crucial in the etiology and maintenance of sexual behavior, including sexual dysfunctions. As we shall see, such principles are reflected in behavioral assessment and treatment strategies of male and female sexual dysfunctions.

Male and Female Sexual Dysfunctions: An Overview and Prevalence Data

The *DSM-IV* (APA, 1994) lists several major sexual dysfunctions, which are characterized by disturbance in sexual desire and changes in psychophysiology associated with the sexual response cycle, as well as interpersonal difficulties associated with changes in the sexual response cycle. Sexual dysfunctions include sexual desire disorders such as hypoactive sexual desire disorder, sexual aversion disorder; sexual arousal disorders such as female sexual arousal disorder and male erectile disorder; orgasmic disorders such as female orgasmic disorder, male orgasmic disorder, and premature ejaculation; sexual pain disorders such as dyspareunia and vaginismus; sexual dysfunction due to a general medical condition; substance-induced sexual dysfunction; and sexual dysfunction not otherwise specified. Classical and operant conditioning play important roles in virtually all of these disorders.

Sexual Desire Disorders

Sexual desire disorders are a recent and controversial addition to the psychiatric taxonomy of sexual dysfunctions. Strictly speaking not a dysfunction, sexual desire disorders are characterized by a lack of sexual desire or interest and/or an aversion to genital sexual activity.

Hypoactive sexual desire disorder is used to refer to people who complain of little or no sexual interest or desire. Other sexual dysfunctions (e.g., arousal disorders, orgasmic disorders) may or may not be present. Several biological and psychological factors have been linked to the development and/or maintenance of this disorder, including testosterone or other hormonal deficiencies, medication side-effects, anxiety, and depression (Kresin, 1993; Letourneau & O'Donohue, 1993). The diagnosis of hypoactive sexual desire typically depends on the presence of associated personal distress and/or relationship difficulties. In other words, there is no accepted standard concerning what qualifies as low sexual desire. Therefore, the "disorder" usually surfaces when an individual becomes disturbed by his or her lack of sexual interest or desire, or when relationship problems are associated with one's partner's lack of interest or desire. Despite this lack of consensus and subjectivity, hypoactive sexual desire disorder has become a commonly diagnosed disorder in clinical settings (Letourneau & O'Donohue, 1993).

Sexual aversion disorder refers to people who express a phobic response to sexual activity. It is characterized by intense fear, dread, and/or revulsion to sexual activity. Physiological symptoms (e.g., sweating, nausea) can also be present. Other sexual dysfunctions can be the cause (e.g., erectile dysfunctions) of sexual aversions (Spark, 1991), as can sexual trauma or other negative sexual experiences (Masters, Johnson, & Kolodny, 1995). Sexual aversions appear to be less common than hypoactive sexual desire disorders (Spark, 1991), though relatively little research exists.

Sexual Arousal Disorders

These disorders occur during the arousal phase of the sexual response cycle. They are characterized by the lack of subjective feelings of sexual excitement and pleasure and/or physiological responses that are associated with sexual arousal (e.g., lubrication, penile tumescence).

Female sexual arousal disorder is characterized by the fact that arousal strength and duration are not sufficient for pleasure to be felt or enjoyed during sexual activities (Arentewicz & Schmidt, 1983). Most typically, these problems with arousal encompass both subjective feelings of sexual excitement and physiological responses such as vaginal lubrication; however, some women report adequate amounts of lubrication, but an absence of sexually arousing feelings (Wincze & Carey, 1991). Unlike men with sexual arousal disorders (e.g., erectile dysfunction), women with arousal dysfunctions can often still engage in coitus. However, most women with arousal dysfunctions have an inadequate amount of lubrication, which may result in painful intercourse (Arentewicz & Schmidt, 1983). Most women with this type of dysfunction show a negative response toward sex, but a few women are still able to enjoy sexual activities. Although female sexual arousal disorder may have physical causes (Graber, 1993), psychosocial causes (e.g., childhood sexual abuse, anger, resentment, anxiety, guilt) are more likely (Morokoff, 1993). Clinical studies of female sexual arousal disorder have been found to have a prevalence rate between 38.1 percent and 51 percent, with community studies estimating the rate at 11.4 percent (Rosen et al., 1993).

Male erectile disorder refers to insufficient duration and strength of penile erection for intercourse. The male's penis does not erect, partially erects, or loses erection before ejaculation occurs, either on attempting insertion or shortly after penetration. These erectile problems seldom occur during masturbation or petting (Arentewicz & Schmidt, 1983). Erectile dysfunction almost always coincides with failure to ejaculate. However, in some cases ejaculation with a flaccid penis does occur. For individuals who are never able to obtain an erect penis, physical examination should ensue (Arentewicz & Schmidt, 1983). Most men with erectile dysfunction have acquired the disorder after previous periods of normal functioning (acquired or secondary erectile disorder), but some men have never had adequate erectile function (lifelong or primary erectile disorder). Physical factors such as diabetes, alcoholism, neurological disorders, infections, hormone deficiences, circulatory problems, and medication side-effects are frequent causes of erectile dysfunction but psychological factors are often intertwined (Masters, Johnson, & Kolodny, 1995). In a review of prevalence data, Spector and Carey (1990) report ranges from 3.5 percent for primary dysfunction to 48 percent for secondary dysfunction (Renshaw, 1988). Furthermore, it has been reported that the prevalence rate of erectile disorder at 53 percent in clinical samples (Spector & Carey, 1990). Community samples of erectile disorder have been lower, with one major study reporting 3.9 percent (Spector & Carey, 1990).

Orgasmic Disorders

Orgasmic disorders are characterized by problems or disruptions associated with the orgasm phase of the sexual response cycle. These problems or disruptions include premature, delayed, or nonexistent orgasm.

Male orgasmic disorder is diagnosed when a man's orgasm is either greatly delayed or doesn't occur despite a firm erection and sufficiently intense and persistent sexual stimulation. This disorder is typically limited to coitus and does not occur with other sexual activities. As with other disorders, this problem can be lifelong or may have developed after a period of relatively normal functioning. Although it is typically generalized, it can occur with one partner and not others. Research on this disorder is minimal, but identified causes include physical factors such as multiple sclerosis or other neurological disorders, medication side-effects and psychological factors such as anxiety, guilt, and hostility. This disorder is seen relatively infrequently in clinical practice (prevalence rates between 3 percent and 8 percent; Renshaw, 1988) and in the community (prevelance rates of 1 percent to 10 percent; Spector & Carey, 1990).

Female orgasmic disorder is characterized by difficulty reaching orgasm or an inability to orgasm despite sufficient stimulation. Orgasmic dysfunction can be either restricted to sexual intercourse and foreplay or affect all other forms of stimulation as well (e.g., masturbation, fantasies, erotic books and films [Arentewicz & Schmidt, 1983]. Some women's orgasmic difficulties are accompanied by arousal problems, but other women have no problems being aroused, yet are still unable to reach orgasm (Wincze & Carey, 1991). A large percent of the women who seek sexual counseling suffer from combined orgasmic and arousal dysfunctions. It has been estimated that 5 to 10 percent of women under the age of forty have never had an orgasm, with 20 to 25 percent experiencing orgasm only occasionally (Arentewicz & Schmidt, 1983). This "disorder" can sometimes be diagnosed inappropriately when the actual cause of the orgasm difficulties is insufficient or ineffective sexual stimulation, but when the diagnosis is applied appropriately the identified causes are usually psychological factors such as performance anxiety or guilt. The most comprehensive epidemiological review and analysis of incidence and prevalence of sexual dysfunction was performed by Spector and Carey (1990), who found that female orgasm disorders were the most common sexual difficulties practitioners encounter. They report that clinical studies indicate a prevalence rate between 15.4 percent and 24 percent, while community studies have found the rate to be around 9 percent (Spector & Carey, 1990).

Premature ejaculation (ejaculation prior to or immediately after vaginal penetration) is the most common orgasmic dysfunction in males (Wincze & Carey, 1991). In most cases premature ejaculation is defined as ejaculation within thirty to sixty seconds after vaginal insertion, whereas at other times it is defined as ejaculation occuring after ten to twenty pelvic movements, though some authors reject both of these definitions (Arentewicz & Schmidt, 1983). Physical (i.e., sexual sensations) and psychological factors (e.g., anxiety, guilt) are often involved in this dysfunction; however, neither are generally considered to be causes of the disorder. Instead this "disorder" is best conceptualized as a man's inability to control or regulate sexual stimulation and hence sexual arousal levels. Although speculative, it is easy to see how conditioning mechanisms (as described above) could be important in the development, maintenance, and elimination of this disorder. Clinical studies of premature ejaculation show a prevalence rate of 21.3 percent (Renshaw, 1988), with community studies estimating 36 percent (Frank et al., 1978). As noted by Spector and Carey (1990), however, these studies are difficult to compare because the researchers were not specific regarding their definitions of premature ejaculation.

Sexual Pain Disorders

Sexual pain disorders are characterized by painful sensations accompanying coitus.

Painful sexual intercourse for females, which is labeled dyspareunia or algopareunia, can have a number of causes, the most common being lack of lubrication. Inadequate lubrication can be a result of menopause or can be a parallel symptom of arousal disturbance (Wincze & Carey, 1991). Painful sexual intercourse is oftentimes described as burning, stinging, or itching on penile insertion, a dull pain inside the vagina, spasms or orgasm similar to labor pains or diffuse abdominal pain, which may require an examination by a gynecologist (Arentewicz & Schmidt, 1983). In some cases pain may continue to exist even after the organic causes have been removed. Generally, women who experience painful intercourse frequently, through the mechanisms of classical conditioning described above, may develop sexual aversions, and arousal and orgasmic disturbances. Dyspareunia prevalence estimates have ranged between 5.1 percent (Renshaw, 1988) and 11.3 percent in clinical studies, with community samples ranging between 8 percent and 23 percent (Spector & Carey, 1990). Lack of lubrication problems in females have been estimated to be 13.6 percent (Rosen et al., 1993).

Painful sexual intercourse is experienced less frequently in men than in women and is most typically associated with genital infections (if involving the penis) or problems with the prostate or seminal vesicles (if felt internally or in the testes). Men may also express nonorganic complaints such as fear of pain when the glans is touched. This psychological fear often results in erectile difficulties or avoidance of intercourse, which may also be a conditioned reaction. As Arentewicz and Schmidt (1983) point out, dyspareunic complaints that are psychogenic rarely occur independently of other dysfunctions, and when evident can usually be removed by systematic desensitization of fear of pain in couple therapy.

Vaginismus generally refers to the constriction of the vaginal orifice due to involuntary spasms of the pelvic musculature and the outer third of the vagina. This constriction may be in response to either a real or imagined attempt at vaginal penetration (Arentewicz & Schmidt, 1983). The severity of the constriction is variable, with some women unable to insert their own finger or a tampon into their vagina, while other women experience problems only during attempted coitus. Vaginismus is typically considered to be a conditioned response with associated fears of penetration rather than a physical defect, injury, or disease (Beck, 1993; LoPiccolo & Stock, 1986). Women with vaginismus often have histories of sexual trauma (Rathus, Nevid, & Fichner-Rathus, 1997). Clinical studies of vaginismus have estimated a general prevalence rate of 5.1 percent (Renshaw, 1988), though no community studies have been conducted in this area.

Behavioral Assessment of Sexual Dysfunction

At the heart of behavioral assessment lies the goal of revealing as much as possible about the three-term contingencies that cause humans to act, think, and feel as they do in different sexual situations. These techniques include direct behavior measurement, situational behavior sampling, verbal behavioral analysis (e.g., the clinical interview), and functional analysis. Behavior is analyzed in terms of its controlling contingencies. Once situations, behaviors, and consequences are identified, behavioral approaches to treatment of sexual dysfunction attempt to modify existing behavioral repertoires.

The behavioral approach is different from psychiatric disease and psychodynamic approaches that stress inferred motives for behavior. The behavioral perspective focuses directly upon the sexually relevant behaviors in question, and views such behavior (even sexually dysfunctional behavior) as the product of environmental and biological contingencies, rather than hypothesized underlying mental diseases or dynamics.

While the focus of behavioral assessment is upon the function of the sexually relevant behavior in question, it is true that studies of males and females have shown comorbidity of sexual dysfunction and other psychiatric diagnoses, such as anxiety and mood disorders (Krause, Herth, Maier, Steiger, Schoneich, & Benkert, 1991), and advances in medical assessment procedures have lead to the easier detection and identification of biological factors related to sexual dysfunction in men and women (Plaud et al., 1997). Sexual dysfunction is often a product of behavioral and biological factors (e.g., anxiety or poor communications complicating a mild organic deficit), therefore the assessment of behavioral factors is considered important in the diagnosis and management of patients regardless of the etiology of the problem (Anderson & Wolf, 1987; Plaud et al., in press; Kaplan, 1983).

Psychological evaluations of sexual dysfunction typically rely heavily on clinical judgement and face-to-face patient and couple interviews (LoPiccolo, 1990; Kaplan, 1983; McConaghy, 1988; Schover & Jensen, 1988). Psychometric testing is also considered a valuable part of sexual dysfunction evaluation because it yields empirical measures that can be compared across time or individuals and because self-report instruments can reduce expensive clinician time (Conte, 1983; Schover & Jensen, 1988). For example, recommendations for testing of men with erectile disorders typically include measures of marital satisfaction and/or marital communications and measures of depression. Emphasis on standardized measures of sexual history and medical and psychological symptoms varies, since these can be valuable for research purposes, but larger batteries of questionnaires may not be tolerated by patients in clinical settings. It is still the case that no single battery of psychometric tests has been widely adopted, and additional validity studies have been recommended for all the test instruments currently used to evaluate sexual functioning (Conte, 1983).

An important source of data for behavior therapy is a detailed sexual history, that can provide for a functional analysis of sexual behavior. As such, antecedents (discriminative stimuli), specific behaviors associated with antecedents, and the consequences of sexual responding, or lack of sexual responding, need to be identified. Since the principles of both operant and classical conditioning, or habituation, may be operating concurrently or in succession, antecedent or environmental stimuli may serve the function of both discriminative (operant) and eliciting (classical) stimuli, especially when physically painful consequences follow sexual behavior.

As an example, important areas of functional assessment of a suspected sexual desire disorder include (1) determining how much sexual activity is the person engaging in currently, (2) how much sexual activity does he or she want to engage in or thinks he or she should engage in, and (3) how much sexual activity does an individual wish to partake of in relation to her or his partner's level of interest (Munjack & Oziel, 1980). According to Munjack and Oziel (1980), once the actual sexual desire dysfunction is determined, questions such as the following can be asked: (1) What is the couple's actual frequency of sexual intercourse? (2) Based on statistical norms, is the individual's desire for sex extremely frequent or infrequent, or is it just frequent or infrequent relative to his partner? (3) Has there been a recent change in the level of sexual interest in one or both partners? (4) Has the situation about which they are complaining existed for some time? If the situation has existed for some time, why is the problem being presented now? (5) Has there been an identifiable crisis or event that would account for a recent change in sexual desire? (6) How has the couple dealt with the loss of sexual desire in one or both partners? and (7) Why have past attempts to solve the problem failed? If there have been no attempts to solve the problem in the past, why not?

When assessing an individual with sexual dysfunction, the behavior therapist should also consider relevant biological domains, and refer to a physician where appropriate. For example, low sex drive can be due to several organic reasons, such as reduced testosterone levels, general weakness, and debilitation, as well as psychological factors relevant to a biological illness (Munjack & Oziel, 1980). Congenital abnormalities that may affect sex drive also include bilateral undescended testicles, or severe hypospadias with rudimentary external genitalia. A variety of neurological disorders (e.g., multiple sclerosis) can also impact sexual functioning as can chronic disorders such as diabetes, circulatory problems, and others. Finally a variety of medications have side effects that impair sexual functioning (e.g., desire, arousal, orgasm).

In the clinical area of male and female sexual dysfunction, the interplay between biological and behavioral variables is always a central consideration in assessment and treatment (Plaud et al., 1997). Substances that decrease the sex drive include alcohol, barbiturates and other hypnotics, hallucinogens, marijuana, amphetamines, and cocaine (even though in small doses such substances are often reported to increase sexual desire and drive). Narcotics such as heroin decrease testosterone levels, and peripherally acting drugs such as antipsychotic drugs also negatively affect sexual arousal (Munjack & Oziel, 1980). On the behavioral side, lack of desire in interpersonal relationships may be a function of reduced physical attractiveness, decreases in marital intimacy, boring sexual routine (recall the effects of short- and long-term sexual habituation), extramarital affairs, situational disturbances, and marital maladjustment (Munjack & Oziel, 1980; Wincze & Carey, 1991).

Behavior Therapy of Sexual Dysfunction

Given the considerations discussed above in terms of the importance of a valid functional analysis of sexually relevant behavior, behavior therapy approaches focus on changing the conditions under which such behaviors are emitted. The relevance of classical and operant conditioning, as well as habituation, is evident in the major behavioral approaches to sexual dysfunction.

One behavioral approach to treating sexual dysfunction has to do with changing the verbal context of sexual behavior, especially when such behavior is seen as negative or related to nonsexual behavior or anxiousness (Wincze & Carey, 1991). Rule-governed behavior is behavior controlled by a verbal specification of environmental contingencies (Cerutti, 1989). Rule-governed behavior has been described as the natural product of verbal behavior (Skinner, 1957). As such, it appears to be a human phenomenon (Plaud, 1995). Late in the 1960s, B. F. Skinner differentiated between two types of operant behavior: contingency-shaped and rule-governed behavior. Much of what humans learn sexually involves contingency-shaped behavior: the consequences of behavior are experienced directly and shape that behavior in the presence of a discriminative stimulus. All organisms, including humans, learn through their contact with environmental contingencies. Only humans, however, can also learn and modify their behavior by using rules, because we have a language. Rule-governed behavior is therefore defined as the behavior controlled by rules, a rule being the specification of a relationship between at least two events. One of the events is a behavior emitted by a human. The other event is a verbal specification of the consequence and the situations, or discriminative stimuli, under which the relationship holds. Such specifications are often referred to as instructions, directions, or principles (Joyce, Joyce, & Chase, 1989). This contrasts with contingency-shaped behavior, which is controlled by the actual events (e.g., reinforcers, punishers) that follow the behavior (Cerutti, 1989).

Rules come to serve as discriminative stimuli themselves (Cerutti, 1989). That is, rules precede behaviors and set the occasion for a behavior or class of behaviors to be emitted. They often do so by specifying a discriminative stimulus a human is likely to encounter. For example, the rule, "you must be able to maintain an erection for an hour to be thought of as a real man" specifies that the behavior of maintaining an erection for an extended period of time will be socially reinforced. In addition, this example shows that the contingency of a response need not be clearly specified by a rule. In fact, the contingencies associated with the behaviors described by rules are often vague and general. An example of this is "be polite," which suggests that if a person is polite he or she will be more successful in dealings with other humans than if the individual is rude.

Humans follow rules despite the lack of specificity in the contingencies rules describe. In exploring this phenomenon, it has been pointed out that rule-following is itself a behavior shaped by its outcome (Galazio, 1979). In the course of a human life, many rules will be encountered. Humans learn that rule-following behavior, overall, often results in positive outcomes, therefore, rule-governed behavior can be conceptualized in part as a product of its consequences, therefore it meets the functional definition of operant behavior. Much of what cognitive therapists label "cognitive restructuring" involves changing the rules under which humans operate (Plaud & Newberry, 1996). In sex therapy, changing dysfunctional rules can be an important component to meaningful behavior change (Wincze & Carey, 1991).

Sensate Focus

Human behavior is usually controlled by both contingencies and rules (Buskist & Miller, 1986). Despite the insensitivity described above, contingencies can shape behavior that originally was rule-governed (Cerutti, 1989). Sensate focus techniques in sex therapy, for example, often result in the modification or discarding of inflexible rules based on their experiences with contingencies. In sensate focus, after a functional analysis, the behavior therapist explains to the couple the functional nature of the problem and the fact that the sexual dysfunction may be maintained by a verbal rule such as the man's concerns about subsequent erectile failure or the woman's concerns about subsequent inability to orgasm, for example. A rule is given to the couple that the "problem" exists between the two of them, and therefore cooperation between both partners is important. The behavior therapist continues by explaining that sensate-focused home-work assignments will be assigned that will help overcome the problem. The focus is on sensations rather than performance (Wincze & Carey, 1991). Explicit instructions (i.e., "rules") for intimacy are developed between the couple. The giving and receiving of pleasure, the absence of the goal of intercourse, and the varieties of intimate interactions restructure the sexual situation for the couple, a direct rule-governed and stimulus control approaches to sexual behavior. Sensate focus is a direct behavioral strategy that changes the context of sexual behavior from performance, anxiety, and control to intimacy, pleasuring, and communication.

In sensate focus, both partners are encouraged to approach each other in a non-threatening manner. A first step is usually "nongenital pleasuring" such as touching while both partners are dressed (Wincze & Carey, 1991). The importance of long-term goals is stressed, as gradual changes in the discriminative control over sexual behavior is the function of sensate-focus exercises. Oftentimes sex therapists discuss some of the myths of human sexuality, which are really rules that are maladaptive. Examples include the necessity of intercourse as a final sexual behavior, the notion that sex equals intercourse (Wincze & Carey, 1991), and that what comes before is "only" foreplay. Next, the couple gradually moves to "genital pleasuring," and the partners caress each other, again without focusing on performance but rather on the pleasurable sensations. Sexual behaviors associated with intercourse are introduced only when the couple is able to engage in nongenital and genital pleasuring behavior. Sensate focus represents an empirically validated behavioral approach to changing the context of sexual behavior, and therefore eliminating the negative consequences of sexual interaction (Munjack & Oziel, 1980).

Stimulus Control and Other Behavioral Techniques in Sex Therapy

There are other stimulus control shortcuts that can be applied to sexual behavior. Other techniques include modeling, physical guidance, and situational inducement, which involves rearranging existing surroundings, moving activities to new locations, relocating people, and changing the time of activities. Counterconditioning approaches, in which a response to a given stimulus is eliminated by eliciting different behavior in the presence of that stimulus, can also be used in behavioral sex therapy. Systematic desensitization reduces anxiety by pairing imagined anxiety-provoking scenes with relaxation. The theoretical basis for this procedure (which resembles counterconditioning in respondent conditioning) is that the relaxation response reciprocally inhibits anxiety, and over repeated exposure allows the anxiety to extinguish. Premature ejaculation may involve anxiety responses as well as sexual or general psychological problems in a relationship (Munjack & Oziel, 1980).

Men have attempted to reduce sexual sensation by applying anesthetic creams to the penis, or by wearing one or more condoms. Another method that has been tried to reduced sexual stimulation is to reduce the actual "thrusting speed" during intercourse (Munjack & Oziel, 1980). Another behavioral approach to premature ejaculation is termed the "start-stop" or "pause" technique (Semans, 1956; Wincze & Carey, 1991) in which just prior to ejaculation the male signals his partner to stop penile stimulation to lessen arousal. After this is tried several times, ejaculation occurs. The squeeze technique (Masters & Johnson, 1970) is similar in that stimulation of the penis continues to a point just before ejaculation, when the man pauses and squeezes the head of his penis, along his coronal ridge, by placing his forefinger and middle finger on one side of his penis, and his thumb opposite. The squeeze should last approximately ten to twelve seconds, and should be repeated several times. In so doing, the man will learn to control his ejaculation (Wincze & Carey, 1991). Drugs which act as a sedative or have a central nervous system depressant effect are often used to delay the onset of sexual stimulation. However, they also delay the entire sexual response. Although premature ejaculation seems to most likely be a result of anxiety, antianxiety medications are of little value in men who suffer from severe cases of premature ejaculation (Munjack & Oziel, 1980).

Although standard sensate focus exercise (as described above) is typically the primary treatment for erectile dysfunction, behavior therapy also may include the identifying and altering of inadequate sexual stimulation as well as education about the sexual response cycle. After ejaculation there is a time period when no amount of stimulation will allow the man to maintain another erection. This time between erections increases with age. As the man becomes aware of this increasing time period he may become fearful and anxious, which can lead to erectile failure. Educating the individual about the refractory period after an erection can be very helpful in this domain (Munjack & Oziel, 1980). In many cases erectile failure is largely a result of performance anxiety. According to Munjack and Oziel (1980), some cases of erectile failure are due to (1) significant marital disturbances or severe and anxious overconcern about their partner's reaction to them, or (2) phobic anxiety about touching, body secretions, impregnation, maladaptive rules, and so forth. Stimulus control and rule-governed behavioral strategies used in combination can be effective in this domain.

Behavior therapy for vaginismus and dyspareunia is more difficult, due to the potential biological complications, which require thorough medical referral. Wincze and Carey (1991) state that the most common nonorganic explanation of vaginismus and dyspareunia involve past sexual trauma and negative sexual messages. Physical traumas affecting the genitalia (e.g., complicated childbirth, genital surgery, diseases such as endometriosis) can trigger fear of pain during coitus and thus enhance the development of vaginismus (Arentewicz & Schmidt, 1983). In some of the most serious cases of vaginismus it is impossible to insert something as small as a finger into the vagina. In order for an exam to be performed a general anesthetic must be administered. A less serious case would allow for the insertion of a finger but not a penis. In even milder cases intercourse is possible but typically involves pain. Most women who suffer with vaginismus can reach orgasm through petting. While vaginismus is not the same thing as a coital phobia, a similar behavioral approach may be employed (Arentewicz & Schmidt, 1983), which may include the use of a series of various-sized plastic dilators that progressively expose and accustom the woman to larger and larger dilators. The progressive use of dilators can recondition the reflex response of the muscles surrounding the outer third of the vagina.

In dyspareunia, pain may continue to exist even after the biological causes have been removed. Women who experience painful intercourse frequently may develop sexual aversions, arousal, and/or orgasmic disturbances, as discussed above. Systematic desensitization may be particularly effective in such cases (Arentewicz & Schmidt, 1983). With regard to trauma, the following areas of focus are important in behavior therapy (McCarthy, 1990):

1. Consider past trauma as something that needs to be dealt with in the context of the present sexual dysfunction.
2. Focus on the present and the future.
3. Integrate trauma in the treatment of the sexual dysfunction instead of treating it separately.
4. Emphasize that trauma not only affects the individual with the problem, but also the bond between the couple, so they both must be treated.
5. An integral component of treatment is individual and couple cognitive and communication exercises to address the traumatic incident.
6. The cognitive-behavioral strategy is to continue with the sexual pleasuring while identifying and dealing with road blocks.
7. Changing cognitions (i.e., "rules") and behavior in the couple's relationship is the therapeutic focus.

Combining Sex and Marital Therapy

According to Metz and Weiss (1992), research suggests that marital dysfunction is clearly involved in one-third or more of sexual dysfunctions. Metz and Weiss argue that therapies that only address the sexual dysfunction or only the marital problems will not be maximally effective, and therefore advocate a combination of the two.

Combinations of sex and marital therapy may involve the following (Metz and Weiss, 1992):

1. One of the goals is to get the client thinking (cognitive), acting (behavior), and feeling (affect) more confidently and skillfully.
2. Consideration of "basic relationship themes" such as relationship identity (cognitive life of the relationship), relationship cooperation (behavioral inter-actions), and intimacy (measure of the emotional bondedness).
3. In the group, the goal is to address and integrate the individual and relationship dimensions.
4. In group, when possible, they attempt to integrate general and sexual dimensions.
5. They have a priority on teaching skills dealing with cognitions, behaviors, and affects.
6. They see the "overriding goal" of the group is to develop cooperation for the couple. They do this by overcoming the barriers to cooperation, and facilitating cooperation through structured exercises.

Given the complex interaction of biological and behavioral processes in the genesis and maintenance of sexual dyfunction for both males and females, it is clear that behavioral approaches add significantly to our understanding of the causes and modification of maladaptive sexual behavior. Consideration of classical and operant conditioning as well as habituation parameters of human sexual arousal in the context of interpersonal and other social contingencies related to sexual responding has led to innovative techniques to treat sexual dysfunction. As our understanding of the learning parameters of human sexuality increases, so too will the repertoire of behavior therapy approaches to effectively address sexual dysfunction, which promises even more advances in this area of behavior modification and therapy.

References

Alford, G., Plaud, J. J., & McNair, T. L. (1995). Conditioning perspectives on sexual behavior and orientation. In L. Diamant & R. McAnulty (Eds.), *The psychology of sexual orientation, behavior and identity: A handbook* (pp. 121–135). Westport, CT: Greenwood.

American Psychiatric Association (1994). *Diagnostic and statistical manual of mental disorders, fourth edition*. Washington, DC: Author.

Anderson, B. J., & Wolf, F. M. (1986). Chronic physical illness and sexual behavior: Psychological issues. *Journal of Consulting and Clinical Psychology, 54,* 168–175.

Arentewicz, G., & Schmidt, G. (1983). *The treatment of sexual disorders*. New York: Basic Books.

Barbaree, H. E., & Marshall, W. L. (1991). The role of male sexual arousal in rape: Six models. Special Section: Theories of sexual aggression. *Journal of Consulting and Clinical Psychology, 59,* 621–630.

Beck, J. G., (1993). Vaginismus. In W. O'Donohue & J. H. Geer (Eds.), *Handbook of sexual dysfunctions: Assessment and treatment* (pp. 381–397). Boston: Allyn & Bacon.

Buskist, W. F., & Miller, H. L. (1986). Interaction between rules and contingencies in the control of human fixed-interval performances. *The Psychological Record, 36,* 109–116.

Cerutti, D. T. (1989). Discrimination theory of rule-governed behavior. *Journal of the Experimental Analysis of Behavior, 51,* 259–276.

Cliffe, M. J., & Parry, S. J. (1980). Matching to reinforcer value: Human concurrent variable-interval performance. *Quarterly Journal of Experimental Psychology, 32,* 557–570.

Conte, H. R. (1983). Development and use of self-report techniques for assessing sexual functioning: A review and critique. *Archives of Sexual Behavior, 12,* 555–576.

Davenport, W. H. (1987). An anthropological approach. In J. Geer & W. O'Donohue (Eds.), *Theories of Human Sexuality* (pp. 197–236). New York: Plenum.

DeLamater, J. (1987). A sociological approach. In J. Geer & W. O'Donohue (Eds.), *Theories of human sexuality* (pp. 237–256). New York: Plenum.

Domjan, M. & Burkhard, B. (1986). *The principles of learning and behavior*. Belmont, CA: Brooks/Cole.

Frank, E., Anderson, C., & Rubenstein, D. (1978). Frequency of sexual dysfunction in "normal" couples. *New England Journal of Medicine, 299,* 111–115.

Galazio, M. (1979). Contingency-shaped and rule-governed behavior: Instructional control of human loss avoidance. *Journal of the Experimental Analysis of Behavior, 31,* 53–70.

Graber, B. (1993). Medical aspects of sexual arousal disorders. In W. O'Donohue & J. H. Geer (Eds.), *Handbook of sexual dysfunctions: Assessment and treatment* (pp. 103–156). Boston: Allyn & Bacon.

Herrnstein, R. J. (1970). On the law of effect. *Journal of the Experimental Analysis of Behavior, 13,* 243–266.

Joyce, B. G., Joyce, J. H., & Chase, P. N. (1989). Considerations for the use of rules in academic settings. *Education and Treatment of Children, 12,* 82–92.

Kaplan, H. S. (1983). *The evaluation of sexual disorders*. New York: Brunner/Mazel.

Krause, J., Herth, T., Maier, W., Steiger, A., Schoneich, S., & Benkert, O. (1991). An interdisciplinary study towards a multiaxial classification of male sexual dysfunction. *Acta Psychiatrica Scandinavica, 84,* 130–136.

Kresin, D. (1993). Medical aspects of inhibited sexual desire disorder. In W. O'Donohue & J. H. Geer (Eds.), *Handbook of sexual dysfunctions: Assessment and treatment* (pp. 15–52). Boston: Allyn & Bacon.

Langevin, R., & Martin, M. (1975). Can erotic responses be classically conditioned? *Behavior Therapy, 6,* 350–355.

Letourneau, E., & O'Donohue, W. (1993). Sexual desire disorders. In W. O'Donohue & J. H. Geer (Eds.), *Handbook of sexual dysfunctions: Assessment and treatment* (pp. 53–81). Boston: Allyn & Bacon.

LoPiccolo, J. (1990). Sexual dysfunction. In A. S. Bellack, M. Hersen, & A. E. Kazdin (Eds.), *International handbook of behavior modification and therapy* (2nd ed.) (pp. 547–564). New York: Plenum.

LoPiccolo, J., & Stock, W. E. (1986). Treatment of sexual dysfunction. *Journal of Consulting and Clinical Psychology, 54,* 158–167.

McCarthy, B. W. (1990). Treating sexual dysfunction associated with prior sexual trauma. *Journal of Sex and Marital Therapy, 16,* 142–146.

McConaghy, N. (1988). Sexual dysfunction and deviation. In A. S. Bellak & M. Hersen (Eds.), *Behavioral assessment: A practical handbook* (3rd ed.) (pp. 490–541). New York: Pergamon.

Masters, W. H., & Johnson, V. E. (1970). *Human sexual inadequacy.* Boston: Little, Brown.

Masters, W. H., Johnson, V. E., & Kolodny, R. C. (1995). *Human sexuality.* New York: HarperCollins College.

Metz, M. E., & Weiss, K. E. (1992). A group therapy format for the simultaneous treatment of marital and sexual syfunctions: A case illustration. *Journal of Sex and Marital Therapy, 18,* 173–187.

Millenson, J. R., & Leslie, J. C. (1979). *Principles of behavioral analysis.* New York: Macmillan.

Morokoff, P. J. (1993). Female sexual arousal disorder. In W. O'Donohue & J. H. Geer (Eds.), *Handbook of sexual dysfunctions: Assessment and treatment* (pp. 157–199). Boston: Allyn & Bacon.

Munjack, D. J., & Oziel, L. J. (1980). *Sexual medicine and counseling in office practice: A comprehensive treatment guide.* New York: Little, Brown.

O'Donohue, W. T., & Geer, J. H. (1985). The habituation of sexual arousal. *Archives of Sexual Behavior, 14,* 233–246.

O'Donohue, W. T., & Plaud, J. J. (1991). The long-term habituation of male sexual arousal. *Journal of Behavior Therapy and Experimental Psychiatry, 22,* 87–96.

O'Donohue, W. T., & Plaud, J. J. (1994). The conditioning of human sexual arousal. *Archives of Sexual Behavior, 23,* 321–344.

Plaud, J. J. (1992). The prediction and control of behavior revisited: A review of the matching law. *Journal of Behavior Therapy and Experimental Psychiatry, 23,* 25–31.

Plaud, J. J. (1995). The formation of stimulus equivalences: Fear-relevant versus fear-irrelevant stimulus classes. *The Psychological Record, 45,* 207–222.

Plaud, J. J., Gaither, G. A., Amato-Henderson, S., & Devitt, M. K. (1997). The long-term habituation of sexual arousal in human males: A crossover design. *The Psychological Record, 47,* 385–398.

Plaud, J. J., & Newberry, D. E. (1996). Rule-governed behavior and pedophilia. *Sexual Abuse: A Journal of Research and Treatment, 8,* 143–159.

Rathus, S. A., Nevid, J. S., & Fichner-Rathus, L. (1997). *Human sexuality in a world of diversity.* Boston: Allyn & Bacon.

Renshaw, D. C. (1988). Profile of 2376 patients treated at Loyola Sex Clinic between 1972 and 1987. *Sexual and Marital Therapy, 3,* 111–117.

Rosen, R. C., Shapiro, D., & Schwartz, G. E. (1975). Voluntary control of penile tumescence. *Psychosomatic Medicine, 37,* 479–483.

Rosen, R. C., Taylor, J. F., Leiblum, S. R., Bachman, G. A. (1993). Prevalence of sexual dysfunction in women: Results of a survey study of 329 women in an outpatient gynecological clinic. *Journal of Sex and Marital Therapy, 19,* 171–188.

Schover, L. R., & Jensen, S. B. (1988). *Sexuality and chronic illness.* New York: Guilford.

Semans, J. H. (1956). Premature ejaculation: A new approach. *Southern Medical Journal, 49,* 353–358.

Skinner, B. F. (1957). *Verbal behavior.* New York: Appleton-Century-Crofts.

Skinner, B. F. (1969). *Contingencies of reinforcement: A theoretical analysis.* New York: Appleton-Century-Crofts.

Skinner, B. F. (1988). The phylogeny and ontogeny of behavior. In A. C. Catania & S. Harnad (Eds.), *The selection of behavior: The operant behaviorism of B. F. Skinner* (pp. 382–400).

Spector, I. P., & Carey, M. P. (1990). Incidence and prevalence of the sexual dysfunctions: A critical review of the empirical literature. *Archives of Sexual Behavior, 19,* 389–408.

Spark, R. F. (1991). *Male sexual health: A couple's guide.* Mount Vernon, NY: Consumer Reports Books.

Watson, J. B. (1925). *Behaviorism.* New York: Norton.

Wincze, J. P., & Carey, M. P. (1991). *Sexual dysfunction: A guide for assessment and treatment.* New York: Guilford.

8

SEXUAL DISORDERS

GEORGE A. GAITHER
Department of Psychology
University of North Dakota

RICHARD R. ROSENKRANZ
Department of Psychology
University of North Dakota

JOSEPH J. PLAUD
Department of Psychology
Judge Rotenberg Educational Center

Many of the most commonly employed therapy techniques in use today with sexual deviations, or the paraphilias, are based on learning principles (Abel & Blanchard, 1976; Langevin & Martin, 1975; McGuire, Carlisle, & Young, 1965; O'Donohue & Plaud, 1994). The hypotheses vary, however, in the extent to which they emphasize the classical conditioning of sexual arousal (i.e., penile responses) or the operant conditioning of deviant sexual behavior patterns (Alford, Plaud, & McNair, 1995; O'Donohue & Plaud, 1994). In fact, Abel and Blanchard (1976) state that: "The problem of deviant sexual behavior was one of the earliest areas of psychopathology to which behavioral techniques were applied, and it continues to be a major area of research and treatment" (p. 99). Unfortunately, however, it seems as though the cart has been placed before the horse. Sexual deviance, in other words, seems to be an area in which the widespread use of behavior therapy techniques has preceded research into the veracity of the hypotheses from which the therapy techniques were said to have been rooted.

Two decades ago, Langevin and Martin (1975) cautioned that "there have been few empirical demonstrations that classical conditioning procedures can be used to elicit penile tumescence" (p. 350). In a recent review of the empirical literature, O'Donohue and Plaud (1994) concluded that the question of whether sexual arousal may be conditioned is still open to debate. The current literature, however, is replete with case studies demonstrating the effectiveness of different types of behavioral techniques, many of which have been developed specifically for use with sexual deviations. Where does this leave us as behavior therapists? Should we use the techniques that are considered effective due to the publication of a number of case studies, or should we hold out for laboratory research or other empirical evidence to demonstrate the veracity of theories that sexual deviations arise from some type of conditioning processes? The authors of this chapter believe that this is a question that needs to be answered by each therapist individually. Behavioral researchers and therapists are working to make this a less difficult decision, however, by continuing to conduct research on the conditioning of human sexual arousal. In this chapter we will discuss one of the more well-developed behavioral theories of the conditioning of sexual deviations on which behavior-therapy techniques have been based. Next, a discussion of some of the more common behavior-therapy techniques used in this area over the years will be presented. Finally, we will present a brief discussion of the published laboratory data that exists, tying theories of human sexual behavior to behavior-therapy approaches in this area.

Behavioral Hypotheses of the Etiology of Sexual Deviance

The earliest behavioral theories of sexual deviations were based upon a classical conditioning paradigm. Theorists such as Binet (1888), Jaspers (1963), and Rachman (1961) believed that these deviations were the result of an accidental pairing. According to Jaspers (1963), "Perversion rises through the accidents of our first experience. Gratification remains tied to the form and object once experienced, but this does not happen simply through the force of simultaneous association with that former experience" (p. 323). An accidental pairing of an abnormal stimulus with sexual arousal or ejaculation, though feasible, leaves much to be explained. For instance, why do only some people whose first sexual experience involved a partner of the same sex practice homosexuality in adulthood while many others do not? Or why would a stimulus such as a shoe gain such erotic value as to become a fetish while other objects in the room at the time of a first ejaculation (e.g., other items of clothing or even pillows, blankets, etc.) do not?

McGuire, Carlisle, and Young (1965) developed one of the most comprehensive hypotheses of the conditioning of sexual deviations to date. According to these authors, the hypothesis grew out of treating several cases of sexual deviations with aversive techniques that were, at the time, the most commonly employed behavioral techniques. McGuire et al. noted that although it is possible that sexual deviance is learned in one trial or one experience, this is probably an oversimplification. In fact, the authors pointed out, not all people who have homosexual experiences in childhood practice homosexuality in adulthood. Therefore, other factors must be involved. Some of the earlier theorists had suggested that a constitutional factor, such as ease of conditionability, may be that something else.

The hypothesis of McGuire et al. (1965) seems to be more parsimonious than earlier theories. These authors suggested that the major difference between their hypothesis and the prevailing theory was that "the learning is postulated to take place more commonly *after* the initial seduction or experience, which plays its part only in supplying a fantasy for later masturbation" (p. 185). McGuire et al. state their hypothesis as follows:

It is in accordance with conditioning theory that any stimulus which precedes ejaculation by the correct time interval should become more and more sexually exciting. The stimulus may be circumstantial (for example, a particular time or place in which masturbation or intercourse is commonly practiced) or it may be deliberate (for example, any sexual situation or a fantasy of it, be it normal intercourse or wearing female apparel). It is hypothesized that the latter process is the mechanism by which most sexual deviations are acquired and developed.

Why some people (sexual deviates) choose to incorporate the deviant stimuli into their masturbatory fantasies is explained in this conditioning hypothesis as a combination of factors. One factor is the stimulus value of "deviant" stimuli, which is continually strengthened through the pairing of these stimuli with ejaculation. Nondeviant stimuli or fantasies, at the same time, are being extinguished or losing their sexual value due to their lack of pairing with ejaculation. Another contributing factor is a common belief held by sexual deviants that a normal sex life is not possible. This belief, according to McGuire et al. (1965), may develop from a number of different sources including aversive adult heterosexual experiences, or feelings of physical or sexual inadequacy. McGuire et al. found that in forty-five cases, all of the patients held this belief before their first deviant sexual encounter. This leads one to the conclusion that the belief (a covert behavior) may play a causal role in the development of sexual deviations (overt behaviors) rather than being an effect of the deviation.

It seems that what McGuire et al. (1965) have proposed is that sexual deviations are learned through a combination of classical and operant conditioning processes. Deviant sexual behavior begins with an accidental pairing of an "abnormal" or deviant stimulus with sexual arousal and/or ejaculation, giving this stimulus a high amount of erotic value. Thus, through a classical conditioning process, the deviant stimulus begins to elicit sexual arousal. The deviant stimulus is then incorporated into sexual fantasies during masturbation that is reinforced by ejaculation. Thus, ejaculation serves as a reinforcer for the covert behavior of deviant fantasizing. Unfortunately, the process by which masturbating to deviant sexual fantasies leads to deviant sexual behavior is unclear.

McGuire et al. (1965) discussed the implications of their hypothesis for the treatment of sexual deviations. First, the authors stated that "since the original conditioning was carried out in most cases to fantasy alone, treatment also need only be to fantasy" (p. 187). Thus, in the treatment of deviations such as pedophilia, it is not necessary to present the subject with children, but only with fantasies involving children. Another implication of this hypothesis is that therapists can warn their patients of the conditioning effects of orgasm on the immediately preceding fantasy. Finally, according to McGuire et al., "positive conditioning to normal heterosexual stimuli can follow the same lines as it is deduced that the deviation followed" (p. 187).

Many early studies of sexual deviance adopted a rather simplistic view that sexual deviance consisted of only an excess of sexual arousal to deviant objects or behaviors (Abel & Blanchard, 1976). Thus, the earliest behavior-treatment techniques, mainly aversive procedures, focused only on the reduction of deviant sexual arousal. Beginning in the 1970s, researchers (e.g., Barlow, 1973; Card, 1977; Rosen & Kopel, 1977) began to recognize that sexual deviations included not only behavioral excesses but also behavioral deficits such as arousal to "appropriate" or nondeviant objects or behaviors (Abel & Blanchard, 1976). Thus, a second class of conditioning procedures were developed (Card, 1982), which had as their function not only a decrease in arousal to deviant stimuli but also an increase in sexual arousal to nondeviant stimuli.

Behavioral-Treatment Techniques

We will next present a discussion of some of the more common behavior therapy techniques that have been employed in the treatment of sexual deviations. We will provide examples from the literature, and attempt to delineate, where possible, whether the technique uses classical or operant conditioning processes or a combination of the two.

Aversion Therapy Techniques

This set of techniques was among the first to be applied to sexual deviations. These techniques have in common a goal of reducing sexual arousal to deviant stimuli through the introduction of aversive events. This set of techniques includes covert sensitization, olfactory aversion, and faradic or electrical aversion therapy.

Covert sensitization is a form of conditioning in which a behavior and its precipitative events are paired with some aversive stimulus in order to promote avoidance of the precipitative events and thereby to decrease the undesirable behaviors. Cautela and Kearney (1990) discussed covert conditioning and defined it as the following:

> *Covert conditioning refers to a family of behavioral therapy procedures which combine the use of imagery with the principles of operant conditioning. Covert conditioning is a process through which private events such as thoughts, images, and feelings are manipulated in accordance with principles of learning, usually operant conditioning, to bring about changes in overt behavior, covert psychological behavior (i.e., thoughts, images, feelings) and/or physiological behavior (e.g., glandular secretions) (p. 86).*

In covert sensitization, the aversive stimulus usually consists of an anxiety-inducing or nausea-inducing image that may be presented verbally by the therapist or imagined by the client. The aversive scene is individually created, and is specific to each client's problem behavior. Covert sensitization has frequently been successfully employed alone (e.g., Brownwell & Barlow, 1976; Curtis & Presley, 1972; Dougher, Crossen, Ferraro, & Garland, 1987; Haydn-Smith, Marks, Buchaya, & Repper, 1987; Hayes, Brownwell, & Barlow, 1978; Hughes, 1977; King, 1990; McNally & Lukach, 1991; Maletzky & George, 1973) as well as in combination with other techniques (Kendrick & McCullough, 1972; Moergen, Merkel, & Brown, 1990; Rangaswamy, 1987; Stava, Levin, & Schwanz, 1993) in the treatment of sexual deviance.

Lamontagne and Lesage (1986) nicely illustrate the use of covert sensitization in the treatment of exhibitionism. The subject in this study was a thirty-seven-year-old male who had been exposing himself several times per week. The treatment consisted of covert sensitization techniques and allowing the client to privately expose himself at home with his wife. Before treatment, this client had fantasized about exhibitionism approximately 60 percent of the time during masturbation and 30 percent of the time during sexual intercourse with his wife. In the covert sensitization sessions, the subject imagined exposing himself to a woman who would then angrily scold him. As another part of the aversive image, he imagined losing his wife because of the exhibitionism. Thus, the deviant fantasy was paired with two powerfully aversive images. In combination with the covert sensitization procedures, the client was allowed to expose himself two times per week at home with his wife. This private exposure was always followed by either masturbation or sexual intercourse without deviant fantasies. Also, the client was instructed not to masturbate unless his wife was present, so that nondeviant sexual fantasy and behavior could be promoted. A post-treatment follow-up indicated that the subject had not publicly exposed himself for two years. It would seem that the treatment rendered the exhibitionism appropriate, and even socially acceptable, since it occurred in the privacy of the home. Interestingly, the couple even reported that their sex life improved following treatment.

As discussed above, the underlying theory of this treatment approach is probably best thought of as a combination of classical and operant conditioning processes. The therapist works with a client to develop an aversive image that will be paired with the precipitative events, and with the image of the deviant behavior itself, according to a classical conditioning paradigm. The aversive image serves as the unconditioned stimulus (UCS). The images of the precipitative events, being continually paired with the UCS, become the conditioned stimulus (CS). Both the conditioned response (CR) and the unconditioned response (UCR) consist of a negative reaction which may be emotional (e.g., fear), physiological (e.g., nausea), or in some other way repulsive. Once the client's deviant behavior has been classically conditioned, the client should begin to actively avoid or escape the situations associated with the deviant behavior. The precipitative events, as well as the behavior itself, should elicit a negative reaction and thus be aversive.

According to the principles of operant conditioning, and specifically of negative reinforcement, the client should behave in ways that would minimize contact with the aversive stimulus; in this case the precipitative events and the deviant behavior. If the client does pursue the deviant behavior further, hopefully the treatments will have at least reduced the effectiveness of the reinforcement for the deviant behavior, which should lead to lower frequency of the behavior. It would also be possible for classical conditioning to work alone, if the CR was so powerful that it rendered the person unable engage in the deviant behavior, or consisted of a response that was incompatible with the deviant behavior. For example, if the CR was extreme anxiety or fear, and the deviant behavior required an erect penis, it may be the case that the CR would preclude the possibility of erection, and thereby preclude the occurrence of the deviant behavior.

In the example discussed above, Lamontagne and Lesage (1986) effectively combined classical conditioning and operant conditioning in their covert sensitization treatment approach. Another important part of their treatment consisted of the operant reinforcement of private exposure through orgasm from masturbation or intercourse, both of which took place with the client's wife. Essentially, only the context of the exhibition behavior changed, not the behavior itself. The client learned that the behavior would be reinforced in one situation (at home with his wife), while it would either be extinguished or punished in any other situations.

Olfactory aversion, or olfactory aversive therapy, is frequently used in the treatment of sexual deviance, to reduce deviant sexual behaviors, arousal, and fantasies (Earls & Castonguay, 1989; Enright, 1989; Marshall, Eccles, & Barbaree, 1991). The aversive stimulus used in treatment may be a presentation of ammonia, valeric acid, or just about any noxious odor. Frequently in this type of therapy, the subject self-administers the aversive stimulus by inhaling from an ampule containing the noxious substance. Another way to administer the aversive odor, which is usually under the therapist's direct control, consists of a device much like a small atomizer, which sprays a small amount of a noxious vapor into the client's nostrils.

Several studies have shown the usefulness of olfactory aversive therapy (e.g., Colson, 1972; Earls & Castonguay, 1989; Enright, 1989; Laws, Meyer, & Holmen, 1978; Marshall et al., 1991; Wolfe, 1992). Earls & Castonguay (1989) successfully employed olfactory aversion in the treatment of a seventeen-year-old male sex offender. The subject of this study was a bisexual pedophile who was plethysmographically assessed, and found to be sexually aroused to male and female children as well as to male and female adults. In subsequent treatment sessions, the client listened to audiotapes and was administered the aversive odor of ammonia with any inappropriate sexual arousal (male and female children). Post-treatment assessment and follow-up showed dramatic decreases in arousal to children and pre-adolescents, with an increase in sexual arousal to adult and adolescent women. Since the client was himself an adolescent close to adulthood, arousal patterns to adolescent women and to adult women were both deemed appropriate. According to these results, the subject apparently learned to discriminate and to become aroused only by the appropriate stimuli, and not to become aroused by inappropriate stimuli.

Like covert sensitization, olfactory aversive therapy is a procedure in which an aversive stimulus is strategically used to reduce an undesirable behavior and its precipitative events. In this case the aversive stimulus is in the form of a noxious odor. The theory underlying olfactory aversive therapy may be either operant or classical conditioning acting alone, or a combination of classical and operant conditioning, depending on the specific procedures used and the results.

In the case described by Earls and Castonguay (1989) above, the client was administered the aversive stimulus only contingent upon his sexual arousal to inappropriate material. Therefore, this would be using a punishment paradigm of operant conditioning. Essentially the inappropriate sexual arousal was being punished by presentation of the noxious odor (provided that it resulted in a decrease of that behavior, which, in this case, it did). Similarly, if the client then pursued the deviant behavior only to experience the aversive consequences of the conditioned response (nausea, repulsion, etc.), and then ceased the behavior, or sought to avoid or escape future deviant behavior situations, then it would be due to operant conditioning as well. However, if the therapist used a different procedure in which the noxious odor was consistently paired with presentations of the inappropriate stimulus material regardless of sexual arousal or other behavior, then it would be operating through classical conditioning alone. Also, if the conditioned response prevented the deviant behavior from being performed by being incompatible with that behavior, or simply not allowing the person to act at all (e.g., being frozen with fear), then classical conditioning would be operating alone.

Faradic aversion, also known as electrical aversive therapy or simply as aversion therapy, is a procedure in which aversive electrical shocks are used to reduce the occurrence of a deviant behavior and its precipitative events (Marshall et al., 1991). Faradic aversion has often been used in the treatment of sexual deviance as well as other problem behaviors (see Wolfe, 1992; Marshall et al., 1991).

Freeman and Meyer (1975) employed faradic aversion in the treatment of three married and six single homosexual males ranging in age from nineteen to forty-three. This study was different from previous papers published in the area of sexual deviance in that it reported results of treatment for more than just a single case study. The treatment consisted of a six-week waiting period in which behavioral diaries were kept, twenty reconditioning sessions (two per week), and an extended follow-up period. In the reconditioning sessions, each client masturbated to orgasm while exposed to a heterosexually oriented slide presentation. Afterwards, each client was exposed to homosexually oriented slides that were paired with electrical shock. Through the follow-up period, seven of the original nine subjects had maintained an exclusive heterosexual orientation for over a year and a half after treatment, and all nine had done so for a year.

Faradic aversion is thought to operate in an almost identical manner as olfactory aversive therapy; it is merely a difference in the form of aversive stimulus used. Of course, in the case of faradic aversion therapy, the aversive stimulus consists of a mildly painful electrical stimulation. The theory underlying faradic aversion may be either operant or classical conditioning acting independently, or a combination of classical and operant conditioning, depending on the specific procedures used and the results. In the cases discussed above (Freeman & Meyer, 1975), it would seem that heterosexually oriented behaviors were being directly positively reinforced, and thus operantly conditioned through masturbation and orgasm. Alternately, the pairing of electrical shocks with the homosexually oriented slides would result in classical conditioning, and an aversive conditioned response to homosexually oriented behaviors. However, the aversive CR associated with homosexually oriented behaviors may operantly result in avoidance or escape of those situations. Finally, the CR may be such that it renders the person incapable of engaging in the deviant behavior altogether, which would be an instance of classical conditioning acting alone.

Masturbatory Retraining Techniques

This next set of techniques, which includes masturbatory satiation, masturbatory extinction, and orgasmic reconditioning, did not surface until the early 1970s. Although the primary goal of these techniques, much like the aversion techniques described above, is the reduction of sexual arousal to deviant stimuli, the process by which this is achieved is much different (Marshall, 1979; Marshall & Barbaree, 1978).

Masturbatory satiation is a technique in which the erotic value attached to deviant stimuli is systematically decreased. This procedure entails having a client masturbate while engaging in deviant fantasies for a much longer time than is pleasurable, usually one to two hours at a time. If the client ejaculates during the time period, which very often happens in the initial sessions, he is instructed to continue masturbating until the time period has ended. Thus, through this process, the deviant stimuli lose their erotic value as they become associated with boredom (Marshall, 1979). This procedure has been shown to be effective by several researchers (Johnston, Hudson, & Marshall, 1992; Marshall, 1979; Marshall & Barbaree, 1978; Marshall & Lippens, 1977).

Marshall (1979) presented a case study in which he was able to successfully treat a pedophile using masturbatory satiation. The subject in this study was a thirty-six-year-old married male who had a long history of offenses with girls ranging in age from three to thirteen years of age. The subject was arrested for having sexual intercourse with his three-year-old daughter and subsequently entered treatment. The results of a pretreatment plethysmographic assessment indicated that the subject displayed high levels of penile tumescence when presented stimuli depicting female children and adult males, and much lower tumescence in the presence of female adults.

Marshall (1979) initiated masturbatory satiation, targeting first the subject's sexual arousal to female children. The subject was instructed to masturbate continuously while verbalizing aloud his deviant fantasies during each of the six one-hour treatment sessions, with the instruction that he continue masturbating each time he ejaculated. Results of the post-treatment plethysmographic assessment showed the subject displayed markedly lower levels of penile tumescence when presented stimuli depicting children, slight decreases for stimuli of adult males, and a slight increase to adult female stimuli. The subject displayed a similar pattern of sexual arousal during a ten month follow-up assessment.

Masturbatory extinction very closely resembles masturbatory satiation in that a primary goal of the technique is to reduce sexual arousal to deviant fantasies. However, unlike masturbatory satiation, masturbatory extinction is further concerned with increasing sexual arousal to nondeviant fantasies (Alford, Morin, Atkins, & Schoen, 1987). This procedure involves having a client masturbate while engaging in nondeviant fantasies until he ejaculates. Next, the client is instructed to masturbate while engaging in nonsexual fantasies until he ejaculates a second time. Finally, the client is instructed to masturbate for an extended period of time while engaging in deviant fantasies without ejaculating.

The reason, as Alford et al. (1987) explain, that the client is instructed to masturbate to nonsexual fantasies is to reduce the possibility that he will orgasm while engaging in deviant fantasies as well as to ensure that nondeviant fantasies are not associated with a less powerful orgasmic experience, which may reduce the erotic value of the nondeviant fantasies (Alford et al., 1987). Alford et al. caution that one limitation of this procedure is that a candidate for this type of treatment must initially show high levels of sexual arousal to nondeviant stimuli.

Alford et al. (1987) presented a case study in which they treated a pedophile with masturbatory extinction. The subject, a twenty-seven-year-old heterosexual male, had been arrested for engaging in sexual activities with young girls. During an initial interview, the subject reported sexual attraction to adolescent, as well as adult, females, although he denied ever having had any sexual contact with adolescent females. The subject displayed high levels of penile tumescence when presented stimuli depicting female children, adolescent females, and adult females during a pretreatment plethysmographic assessment.

During each of forty treatment sessions, which lasted approximately 90 to 120 minutes each, the subject was instructed to masturbate to orgasm while viewing slides or listening to audiotaped stimuli depicting nondeviant sexual activities. Next, the subject was instructed to masturbate to orgasm while listening to a relaxation tape. Finally, the subject masturbated for the remainder of the session, without achieving orgasm, while being presented deviant stimuli.

Results of a post-treatment plethysmographic assessment indicated that the researchers had successfully increased the subject's arousal levels in the presence of nondeviant stimuli while markedly decreasing his arousal to deviant stimuli. Results from a twelve month follow-up assessment indicated that the effects had been maintained.

According to Marquis (1970), *orgasmic reconditioning*, much like masturbatory satiation and masturbatory extinction, "attaches sexual arousal and rehearses sexual behavior in response to socially acceptable stimuli" (p. 267). Marquis further described that the technique

> *extinguishes sexual responses to the deviant stimulus by preventing them from being paired with orgasm and eventually decreasing to zero the amount of arousal with which they are paired (p. 267).*

Through the use of orgasmic reconditioning, sexual arousal to nondeviant stimuli is increased while, at the same time, sexual arousal to the deviant stimulus is decreased or extinguished. Several different forms of this technique have been reported (Foote & Laws, 1981; Keller & Goldstein, 1978; Kremsdorf, Holmen, & Laws, 1980; Laws, 1985). In the original form proposed by Marquis (1970), however, the patient was instructed to masturbate while engaging in deviant fantasies and then, five seconds before orgasm, he was instructed to switch to a nondeviant fantasy, so that the nondeviant fantasy was associated with the reinforcing orgasm. After several sessions of this procedure, it has been proposed, the patient should be able to move the point at which he switches to the nondeviant fantasy backward in time, until, ultimately, he is able to become aroused by the nondeviant fantasy alone.

This procedure differs from masturbatory extinction in the sense that the patient need not necessarily be sexually aroused by nondeviant fantasies at the onset of treatment. Several researchers have reported great success with orgasmic reconditioning alone (Davison, 1968; Jackson, 1969; Kremsdorf et al., 1980; Thorpe, Schmidt, & Castell, 1963; Thorpe, Schmidt, Brown, & Castell, 1964; Van Deventer & Laws, 1978) as well as in combination with other treatment techniques (Johnston, Hudson, & Marshall, 1992; LoPiccolo, Stewart, & Watkins, 1972; Marshall, 1973, 1979). Leonard and Hayes (1983) cautioned, however, that the effect of orgasmic reconditioning "seems to be sensitive to the rapidity of fantasy alternation" (p. 241), and, thus, that this procedure should not be used in isolation but as a part of a broader treatment package.

Kremsdorf et al. (1980) described a case in which a modification of orgasmic reconditioning was used to treat a twenty-year-old pedophile. The subject, who was confined to a state hospital for child molestation, reported primarily being sexually aroused by female children between the ages of one and twelve. In the pretreatment interview the subject also stated that he had little sexual experience with adult females and did not find them very sexually appealing.

Treatment for this subject lasted eight weeks. During the treatment sessions, the subject engaged in directed masturbation. The procedure was altered from its original form in that the subject was instructed to masturbate solely to nondeviant fantasies throughout each of the sessions. Results from a post-treatment plethysmographic assessment indicated a marked increase in sexual arousal to stimuli depicting adult females as well as a marked decrease in arousal to stimuli depicting children.

The treatment techniques discussed above are only a sample of all of the techniques that have been used to eliminate sexual arousal to deviant stimuli. Other behavioral techniques that have been employed, but which are no longer practiced regularly, include anticipatory avoidance (Feldman & MacCulloch, 1965; Larson, 1970), aversion relief (Clark, 1965; Pinard & Lamontagne, 1976; Thorpe, Schmidt, Brown, & Castell, 1964; Thorpe, Schmidt, & Castell, 1964), and fading (Barlow & Agras, 1973; McCrady, 1973). A relatively new technique, biofeedback, capitalizes on the aspect of voluntary control over penile responses. Researchers using this technique provide the subject with auditory or visual feedback regarding his level of penile tumescence in order to teach him ways to bring this autonomic response (penile erection) under voluntary control. This technique has been employed by several researchers with mixed results (Barlow, Agras, Abel, Blanchard, & Young, 1975; Card, 1982; Csillag, 1976; Keltner, 1977; Laws, 1977; Rosen, 1973; Rosen & Kopel, 1977).

Although the treatment techniques that have been discussed focus solely on changing sexual arousal patterns, many researchers have realized that other behavioral excesses and deficits may either cause, or at least maintain, sexual deviations. For instance, a lack of social skills in dealing with appropriate sexual partners may lead a person to seek out individuals with whom these skills are not required (e.g., children). Thus, other techniques such as social skills training (e.g., Josiassen, Fantuzzo, & Rosen, 1980; Moergen et al., 1990; Turner & Van Hasselt, 1979), assertiveness training (Keltner, Scharf, & Schell, 1979), relaxation training (e.g., Blitch & Haynes, 1972), and systematic desensitization (e.g., Hanson & Adesso, 1972) have been included in more comprehensive treatment approaches.

Laboratory Research

As can be seen from above, many articles have been published regarding treatment methods of sexual deviations, outcome of such treatment, characteristics and behavior of sexual deviants, as well as numerous case studies and interviews with sex offenders. Unfortunately, however, there has been a relative paucity of research published concerning the underlying fundamentals of learning theory in the etiology of sexual deviations (Alford, Plaud, & McNair, 1995; O'Donohue & Plaud, 1994). Since many treatment methods seem to rest on the assumption that sexual arousal and sexual behavior are in some way learned, it is important to continue to conduct research concerning these theories, and to analyze the empirical evidence supporting or contradicting this position. Below, we will briefly cover some of the important articles and studies concerning the conditioning of sexual deviations.

O'Donohue and Plaud (1994) reviewed the literature on conditioning of human sexual arousal in several areas including classical conditioning and operant conditioning.

The authors concluded that while there has been a progression in sophistication of the research on classical conditioning and operant conditioning, most of the studies had some potential methodological confounds, or provided only limited support for the theories.

Classical Conditioning

One of the earliest studies on the classical conditioning of sexual arousal was conducted by Rachman (1966). In this study, a photographic slide of a pair of black boots was paired with slides of attractive nude women. Results indicated that a conditioned penile arousal response developed to the slide of the boots, essentially resulting in what might be termed a sexual fetish. Consistent with behavioral accounts of sexual deviation, it was concluded that sexual arousal could be conditioned to previously neutral stimuli. Further, it provided an analogue experiment that sexual deviance may result from the pairing of sexual arousal with some previously neutral stimuli.

Rachman and Hodgson (1968) attempted to replicate Rachman's (1966) original study, and to avoid the potential confounds in the previous study. The authors again reported results of a conditioned penile response, and concluded that they had established an experimental model of sexual fetishism. Unfortunately, their sample size was small, and there were other methodological flaws in the study. For instance, they apparently did not assess the subjects' response to the conditioned stimulus before initiating conditioning, nor did they use random control procedures, or assess for unconditioned effects of the CS. Because of this, effects cannot be determined with certainty. Though both of these studies had some methodological flaws, they were both important steps in discovering the roles of classical conditioning on sexual arousal.

McConaghy (1967) conducted a classical conditioning experiment similar to Rachman's (1966) study, but using motion-picture stimuli instead of static slides. In this study, green and red geometrical figures were paired with the unconditioned stimulus of motion picture films. The results showed that the geometric shapes came to elicit conditioned tumescent responding in the subjects. Unfortunately, this study did not allow for detumescence periods between trials to allow the subjects to return to baseline, which could have accounted for some of the results. This study also suffered from similar problems as Rachman's first study in the area of random control procedures, and so forth.

To date the only laboratory classical conditioning study of male sexual arousal employing appropriate control conditions was conducted by Plaud and Martini (in press). In this study of the conditioning of male sexual arousal nine subjects participated in three sessions. Each session was composed of fifteen stimulus periods and fifteen detumescence periods. Three subjects participated in each of three different experimental conditioning procedures. Sexually explicit visual stimuli preselected by each subject were utilized as the unconditioned stimuli (US), and a neutral slide of a penny jar was employed as the conditioned stimulus (CS). In the first procedure, short delay conditioning, the CS was presented for fifteen seconds, followed immediately by the US for thirty seconds (with a CS/US overlap interval of one second). Interspersed in the fifteen trials were five probe trials in which the CS was presented alone. Following each trial a two-minute detumescence period permitted a return to baseline. The second procedure was a backward conditioning procedure, in which the US was presented before the CS to control for any effects of temporal ordering. In the third procedure, a random control condition, the presentation of CS and US was determined randomly in order to test for nonassociative effects (i.e., a random combination of the first two procedures). Therefore, Plaud and Martini employed two control procedures in order to control for the possibility of pseudoconditioning. Results indicated that subjects showed systematic increases in penile tumescence from baseline in the short delay conditioning procedure, but not in the other two control procedures. Results of this study are presented in Figure 8-1, and highlight the potentially significant role of classical conditioning in the expression of human sexual behavior.

Operant Conditioning

Researchers have demonstrated that it may be possible to condition sexual arousal using an operant conditioning paradigm. Two studies demonstrated that sexual arousal can be increased using reinforcement such as money (Rosen, Shapiro, & Schwartz, 1975), lime juice (Quinn, Harbisan, & McAllister, 1970), and ejaculation (Schaefer & Colgan, 1977). Other researchers have demonstrated that sexual arousal may be decreased using punishment such as an aversive noise (Rosen & Kopel, 1977). Each of these studies, however, had rather severe methodological flaws as to warrant the conclusions questionable (O'Donohue & Plaud, 1994).

Quinn et al. (1970) conducted one of the earliest studies of operant conditioning of sexual arousal with a single homosexual subject. The subject, placed on a water-deprivation schedule, was given sips of lime juice for increases in penile tumescence in the presence of slides depicting nude females. Results of this study indicated that the subject emitted increased levels of penile tumescence in the presence of the female slides at the end of the study relative to his baseline tumescence levels to the same stimuli. Thus, the researchers were successful in establishing a direct contingent relationship between penile tumescence and lime juice (the reinforcing event). Due to the design of this study, however, these researchers could not rule out the possibility that the subject was engaging in homosexual fantasies while viewing the slides of nude females. Finally, since a continuous reinforcement schedule was used in this study, the researchers were not able to test for sensitivity to intermittent reinforcement.

Rosen et al. (1975), using a paradigm somewhat similar to Quinn et al. (1970), demonstrated increased sexual arousal (i.e., penile tumescence) contingent upon monetary reinforcement in a group of twelve male college students compared to twelve subjects in a yoked control group who were provided noncontingent reinforcement. Again, however, the researchers did not test for sexual fantasizing, nor did they test for sensitivity to intermittent reinforcement.

Schaefer and Colgan (1977) demonstrated that ejaculation could be used as reinforcement to operantly condition increases in penile tumescence. Subjects in this study were divided into two groups. Subjects in both groups read a number of pages of erotic scripts individually while their sexual arousal was measured with a penile plethysmograph. One group of subjects (the experimental group) was instructed to masturbate to

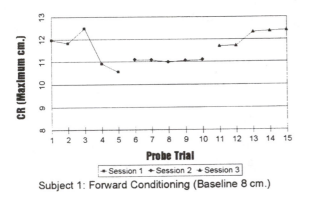

Subject 1: Forward Conditioning (Baseline 8 cm.)

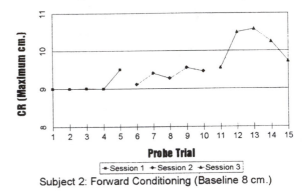

Subject 2: Forward Conditioning (Baseline 8 cm.)

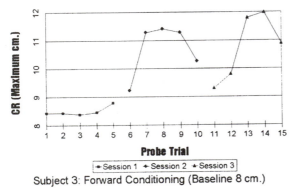

Subject 3: Forward Conditioning (Baseline 8 cm.)

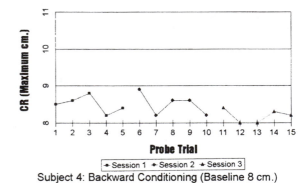

Subject 4: Backward Conditioning (Baseline 8 cm.)

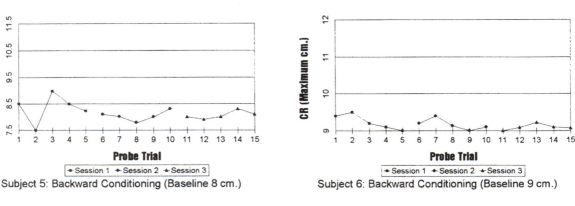

Subject 5: Backward Conditioning (Baseline 8 cm.)

Subject 6: Backward Conditioning (Baseline 9 cm.)

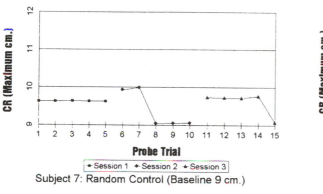

Subject 7: Random Control (Baseline 9 cm.)

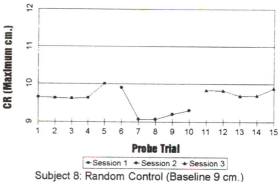

Subject 8: Random Control (Baseline 9 cm.)

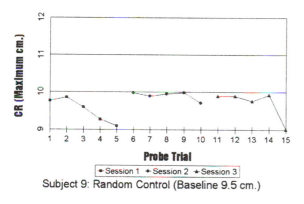

Subject 9: Random Control (Baseline 9.5 cm.)

FIGURE 8-1. Respondent Conditioning and Control Procedures trial data for all subjects in the Plaud and Martini (in press) study. The abscissa plots the five probe trials for each of the three sessions in each procedure. The ordinate represents the maximum penile circumference (in centimeters) for each subject in each trial. The minimum ordinate value is within 0.5 centimeters of each subject's penile baseline circumference, therefore the data in show any penile responding above baseline.

orgasm after reading the scripts, thereby reinforcing the penile response. A control group was instructed to read more nonerotic material until their level of arousal had decreased to within 25 percent of full erection. The results of this study indicated that the experimental group emitted increased penile responses while the control group emitted decreased penile responses. Schaefer and Colgan concluded that this study demonstrated evidence for the hypothesis of McGuire et al. (1965) that sexual reinforcement (ejaculation) may create or at least maintain sexual arousal. The researchers also concluded, however, that the decreased responding by the control group was due to either a punishment of arousal—reading nonerotic material for a longer time for emitting greater levels of arousal (since it takes longer to decrease back to within 25 percent erection when the subject had attained a greater level of arousal)—or habituation. Schaefer and Colgan suggested that habituation was the more parsimonious of the two alternative explanations, though this could not be directly tested.

Other researchers (e.g., Koukounas & Over, 1993; Meuwissen & Over, 1990; O'Donohue & Geer, 1985; O'Donohue & Plaud, 1991; Plaud, Gaither, Amato-Henderson, & Devitt, 1997) have provided evidence of the habituation of sexual arousal that could be seen as a confirmation of this. Figure 8-2 shows the results obtained by Plaud et al. (1997) in demonstrating long-term habituation processes in males.

Rosen and Kopel (1977) successfully established a contingent relationship between decreases in penile tumescence and an aversive noise using a punishment paradigm. Subjects in this study were presented with video stimuli that depicted their sexual preferences while their sexual arousal was measured with a penile plethysmograph. As

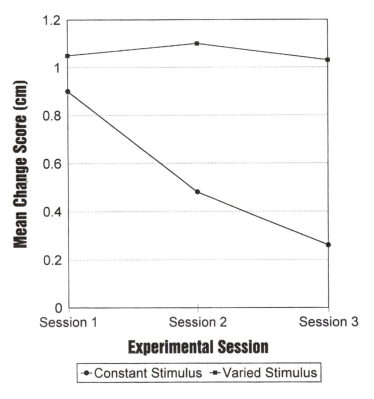

FIGURE 8-2. Physiological arousal (mean change scores in centimeters) by condition across sessions in the Plaud, Gaither, Amato-Henderson, and Devitt (1997) study of long-term habituation. Penile responding only decreased systematically in the constant stimulus condition, providing evidence for the long-term habituation of sexual arousal in human males.

arousal increased, the loudness of the aversive noise (an alarm clock buzzer) also increased. The researchers in this case found that the subjects' levels of penile tumescence decreased while this contingency was in effect. Once again, however, the effects of fatigue or habituation were not ruled out.

Cliffe and Parry (1980) presented the most methodologically complex study of operant conditioning and human sexual arousal to date. The study represented a test of the matching law using a single male pedophile as a subject. The matching law (Hernstein, 1970) basically states that as long as two or more variable-interval schedules of reinforcement are in effect concurrently, a matching relationship will exist between the relative overall number of responses and the relative overall number of reinforcement presentations (O'Donohue & Plaud, 1994). The reinforcement presentations in this study were slides of either children, men, or women.

The subject was tested in three conditions in this study. In each condition, he was presented two boxes each with a number of different colored keys—one box on his left and one box on his right. The two boxes represented two concurrent variable-interval schedules of reinforcement. The variable that was manipulated in this study was the operant choice in which the subject had to make. In one condition, pressing keys on one box resulted in a brief presentation of slides of women, while pressing keys on the opposite box resulted in a brief presentation of slides of children. Thus, the subject was forced to choose which box to spend his time pressing keys on to receive slide presentations. In the second condition the choice involved men versus children, while in the third condition the choice was women versus men.

Cliffe and Parry (1980) hypothesized that the subject would choose behaviors that resulted in presentations of slides of children whenever this was a choice. They further hypothesized that they would be able to use regression analyses to predict how the subject would respond in the third condition (women versus men). Results of the study indicated that although the matching law had correctly described the subject's behavior in all three conditions, the subject chose behaviors which resulted in slides of women over slides of children or men. Cliffe and Parry presented several hypotheses as to why the subject chose the slides of females over slides of children, such as the fact that the subject had recently begun making advances toward women and that the slides of children were of a much lower quality than those of men and women. Whatever the reason, the result of importance here is that the matching law was able to correctly describe the subject's behavior.

Conclusion

Although this chapter has not been an exhaustive review of the laboratory research conducted on the conditioning of sexual arousal, it does seem safe to conclude that there has yet to be a study showing definite support for the conditioning of sexual arousal and/or sexual behavior that is completely free of methodological flaws. Currently, in the psychophysiology laboratory at the University of North Dakota, the present authors are conducting studies in both classical conditioning and operant conditioning of sexual arousal. These studies have been designed to correct for the methodological flaws discovered in the studies discussed above and to provide the evidence necessary to support the conditioning theories of sexual arousal.

While the majority of this chapter has discussed research on and treatment of sexual deviations within the framework of classical or operant conditioning processes, it is very possible that this may be an overly simplistic view of such a complex set of behavioral patterns. To address this possibility, perhaps future research should follow the lead of Cliffe and Parry (1980) by subjecting deviant sexual arousal and/or behavior to analysis under such models as the matching law (Hernstein, 1970), stimulus equivalence (e.g., Plaud, 1995) and behavioral momentum (Nevin, Mandell, & Atak, 1983). These models may lead to the development of innovative treatment techniques for altering deviant sexual behavior patterns.

References

Abel, G. G., & Blanchard, E. B. (1976). The measurement and generation of sexual arousal in male sexual deviates. In M. Hersen, R. Eisler, and R. M. Miller (Eds.), *Progress in Behavior Modification, Vol. 2* (pp. 99–133). New York: Academic Press.

Alford, G. S., Morin, C., Atkins, M., & Schoen, L. (1987). Masturbatory extinction of deviant sexual arousal. *Journal of Behavior Therapy and Experimental Psychiatry, 1,* 59–66.

Alford, G., Plaud, J. J., & McNair, T. L. (1995). Conditioning perspectives on sexual behavior and orientation. In L. Diamant & R. McAnulty (Eds.), *The psychology of sexual orientation, behavior and identity: A handbook* (pp. 121–135). Westport, CT: Greenwood.

Barlow, D. H. (1973). Increasing heterosexual responsiveness in the treatment of sexual deviation: A review of clinical and experimental evidence. *Behavior Therapy, 4,* 655–671.

Barlow, D. H., & Agras, W. S. (1973). Fading to increase heterosexual responsiveness in homosexuals. *Journal of Applied Behavior Analysis, 6,* 355–366.

Barlow, D. H., Agras, W. S., Abel, G. G., Blanchard, E. B., & Young, L. D. (1975). Biofeedback and reinforcement to increase heterosexual arousal in homosexuals. *Behavior Research and Therapy, 13,* 45–50.

Binet, A. (1888). *Le fetichisme dans l'amour.* Paris: Parvot.

Blitch, J. W., & Haynes, S. N. (1972). Multiple behavioral techniques in a case of female homosexuality. *Journal of Behavioral Therapy and Experimental Psychiatry, 3,* 319–322.

Brownwell, K. D., & Barlow, D. H. (1976). Measurement and treatment of two sexual deviations in one person. *Journal of Behavior Therapy and Experimental Psychiatry, 7,* 349–354.

Card, R. D. (1977). A preliminary report of a treatment program for working with various forms of sexual deviancy. *Journal of Sex Education and Therapy, 3,* 5–7.

Card, R. D. (1982). Biofeedback in the treatment of sexual deviation. *American Journal of Clinical Biofeedback, 5,* 31–42.

Cautela, J. R., & Kearney, A. J. (1990). Behavior analysis, cognitive therapy and covert conditioning. *Journal of Behavior Therapy and Experimental Psychiatry, 21,* 83–90.

Clark, D. F. (1965). A note on the avoidance conditioning techniques in sexual disorder. *Behavior Research and Therapy, 3,* 203–206.

Cliffe, M. J., & Parry, S. J. (1980). Matching to reinforcer value: Human concurrent variable-interval performance. *Quarterly Journal of Experimental Psychology, 32,* 557–570.

Colson, C. E. (1972). Olfactory aversion therapy for homosexual behavior. *Journal of Behavior Therapy and Experimental Psychiatry, 3,* 185–187.

Csillag, E. R. (1976). Modification of erectile response. *Journal of Behavior Therapy and Experimental Psychiatry, 7,* 27–29.

Curtis, R. H., & Presley, A. S. (1972). The extinction of homosexual behaviour by covert sensitization: A case study. *Behavior Research and Therapy, 10,* 81–83.

Davison, G. C. (1968). Elimination of a sadistic fantasy by a client-controlled technique: A case study. *Journal of Abnormal Psychology, 73*, 84–90.

Dougher, M. J., Crossen, J. R., Ferraro, D. P., & Garland, R. (1987). The effects of covert sensitization on preference for sexual stimuli. *Journal of Behavior Therapy and Experimental Psychiatry, 18*, 337–348.

Earls, C. M., & Castonguay, L. G. (1989). The evaluation of olfactory aversion for a bisexual pedophile with a single-case multiple baseline design. *Behavior Therapy, 20*, 137–146.

Enright, S. J. (1989). Pedophilia: A cognitive/behavioral treatment approach in single case. *British Journal of Psychiatry, 155*, 399–401.

Feldman, M. P., & MacCulloch, M. J. (1965). The application of anticipatory avoidance learning to the treatment of homosexuality. *Behavior Research and Therapy, 2*, 165–186.

Foote, W. E., & Laws, D. R. (1981). A daily alternation procedure for orgasmic reconditioning with a pedophile. *Journal of Behavior Therapy and Experimental Psychiatry, 12*, 267–273.

Freeman, W., & Meyer, R. G. (1975). A behavioral alteration of sexual preferences in the human male. *Behavior Therapy, 6*, 206–212.

Hanson, R. W., & Adesso, V. J. (1972). A multiple behavioral approach to male homosexual behavior: A case study. *Journal of Behavior Therapy and Experimental Psychiatry, 3*, 323–325.

Haydn-Smith, P., Marks, I., Buchaya, H., & Repper, D. (1987). Behavioral treatment of life threatening masochistic asphyxiation: A case study. *British Journal of Psychiatry, 150*, 518–519.

Hayes, S. C., Brownell, K. D., & Barlow, D. H. (1978). The use of self-administered covert sensitization in the treatment of exhibitionism and sadism. *Behavior Therapy, 9*, 283–289.

Hernstein, R. J. (1970). On the law of effect. *Journal of the Experimental Analysis of Behavior, 13*, 243–266.

Hughes, R. C. (1977). Covert sensitization treatment of exhibitionism. *Journal of Behavior Therapy and Experimental Psychiatry, 8*, 177–179.

Jackson, B. (1969). A case of voyeurism treated by counter conditioning. *Behavior Research and Therapy, 7*, 133–134.

Jaspers, K. (1963). *General psychopathology.* Manchester, England: Manchester University Press.

Johnston, P., Hudson, S. M., & Marshall, W. L. (1992). The effects of masturbatory reconditioning with nonfamilial child molesters. *Behavior Research and Therapy, 30*, 559–561.

Josiassen, R. C., Fantuzzo, J. W., & Rosen, A. C. (1980). Treatment of pedophilia using a multistage aversion therapy and social skills training. *Journal of Behavior Therapy and Experimental Psychiatry, 11*, 55–61.

Keller, D. J., & Goldstein, A. (1978). Orgasmic reconditioning reconsidered. *Behavior Research and Therapy, 16*, 299–301.

Keltner, A. A. (1977). The control of penile tumescence with biofeedback in two cases of pedophilia. *Corrective and Social Psychiatry and Journal of Behavior Technology, Methods and Therapy, 23*, 117–121.

Keltner, A., Scharf, N., & Schell, R. (1979). The assessment and training of assertive skills with sexual offenders. *Corrective and Social Psychiatry and Journal of Behavior Technology, Methods and Therapy, 23*, 88–92.

Kendrick, S. R., & McCullough, J. P. (1972). Sequential phases of covert reinforcement and covert sensitization in the treatment of homosexuality. *Journal of Behavior Therapy and Experimental Psychiatry, 3*, 229–213.

King, M. B. (1990). Sneezing as a fetishistic stimulus. *Sexual and Marital Therapy, 5*, 69–72.

Koukounas, E., & Over, R. (1993). Habituation and dishabituation of male sexual arousal. *Behavior Research and Therapy, 31*, 575–585.

Kremsdorf, R. B., Holmen, M. L., & Laws, D. R. (1980). Orgasmic reconditioning without deviant imagery: A case report with a pedophile. *Behavioral Research and Therapy, 6.* 203–207.

Lamontagne, Y., & Lesage, A. (1986). Private exposure and covert sensitization in the treatment of exhibitionism. *Journal of Behavior Therapy and Experimental Psychiatry, 17*, 197–201.

Langevin, R., & Martin, M. (1975). Can erotic responses be classically conditioned? *Behavior Therapy, 6*, 350–355.

Larson, D. E. (1970). An adaptation of the Feldman and MacCulloch approach to treatment of homosexuality by the application of anticipatory avoidance learning. *Behavior Research and Therapy, 8*, 209–210.

Laws, D. R. (1977). Treatment of bisexual pedophilia by a biofeedback assisted self-control procedure. *Behavior Research and Therapy, 1980*, 207–211.

Laws, D. R. (1985). Sexual fantasy alternation: Procedural considerations. *Journal of Behavior Therapy and Experimental Psychiatry, 16*, 39–44.

Laws, D. R., Meyer, J., & Holmen, M. L. (1978). Reduction of sadistic sexual arousal by olfactory aversion: A case study. *Behavior Research and Therapy, 16,* 281–285.

Leonard, S. R., & Hayes, S. C. (1983). Sexual fantasy alternation. *Journal of Behavior Therapy and Experimental Psychiatry, 14,* 241–249.

LoPiccolo, J., Stewart, R., & Watkins, B. (1972). Treatment of erectile failure and ejaculatory incompetence of homosexual etiology. *Journal of Behavior Therapy and Experimental Psychiatry, 3,* 233–236.

McConaghy, N. (1967). Penile volume change to moving pictures of male and female nudes in heterosexual and homosexual males. *Behavior Research and Therapy, 5,* 281–284.

McCrady, R. E. (1973). A forward-fading technique for increasing heterosexual responsiveness in male homosexuals. *Journal of Behavior Therapy and Experimental Psychiatry, 4,* 257–261.

McGuire, R. J., Carlisle, J. M., & Young, B. G. (1965). Sexual deviation as conditioned behavior. *Behavior Research and Therapy, 2,* 185–190.

McNally, R. J., & Lukach, B. M. (1991). Behavioral treatment of zoophilic exhibitionism. *Journal of Behavior Therapy and Experimental Psychiatry, 22,* 281–284.

Maletzky, B. M., & George, F. S. (1973). The treatment of homosexuality by "assisted" covert sensitization. *Behavior Research and Therapy, 11,* 655–657.

Marquis, J. N. (1970). Orgasmic reconditioning: Changing sexual object choice through controlling masturbation fantasies. *Journal of Behavior Therapy and Experimental Psychiatry, 1,* 263–271.

Marshall, W. L. (1973). The modification of sexual fantasies: A combined treatment approach to the reduction of deviant sexual behavior. *Behavior Research and Therapy, 11,* 557–564.

Marshall, W. L. (1979). Satiation therapy: A procedure for reducing deviant sexual arousal. *Journal of Applied Behavior Analysis, 12,* 377–389.

Marshall, W. L., & Barbaree, H. E. (1978). The reduction of deviant arousal: Satiation treatment for sexual aggressors. *Criminal Justice and Behavior, 5,* 294–303.

Marshall, W. L., Eccles, A., & Barbaree, H. E. (1991). The treatment of exhibitionists: A focus on sexual deviance versus cognitive and relationship features. *Behavior Research and Therapy, 29,* 129–135.

Marshall, W. L., & Lippens, K. (1977). The clinical value of boredom: A procedure for reducing inappropriate sexual interests. *Journal of Nervous and Mental Disease, 165,* 283–287.

Meuwissen, I., & Over, R. (1990). Habituation and dishabituation of female sexual arousal. *Behavior Research and Therapy, 28,* 281–284.

Moergen, S. A., Merkel, W. T., & Brown, S. (1990). The use of covert sensitization and social skills training in the treatment of an obscene telephone caller. *Journal of Behavior Therapy and Experimental Psychiatry, 21,* 269–275.

Nevin, J. A., Mandell, C., & Atak, J. R. (1983). The analysis of behavioral momentum. *Journal of the Experimental Analysis of Behavior, 39,* 49–59.

O'Donohue, W. T., & Geer, J. H. (1985). The habituation of sexual arousal. *Archives of Sexual Behavior, 14,* 233–246.

O'Donohue, W. T., & Plaud, J. J. (1991). The long-term habituation of human sexual arousal. *Journal of Behavior Therapy and Experimental Psychiatry, 22,* 87–96.

O'Donohue, W. T., & Plaud, J. J. (1994). The conditioning of human sexual arousal. *Archives of Sexual Behavior, 23,* 321–344.

Pinard, G., & Lamontagne, Y. (1976). Electrical aversion, aversion relief, and sexual retraining in treatment of fetishism with masochism. *Journal of Behavior Therapy and Experimental Pyschiatry, 7,* 71–74.

Plaud, J. J. (1995). The formation of stimulus equivalences: Fear-relevant versus fear-irrelevant stimulus classes. *The Psychological Record, 45,* 207–222.

Plaud, J. J., Gaither, G. A., Amato-Henderson, S., & Devitt, M. K. (1997). The long-term habituation of sexual arousal in human males: A crossover design. *The Psychological Record, 47,* 385–398.

Plaud, J. J., & Martini, J. R. (In press). The respondent conditioning of male sexual arousal. *Behavior Modification.*

Quinn, J. T., Harbisan, J. J., & McAllister, H. (1970). An attempt to shape human penile responses. *Behavior Research and Therapy, 8,* 213–216.

Rachman, S. (1961). Sexual disorders and behavior therapy. *American Journal of Psychiatry, 118,* 235–240.

Rachman, S. (1966). Sexual fetishism: An experimental analogue. *Psychological Record, 16,* 293–293.

Rachman, S., & Hodgson, R. J. (1968). Experimentally-induced "sexual fetishism": Replication and development. *Psychological Record, 18,* 25–27.

Rangaswamy, K., (1987). Treatment of voyeurism by behavior therapy. *Child Psychiatry Quarterly, 20,* 73–76.

Rosen, R. C. (1973). Suppression of penile tumescence by instrumental conditioning. *Psychosomatic Medicine, 35,* 509–514.

Rosen, R. C., & Kopel, S. A. (1977). Penile plethysmography and biofeedback in the treatment of a transvestite-exhibitionist. *Journal of Consulting and Clinical Psychology, 45,* 908–916.

Rosen, R. C., Shapiro, D., & Schwartz, G. E. (1975). Voluntary control of penile tumescence. *Psychosomatic Medicine, 37,* 479–483.

Schaefer, H. H., & Colgan, A. H. (1977). The effect of pornography on penile tumescence as a function of reinforcement and novelty. *Behavior Therapy, 8,* 938–946.

Stava, L., Levin, S. M., & Schwanz, C. (1993). The role of aversion in covert sensitization treatment of pedophilia: A case report. *Journal of Child Sexual Abuse, 2,* 1–13.

Thorpe, J. G., Schmidt, E., Brown, P. T., & Castell, D. (1964). Aversion-relief therapy: A new method for general application. *Behavior Research and Therapy, 2,* 71–82.

Thorpe, J. G., Schmidt, E., & Castell, D. (1963). A comparison of positive and negative (aversive) conditioning in the treatment of homosexuality. *Behavior Research and Therapy, 1,* 357–362.

Thorpe, J. G., Schmidt, E., & Castell, D. (1964). Aversion-relief therapy: A new method for general application. *Behavior Research and Therapy, 2,* 71–82.

Turner, S. M., & Van Hasselt, V. B. (1979). Multiple behavioral treatment in a sexually aggressive male. *Journal of Behavior Therapy and Experimental Psychiatry, 10,* 343–348.

Van Deventer, A. D., & Laws, D. R. (1978). Orgasmic reconditioning to redirect sexual arousal in pedophiles. *Behavior Therapy, 9,* 748–765.

Wolfe, R. W. (1992). Video aversive satiation: A hopefully heuristic single-case study. *Annals of Sex Research, 5,* 181–187.

9

CHILD CONDUCT AND DEVELOPMENTAL DISABILITIES: FROM THEORY TO PRACTICE IN THE TREATMENT OF EXCESS BEHAVIORS

JOSEPH R. SCOTTI
Department of Psychology
West Virginia University

KIMBERLY B. MULLEN
Department of Psychology
West Virginia University

ROBERT P. HAWKINS
Department of Psychology
West Virginia University

The practice of behavior analysis and therapy is closely linked with the treatment of excess behaviors of children and persons with developmental disabilities. It is with these populations (in addition to persons with chronic psychiatric disorders, see Scotti, McMorrow, & Trawitzki, 1993) that behavioral principles were first used during the period in the 1950s to 1960s when behavior analysis was moving from the operant laboratory to the clinical setting (see also Salzinger, Chapter 5, this volume). According to Wolpe (1982), Skinner and Lindsley, in 1954, first offered the term "behavior therapy" for the application of "experimentally established principles and paradigms" (p. 1) to clinical problems. In this chapter, we briefly discuss the development of applied behavior analysis and behavior therapy from a set of laboratory procedures to established clinical techniques, emphasizing work with children and persons with developmental dis-

Preparation of this manuscript was partially funded by a grant to the first author from the West Virginia Developmental Disabilities Planning Council, which is gratefully acknowledged. We would also like to acknowledge "Ignatius," whose behavior confounded, and whose passing saddened, those around him.

abilities. We then review current strategies for intervening with these populations, pointing out links to basic theory and principles. Finally, we contrast the approaches taken in these two areas, as it will be seen that although both link behavior theory to behavior therapy, they do so in rather different ways.

Early Development of Behavior Analysis

Behavior analysis can be described as an attempt to reinvent psychology—or rather behavioral science—taking a natural science approach, the kind of objective approach taken in biology, chemistry, or geology. The beginning of this "reinvention" is best attributed to Skinner (1938, 1945, 1953, 1974, 1981), but in the past fifty years it has engaged an ever-increasing number of scientists and practitioners worldwide. A fundamental premise of this group is that the best strategy for a science of behavior is to view the science as a study of the relation between environment and behavior.

Applied behavior analysis thus refers to the application of the natural science of behavior to issues of practical importance to individuals and society (Baer, Wolf, & Risley, 1968; Hawkins, 1991; Wolf, 1978). However, the initial applications of these principles were only approximations of this, because the results did not have directly valuable effects. For example, Fuller (1949) showed that a man with profound retardation and multiple handicaps, who was considered totally beyond learning, could be taught to raise his arm by making squirts of sweetened milk contingent upon small arm movements. This could hardly be called a "significant habilitative step" for that particular man, because it did not lead to further training (although had such training followed, it might have been important; see Black & Meyer, 1992); but it did demonstrate that the basic principles and procedures discovered in the infrahuman laboratory were applicable to potentially important human behavior (see Evans & Scotti, 1989, for other examples).

Many other "classic" early studies typify the laboratory research approach involving often arbitrary responses with clinical patients and children in order to demonstrate that their behavior was controlled by the arranged contingencies—a dramatic revelation at the time (e.g., Ayllon, Haughton, & Hughes, 1965; Azrin & Lindsley; 1956; Hutchinson & Azrin, 1961; Issacs, Thomas, & Goldiamond, 1960; Lindsley, 1956; Staats, 1964; Staats & Staats, 1963). However, by the late 1950s, behavior analysts around the country were beginning to apply behavior principles and procedures to the production of *significant* behavior changes. One of the first data-based examples involved the elimination of the bedtime tantrums of a small child through a simple extinction procedure conducted by the parents (Williams, 1959). Other early examples involving children at the University of Washington preschool included the use of extinction and differential reinforcement to reduce the crying of two boys (Hart, Allen, Buell, Harris, & Wolf, 1964), the reinstatement of walking in a child who had regressed to crawling (Harris, Johnston, Kelley, & Wolf, 1964), teaching mothers to manage the tantrum and uncooperative behavior of their children (Hawkins, Peterson, Schweid, & Bijou, 1966; Wahler, Winkel, Peterson, & Morrison, 1965), and work with children with developmental disabilities (Risley & Wolf, 1966; Wolf, Birnbrauer, Williams, & Lawler, 1965; Wolf, Risley, & Meese, 1964).

As behavior problems are conceptualized as having been learned from the environments in which the person has lived, the natural progression for behavior analysts was to involve persons indigenous to the child's natural environment in interventions. This led to studies involving parents and teachers as both change agents and as the targets of change—an important facet of behavioral intervention that continues today. Some early examples include the work of Hawkins et al. (1966), and Tharp and Wetzel (1969) with parents; teacher-initiated interventions such as by Allen, Hart, Buell, Harris, and Wolf (1964), and Hawkins and colleagues (Hawkins, 1971; Hawkins & Hayes, 1974); and joint home–school collaborations (Hawkins, Sluyter, & Smith, 1972). Within a few years, numerous studies with a similar focus were appearing, especially in the *Journal of Applied Behavior Analysis*, and several conferences were held at the University of Kansas on behavior analysis in education (e.g., Brigham, Hawkins, Scott, & McLaughlin, 1976; Ramp & Hopkins, 1971; see also Klein, Hapkiewicz, & Roden, 1973), with broad impact continuing to be evident in many departments of special education and school programs (Becker, 1978; Greer, 1992; Johnson & Layng, 1992).

From Established Principles to Best Practices

These research and clinical developments provide only a meager sample of efforts to apply principles and procedures from the basic laboratory to clinically meaningful problems, as would easily be discovered by a perusal of bibliographies containing hundreds of studies from this period in applied behavior analysis (e.g., Scotti, Trawitzki, Vittimberga, & McMorrow, 1991; Scotti, Walker, Evans, & Meyer, 1991b). This early body of work was very exciting and attracted a great deal of interest in psychology and related fields, leading to the development of numerous intervention strategies for children, adult psychiatric patients, and persons with developmental disabilities (see Bellack & Hersen, 1985; Martin & Pear, 1996).

Clearly, many of the most common behavioral intervention strategies are directly based on operant principles derived from the laboratory. Examples include reward systems that use positive reinforcement (e.g., food, tokens, "star charts"); punishment in the form of response-cost programs (e.g., loss of tokens) or presentation of aversive events (e.g., scolding); extinction, through "planned ignoring" or escape extinction (see Iwata, 1987); and stimulus control and fading procedures, such as the systematic fading of instructional prompts. Any reasonably complete text on operant principles can provide multiple examples of infrahuman research demonstrating these basic processes, and a thorough text on behavior analysis, modification, or therapy can show the application of these processes to the clinical setting. Thus, we need not take time to delineate examples at this more basic level of application. However, as the field of applied behavior analysis developed, it became evident that certain strategies could be considered best practices. Although not immediately obvious, these best practices have much in common with the experimental literature in terms of basic principles and methods. For instance, a cornerstone of the current approach to intervention with excess behaviors of persons with developmental disabilities is the *functional analysis,* defined by Haynes and O'Brien (1990) as "the identification of important, controllable, causal functional relationships applicable to a specified set of target behaviors for an individual" (p. 654). A functional analysis may be either descriptive or data-based and will consider those variables that can be controlled or manipulated, including antecedents, consequences, and contextual variables (e.g., Iwata, Dorsey, Slifer, Bauman, & Richman, 1982; O'Neill, Horner, Albin, Storey, & Sprague, 1990).

Functional Analysis

In the operant chamber, functional relations among antecedent stimuli, responses, and consequent events were readily identified and controlled by the experimenter. As a result, early applications to the behavior and clinical problems of humans either assumed that a similar degree of control was available or it was obtained in ways that were often naive and unproductive when compared to the complex and multi-determined nature of human behavior, typical and abnormal. The functional relation of interest in early behavior analytic studies was between a clinician-controlled antecedent and/or consequent stimulus (primarily the latter) and the response of the client. Demonstration of control exerted by stimuli through such manipulations, and the measurement of attendant outcome, is the essence of good experimental design (Johnston & Pennypacker, 1980); however, this emphasis on consequences may well have lead to the proliferation of ever more inventive ways to punish undesirable behavior, obtaining control by merely directly decelerating (and rarely eliminating) the response of interest. As noted by Scotti et al. (1991b), the apparent strategy often was to use a sufficiently powerful intervention—generally a punishing consequence—under the assumption that the target behavior could be controlled *without* considering either the original or the maintaining causes of that behavior, thus, in a sense, "overwhelming the controlling variables, regardless of what they were" (p. 252; see also Hawkins, 1975, 1986; Iwata, 1994). However, as demonstrated by several reviews of the developmental disabilities literature (e.g., Lennox, Miltenberger, Spengler, & Erfanian, 1988; Scotti et al., 1991b), this strategy did not always stand up to empirical test.

This lack of complete success is perhaps because of a crucial difference in the analysis of functional relations in basic versus applied work. In the laboratory, one proceeds by asking "Of what variables can I make behavior a function?" That is, "If variable X is manipulated, will there be a predictable change in behavior Y?" This is clearly the form of functional analysis to be found in early applied studies: "If reinforcement is withheld, will the behavior decrease in frequency?" This form of functional analysis is actually a post hoc description of outcome—a functional relation between variables. This approach also implicitly assumes a "naive" organism; that is, an organism with no "experimental history" that might confound the interpretation of the outcome—clearly a hold-over from the animal laboratory.

On the other hand, applied behavior analysts—recognizing that clients come to the intervention context with a learning history—have begun to apply functional analysis in an a priori fashion. That is, functional analysis is employed prior to initiating an intervention to ascertain the current controlling variables so that these may then be systematically manipulated. Such a pre-intervention analysis of the function of the target behavior is now an accepted standard of practice in behavior analysis and therapy, particularly in developmental disabilities, along with matching the subsequent intervention to the identified function of the behavior (see Scotti, Ujcich, Weigle, Holland, & Kirk, 1995). Studies are even beginning to demonstrate the differential efficacy of interventions selected on the basis of a *function-treatment match* (Eifert, Evans, & McKendrick, 1990; Repp, Karsh, Munk, & Dahlquist, 1995), versus a *mismatch* (Iwata et al., 1994; Repp, Felce, & Barton, 1988), a crucial step in demonstrating the validity and utility of such an approach.

Additional Best Practices

The functional analysis, then, essentially returns us to our roots in the operant laboratory as we again examine closely the variables of which behavior is a function and manipulate those variables, rather than ignoring them and relying on "powerful" procedures. The return to a functional analysis of behavior is only the most recent of several practices to be emphasized in the disabilities literature; however, it has also served to heighten awareness of other model intervention components. These other features include (1) target behavior and intervention selection based on a constructional or educative approach, (2) monitoring of collateral behavior changes, (3) intervention context and generalization of gains, and (4) fading of intervention procedures. Each of these practices has a link to established principles and procedures in the experimental literature and bears a particular relation to the process of functional analysis, as will be shown below.

The current emphasis on *fully inclusive environments* as a best practice—versus "integration" or "mainstreaming," which has often meant parallel services and settings, rather than provision of services for all children in the regular education classroom (see Giangreco & Putnam, 1991)—brings to a new level the importance, in applied work, of context, generalization, and fading. Inclusion of children with disabilities in typical environments is not just a best practice in the sense of being ethical and humane, but it is also a sound practice from the point of view of being good behavior analysis. First, it has long been thought that excess behaviors of persons with developmental disabilities may be attributed to the *deficit environments* into which they are segregated, with restricted opportunities for typical routines and activities, and with peers who model undesired rather than socially acceptable behavior (see Bruininks, Meyers, Sigford, & Lakin, 1981; Emerson, McGill, & Mansell, 1994; Nisbet, Clark, & Covert, 1991). Second, the typical strategy in disabilities has been an "eliminative" model in which the focus is first on the deceleration of excess behaviors—in the very environments that likely maintain them (Meyer & Evans, 1989). The eliminative view is that once excess behaviors are reduced, the person is ready for training to remedy skill deficits, after which they can finally enter the real world outside the walls of the segregated setting.

However, applying basic principles, it is sensible to take an "educative" approach and teach skills to replace excess behaviors, and to do so in the very environments in which they will be used, such as the regular education classroom (Meyer & Evans, 1989). Such an inclusive, educative approach also takes advantage of typical peers as models of acceptable behavior and provides a context of "natural" (i.e., typical) reinforcers and punishers for desired and undesired behavior within which any specific intervention strategy can be faded (see Scotti, Evans, Meyer, & DiBenedetto, 1991a). Thus, both learning and the generalization of interventions are enhanced by an inclusive environment as the similarity between the training and performance environments is maximized, the full range of relevant stimuli and response variations naturally arise, and incidental opportunities arise in the normal course of the daily routine (rather than being artificially created)—all basic principles of generalization that are thus explicitly created rather than implicitly expected (see O'Neill & Reichle, 1993; Meyer & Evans, 1989; Stokes & Baer, 1977).

The importance of functional analysis here is in the recognition of deficit environments as being antecedents or setting events for excess behaviors, and as providing reinforcement for those excess behaviors, while at the same time failing to reinforce socially desirable skills. Given this understanding, it follows that persons should be placed into typical environments that naturally create the occasion for, reinforce, and support desirable behavior. However, a primary concern in such an educative approach is that of response relations and functional equivalence, to which we now turn.

Response Relations

The concept of response relations (i.e., response classes, hierarchies, and chains; concurrent operants) is an old one in behavior analysis, reaching back to the earliest writings in this field (Keller & Schoenfeld, 1950; Skinner, 1938, 1953; Staats & Staats, 1963). However, in recent years, response relations has become an increasingly important focus in the behavioral analysis of intervention side effects—notably surrounding the controversy over the use of aversive procedures (e.g., overcorrection, electric shock). The issue has been one of whether interventions cause side effects, that is, unplanned or unconsidered changes in other than the targeted response. It would appear that such effects do occur (Newsom, Favell, & Rincover, 1983), and this is well predicted by the basic infrahuman literature (see Azrin & Holz, 1966; Catania, 1968). However, the problem has repeatedly been one of grossly inadequate documentation of such effects, either positive or negative (Scotti et al., 1991b, 1996).

Still, recognition of the problem of side effects has brought a new appreciation for response class phenomena and an understanding that interventions can be structured so as to take advantage of response organization, rather than bemoan it (Scotti et al., 1991a). The human and infrahuman experimental literatures suggest that "to decrease an undesired response, increase a desired one" by providing evidence of the relations between responses within a system (e.g., Azrin & Holz, 1966; see also Crosbie, 1993; Dunham, 1972; Dunham & Grantmyre, 1982). Initially conceptualized as the "fair-pair" rule, this strategy called for reinforcing some other response while decelerating the undesired target behavior. However, it is simply *not* sufficient to employ differential reinforcement strategies where the *O* in DRO (Differential Reinforcement of Other Behavior) is *any* response other than the target (Vittimberga, Weigle, &, Scotti, in press); this is a potentially useful procedure, but is comparatively weak clinically (see Carr, Robinson, & Palumbo, 1990; Carr, Robinson, Taylor, & Carlson, 1990; Scotti et al., 1991b). Thus, the process has been refined as the teaching of *functionally equivalent* responses, that is, a response with the same function, or in the same response class, as the targeted excess behavior (see Carr et al., 1994; Reichle & Wacker, 1993). This, we are finding, is leading more often to both the increase in nonaversive forms of intervention and the decreased need to provide any form of consequence for the targeted behavior other than extinction (see Iwata, 1994; Iwata et al., 1994; Scotti et al., 1991a, 1991b, 1996).

The functional analysis plays an important role in determining not only the function(s) of targeted excess behaviors (e.g., self-injury), but in identifying potential replacement behaviors for the targeted excess (e.g., hand raising). In the best of cases, assessment would determine the presence in the repertoire of functionally equivalent skills. These would then be selectively reinforced to the exclusion of the excess behavior. On the other hand, assessment may determine the presence of other excess behaviors with the same function as the targeted excess (i.e., both self-injury and aggression may obtain attention from a teacher). The situation then becomes one of multiple behaviors (i.e., several excesses and one desired skill) serving the same function—a response class. A simple consequence-based intervention might then be to punish self-injury when it occurred. However, this leaves to chance whether the other behaviors in the response class will also decrease in frequency (i.e., generalization) or may actually increase. The latter might occur if attention continues to result from aggression or hand-raising (an outcome that looks like what has been called symptom-substitution, see Kazdin, 1982). An educative approach to this situation would involve differentially attending to hand-raising and ignoring self-injury *and* aggression—an intervention plan that could only be specified on the basis of a pre-intervention functional analysis and a knowledge of response relations.

Although much of the early work in applied behavior analysis was directly based on principles of learning derived from the operant laboratory, target behaviors were viewed in only the most simple of ways—as a single, isolated operant. This unsophisticated conceptualization is clearly derived from the status of laboratory work at the time of the emergence of applied behavior analysis from the lab. However, viewing clinically relevant target behaviors as comparable to the lever-press or key-peck response in the operant chamber can only go so far. The point here is that, at long last, a more complete conceptualization of human behavior in the clinical situation has arisen from a return to basic principles. One caution, however, is that this return to principles has been slow in coming and is not yet complete, at least as judged by the consistency with which those principles are applied in the intervention literature. As a case in point, we turn to the applied literature on child conduct disorders.

Current Application: Child Conduct and Oppositional Defiant Disorders

The past three decades have seen a progressive advancement of behavioral technology for the remediation of childhood conduct and oppositional defiant disorders. Children with conduct disorder are those who engage in a persistent pattern of behavior in which the basic rights of others, or major age-appropriate societal norms or rules are violated, including such behaviors as aggression, property damage, theft, and serious rule violations. A less severe disorder, but one that might presage conduct disorder, is oppositional defiant disorder, which involves a recurrent pattern of negativistic, defiant, disobedient, and hostile behavior toward authority figures (see American Psychiatric Association, 1994, for the full diagnostic criteria). The occurrence of oppositional defiant and conduct disorder behavior is considered a serious childhood problem as it may result in placement in restrictive or segregated environments, such as group homes, special classrooms, or institutions. Further, exhibition of these behaviors in childhood has been correlated with adulthood psychopathology, including alcoholism, drug abuse, and criminal activity (Forehand & McMahon, 1981; Webster-Stratton, 1994).

An Overview of Parent-Intervention Packages

A common intervention used to address the excess behavior of children with conduct or oppositional disorders involves teaching parents to apply procedures that change the environmental variables influencing their child's behavior, on the assumption that parental skills deficits are contributing factors to the development and maintenance of child behavior problems (McMahon & Wells, 1989; Webster-Stratton, 1994). Thus, the aim of such programs is to indirectly change child behavior by directly changing parenting behavior (Patterson, 1982). Although a wealth of parent-training packages exist, few have been empirically studied for their clinical effects, with most of these being packages modified from a two-stage parenting skills model developed by Hanf (1969; e.g., Barkley, 1987; Eyberg, 1988; Forehand & McMahon, 1981; Webster-Stratton, 1982b; cf. Patterson, Reid, Jones, & Conger, 1975). In this section, we will first present the Forehand and McMahon (1981) parent-intervention package, and then highlight the differences between that package and those of Eyberg (1988), Webster-Stratton (1982b), and Patterson et al. (1975).

The Forehand Model of Parent Training

Formulation of Noncompliant Behavior

The Forehand and McMahon (1981) program is designed to teach parents skills for decreasing noncompliant behavior of children ages three to eight years, the focus being on how parents interact with their children. Noncompliant behavior is defined as refusal to initiate or complete a request, or failure to cooperate with a rule that has either been directly stated (e.g., "No jumping on the furniture") or is implicitly understood (e.g., no fighting). Thus, nearly all child excess behavior can be conceptualized as "noncompliant behavior" (Forehand & McMahon, 1981). The Patterson (1976a) "coercion hypothesis," which gives a pivotal role to negative reinforcement, is the primary model for conceptualizing the development and maintenance of noncompliant behavior. In the Patterson model, parental directives represent aversive stimuli for the child that are responded to in an aversive, counter-controlling manner (i.e., noncompliance). To this counter-controlling response, the parent may terminate the command, thus negatively reinforcing the child's noncompliant behavior. Occasionally, the parent may respond to the child's noncompliance with further coercive behavior of their own (e.g., yelling, threatening, punishment), to which the child may respond by terminating their noncompliance. Thus, on some occasions the parent's coercive behavior is negatively reinforced, and at other times the child's coercive behavior is negatively reinforced. Over time, the coercive behavior of both parent and child escalates in intensity. Forehand and McMahon (1981) recognize another contributor to the development and maintenance of noncompliant behavior: the "positive reinforcement trap" (Wahler, 1975). In this situation, noncompliance is positively reinforced by parental attention, such as the parent talking with the child about their behavior (Wahler, 1975), or, for some children, the negative attention provided by parents during a coercive interaction (Patterson, 1976a).

Assessment

Assessment, in the Forehand and McMahon (1981) program, focuses on analyzing the nature of the parent-child interaction—the actual behaviors exhibited by both parties. Multiple methods are used to determine parent and child behaviors that constitute antecedents, responses, and consequences of coercive parent-child interactions. Components of the initial assessment are included both during and following intervention to assess behavior change in terms of (a) the quality and quantity of the parent's attending, command deliverance, and implementation of time-out; and (b) the frequency of the child's compliance to commands and rates of excess behavior. Additionally, parent perception of parent and child overall adjustment and marital satisfaction (when appropriate) are identified, and reassessed at postintervention and follow-up.

These goals are accomplished during the assessment process through direct observation in a clinic playroom, with the parent being instructed to interact with the child in two ways: (1) participating in any activity that the child chooses, with the child determining the rules of the play (simulating a free-play situation); and (2) engaging the child in activities whose nature and rules are determined by the parent (simulating a command situation). Similar naturalistic observations are also made in the home. Finally, a series of questionnaires are completed by the parents, supplementing the clinical interview, followed by in-home data collection of parent-identified target behaviors.

Intervention

In accordance with the basic assumptions of the Forehand and McMahon (1981) model, the focus of intervention involves changing the interactions between parent and child. Two principal techniques are taught to parents, using clinic-based didactic instruction, modeling, role-play, and observational feedback: (1) *differential attention*, so the parent becomes a better reinforcing agent and can increase positive child behaviors; and (2) *effective commands and disciplinary techniques* to decrease the rate of child excess behavior. It is important that the positive techniques are taught first, as some parents will discontinue the program prior to learning the positive strategies if discipline techniques are taught first.

Teaching differential reinforcement.   The differential reinforcement phase of the package teaches parents how to reinforce appropriate behaviors, while ignoring minor inappropriate ones. A necessary prerequisite to this is being able to provide meaningful positive attention to the child, thus parents are first instructed in the "Child's Game." During this game, parents refrain from commands, questions, and criticisms, and provide positive attention via ongoing verbal description of the child's appropriate behaviors ("labeled praise"; see Bernhardt & Forehand, 1975). The purpose is to teach the parent to observe the child's behavior and identify behaviors that the child engages in appropriately, and provide a context for the child within which appropriate behavior is reinforced and thus comes under stimulus control of the parent (also increasing the parent's value as a conditioned positive reinforcer). After learning the reward component, parents are taught how to effectively ignore (e.g., avoiding eye contact, physical contact, other nonverbal responses, and verbal comments about the behavior) mild inappropriate behavior—behavior that does not have the potential to damage themselves, others, or property. These skills are practiced during clinic sessions, with feedback to the parents.

Teaching skills to decrease noncompliance.   The second phase of the program teaches parents how to decrease any continuing noncompliant behavior by altering the antecedents and consequences of the command situation. Parents are taught to provide effective commands (antecedents), and how to reward compliance and discipline noncompliance (consequences). Parents are educated about research demonstrating that some children do not comply when commands are vague, lengthy, or confusing (Forehand & Scarboro, 1975; Roberts, McMahon, Forehand, & Humphreys, 1978; Williams & Forehand, 1984). Thus, they are taught to make commands that are direct, single statements, easily understood by their child, with praise following compliance to such commands.

Parents are also taught to enforce all commands so that noncompliant behavior is not negatively reinforced by termination of the demand. This involves implementing a time-out procedure if the child does not begin to comply with a command within five seconds. The time-out procedure is based on empirical research demonstrating which components are associated with the greatest subsequent compliant behavior (Hobbs & Forehand, 1975; Hobbs, Forehand, & Murray, 1978; Scarboro & Forehand, 1975). Only after parents have demonstrated the proper use of time-out in the clinic is it implemented in the home setting.

Outcome Research

A number of studies have investigated the effectiveness and generalizability of the Forehand and McMahon parent training package. Short-term effectiveness has been demonstrated for both child and parent behaviors in two early studies (Forehand & King, 1974, 1977). In addition, generalization from the clinic to home settings was demonstrated by Peed, Roberts, and Forehand (1977); however, two other studies failed to find generalization of gains from clinic to school settings (Breiner & Forehand, 1981; Forehand et al., 1979). Studies of maintenance over a period of six months up to five years are also qualified in their results. Forehand et al. (1979) showed maintenance of positive changes in parent and child behavior and maternal reports, despite decreased maternal use of contingent attention. However, Baum and Forehand (1981) demonstrated that child noncompliant behavior remained less frequent at follow-up despite some decreases in parental skills.

Maintenance over even longer periods has also been studied. For instance, Forehand and Long (1988) did a follow-up of adolescents who had participated in the Forehand and McMahon (1981) program four to ten years previously, finding that, on most measures of adolescent function, parent-intervention children were indistinguishable from a comparison group of non clinic adolescents. Finally, Long, Forehand, Wierson, and Morgan (1994) evaluated the functioning (in terms of relationship with parents, delinquency, emotional adjustment, and academic performance) of twenty-six late adolescents whose families had participated in parent training approximately fourteen years earlier. In comparison to a matched community sample, the parent-training group was no different than the control group on any measure. Despite a number of methodological concerns (see below), these studies provide impressive evidence for the effectiveness of parent-training programs with this population.

Additional Parent-Training Packages

Parent-Child Interaction Therapy

The Parent-Child Interaction Therapy (PCIT) program, developed by Sheila Eyberg, a colleague of Constance Hanf, is another two-stage model of parent intervention that addresses preschool-aged child noncompliance and conduct disorder. The essential difference between the Eyberg (1988) model and the Forehand and McMahon program (1981) is the further development of, and emphasis on, teaching parents effective play-therapy skills for use during the child-directed interaction component, including: (a) following the child's lead; (b) omission of commands, questions, and criticisms; and (c) a high rate of description and imitation of the child's motor behavior, with reflection of the child's verbal behavior. Eyberg (1988) suggests that effective play skills are important social behaviors for parents to teach to their children, and parental utilization of play-therapy skills should lead to relationship enhancement—making "time-in" more valuable to the child and time-out more potent in its effects. A second important difference between the Forehand and McMahon (1981) and Eyberg (1988) packages is the addition of a standardized behavioral rating scale, the Eyberg Child Behavior Inventory (ECBI; Robinson, Eyberg, & Ross, 1980), to the assessment phase. The ECBI provides evaluation of (a) the child's behavior with respect to standardized norms, (b) whether parental expectations of child behavior are too high or low, and (c) intervention effects.

Outcome studies with parent–child dyads completing PCIT have indicated a change in child behavior on the ECBI from outside of normal limits at pretreatment assessment to within normal limits at post-treatment (Eisenstadt, Eyberg, McNeil, Newcomb, & Funderburk, 1993; Eyberg & Robinson, 1982; Eyberg & Ross, 1978). Similar improvements in other measures of compliance, problem behavior, and activity level, as well as maternal stress and direct observation of parent–child behaviors have been noted (Eisenstadt et al., 1993; Eyberg & Matarazzo, 1980). Furthermore, McNeil, Eyberg, Eisenstadt, Newcomb, and Funderburk (1991) found postintervention generalization of intervention gains from the home to school setting in children exhibiting conduct problems in both settings.

Videotape Modeling and Group Discussion Program

A parent-intervention program for young (three to eight years old) children with a unique method of delivery was developed by Webster-Stratton (1982b). This program involves many of the same strategies employed by Forehand and McMahon, however it has a self-contained educational package that can be conducted with groups of parents (as compared to the individual case focus of the other packages). The program utilizes ten videotaped vignettes to demonstrate effective and ineffective parenting skills for groups of parents, and the therapist leads a discussion of the relevant treatment components after each vignette. Parents are then instructed to practice their new skills at home. The authors note that videotaped modeling offers a relatively cost-effective training technique and has the potential to facilitate mass distribution. Outcome studies demonstrate the effectiveness of this video-modeling approach, with a number of variants apparently being equally effective (Webster-Stratton, 1982a, 1982b, 1984; Webster-Stratton, Hollinsworth, & Kolpacoff, 1989; Webster-Stratton, Kolpacoff, & Hollinsworth, 1988).

A Social Learning Approach to Families with Aggressive Children

Patterson and his colleagues (1975) have designed a program that, unlike the other packages discussed here, is not based on Hanf's two-stage model. This program consists of three phases of parent intervention. First, parents are taught the basic concepts of social learning theory, and must read and demonstrate mastery of material in one of two books, *Families* (Patterson, 1975) or *Living with Children* (Patterson, 1976b). In the second phase, parents are taught to define and monitor specific child target behaviors (two excess behaviors and two prosocial behaviors). The third phase teaches parents to implement a reinforcement system using points (exchanged daily for child-selected items) and labeled praise contingent on the identified positive behaviors. When the reinforcement system is well-established, the parents are taught to implement a five-minute time-out procedure for noncompliant or aggressive behavior (a response-cost procedure is used with older children). As parents learn these skills, they become increasingly responsible for applying them to various child conduct problems. Finally, parents are taught problem-solving and negotiation skills to address marital difficulties, family crises, and parental adjustment difficulties. Outcome studies with the Patterson et al. (1975) program have demonstrated short-term effectiveness (Patterson, 1974; Patterson, Cobb, & Ray, 1973; Patterson & Reid, 1973), and evidence for setting, behavior, and temporal (one year post-treatment) generalization of treatment gains (Arnold, Levine, & Patterson, 1975; Patterson, 1974; Patterson, Chamberlain, & Reid, 1982).

Summary of Parent-Intervention Packages

In summarizing the parent-intervention packages, it is useful to review them in terms of the philosophy, assessment procedures, treatment strategies, and outcome research, linking these back to basic principles of behavior.

Philosophy

These programs conceptualize child noncompliance and conduct disordered behavior as the result of a coercive pattern of interaction between the parent and child that escalates through a repeated cycle of negative and positive reinforcement. Thus, the goal of intervention is to alter—indirectly—the parent–child interaction via teaching parents new interactional skills. Child excess behavior is conceptualized as being under stimulus control, such that parental commands set the occasion for noncompliance that, when intense enough, will result in removal of the demands. Additionally, these programs recognize a deficiency in the frequency of parental positive reinforcement for appropriate behavior.

Assessment

The primary goal of assessment within these packages is to identify and describe the problem behaviors of the child within an environmental system that includes the parent. Parent and child behaviors are identified through multiple methods, creating an analysis of the relation between the two participants in the interaction. Emphasis is placed on measuring levels of child noncompliant or conduct disordered behavior with standardized instruments, allowing a comparison to a normal sample and permitting the clinician to (a) judge whether the child's behavior is statistically outside of normal limits, (b) obtain a baseline level of disruptive behavior, and (c) facilitate communication about the severity of the problem behavior. However, the direct target of intervention is parental behavior—the context within which child behavior occurs.

Intervention

The assessment described above is not a true functional analysis in the sense that the motivation of an *individual* child's behavior is not systematically determined; instead the parent and child are compared to group norms to see if they fit the "coercive family process model." Once the family is determined to be a good fit to the model, parents are taught a systematic, "packaged" set of procedures designed to modify maintaining antecedents and consequences. The goal is to change the stimulus control of parental demands from setting the occasion for noncompliant behavior to that of compliant behavior. This requires parental consistency in following through with directives, thus removing the negatively reinforcing consequences (i.e., escape extinction). Punishment is applied if warranted, in the form of time-out. However, to ensure that time-out serves as a removal from a desirable situation (rather than removal from an undesirable situation, such as a demand), the parent is taught ways to interact in a positive manner with the child. This pairing of the parent with positive events is conditioned reinforcement; making the removal of the parent's attention during time-out an undesired (i.e., punishing) event.

Outcome Research

Considerable empirical evidence supports the short-term behavioral change in both children and parents following participation in a parent-training package. Although studies of maintenance have generally reported durability of intervention gains, conclusions from these studies must be tempered by several methodological concerns, including (a) lack of detailed information about the severity of problem behaviors (e.g., Baum & Forehand, 1981), (b) questionable clinical significance of pre- to post-intervention changes (e.g., Baum & Forehand, 1981), (c) families using other therapeutic services following their participation in parent training (i.e., Forehand & Long, 1988), and (d) the exclusive use of adolescent self-report data to determine current functioning (Long et al., 1994). Finally, although parents have been found to generalize their skills to the home and other settings, generalization of child gains to school settings has not been consistently demonstrated.

To conclude, parent-intervention packages have been shown to be a promising method for reducing child excess behavior associated with conduct and oppositional defiant disorders. These standardized packages teach persons indigenous to the child's natural environment to use several of the basic principles and procedures that flow from laboratory research, including reinforcement and punishment, conditioned and differential reinforcement, and extinction. It should be noted that the use of individualized functional analysis is lacking from these packages, a deficiency also common to the attention-deficit hyperactivity literature (Kirk, in press), as well as the developmental disabilities literature, to which we now return.

Current Application: Excess Behavior of Persons with Developmental Disabilities

Use of Best Practices

A number of reviews of the intervention literature on the excess behaviors of persons with developmental disabilities have been conducted; the most recent and inclusive being those of Lennox et al. (1988) and Scotti and colleagues (1991b). These reviews were statistical meta-analyses that shared the goal of investigating the use and differential efficacy of aversive and nonaversive intervention strategies. Although Scotti et al. (1991b) covered a longer time period and more journals than did Lennox et al., both reviews similarly concluded that there was little evidence for a claim of differential efficacy of any particular group of procedures. Complicating the findings, both reviews revealed a disappointingly low level of adherence to commonly accepted standards of practice, particularly with regard to the use of functional analysis. For example, Lennox et al. found that only one-third of studies employed a pretreatment functional analysis, with 18 percent referring to some form of Antecedent-Behavior-Consequence (A-B-C) analysis and only 6 percent having conducted more intensive empirical analyses (e.g., analog manipulations).

Scotti and his colleagues (1991b) also reported the rates of other standards of practice in some 403 studies published in 1976 through 1987. These practices included (a) active programming (i.e., a background context of typical and useful activities) in 35 percent of studies, (b) generalization strategies (30 percent of studies), (c) follow-up data (50 percent, equally split between those of less than versus those of greater than six months duration), (d) change in collateral (i.e., nontargeted) behaviors (one-third of studies), (e) normalized settings (i.e., integrated community settings; fewer than 5 percent of studies), (f) nonintrusive strategies (about 40 percent of studies, with no evidence of employing a hierarchy from least to most intrusive interventions), and (g) skill-building as a primary intervention component (less than 10 percent of studies).

Although these findings are discouraging with regard to the fidelity with which investigators incorporate certain standards into their practices, a subsequent review by Scotti et al. (1996) of 179 studies suggests some improvement in the published literature over the subsequent years (1988 through 1992). For instance, Scotti et al. (1996) noted increased active programming (53 percent of studies), a greater focus on generalization (59 percent) and monitoring of collateral behavior change (61 percent, with a dramatic increase in *data-based* monitoring), an increased use of functional analysis (48 percent), and a greater proportion of nonaversive strategies (especially reinforcement-based and skill-building approaches). Still, only 10 percent of studies in the 1996 review provided evidence of having performed all five of the most central best practices (i.e., functional analysis, monitoring collateral behaviors, active programming, generalization, follow-up), a figure similar to the 1991 review. Additionally, the context of studies remained almost exclusively segregated settings.

Functional Analysis and Treatment-Function Matching

Evolving from the concept of excess behaviors being functional, the matching of treatment to the function of targeted excess behaviors has arisen as perhaps the single most important best practice in the literature. Because the analysis by Scotti et al. (1991b) suggested that performance of a functional analysis was a critical contributor to intervention effectiveness scores, it was heartening to note that not only did the rate of performing pre-intervention functional analyses more than double by the time of the 1996 review, but more of the analyses were data-based. The 1996 review found that over half of those studies performing a functional analysis employed empirical procedures, such as direct observation (e.g., A-B-C), experimental analogs (e.g., Iwata et al., 1982), interviews, or questionnaires prior to the intervention, with one-third reporting two or more of these methods. However, although the identified functions (e.g., escape, attention, access to tangibles) did appear to vary by targeted excess behavior, there remained little evidence that either the identified function or the target behavior itself (i.e., the topography) bore any relation to the final selection of an intervention. That is, neither *function* nor *structure* formed the basis for a differential selection of interventions, a discouraging result for several reasons besides the violation of current best practices.

First, this finding is contrary to a small but steadily growing data-base that suggests the differential efficacy of function-based interventions (Iwata et al., 1994; Repp et al., 1988). Second, it has been suggested that a focus on function will lead to (a) a reduced use of aversive interventions and a greater emphasis on nonaversive and skill-building strategies (Axelrod, 1987), and (b) increased intervention effectiveness at the time of follow-up with greater ease of generalization (Carr et al., 1994; Durand, 1990; Reichle & Wacker, 1993). Finally, it has been suggested that greater attention to the function of target behaviors will result in an increased focus on the multiple behaviors—both excessive and desirable—within a person's repertoire, and how those responses are interrelated (Scotti et al., 1991a). This latter point in particular holds hope for reducing multiple excess behaviors by increasing the efficacy of current skills, thereby also reducing the problem of treatment side effects. Each of these issues has been touched upon in earlier sections of this chapter. We turn now, however, to a further explication of the evidence for response relations and then provide actual case data as a means of demonstrating several of the attendant points.

Response Class Relations, Assessment, and Intervention

The continuing "problem" of side effects. A number of reviews have focused on an explication of behavioral interrelations and the problem of side effects in both the child behavior therapy (Evans, Meyer, Kurkjian, & Kishi, 1987; Voeltz & Evans, 1982) and developmental disabilities literatures (Matson & Taras, 1989; Newsom et al., 1983; Scotti et al., 1991b, 1996). Depending on one's position in the debate over intrusive interventions, it has often been assumed that aversive procedures either cause many undesirable side effects (i.e., increases in other excess behaviors, decreases in desirable skills) or many desirable side effects (i.e., concomitant decreases in non targeted excess behaviors, increases in desirable skills). Unfortunately, there are few studies that have empirically documented the effects of an intervention on other than the targeted excess behavior. Reviews (Matson & Taras, 1989; Newsom et al., 1983; Scotti et al., 1991b) do suggest that side effects tend to be predominantly "positive" rather than "negative" as a result of intervention—whether that intervention is an aversive or nonaversive one. But, as Scotti and colleagues (Scotti et al., 1991b, 1996) have repeatedly pointed out, there is little empirical basis for such statements, as the few studies that do address collateral effects usually do so only anecdotally and without empirical data. Scotti et al. (1996) noted that over half of published studies are now providing information on collateral intervention effects (an increase from 37 percent noted by Scotti et al., 1991b). Even more encouraging is that over two-thirds of these reports are data-based; however, this often means that simple percentages, and not graphic displays, are provided, thus severely limiting the interpretation of effects.

Still, this improving data-base continues to suggest a preponderance of positive over negative side effects, a result that remains questionable, however, because there is no a priori basis for deciding which collateral behaviors should be monitored (i.e., authors can decide to emphasize positive over negative effects). The problem remains that, despite an improving data-base, the theoretical basis for analyzing collateral effects is weak. Researchers generally do not discuss collateral effects as a response class phenomenon, with a common function(s) across multiple behaviors (Scotti et al., 1996); nor do they conduct pre-intervention functional analyses of the collateral behaviors, including potential replacement skills.

Overlap of response classes and functions.   Since the classic paper by Carr (1977), it has been increasingly recognized and documented that excess behavior is a function of environmental variables. Thus, when we speak of the function of a behavior as being, say, to escape a demand, we mean that removal of the demand is an event that frequently follows the occurrence of the excess behavior, thus negatively reinforcing it. As researchers move away from the earlier emphasis on single, isolated operants (Evans & Scotti, 1989; Scotti et al., 1991a) and begin to look at repertoires of behavior, it has become evident that (a) a single excess behavior may have more than one function, such as a history of being followed sometimes by attention and sometimes by removal of demands; (b) that several behaviors may have the same function, such as self-injury and aggression both leading to removal of demands; and (c) that the same topography of behavior *across individuals* does not imply the same function for that behavior for each of those individuals. Adding to these observations, it is now recognized that other behaviors within a person's repertoire that are desirable skills, and not excesses, may also have functions similar to some excess behavior. Thus, a student might raise his hand to get the attention of the teacher (a desirable skill), but failing to do so, hit the classmate next to him (an excess behavior). These more elaborate response class relations between excesses and desired skills hold specific implications for assessment and intervention that have not been well addressed in the literature (Evans & Meyer, 1985; Meyer & Evans, 1989; Scotti et al., 1991a).

A number of published studies well document these points. For example, in an analog functional analysis of the self-injury of nine persons with developmental disabilities, Iwata et al. (1982) demonstrated that for any one individual self-injury might serve one function (e.g., escape) or multiple functions (e.g., escape and attention). Day, Horner, and O'Neill (1994) obtained similar results for the self-injurious behavior of two individuals, as well as the aggressive behavior of a third person. Of course, a single individual may exhibit several excess behaviors, with several possible relations among them. First, different topographies of behavior may have different functions. This result is seen in a study by Derby et al. (1994), in which, for one individual, self-injury had the function of access to attention and stereotypic behavior functioned to escape demands; the opposite pattern was observed for a second individual. Lastly, multiple behaviors within the repertoire of a single individual may serve the same function, as shown by Sprague and Horner (1992) in an analysis of the tantrum behavior of two students. The tantrums consisted of multiple behaviors (e.g., yelling, hitting others, head/body shaking, hitting objects) that covaried with each other and functioned to escape from demands. Sprague and Horner demonstrated that as one member of the response class decreased, other behaviors would increase if not also consequated.

Functional Assessment: Single versus Multiple Behaviors

It is beyond the scope of this chapter to provide even a brief discussion of the methodology of functional assessment; however, a brief listing with appropriate references might assist the unfamiliar reader at this point. The major categories of functional analysis methods are (a) interviews (O'Neill et al., 1990; Willis, LaVigna, & Donnellan, 1987), (b) questionnaires (e.g., Motivation Assessment Scale; Durand & Crimmins, 1988; Durand & Kishi, 1987), (c) direct observation in natural environments using an A-B-C (Bijou, Peterson, & Ault, 1968/1973; Lerman & Iwata, 1993; O'Neill et al., 1990; Repp & Karsh, 1990) or similar format (Touchette, MacDonald, & Langer, 1985), and (d) analog experimental manipulations (Evans, 1971; Iwata et al., 1982). All of these strategies, with the exception of the last, employ a descriptive or correlational methodology; only analogs employ direct experimental manipulation of setting events and consequences in order to ascertain the effect on the targeted behavior. Typically, each of these methods is employed with a small number of excess behaviors—generally one. The focus is on determining the function of only the excess behavior. Existing skills are considered with regard to their availability as alternative responses; however, the function of these skills is more often assumed than actually assessed.

Analog Assessment of Multiple Behavior and Functions: An Example
At this point, a case example might help clarify both the method of analog assessment, the multiple functions of behaviors, and the incorporation of alternative skills into the functional assessment process. In this example, Ignatius, a fourteen-year-old male with profound mental retardation, was assessed due to severe, chronic self-injurious head-hitting. He also exhibited related aggression (hitting, grabbing clothing) and property

destruction (turning over furniture, throwing objects), and several potential replace-ment skills: touching others on the upper arm (physical contact) and manual signing ("juice," "cracker," "walk").

The analog assessment proceeded by creating three conditions: (1) *Control,* during which Ignatius was alone in a room and leisure materials were freely available; (2) *Attention,* during which Ignatius was ignored until he exhibited a target behavior, with this being followed by twenty seconds of interaction with the investigator; and (3) *Task,* during which a task was presented and Ignatius was guided to participate until he exhibited a target behavior, which then terminated the task for twenty seconds. Each of these fifteen-minute conditions was repeated ten times; however, in a variation from usual procedures, the conditions were alternately conducted such that the target response was either an excess behavior (self-injury, aggression, destruction) or an alternative skill (engaged with materials, physical contact, signing). This procedure allowed an empirical demonstration of the function of both the excess and alternative behaviors in conditions during which they were alternately reinforced (attention or escape) or ignored (see Scotti et al., 1991a).

Figure 9-1 presents the results of the analog assessment for the excess behaviors. It can be seen that the rates of self-injury are high in all conditions, reflecting an ongoing rate of several times per minute regardless of the condition. However, relative to the

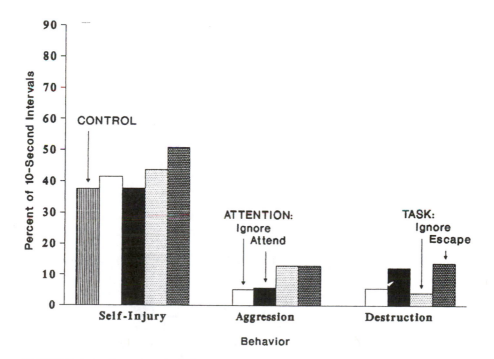

FIGURE 9-1   Results of analog assessment of *excess behaviors.* Contingen-cies were in effect for excess behaviors under the Task and Attention condi-tions. Alternative behaviors were ignored in all conditions.

baseline Control condition, self-injury occurred most often when it resulted in escape from an ongoing task. Aggression was higher under the two Task conditions, even when it did not directly result in task removal. Destruction, however, had two functions, that of escape from task and obtaining attention. Thus, these data provide an example of several excess behaviors having the same function, and one behavior having two functions.

Figure 9-2 presents the results of the analog for the alternative skills. Engagement with materials was highest under the baseline Control condition, suggesting a stimulatory or automatic reinforcement function, with the rates of engagement decreasing as attention or task removal were made contingent on being engaged. Physical contact was highest when it resulted in attention, and lowest under the Task conditions. Finally, signing occurred at low rates, if at all, in each condition, appearing to function primarily for attention. Again, a case of multiple behaviors with a similar function. Here, however, it has been demonstrated that desirable skills have functions similar to those of the identified excess behaviors.

Although it is only partially evident in these two figures, the targeted excess and alternative behaviors are related in additional ways: response covariation and chains. For example, a chain of behaviors with the function of obtaining attention became evident during the assessment. Ignatius would be engaged with materials, signing, and making physical contact. This would be followed, however, by self-injury and destruction, and finally by aggression, when attention (interaction with the investigator) was not forth-

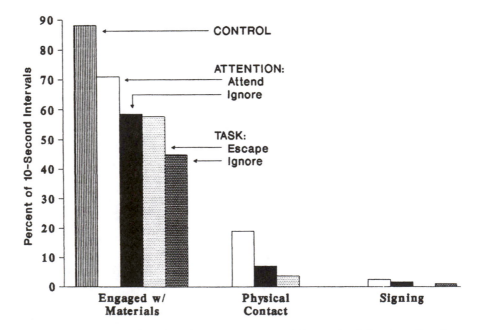

FIGURE 9-2   Results of analog assessment of *alternative behaviors*. Contingencies were in effect for alternative behaviors under the Task and Attention conditions. Excess behaviors were ignored in all conditions.

coming. Similarly, during task conditions, Ignatius would alternately engage in self-injury and signing—this latter response primarily being requests for food or a walk—thus effectively interrupting the task (this alternation is an example of concurrent operants; Catania, 1968; Ferster & Skinner, 1957). Continuation of the task was then likely to result in aggressive and/or destructive behavior. These distinct chains of responses might also be considered conceptually as representing response hierarchies, where more probable responses occur first and are followed by other responses in the class when these earlier responses do not result in attention or escape.

Finally, evidence of response covariation is seen in the analog assessment when comparing the differential rates of responding under the analogs that focused on the targeted excess behaviors versus those focusing on the alternative behaviors. For example, the behaviors of physical contact and destruction of property both function to obtain attention. Thus, under the Attention condition, when physical contact results in attention and destruction is ignored, the rates of physical contact are higher than destruction. When the contingencies are reversed (i.e., ignore contact and attend to destruction), the relative rates of the two behaviors also reverse. Such an analysis of response covariation adds further information regarding the function of physical contact, previously suggested to function to obtain attention. Yet it may be seen that physical contact alternates in frequency with destructive behavior, occurring when destruction was ignored and failing to occur when destruction results in escape. Thus, based on the prevailing contingencies, two behaviors (physical contact and destruction) covary, within a response class with a common function of escape.

Formulating an intervention based on function and response relations.   The above analysis of the function of both excess and alternative behaviors and their response interrelations provides information that easily leads into an intervention plan. Some immediate reduction in excess behavior should be attainable merely by differentially reinforcing selected members of the escape and attention response classes, under the appropriate conditions. Thus, under Task conditions, physical contact and signing would be allowed to result in a brief suspension of demands, with an expected decrease in self-injury and destruction. Furthermore, under situations of low rates of social interaction, independent initiation of social interactions by Ignatius (through physical contact and signing) would be responded to with brief periods of interaction and compliance with his requests for food or a walk; a decrease in destructive behavior would then be expected.

Once begun, such a strategy would be modified in two ways. First, the alternative behaviors of physical contact and signing would be shaped into more and more socially acceptable responses. Thus, physical contact, initially consisting of touching another person on the arm, would be shaped into a handshake and then hand raising, such as students do to gain a teacher's attention in a typical classroom. Signing would also be shaped, but in a different way. The signs for "juice," "cracker," and "walk" would continue to be useful signs, and additional signs would be introduced, such as "stop," "help," "work," and "play," so that Ignatius could directly request either a break from or assistance with a task, rather than signing for "juice" (which results in a break from the task but is a less direct communication).

The second modification would be to fade-in natural contingencies. Ignatius would be required to wait for increasing periods of time to take a break or engage in a social interaction, until the schedule of reinforcement more closely resembled that seen in typical work and social settings (i.e., not every request for a break or an interaction is responded to immediately). As the form and timing of requests became more similar to those of typical environments, the natural social contingencies would increasingly strengthen these desirable behaviors, allowing for maintenance and generalization of the skills. At the same time, rates of excess behaviors should continue to be low and decelerating—if indeed they occur at all within such an intervention—one that does not include direct consequences for excess behaviors.

Does This Strategy Work?

Although the literature on the challenging behavior of persons with developmental disabilities is replete with examples of consequence-based interventions that are often punitive and not based upon the function of the targeted behavior, a dramatic shift in the general approach to challenging behavior is well under way. This change in approach might even be considered a paradigm shift because of the considerable difference in emphasis on proactive, constructional, or educative procedures that are function-based and involve teaching functionally equivalent skills, as opposed to the simple deceleration of excess behaviors through often heavy-handed consequences.

Without a doubt, the overarching paradigm remains the behavior analytic framework with a focus on the relation between behavior and environment, as well as its distinct single-subject methodology (Johnston & Pennypacker, 1980). But if a paradigm is in part defined by its methodology and theoretical concepts (Kuhn, 1970; Staats, 1990), it should be clear that a new (or perhaps only a *renewed*) focus on function and response-relations has arisen, with a concurrent alteration in the approach to modifying behavior. Clearly, a focus on functional relations was a key theme and achievement in Skinner's "radical" behaviorism (Delprato & Midgley, 1992; Moxley, 1992). However, the shift noted earlier in this paper—and of essential importance to clinical intervention—is from a focus on demonstrating functional relations (i.e., experimental control) to assessing and then employing those relations in a subsequent manipulation of environmental events (i.e., therapy). Furthermore, a shift has occurred in the desired outcome of interventions, from that of the simple deceleration of excess behaviors to meaningful lifestyle changes, including the acquisition of new skills, the absence of negative side effects, movement to less restrictive placements, improvements in subjective quality of life for the target persons and significant others, and expanded social relationships (Meyer & Evans, 1989; 1993).

It is perhaps too early to determine whether the function-based educative approach to intervention will succeed any better than its predecessor, the eliminative approach. However, the literature reviews discussed earlier suggest ever more examples of the approach are being published. The most recognized approach within this paradigm is *functional communication training*, which has its roots in the seminal analysis of Ted Carr (1977), with multiple case examples and theoretical treatments by Carr and Mark Durand. Parrish and Roberts (1993) provide a chronology of the development of this specific approach, but some key references include Carr and Durand (1985a, 1985b), Durand and Carr (1987, 1991), Durand (1990), and Carr et al. (1994). The approach has gained many adherents too numerous to mention here, but a good start on such a list might begin by scanning the contents of recent issues of the *Journal of Applied Behavior Analysis* and the *Journal of the Association for Persons with Severe Handicaps,* as well as several recent books (Koegel, Koegel, & Dunlap, 1996; Reichle & Wacker, 1993, among others). In these sources, the accumulating evidence for this approach is to be found. However, while the function-based approach can be shown to work, the literature remains light on evidence that supports the differential efficacy over more traditional eliminative approaches, as noted earlier.

Indeed, there remain problems with the very heart of this approach—the functional analysis. A thorough functional analysis may not always result in hypotheses that are valid or which lead to interventions that produce a successful outcome (Anderson, 1995; Scotti, Schulman, & Hojnacki, 1994). Alternately, an inconclusive functional analysis does not mean that treatment will be unsuccessful (Vollmer, Marcus, & LeBlanc, 1994). A perusal of any number of studies on functional analysis will reveal a wide range in the methods employed (e.g., interview, questionnaire, A-B-C, analog) and even in the manner in which similar methods are implemented. For example, there are few guidelines as to which conditions should be included in an analog functional analysis (e.g., O'Neill et al., 1990), or how long such assessment should be (i.e., a single one-hour session versus repeated fifteen-minute sessions). In fact, there appears to be poor agreement, in terms of the derived function, between different methods of functional analysis (Scotti, Weigle, et al., 1993) and between brief versus extended versions of analogs (Scotti, Kirk, et al., 1993). Additionally, the more structured and removed from the natural environment the assessment is, the more likely there will be a problem with generalizing the assessment results to the treatment setting (Scotti et al., 1994). Furthermore, the assessment of function has focused heavily on the relation of behavior to its immediate consequences, almost to the exclusion of both proximal (e.g., room temperature, social context, physical pain and illness) and distal (i.e., hunger, fatigue) setting events (see Evans, 1971; Halle & Spradlin, 1993). Still, the approach holds great promise, especially when a hypothesis-testing approach can be integrated into the assessment and intervention process (see Repp et al., 1995; Scotti et al., 1994).

Conclusions

In concluding this chapter, there are two points that summarize both the literatures on child behavior disorders and excess behaviors in developmental disabilities and their relation to behavior theory and therapy—the theme of this book. First, it should be noted that both of the literatures discussed here, and their attendant therapeutic approaches, are well backed by behavioral principles drawn from theoretical models that owe much to the basic research emanating from the human and infrahuman research laboratories of the earlier part of this century. They, in short, both embody the movement from basic theory to clinical application, holding consistent to that theory in the process of adapting to a variety of clinical behaviors and settings. In fact, in holding true to basic principles, it is most amazing how the two literatures have departed in their approaches to often similar behaviors and circumstances.

The departure we note here (described more fully elsewhere; Mullen, 1995) is a difference in the strategies taken during the assessment and intervention processes. First, it should be clear that the child behavior therapy literature has largely held to the eliminative approach to intervention. The various intervention packages focus on consequences to excess behavior (note that where reinforcement of skills is employed, this is primarily of the skill of "compliance," which is *not* a functionally equivalent replacement for excess behavior). The developmental disabilities literature, although clearly strongly immersed in the eliminative approach until recently, has instead begun to endorse a more educative or constructional approach to intervention. These two approaches to intervention are also linked to two disparate forms of assessment. In parent-intervention packages, the assessment is largely to confirm the occurrence of problematic behavior by reference to group norms that establish what behavior, or frequency of behavior, is outside of normal limits. In the disabilities literature, on the other hand, we see a nearly exclusive focus on the individual—without direct reference to group norms—and a focus on the individualized functional analysis.

These two models are thus diverging in an interesting way that could be described as a focus on *structure* versus *function* (Scotti, Morris, McNeil, & Hawkins, 1996). In focusing on structure, the parent-intervention programs establish the occurrence of certain behavior, and then apply an intervention package that is based on a theory of why conduct problems occur. Thus, these packages are largely applied in the same, rather prescriptive manner, for each child meeting the diagnostic criteria. The functional analysis model employed in the disabilities literature, however, may make some basic theoretical assumptions about the maintaining causes of excess behavior, but the process is an attempt to determine the specific function and causes for each person individually, and only then create a tailor-made intervention. Although basic strategies may be similar (i.e., conduct a functional analysis, teach functionally equivalent replacement skills, modify aspects of the setting), how these are accomplished will vary from person to person, based on the functional assessment.

We will note, however, that both the package approach and the function-based approach have had their successes, they are not mutually exclusive procedures (Arndorfer & Miltenberger, 1993; Luiselli, 1991), and both remain theory driven and data-based. Yet there remain many questions to address in both areas, including the relative benefits of function-treatment matching versus packaged approaches; the differential efficacy of specific function-based interventions; the role of specific intervention components in outcome and maintenance, especially that of teaching functionally equivalent replacement skills; and the role of education and training for parents, teachers, and other care providers in the success of these interventions. These and other assessment-related issues will remain to be addressed and will become increasingly important in both the current managed health-care environment and the move toward empirical validation of psychological treatments (American Psychological Association, 1995).

References

Allen, E. K., Hart, B. M., Buell, J. S., Harris, F. R., & Wolf, M. M. (1964). Effects of social reinforcement on isolate behavior of a nursery school child. *Child Development, 35,* 511–518.

American Psychiatric Association. (1994). *Diagnostic and statistical manual of mental disorders* (4th ed.). Washington, D C: Author.

American Psychological Association: Task Force on Promotion and Dissemination of Psychological Procedures, D. L. Chambless (Chair). (1995). Training in and dissemination of empirically-validated psychological treatments: Report and recommendations. *The Clinical Psychologist, 48*(1), 3–23.

Anderson, C. M. (1995). *Functionally-derived treatments: An empirical validation.* Unpublished master's thesis, Department of Psychology, West Virginia University, Morgantown.

Arndorfer, R. E., & Miltenberger, R. G. (1993). Functional assessment and treatment of challenging behavior: A review with implications for early childhood. *Topics in Early Childhood Special Education, 13,* 82–105.

Arnold, J. E., Levine, A. G., & Patterson, G. R. (1975). Changes in sibling behavior following family intervention. *Journal of Consulting and Clinical Psychology, 43,* 683–688.

Axelrod, S. (1987). Functional and structural analyses of behavior: Approaches leading to reduced use of punishment procedures. *Research in Developmental Disabilities, 8,* 165–178.

Ayllon, T., Haughton, E., & Hughes, H. B. (1965). Interpretation of symptoms: Fact or fiction. *Behaviour Research and Therapy, 3,* 1–7.

Azrin, N. H., & Holz, W. C. (1966). Punishment. In W. K. Honig (Ed.), *Operant behavior: Areas of research and application* (pp. 380–447). New York: Appleton-Century-Crofts.

Azrin, N. H., & Lindsley, O. R. (1956). The reinforcement of cooperation between children. *Journal of Abnormal and Social Psychology, 52,* 100–102.

Baer, D. M., Wolf, M. M., & Risley, T. R. (1968). Some current dimensions of applied behavior analysis. *Journal of Applied Behavior Analysis, 1,* 91–97.

Barkley, R. A. (1987). *Defiant children: A clinician's manual for parent training.* New York: Guilford.

Baum, C. G., & Forehand, R. (1981). Long term follow-up assessment of parent training by use of multiple outcome measures. *Behavior Therapy, 12,* 643–652.

Becker, W. C. (1978). The national evaluation of Follow Through: Behavior-theory-based programs come out on top. *Education and Urban Society, 10,* 431–458.

Bellack, A. S., & Hersen, M. (1985). *Dictionary of behavior therapy techniques.* New York: Pergamon.

Bernhardt, A. J., & Forehand, R. (1975). The effects of labeled and unlabeled praise upon lower and middle class children. *Journal of Experimental Child Psychology, 19,* 536–543.

Bijou, S. W., Peterson, R. F., & Ault, M. H. (1973). A method to integrate descriptive and experimental field studies at the level of data and empirical concept. In R. D. Klein, W. G. Hapkiewicz, & A. H. Roden (Eds.), *Behavior modification in educational settings* (pp. 44–77). Springfield, IL: Charles C. Thomas. (Reprinted from *Journal of Applied Behavior Analysis, 2,* 175–191, 1968.)

Black, J. W., & Meyer, L. H. (1992). But . . . is it really work? Social validity of employment training for persons with very severe disabilities. *American Journal on Mental Retardation, 96,* 463–474.

Breiner, J., & Forehand, R. (1981). An assessment of the effects of parent training on clinic-referred children's school behavior. *Behavioral Assessment, 3,* 31–42.

Brigham, T. A., Hawkins, R., Scott, J. W., & McLaughlin, T. F. (1976). *Behavior analysis in education: Self-control and reading.* Dubuque, IA: Kendall/Hunt.

Bruininks, R. H., Meyers, C. E., Sigford, B. B., & Lakin, K. C. (Eds.). (1981). *Deinstitutionalization and community adjustment of mentally retarded people* (Monograph #4). Washington, DC: American Association on Mental Deficiency.

Carr, E. G. (1977). The motivation of self-injurious behavior: A review of some hypotheses. *Psychological Bulletin, 84,* 800–816.

Carr, E. G., & Durand, V. M. (1985a). Reducing behavior problems through functional communication training. *Journal of Applied Behavior Analysis, 18,* 111–126.

Carr, E. G., & Durand, V. M. (1985b). The social-communicative basis of severe behavior problems in children. In S. Reiss & R. R. Bootzin (Eds.), *Theoretical issues in behavior therapy* (pp. 219–254). New York: Academic Press.

Carr, E. G., Levin, L., McConnachie, G., Carlson, J. I., Kemp, D. C., & Smith, C. E. (1994). *Communication-based intervention for problem behavior: A user's guide for producing positive change.* Baltimore: Paul H. Brookes.

Carr, E. G., Robinson, S., & Palumbo, L. W. (1990). The wrong issue: Aversive versus nonaversive treatment. The right issue: Functional versus nonfunctional treatment. In A. C. Repp & N. N. Singh (Eds.), *Perspectives on the use of nonaversive and aversive interventions for persons with developmental disabilities* (pp. 361–379). Sycamore, IL: Sycamore Press.

Carr, E. G., Robinson, S., Taylor, J. C., & Carlson, J. I. (1990). Positive approaches to the treatment of severe behavior problems in persons with developmental disabilities: A review and analysis of reinforcement and stimulus-based procedures. *Monographs of the Association for Persons with Severe Handicaps, 4.*

Catania, A. C. (Ed.). (1968). *Contemporary research in operant behavior.* Glenview, IL: Scott, Foresman.

Crosbie, J. (1993). The effects of response cost and response restriction on a multiple-response repertoire in humans. *Journal of the Experimental Analysis of Behavior, 59,* 173–192.

Day, H. M., Horner, R. H., & O'Neill, R. E. (1994). Multiple functions of problem behaviors: Assessment and intervention. Special issue: Functional analysis approaches to behavioral assessment and treatment. *Journal of Applied Behavior Analysis, 27,* 279–289.

Delprato, D. J., & Midgley, B. D. (1992). Some fundamentals of B. F. Skinner's behaviorism. Special issue: Reflections on B. F. Skinner and psychology. *American Psychologist, 47,* 1507–1520.

Derby, K. M., Wacker, D. P., Peck, S., Sasso, G., DeRaad, A., Berg, W., Asmus, J., & Ulrich, S. (1994). Functional analysis of separate topographies of aberrant behavior. Special issue: Functional analysis approaches to behavioral assessment and treatment. *Journal of Applied Behavior Analysis, 27,* 267–278.

Dunham, P. J. (1972). Some effects of punishment upon unpunished responding. *Journal of the Experimental Analysis of Behavior, 17,* 443–450.

Dunham, P. J., & Grantmyre, J. (1982). Changes in a multiple-response repertoire during response-contingent punishment and response restriction: Sequential relationships. *Journal of the Experimental Analysis of Behavior, 37,* 123–133.

Durand, V. M. (1990). *Severe behavior problems: A functional communication training approach.* New York: Guilford.

Durand, V. M., & Carr, E. G. (1987). Social influences on "self-stimulatory" behavior: Analysis and treatment application. *Journal of Applied Behavior Analysis, 20,* 119–132.

Durand, V. M., & Carr, E. G. (1991). Functional communication training to reduce challenging behavior: Maintenance and application in new settings. *Journal of Applied Behavior Analysis, 24,* 251–264.

Durand, V. M., & Crimmins, D. B. (1988). Identifying the variables maintaining self-injurious behavior. *Journal of Autism and Developmental Disorders, 18,* 99–117.

Durand, V. M., & Kishi, G. (1987). Reducing severe behavior problems among persons with dual sensory impairments: An evaluation of a technical assistance model. *Journal of the Association for Persons with Severe Handicaps, 12,* 2–10.

Eifert, G. H., Evans, I. M., & McKendrick, V. G. (1990). Matching treatments to client problems not diagnostic labels: A case for paradigmatic behavior therapy. *Journal of Behavior Therapy and Experimental Psychiatry, 21,* 163–172.

Eisenstadt, T. H., Eyberg, S., McNeil, C. B., Newcomb, K., & Funderburk, B. (1993). Parent-child interaction therapy with behavior problem children: Relative effectiveness of two stages and overall treatment outcome. *Journal of Clinical Child Psychology, 22,* 42–51.

Emerson, E., McGill, P., & Mansell, J. (1994). *Severe learning disabilities and challenging behaviours: Designing high quality services.* London: Chapman & Hall.

Evans, I. M. (1971). Theoretical and experimental aspects of the behaviour modification approach to autistic children. In M. Rutter (Ed.), *Infantile autism: Concepts, characteristics and treatment* (pp. 229–251). London: Churchill Livingstone.

Evans, I. M., & Meyer, L. H. (1985). *An educative approach to behavior problems: A practical decision model for interventions with severely handicapped learners.* Baltimore: Paul H. Brookes.

Evans, I. M., Meyer, L. H., Kurkjian, J. A., & Kishi, G. S. (1988). An evaluation of behavioral interrelationships in child behavior therapy. In J. C. Witt, S. N. Elliott, & F. N. Gresham (Eds.), *Handbook of behavior therapy in education* (pp. 189–216). New York: Plenum.

Evans, I. M., & Scotti, J. R. (1989). Defining meaningful outcomes for persons with profound disabilities. In F. Brown & D. H. Lehr (Eds.), *Persons with profound disabilities: Issues and practices* (pp. 83–107). Baltimore: Paul H. Brookes.

Eyberg, S. (1988). Parent-child interaction therapy: Integration of traditional and behavioral concerns. *Child and Family Behavior Therapy, 10,* 33–46.

Eyberg, S. M., & Matarazzo, R. G. (1980). Training parents as therapists: A comparison between individual parent-child interaction training and parent group didactic training. *Journal of Clinical Psychology, 36,* 492–499.

Eyberg, S. M., & Robinson, E. A. (1982). Parent-child interaction training: Effects on family functioning. *Journal of Clinical Child Psychology, 11,* 130–137.

Eyberg, S. M., & Ross, A. W. (1978). Assessment of child behavior problems: The validation of a new inventory. *Journal of Clinical Child Psychology, 7,* 113–116.

Ferster, C. B., & Skinner, B. F. (1957). *Schedules of reinforcement.* Englewood Cliffs, NJ: Prentice-Hall.

Forehand, R., & King, H. E. (1974). Pre-school children's noncompliance: Effects of short-term behavior therapy. *Journal of Community Psychology, 2,* 42–44.

Forehand, R., & King, H. E. (1977). Noncompliant children: Effects of parent training on behavior and attitude change. *Behavior Modification, 1,* 93–108.

Forehand, R., & Long, N. (1988). Outpatient treatment of the acting out child: Procedures, long-term follow-up data, and clinical problems. *Advances in Behaviour Research and Therapy, 10,* 129–177.

Forehand, R., & McMahon, R. J. (1981). *Helping the noncompliant child: A clinician's guide to effective parent training.* New York: Guilford.

Forehand, R., & Scarboro, M. E. (1975). An analysis of children's oppositional behavior. *Journal of Abnormal Child Psychology, 3,* 27–31.

Forehand, R., Sturgis, E. T., McMahon, R. J., Aguar, D., Green, K., Wells, K. C., & Breiner, J. (1979). Parent behavioral training to modify child noncompliance: Treatment generalization across time and from home to school. *Behavior Modification, 3,* 3–25.

Fuller, P. R. (1949). Operant conditioning of a vegetative human organism. *American Journal of Psychology, 62,* 587–590.

Giangreco, M. F., & Putnam, J. W. (1991). Supporting the education of students with severe disabilities in regular education environments. In L. H. Meyer, C. A. Peck, & L. Brown (Eds.), *Critical issues in the lives of people with severe disabilities* (pp. 245–270). Baltimore: Paul H. Brookes.

Greer, R. D. (1992). *L'enfant terrible* meets the educational crisis. *Journal of Applied Behavior Analysis, 25,* 65–69.

Halle, J. W., & Spradlin, J. E. (1993). Identifying stimulus control of challenging behavior (pp. 83–109). In J. Reichle & D. P. Wacker (Eds.), *Communicative alternatives to challenging behavior: Integrating functional assessment and intervention strategies* (pp. 83–109). Baltimore: Paul H. Brookes.

Hanf, C. (1969). *A two-stage program for modifying maternal controlling during mother-child (M-C) interaction.* Paper presented at the meeting of the Western Psychological Association, Vancouver, BC.

Harris, F., Johnston, M., Kelley, C., & Wolf, M. (1964). Effects of social reinforcement on regressed crawling of a nursery school child. *Journal of Educational Psychology, 55,* 35–41.

Hart, B., Allen, E., Buell, J., Harris, F., & Wolf, M. (1964). Effects of social reinforcement on operant crying. *Journal of Experimental Child Psychology, 1,* 145–153.

Hawkins, R. P. (1971). The School Adjustment Program: Individualized intervention for children with behavior disorders. In E. A. Ramp & B. L. Hopkins (Eds.), *A new direction for education: Behavior analysis* pp. 235–267. Lawrence: Support and Development Center for Follow Through, University of Kansas.

Hawkins, R. P. (1975). Who decided *that* was the problem? Two stages of responsibility for applied behavior analysts. In W. S. Wood (Ed.), *Issues in evaluating behavior modification: Proceedings of the first Drake conference on professional issues in behavior analysis, March, 1974* (pp. 195–214). Champaign, IL: Research Press.

Hawkins, R. P. (1986). Selection of target behaviors. In R. O. Nelson & S. C. Hayes (Eds.), *Conceptual foun-*

dations of behavioral assessment (pp. 331–385). New York: Guilford.

Hawkins, R. P. (1991). Is social validity what we are interested in? Argument for a functional approach. *Journal of Applied Behavior Analysis, 24,* 205–213.

Hawkins, R. P., & Hayes, J. E. (1974). The School Adjustment Program: A model program for treatment of severely maladjusted children in the public schools. In R. Ulrich, T. Stachnik, & J. Mabry (Eds.), *Control of human behavior, Vol. III: Behavior modification in education.* Glenview, IL: Scott, Foresman.

Hawkins, R. P., Peterson, R. F., Schweid, E., & Bijou, S. W. (1966). Behavior therapy in the home: Amelioration of problem parent-child relations with the parent in a therapeutic role. *Journal of Experimental Child Psychology, 4,* 99–107.

Hawkins, R. P., Sluyter, D. J., & Smith, C. D. (1972). Modification of achievement by a simple technique involving parents and teacher. In M. B. Harris (Ed.), *Classroom uses of behavior modification* (pp. 101–119). Columbus, OH: Charles E. Merrill.

Haynes, S. N., & O'Brien, W. H. (1990). Functional analysis in behavior therapy. *Clinical Psychology Review, 10,* 649–668.

Hobbs, S. M., & Forehand, R. (1975). Effects of differential release from time-out on children's behavior. *Journal of Behavior Therapy and Experimental Psychiatry, 6,* 256–257.

Hobbs, S. M., Forehand, R., & Murray, R. G. (1978). Effects of various durations of time-out on the noncompliant behavior of children. *Behavior Therapy, 9,* 652–656.

Hutchinson, R. R., & Azrin, N. H. (1961). Conditioning of mental-hospital patients to fixed-ratio schedules of reinforcement. *Journal of the Experimental Analysis of Behavior, 4,* 87–95.

Issacs, W., Thomas, J., & Goldiamond, I. (1960). Application of operant conditioning to reinstate verbal behavior in psychotics. *Journal of Speech and Hearing Disorders, 25,* 8–12.

Iwata, B. A. (1987). Negative reinforcement in applied behavior analysis: An emerging technology. *Journal of Applied Behavior Analysis, 20,* 361–378.

Iwata, B. A. (1994). Functional analysis methodology: Some closing comments. Special issue: Functional analysis approaches to behavioral assessment and treatment. *Journal of Applied Behavior Analysis, 27,* 413–418.

Iwata, B. A., Dorsey, M. F., Slifer, K. J., Bauman, K. E., & Richman, G. S. (1982). Toward a functional analysis of self-injury. *Analysis and Intervention in Developmental Disabilities, 2,* 3–20.

Iwata, B. A., Pace, G. M., Dorsey, M. F., Zarcone, J. R., Vollmer, T. R., Smith, R. G., Rodgers, T. A., Lerman, D. C., Shore, B. A., Mazaleski, J. L., Goh, H. L., Cowdrey, G. E., Kalsher, M. J., McCosh, K. C., & Willis, K. D. (1994). The functions of self-injurious behavior: An experimental-epidemiological analysis. Special issue: Functional analysis approaches to behavioral assessment and treatment. *Journal of Applied Behavior Analysis, 27,* 215–240.

Johnson, K. R., & Layng, T. V. J. (1992). Breaking the structuralist barrier: Literacy and numeracy with fluency. *American Psychologist, 47,* 1475–1490.

Johnston, J. M., & Pennypacker, H. S. (1980). *Strategies and tactics of human behavioral research.* Hillsdale, NJ: Erlbaum.

Kazdin, A. E. (1982). Symptom substitution, generalization, and response covariation: Implications for psychotherapy outcome. *Psychological Bulletin, 91,* 349–365.

Keller, F. S., & Schoenfeld, W. N. (1950). *Principles of psychology: A systematic text in the science of behavior.* New York: Appleton-Century-Crofts.

Kirk, K. S. (in press). Issues in selecting intervention strategies for persons with attention deficit hyperactivity disorder. In J. R. Scotti & L. H. Meyer (Eds.), *Behavioral intervention: Principles, models, and practices.* Baltimore: Paul H. Brookes.

Klein, R. D., Hapkiewicz, W. G., & Roden, A. H. (Eds.). (1973). *Behavior modification in educational settings.* Springfield, IL: Charles C. Thomas.

Koegel, L. K., Koegel, R. L., & Dunlap, G. (1996). *Positive behavioral support: Including people with difficult behavior in the community.* Baltimore: Paul H. Brookes.

Kuhn, T. S. (1970). *The structure of scientific revolutions* (2nd ed.). Chicago: University of Chicago Press.

Lennox, D. B., Miltenberger, R. G., Spengler, P., & Erfanian, N. (1988). Decelerative treatment practices with persons who have mental retardation: A review of five years of the literature. *American Journal on Mental Retardation, 92,* 492–501.

Lerman, D. C., & Iwata, B. A. (1993). Descriptive and experimental analyses of variables maintaining self-injurious behavior. *Journal of Applied Behavior Analysis, 26,* 293–319.

Lindsley, O. R. (1956). Operant conditioning methods applied to research in chronic schizophrenia. *Psychiatric Research Reports, 5,* 118–139.

Long, P., Forehand, R., Wierson, M., & Morgan, A. (1994). Does parent training with young noncompliant children have long-term effects? *Behaviour Research and Therapy, 32,* 101–107.

Luiselli, J. K. (1991). Assessment-derived treatment of children's disruptive behavior disorders. *Behavior Modification, 15,* 294–209.

McMahon, R. J., & Wells, K. C. (1989). Conduct disorders. In E. J. Mash & R. A. Barkley (Eds.), *Treatment of childhood disorders* (pp. 73–132). New York: Guilford.

McNeil, C. B., Eyberg, S. M., Eisenstadt, T. H., Newcomb, K., & Funderburk, B. (1991). Parent-child interaction therapy with behavior problem children: Generalization of treatment effects to the school setting. *Journal of Clinical Child Psychology, 20,* 140–151.

Martin, G., & Pear, J. (1996). *Behavior modification: What it is and how to do it* (5th ed.). Upper Saddle River, NJ: Prentice-Hall.

Matson, J. L., & Taras, M. E. (1989). A 20-year review of punishment and alternative methods to treat problem behaviors in developmentally delayed persons. *Research in Developmental Disabilities, 10,* 85–104.

Meyer, L. H., & Evans, I. M. (1989). *Nonaversive intervention for behavior problems: A manual for home and community.* Baltimore: Paul H. Brookes.

Meyer, L. H., & Evans, I. M. (1993). Meaningful outcomes in behavioral intervention: Evaluating positive approaches to the remediation of challenging behaviors. In J. Reichle & D. P. Wacker (Eds.), *Communicative alternatives to challenging behavior: Integrating functional assessment and intervention strategies* (pp. 407–428). Baltimore: Paul H. Brookes.

Moxley, R. A. (1992). From mechanistic to functional behaviorism. Special issue: Reflections on B. F. Skinner and psychology. *American Psychologist, 47,* 1300–1311.

Mullen, K. B. (1995). *The educative approach to child excess behavior: Toward an application to parent intervention packages.* Unpublished manuscript, Department of Psychology, West Virginia University, Morgantown.

Newsom, C., Favell, J. E., & Rincover, A. (1983). The side effects of punishment. In S. Axelrod & J. Apsche (Eds.), *The effects of punishment on human behavior* (pp. 285–316). New York: Academic Press.

Nisbet, J., Clark, M., & Covert, S. (1991). Living it up! An analysis of research on community living. In L. H. Meyer, C. A. Peck, & L. Brown (Eds.), *Critical issues in the lives of people with severe disabilities* (pp. 115–144). Baltimore: Paul H. Brookes.

O'Neill, R. E., Horner, R. H., Albin, R. W., Storey, K., & Sprague, J. R. (1990). *Functional analysis of problem behavior: A practical assessment guide.* Sycamore, IL: Sycamore Press.

O'Neill, R., & Reichle, J. (1993). Addressing socially motivated challenging behaviors by establishing communicative alternatives: Basics of a general-case approach. In J. Reichle & D. P. Wacker (Eds.), *Communicative alternatives to challenging behavior: Integrating functional assessment and intervention strategies* (pp. 205–235). Baltimore: Paul H. Brookes.

Parrish, J. M., & Roberts, M. L. (1993). Interventions based on covariation of desired and inappropriate behavior. In J. Reichle & D. P. Wacker (Eds.), *Communicative alternatives to challenging behavior: Integrating functional assessment and intervention strategies* (pp. 135–173). Baltimore: Paul H. Brookes.

Patterson, G. R. (1974). Interventions for boys with conduct problems: Multiple settings, treatments, and criteria. *Journal of Consulting and Clinical Psychology, 42,* 471–481.

Patterson, G. R. (1975). *Families: Applications of social learning to family life.* Champaign, IL.: Research Press.

Patterson, G. R. (1976a). The aggressive child: Victim and architect of a coercive system. In E. G. Mash, L. A. Hammerlynck, & L. C. Handy (Eds.), *Behavior modification and families* (pp. 267–316). New York: Brunner/Mazel.

Patterson, G. R. (1976b). *Living with children* (Rev. ed.). Champaign, IL: Research Press.

Patterson, G. R. (1982). *Coercive family process: A social learning approach,* Vol. 3. Eugene, OR: Castalia.

Patterson, G. R., Chamberlain, R., & Reid, J. B. (1982). A comparative evaluation of a parent training program. *Behavior Therapy, 13,* 638–650.

Patterson, G. R., Cobb, J. A., & Ray, R. S. (1973). A social engineering technology for retraining the families of aggressive boys. In H. E. Adams & I. P. Unikel (Eds.), *Issues and trends in behavior therapy* (pp. 139–224). Springfield, IL.: Charles C. Thomas.

Patterson, G. R., & Reid, J. B. (1973). Intervention for families of aggressive boys: A replication study. *Behaviour Research and Therapy, 11,* 383–394.

Patterson, G. R., Reid, J. B., Jones, R. R., & Conger, R. E. (1975). *A social learning approach to family intervention: Families with aggressive children.* Eugene, OR.: Castalia.

Peed, S., Roberts, M., & Forehand, R. (1977). Evaluation of the effectiveness of a standardized parent training program in altering the interaction of mothers and their noncompliant children. *Behavior Modification, 1,* 323–350.

Ramp, E. A., & Hopkins, B. L. (1971). *A new direction for education: Behavior analysis.* Lawrence: Support and Development Center for Follow Through, University of Kansas.

Reichle, J., & Wacker, D. P. (Eds.). (1993). *Communicative alternatives to challenging behavior: Integrating functional assessment and intervention strategies.* Baltimore: Paul H. Brookes.

Repp, A. C., Felce, D., & Barton, L. E. (1988). Basing the treatment of stereotypic and self-injurious behaviors on hypotheses of their causes. *Journal of Applied Behavior Analysis, 21,* 281–289.

Repp, A. C., & Karsh, K. G. (1990). A taxonomic approach to the nonaversive treatment of maladaptive behavior of persons with developmental disabilities. In A. C. Repp & N. N. Singh (Eds.), *Perspectives on the use of nonaversive and aversive interventions for persons with developmental disabilities* (pp. 331–347). Sycamore, IL: Sycamore Press.

Repp, A. C., Karsh, K. G., Munk, D., & Dahlquist, C. M. (1995). Hypothesis-based interventions: A theory of clinical decision making. In W. O'Donohue & L. Krasner (Eds.), *Theories of behavior therapy: Exploring behavior change* (pp. 585–608). Washington, DC: American Psychological Association.

Risley, T., & Wolf, M. M. (1966). Experimental manipulation of autistic behaviors and generalization into the home. In R. Ulrich, T. Stachnik, & J. Mabry (Eds.), *Control of human behavior* (pp. 193–198). Glenview, IL: Scott, Foresman.

Roberts, M., McMahon, R., Forehand, R., & Humphreys, L. (1978). The effect of parental instruction-giving on child compliance. *Behavior Therapy, 9,* 793–798.

Robinson, E. A., Eyberg, S. M., & Ross, A. W. (1980). The standardization of an inventory of child conduct problem behavior. *Journal of Clinical Child Psychology, 9,* 22–28.

Scarboro, M. E., & Forehand, R. (1975). Effects of two types of response-contingent time-out on compliance and oppositional behavior of children. *Journal of Experimental Child Psychology, 19,* 252–264.

Scotti, J. R., Evans, I. M., Meyer, L. H., & DiBenedetto, A. (1991a). Individual repertoires as behavioral systems: Implications for program design and evaluation. In B. Remington (Ed.), *The challenge of severe mental handicap: A behavior analytic approach* (pp. 139–163). London: Wiley.

Scotti, J. R., Evans, I. M., Meyer, L. H., & Walker, P. (1991b). A meta-analysis of intervention research with problem behavior: Treatment validity and standards of practice. *American Journal on Mental Retardation, 3,* 233–256.

Scotti, J. R., Kirk, K. S., Weigle, K. L., Cuddihy, K., Lumley, V., Magruda, A., Rasheed, S., & Cohen, T. (1993). *Analog functional assessments and nonaversive interventions in special education classrooms: A comparison of brief versus extended assessments.* Poster presented at the 19th Annual Convention of the Association for Behavior Analysis, Chicago, IL, May 1993.

Scotti, J. R., McMorrow, M. J., & Trawitzki, A. L. (1993). Behavioral treatment of chronic psychiatric disorders: Publication trends and future directions. *Behavior Therapy, 24,* 527–550.

Scotti, J. R., Morris, T. L., McNeil, C. B., & Hawkins, R. P. (1996). DSM-IV and disorders of childhood and adolescence: Can structural criteria be functional? Special issue on the DSM-IV. *Journal of Consulting and Clinical Psychology, 64,* 1177–1191.

Scotti, J. R., Schulman, D. E., & Hojnacki, R. M. (1994). Functional analysis and unsuccessful treatment of Tourette's syndrome in a man with profound mental retardation. *Behavior Therapy, 25,* 721–738.

Scotti, J. R., Trawitzki, A. L., Vittimberga, G., & McMorrow, M. J. (1991). *Applied behavior analysis in the treatment of severe psychiatric disorders: A bibliography.* (ERIC Document Reproduction Service No. ED 325 759).

Scotti, J. R., Ujcich, K. J., Weigle, K. L., Holland, C. M., & Kirk, K. S. (1996). Interventions with challenging behavior of persons with developmental disabilities: A review of current research practices.

Journal of the Association for Persons with Severe Handicaps, 21, 123–134.

Scotti, J. R., Walker, P., Evans, I. M., & Meyer, L. H. (1991). *A bibliography of the developmental disabilities literature focusing on the deceleration of excess behaviors.* (ERIC Document Reproduction Service No. ED 329 090).

Scotti, J. R., Weigle, K. L., Kirk, K. S., Ellis, J. T., Jackson, S., Kennedy, C., & Schreiber, R. (1993). *A comparison of three functional assessment strategies with the excess and positive behaviors of students with developmental disabilities.* Poster presented at the 19th Annual Convention of the Association for Behavior Analysis, Chicago, IL., May 1993.

Skinner, B. F. (1938). *The behavior of organisms: An experimental analysis.* New York: Appleton-Century-Crofts.

Skinner, B. F. (1945). The operational analysis of psychological terms. *Psychological Review, 52,* 270–277, 291–294.

Skinner, B. F. (1953). *Science and human behavior.* New York: The Free Press.

Skinner, B. F. (1974). *About behaviorism.* New York: Knopf.

Skinner, B. F. (1981). Selection by consequences. *Science, 213,* 501–504.

Sprague, J. R., & Horner, R. H. (1992). Covariation within functional response classes: Implications for treatment of severe problem behavior. *Journal of Applied Behavior Analysis, 25,* 735–745.

Staats, A. W. (1964). *Human learning: Studies extending conditioning principles to complex behavior.* New York: Holt, Rinehart, & Winston.

Staats, A. W. (1990). Paradigmatic behavior therapy: A unified framework for theory, research, and practice. In G. H. Eifert & I. M. Evans (Eds.), *Unifying behavior therapy: Contributions of paradigmatic behaviorism* (pp. 14–54). New York: Springer.

Staats, A. W., & Staats, C. K. (1963). *Complex human behavior: A systematic extension of learning principles.* New York: Holt, Rinehart, & Winston.

Stokes, T., & Baer, D. (1977). An implicit technology of generalization. *Journal of Applied Behavior Analysis, 10,* 349–367.

Tharp, R. G., & Wetzel, R. J. (1969). *Behavior modification in the natural environment.* New York: Academic Press.

Touchette, P. E., MacDonald, R. F., & Langer, S. N. (1985). A scatter plot for identifying stimulus control of problem behavior. *Journal of Applied Behavior Analysis, 18,* 343–351.

Vittimberga, G. L., Weigle, K. L., & Scotti, J. R. (In press). Standards of practice in behavioral intervention with persons with developmental disabilities and chronic psychiatric disorders. In J. R. Scotti & L. H. Meyer (Eds.), *Behavorial intervention: Principles, models, and practices.* Baltimore: Paul H. Brookes.

Voeltz, L. M., & Evans, I. M. (1982). The assessment of behavioral interrelationships in child behavior therapy. *Behavioral Assessment, 4,* 131–165.

Vollmer, T. R., Marcus, B. A., & LeBlanc, L. (1994). Treatment of self-injury and hand mouthing following inconclusive functional analyses. Special issue: Functional analysis approaches to behavioral assessment and treatment. *Journal of Applied Behavior Analysis, 27,* 331–344.

Wahler, R. G. (1975). Some structural aspects of deviant child behavior. *Journal of Applied Behavior Analysis, 8,* 27–42.

Wahler, R. G., Winkel, G. H., Peterson, R. F., & Morrison, D. C. (1965). Mothers as behavior therapists for their own children. *Behaviour Research and Therapy, 3,* 113–124.

Webster-Stratton, C. (1982a). Long-term effects of videotape modeling parent education program: Comparison of immediate and one-year followup results. *Behavior Therapy, 13,* 702–714.

Webster-Stratton, C. (1982b). Teaching mothers through videotape modeling to change their children's behavior. *Journal of Pediatric Psychology, 7,* 279–294.

Webster-Stratton, C. (1984). Randomized trial of two parent-training programs for families with conduct disordered children. *Journal of Consulting and Clinical Psychology, 52,* 666–678.

Webster-Stratton, C. (1994). *Troubled families—problem children: Working with parents: A collaborative process.* Chichester, England: Wiley.

Webster-Stratton, C., Hollinsworth, T., & Kolpacoff, M. (1989). The long-term effectiveness and clinical significance of three cost-effective training programs for families with conduct-problem children. *Journal of Consulting and Clinical Psychology, 57,* 550–553.

Webster-Stratton, C., Kolpacoff, M., & Hollinsworth, T. (1988). Self-administered videotape therapy for families with conduct-problem children: Comparison with two cost-effective treatments and a control group. *Journal of Consulting and Clinical Psychology, 55*, 558–566.

Williams, C. D. (1959). The elimination of tantrum behavior by extinction procedures. *Journal of Abnormal and Social Psychology, 59*, 269.

Williams, C. A., & Forehand, R. (1984). An examination of predictor variables for child compliance and noncompliance. *Journal of Abnormal Child Psychology, 12*, 491–504.

Willis, T. J., LaVigna, G. W., & Donnellan, A. M. (1987). *Behavior assessment guide.* Los Angeles: Institute for Applied Behavior Analysis.

Wolf, M. M. (1978). Social validity: The case for subjective measurement, or how applied behavior analysis is finding its heart. *Journal of Applied Behavior Analysis, 11*, 315–329.

Wolf, M. M., Birnbrauer, J. S., Williams, T., & Lawler, J. (1965). A note on apparent extinction of the vomiting behavior of a retarded child. In L. P. Ullmann & L. Krasner (Eds.), *Case studies in behavior modification* (pp. 364–366). New York: Holt, Rinehart, & Winston.

Wolf, M., Risley, T., & Meese, H. (1964). Application of operant conditioning procedures to the behaviour problems of an autistic child. *Behaviour Research and Therapy, 1*, 305–312.

Wolpe, J. (1982). *The practice of behavior therapy* (3rd ed.). New York: Pergamon.

10

CHILDHOOD ANXIETY, OBSESSIVE-COMPULSIVE DISORDER, AND DEPRESSION

ANNE MARIE ALBANO
Department of Psychology
University of Louisville

TRACY L. MORRIS
Department of Psychology
West Virginia University

The assessment and treatment of fears and anxieties in children and adolescents owns a long and rich tradition within the field of behavior therapy. Indeed, the extant literature of case studies of phobic children examining applications of learning theory and behaviorism have "served to shape and validate the paradigm, theories, and techniques of behavior therapy" (Barrios & O'Dell, 1989, p. 167). For example, Mary Cover Jones is credited with using conditioning techniques and an early precursor of modeling to alleviate childhood fears. In the historic case study of Peter, a three-year-old boy with an intense fear of rabbits, Jones combined observational learning with graduated desensitization (Jones, 1924). Initially, Peter observed other children playing with a rabbit. Next, during a time when Peter was eating his favorite food and not demonstrating any fear, a caged rabbit was introduced into the room. Gradually and in systematic steps, the rabbit was moved closer to Peter until he was able to pet and play with the rabbit comfortably. Essentially, this landmark study set the stage for the development of modeling paradigms and graduated in vivo exposure. Since then, a variety of behavioral treatment modalities targeting childhood fears and anxieties have been evaluated, including methods grounded in theories of classical conditioning, respondent conditioning, and two-factor theory. Although the advent of cognitive-behavioral therapy dates back to the early 1970s, cognitive-behavioral treatment approaches targeting disorders such as depression, social phobia, and generalized anxiety disorder in youth have only emerged in the 1990s. Overall, there is a considerable literature consisting mainly of uncontrolled studies attesting to the relative effectiveness of behavioral and cognitive-behavioral methods for treating the range of anxiety disorders and depression in children and adolescents. In this chapter, we provide an overview of the most prominent contemporary behavioral models accounting for the development of anxiety and depression in youth. We then describe current developments in the application of treatment protocols for specific disorders.

Theoretical Formulations

Although there is no one behavioral theory to account for anxiety and depression in children and adolescents, several behavioral models have been proposed to explain the development and maintenance of these internalizing disorders in children. The major tenets of each model reflect the general trend within the field of behavior theory at the time the model was proposed. Hence, early models reflected conditioning paradigms with little (if any) reference to cognitive behavior, whereas contemporary models incorporate cognitive, biologicial, and environmental factors from a behavioral perspective. Although a detailed review of each behavioral and cognitive-behavioral model is beyond the scope of this chapter, below we present the most popular conceptualizations for the development of anxiety and depression in youth. For additional models and greater detail, the reader is referred to Mash and Barkley (1989), Ollendick, King, and Yule (1994), and Reynolds and Johnston (1994).

Behavioral Models of Anxiety

Classical Conditioning
The infamous case study of Little Albert (Watson & Rayner, 1920) best illustrates the mechanisms involved in the classical conditioning of fear. Although initially unafraid of white, furry animals, young Albert learned to become afraid through the process of repeated pairings of a white rabbit with an unexpected, loud, noxious noise resulting in a startle and fear response. Anxiety from a classical conditioning perspective involves learning through the process of associating neutral with nonneutral stimuli. Initially conditioned to fear a white rabbit, Albert also became fearful of other furry animals and stimuli. Thus, generalization of the fear may occur to similiar stimuli, such that direct conditioning of fear to these stimuli is unnecessary. However, discrimination has also been observed in persons with circumscribed fears and anxieties, such that the fear response is limited to only particular stimuli. A number of criticisms of the classical conditioning explanation for the development of anxiety have been noted. For example, anxiety and phobias may develop in the absence of any direct contact with a particular stimulus. Moreover, classical conditioning assumes, at least in part, that all neutral stimuli have equal potential to become feared through the process of association (equipotentiality). However, Watson and Rayner's findings have been criticized on the grounds that later studies could not replicate or demonstrate fear conditioning in young children

to more neutral stimuli (e.g., wooden blocks) (cf. Morris & Kratochwill, 1983). Methodological differences and shortcomings are offered as reasons for the failure to replicate and extend Watson and Rayner's work (see Delprato, 1980). In addition, the notion of equipotentiality does not address the possibility of a biological predisposition (presumably related to survival mechanisms) towards fear of certain stimuli (Seligman, 1971). In general, classical conditioning is useful for explaining the development of some fears and anxieties. For further explanation of classical conditioning theory and criticisms of such, the reader interested in a detailed review is referred to Barrios and O'Dell (1989) and Eisen and Kearney (1995).

Operant Conditioning

The development of fear and anxiety from a Skinnerian or operant conditioning perspective assumes that behavior is learned as a function of its consequences. Thus, positive consequences will increase the frequency of a behavior, whereas negative consequences or a lack of positive reinforcement (extinction) will decrease the frequency of a behavior. Therefore, all behavior is subject to these contingencies of reinforcement, such that inappropriate or maladaptive behaviors will increase if followed by positive consequences, or if such behavior results in removal from or termination of an aversive situation (negative reinforcement). The operant conditioning paradigm fits well in explaining the development and maintenance of anxiety disorders in youth. Research has demonstrated that all children experience normal, developmentally appropriate fears that are relatively circumscribed, of short duration, and dissipate with time (cf. Ollendick, Matson, & Helsel, 1985). Such fears may be accompanied by a range of behaviors including whining, crying, or attempts to avoid the feared stimulus or situation. In an attempt to comfort the child, and perhaps not recognizing the developmentally appropriate nature of the complaint, parents may inadvertently reinforce inappropriate fearful or avoidant behavior in their children, resulting in the development of consistent expressions of fear and anxiety (cf. Albano, Chorpita, & Barlow, 1996). For example, intermittent requests to sleep with the parents can develop into consistent nighttime patterns for children with separation anxiety disorder, parents who order food in restaurants for their adolescents may be reinforcing the adolescent's social phobia of speaking to others, and allowing a fearful child to stay home from school reinforces the serious behavioral concomitant of school refusal behavior which often accompanies the anxiety disorders (Albano et al., 1996; Eisen & Kearney, 1995).

The operant conditioning model, similar to the classical condition paradigm, cannot explain the development of all fears and anxieties, such as in cases where anxiety and phobic reactions persist in the absence of any direct reinforcement. Nevertheless, the usefulness of this model cannot be overemphasized, especially when considering the role of reinforcement in the maintenance of anxiety. Later in this chapter we describe several treatment protocols that directly address reinforcement contingencies and the role of parents in the process of therapeutic change.

Two-Factor Theory

Mowrer (1947, 1960) proposed a two-factor learning theory for the development and maintenance of anxious avoidant behavior. This two-factor theory proposes that both respondent and operant conditioning are involved in the development of anxiety disorders. Lyons and Scotti (1995) present a concise overview of the two-factor learning theory model. Essentially, the theory states that in the face of an aversive event (UCS), the organism responds with increased physiological reactivity and subjective distress (UCR). These responses become associated with otherwise benign cues (CS) present at the time of the aversive event. Subsequently, presentation of CS (including external environmental cues and internal cognitive cues serving as reminders of the aversive event) results in physiological reactivity and subjective distress (CR). As these CR are aversive, escape and/or avoidance of CS is negatively reinforced. The problem becomes compounded when additional cues lead to increased avoidance over time through the process of stimulus generalization. According to Levis (1985), "Inherent in the development of psychopathology is the learning of two response classes. The first response class involves the conditioning of an aversive emotional state and the second involves learned behavior designed to reduce the negative effects of the first response class" (p. 53). Eisen and Kearney (1995) describe a case study of a seven-year-old child who was fearful of giving oral presentations. Although the child may have initially learned to associate public speaking with increased somatic sensations and fear, the resultant avoidance of giving oral reports resulted in a reduction of the fear and maintenance of the avoidance. Several criticisms of the two-factor theory have been noted (see Barrios & O'Dell, 1989), among which is the observation that fear may be acquired and maintained without the development of concomitant avoidance behavior.

Behavioral Models of Depression

Early behavioral models of depression in adults focused on a person's inability to access positive reinforcement from the environment (Ferster, 1966; Skinner, 1953). This leads to a reduction in the frequency of behaviors that previously led to reinforcement. This decrease in the frequency of these behaviors can be brought on by (a) a sudden large environmental change, (b) a punishing situation with no escape or being in a constant process of escape, and (c) exerting excessively large amounts of adaptive behavior before reinforcement is available (Ferster, 1966, 1973). From this view, depression is categorized as a condition of the entire repertoire, and therefore a single underlying psychological process or single cause cannot be expected to define all instances of depression. Although depression involves broad changes in repertoire, the main observed behaviors are verbal. Assessment and treatment focus mainly on verbal descriptions by the client. The main diagnostic symptomatology—negative self-talk and pessimism—are actually verbal tacts under discriminative control of private events (Skinner, 1957; see also Forsyth & Eifert, Chapter 3, this volume). These verbal behaviors block the cumulative development of an adaptive repertoire.

Expanding on this theory, Lewinsohn and colleagues proposed that depressed persons lack adequate social skills that are necessary for accessing reinforcement from others, resulting in a low rate of response-contingent positive reinforcement (Lewinsohn, 1974; Lewinsohn, Biglan, & Zeiss, 1976; see also Eifert, Beach, & Wilson, Chapter 4, this volume). In general, research supports this model as applied to youth. Depressed children demonstrate impaired social and interpersonal functioning with peers, family members, and teachers (e.g., Altmann & Gotlib, 1988; Blechman, McEnroe, Carella, &

Audette, 1986; Kazdin, Esveldt-Dawson, Sherick, & Colbus, 1985; Sacco & Graves, 1984). Moreover, depressed youngsters report wanting to be alone, spend less time in public situations, view others as less friendly (Larson et al., 1990), and perceive themselves as less socially competent than their peers (Altmann & Gotlib, 1988; Sacco & Graves, 1984).

Cognitive Models of Anxiety and Depression

Central to the cognitive models of anxiety and depression is the role of negative and distorted cognitions in the etiology, maintenance, and treatment of these disorders (Kendall, 1992; Kendall & Ingram, 1989). Hence, from the cognitive-behavioral perspective, an understanding of cognitive mediation is essential for a complete functional analysis of an individual's pathological behavior. Briefly, we review the main cognitive conceptualizations of these emotional disorders.

Cognitive Models of Anxiety

The basic premise underlying the cognitive approach is that anxiety results from an individual's tendency to interpret all events and experiences in a negative, catastrophic, and irrational manner, such that the individual overestimates the probability of threat and underestimates his or her ability to cope with a situation. According to Beck and colleagues (Beck, 1976; Beck & Emery, 1985), individuals with anxiety disorders have overdeveloped and hypersensitive *schemata* for perceiving threat in their environment. The content of prior experiences and the storage of such experience in memory form "anxious schemata" that comprise themes of danger, threat, embarrassment, and harm. As schemata provide a "mental template" for viewing the world, they are deemed to account for the consistency that we see in a person's thoughts, behavior, and emotions (Spence, 1994). This template serves as the filter for what is perceived and how events are experienced and processed (see Kendall, 1992). Thus, individuals with threat schemata view the world with a hypervigilance and heightened sense of threat, and are overly sensitive to perceptions of danger to the self. Children with anxiety disorders process information through a negative bias comprised of "What if" statements: What if I fail this test? What if they don't like me? What if Mom gets in a car accident? What if I get lost? What if someone tries to kidnap me? The content of this self-questioning is centered around the particular focus of the situation. For example, separation anxious children focus on issues of loss, harm to self or family members, and fears of getting lost, while children with social phobias focus on negative evaluation and embarrassment. Overall, a negative, internal dialogue or self-talk occurs that is mainly focused on catastrophic events occurring in the immediate or distant future (Kendall & Ingram, 1989).

Cognitive Models of Depression

Learned helplessness theory (Seligman, 1975) was originally proposed to explain depression in terms of the motivational, cognitive, and emotional disturbances that result when there is a lack of correspondence between responding and outcome. Depressed affect is the emotional deficit that the model claims is a further consequence of learning that outcomes are uncontrollable. A number of criticisms led to reformulations of the learned helplessness model (see Abramson, Seligman, & Teasdale, 1978; Alloy,

Clements, & Kolden, 1985) based on attribution theory. Essentially, the type of causal attributions people make for experience with lack of control will determine whether depression or some more adaptive response will follow.

The extant literature examining the attributional hypothesis of depression in children and adolescents suggests that depressed youngsters evidence a more internal, stable, and global attributional style for negative events, and a more external, unstable, and specific attributional style for positive events relative to their nondepressed peers (Kaslow, Brown, & Mee, 1994). Internal, stable, and global attributions for failure have been found to correlate with high scores on the Children's Depression Inventory (CDI; Kovacs, 1981) (e.g., Kaslow et al., 1984; Nolen-Hoeksema et al., 1986; Saylor et al., 1984), although the influence of other mediating factors on depression (e.g., school problems, socioeconomic factors) may decrease the amount of variance uniquely accounted for by attributional style (see Kaslow et al., 1994). Overall, the research examining attributional style is equivocal and warrants further investigation.

The self-control model of depression proposed by Rehm (1977) proposes that deficits in self-control behaviors underlie the development of depressive symptomatology. This model is an outgrowth of Kanfer's (1971) more general self-control model that proposes that individuals use three sequential processes—self-monitoring, self-evaluation, and self-reinforcement—to acquire and maintain the behaviors necessary to attain their goals. Depressed persons are hypothesized to exhibit deficits in each of these phases in the self-control process. In the self-monitoring phase, depressed individuals selectively attend to negative events and cannot delay gratification or outcomes. At the self-evaluation phase, the self-monitored behaviors are compared to an unrealistic internal criterion or standard. These unattainable standards set the depressed person up for perceived failures, and discouragement from goal seeking. Finally, self-punishment is posited as the result of discrepencies between observed behaviors and performance standards. The self-punishment serves to discourage future goal-directed behaviors and is hypothesized to account for psychomotor retardation, inhibition, and low response rates characteristic of depressed individuals. Consistent with this model, depressed children have been found to evidence deficits in self-monitoring, attribution, self-evaluation, and self-reinforcement (e.g., Cole & Rehm, 1986; Kaslow et al., 1984, 1988).

Beck's (1967) *cognitive theory of depression* proposes that depression is viewed in terms of the activation of three major cognitive patterns (the "cognitive triad") that induce the individual to regard himself, his experiences, and his future in an unrealistically negative manner. From this perspective, depressed persons regard themselves as unworthy, undesirable, and incapable, and thus they expect failure and rejection, and perceive most experiences as confirming this negative bias. Beck's theory is also conceptualized as a diathesis-stress model. Early life experiences shape a child's attitudes about herself and the environment. Depressogenic cognitive schemas remain latent until activated by precipitating factors (significant stressors) to which the individual is sensitized. Cognitive distortions are considered causally related to the depressed individual's tendency to interpret events in extreme, negative, categorical, absolute, and judgemental ways and reflect more primitive, immature levels of cognitive processing (Beck, Rush, Shaw, & Emery, 1979). Depressed children have reported significantly more negatively distorted cognitions on self-report measures, have low self-esteem, feel hopeless about their future, and are at higher risk for suicidal behavior (Kaslow et al., 1994).

Barlow's Integrative Theory of Emotional Disorders

As an alternative to the conceptualization of anxiety and depression as distinct and separate constructs, recent conceptualizations propose that anxiety and depression should be viewed as part of a larger, more general category called *internalizing syndrome* or *negative affectivity* (see Brady & Kendall, 1992; Watson & Clark, 1984). Evidence in support of the broad construct of negative affectivity comes from psychopathology studies of adults and children, which consistently report findings of high comorbidity between these two disorders (e.g., Barlow et al., 1986; Last et al., 1987). Barlow (1991) proposed an integrative model of emotional disorders, conceptualizing anxiety as a "blending" of cognitive and affective elements. Components of the aforementioned models of anxiety and depression that have received empirical support are evident in this model. Specifically, anxiety is conceptualized by its state of helplessness resulting from an individual's inability to predict, control, or obtain desired results in anticipated future situations or contexts (Barlow, 1991). As such, the elements necessary for the development of anxiety are high negative affect, a sense of uncontrollability, and an attentional shift to a negative self-focus. In this model, depression shares the same affective properties as anxiety, but involves a greater measure of uncontrollability on the cognitive dimension (cf. Albano, Chorpita, & Barlow, 1996). Anxiety can be distinguished from depression by a marked shift from a sense of limited control (resulting in autonomic arousal and anxious apprehension) to a sense of no control (characterized by anhedonia, psychomotor retardation, dysphoria). Given that perception of control is proposed as the core feature of anxiety (Barlow, 1988), Barlow and colleagues suggest that early experience with uncontrollability contributes to the development of anxiety in children, along with an increased vulnerability to depression (Barlow, Chorpita, & Turovsky, in press; Chorpita & Barlow, 1995).

Evidence in support of this model are found in conditioning studies (see Mineka & Zinbarg, in press), studies of infant temperament (e.g., Kagan et al., 1987), and examination of mother-infant interactions (e.g., Sroufe, 1990). Also consistent with this model, research suggests that family factors exert a potent influence on the maintenance of child psychopathology, and although less clear, on the development of depression or anxiety. For example, parents of depressed children are more likely to give contingent attention to the child for failure, and to make matters worse, they ignore the child's success experiences (Cole & Rehm, 1986). In a study examining differences in family interaction between conduct disordered (CD) and depressed children, Dadds et al. (1992) found a high level of parental hostility directed towards the depressed children, and these children were less likely than CD children to respond with their own hostility. Similarly, several studies have investigated family processes in childhood anxiety (Chorpita, Albano, & Barlow, 1996; Dadds & Barrett, 1996). These studies typically involve presenting the child with an ambiguous situation such as: "You wake up in the middle of the night, everyone is asleep, and you hear a noise coming from the hallway. What do you think is happening? What would you do? How anxious or afraid would you be?" After the child presents his or her response, the parents are brought in, the situation is repeated, and the family is left to discuss the situation for several minutes. These situations are typically videotaped for coding of content. Finally, the parents are excused, and the child is again presented with the situation and asked for an interpretation, plan, and anxiety rating. In response to such an ambiguous situation, an anxious interpretation would be, "It could be a robber, or maybe someone is really sick and dying!" Nonanxious interpretations would be things such as, "It could be the refrigerator or air conditioner, or maybe someone went for a drink of water." Using such a paradigm, Dadds, Barrett, Rapee, and Ryan (in press) showed that as compared with parents of nonclinical and aggressive children, parents of anxious children are more likely to model and reinforce anxious interpretations, along with escape and avoidance plans, rather than assist the child in developing a proactive interpretation and solution. Such family processes, whether expressed as direct reinforcement, modeling of overt avoidance behavior, or public tacts, certainly figure prominently in the development of learned avoidance, perceptions of uncontrollability, and psychopathology.

Treatment Applications

Recent years have witnessed increased attention toward addressing the treatment of anxiety in youth, although evaluations of protocols for childhood depression continue to remain relatively sparse. In the remainder of this chapter, we review current treatment approaches for these disorders in youth. Although well controlled empirical studies for anxiety and depression in youth are just beginning to emerge, behavior therapists have at their advantage the extant literature validating the effectiveness of specific techniques and a mounting literature supporting the use of prescriptive treatment protocols for these disorders. We first review specific techniques from a respondent conditioning paradigm, and then turn our attention to focus on protocol-driven treatments for childhood internalizing disorders.

Treatment from a Respondent Conditioning Paradigm

The behavioral treatment of fear and anxiety in children dates back to the classic work of Jones and the elimination of a fear of rabbits in a small boy referred to as "Peter" (Jones, 1924). Treatment consisted of progressive exposure of the rabbit to the child while the child was engaged in a pleasurable response (eating) incompatible with fear. Following treatment, Peter's fear dissipated to the rabbit as well as to other similar stimuli to which the fear had generalized. The case of Peter is typically presented as an example of "deconditioning" through principles of respondent conditioning.

Systematic Desensitization
Building upon Jones's early work, Wolpe (1958) developed a "graduated deconditioning" technique he called "systematic desensitization" (SD). The rationale for SD is that anxiety is a set of classically conditioned responses that can be unlearned or counterconditioned through associative pairing with anxiety-incompatible stimuli and

responses. In SD, anxiety-arousing stimuli are systematically and gradually paired (imaginally or in-vivo) with competing stimuli such as food, praise, imagery, or cues generated from muscular relaxation. Imaginal presentation of fearful stimuli was used predominantly in the initial work with SD.

SD with children consists of three basic steps: (1) training in progressive muscle relaxation, (2) rank ordering of fearful situations from lowest to highest, and (3) hierarchical presentation of fear stimuli via imagery while the child is in a relaxed state (see Eisen & Kearney, 1995, for a detailed review and example of procedures). Systematic desensitization appears to work well with older children and adolescents (see Barrios & O'Dell, 1989, for a review). Younger children, however, often have difficulty with both obtaining vivid imagery and acquiring the incompatible muscular relaxation response (Ollendick & Cerny, 1981). Strategies such as using developmentally appropriate imagery and adjunctive use of workbooks (see Kendall, 1990) may boost the effectiveness of these procedures with children.

Although SD is regarded as an effective treatment for reducing fear and anxiety, considerable disagreement exists regarding mechanism of effect. Systematic desensitization is said to operate through reciprocal inhibition whereby anxiety (sympathetic arousal) is inhibited by an incompatible response (relaxation). An alternative explanation is that rather than counterconditioning, the effective mechanism in SD is extinction. In an extinction paradigm, repeated pairing of conditioned fear stimuli in the absence of any adverse consequence results in a decay of the conditioned response.

Exposure-Based Treatments

Exposure-based treatments include graduated exposure and flooding (response prevention). These treatments are based on respondent conditioning and the classic extinction paradigm. Typically, individuals do not remain in the presence of anxiety-arousing stimuli for a sufficient duration to allow for extinction to occur in the natural environment. Moreover, escape and avoidance behaviors are negatively reinforced by cessation of anxiety. Exposure-based procedures require extended presentation of fear stimuli with concurrent prevention of escape and avoidance behaviors for the extinction of the conditioned responses to occur (see Morris & Kratochwill, 1983; Eisen & Kearney, 1995), thus addressing both components of two-factor theory. Emotive imagery is a variation of systematic desensitization, developed by Lazarus and Abramovitz (1962), to be developmentally appropriate for the treatment of childhood anxiety problems. This technique involves presenting a graduated series of increasingly potent feared stimuli to the child through imaginal exposure; however, the child's favorite "superhero" is described as supporting or assisting the child during the scenario. In a recent study, twenty-four children (aged seven to ten) who met criteria for simple phobia of the dark were randomly assigned to a wait list or emotive imagery condition (Cornwall, Spence, & Schotte, 1996). Individual treatment was conducted once weekly over six weeks, with sessions lasting forty minutes. Participants were exposed in nine scripts, presented sequentially in order of increasing potency. During the exposure each child's favorite superhero (e.g., Bart Simpson, Batman, Mickey Mouse) was incorporated into the images to invoke positive emotions that were proposed to inhibit the anxiety triggered by the scene (much like systematic desensitization). Results showed that, as compared with wait-list children, emotive imagery participants demonstrated decreased fear on a behavioral task, along with reduction in both self- and parent-reported fear and anxiety. Effects were maintained at the three-month follow-up. Wait-list children demonstrated maintenance of their fears at twenty weeks, lending further support to the stability and intractability of childhood anxiety problems.

In contrast to graduated exposure procedures, flooding involves sustained exposure (imaginally or in vivo) to fear stimuli. In this technique, the individual is required to remain in the presence of fear stimuli until his or her self-reported anxiety level dissipates. Graduated exposure refers to progressive in vivo exposure to hierarchically presented fear stimuli. Unlike systematic desensitization, stimulus presentation is not accompanied by progressive muscle relaxation or calming stimuli such as a superhero. Reinforced practice is often used in conjunction with graduated exposure whereby positive reinforcement is provided for progressively longer exposure to fear stimuli (Leitenberg & Callahan, 1973). Graduated exposure is generally considered to produce less stress for the client (and therapist) and thus is often preferred over the use of flooding with younger children.

Protocol-Driven Treatment Packages

Behavioral Treatment of Childhood Depression
Several treatment approaches have been evaluated for depressed children, including social skills training, strategies to increase activity level, reattribution training, and self-control techniques. Stark, Rouse, and Kurowski (1994) propose a cognitive-behavioral treatment model intervening at the affective (emotional), cognitive, and behavioral levels with the child. The primary goal of this approach is to provide the child with (1) coping skills to moderate depressive symptoms, (2) a problem-solving approach toward managing daily life problems and difficulties, and (3) an alternative way of processing information, especially regarding the self. In addition to teaching contingency management procedures, parents are engaged in the therapeutic process and provided with alternative, effective methods for parenting and creating a more positive family environment. Moreover, family interactions are targeted directly to shape and reinforce effective communication, interactions, and increase pleasant activities and positive affect. Preliminary results for this multicomponent package are promising (Stark et al., 1994).

Kendall's Cognitive-Behavioral Treatment
Kendall and colleagues (Kendall, 1990, 1991, 1992; Kendall et al., 1992) developed a comprehensive cognitive-behavioral protocol for anxious youth, focused on transmitting coping skills to children in need. Based on the premise that anxious children view the world through a "template" of threat, automatic questioning (e.g., "What if . . . "), and behavioral avoidance, treatment is focused on providing educational experiences to build a new "coping template" for the child. Therapists assist the children to reconceptualize anxiety-provoking situations as problems to be solved or situations to be coped with. A variety of cognitive-behavioral components assist the therapist and child in building the coping template: relaxation training, imagery, correcting maladaptive self-

talk, problem-solving skills, and managing reinforcers. Therapists use coping modeling, role-play rehearsals, in vivo exposure, and a collaborative therapeutic relationship with the child to facilitate the treatment progress. Parents are actively involved in all facets of treatment as collaborators in the change process. Moreover, this treatment program incorporates an innovative relapse prevention component, where the child assumes the role of an expert and produces a video or audiotaped "commercial" for the management of anxiety and fear.

In the first reported randomized clinical trial of a psychosocial intervention for anxious youth, Kendall (1994) presented impressive results supporting his sixteen-session treatment protocol. Relative to wait-list controls, 64 percent of the treated children demonstrated diagnostic remission with maintenance of results at one-year follow-up. Behavioral, self-reported, and parent-reported dependent measures showed marked superiority for the cognitive-behavioral group. This protocol is available in manual form ("The Coping Cat"), with an equally effective version adapted for Australian children ("The Coping Koala"; Heard, Dadds, & Rapee, 1992).

Family-Based Behavioral Interventions

Recognizing the impact of anxiety on the family system (see Albano, Chorpita & Barlow, 1996), and the potential for family members to inadvertently participate in the maintenance of an anxiety disorder, several investigators have developed behavioral treatment protocols directly incorporating family members in treatment.

Parental involvement in the treatment of OCD.   Research has documented the insidious nature of obsessive-compulsive disorder (OCD), its debilitating impact on a child's social and emotional functioning, and the chronicity of the disorder despite potent pharmacological intervention (Albano, Knox, & Barlow, 1995; March et al., 1995). Moreover, investigators have observed family members to become drawn into the child's rituals, either by participating in the performance of rituals, or by accommodating the child's rituals by rearranging schedules, activities, and otherwise making attempts to keep the child from exposure to fear-eliciting stimuli (see Albano et al., 1995; Albano, Chorpita, & Barlow, 1996). From a behavioral perspective, it is hypothesized that parents and family members become involved in the psychopathology of the OCD through their attempts to decrease or prevent the child's anxiety from escalating. For example, if exposure to touching the beloved family dog cues a child to become obsessed with fears of germs and contamination, resulting in the child's attempts to alleviate the obsession through repeated hand washing, then family members may attempt to prevent this exposure by keeping the dog in a pen and away from physical contact with the child. Although well intentioned, this seemingly helpful behavior serves to reinforce avoidance of the feared stimuli and perpetuate the catastrophic obsession of contamination and germs. By attempting to "protect" the child from his or her own catastrophic obsession, the family never lets the child learn that exposure to petting the dog will not lead to the feared consequence, and that excessive hand washing is unnecessary and serves to perpetuate the obsession. In effect, the family inadvertently conducts "anti-exposures" and reinforces the cycle of anxiety and avoidance. Habituation to the anxiety response is thus prevented by distressed and caring family members.

Recently, investigators examined the relative effectiveness of involving parents directly in the treatment of childhood OCD (Knox, Albano, & Barlow, 1996), with the goal to break the family's participation in maintaining the disorder, and also to incorporate parents as active agents of change. Following closely the methods found effective for the treatment of OCD in adults (Riggs & Foa, 1993), an eighteen-session exposure and response prevention (ERP) protocol with a parent component (ERP-P) was evaluated in a multiple-baseline design. ERP is based on the premise that the emotional processing of the anxiety state (upon exposure to the fear stimuli), combined with habituation to anxiety over the course of repeated exposure with prevention of the neutralizing compulsion, teaches the child that anxiety dissipates naturally and feared consequences are not directly tied to failure to perform a ritual. ERP requires sustained exposure, first imaginal followed by in vivo, to feared stimuli and prevention of the ritual continuously until habituation occurs. Typically, each ERP trial lasts upwards of forty-five minutes, and as many as two or three trials may be repeated in one session. Parents are trained in conducting both imaginal and in vivo exposures through therapist modeling, guided participation, and direct feedback. In addition, parents are given instruction in contingency management procedures (reinforcement, ignoring) and psychoeducation about the nature of anxiety and OCD from a behavioral perspective. Systematic homework is assigned to facilitate the treatment process, whereby between-session exposures are conducted twice daily. During the acute phase of treatment, sessions are held three times a week (weeks one through twelve), followed by a maintenance phase of four weekly sessions (weeks thirteen through sixteen), and two biweekly sessions to termination. A particular emphasis is placed on the child during the maintenance phase for conducting home-based ERP.

A controlled evaluation of the ERP-P protocol revealed promising results (Knox et al., 1996). Four children (ages eight to thirteen) were treated in a multiple baseline design examining the efficacy of ERP and the relative contribution of parental involvement (ERP-P) in the treatment protocol. Baseline measures were recorded for each child in a staggered baseline fashion ranging from one to four weeks, with the ordering of the children randomized. The first treatment phase consisted of therapist-assisted imaginal and in vivo exposure and response prevention. The initiation of the second phase of treatment, parent involvement in the exposure and response prevention, was staggered across participants approximately two weeks after the initiation of the first phase. Maintenance treatment began approximately two weeks after the initiation of the parent phase. In this study, results demonstrated that ERP alone was insufficient to produce any discernable change in the frequency of the children's compulsions; however, a significant decrease in compulsions occurred after the initiation of the parent component for the first two children randomized to the protocol. Effects were less clear for the third and fourth participants; however, the authors point to the comorbidity of externalizing problems as confounding these results. Children's daily self-ratings of anxiety decreased steadily throughout treatment. Several factors were discussed as potentially contributing to the obtained results: (1) parents may have disengaged from participating in rituals as a function of becoming involved in exposures and trained in the use of positive reinforcement principles, (2) positive reinforcement may have prompted motivation and compliance with exposures, and (3) treatment effects may have been delayed from the first phase of therapist-only treatment. These results hold promise for the continued development of parent-based treatment protocols for children with anxiety disorders in general. Future research should use group comparisons of children treated with and without parental involvement in a randomized controlled trial.

Family anxiety management. Family Anxiety Management (FAM; Heard, Dadds, & Rapee, 1992) was developed as a parallel program to Kendall's cognitive-behavioral program, and is based on behavioral family intervention strategies found effective for the treatment of externalizing disorders in youth (Sanders & Dadds, 1992). Following the completion of each child's session with the therapist, the child and parents would participate in a FAM session with the therapist. The main focus of the program is to empower parents and children by forming an "expert team" to overcome and master anxiety. Parents are trained in reinforcement strategies, with emphasis on differential reinforcement and systematic ignoring of excessive complaining and anxious behavior. Contingency management strategies are the main methods for reducing conflict and increasing cooperation and communication in the family. Moreover, parents are provided training in communication and problem-solving skills so that they will be better able to function as a team in solving future problems.

Barrett, Dadds, and Rapee (1996) report on a controlled investigation comparing children treated with Kendall's cognitive behavioral treatment (CBT) to a group treated with CBT+FAM, and a wait-list control. Across treatment conditions, 69.8 percent of children no longer met diagnostic criteria for an anxiety disorder as compared to 26 percent of children in the control condition. At one-year follow-up, 70.3 percent of children in the CBT group did not meet criteria for diagnosis, as compared to 95.6 percent of the CBT+FAM group. Self-report and clinician ratings supported the increased effectiveness of the family intervention relative to CBT alone. Interestingly, younger children and females responded better to the CBT+FAM condition.

Protocols for Social Phobia and Related Social Interaction Problems
Peer-pairing. Peer interaction plays a crucial role in children's social and emotional development. As such, disturbances in peer relationships constitute a risk factor for subsequent psychopathology (Parker & Asher, 1987). Peer-neglected children are those who are neither rated as liked nor disliked by their peers and are typically characterized as shy and withdrawn. Peer-neglected children have been found to report higher levels of social anxiety (LaGreca et al., 1988) and depression (Kupersmidt & Patterson, 1991) than popular and peer-rejected children. Furthermore, children with an anxiety disorder were more likely to be classified as peer-neglected than both psychiatric and nonpsychiatric controls (Strauss, Lahey, Frick, Frame, & Hynd, 1988).

The utility of a peer-pairing procedure in improving the peer acceptance and positive social interaction rate of peer-neglected children was addressed in a recent study by Morris, Messer and Gross (1995). Twenty-four peer-neglected children and twenty-four popular children (matched for sex, age, and classroom) were identified via sociometric nominations from an initial pool of 390 first- and second-grade children. Playground observations of social interaction during recess were also obtained. Twelve of the peer-neglected children (and their matched popular peer) were assigned at random to the peer-pairing intervention. The remaining children were assigned to a no-treatment, control condition. Peer-pairing consisted of one-on-one interaction sessions, with each peer-neglected child paired with a same-sex, popular child from his or her own classroom. During the peer-pairing sessions, children engaged in joint-task activities requiring interaction (e.g., card games). Twelve sessions (fifteen to twenty minutes each) were conducted across a four-week period.

Following the peer-pairing intervention, substantial improvements in peer acceptance and positive interaction rate were noted. With regard to social status, 75 percent of target children in the treatment group shifted from a neglected to an average or popular sociometric classification (only 17 percent of controls demonstrated improvement in social status). Individual gains in absolute percentage of time spent in positive interaction on the playground during recess ranged from 13 percent to 45 percent over baseline levels (average gain = 28 percent). Prior to intervention all peer-neglected children were found to have positive interaction rates significantly below the mean rates of average- and popular-status children. Following the peer-pairing intervention, 50 percent of the treatment group had positive interaction rates *above* the mean rate obtained for average- and popular-status children. No increase in positive interaction rate was observed for the control group. Gains in peer acceptance and positive social interaction remained constant at a one-month follow-up.

The authors suggest that peer-pairing intervention may be conceptualized as the provision and structuring of a facilitative environment conducive to mutually reinforcing social interaction influences. Changes in behavior follow from changes in social reinforcement contingencies. Improvements in observed behavior among peer-neglected children may be explained by reinforcement mechanisms operating in the peer-pairing condition. In addition, changes in peer perceptions may derive largely from the altered perceptions and behavior of the peer confederates as a result of social interaction effects. Put simply, children in the peer-pairing intervention appeared to enjoy playing together, which may have increased the probability that they would play together at their next regular recess period. Other children could then witness the pair playing together, which may have increased the probability that they too would interact with the target child. Such processes may lead to peer-neglected children becoming integrated in the popular peer's social group.

Social effectiveness therapy for children.   Social Effectiveness Therapy for Children (SET-C; Beidel, Turner, & Morris, 1994) is a multicomponent behavioral treatment program for childhood social phobia. SET-C is a comprehensive treatment program designed to reduce social anxiety, enhance social skill, increase participation in social activities, and improve self-confidence. Components of the SET-C program include Parent Education, Social Skills Training and Peer Generalization, Graduated In Vivo Exposure, and Programmed Practice. The length of the treatment program is sixteen weeks. The Parent Education component consists of one session on the nature of social anxiety and an overview of the treatment program. Subsequent to the parent education component, treatment sessions are held twice weekly for twelve weeks: one small group session (Social Skills Training) and one individual session (Graduated In Vivo Exposure).

Group sessions are 180 minutes in length (60 minutes social skills training and 120 minutes peer generalization experiences). Strategies used to teach and reinforce appropriate social behavior include instruction, modeling, behavior rehearsal, feedback, and social reinforcement. SET-C targets five major topic areas: nonverbal social skills, initiating and maintaining conversations, joining groups of children, friendship establishment and maintenance, positive assertion, and negative assertion. A unique and essential component of SET-C is the use of formalized peer interaction experiences to assist in the generalization of social skills to situations outside the clinic. "Normal" child volunteers are recruited from the community to serve as peer facilitators in the peer generalization experiences (developmentally appropriate group recreational activities, e.g., roller skating). Following completion of the group social skills training and individual graduated exposure components, four additional weekly sessions are devoted to programmed practice. Program practice consists of individualized therapist-directed exposure activities that the child completes in the natural environment, unaccompanied by the therapist. Although a three-year NIH-funded study is in progress to empirically assess the efficacy of SET-C in treating childhood social phobia, initial results have been extremely promising.

Cognitive-behavioral group treatment for adolescent social phobia (CBGT-A).   Albano and colleagues (Albano, 1995; Albano, DiBartolo, Heimberg, & Barlow, 1995; Albano, Marten, Holt, Heimberg, & Barlow, 1995) developed a sixteen-session, cognitive-behavioral group treatment protocol for social phobia in adolescents. Based upon Heimberg's (Heimberg, Dodge, Hope, et al., 1990; Hope & Heimberg, 1993) successful treatment program for adult social phobia, and combining procedures found to be effective in the treatment of shy adolescents (Christoff, Scott, Kelley et al., 1985; Franco, Christoff, Crimmins, et al., 1983), CBGT-A was developed to meet the clinical and developmental needs of adolescents with social phobia. Appropriate for adolescents ages thirteen through seventeen, CBGT-A combines psychoeducation, skills training (cognitive restructuring, problem-solving, social and assertiveness skills) and systematic behavioral exposures both within session and in vivo. Therapists rely heavily on modeling, role-playing, positive reinforcement, and skill rehearsal as mechanisms of treatment. Parents are involved in a limited number of sessions in order to present the treatment rationale and cognitive-behavioral conceptualization of the disorder, and to enlist the parents as "coaches" to assist with the between-session exposure homework. Given the adolescents' developmental task of individuation and independence (see Albano & Barlow, 1996), parental involvement was kept to a minimum to encourage independent functioning and place greater responsibility for change directly on the adolescents. Detailed descriptions of the protocol and clinical case examples can be found elsewhere (Albano, 1995; Albano & Barlow, 1996; Albano, DiBartolo, et al., 1995). A preliminary study of five adolescents who completed the protocol offered promising results (Albano, Marten, et al., 1995). Despite high comorbidity with overanxious disorder and mood disorders, diagnostic and behavioral test data indicate remission of the disorder and decreased levels of anxiety and depression through one-year follow up. A controlled, NIMH-funded investigation of this protocol is currently in progress.

Conclusions

Anxiety and depression in children and adolescents has been the topic of considerable interest from a theoretical standpoint, yet advances in the behavioral treatment of these disorders is still in its infancy. Nevertheless, the treatment of children and adolescents is a fertile area for bridging the gap between theory and therapy, and one where behavioral models are at the forefront. Although other treatment modalities exist and are fairly widely used for treating depression and anxiety in children (e.g., pharmacotherapy, play therapy, family interventions), controlled evidence in support of these treatments is practically nonexistent. Behavioral treatment approaches, and multicomponent cognitive-behavioral packages, hold much promise for addressing conditions of negative affectivity in youth, with empirical support for specific strategies and techniques mounting. Of particular note is the approach taken by the aforementioned investigators to intervene in ways that are sensitive to the developmental level of the child (e.g., Cornwall et al., 1996) or adolescent (Albano et al., 1995), while attending to the unique cognitive-developmental and familial factors inherent in these emotional disorders. Thus, adult interventions are not simply applied to children, rather, efforts are made to understand the mechanisms of action exerting influence over the etiology and maintenance of these disorders such that developmentally appropriate treatments can be devised and applied. As behavior therapists we have a strong tradition of empirical validation through rigorous experimentation of our models of behavior and intervention. Our tasks with regard to the childhood internalizing disorders is to further our understanding of the risk and protective factors operating in the etiology and maintenance of these disorders, and to increase our focus on developing and validating effective treatment protocols that are grounded in behavioral theory. We hope that this chapter will spark interest and enthusiasm in these pursuits.

References

Abramson, L. Y., Seligman, M. E. P., & Teasdale, J. (1978). Learned helplessness in humans: Critique and reformulation. *Journal of Abnormal Psychology, 87,* 49–74.

Albano, A. M. (1995). Treatment of social anxiety in adolescents. *Cognitive and Behavioral Practice, 2,* 271–298.

Albano, A. M., & Barlow, D. H. (1996). Breaking the vicious cycle: Cognitive-behavioral group treatment for adolescent social phobia. In E. D. Hibbs & P. Jensen (Eds.), *Psychosocial treatment research for child and adolescent disorders* (pp. 43–62). Washington, DC: American Psychological Association.

Albano, A. M., Chorpita, B. F., & Barlow, D. H. (1996). Anxiety disorders. In E. J. Mash & R. A. Barkley (Eds.), *Child Psychopathology* (pp. 196–241). New York: Guilford.

Albano, A. M., DiBartolo, P. M., Heimberg, R. G., & Barlow, D. H. (1995). Children and adolescents: Assessment and treatment. In R. G. Heimberg, M. R. Liebowitz, D. A. Hope, & F. Schneier (Eds.), *Social phobia: Diagnosis, assessment, and treatment* (pp. 387–425). New York: Guilford.

Albano, A. M., Knox, L. S., & Barlow, D. H. (1995). Obsessive-compulsive disorder. In A. R. Eisen, C. A. Kearney, & C. E. Schaefer, (Eds.)., *Clinical handbook of anxiety disorders in children and adolescents* (pp. 282–316). Northvale, NJ: Jason Aronson.

Albano, A. M., Marten, P. A., Holt, C. S., Heimberg, R. G., & Barlow, D. H. (1995). Cognitive-behavioral group treatment for social phobia in adolescents: A preliminary study. *Journal of Nervous and Mental Disease, 183,* 685–692.

Altmann, E. O., & Gotlib, I. H. (1988). The social behavior of depressed children: An observational study. *Journal of Abnormal Child Psychology, 16,* 29–44.

Barlow, D. H. (1988). *Anxiety and its disorders.* New York: Guilford.

Barlow, D. H. (1991). Disorder of emotion. *Psychological Inquiry, 2,* 58–71.

Barlow, D. H., Chorpita, B. F., & Turovsky, J. (In press). Fear, panic, anxiety, and the disorders of emotion. In D. A. Hope (Ed.), *Nebraska symposium on motivation: Integrated views of motivation and emotion, Vol. 43.* Lincoln: University of Nebraska Press.

Barlow, D. H., DiNardo, P. A., Vermilyea, J. A., & Blanchard, E. B. (1986). Comorbidity and depression among the anxiety disorders: Issues in diagnosis and classification. *Journal of Nervous and Mental Disease, 174,* 63–72.

Barrett, P. M., Dadds, M. R., & Rapee, R. M. (1996). Family intervention for childhood anxiety: A controlled trial. *Journal of Consulting and Clinical Psychology, 64,* 333–342.

Barrios, B., & O'Dell, S. (1989). Fears and anxieties. In E. J. Mash & R. A. Barkley (Eds.), *Treatment of childhood disorders* (pp. 167–221). New York: Guilford.

Beck, A. T. (1967). *Depression: Clinical, experimental, and theoretical aspects.* New York: Harper & Row.

Beck, A. T., (1976). *Cognitive therapy and the emotional disorders.* New York: International Universities Press.

Beck, A. T., & Emery, G. (1985). *Anxiety disorders and phobias: A cognitive perspective.* New York: Basic Books.

Beck, A. T., Rush, A. J., Shaw, B. F., & Emery, G. (1979). *Cognitive therapy for depression: A treatment manual.* New York: Guilford.

Beidel, D. C., Turner, S. M., & Morris, T. L. (1994). *Social Effectiveness Training for Children—Treatment Manual.* Unpublished manuscript.

Blechman, E. A., McEnroe, M. J., Carella, E. T., & Audette, D. P. (1986). Childhood competence and depression. *Journal of Abnormal Psychology, 95,* 223–227.

Brady, E. U., & Kendall, P. C., (1992). Comorbidity of anxiety and depression in children and adolescents. *Psychological Bulletin, 111,* 244–255.

Christoff, K. A., Scott, W. O. N., Kelley, M. L., Schlundt, D., Baer, G., & Kelly, J. A. (1985). Social skills and social problem-solving training for shy young adolescents. *Behavior Therapy, 16,* 468–477.

Chorpita, B. F., Albano, A. M., & Barlow, D. H. (1996). Cognitive processing in anxious children: Relation to anxiety and family influences. *Journal of Clinical Child Psychology, 25,* 170–176.

Chorpita, B. F., & Barlow, D. H. (1995). *Control in the early environment: Implications for the development of childhood anxiety.* Unpublished manuscript, State University of New York at Albany.

Cole, D. A., & Rehm, L. P. (1986). Family interaction patterns and childhood depression. *Journal of Abnormal Psychology, 14,* 297–314.

Cornwall, E., Spence, S. H., & Schotte, D. (1996). The effectiveness of emotive imagery in the treatment of darkness phobia in children. *Behaviour Change, 13,* 223–229.

Dadds, M. R., Barrett, P. M., Rapee, R. M., & Ryan, S. (In press). Family process and child anxiety and aggression: An observational analysis. *Journal of Abnormal Child Psychology.*

Dadds, M. R., & Barrett, P. M. (1996). Family processes in child and adolescent anxiety and depression. *Behaviour Change, 13,* 231–239.

Dadds, M. R., Sanders, M. R., Morrison, M., & Regbetz, M. (1992). Childhood depression and conduct disorder: An analysis of family interaction patterns in the home. *Journal of Abnormal Psychology, 101,* 505–513.

Delprato, D. J. (1980). Hereditary determinants of fears and phobias: A critical review. *Behavior Therapy, 11,* 79–103.

Eisen, A. R., & Kearney, C. A. (1995). *Practitioner's guide to treating fear and anxiety in children and adolescents: A cognitive-behavioral approach.* Northvale, NJ: Jason Aronson.

Ferster, C. B. (1966). Arbitrary and natural reinforcement. *Psychological Record, 17,* 341–347.

Ferster, C. B. (1973). A functional analysis of depression. *American Psychologist, 28,* 857–870.

Franco, D. P., Christoff, K. A., Crimmins, D. B., et al. (1983). Social skills training for an extremely shy young adolescent: An empirical case study. *Behavior Therapy, 14,* 568–575.

Heard, P. M., Dadds, M. R., & Rapee, R. M. (1992). *The role of family intervention in the treatment of child anxiety disorders.* Paper presented at the World Congress on Behavioural Therapy, Gold Coast, Australia, July 1992.

Heimberg, R. G., Dodge, C. S., Hope, D. A., Kennedy, C. R., Zollo, L., & Becker, R. E. (1990). Cognitive behavioral group treatment for social phobia: Comparison with a credible placebo control. *Cognitive Therapy and Research, 14,* 1–23.

Hope, D. A., & Heimberg, R. G. (1993). Social phobia and social anxiety. In D. H. Barlow (Ed.), *Clinical handbook of psychological disorders* (2nd ed.) (pp. 99–136). New York: Guilford.

Jones, M. C. (1924). The elimination of children's fears. *Journal of Experimental Psychology, 7,* 382–390.

Kagan, J., Reznick, J. S., & Snidman, N. (1987). The physiology and psychology of behavioral inhibition. *Child Development, 58,* 1459–1473.

Kaslow, N. J., Brown, R. T., & Mee, L. L. (1994). Cognitive and behavioral correlates of childhood depression: A developmental perspective. In W. M. Reynolds & H. F. Johnston (Eds.), *Handbook of depression in children and adolescents* (pp. 97–121). New York: Plenum.

Kaslow, N. J., Rehm, L. P., Pollack, A., & Siegel, A. W. (1988). Attributional style and self-control behavior in depressed and nondepressed children and their parents. *Journal of Abnormal Child Psychology, 16,* 163–177.

Kaslow, N. J., Rehm, L. P., & Siegel, A. W. (1984). Social cognitive and cognitive correlates of depression in children. *Journal of Abnormal Child Psychology, 12,* 605–620.

Kazdin, A. E., Esveldt-Dawson, K., Sherick, R. B., & Colbus, D. (1985). Assessment of overt behavior and childhood depression among psychiatrically disturbed children. *Journal of Consulting and Clinical Psychology, 53,* 201–210.

Kendall, P. C. (1990). *Coping cat workbook.* Available from author, 238 Meeting House Lane, Merion Station, PA, 19066.

Kendall, P. C. (1991). Guiding theory for treating children and adolescents. In P. C. Kendall (Ed.), *Child and adolescent therapy: Cognitive-behavioral procedures* (pp. 3–24). New York: Guilford.

Kendall, P. C. (1992). Healthy thinking. *Behavior Therapy, 23,* 1–11.

Kendall, P. C. (1994). Treating anxiety disorders in children: Results of a randomized clinical trial. *Journal of Consulting and Clinical Psychology, 62,* 100–110.

Kendall, P. C., Chansky, T. E., Kane, M. T., Kim, R., Kortlander, E., Ronan, K. R., Sessa, F.M., & Siqueland, L. (1992). *Anxiety disorders in youth: Cognitive-behavioral interventions.* Boston: Allyn & Bacon.

Kendall, P. C., & Ingram, R. (1989). Cognitive-behavioral perspectives: Theory and research on depression and anxiety. In P. C. Kendall & D. Watson (Eds.), *Anxiety and depression: Distinctive and overlapping features* (pp. 27–53). New York: Academic Press.

Knox, L. S., Albano, A. M., & Barlow, D. H. (1996). Exposure and response prevention in the treatment of childhood obsessive-compulsive disorder: A multiple-baseline examination incorporating parents. *Behavior Therapy, 27,* 93–115.

Kovacs, M. (1981). Rating scales to assess depression in school-aged children. *Acta Paedopsychiatrica, 46,* 305–316.

Kupersmidt, J. B., & Patterson, C. J. (1991). Childhood peer rejection, aggression, withdrawal, and perceived competence as predictors of self-reported behavior problems in preadolescence. *Journal of Abnormal Child Psychology, 19,* 427–447.

LaGreca, A. M., Dandes, S. K., Wick, P., Shaw, K., & Stone, W. L. (1988). Development of the Social Anxiety Scale for Children: Reliability and concurrent validity. *Journal of Clinical Child Psychology, 17,* 84–91.

Last, C. G., Hersen, M., Kazdin, A. E., Finkelstein, R., & Strauss, C. C. (1987). Comparison of DSM-III separation anxiety and overanxious disorders: Demographic characteristics and patterns of comorbidity. *Journal of the American Academy of Child and Adolescent Psychiatry, 26,* 527–531.

Larson, R. W., Raffaelli, M., Richards, M. H., Ham, M., & Jewell, L. (1990). Ecology of depression in late childhood and early adolesence: A profile of daily states and activities. *Journal of Abnormal Psychology, 99,* 92–102.

Lazarus, A. A., & Abramovitz, A. (1962). The use of "emotive imagery" in the treatment of children's phobias. *Journal of Mental Science, 108,* 191–195.

Leitenberg, H., & Callahan, E. (1973). Reinforced practice and reduction of different kinds of fears in adults and children. *Behaviour Research and Therapy, 11,* 19–30.

Levis, D. J. (1985). Implosive therapy: A comprehensive extension of conditioning theory of fear/anxiety to psychopathology. In S. Reiss & R. R. Bootzin (Eds.), *Theoretical issues in behavior therapy* (pp. 49–82). New York: Academic Press.

Lewinsohn, P. M. (1974). A behavioral approach to depression. In R. M. Friedman & M. M. Katz (Eds.),

The psychology of depression: Contemporary theory and research (pp. 157–185). New York: Wiley.

Lewinsohn, P. M., Biglan, A., & Zeiss, A. M. (1976). Behavioral treatment of depression. In P. O. Davidson (Ed.), *Behavioral management of anxiety, depression, and pain* (pp. 91–146). New York: Brunner/Mazel.

Lyons, J. A., & Scotti, J. R. (1995). Behavioral treatment of a motor vehicle accident survivor: An illustrative case of direct therapeutic exposure. *Cognitive and Behavioral Practice, 2,* 343–364.

March, J. S., Leonard, H. L., & Swedo, S.E. (1995). In J. S. March (Ed.), *Anxiety disorders in children and adolescents* (pp. 251–275) New York: Guilford.

Mash, E. J., & Barkley, R. A. (Eds.). (1989). *Treatment of childhood disorders.* New York: Guilford.

Mineka, S., & Zinbarg, R. (In press). Conditioning and etiological models of anxiety disorders. In D. A. Hope (Ed.), *Nebraska symposium on motivation: Integrated views of motivation and emotion, Vol. 43.* Lincoln: University of Nebraska Press.

Morris, R. J., & Kratochwill, T. R. (1983). Childhood fears and phobias. In R. J. Morris & T. R. Kratochwill (Eds.), *The practice of child therapy* (pp. 53–86). New York: Pergamon.

Morris, T. L., Messer, S. C., & Gross, A. M. (1995). Enhancement of the social interaction and status of neglected children: A peer-pairing approach. *Journal of Clinical Child Psychology, 24,* 11–20.

Mowrer, O. H. (1947). On the dual nature of learning—a reinterpretation of "conditioning" and "problem-solving." *Harvard Educational Review, 17,* 102–148.

Mowrer, O. H. (1960). *Learning theory and behavior.* New York: Wiley.

Nolan-Hoeksema, S., Girgus, J. S., & Seligman, M. E. P. (1986). Learned helplessness in children: A longitudinal study of depression, achievement, and explanatory style. *Journal of Personality and Social Psychology, 51,* 435–442.

Ollendick, T. H., & Cerny, J. A. (1981). *Clinical behavior therapy with children.* New York: Plenum.

Ollendick, T. H., King, N. J., & Yule, W. (Eds.). (1994). *International handbook of phobic and anxiety disorders in children and adolescents.* New York: Plenum.

Ollendick, T. H., Matson, J. L., & Helsel, W. J. (1985). Fears in children and adolescents: Normative data. *Behaviour Research and Therapy, 23,* 465–467.

Parker, J. G., & Asher, S. R. (1987). Peer relations and later personal adjustment: Are low accepted children at risk? *Psychological Bulletin, 102* (3), 357–389.

Rehm, L. P. (1977). A self-control model of depression. *Behavior Therapy, 8,* 787–804.

Reynolds, W. M., & Johnston, H. F. (Eds.). (1994). *Handbook of depression in children and adolescents.* New York: Plenum.

Riggs, D., & Foa, E. (1993). Obsessive-compulsive disorder. In D. H. Barlow (Ed.), *Clinical handbook of psychological disorders* (pp. 189-239). New York: Guilford.

Sacco, W. P., & Graves, D. J. (1984). Childhood depression, interpersonal problem-solving, and self-ratings of performance. *Journal of Clinical Child Psychology, 13,* 10–15.

Sanders, M., & Dadds, M. R. (1992). *Behavioral family intervention.* New York: Pergamon.

Saylor, C. F., Finch, A. J., Spirito, A., & Bennett, B. (1984). The Children's Depression Inventory: A systematic evaluation of psychometric properties. *Journal of Consulting and Clinical Psychology, 52,* 955–967.

Seligman, M. E. P. (1970). Phobias and preparedness. *Behavior Therapy, 2,* 307–320.

Seligman, M. E. P. (1975). *Helplessness: On depression, development and death.* San Francisco: Freeman.

Seligman, M. E. P. (1981). A learned helplessness point of view. In L. P. Rehm (Ed.), *Behavior therapy for depression* (pp. 123–141). New York: Academic Press.

Skinner, B. F. (1953). *Science and human behavior.* New York: Macmillan.

Skinner, B. F. (1957). *Verbal behavior.* Englewood Cliffs, NJ: Prentice-Hall.

Spence, S. H. (1994). Practitioner review: Cognitive therapy with children and adolescents: From theory to practice. *Journal of Child Psychology and Psychiatry, 35,* 1191–1228.

Sroufe, L. A. (1990). Considering the normal and abnormal together: The essence of developmental psychopathology. *Development and Psychopathology, 2,* 335–347.

Stark, K. D., Rouse, L. W., & Kurowski, C. (1994). Psychological treatment approaches for depression in children. In W. M. Reynolds & H. F. Johnston (Eds.), *Handbook of depression in children and adolescents* (pp. 275–307). New York: Plenum.

Strauss, C. C., Lahey, B. B., Frick, P., Frame, C. L., & Hynd, G. W. (1988). Peer social status of children with anxiety disorders. *Journal of Consulting and Clinical Psychology, 56,* 137–141.

Watson, D., & Clark, L. A. (1984). Negative affectivity: The disposition to experience aversive emotional states. *Psychological Bulletin, 96,* 465–490.

Watson, J. B., & Rayner, P. (1920). Conditioned emotional reactions. *Journal of Experimental Psychology, 3,* 1–14.

Wolpe, J. (1958). *Psychotherapy by reciprocal inhibition.* Stanford, CA: Stanford University Press.

11

ALZHEIMER'S DISEASE AND BEHAVIORAL GERONTOLOGY

JOSEPH J. PLAUD
Department of Psychology
Judge Rotenberg Educational Center

THOMAS H. MOSLEY
Department of Medicine
University of Mississippi School of Medicine

MARCIA MOBERG
Department of Psychology
University of North Dakota

Behavior therapy, as a direct application of behavioral theory and science, represents one of the major attempts to show lawful relationships among behavioral events, and to understand the behavioral factors that are associated with major age-related phenomenon. Skinner (1961) proposed two relevant independent variables of which behavior is a function: environmental and genetic/physiological variables. The experimental analysis of behavior has been primarily concerned with the study of environmental events on the acquisition and maintenance of behavior, largely because of the difficulty of manipulating genetic or biological variables directly (Skinner, 1988). Progressive dementing illnesses such as Alzheimer's disease (AD) present the behavioral researcher and clinician with the ability to study the effects of organic disease on behavior in order to examine the functional relationship between a particular physiological state and behavior (Plaud, Moberg, & Ferraro, in press).

A basic understanding of the behavioral effects of dementing illnesses such as AD will help to identify environmental influences that may lead to a mitigation of the impairment of memory and intellectual functioning seen in victims of AD (Gatz, 1990). A central question is whether age-related phenomena systematically affect learning parameters such as operant conditionability of humans; and if so, what kinds of effects are evidenced? Answers to this question have implications for the development and implementation of behavior therapy strategies for geriatric populations (e.g., stimulus control interventions, differential reinforcement strategies, and so on). This chapter will focus on issues related to behavioral gerontology, focusing on etiological and epidemiological issues relating to dementia and more specifically AD. We will then review basic and applied behavioral studies of the aging process, with special consideration given to behavioral studies concerned with the impact of dementia and AD on behavior, and how such behavior can be modified through applications of the principles of behavior therapy.

Epidemiology

AD has become a major health concern in the United States and other Western countries. Persons afflicted with AD become mentally and physically disabled, usually resulting in the necessity of institutional care and death within fifteen years of the onset of symptoms. AD is the fourth leading cause of death in the United States, resulting in more than 100,000 deaths per year (The Alzheimer's Disease and Related Disorders Association, 1992). Incident rates have been estimated at 127 cases per 100,000 persons per year, and prevalence rates estimated at 5.8 cases per 100 persons per year.

AD is the most common cause of senile dementia and the principle cause of institutionalization for the elderly (Terry & Katzman, 1992). Prevalence rates for AD have been strongly correlated with age, particularly after the age of seventy-five years. In a community population study conducted in East Boston, Evans et al. (1989) reported a prevalence rate for AD of 10.3 percent in individuals over age sixty-five. Estimates rose with the age of the cohort examined (e.g., 3 percent, sixty-five to seventy-four; 18.7 percent, seventy-five to eighty four; and 47.2 percent, over eighty-five). Total costs associated with treating AD and related medical complications have been estimated at $90 billion dollars per year in the U.S. alone. AD therefore is a growing problem that exerts a tremendous burden upon the victims of AD, the families of AD patients, and upon the social networks supporting the care of AD patients. Given the phenomenal personal and societal costs associated with AD, the past decade has seen a marked growth in basic research into the many problems associated with AD (Roth, 1986).

Etiology

Prichard (1835) described a syndrome he called senile dementia (or incoherence), characterized by the forgetting of recent impressions, while impressions formed in the long past remained unhindered (Henderson, 1986). Seventy-two years later, Alois Alzheimer (Alzheimer, 1907) published a case report of a woman who had died prematurely at age fifty-one of dementia. Alzheimer noted the presence of abnormal and degenerative neurons in the cerebral cortex. The disease that now bears his name, senile dementia of the Alzheimer's type or Alzheimer's disease, was used to describe a presenile onset of dementia until 1970, when Tomlinson, Blessed, and Roth reported similar symptomatology in patients with both early and late onset of dementia (Crook, 1987).

At present, the diagnosis of AD can only be confirmed through microscopic autopsy of brain tissue (Crook, 1987). Blessed, Tomlinson, and Roth (1968) found evidence for the existence of two types of dementia, noting the correlation between mental functioning (up to nine months prior to death) and autopsy pathology reports. One type was associated with decreasing mental functioning as a function of increased numbers of senile plaques (i.e., spherical lesions containing amyloid beta-protein surrounded by degenerated cellular fragments). The second type was produced by arteriosclerotic changes with multiple areas of infarction. The amount of infarcted brain tissue correlated with the severity of dementia. This second type is not considered AD, but rather multi-infarct (now termed vascular) dementia.

Autopsies of AD patients have also revealed the presence of neurofibrillary tangles (i.e., a number of pairs of neuronal filaments wrapped in a helical manner), the density of which is related to the severity of the dementia (Farmer, Peck, & Terry, 1976). A third neuropathological change (Crook, 1987) seen in autopsies of AD patients is the granulo-vacuolar degeneration of neurons in the cerebral cortex (i.e., hippocampal cellular degeneration resulting in fluid-filled intracellular vacuoles). Other organic changes include neuron degeneration within subcortical areas of the brain (Whitehouse, Price, Clark, Coyle, & Delong, 1981), widespread atrophy of various brain regions (e.g., hippocampus and the basal nucleus of Meynert; Crook, 1987), and reduction in levels of cerebral RNA (Sajdel-Sulkowska & Marotta, 1984).

To date, a stronger case has been made for a genetic etiology in early onset (occurring before age sixty-five) compared to late-onset cases of AD. This apparent distinction has given rise to the terms familial AD and sporadic AD (without known familial predisposition). Late-onset cases may also have a genetic component; however, this relationship may be harder to demonstrate in late-onset patients as family members with the faulty gene are more likely to be deceased from other causes. Familial AD has been related to an inherited autosomal dominant trait with linkage to several chromosomes, including chromosomes 21, 19, and 14. Interestingly, patients with Down's syndrome (trisomy 21), begin to show neuropathologic and neurochemical changes after the age of forty similar to those of AD patients (Barnes, 1987; Perry, 1986). The potential importance of nongenetic factors should also be noted (e.g., the majority of AD patients have no family history of AD; and the concordance rate for identical twins is only 50 percent).

Perry (1986) discussed structures that morphologically resemble plaques in AD that occur in a group of rare CNS diseases known to be associated with infective agents and assumed to be slow viruses (e.g., scrapie [in animals], kuru, and Creutzfeldt-Jakob disease). All may be transmitted to the same or other species from affected brain tissue. Thus far, attempts to transmit AD to animals have been unsuccessful. The presence of plaques in the brains of most elderly and many middle-aged individuals suggests that if any such putative slow virus causes AD, it must infect almost the entire human population and other mammalian species known to develop plaques in old age. To date, no such infectious agent has been identified.

A possible etiological relationship between enhanced aluminum exposure and impaired cognition has been suggested for residents in Guam (in a region where high contents of aluminum are found in the water) and for hemodialysis patients exposed to high doses of aluminum in medications and in dialysate fluid. Although aluminum salts appear to accumulate in the brains of AD patients, aluminum exposure does not appear to lead to Alzheimer's-type lesions. Longer-term studies will have to determine the possible effects of life-long exposure to aluminum in the environment and its potential for cumulative toxicity (Meiri, Banin, & Roll, 1991; Perry, 1986).

Biochemical abnormalities in specific neurotransmitter systems (e.g., cholinergic) and neuropeptides (e.g., somatostatin) have also been associated with clinical and pathologic markers of AD. The frontal cortex, hippocampus, and the nucleus basalis are areas rich in cholinergic projections and areas that have been consistently implicated in AD dysfunction (Sparks et al., 1992). Reductions of choline acetyltransferase (ChAT), acetylcholinesterase (AchE), and acetylcholine (Ach) have been strongly associated with cognitive impairment and memory loss in AD (Sparks et al., 1992). Noradrenaline and serotonin have also been implicated in cognition and the behavioral symptoms associated in AD (Whitehouse, 1992; Whitehouse, Struble, Uhl, & Price, 1985). Noradrenergic abnormalities may be more closely linked to noncognitive symptoms of AD, such as pacing, agitation, or depression.

Classification of Alzheimer's Disease

Dementia is a term used to describe a variety of organic disorders rather than a specific disease (Crook, 1987). It describes a "syndrome of intellectual impairment produced by brain dysfunction" (Cummings & Benson, 1983). Although efforts to arrive at a singular definition of dementia have met with controversy (Fliers, Lisei, & Swaab, 1983), current descriptions of dementia have focused on a syndrome of symptomatology, though idiographic instances may differ widely (Van Crevel, 1986). The term *dementia* made its first recorded appearance in the first two centuries A.D. in the works of the Romans Aurelius Cornelius Celsus and Galen (Crook, 1987). The first signs of progress in the conceptualization or treatment of dementia did not appear until the end of the eighteenth century, when the French physician Pinel became superintendent of the Bicetre (Mora, 1985; Crook, 1987). Pinel and his student Esquirol developed a descriptive system of psychopathology that included melancholia, mania, idiocy, and dementia. The latter was subdivided into three types: acute, chronic, and senile dementia (Crook, 1987). It was not until the twentieth century that the term *dementia* defined mental disturbances arising from organic rather than functional etiologies (Crook, 1987).

Criteria for the diagnosis of dementia and AD have been developed by three primary groups: the Consortium to Establish a Registry for Alzheimer's Disease (CERAD, 1987); the American Psychiatric Association Diagnostic and Statistical Manual of Mental Disorders, Fourth Edition (DSM-IV; APA, 1994); and a joint workgroup representing the National Institute of Neurological and Communicative Disorders and Stroke (NINCDS) and the Alzheimer's Disease and Related Disorders Association (ADRDA; McKhann, Drachman, Folstein, Katzman, Price, & Stadlan, 1984).

NINCDS-ADRDA criteria for the clinical diagnosis of "probable" AD requires (1) dementia to be established by clinical examination, documented by a mental status examination, and confirmed by neuropsychological testing; (2) deficits in two or more areas of cognitive functioning; (3) progressive worsening of memory and other cognitive functions (e.g., problem solving, language, motor skills, perception); (4) no disturbance of consciousness; (5) onset between the ages of forty and ninety; and (6) absence of systemic disorders or other brain diseases that may account for the decline in functioning. Typically AD involves an insidious onset with a gradual and steady deteriorating course (Crook, 1987). CERAD criteria are similar to those of the NINCDS-ADRDA except that the CERAD criteria require a symptom progression of twelve months rather than six months as outlined by the NINCDS-ADRDA.

DSM-IV criteria require (1) the development of multiple cognitive deficits, one of which must be memory impairment, and at least one of the following: aphasia, apraxia, agnosia, or disturbance in executive functioning; (2) these deficits must cause significant impairment in social or occupational functioning and must represent a significant decline from previous functioning; (3) gradual onset and progressive cognitive decline; (4) cognitive deficits are not attributable to other central nervous system conditions (e.g., Parkinson's disease, Huntington's disease), systemic conditions (e.g., hyperthyroidism, HIV infection), substance-induced conditions, or other psychiatric disorders (e.g., depression, schizophrenia); and (5) the deficits do not occur exclusively during the course of a delirium.

As noted above, a definitive diagnosis of AD can be made only with cerebral biopsy or autopsy. Using specific clinical and laboratory criteria as those described, however, has made it possible to obtain a highly accurate clinical diagnosis.

Assessment of Alzheimer's Disease

In the elderly, diagnosis of cognitive impairment is often complicated by concomitant chronic illness, polypharmacy, psychiatric disorders (e.g., depression), and normal aging. Disentangling these factors from AD requires a comprehensive physical, laboratory, neurological, and neuropsychological evaluation. The medical evaluation of dementia typically consists of (1) a complete history including the nature of the earliest symptoms, onset, and course of the symptoms; (2) a physical examination, including sensory and motor tests; (3) laboratory investigations, including thyroid and liver function tests, serologic tests for syphilis and HIV, complete blood count, electrolyte panel, metabolic panel, and urinalysis; (4) mental status examination; and (5) other tests, such as chest X-ray, electrocardiogram, electroencephalogram, and Neuroimaging (Huppert & Tym, 1986; Kane, Ouslander, & Abrass, 1989; NIH, 1987). Computed tomography (CT) and magnetic resonance imaging (MRI) are particularly helpful for ruling out subdural hematomas, tumors, and vascular pathologies.

The marked cholinergic deficits observed in postmortem studies are reflected in the cerebral spinal fluid (CSF) of AD patients, and it is conceivable that CSF measures may some day prove useful in discriminating between AD and other conditions. Similarly, studies of Auditory Evoked Potential (AEP) show preliminary signs of successful discrimination of AD patients from controls. Expansion of AEP work will reveal if this test is capable of discriminating AD patients from those of other etiologies. Other sophisticated imaging techniques such as single-photon emission tomography (SPECT), positron emission tomography (PET), and nuclear magnetic resonance (NMR) are capable of yielding information about brain morphology and physiology and may discriminate between AD, normal aging, and other pathologies. All three procedures have been applied to AD, but their utility as diagnostic indicators remains controversial (Bennett & Evans, 1992; Benson, 1987).

The mental status examination (MSE) typically measures several domains of cognition including orientation (to person, place, and time), attention, memory, language, abstract reasoning, and visuospatial skills (Thompson et al., 1987; Tranel, 1992). Although the MSE is an important and efficient device for screening cognition, it should never be used as the sole criteria for the diagnosis of dementia. The MSE may over- or underestimate deficits depending on a variety of factors such as the patient's educational status, medication intake, psychological state, or level of sensory deficit. Widely used MSE exams include the Mini-Mental State Exam (Folstein, Folstein, & McHugh, 1975), the Cognitive Capacity Screening Exam (Jacobs et al., 1977), the Short Portable Mental Status Questionnaire (Pfieffer, 1975), and the Blessed Dementia Scale (Blessed, Tomlinson, & Roth, 1968). Other short tests that provide a more detailed examination of mental status include the Brief Cognitive Rating Scale (BCRS; Reisberg et al., 1982), the Alzheimer's Disease Assessment Scale (ADAS; Rosen, Mohs, & Davis, 1984), and the Mattis Dementia Rating Scale (Mattis, 1976).

Neuropsychological assessment plays an essential part in the diagnosis and treatment planning of patients with dementia. A comprehensive neuropsychologic assessment may assist in early diagnosis in differentiating between dementias of various etiologies and deficits associated with normal aging, and provides important information about the relative strengths and weaknesses of the patient. The diagnosis of dementia requires the assessment of a wide range of cognitive abilities. Albert and Kaplan (1980) delineated several broad areas of cognitive function that should be assessed: (1) attention—the ability to track information both visually and auditorially; (2) language—comprehension, reading, writing, naming, and repetition; (3) memory—including visual and verbal memory as well as immediate, recent, and remote encoding, retention, and retrieval; (4) visuospatial skills, such as the ability to organize perceptually and act accurately on spatial demands; (5) cognitive flexibility—including the ability to orient to a new stimulus, maintain strategies, and fluidly shift between cognitive sets; and (6) abstract reasoning, such as the ability to determine the meaning of concepts.

Numerous neuropsychological instruments are available to assess each of these domains. Moreover, specific test batteries have been developed by various research groups (e.g., the University of California, San Diego, Alzheimer's Disease Center; and Washington University Alzheimer's Disease Research Center), which have proven useful for differentiating between dementias of various causes (Salmon & Butters, 1992; Storandt, Botwinick, Danziger, Berg, & Hughes, 1984). Although improvements have been made with respect to use of age-appropriate norms, normative data that takes into account gender and educational attainment remains relatively sparse (Heaton, Grant, & Matthews, 1986; McKhann et al., 1984).

Although AD affects a wide range of cognitive abilities, some are disrupted more than others depending on the stage of illness. Monsch, Bondi, Butters, Salmon, Katzman, and Thal (1992) examined four commonly used verbal fluency tasks in the detection of AD. Eighty-nine outpatients with a diagnosis of probable AD and fifty-three neurologically intact, normal control subjects were compared on four verbal fluency measures (category, letter, first names, and supermarket fluency). Category fluency demonstrated the greatest degree of discrimination between patients with AD and normal control subjects. Letter fluency was the least accurate. Separation of patients with AD by gender revealed similar findings. In further analyses with a subgroup of twenty-one mildly impaired patients with AD, category fluency lost none of its discriminative capabilities, whereas all other fluency measures showed marked reductions in discriminability. The superiority of category fluency is possibly due to its dependence on semantic memory, which deteriorates in the early stages of AD. Letter fluency, which depends to a degree on information processing speed, may be more affected in subcortical pathologies.

In general, AD has been characterized by problems in the consolidation and storage of new information, numerous perseverative and intrusion errors, rapid forgetting, severe and temporally graded retrograde amnesia, and severe deficits in category fluency (Butters, Salmon, & Butters, 1994). In contrast to episodic memory, procedural or motor learning appears better preserved, at least in the early stages of the disease. Disturbances of language become more apparent as the disease progresses. Although there have been few studies of apraxia in AD, it is reportedly highly prevalent (70 percent to 80 percent) in moderately advanced stages. In the advanced stages of AD, agnosias and psychic blindness (Balint's syndrome) may be observed; however, by this time severe inattention, amnesia, aphasia, and apraxia complicate investigation. In contrast to other dementias such as Pick's disease, social skills and appropriateness are generally well preserved well into the course of AD (Chui, 1989).

Global staging instruments are useful to track the course of AD and to provide additional prognostic information to families as the disease course progresses. Two common instruments employed for staging AD are the Global Deterioration Scale (GDS; Reisberg, Ferris, deLeon, & Crook, 1982) and the Clinical Dementia Rating Scale (Hughes, Berg, Danziger, Coben, & Martin, 1982). Each of these scales appears to be adequate for staging, with acceptable reliability and validity coefficients. Such properties would obviously be strengthened with longitudinal studies.

Behavior Problems in Alzheimer's Disease

In addition to deterioration of memory and other cognitive abilities, AD is associated with profound disturbances of behavior and emotion. These worrisome, disruptive, or even dangerous behaviors are a major source of caregiver distress and may hasten or necessitate institutionalization (Rabins, Mace, & Lucas, 1982). The management of behavioral disturbances, therefore, is frequently the principle focus of clinical care.

Although the behavioral changes associated with AD have been recognized since Alois Alzheimer's original case report (Crook, 1987), subsequent clinical research has primarily focused on the memory and cognitive deficits of the disease. Prevalence estimates of behavioral problems in AD are high, varying from 48 percent to 90 percent, depending upon the types of problems studied and the patient setting (Reisberg et al., 1987; Rovner et al., 1990; Swearer, Drachman, O'Donnell, & Mitchell, 1988; Teri et al., 1992). Deutsch and Rovner (1991) found that at least 50 percent of patients attending outpatient dementia clinics and 75 percent of demented nursing home patients exhibit problem behaviors. A broad range of problem behaviors have been identified, including agitation, aggression, wandering, mood disturbance (depression, anxiety, irritability, apathy), vegetative disturbance (sleep/wake disruption, eating changes, inappropriate sexual behaviors), incontinence, motor restlessness, compulsive/ritualistic behaviors, self-care deficits (personal hygiene, dressing, etc.), and psychotic symptoms (delusions, hallucinations). Although a wide range of problems have been catalogued, there is little consensus (empirical or theoretical) concerning the definition and assessment of many of these behaviors.

A number of rating scales have been developed over the past few years for assessing behavior problems. Many of these also include some assessment of the caregiver's reaction or distress associated with the problem. Examples of these instruments include the Index of Activities of Daily Living Scale (Katz, Downs, Cash, & Grotz, 1970), Instrumental Activities of Daily Living Scale (Lawton & Brody, 1969), Blessed Dementia Scale (Blessed, Tomlinson, & Roth, 1968), Alzheimer's Disease Assessment Scale (Rosen, Mohs, & Davis, 1984), Revised Memory and Problem Behavior Checklist (Teri, Truax, Logsdon, Uomoto, Zarit, & Vitaliano, 1992), Behavior and Mood Disturbance Scale and the Relative's Stress Scale (Greene, Smith, Gardiner, & Timbury, 1982), Disruptive Behavior Scale (Mungas, Weiler, Franz, & Henry, 1989), Behavioral Pathology in Alzheimer's Disease Rating Scale (Reisberg et al., 1987), Cognitive Behavior Rating Scale (Williams, 1987), and the Geriatric Depression Scale (Brink et al., 1982). Adequate psychometric properties have been demonstrated for most of these measures. The composite score yielded by most of these measures, however, may not adequately capture important dimensions of certain behaviors and may be insensitive to change related to treatment or disease progression.

In general, studies have found a positive relationship between level of cognitive impairment and the prevalence or severity of behavior problems. Cooper, Mungas, and Weiler (1990) examined the relationship between cognitive loss and abnormal behaviors in 680 patients with probable AD. Cognitive functioning was assessed with the Folstein Mini-Mental State Examination (MMSE). Six behaviors were assessed: agitation/anger, personality change, wandering, hallucinations/delusions, insomnia, and depression. Both the prevalence and severity of behaviors (except depression) were associated with lower MMSE scores. Hallucinations/delusions were found to be associated with age and race, agitation/anger was related to male gender, and wandering was associated with increased age. Correlations between the increasing behaviors and increasing cognitive loss, however, were small, and it is suggested that other as yet unproven factors may play a greater role than MMSE scores in predicting such behaviors.

Swearer, Drachman, O'Donnell, and Mitchell (1988) also found a relationship between the prevalence of behavior problems and severity of AD. They evaluated behavioral disturbances in three groups of dementia patients (AD, multi-infarct dementia, and mixed AD and multi-infarct). Disruptive behaviors were clustered into three categories: aggressive, ideational, and vegetative. The prevalence and severity of behaviors was found to increase with the global severity of dementia. No differences were observed in the frequency or type of behaviors displayed between diagnostic groups.

The relationship between cognitive impairment and behavior may not be so straightforward. Gilley, Wilson, Bennett, Bernard, and Fox (1991) conducted three studies that looked at the relationship of behavioral disturbances in AD to disease severity, age at onset, and the presence of extrapyramidal signs. In the first study, 146 patients referred for treatment were used. The primary caregivers were interviewed about the presence or absence and frequency or severity of thirty-six specific behaviors in the preceding month. Results suggest that the severity of behavioral disturbances was more closely associated with the level of functional disability than to cognitive impairment. In addition, those with an early onset of AD symptoms were more agitated.

In the second study conducted by Gilley et al. (1991), the interaction between extrapyramidal symptoms (EPS) and dementia severity was examined. The authors found that there was an interaction between EPS and dementia severity on the Psychotic Symptoms and Irritability Scales. The final study investigated the possible interaction of age at onset (AAO) and dementia severity for behavioral disturbances. The results indicated that early AAO patients had higher agitation scores. Also, early AAO patients' Psychotic Symptoms and Irritability scores were more pronounced, whereas higher apathy scores were seen in late AAO patients. With severe dementia, AAO appears to moderate the association between behavioral disturbance and disease severity but does so differentially within specific behavioral domains.

The relationship between behavioral problems and cognitive impairment may also be behavior-specific or idiosyncratic. For example, Burns, Jacoby, and Levy (1990) found that wandering behavior was significantly associated with dementia severity but that binge eating was not. In another study, Teri, Larson, and Reifler (1988) examined several behaviors in 127 patients diagnosed with AD. Wandering, agitation, incontinence, and hygiene were associated with cognitive impairment. Hallucinations, suspiciousness, falls, and restlessness were not associated with cognitive impairment. No relationship was found between occurrence of specific problems and patient age (except falling), gender, disease duration, or age of onset of AD (except falling). Teri and colleagues (1988) concluded that behaviors associated with cognitive impairment may be more characteristic of AD than behaviors that appeared to be unrelated to disease progression. The former may be anticipated at various stages in the course of the disease and therefore incorporated into standard educational and treatment programs, whereas the latter may be viewed as idiosyncratic behaviors, to be addressed on an individual, as needed basis.

Behavioral problems may also be more prevalent in the presence of specific key behaviors, such as agitation or delusions. Lachs, Becker, Siegal, Miller, and Tinetti (1992), for example, reported that several behaviors were more common in patients suffering from delusions (i.e., agitation, angry or hostile outbursts, urinary incontinence, wandering or pacing, and insomnia) than in those without delusions. Further studies are needed to clarify the role of cognitive impairment in delusions and the role of delusions in the development of disruptive behaviors.

The possible association of premorbid behaviors to the development of problems following disease onset have been seldom examined. Using family interviews and records of nine AD patients (ages sixty to ninety), Shomaker (1987) found a continuity of behavior from predementia to postdementia, with the intensity and frequency of certain behaviors increasing and decreasing as a function of the progression of the dementia. More research in this area is clearly needed. Basic studies of etiology, prevention, and epidemiology of AD have progressed in the past several years. The long-term care and management of AD patients also necessitates behavioral treatment and research designed to understand the effects of AD on the behavior of patients. More theoretical and empirical research is needed to guide assessment and to disentangle relationships between the varied and frequently overlapping behavioral problems discussed. Although the literature suggests only modest improvements for pharmacologic treatments, the management of problem behaviors is most frequently through neuroleptic drugs. An increased understanding of the behavioral effects of AD may offer answers to questions concerning the development of environments that maximize the functioning of AD patients. We now turn to a review of behavioral research and applied behavior analysis concerning AD and dementia.

Issues Affecting Treatment: Basic Behavior Analysis

A review of the behavioral literature indicates that few studies have directly examined the relationship between operant conditionability and AD. As Lawton (1989) stated, "[environmental] design for the aged is, in fact, a rare phenomenon" (p. 343). Lawton (1989) specified three criteria for evaluating the suitability of environments for the AD patient: (1) Does the environmental aspect demand behavior that the AD patient can realistically emit in an adaptive manner? (2) Does the environmental aspect add some resource to the possible resources present in the overall environment? (3) Does or can the environment provide "leading stimuli" that can continually motivate the AD patient to emit a variety of adaptive behaviors? A natural empirical question for the behavioral scientist is whether the behavior of persons with AD is under the same type of environmental contingency control characteristic of nondemented persons. In other words, "an important question that has not been resolved is whether the behavioral paradigm is applicable to diseases that affect the ability to learn" (Rabins, 1989, p. 323).

One study which addresses this issue was conducted by Duchek, Cheney, Ferraro, and Storandt (1991). Explicit learning ability in AD patients was examined as a function of the difficulty of material to be remembered and dementia severity. The Associate Learning task from the Wechsler Memory Scale was administered to a group of healthy older adults and to individuals with questionable, mild, and moderate AD. AD individuals showed poorer learning performance across trials than did healthy older adults even when the to-be-remembered material was relatively easy. However, despite their overall lower level of performance, individuals with questionable and mild AD did show evidence for learning across trials for easy paired associates. This study provides evidence that individuals with AD can acquire new information, provided that it is relatively undemanding.

Dementia may also produce deficiencies in stimulus-response relations to control behavior (i.e., specific nervous system dysfunction preventing certain stimulus modalities to gain control of behavior; Perez, 1980). Also implicated are the potential effects of memory deficits on stimulus-behavior-consequence relationships. A basic study employing a matching-to-sample task points up these issues.

Sahgal et al. (1992) compared short-term recognition memory in patients with AD and patients with senile dementia of the Lewy body type (SDLT). Sixteen healthy elderly volunteers, ten patients with probable AD, and seven patients diagnosed with SDLT were tested on a matching-to-sample task involving nonverbal visual recognition memory. Latency analyses indicated that both patient groups responded more slowly than the control group in the simultaneous matching-to-sample task, but were not different from each other. In the delayed matching-to-sample, latencies increased with delay, but no group-by-delay interaction was found. The pattern of errors suggests that when errors were made, subjects tended to remember the correct colors but not the shapes. However, the increased number of errors made by patients to the distractor stimulus, which had neither shape nor color in common with the sample stimulus, suggests an impairment of encoding mechanisms (ability to categorize stimuli according to their specific properties before committing them to memory). These findings show that AD produces deficiencies in stimulus categorization. Moreover, the findings may have implications for behavioral approaches to treatment. Basic research in this area has just begun to address some of the more important questions concerning the effects of AD on operant conditionability.

Basic Research in the Experimental Analysis of Aging: Foundations of Behavioral Gerontology

More research has been conducted into the operant conditionability of normal elderly adults. In an effort to study the normal effects of aging on behavior in nondemented subjects, Perone and Baron (1982) studied response speed in three younger and three older men. A predetermined sequence of ten responses on four keys was reinforced monetarily. Two conditions were set up. In the first condition, the correct sequence changed each session, while in the other, the sequence remained the same. During self-paced responding (i.e., no penalty for slow responding), stable patterns of acquisition and performance emerged for both groups of subjects. However, introduction of a pacing schedule (i.e., the time available for each key press had to be between 0.5 to 3 seconds across sessions) disrupted the behavior of the older subjects. Over the course of sessions, the older subjects did evidence adjustment to the pacing schedule, thereby implicating adaptive functioning in elderly subjects, although at a slower pace than that evidenced by younger subjects. These findings were replicated in another study by Perone and Baron (1983a), including the finding that disruption of behavior in the elderly men was greater in acquisition of novel sequences than in the performance of established sequences.

Perone and Baron (1983b) extended this line of analysis. Using similar groups of male subjects (median young age nineteen, median old age seventy), the researchers implemented chained schedules of reinforcement. An initial link response produced a terminal link where ten key presses were monetarily reinforced. The time available for each key press (IRT) was varied between 0.5 seconds to an unlimited period of time. They found that initial link response rate increased with increasing reinforcement, especially when the elderly subjects had difficulty with the pacing requirements. The researchers interpreted these results by hypothesizing that extra-experimental variables (e.g., lights signaling correct responses, pleasing the experimenters, mastering the task) served to reinforce slower paced behavior. Once the subjects became competent at the experimental task, even when small IRTs were in effect, these sources of reinforcement were lost and the subjects' behavior came under the control of the extraneous variables. However, as in the above study, even the elderly subjects adjusted over time to the pacing schedules in force.

Baron, Menich, and Perone (1983) used a chained schedule of reinforcement with variable-interval (VI) initial links and terminal links involving reaction time measurements to either matching-to-sample or oddity matching in a conditional discrimination procedure. Two groups of men (young mean 20.3, elderly mean 69.7) were studied, in line with the above studies. Increasingly shorter time limits were placed on the conditional discrimination phase. As a result of this contingency, both sets of subjects evidenced decreased reaction times, with the younger men generally responding the fastest. As in the previous studies, however, the elderly subjects also adapted to the experimental contingencies.

Finally, Baron and Menich (1985) studied two groups of men in a series of delayed matching-to-sample discriminations with sample-choice intervals of zero, five, ten, and fifteen seconds. The ages and physical conditions of the subjects were similar to those reported by Perone and Baron above. Following baseline, correct responses were reinforced only if they occurred within a specified time range that was also manipulated (0.5 to 2.5 seconds). Response rate was shown to correspond to these requirements (i.e., as time restraints became more stringent, response rate increased). Also, response was slower when the choice stimuli were delayed and involved more stimuli in the stimuli pool. The groups did not differ appreciably in performance, adding further support to the abilities of the elderly subjects studied.

The effect of the manipulation of stimulus quality was investigated by Ferraro and Kellas (1992). Twenty-four undergraduates (mean twenty-one years) and twenty-four retired faculty (mean seventy-two years) were tested. Four main results were found: (1) rotation effects were greater in elderly adults, (2) semantic priming was greater in elderly adults, (3) semantic priming increased with increasing Target Orientation, and (4) semantic priming increased more for elderly adults as Target Orientation increased. These results offer continuing support for the interactive compensatory nature of elderly adults' word recognition performance.

Overall analysis of whole latencies and durations of component processes on lexical decision tasks provides converging evidence for a general slowing factor for older adults of approximately 1.5 times that of younger adults for lexical information processing. Specifically, analyses of lexical decision studies revealed that older adults' mean semantic priming effect was 1.44 times that of younger adults. Analyses of delayed pronunciation data revealed that word recognition was 1.47 times slower in older adults, whereas older adults output processes were only 1.26 times slower (Myerson, Ferraro, Hale, & Lima, 1992).

The above studies offer support to the adaptive functioning and seemingly normal patterns of operant acquisition and steady state behavior in healthy elderly subjects. We now turn to a brief review of studies examining stimulus control of behavior in AD.

The Stimulus Control of the Behavior of Alzheimer's Patients: Experimental Research

In an early study of the effects of discriminative stimuli on behavior, Steffes and Thralow (1985) investigated the correlation between the color of nurses' uniforms and the amount of disturbed nighttime behavior in twenty-five male patients. Subjects included some with AD as well as victims of cerebral vascular accidents, alcohol abuse, organic dementia, Huntington's chorea, and schizophrenia. Nursing staff wore dark brown or white uniforms at random during a four-week period. The researchers found that subjects who had impaired vision and cognitive impairment were affected by the use of white uniforms. The nurses who wore white uniforms were described as taking on a ghostlike appearance in darkened patient rooms. The researchers found that these patients had an increase in disturbed behavior after nursing rounds were made. This study provides data that increases in disturbed behavior in AD patients can partly result from the stimulus situation in which the patients are placed. Cognitive and biological deficits can interact with discriminative stimuli to produce an increased frequency of certain types of behaviors.

Although control of behavior through the modification of reinforcement schedules has been studied in normal elderly adults (Baron & Menich above), few studies have examined reinforcement schedule control of behavior in dementia patients. Mackay (1965) studied a small sample of psychiatric patients described as memory disordered. Implementing fixed ratio, fixed interval, and variable interval schedules of reinforcement, he found that only one of six subjects emitted fixed ratio responding. However, no systematic method of assessing the value of reinforcers was implemented, and the study was poorly controlled. Ankus and Quarrington (1972) also showed that fixed ratio responding could be obtained in memory disordered patients providing that reinforcers were identified for individual subjects.

A more sophisticated study that attempted to investigate the relationship between AD and operant conditionability was performed by Fisher and Carstensen (1988). Subjects were matched on age and educational level. Following a neuropsychological evaluation, three groups of women were studied: Early Stage AD ($n = 4$), Middle Stage AD ($n = 4$), and Normal controls (also matched for age and education level, $n = 5$). Subjects were trained on each of three different concurrent VI VI reinforcement schedules (using monetary reinforcers) of eight sessions each in a matching law paradigm. The matching law is an empirical behavioral law that essentially states that given two or more concurrent sources of reinforcement in an experimental situation, response rates will equal (or match) their corresponding reinforcer rates. Results of this study showed that as the dementia progressed, performances expected given the established matching relation-ship (i.e., response ratios approximately equal to corresponding reinforcement ratios over sessions) deviated progressively more from the matching relation.

Several potential methodological problems were noted. First, the researchers used a limited number of reinforcement schedules in order to study reinforcement and re-sponse relationships. In operant matching research, many more reinforcement distribu-tions are typically studied, so that a valid range of reinforcer values may be tested. Use of limited schedules would not provide enough range of reinforcer/response values, and therefore matching would be hard to obtain even if the effects of AD were negligi-ble. Moreover, the scheduled rather than the obtained reinforcement rates were plotted as the independent variable. If these two values are discrepant, the scheduled values may be irrelevant. If the data were plotted in terms of scheduled values, then deviations from matching would also be produced as experimental artifact. Finally, adequate steady-state performance by the subjects was not established, which may also bias the data in favor of deviations from matching. These confounds may account for the results obtained in this study.

Despite these apparent problems, the rationale for the study as well as the results have direct implications for the operant conditionability of AD patients. Sensitivity to changes in reinforcement contingencies is integral to behavior-consequence relation-ships in the functional analysis of behavior. More empirical studies along this line are overdue. Plaud, Gillund, and Ferraro (in press) conducted a study to determine whether the aging process itself systematically affects operant conditionability (i.e., the ability of humans to operate on their environments, and be responsive to consequences). The pri-mary research question of the study was whether aging subjects respond to the contin-gencies of reinforcement such that they allocate their behavior as predicted by the reinforcement contingencies and discriminative stimuli programmed by the experi-menters. Six subjects ranging in age from sixty-two to seventy-four participated in fif-teen experimental sessions. Subjects were instructed to press the *a* key when they saw a white circle, and to press an alternate key when they saw a red letter *A*. Responses on the first key were reinforced on a VI 30-s schedule (i.e., a variable-interval schedule of reinforcement with eleven arithmetically spaced intervals with a mean of thirty sec-onds); and alternative key responses were reinforced on a VI 60-s schedule (i.e., a vari-able-interval schedule of reinforcement with eleven arithmetically spaced intervals with a mean of sixty seconds). Reinforcers included monetary units (ten cents) and verbal praise. Results indicated positive effects of stimulus control of behavior. Collective false alarms and miss rates represented only 0.05 percent of the total responses. Also, two-thirds of the subjects allocated behavior consistent with the second hypothesis that the more dense reinforcement schedule (i.e., the VI 30-s) would cause subjects to respond more quickly to this condition. This study provides further evidence for the critical nature of understanding how behavioral contingencies interact with the aging process to produce stable behavior patterns. The extension of this paradigm to AD patients rep-resents a logical next step in understanding how dementia affects operant condition-ability.

There have been a few other basic studies of the stimulus control of the behavior of AD patients. Mayers and Griffin (1990) studied five male patients diagnosed with AD.

The researchers also studied four male patients who had a diagnosis of dementia secondary to alcohol abuse. Mayers and Griffin found that their subjects engaged in stimulus-seeking and exploratory behaviors, especially for mechanical toys that were originally devised for the use of children. The researchers concluded that AD patients are indeed responsive to environmental stimuli. Stimuli such as objects that can be manipulated could therefore be used to sustain positive exploratory behavior by AD patients, leading to a possible decline in negative behaviors such as agitation and combativeness. This study provides some preliminary evidence that AD patients can operate on their environments, and therefore social behaviors and interactions may be directly shaped.

The effect of social stimuli on the behavior of AD patients was also investigated by Kongable, Buckwalter, and Stolley (1989). Twelve AD patients were observed to see whether the introduction of a social stimulus affected the patients' social behavior. The researchers used specific definitions of social behaviors such as frequency of smiles, laughs, looks, leans, touches, verbalizations, and name-calling. Using multiple observation periods, they found that the introduction of a pet dog (i.e., the social stimulus) increased the number of social behaviors by the AD patients, indicating that the addition of a discriminative social stimulus had a definite positive effect on the behavior of the AD patients. This study reinforces the possibility that AD patients may be responsive to the manipulation of discriminative stimuli.

Olderdog-Millard and Smith (1989) studied ten patients with AD. Using behavioral checklists to collect data, the researchers found that the introduction of therapeutic singing (which may be conceptualized as a social discriminative stimulus) significantly increased social behaviors with others (e.g., walking with others) when compared with baseline responding. The researchers also found that when therapeutic singing was introduced, AD patients engaged in significantly more positive verbalizations with others. This study provides more basic evidence that the introduction of social stimuli can positively affect the behavior of AD patients by leading to an increase in prosocial behaviors and a concomitant decrease in combative and isolative behaviors.

Hanley (1981) found that a combination of verbal discriminative cues and visual discriminative cues, termed *signposts,* significantly increased ward orientation in eight females evidencing moderate to severe dementia. This study is a direct test of the efficacy of the use of discriminative stimuli in the modification of behavior in demented subjects. Hanley, McGuire, and Boyd (1981) replicated these results by finding that ward behavior orientation significantly enhanced the orientation behavior of fifty-seven subjects drawn from either a psychogeriatric hospital or a home for the aged. Bergert and Jacobsson (1976) found that explicit orientation training using distinctive stimuli to orient subjects to time, place, room, and person not only increased proper orienting behaviors but also led to a general increase in activities in five subjects diagnosed with AD.

This collection of studies provides clear support for the ability of behavioral approaches based on stimulus manipulation to have a direct and efficacious effect on demented behavior. As we have discussed above, it has been found that AD patients also engage in stimulus-seeking exploratory behavior (Mayers & Griffin, 1990). The significance of this phenomenon is that exploratory behavior allows the behavior analyst to selectively reinforce target behaviors. As we have seen in the above studies pertaining to orientation behavior, the use of discriminative stimuli had a positive effect on the emission of appropriate behaviors in demented subjects.

Another empirical test of the efficacy of stimulus manipulation was performed by Hussian (1982). This behavioral researcher studied the effects of discriminative stimuli (i.e., color hues) on wandering, self-stimulatory, and inappropriate sexual behavior of geriatric patients, including several patients with AD. The author also reported the effective use of fading techniques. The single-subject studies reported are a direct test of contingency management/behavior modification intervention techniques with chronically institutionalized geriatric patients, including patients diagnosed with AD. Larger studies of this kind, with more AD patients, would provide valuable information on the conditionability of AD patients. Hussian (1988) also reported the effectiveness of what he termed *stimulus enhancement techniques* designed to reduce inappropriate behaviors such as wandering. Subjects in this study were five demented males. Hussian found that using discriminative stimuli for each target behavior increased desired behaviors by 86 percent, even in the absence of explicit reinforcement for the execution of targeted behaviors. This study shows that the use of discrete, discriminative stimuli themselves may exert control over behavior even when direct positive reinforcement is not used.

Behavior Therapy Approaches to Alzheimer's Disease

Research conducted in the applied behavior analysis of AD and dementia has been an emerging investigative field. According to Carstensen (1988), practical problems, such as special concerns related to working with elderly populations, have led researchers away from the field of behavioral gerontology. However, Carstensen writes that "one common theme that permeates the entire body of intervention research is that the basic procedures that work with the young also work with the old. Only recently has the systematic study of the effects of behavior therapy with the aged been undertaken, and in most cases research programs are in rudimentary stages" (Carstensen, 1988, pp. 272–274).

Previous reviews (e.g., Rabins, 1989; Teri et al., 1992) have concluded that behavioral treatment approaches may be effective for treating or managing a wide range of problems encountered in demented patients. Behavioral interventions attempt to change the frequency, intensity, or duration of specific behaviors by identifying and systematically varying antecedent and consequent events. Environments may be structured such that simplified step-by-step instruction is in effect, and desired behavior reinforced. A selected review of this applied literature will be discussed.

Burnand, Richard, Tissot, and de Ajuriaguerra (1977) studied sixteen patients with severe memory deficits. The patients were diagnosed either with Korsakoff's syndrome or degenerative dementia of the aged. The researchers found that when they directly reinforced organized responses, all subjects demonstrated continued capacity for what the researchers termed *sensorimotor organization*. Schonfeld and McEvoy (1989) reported a successful attempt to restore memory deficits in a fifty-three-year-old female with pseudodementia through the use of structured reinforcement principles and shaping. Although this report is encouraging, it is limited as a case study.

Peppard (1986) described a behavioral management nursing home unit for AD patients. Contingency management was targeted for each patient individually, in an environment that the author termed "holistic." Peppard reported that the patients' care was rated as better than other nursing home units, and that there was a higher level of job satisfaction and lower turnover of staff. Although this report is also encouraging, not enough data are presented in terms of effective behavioral change in the unit patients, including elaboration of the specific contingency management techniques and their effects on patient behaviors.

Behavior therapy techniques were shown to be effective in treating anger in a demented patient. Wisner and Green (1986) reported the results of a case study of a seventy-three-year-old demented male. Using a two-week baseline to measure the subject's outbursts of anger, behavioral techniques were used to modify the conditions under which the subject displayed anger responses and the topography of the anger responses. A three-month follow-up showed that the treatment significantly diminished the subject's anger responses relative to the baseline period. Block, Boozkowski, and Hansen (1987) showed that training staff members in operant principles of reinforcement and discriminative stimulus manipulation significantly decreased dependent and abusive behaviors of a sixty-eight-year-old male with dementia and a seventy-eight-year-old male with numerous medical ailments.

Donat (1984) implemented basic operant behavioral techniques to modify the wandering behavior of a seventy-nine-year-old demented patient. The researcher found that manipulating discriminative stimuli and reinforcing appropriate behaviors significantly changed the patient's behaviors without affecting reinforcement contingencies in other patients.

An innovative approach to dealing with wanderers at a nursing home was developed by McGrowder-Lin and Bhatt (1988). Each afternoon patients were taken to a lounge for 1.5 to 2 hours. Music, exercise, sensory stimulation, nourishment, and dancing were part of each day's program. The researchers reported that wandering behaviors on the unit decreased, presumably because patients were tired. It was also noted that group members sought each other out when not in the lounge. Weight gain was noted in some patients because of improvements in appetite and the ability to feed themselves finger food.

Negley and Manley (1990) used a rudimentary behavioral approach to decrease the frequency of assaultive behaviors by patients on an AD hospital unit. Building upon basic research in the stimulus control of behavior, the researchers implemented a change in dining room location where forty-seven separate assaults had taken place. The researchers found that a simple change in environmental location produced an immediate decrease in the frequency of assaultive behavior. The researchers concluded that environmental manipulations can produce subsequent (in this case positive) change in the behavior of confused and disorganized patients. In a somewhat different behavioral direction, Welden and Yesavage (1982) evaluated the effectiveness of relaxation training on forty-eight dementia patients who had a probable diagnosis of either AD or multi-infarct dementia (ages fifty-two to ninety-three). The researchers found that patients were able to effectively use the relaxation strategies to decrease aggressive and agitated behaviors.

Bourgeois (1990) reported the results of a study designed to test the effectiveness of teaching three female AD patients (ages fifty-nine to sixty-six) to use a prosthetic memory aid when engaging in conversation. The researcher used the husbands of the patients as caregiver trainers, and three women (two neighbors and one daughter) as the familiar conversational partners. Different subject matters were chosen, such as "my day" or "myself," and the subject was shown facts about the topic along with photographs by the caregiver trainers. The patients were verbally praised for accurately reading the sentences and elaborating on the stimulus items. Daily and weekly probes indicated that all three patients used the memory aids to enhance conversation with the familiar conversational partners. Patients made significantly more elaborative statements while also generating novel statements with both the caregiver trainers and familiar conversational partners. This study demonstrates the possibility that contingency-shaped skills training techniques can have a positive effect on the communication deficits seen in the progression of AD.

Teri and Gallagher-Thompson (1991) have shown that depressive symptoms seen in AD patients can be successfully treated with cognitive-behavioral strategies. The authors found that cognitive therapy for depression can be efficacious with mildly impaired patients, while more severely impaired AD patients can be helped by more direct behavioral methods, such as increasing the level of positive experiences in the patients' environments while at the same time decreasing the number of negative experiences (which could be accomplished through the manipulation of stimulus control as reviewed above). Teri and Gallagher-Thompson (1991) report that the use of cognitive-behavioral therapies for depression has been shown to significantly alleviate the clinical symptoms of depression that are seen in up to 30 percent of AD patients.

The treatment of AD encompasses more than merely the treatment of the AD patient individually. Treatment also includes the education and support given to the family members of the AD patient and/or the primary caregiver. Deutsch and Rovner (1991) propose the formation of AD units in nursing homes and education of the family as important strategies for reducing behavioral problems in AD patients. Family members of AD patients are less likely to interpret behavioral changes as deliberate and hostile if they understand the general features of AD that contribute to problem behavior. Targeting caregivers may reduce caregiver stress and prevent premature institutionalization of patients.

Separation-individuation conflicts can also occur in AD patients' caregivers. These conflicts in caregivers can be divided into two categories: (1) behavior under the dual control of the nonverbal and verbal antecedents and consequences of others (i.e., care receiver and professional staff), and (2) the dysfunctional self-rules of the caregiver. Two types of treatment are described by Lewin and Lundervol (1990): the first type of treatment involved changing the care receiver's problem behaviors by training the nursing home staff in applied behavior analysis procedures, and the second type involved teaching the caregiver to critically examine his or her self-rules by more accurately describing his or her own and others' behavior.

Although the studies mentioned above are promising, they are sparse. Further research with more clearly defined patient groups (accurately diagnosed and staged) and specified procedures are clearly needed to determine the efficacy of behavioral therapies for improving function and behavior.

Conclusion: Behavior Analysis and Therapy in Alzheimer's Disease

We have reviewed the prominent features of AD and dementia, including a brief description of the epidemiology, etiology, and clinical assessment of AD. A broad range of problem behaviors were shown to be prevalent in AD; however, a number of issues remain to be investigated in this area, such as further specification of definitions for behaviors, determining the degree to which behaviors covary or cluster, determining whether any behaviors are stage specific, and examining the relationship of premorbid behavior patterns to post-disease patterns.

Behavioral analysis and behavior therapy strategies in the context of both normal aging and AD were also reviewed. The picture that emerges is a complex one. Although advances are being made in the biological understanding of AD, including genetic linkage studies and biochemical findings, investigators in the behavioral sphere are still trying to answer basic questions concerning the effects of a dementing disease on behavioral processes.

The Fisher and Carstensen (1988) study is the only attempt thus far to study basic behavioral allocation and choice using a matching law paradigm with AD patients. An understanding of the degree to which AD patients remain sensitive to changes in reinforcement contingencies is critical to determining whether behavior can be altered through behavior-consequence treatment procedures. Further study is needed to address this question. More behavioral studies have been performed with normal elderly subjects, as illustrated by the research programs of Perone and Baron et al. reviewed above; however, we are just beginning to see the influence of basic operant research in the study of AD and dementia in general.

Likewise, the Hussian studies showed the direct implications of applied behavior analysis with AD patients. These studies, along with others discussed, provide important empirical findings with regard to the effects of stimulus control of patients with AD.

Behavior therapy approaches hold promise to improve the quality of life of AD patients, decrease caregiver burden, and prevent premature institutionalization. However, more applied research with more clearly defined patient samples, well-defined behavioral targets, and detailed procedures is still needed to demonstrate the efficacy of behavioral approaches.

References

Albert, M. S., & Kaplan, E. (1980). Organic implications of neuro-psychological deficits in the elderly. In L. W. Poon, J. L. Fozard, L. S. Cermak, D. Arenberg, & L. W. Thompson (Eds.), *New directions in memory and aging: Proceedings of the George E. Talland conference.* Hillsdale, NJ: Erlbaum.

Alzheimer, A. (1907). Uber eine eigenartige Erkankung der Hirnrinde. *Allgemeine Zeitschrift Fur Psychiatrie und Psychisch-Gerichtiliche Medicin, 64,* 146-148.

American Psychiatric Association (1994). *Diagnostic and Statistical Manual of Mental Disorders* (4th Ed.). Washington, DC: Author.

The Alzheimer's Disease and Related Disorders Association, Inc. (1992). Statistical Data on Alzheimer's Disease.

Ankus, M., & Quarrington, B. (1972). Operant behavior in the memory-disordered. *Journal of Gerontology, 27,* 500–510.

Barnes, D. M. (1987). Defect in Alzheimer's is on chromosome 21. *Science, 235,* 846–847.

Baron, A., & Menich, S. R. (1985). Age-related effects of temporal contingencies on response speed and memory: An operant analysis. *Journal of Gerontology, 40,* 60–70.

Baron, A., Menich, S. R., & Perone, M. (1983). Reaction times of younger and older men and temporal contingencies of reinforcement. *Journal of the Experimental Analysis of Behavior, 40,* 275–287.

Bennett D.A. & Evans, D.A. (1992). Alzheimer's disease. *Disease-a-Month, 38,* 1–64.

Benson, D. F. (1987). Clinical diagnosis of Alzheimer's disease. In G. G. Glenner & R. J. Wurtmen (Eds.), *Advancing Frontiers in Alzheimer's Disease Research* (pp. 235–248). Austin: University of Texas Press.

Bergert, L., & Jacobsson, F. (1976). Reality orientation training in a group of patients with senile dementia. *Scandinavian Journal of Behaviour Therapy, 5,* 191–200.

Blessed, G., Tomlinson, B. E., & Roth, M. (1968). The association between quantitative measures of dementia and of senile change in the cerebral grey matter of elderly subjects. *British Journal of Psychiatry, 114,* 797–811.

Block, C., Boozkowski, J. A., & Hansen, N. (1987). Nursing home consultation: Difficult residents and frustrated staff. *Gerontologist, 27,* 443–446.

Bourgeois, M. S. (1990). Enhancing conversation skills in patients with Alzheimer's disease using a prosthetic memory aid. *Journal of Applied Behavior Analysis, 23,* 29–42.

Brink, T. L, Yesavage, J. A., Owen, L., Heersema, P. H., Adey, M., & Rose, T. L. (1982). Screening tests for geriatric depression. *Clinical Gerontologist, 1,* 37–43.

Burnand, Y., Richard, J., Tissot, R., & de Ajuriaguerra, J. (1977). Acquisition of sensorimotor schema by patients suffering from fixation amnesia (anterograde amnesia): Memory in the strict and in the broad sense, according to Piaget. *Annales-Medico-Psychologiques, 1,* 427–441.

Burns, A., Jacoby, R., & Levy, R. (1990). Behavioral abnormalities and psychiatric symptoms in Alzheimer's disease: Preliminary findings. *International Psychogeriatrics, 2,* 25–36.

Butters, M. A., Salmon, D. P., & Butters, N. (1994). Neuropsychological assessment of dementia. In M. Storandt & G. R. VandenBos (Eds.), *Neuropsychological assessment of dementia and depression in older adults: A clinician's guide* (pp. 33–59). Washington, DC: American Psychological Association.

Carstensen, L. L. (1988). The emerging field of behavioral gerontology. *Behavior Therapy, 19,* 259-281.

CERAD. (1987). The Consortium to Establish a Registry for Alzheimer's Disease Assessment Packet for Probable Alzheimer's Disease.

Chui, H. C. (1989). Dementia: A review emphasizing clinicopathologic correlation and brain-behavior relationships. *Archives of Neurology, 46,* 806–814.

Cooper, J. K., Mungas, D., & Weiler, P. G. (1990). Relation of cognitive status and abnormal behaviors in Alzheimer's disease. *Journal by the American Geriatric Society, 38,* 867–870.

Crook, T. (1987). Dementia. In L. L. Carstensen & B. A. Edelstein (Eds.), *Handbook of clinical gerontology,* (pp. 96–111). New York: Pergamon.

Cummings, J., & Benson, D. (1983). *Dementia: A clinical approach.* London: Butterworths.

Deutsch, L. H. & Rovner, B. W. (1991). Agitation and other noncognitive abnormalities in Alzheimer's disease. *The Psychiatric Clinics of North America, 14,* 341–351.

Donat, D. C. (1984). Modifying wandering behavior: A case study. *Clinical Gerontologist, 3,* 41–43.

Duchek, J. M., Cheney, M., Ferraro, F. R., & Storandt, M. (1991). Paired associate learning in senile dementia of the Alzheimer type. Archives of Neurology, 48, 1038–1040.

Evans, D. A., Funkenstein, H. H., Albert, M. S., Scherr, P. A., Cook, N. R., Chown, M. J., Hebert, L. E., Hennekens, C. H., & Taylor, J. O. (1989). Prevalence of Alzheimer's disease in a community population of older persons: Higher than previously reported. *Journal of the American Medical Association, 262,* 2551–2556.

Farmer, P. M., Peck, A., & Terry, R. D. (1976). Correlations among neuritic plaques, neurofibrillary tangles, and the severity of senile dementia. *Journal of Neuropathology and Experimental Neurology, 35,* 367–376.

Ferraro, F. R., & Kellas, G. (1992). Age-related changes in the effects of target orientation of word recognition. *Journal of Gerontology, 47,* 279–280.

Fisher, J. E., & Carstensen, L. L. (1988). *The effects of Alzheimer's disease on operant conditionability.* Paper presented at the 41st Annual Scientific Meeting of the Gerontological Society of America, San Francisco, May 1988.

Fliers, E., Lisei, A., & Swaab, D. (1983). *Dementia: Some current concepts and research in the Netherlands.* Amsterdam: Institute for Gerontology, Netherlands Institute for Brain Research.

Folstein, M., Folstein, S., & McHugh, P. (1975). Mini-mental state: A practical method for grading the cognitive state of patients for the clinician. *Journal of Psychiatric Research, 12,* 189–198.

Gatz, M. (1990). Interpreting behavioral genetic results: Suggestions for counselors and clients. *Journal of Counseling and Development, 68,* 601–605.

Gilley, D. W., Wilson, R. S., Bennett, D. A., Bernard, B. A. & Fox, J. H. (1991). Predictors of behavioral disturbance in Alzheimer's disease. *Journal of Gerontology: Psychological Sciences, 46,* 362–371.

Greene, J. G., Smith, R., Gardiner, M., & Timbury, G. C. (1982). Measuring behavioral disturbance of elderly demented patients in the community and its effects on relatives: A factor analytic study. *Age and Ageing, 11,* 121–126.

Hanley, I. (1981). The use of signposts and active training to modify ward disorientation in elderly patients. *Journal of Behavior Therapy and Experimental Psychiatry, 12,* 241–247.

Hanley, I., McGuire, R. J., & Boyd, W. D. (1981). Reality orientation and dementia: A controlled trial of two approaches. *British Journal of Psychiatry, 138,* 10–14.

Heaton, R. K., Grant, I., & Matthews, C. G. (1986). Differences in neuropsychological test performance associated with age, education, and sex. In I. Grant & K. M. Adams (Eds.), *Neuropsychological assessment of neuropsychiatric disorders.* New York: Oxford University Press.

Henderson, A. S. (1986). The epidemiology of Alzheimer's disease. *British Medical Bulletin, 42,* 3–10.

Hughes, C. P., Berg, L., Danziger, W. L., Coben, L. A., & Martin, R. L. (1982). A new clinical scale for staging of dementia. *British Journal of Psychiatry, 140,* 566–572.

Huppert, F. A., & Tym, E. (1986). Clinical and neuropsychological assessment of dementia. *British Medical Bulletin, 42,* 11–18.

Hussian, R. A. (1982). Stimulus control in the modification of problematic behavior in elderly institutionalized patients. *International Journal of Behavioral Pediatrics, 1,* 33–42.

Hussian, R. A. (1988). Modification of behaviors in dementia via stimulus manipulation. *Clinical Gerontologist, 8,* 37–43.

Jacobs, J. W., Bernhard, M. R., Delgado, A., & Strain, J. J. (1977). Screening for organic mental syndromes in the medically ill. *Annals of Internal Medicine, 86,* 40–46.

Kane, R. L., Ouslander, J. G., & Abrass, I. B. (1989). *Essentials of Clinical Geriatrics* (2nd ed.) (pp. 47–111). New York: McGraw-Hill.

Katz, S., Downs, T. D., Cash, H. R., & Grotz, R. C. (1970). Progress in development of the Index of ADL. *The Gerontologist, 10,* 20–30.

Kongable, L. G., Buckwalter, K. C., & Stolley, J. M. (1989). The effects of pet therapy on the social behavior of institutionalized Alzheimer's clients. *Archives of Psychiatric Nursing, 3,* 191–198.

Lachs, M. S., Becker, M., Siegal, A. P., Miller, R. L., & Tinetti M. E. (1992). Delusions and behavioral disturbances in cognitively impaired elderly persons. *JAGS, 40,* 768–773.

Lawton, M. P. (1989). Environmental approaches to research and treatment of Alzheimer's disease. In *Alzheimer's disease treatment and family stress: Directions for research,* (pp. 340–362). Washington, DC: NIMH.

Lawton, M. P., & Brody, E. M. (1969). Assessment of older people: Self-maintaining and instrumental activities of daily living. *The Gerontologist, 9,* 179–186.

Lewin, L. M. & Lundervol, D. A. (1990). Behavioral analysis of separation-individuation conflict in the spouse of an Alzheimer's disease patient. *The Gerontologist, 30,* 703–705.

McGrowder-Lin, R., & Bhatt, A. (1988). Wander's lounge program for nursing home residents with Alzheimer's disease. *The Gerontologist, 28,* 607–609.

Mackay, H. A. (1965). Operant techniques applied to disorders of the senium. Queens College. Unpublished doctoral dissertation.

McKhann, G., Drachman, D., Folstein, M., Katzman, R., Price, D., & Stadlan, E. M. (1984). Clinical diagnosis of Alzheimer's disease: Report of the NINCDS-ADRDA Work Group under the auspices of Department of Health and Human Services task force on Alzheimer's disease. *Neurology, 34,* 939–944.

Mattis, S. (1976). Mental status examination for organic mental syndrome in the elderly patient. In L. Bellak & T. B. Karasu (Eds.), *Geriatric Psychiatry* (pp. 77–120). New York: Grune & Stratton.

Mayers, K., & Griffin, M. (1990). The play project: Use of stimulus objects with demented patients. *Journal of Gerontological Nursing, 16,* 32–37.

Meiri, H., Banin, E., & Roll, M. (1991). Aluminum ingestion—Is it related to dementia? *Reviews on Environmental Health, 4,* 191–205.

Monsch, A. U., Bondi, M. W., Butters, N., Salmon, D. P., Katzman, R., & Thal, L. J. (1992). Comparisons of verbal fluency tasks in the detection of dementia of the Alzheimer type. *Archives of Neurology, 49,* 1253–1258.

Mora, G. (1985). History of psychiatry. In H. I. Kaplan & B. J. Sadock (Eds.), Comprehensive textbook of psychiatry/IV, (pp. 2034–2054). Baltimore: Williams & Wilkins.

Mungas, D., Weiler, P., Franz, C., & Henry, R. (1989). Assessment of disruptive behavior associated with dementia: The Disruptive Behavior Rating Scales. *Journal of Geriatric Psychiatry and Neurology, 2,* 196–202.

Myerson, J., Ferraro, F. R., Hale, S., & Lima, S. D. (1992). General slowing in semantic priming and word recognition. *Psychology and Aging, 2,* 257–270.

Negley, E., & Manley, J. T. (1990). Environmental interventions in assaultive behavior. *Journal of Gerontological Nursing, 16,* 29–33.

NIH. (1987). Consensus Conference: Differential diagnosis of dementing disease. *Journal of the American Medical Association, 258,* 3411–3416.

Olderdog-Millard, K. A., & Smith, J. M. (1989). The influence of group singing therapy on the behavior of Alzheimer's disease patients. *Journal of Music Therapy, 26,* 58–70.

Peppard, N. R. (1986). Special nursing home units for residents with primary degenerative dementia: Alzheimer's Disease. *Journal of Gerontological Social Work, 9,* 5–13.

Perez, F. I. (1980). Behavioral studies of dementia: methods of investigation and analysis. In J. O. Cole & J. E. Barrett (Eds.), *Psychopathology in the aged,* pp. 81–95. New York: Raven Press.

Perone, M., & Baron, A. (1982). Age-related effects of pacing on acquisition and performance of response sequences: An operant analysis. *Journal of Gerontology, 37,* 443–449.

Perone, M., & Baron, A. (1983a). Reduced age differences in omission errors after prolonged exposure to response pacing contingencies. *Developmental Psychology, 19,* 915–923.

Perone, M., & Baron, A. (1983b). Age-related preferences for paced and unpaced tasks in chained schedules of reinforcement. *Experimental Aging Research, 9,* 165–168.

Perry, R. H. (1986). Recent advances in neuropathology. *British Medical Bulletin, 42,* 34–41.

Pfeiffer, E. (1975). A short portable mental status questionnaire for the assessment of organic brain deficit in elderly patients. *Journal of the American Geriatrics Society, 23,* 433–441.

Plaud, J. J., Gillund, B. E., & Ferraro, F. R. (In press). A signal detection analysis of choice behavior and aging. *Journal of Clinical Geropsychology.*

Plaud, J. J., Moberg, M., & Ferraro, F. R. (In press). A review of Alzheimer's disease and dementia: Applied behavioral assessment and treatment approaches. *Journal of Clinical Geropsychology.*

Prichard, J. C. (1835). *A treatise on insanity and other disorders affecting the mind.* London: Sherwood, Gilbert, & Piper.

Rabins, P. V. (1989). Behavior problems in the demented. In *Alzheimer's disease treatment and family stress: Directions for research,* (pp. 322–339). Washington, DC: NIMH.

Rabins, P. V., Mace, N. L., Lucas, M. J. (1982). The impact of dementia on the family. *Journal of the American Medical Association, 248,* 333–335.

Reisberg, B., Borenstein, J., Salob, S. P., Ferris, S. H., Franssen, E., & Georgotas, A. (1987). Behavioral symptoms in Alzheimer's disease: Phenomenology and treatment. *Journal of Clinical Psychiatry, 48* (Suppl.), 9–15.

Reisberg, B., Ferris, S., deLeon, M., & Crook, T. (1982). The global deterioration scale for assessment of primary degenerative dementia. *American Journal of Psychiatry, 139,* 1136–1139.

Rosen, W., Mohs, R., & Davis, K. (1984). A new rating scale for Alzheimer's disease. *American Journal of Psychiatry, 141,* 1356–1364.

Roth, M. (1986). Introduction. *British Medical Bulletin, 42,* 1–2.

Rovner, B. W., German, P. S., Broadhead, J., Morriss, R. K., Brant, L. J., Blaustein, J., & Folstein, M. F. (1990). The prevalence and management of dementia and other psychiatric disorders in nursing homes. *International Psychogeriatrics, 2,* 13–24.

Sahgal, A., Galloway, P. H., McKeith, I. G., Lloyd, S., Cook, J. H., Ferrier, N., & Edwardson, J. A. (1992). Matching-to-sample deficits in patients with senile dementias of the Alzheimer and Lewy Body types. *Archives of Neurology, 49,* 1043–1046.

Sajdel-Sulkowska, E. M., & Marotta, C. A. (1984). Alzheimer's disease brain: Alterations in RNA levels and in ribonuclease inhibitor complex. *Science, 255,* 947–949.

Salmon, D. P., & Butters, N. (1992). Neuropsychologic assessment of dementia in the elderly. In R. Katzman & J. W. Rowe (Eds.), *Principles of Geriatric Neurology* (pp. 144–163). Philadelphia: F. A. Davis.

Schonfeld, L., & McEvoy, C. L. (1989). Behavioral approaches to pseudodementia-related memory problems. *Clinical Gerontologist, 9,* 40–43.

Shomaker, D. (1987). Problematic behavior and the Alzheimer patient: Retrospection as a method of understanding and counseling. *Gerontologist, 27,* 370–375.

Skinner, B. F. (1961). *Cumulative record.* New York: Appleton-Century-Crofts.

Skinner, B. F. (1988). The phylogeny and ontongeny of behavior. In A. C. Catania & S. Harnad (Eds.), *The selection of behavior: The operant behaviorism of B. F. Skinner,* (pp. 382–4000). Cambridge: Cambridge University Press.

Sparks, D. L., Hunsaker, J. C., III, Slevin, J. T., DeKosky, S. T., Kryscio, R. J., Markesbery, W. R. (1992). Monoaminergic and cholinergic synaptic markers in the nucleus basalis of Meynert (nbM): Normal age-related changes and the effect of heart disease and Alzheimer's disease. *Annals of Neurology, 31,* 611–620.

Steffes, R., & Thralow, J. (1985). Do uniform colors keep patients awake? *Journal of Gerontological Nursing, 11,* 6–9.

Storandt, M., Botwinick, J., Danziger, W. L., Berg, L., & Hughes, C. P. (1984). Psychometric differentiation of mild senile dementia of the Alzheimer type. *Archives of Neurology, 41,* 497–499.

Swearer, J. M., Drachman, D. A., O'Donnell, B. F., & Mitchell, A. L. (1988). Troublesome and disruptive behaviors in dementia relationships to diagnosis and disease severity. *JAGS, 36,* 784–790.

Teri, L., & Gallagher-Thompson, D. (1991). Cognitive-behavioral interventions for treatment of depression in Alzheimer's patients. *The Gerontologist, 31,* 413–416.

Teri, L., Larson, E. B. & Reifler, B. V. (1988). Behavioral disturbance in dementia of the Alzheimer's type. *Journal of the American Geriatrics Society, 36,* 1–6.

Teri, L., Rabins, P., Whitehouse, P., Berg, L., Reisberg, B., Sunderland, T., Eichelman, B., & Creighton, P. (1992). Management of behavior disturbance in Alzheimer disease: Current knowledge and future directions. *Alzheimer Disease and Associated Disorders, 6,* 77–88.

Teri, L. Truax, P., Logsdon, R., Uomoto, J., Zarit, S., & Vitaliano, P. (1992). Assessment of behavioral problems in dementia: The Revised Memory and Problem Behavior Checklist. *Psychology and Aging, 7,* 622–631.

Terry, R., & Katzman R. (1992). Alzheimer's disease and cognitive loss. In R. Katzman & J. W. Rowe (Eds.), *Principles of Geriatric Neurology* (pp. 207–265). Philadelphia: F. A. Davis.

Thompson, L., Gong, V., Haskins, E., & Gallagher, D. (1987). Assessment of depression and dementia during the late years. In K. Schaie (Ed.), *Annual review of gerontology and geriatrics.* New York: Springer.

Tranel, D. (1992). Neuropychological assessment. *The Psychiatric Clinics of North America, 15,* 283–299.

Van Crevel, H. (1986). Clinical approach to dementia. In D. Swaab (Ed.), *Progess in brain research.* New York: Elsevier.

Welden, S., & Yesavage, J. A. (1982). Behavioral improvement with relaxation training in senile dementia. *Clinical Gerontologist, 1,* 45–49.

Whitehouse, P. J. (1992). Alzheimer's disease: Relationship of cognition and behavior to neurochemistry. *International Psychogeriatrics, 4,* 71–77.

Whitehouse, P. J., Price, D. L., Clark, A. W., Coyle, J. T., & Delong, M. R. (1981). Alzheimer's disease: Evidence for selective loss of cholinergic neurons in the nucleus basalis. *Annals of Neurology, 10,* 122–126.

Whitehouse, P. J., Struble, R. G., Uhl, G. R., & Price, D. L. (1985). In J. T. Hutton & A. D. Kenny (Eds.), *Dementia: Bridging the brain-behavior barrier,* (pp. 221–229). Liss.

Williams, J. M. (1987). *Cognitive Behavior Rating Scales.* Odessa, FL: Psychological Assessment Resources.

Wisner, E., & Green, M. (1986). Treatment of a demented patient's anger with cognitive-behavioral strategies. *Psychological Reports, 59,* 447–450.

12

BEHAVIOR THEORY IN BEHAVIORAL MEDICINE

ALICE G. FRIEDMAN
Department of Psychology
Binghamton University

JILL S. GOLDBERG
Department of Psychology
Binghamton University

AKIKO OKIFUJI
Department of Psychology
Binghamton University

In its brief history, behavioral medicine has established itself as one of the fastest growing sub-specialties in psychology (Epstein, 1992; Kaplan, 1990). Growth in the field during the past two decades is suggested by the number of new journals and texts devoted to the topic, the increase in the number of psychologists employed by medical centers, and expanding memberships in societies dedicated to behavioral medicine. Empiricism and accountability are hallmarks of the field that has been profoundly influenced by the behavioral movement within psychology. A large percentage of psychologists who specialize in behavioral medicine, and particularly those in major university-affiliated medical centers, identify their theoretical orientation as behavioral or cognitive-behavioral. In fact, in an early reference to the field, Blanchard (1977) defined behavioral medicine as being a "primarily experimental, or at least empirical, psychology which has its roots in the psychology of learning, social psychology, and to a lesser degree physiological psychology" (p. 2).

Ideally, behavioral medicine serves as a prototype for the successful integration of research, theory, and clinical practice. Historically, behavioral medicine has been closely tied to behavior theory. Experimental learning theory served as the foundation for the development of assessment techniques and intervention strategies geared toward improving health and psychological well-being. In recent years, however, the gap between behavioral science and the field of behavioral medicine has widened. While common intervention strategies may give the appearance of being closely tied to theory, this impression is often more illusion than reality.

In this chapter, we discuss the relation between behavior theory and the practice of behavior therapy in the medical setting. We discuss what we believe to be challenges to maintaining behavioral medicine's ties to behavior theory. These challenges are related to the organization of the field, practical limitations and pressures from outside the field, and confusion within the field about what constitutes behavior therapy. We have included a discussion of historic influences, as they have been critical in shaping the current role of the behavior therapist in medical settings. A comprehensive review of behavior therapy's contribution to medical practice is beyond the scope of this chapter. We have therefore opted not to attempt a survey of behavior therapy's impact on specific medical specialty areas (for a more thorough analysis, the reader should consult one of the many new texts on the topic). Instead, we discuss particular content areas only as they illustrate our points.

Before proceeding, a word about the use of the term *behavioral medicine* is warranted. In this chapter we use the term *behavioral medicine* to refer to psychology's contribution to the interdisciplinary field of behavioral medicine—the development, integration, and application of behavioral and biomedical science to the prevention, diagnosis, treatment, and rehabilitation of disease (Schwartz & Weiss, 1978). This use may not be entirely accurate, and one could argue that the term *health psychology* (as defined by Matarazzo, 1980) more aptly describes the scope of this chapter. Belar and Deardorff (1995) make the point that psychology, not behavioral medicine, is the professional activity of the psychologist. We agree, but we wish to emphasize our focus on the practice of clinical psychology within medical settings and the relation between such practice and behavior theory. The term *behavioral medicine* seems to connote that focus better than health psychology. In this chapter we have adopted the definition of behavioral medicine as offered by Pomerleau and Brady (1979):

> (a) the clinical use of techniques derived from the experimental analysis of behavior— behavior therapy and behavior modification—for the evaluation, prevention, management, or treatment of physical disease or physiological dysfunction; and (b) the conduct of research contributing to the functional analysis and understanding of behavior associated with medical disorders and problems in health care (p. xii).

Pediatric psychology, which refers to the activities of psychologists working with children in medical settings, has developed in parallel with behavioral medicine. Its existence as a separate subspecialty area is more a function of its historical influences than the existence of fundamental differences in its concepts, constructs, or current focus. For the purpose of this chapter, we have subsumed pediatric psychology within our discussions of behavioral medicine.

Impact of Behavior Theory on Behavioral Medicine

Current Interest in Behavioral Medicine

The relationship between psychology and medicine can be traced back to at least Descartes, but the formalization of this relationship has never been quite so successful as it is today. This explicit union is evidenced by the proliferation of new books and journals specializing in health psychology, behavioral medicine, and neuropsychology. There are a host of new national and international journals devoted to the topic, and the number of pages devoted to health-related articles in APA journals rival more traditional areas of psychology. Popularity of the field is evidenced by the growing number of training programs (doctoral level, APA-accredited internships, and postdoctoral fellowships) offering specific training experiences or tracks in behavioral medicine. There has also been a steady increase in the number of APA members who belong to health-related divisions. Membership in Division 38-Health Psychology increased 38 percent (from 2,303 to 3,178) during the ten-year period between 1983 and 1993. During the same period, Division 40-Neuropsychology membership increased by 242 percent (from 1,009 to 3,449) and Division 22-Rehabilitation membership nearly doubled (from 881 to 1,318). In 1989 (the latest available statistics), the National Science Foundation estimated that over 25 percent of practicing psychologists identified themselves as working in medical settings. The 1993 APA membership profile report indicates that 1,525 members are employed full time by a medical school. When nonmembers are also considered, the number employed is at least double (Clayson & Mensh, 1987). Over half of the members of the Society of Behavioral Medicine are psychologists (1,774 of a total of 3,372) and the vast majority of their 600 trainee members are students of psychology.

Psychologists are involved in diverse roles and activities within the medical setting. The scope of involvement ranges from designing strategies to promote healthy behavior to implementing interventions that alleviate physical symptoms and improve psychological well-being of medically ill patients. The focus of intervention may be related directly to patient care or indirectly, by improving communication between health care providers and patients. Targets for intervention include individuals and their families, physicians and other health care providers, the hospital setting itself, and the community at large. The scope of the psychologist's activities is similarly broad and includes assessment/diagnosis, prevention, consultation, therapy, and teaching/supervision (Sweet, Rozensky, & Tovian, 1991).

Historical Roots

Accounts of the early influences on the development of behavioral medicine as an interdisciplinary field vary depending upon the perspective or discipline of the historian, some citing forces within psychology while others focus on changes within medicine. It is likely that behavioral medicine's early growth is attributable to forces relevant to both fields. At a conference sponsored by NIMH, Blumenthal (1994) noted that the first research grant awarded by NIMH in 1948 supported a project designed to examine the relation between psychological factors and cardiovascular physiology. Two years later

Robert Felix, a physician and director of the Institute of Mental Health of the U.S. Public Health Service, asserted that many fields of psychology are pertinent to dealing with the problems confronting public health. He stressed the need to advance knowledge through research and to translate the research findings into the "life patterns of people." At the same time, there was growing interest in the relation between psychological traits and illness that was a focus of study within psychosomatic medicine. Finally, growth in behavioral medicine has been stimulated by reports from federal agencies linking behavior and health (such as the U.S. Surgeon General's report on smoking) and by conferences geared toward integrating biomedical findings and behavioral science.

The emergence of behavioral medicine as a bona fide subspecialty *within psychology* is generally traced to the mid- to late 1970s and, in part, to the early debates among learning theorists about the generality of conditioning principles. During the early 1960s the question of whether autonomic and instrumental behavior were governed by the same or different sets of learning principles was still a central question. Studies demonstrating operant conditioning of responses such as heart rate and vasoconstriction of skin among curarized rats (DiCara & Miller, 1968; Miller & DiCara, 1967) appeared to confirm Hull's contention that autonomic and central nervous system processes were controlled by one set of learning principles (Hilgard & Bower, 1975; Dienstfrey, 1991). Also during this period, Kamiya (1969) demonstrated that changes in EEG alpha rhythms could be achieved in humans with operant conditioning. Until this point, most investigators generally accepted the assumption that the autonomic nervous system was beyond voluntary control.

This research generated considerable interest and by the mid 1970s there was speculation that the combination of the potential for gaining control of visceral responses along with the new technology of biofeedback could lead to behavioral cures for a host of arousal-based medical disorders. (Hilgard & Bower, 1975). The early findings were met with great enthusiasm and a flurry of studies were conducted with the anticipation that behavioral interventions could be instrumental for the prevention and treatment of stress-related physical problems. Twenty years ago Hilgard and Bower (1975) projected that the " . . . techniques of visceral learning combined with biofeedback . . . hold out the prospects for helping to cure patients suffering from such disorders as cardiac arrhythmia, high blood pressure, tension headaches, and epileptic seizures." (p. 556).

Early examples of direct application of behavioral principles to medically related symptoms tended to use isolated strategies to eliminate specific physical symptoms, most of which were presumed to be related to maladaptive learning. For example, Yates (1958) used massed practice as a treatment for tics. Wright, Nunnery, Eichel, and Scott (1969) used classical conditioning to wean a young child of tracheostomy addiction (reliance upon a tracheostomy after breathing through normal air passages is possible). In this early study, occlusion of the cannula was paired with pleasurable activities. The occlusion sessions were gradually increased each day until normal breathing patterns were established. These early studies were notable because the targets for intervention were alterations in physiological responses—a territory previously considered outside the scope of psychological practice.

Current Forces

Current interest in behavioral medicine is fueled by the convergence of a number of interrelated factors (Gentry, 1984; Blumenthal, 1994) linking behavior to health outcomes. A major factor is the changing health profile of the nation. Antibiotics and vaccines have eradicated, or at least reduced, many of the most common causes of premature death and morbidity of the first half of the century. Many of the remaining health threats are related to behavior (U.S. Department of Health and Human Services, 1991). There is now overwhelming empirical support linking the most common causes of death (such as cancer, heart disease, diabetes, accidental injury) to specific patterns of behavior such as smoking, risk-taking, poor diet, and lack of exercise (Hirayama, 1994). Behavioral research has demonstrated that these behaviors are modifiable and that modification can improve health outcomes.

Recognition that major illnesses may be preventable has been accompanied by a gradual shift in how these health-related problems are perceived; increasing responsibility for health is placed on the individual. Smoking, for example, is now recognized as a major contributor to heart disease (Orleans, Kristeller, & Gritz, 1993) and lung cancer (Colby, Linsky, & Straus, 1994). Public attitude is increasingly opposed to such behavior. It is not unusual to hear a person inquire about the smoking status of a person reported to have lung cancer. Twenty years ago, motor vehicle deaths and accidental injury were considered random, uncontrollable events. Today we consider them both predictable and preventable (Peterson & Schick, 1993; Jacquess & Finney, 1994). Newspapers now regularly report the seatbelt status of an individual involved in a fatal motor vehicle accident.

While certainly less blatant, the onus for early detection and control of disease is also generally placed on the individual. For example, women are advised to conduct regular breast examinations (Stevens, Hatcher, & Bruce, 1994) and diabetics are instructed to monitor insulin levels, adhere to prescribed diet and exercise regimens (Glasgow, Toobert, Hampson, & Wilson, 1995). Even susceptibility to and management of stress is considered the individual's responsibility (Aikens, Wallander, Bell, & McNorton, 1994).

Since the beginning of this century, our ability to control and prevent medical illness has increased the average life span by approximately twenty-five years. This longevity has been accompanied by an increase in the number of individuals living with chronic disease (Blumenthal, 1994). There is growing evidence that psychological interventions can improve the health status and quality of life of individuals with medical disorders.

Finally, with changes in the health care delivery services in this country there is increasing interest in finding ways to reduce health care costs. Mounting evidence suggests that behavioral interventions may reduce over-dependence on and inappropriate usage of medical services (Budman, Demby, & Feldstein, 1984; Sobel, 1994). Cost containment is now an overriding factor in decision-making about health care. No segment of psychology will be shielded from these concerns, but behavioral therapists are in a better position than other practitioners to demonstrate their efficacy.

State of Behavior Theory in the Medical Arena

In some ways the early optimism about the potential importance of behavior therapy to health has been quickly realized. It would be difficult to think of another area in psychology where behavioral approaches have had such a rapid impact. Today there are few medical specialty areas that have been unaffected by advances made by psychology and particularly by behavior therapists. Behavior therapy has figured strongly in most levels of intervention, from explicating and reducing behavioral factors associated with poor medical outcome to designing interventions that improve quality of life among the medically ill. Interventions based on principles derived from behavioral theories have gained wide acceptance.

Behavior therapists involved in pediatric settings provide some of the clearest examples of a direct translation of behavioral principles to effective treatments for medically ill children. Logan Wright, who coined the phrase *pediatric psychology,* set the stage for behavior therapy's influence in pediatric settings in the mid 1960s. In a visionary paper published in the *American Psychologist,* Wright (1967) stressed the need for the developing field of pediatric psychology to design research methods for use in medical settings with the goal of generating new understanding of medical problems of children. Noting that basic research might initially take a backseat to applied questions, Wright felt that the emergence of basic knowledge is a necessity for the area to remain viable. He also noted that the medical setting did not lend itself to long-term individual psychotherapy. Thus, behaviorally trained psychologists were well suited to accomplish Wright's goal because they were equipped with treatment strategies known to effect behavioral change in a relatively short time period and with assessment tools focused on behavior and measurable outcomes. Further, the focus on measurable outcomes was welcomed by pediatricians unimpressed with the previous generation of insight-oriented medical psychologists.

Behavioral science has an impact on many aspects of current hospital practice. An obvious example of this is how children are now prepared for medical procedures. Most hospitals offer parents an opportunity to acquaint their child with hospital procedures prior to hospitalization for elective surgery. Children are routinely shown films or given books depicting other children undergoing similar procedures. While this may seem based more on common sense than concepts from social learning theory, it was only after research demonstrated positive outcomes following exposure to filmed models that hospitalized children received any information at all. Prior to the 1960s, and the dissemination of relevant behavioral research findings, the medical community believed that providing children with information would simply heighten their anxiety.

Vernon and colleagues (Vernon, Schulman, & Foley, 1966) documented negative consequences of hospitalization, particularly for children between six months and four years of age. This research was followed by studies (Vernon & Bailey, 1974) demonstrating that children experience less distress when exposed to modeling films depicting children coping well with similar procedures. In a series of systematic studies, Melamed, Siegel, and colleagues (Melamed & Siegel, 1975; Melamed, Meyer, Gee, & Soule, 1976) examined the question of what sort of intervention is best for what age child. The systematic nature of the research was critical for revealing that preparatory information is not always helpful. Younger children do not appear to benefit if information is given to them too far in advance of the surgery (Melamed et al., 1976). In fact, information given too far in advance may actually heighten anxiety.

Challenges

The 1980s and early 1990s will probably be remembered as the heyday of behavioral medicine. By the 1980s the field was so well accepted that the term *behavioral medicine* had become a buzzword (Agras, 1992). Interest in behavioral medicine continues to grow. However, we believe that this is a particularly vulnerable time for psychology and behavior therapy in the medical setting. Behavior theory's influence on practice in the medical setting is subject to most of the same challenges faced by behavior therapy in traditional mental health settings. Confusion and disagreement about the core nature of behavior therapy have the potential for eroding its future impact. In addition, changes in the nation's health care delivery system are exerting tremendous pressures on psychologists in medical settings, as they are on psychologists practicing in the community. Epstein (1992) notes that behavioral medicine shares the strengths and weaknesses of psychology and medicine. Current and future influences on both of these fields will have an impact on trends in behavioral medicine, and both these fields are currently undergoing rapid change. The following is a review of some of the issues and concerns that we believe will need to be addressed during the next decade if behavioral theory and therapy are to remain prominent forces in the medical arena. Among the major threats are the atheoretical focus of the field, its focus on specific disease entities, inefficient modes for disseminating new information, and reliance upon a collection of techniques loosely related to behavioral theory, rather than careful construction of treatment based on sound behavioral principles.

Atheoretical Focus

Initially, excitement about behavioral medicine was generated by laboratory findings and their potential impact. The factors that have stimulated this excitement and growth, however, have been primarily pragmatic rather than theoretical, and theory-driven research is rare (Drotar, 1994; Glasgow & Anderson, 1995; Mulhern & Bearison, 1994). The movement away from theory has mirrored that of clinical psychology in general, a concern expressed throughout this book. Omer and Dar (1992) compared research on psychotherapy conducted during the sixties, seventies, and eighties and noted a marked decline in theory-guided studies and a corresponding rise in pragmatic, clinically oriented research. The change is beyond that which could be accounted for by the increase in research in behavioral medicine. Rather, the focus by clinical psychology on applied questions is probably attributable to the increase in the number of scientist-practitioners (many of whom conduct research in applied settings) whose primary interests are developing effective treatments rather than understanding the mechanisms underlying their efficacy. As a result, treatment studies focus more on issues such as magnitude of improvement associated with different treatments rather than on the relation between models of psychopathology and response to treatment. This shift reflects a movement by the field of clinical psychology away from theory building and towards empirically based eclecticism (see Norcross & Newman, 1992). Behavioral medicine has reflected this trend.

Orientation around Disease Entities

A unique aspect of behavioral medicine is its orientation around disease entities rather than psychological constructs or disorders. Psychologists specializing in behavioral medicine, and particularly those working in university-affiliated medical centers, specialty clinics, or large regional hospitals, tend to specialize in specific medical disorders. For example, a psychologist may specialize in oncology, cardiology, or gastroenterology but rarely all three. Within their own specialty, they typically treat patients for a wide range of behavioral/psychosocial problems that arise and conduct research on the most pressing psychological questions. The identity of the psychologist within the medical setting reflects the practitioner's medical affiliation rather than a particular expertise within psychology.

Both research and practice are influenced by the medical affiliation. The organization of texts and journals within behavioral medicine reflects this influence. For instance, a 1992 special issue of the *Journal of Consulting and Clinical Psychology* included separate reviews of psychology's impact on topics such as benign headaches and gastrointestinal disorders. Likewise, most texts in behavioral medicine include chapters on cardiovascular disease, asthma, cancer, and the like. Investigators in some specialty areas have coined new terms to refer to the integration of psychological and biomedical research in their particular disease specialty, such as *psychoimmunology* or *psychoneuroimmunology* (Kiecolt-Glaser & Glaser, 1992) and *psychooncology* (Mulhern & Bearison, 1994).

The disease-related focus is pragmatic. Concentrating on one or two medical disorders makes it possible to remain current about biomedical and psychological research within the specialty areas (Epstein, 1992). It also facilitates communication by enabling the psychologist to become familiar with the language of a particular medical specialty. Collaborative relationships among other health care providers are enhanced since other health care specialties are also organized around particular diseases. Thus, the behavior therapist is more likely to be perceived as a member of the treatment team.

Other pragmatic benefits to the disease orientation are related to the administrative structure of hospitals and their primary focus on physical health as *the* outcome of importance. While psychological research may not be actively discouraged, its value is not germane to the medical setting unless it answers questions pertinent to the medical team. Administrative decisions about salary, retention, and promotion are typically made by administrators far more familiar with medicine than psychology. These decisions are often tied to such factors as publication in well-respected medical journals and grantsmanship—both of which are dependent on demonstrating a well-established programmatic line of research within a medical specialty area.

A major problem with the disease-specific orientation is that it encourages fragmentation of the field both from other content areas within behavioral medicine as well as from other basic areas of psychology. For every medical disease specialty, there is now a body of psychologically relevant research addressing a myriad of problems. Programmatic research within each medical field is conducted parallel to, rather than in collaboration with, research in other medical areas. Research conducted within one particular medical population does not draw on, and often neglects to even reference, similar research conducted with a different medical group. As a result, there is considerable redundancy across medical specialty areas and little theory building. For example, until quite recently research on coping among hospitalized children neglected to discuss the large literature on coping during dental procedures or the growing literature on how children cope with everyday stressors (see Compas, 1987). Another striking example is research on compliance with physician recommendations. Compliance is a general issue relevant to most treatment modalities, medical as well as psychotherapeutic. Research explicating factors that enhance compliance—in terms of patient and/or physician characteristics, patient–physician communication, medical variables, and setting factors—ought to be relevant across medical specialty areas. Yet research on compliance in diabetes has not typically informed research (or clinical practice) on treatment for cancer. This fragmentation is particularly striking in HIV-related research. Here, many of the research questions were not unlike those asked about other behavior-related health problems that had often been already answered decades ago. We have known for quite some time, for example, that simply providing education does not result in long-term behavior change. Yet early in the evolution of HIV-related psychological research there was a flood of studies examining whether information provision and type of dispersal can result in positive behavior change (see Kelly & Murphy, 1992).

Another example of fragmentation is that which occurs between behavioral medicine and basic psychological research. This criticism has also been levied against psychology as a field, as it has become increasingly specialized. The problem is magnified in behavioral medicine because of its focus on medical concerns. Returning to our example of compliance, debate about the mechanisms behind self-regulation or self-control have been central to psychology, particularly within behavior therapy, and should be relevant to understanding how to improve compliance among medical patients. As noted by Karoly (1995), concepts related to self-control have been incorporated into the larger domain of cognitive-behavioral therapy in the form of a host of specific techniques, and in the medical arena they appear in the form of strategies designed to improve compliance. Yet the rationale behind selecting a particular approach is rarely tied to the theoretical discussions about behavior change in general. Instead, the issue of compliance is addressed primarily as it relates to a medical problem. The result is that findings generated by research conducted within the medical specialty is not viewed as relevant to research on more general issues of behavior.

Finally, the disease-specific orientation of the field leads to isolation of psychologists from each other. In most medical settings psychologists are (administratively) members of psychiatry departments or are affiliated with specific medical specialties. Neither placement is ideal for fostering collaborations among psychologists. The placement of psychologists within medical specialties isolates them from other psychologists. This organization places primary focus on the biological processes involved in the medical disease while minimizing the importance of issues related to mental health. Psychologists housed in medical specialities rather than with other psychologists also have less opportunity to impact on clinical practice or to have a voice within the administrative structure of the medical setting. On the other hand, housing divisions of psychology within departments of psychiatry has other drawbacks. Agras (1992) points out that when psychology was concerned primarily with traditional mental health problems, or psychosomatic medicine, its fit with psychiatry was good. This was particularly true when psychiatry focused on treating individuals with neurosis. However, during the past few decades psychiatry has concerned itself more with pharmacological approaches for severely debilitating forms of psychopathology (reflecting what Dana and May [1986] termed the "remedicalization" of psychiatry). As a result, there is now little common ground between the two fields.

While behavioral therapists have successfully established themselves within the medical arena, the very nature and structure of the medical community impose certain challenges that discourage integration of behavior theory and practice. However, there are also factors within psychology that contribute to gaps between theory, research findings, and practice. In the following section we discuss how well-established methods within psychology contribute to the problem.

Gaps in Dissemination of New Findings

Psychology has a well-established method of disseminating new information to its academic community. Findings are typically presented at scientific conferences and later dispersed more formally through publication in journal articles. This method is less ideal for psychologists working in applied settings, and particularly for those employed in medical settings. Journals tend to be geared toward academicians rather than practitioners, and findings are rarely discussed in terms of their relevance to applied work (Roberts, McNeal, Randall, & Roberts, 1996). New lab-based findings, particularly those based on research with infrahumans, are often published in journals geared towards other researchers with similar interests. It may be many years before findings from the lab are included in books, chapters, or articles geared towards the practitioner.

A related concern, therefore, is the ability of the practicing psychologists to remain current in contemporary behavior theory. The issue of how to keep psychologists apprised of current knowledge has been the topic of numerous articles. Rescorla (1988) warned that psychologists, even those in academic settings, are often unaware of recent advances in understanding about associative learning. Viken and McFall (1994) mirrored this concern but discussed it in relation to operant principles. Epstein (1992) discussed the relevance of concepts such as behavioral economics and behavioral momentum to understanding behavior change (or lack thereof) in the medical arena. As practitioners become distanced from new findings, or view behavioral science as irrelevant, there is increased likelihood that they abandon learning theory completely. Alternatively, they are designing interventions based on obsolete ideas. While this is a general problem in the field, it is particularly critical in the medical arena, where psychologists experience pressure to keep up with current medical treatments as well. There is simply less opportunity and available time to remain current in both fields.

There are few efficient mechanisms for dispensing new research findings to applied settings. This reflects, in part, the nature of the field of psychology and the scientific endeavor. Our cautious research methodology ensures that it is never quite clear when findings have been substantiated as findings or are endorsed generally as being true. Rescorla (1988) contends that the notion that Pavlovian conditioning as the acquired ability of one stimulus to evoke the original response to another is outdated. Pavlovian conditioning is now understood to involve the learning of relations among various events in the environment. However, it would be difficult to pinpoint exactly when this transformation actually occurred. It is unclear at what point the field agreed that the old notion was obsolete. Recent movements to establish "validated treatment protocols" are an attempt to circumvent this problem by evaluating and endorsing certain approaches collectively. Discussion of the possible pitfalls of this approach are beyond the scope of the current chapter (cf. Eifert, Schulte, Zvolensky, Lejuez, & Lau, 1997; Evans, 1996). However, one obvious problem is that many of the difficulties experienced by patients in medical centers fall outside the realm of typical mental health problems and may not have a corresponding protocol. Since validated treatment protocols do not necessarily contribute to theory building, they also do not provide a guide for situations that fall outside the scope of traditional mental health problems. We are still left with the problem of keeping practitioners current with contemporary behavior theory.

Related to the problem of establishing new findings as "facts" is the inability to "take back" or withdraw old information and discontinue related strategies once it is established that they are obsolete. Sometimes the difficulty lies in the unwillingness of psychologists to use new empirical information to alter their practice. The continued use of projective tests is an example of this problem. Projective assessment strategies continue to be used despite the lack of empirical support for their efficacy and the availability of better approaches. Sometimes the outdated strategy is no longer under the control of the field. An example of this problem is how hospitals now prepare children for hospitalization. The medical community responded to the initial studies documenting the benefit of preparatory video tapes by incorporating various forms of preparation into its standard intake procedures. In many hospitals all children are given preparatory information and hospital tours a few days before surgery. Subsequent studies, demonstrating that preparatory information is contraindicated for some children under certain circumstances, went virtually ignored.

This problem is not unique to psychology. There is usually a flurry of interest in new medical findings, and the findings of subsequent investigations rarely command the same level of interest. In medicine, however, there are more obvious indicators of success and more scrutiny. Quality assurance committees, whose job it is to ensure that medical practitioners are using the latest techniques, have a clearly delineated role within medical settings. There is no similar entity within psychology to ensure quality control. As a result, we lack a formalized way for ensuring that practitioners abandon dated procedures.

Behavioral Treatment: A Collection of Techniques?

The merging of values and procedures from psychology and medicine has, in some instances, resulted in an odd blend of the two with the outcome being psychotechnology.

Rather than the careful integration of approaches based on a guiding theoretical framework, psychotechnology is an assortment of strategies used together or individually, often in a haphazard manner. This is the psychological equivalent of the physician's medicine bag. Biofeedback is one of the most prominent "treatments" in the psychologist's bag, so we will discuss it in some detail.

Biofeedback, a behavioral strategy with roots in learning theory, refers to the process of teaching physiological self-regulation by providing individuals with visual or auditory signals in response to changes in a target response (for example, muscle tension, temperature, pulse amplitude). The underlying premise is that the signal serves to reinforce the desired change and that change in the particular response mode is related to positive change in the target problem.

Biofeedback has become a popular technique for treating a variety of disorders. Specialty clinics, which offer biofeedback training programs geared towards certifying health professionals, are now fairly mainstream. Biofeedback is probably best known for its use with patients with headaches, but it has gained acceptance as a treatment for a variety of disorders, including such diverse problems as urinary incontinence (Skelly & Flint, 1995), psoriasis (Goodman, 1994), stuttering (Blood, 1995), scoliosis (Birbaumer, Flor, Cevey, Dworkin, & Miller, 1994), temporomandibular disorders (Rudy, Turk, Kubinski, & Zaki, 1995), and hypertension (Dubbert, 1995). Most research on autogenic biofeedback has focused on its application to patients with cardiovascular disease and headaches. They also speculate that it is a strategy that is used clinically for a far broader range of applications than reported in the literature. This also means it is being used for difficulties for which it has not been validated and for which there is little to no support.

The popularity of biofeedback and its broad acceptance by health professionals, psychologists, and patients is not surprising. First, it appears to be an effective means for altering behavior. Both clinical impression and research findings provide support that patients show improvement in symptoms after a course of biofeedback. Second, biofeedback fits well into what most people expect from modern state-of-the-art health care. Complete with graphics, lights, bells, or buzzers, it appears technologically sophisticated and to require more expertise on the part of the technician than other behavioral strategies. In other words, it seems and looks like science. In fact, in a practitioner's guide written for psychologists interested in developing expertise in clinical health psychology, Belar and Deardorff (1995) note that "The technology associated with biofeedback interventions makes it quite acceptable as a psychological intervention in our technologically-oriented society" (p. 87).

Although its appearance as technology is no reason for rejecting its use, it is also not a compelling reason to endorse it. And, interestingly, the continued popularity of biofeedback among practitioners and patients contrasts with waning interest and increased skepticism among researchers (Johnston & Martin, 1991), including those who have been most influential in the biofeedback arena (Blanchard et al., 1994). There is mounting evidence contradicting the notion that biofeedback works by teaching individuals how to alter the physiological mechanisms underlying pathology. Some investigators have concluded that biofeedback effects are attributable to nonspecific treatment effects (Roberts, 1994). Patients can learn to alter certain autonomic responses, such as blood pressure and heart rate, but the extent to which they can decrease these responses is probably not clinically meaningful. Further, it is doubtful that the magnitude of change that is possible would result in clinically meaningful change in the original complaint of the patient. The causes of tension headaches, for example, remain unclear, but are probably not due to muscular tension in the forehead skeletal muscles as was previously assumed. Reduction in muscle tension would not be an effective treatment (Johnston & Martin, 1991).

Biofeedback is one of the most obvious examples of a technology which has gained widespread popularity in the medical setting despite disappointing research findings. Relaxation training is another. Although there certainly are empirical justifications for its use, it has become the "chicken soup" of psychological technique—good for whatever ails you (Miller, 1994). When one of us was working in a pediatric oncology setting, nurses routinely requested that relaxation tape be provided to distressed children undergoing painful medical procedures. The prevailing perception was that relaxation training was the active ingredient in treatments dispensed by psychologists and tapes would serve as well. Indiscriminate use of relaxation training in this manner would have been a disservice to the children. The children would not have received an appropriate assessment, thereby precluding the development of an intervention more carefully tailored to their needs.

Using behavioral strategies outside a guiding theoretical framework introduces a number of additional problems. There is some evidence, for example, that relaxation training may be contraindicated for some problems and some people. Some individuals respond poorly to relaxation training. Miller (1994) questions the basic assumption that psychological relaxation implies or leads to physiological relaxation. In support of this concern he points to a number of studies suggesting that relaxation training may sometimes have a detrimental impact, such as impeding rather than facilitating recovery from surgery. Both relaxation training and biofeedback fall into the category of manipulations designed to enhance feelings of psychological control. Taylor (1990) notes that under some circumstances such strategies can exacerbate problems by increasing feelings of responsibility and blame. Finally, we concur with Miller's (1994) argument that behavioral medicine techniques cannot by themselves foster transformative changes in a person's coping style and personality integration that will make him or her more capable of responding like a tough, hardy, or coherent person.

Limitations of Behavioral Models

The acceptance of behavior therapy within the medical setting is due to its focus on observable, measurable, and objective outcomes. This was in contrast to the relative failure of dynamic therapists who dominated the medical arena a few decades ago. On the other hand, many behavioral therapists have become discouraged by the perceived narrowness of behavioral models that seem to neglect to incorporate, consider, or integrate the full scope of behavioral, physiological, environmental variables that impact on health. For example, there is considerable evidence to suggest that operant-based feeding programs for infants with failure to thrive result in immediate improvement of the most obvious target for change, food intake. But children with failure to thrive typically have difficulties which go beyond food intake. Inadequate parenting may be the basis for the initial feeding problem. However, due to the lack of a unified behavior theory to guide selection of targets for change and integration of strategies, it is left to the therapist to figure out how to integrate well-delineated operant and respondent-based behavioral protocols for specific behaviors with other likely targets for change within the same individual (or, in this example the parent–child dyad).

Apparent limitations of behavior theory have contributed to a movement away from behavior theory and toward cognitive and cognitive-behavioral explanations of behavior. Chronic pain serves as a powerful example of the potential of behavior therapy to enhance understanding and treatment of a common physical complaint, but it also illustrates the movement of the field away from treatments tied closely to behavior theory and toward techniques vaguely related to theory. We will therefore discuss it in some detail.

Chronic pain is a common disabling condition that has been costly to society and an enigma to the medical profession. Of particular interest to psychologists is the relation between psychopathology, particularly depression, and chronic pain. Chronic pain is resistant to traditional medical approaches (typically surgery and/or medication) and patients have historically been considered "treatment failures" by the medical community. Patients are often discharged from their physician's care with advice to rest, take pain medications, and learn to live with their pain. This advice often results in further debilitation.

While medicine has had relatively little to offer for treating and understanding chronic pain, treatments, or rather management programs, based on behavioral models have shown success. Operant models of pain typically place primary emphasis on quantifiable and observable pain behaviors rather than on the subjective private experience of pain (Rachlin, 1985). According to an operant model, pain behaviors are initially responses to specific nociceptive input, perhaps from tissue damage due to injury or illness. An individual lifting a box may, for example, experience a sharp stabbing pain due to a strained muscle. In response, she may wince, and limp to a chair. The specific behaviors emitted may be influenced by previous learning, but without reinforcement they dissipate as the tissue heals. In the case of a patient with chronic pain these behaviors are maintained by environmental factors. Potential sources of reinforcement for pain behavior may include helpful behaviors from others, sympathy, rest, and avoidance of unpleasant tasks. Narcotics taken to relieve pain may actually have a paradoxical effect of increasing pain. Taken on an as-needed basis they can serve as operants and reinforce pain behavior. Pain behavior is conceptualized in the same manner as other behavior and therefore subject to the same principles of learning. Thoughts and images and other "internal events" are considered covert instances of behavior influenced by similar mechanisms (although for a discussion of alternative views see Novy, Nelson, Francis, & Turk, 1995).

Support for the importance of conditioning on maintaining pain behaviors among chronic pain patients comes from both research in clinical settings and laboratory studies. Pain behaviors are clearly affected by contextual cues, occuring more frequently while individuals discuss pain-related issues than while discussing nonpain related issues (Cincirpini & Floreen, 1983). Solicitous behaviors from significant others serve to increase pain behaviors and patients' report of pain severity (Anderson & Rehm, 1984; Romano et al., 1992). Patients who receive compensation payments for their disability appear to have longer hospital stays, exhibit more pain behaviors, and rate their pain as more severe then those who are not being compensated (Block, Kremer, & Gaylor, 1980; Kleinke & Spangler, 1988).

The first behavioral pain-management programs relied heavily upon operant techniques. Shaping of health-promoting behavior was accomplished by establishing goals for exercises and activities and increasing the criteria for success. Social reinforcement was provided contingent on the absence of pain behavior and presence of well behaviors. Pain cocktails (mixtures of medications with gradual reduction in levels of narcotics) were provided on a time-contingent rather than as-needed basis. Spouses were instructed to use the same principles at home. Programmed rest periods were used as rewards for gains in physical and occupational therapy. Positive results from these and other studies included decrease in narcotics usage, increase in activity level, and overall improvement in functioning (see Fordyce, 1976).

Operant-based programs did not address aberrations in mood among pain patients despite the fact that disorders of mood, particularly depression, are almost ubiquitous among chronic pain populations. As a result, pain-rehabilitation programs have moved away from the operant models of pain toward cognitive-behavioral approaches to treatment. According to this perspective, behavioral, affective, cognitive and sensory-physical aspects of the individual's experience are interactive. The individual is an active processor of information. The resulting thoughts (e.g. appraisals, attributions, expectancies) play a critical role in influencing mood, affecting physiological processes, impacting on the environment, and determining behavior. Pain behaviors are still regarded as essential parameters for understanding the chronic pain experience but are not the sole parameter. (Turk, Meichenbaum, & Genest, 1983; Turk and Rudy, 1987).

Cognitive-behavioral-based treatments for pain incorporate many of the principles central to behavioral treatment, but place great emphasis on altering the individual's verbal behavior, replacing maladaptive thoughts and statements with more adaptive ones. Strategies based on a variety of cognitive-behavioral conceptualizations of depression, anxiety, and pain are therefore now included in most comprehensive pain-management programs. Behavioral and cognitive-behavior therapy are now well-established treatments for individuals with chronic pain. Cognitive-behavioral therapy for chronic pain is one of the few empirically supported psychological interventions by the APA Division 12 Task Force on Promotion and Dissemination of Psychological Principles (Chambless et al., 1996).

The shift toward cognition may be viewed as an improvement on the narrowness of the earlier approach. Unfortunately, the inclusion of cognitive-behavioral strategies has not been systematic. Based on informal inquires and program descriptions in treatment-outcome research, there appears to be little consistency in treatment approaches among programs claiming to offer cognitive-behavioral treatment. Different centers use vastly different mixtures of therapeutic techniques. Treatment may include relaxation training, biofeedback, problem-solving, instruction in coping strategies, and cognitive restructuring. Instruction in coping may be designed around principles borrowed from social learning theory, attributional theory, learned helplessness, and Beck's (1987) theory of dysfunctional thinking. The overall goal of these approaches is to provide the patient with an enhanced sense of control and self-efficacy, and reduction in feelings of hopelessness. The sequence, timing, or combination of techniques varies greatly across treatment programs, although most are described as "cognitive-behavioral." The term *cognitive-behavioral treatment* for pain does not refer to any particular approach and treatment strategy. In contrast to the early pain-treatment programs that used clearly delineated techniques, current programs are much more variable, less well defined, and only loosely tied to behavioral principals. As a result, the mechanisms behind the apparent success of these programs are unclear.

Future Directions

Oncology stands out as a shining example of a medical specialty that has fostered a successful collaboration between medicine and psychology, a strong link between research and clinical practice, and a reciprocal relation between research conducted in the clinical setting and lab-based research. Psychologists are critical members of the treatment team in the most well-known oncology centers, and often in smaller regional hospitals. Among centers where practitioners are conducting research, joint ventures between physicians and psychologists are common. Redd (1995) suggests that behavioral research in cancer can serve as a model for understanding the psychological processes associated with health and illness.

There are a number of unique aspects of oncology that have helped foster a close collaboration between psychology and oncology. First, oncologists and psychologists share similar values about the importance of research. The remarkable advances in cancer treatment during the past few decades are attributable to aggressive clinical trials that have been accomplished through large collaborative research projects. While only a small group of oncologists are involved in developing the protocols, oncologists throughout the country participate in the studies by enrolling their patients, following the protocol treatment plan, and conducting diagnostic evaluations according to the protocol schedule. Therefore, even oncologists in small community hospitals are involved in the scientific endeavor.

Oncologists may also be more aware of the psychosocial impact of disease than their counterparts in other medical specialty areas. Due to the aggressive nature of its treatment and the catastrophic nature of the disease itself, there is high potential for what Derogatis (1986) termed *psychological morbidity* (or negative behavioral and neuropsychological sequelae). Psychological assessment is therefore critical and often a required part of the ongoing diagnostic evaluations of the patient.

Further, there is now clear-cut evidence that psychological interventions are beneficial to cancer patients for a host of difficulties (Redd, 1995). One shining example is in the area of alleviating distressful side effects associated with chemotherapy. Some of the symptoms particularly troublesome to patients and their physicians fit well into methodologies established in learning labs. Anticipatory nausea and vomiting (ANV) and learned taste aversions (LTA) are two problems that could be predicted by behavioral scientists on the basis of general laws of learning. ANV refers to nausea and vomiting that occurs in patients prior to chemotherapy. It appears that cues associated with chemotherapy set the stage for the development of nausea and vomiting. Patients also develop aversions to foods that have become associated with the noxious side effects of treatment. The circumstances surrounding the development of these aversions so closely mimic conditions engineered in learning labs that Andrykowski and Otis (1990) termed chemotherapy a "natural laboratory" for investigating learned food aversions.

Behavioral formulations of ANV and LTA have had an impact in applied settings, and the information generated by research conducted in learning labs has been translated directly into effective interventions. Information provided in the clinical setting has also been influential in directing lab-based research. For example, in a series of studies conducted over the past twenty years, Bernstein and colleagues (Bernstein, 1978; Carrell, Cannon, Best, & Stone, 1986) demonstrated that novel flavors can become aversive when ingestion is followed by chemotherapy or radiation therapy. In the initial study (Bernstein, 1978), children were given a novel-flavored ice cream prior to receiving GI-toxic chemotherapy. Compared to controls who were not exposed to this experience, these children were significantly less likely to choose the ice cream when it was later offered to them. It appeared that one experience with the pairing of the ice cream and chemotherapy-induced GI distress was sufficient to form an association. Subsequent studies replicated these findings with adults and suggested similar phenomena can occur with patients toward their regular diet (Bernstein, Webster, & Bernstein, 1982).

As expected based on lab studies (Bernstein, Goehler, & Bouton, 1983), overshadowing can be effective for attenuating acquisition of CTA in humans (Broberg & Bernstein, 1987; Mattes, Arnold, & Borass, 1987). Ingestion of a novel taste prior to emetogenic treatment but after a meal interferes with the acquisition of aversions to the food eaten earlier. The conditions that facilitate acquisition of ANV are also consistent with associative laws of learning. Acquisition of ANV is associated with level of post-treatment nausea and vomiting (Cohen, Blanchard, Ruckdeschel, & Smolen, 1986; Morrow, Lindke, & Black, 1991) and number of previous trials/drug infusions (Nesse et al., 1980). Lab-based research supports the notion that heightened anxiety may facilitate aversive conditioning. For example, Bitterman and Holtzman (1952) reported that galvanic skin responses of anxious individuals were more readily conditioned than those of less-anxious individuals. In the oncology setting, high levels of anxiety and susceptibility to ANV also appear to be related.

Not all patients experience ANV or LTA. The search for variables that increase susceptibility has focused primarily on the set of variables explored in lab studies with infrahumans, such as toxicity of the drug, level of anxiety, frequency and duration of post-treatment NV, and number of trials. This focus may reveal some associations but will probably not result in a level of understanding sufficient to predict which individuals are most susceptible. The search is based on a somewhat simplistic notion of conditioning. Rescorla (1988) notes that emotions and motivations are central to conditioning, and associations are not formed through a process of passive contiguity. Rather the organism actively interprets its environment using "logical and perceptual relations among events, along with its own preconceptions, to form a sophisticated representation of its world" (p. 154). If ANV is a learned response, relevant factors may include the full range of emotions experienced by the patient. The type of information used to make new associations is apt to be considerably wider among humans than infrahumans. Likewise, the range of emotions, complexity, and heterogeneity of previous learning histories are greater in humans. It is therefore inadequate to limit investigations with humans to those variables explored with infrahumans.

Conclusions and Outlook

A decade ago psychologists tended to be unaware of their status on hospital staff, uninvolved with the administrative and fiscal activities in medical settings, and had little knowledge of regulations related to mental health services for patients with Medicare or Medicaid (Carr, 1987; Wright & Friedman, 1992). Things have changed radically since then. Today, psychologists are painfully aware of how the political and sociocultural environment of the medical setting impact on their practice; the pendulum may have swung to the other extreme. It is often from behavioral science that psychologists have become "expatriates" (Carr, 1987). Professional and guild issues tend to eclipse questions more germane to the field of clinical psychology.

Many of the concerns expressed in this chapter are not specific to medical settings but relevant to the field in general. Behavioral therapists specializing in a particular mental health problem rather than a medical entity may also be uninformed about relevant empirical findings derived from other specialty areas. Likewise texts organized around mental health difficulties (depression, anxiety, obsessive-compulsive disorder) impose some of the same difficulties as those organized around medical disease entities. However, the interdisciplinary nature of behavioral medicine and characteristics of the medical setting introduce additional challenges.

A major challenge is preserving an identity as a behavior therapist while gaining acceptance within the medical arena. This means preserving one's ties to behavior therapy and psychology while also educating medical-setting colleagues about the unique skills behavior therapists bring to the setting. Given the contingencies in medical settings, maintaining one's identify can be the more difficult task and may require some changes in how we train behavior therapists and conduct our research.

One suggestion is to establish better methods for encouraging collaborations by behavior therapists across hospitals and between those employed in university settings and those in medical settings. Faculty in psychology departments have great freedom to direct research on a variety of topics, while those in medical settings may be restricted to research on medically driven questions. On the other hand, psychologists in universities often have limited access to the populations needed to best answer their questions. Joint ventures address both problems. Questions arising in the medical setting may be explored systematically in the lab and with undergraduate populations, and subsequently examined with clinical populations with additional questions brought back to the lab. Collaborations of this sort are not unusual but no formal mechanisms exist for facilitating them. Research-based practica or internships may be an effective way of encouraging joint ventures. Training programs with a commitment to Boulder-model training could establish small consortiums focused on common issues or questions. The consortium could serve as a formal mechanism for shared ideas, research collaborations, and coordinated training opportunities. The potential for this type of collaboration would be enhanced if funding sources favored such collaborations.

Educating other health care professionals about the unique contributions of behavior therapy is another important avenue for reinforcing and promoting the identity of the behavior therapist. Education can be accomplished through formal presentations at grand rounds or, less formally, by using informal interactions as opportunities to educate. This may entail including brief, concise discussions of pertinent clinical or research findings in responses to requests for consultation about a case or using a social occasion to discuss the relevance of behavior therapy to health.

A critical aspect of education is dispelling outdated notions other health care professionals have about psychology, as well as discontinuing the use of techniques known to lack validity, and replacing them with techniques based on a more current understanding of behavior therapy. Psychologists who continue to use techniques lacking in validity discredit the field and contribute to the reputation of psychology as lacking in scientific foundation. Complacency on the part of the field has contributed to this problem. New graduates, equipped with knowledge about the validity of certain approaches (e.g., projective tests), are often ill-equipped to reply to supervisors requesting their use. Behavior therapists will have to find more effective ways to use their knowledge to impact on their training settings instead of allowing themselves to be pressured into the use of outdated methods.

We continue to be optimistic about the future of behavior therapy in medical settings. Recent changes in health care, particularly the increased pressure to demonstrate efficacy, have been advantageous to behavior therapists. A threat, however, is that forces from inside the medical setting may encourage behavior therapists to adopt an atheoretical, pragmatic approach towards treatment and focus exclusively on physiological indices as the outcome of importance. Once behavior therapists are employed in medical settings, most contingencies currently favor adoption of the values of, and identification with, their physician colleagues. With increasing interest in behavioral medicine, the field will have to find ways to address these concerns. Simply including more topics relevant to behavioral medicine in the usual clinical curriculum has not been an adequate solution. Establishing more formal avenues for collaboration between academic psychology departments and medical settings—for the purpose of training, research, and clinical practice—will be a necessary step to linking behavior theory to the practice of behavior therapy in medical settings.

References

Agras, W. S. (1992). Some structural changes that might facilitate the development of behavioral medicine. *Journal of Consulting and Clinical Psychology, 60,* 499–504.

Aikens, J. E., Wallander, J. L., Bell, D. S. H., & McNorton, A. (1994). A nomothetic-idiographic study of daily psychological stress and blood glucose in women with Type 1 diabetes mellitus. *Journal of Behavioral Medicine, 17,* 535–548.

Anderson, L. P., & Rehm, L. P. (1984). The relationship between strategies of coping and perception of pain in three chronic pain groups. *Journal of Clinical Psychology, 40,* 1170–1177.

Andrykowski, M., & Otis, M. L. (1990). Development

of learned food aversions in humans: Investigation in a "natural Laboratory" of cancer chemotherapy. *Appetite, 14,* 145–158.

Beck, A. T. (1987). Cognitive models of depression. *Journal of Cognitive Psychotherapy, 1,* 5–37.

Belar, C. D., & Deardorff, W. W. (1995) *Clinical health psychology in medical settings.* Washington, DC: American Psychological Association.

Bernstein, I. L. (1978). Learned taste aversions in children receiving chemotherapy. *Science, 200,* 1302–1303.

Bernstein, I. L., Goehler, L. E., & Bouton, M. E. (1983). Relative potency of foods and drinks as targets in aversion conditioning. *Behavioral and Neural Biology, 37,* 134–148.

Bernstein, I. L., Webster, M. M., & Bernstein, I. D. (1982). Food aversions in children receiving chemotherapy. *Cancer, 50,* 2960–2863.

Birbaumer, N., Flor, H., Cevey, B., Dworkin, B., & Miller, N. E. (1994). Behavioral treatment of scoliosis and kyphosis. *Journal of Psychosomatic Research, 38,* 623–628.

Bitterman, M. E., & Holtzman, W. H. (1952). Conditioning and extinction of the galvanic skin response as a function of anxiety. *Journal of Abnormal and Social Psychology, 47,* 615–623.

Blanchard, E. B. (1977). Behavioral medicine: A perspective. In R. B. Williams & W. D. Gentry (Eds.), *Behavioral approaches to medical treatment* (pp. 1–6). Cambridge, MA: Ballinger.

Blanchard, E. B., Kim, M., Hermann, C., Steffek, B. D., Nichelson, N. L., & Taylor, A. G. (1994). The role of perception of success in the thermal biofeedback treatment of vascular headache. *Headache Quarterly, 5,* 231–236.

Block, A. R., Kremer, E., & Gaylor, M. (1980). Behavioral treatment of chronic pain: Variables affecting treatment efficacy. *Pain, 8,* 367–375.

Blood, G. W. (1995). A behavioral-cognitive therapy program for adults who stutter: Computers and counseling. *Journal of Communications Disorders, 28,* 165–180.

Blumenthal, S. (1994). An overview of NIH behavioral medicine research programs. In S. J. Blumenthal, K. Matthews, & S. W. Weiss (Eds.), *New frontiers in behavioral medicine: Proceedings of the National Conference* (pp. 41–60). Washington, DC: U.S. Government Printing Office.

Broberg, D. J., & Bernstein, I. L. (1987). Candy as a scapegoat in the prevention of food aversions in children receiving chemotherapy. *Cancer, 60,* 2344–2347.

Budman, S. H., Demby, A., & Feldstein, M. L. (1984). Insight into reduced use of medical services after psychotherapy. *Professional Psychology Research and Practice, 15,* 353–361.

Carr, J. E. (1987). Federal impact on psychology in medical schools. *American Psychologist, 42,* 869–872.

Carrell, L. E., Cannon, D. S., Best, M. R., & Stone, M. J. (1986). Nausea and radiation-inducted taste aversions in cancer patients. *Appetite, 7,* 203–208.

Chambless, D. L., Sanderson, W. C., Shoham, V., Bennett-Johnson, S., Pope, K. S., Crits-Christoph, P., Baker, M., Johnson, B., Woody, S. R., Sue, S., Beutler, L., Williams, D. A., & McCurry, S. (1996). An update on empirically validated therapies. *The Clinical Psychologist, 49,* 5–18.

Cincirpini, P. M., & Floreen, A. (1983). An assessment of chronic pain behaviors in a structured interview. *Journal of Psychosomatic Research, 27,* 117–123.

Clayson, D., & Mensh, I. N. (1987). Psychologists in medical schools: The trials of emerging political activism. *American Psychologist, 42,* 859–862.

Cohen, R. E., Blanchard, E. B., Ruckdeschel, J. C., & Smolen, R. C. (1986). Prevalence and correlates of post-treatment and anticipatory nausea and vomiting in cancer chemotherapy. *Journal of Psychosomatic Research, 30,* 643–654.

Colby, J. P., Linsky, A. S., & Straus, M. A. (1994). Social stress and state-to-state differences in smoking and smoking related mortality in the United States. *Social Sciences and Medicine, 38,* 373–381.

Compas, B. (1987). Coping with stress during childhood and adolescence. *Clinical Psychology Review, 7,* 275–302.

Dana, R. H., & May, W. T. (1986) Health care megatrends and health psychology. *Professional Psychology, 17,* 251–255.

Derogatis, L. R. (1986). Psychology in cancer medicine: A perspective and overview. *Journal of Consulting and Clinical Psychology, 54,* 632–638.

DiCara, L. V., & Miller, N. E. (1968). Instrumental learning of vasomotor responses by rats: Learning to respond differentially in the two ears. *Science, 159,* 1484–1486.

Dienstfrey, H. (1991). Neal Miller, the dumb autonomic nervous system, and biofeedback. *Advances, 7,* 33–44.

Drotar, D. (1994). Psychological research with pediatric conditions: If we specialize can we generalize? *Journal of Pediatric Psychology, 19,* 403–414.

Dubbert, P. M. (1995). Behavioral (life-style) modification in the prevention and treatment of hypertension. *Clinical Psychology Review, 15,* 187–216.

Eifert, G. H., Schulte, D., Zvolensky, M. J., Lejeuz, C. W., & Lau, A. W. (1997). Manualizing behavior therapy: Merits and challenges. *Behavior Therapy, 28,* 499–509.

Epstein, L. H. (1992). Role of behavior therapy in behavioral medicine. *Journal of Consulting and Clinical Psychology, 60,* 493–498.

Evans, I. M. (1996). Individualizing therapy, customizing clinical science. *Journal of Behavior Therapy and Experimental Psychiatry, 27,* 99–105.

Farquhar, J. W. (1991). The Stanford cardiovascular disease prevention programs. *Annals of the New York Academy of Sciences, 623,* 327–331.

Fordyce, W. E. (1976). *Behavioral methods for chronic pain and illness.* St. Louis, MO: Mosby.

Gentry, W. D. (1984). Behavioral medicine: A new research paradigm. In W. D. Gentry (Ed.), *Handbook of behavioral medicine* (pp. 1–12). New York: Guilford.

Glasgow, R. E., & Anderson, B. J. (1995). Future directions for research on pediatric chronic disease management: Lessons from diabetes. *Journal of Pediatric Psychology, 20,* 389–402.

Glasgow, R. E., Toobert, D. J., Hampson, S. E., & Wilson, W. (1995) Behavioral research on diabetes at the Oregon Research Institute. *Annals of Behavioral Medicine, 17,* 32–40.

Goodman, M. (1994). An hypothesis explaining the successful treatment of psoriasis with thermal biofeedback: A case report. *Biofeedback and Self Regulation, 19,* 347–352.

Hilgard, E. R. & Bower, G. H. (1975). *Theories of learning.* Englewood Cliffs, NJ: Prentice-Hall.

Hirayama, T. (1994). Lifestyle and mortality: The healthiest way to live. *Homeostasis in Health and Disease, 35,* 168–179.

Jaquess, D. L., & Finney, J. W. (1994). Previous injuries and behavior problems predict children's injuries. *Journal of Pediatric Psychology, 19,,* 79–89.

Johnston, D. W., & Martin, P. R. (1991). Psychophysiological contributions to behavior therapy. In P. R. Martin (Ed.), *Handbook of behavior therapy and psychological science* (pp. 383–409). New York: Pergamon.

Kamiya, J. (1969). Operant control of the EEG alpha rhythm and some of its reported effects on consciousness. In C. T. Tart (Ed.), *Altered states of consciousness* (pp. 507–517). New York: Wiley.

Kaplan, R. M. (1990). Behavior as the central outcome in health care. *American Psychologist, 45,* 1211–1220.

Karoly, P. (1995). Self-control theory. In W. O'Donohue & L. Krasner. (Eds.), *Theories of behavior therapy* (pp. 259–285). Washington, DC: American Psychological Association.

Kelly, J. A. & Murphy, D. A. (1992). Psychological interventions with AIDS and HIV: Prevention and treatment. *Journal of Consulting and. Clinical Psychology, 60,* 576–585.

Kiecolt-Glaser, J. K., & Glaser, R. (1992). Psychoneuroimmunology: Can psychological interventions modulate immunity? *Journal of Consulting and Clinical Psychology, 60,* 569–575.

Kleinke, C. L., & Spangler, A.S.J. (1988). Predicting treatment outcome of chronic back pain patients in a multidisciplinary pain clinic: Methodological issues and treatment implications. *Pain, 33,* 41–48.

Matarazzo, J. D. (1980). Behavioral health and behavioral medicine. *American Psychologist, 35,* 807–817.

Mattes, R. D., Arnold, C., & Borass, M. (1987). Management of learned food aversion in cancer patients receiving chemotherapy. *Cancer Treatment Reports, 71,* 1071–1078.

Melamed, B. G., Meyer, R., Gee, C., & Soule, L. (1976). The influence of time and type of preparation on children's adjustment to hospitalization. *Journal of Pediatric Psychology, 1,* 31–37.

Melamed, B. G., & Siegel, L. J. (1975). Reduction of anxiety in children facing hospitalization and surgery by use of filmed modeling. *Journal of Consulting and Clinical Psychology, 43,* 411–521.

Miller, L. (1994). Biofeedback and behavioral medicine: Treating the symptom, the syndrome, or the person? *Psychotherapy, 31,* 161–169.

Miller, N. E., & DiCara, L. (1967). Instrumental learning of heart rate changes in curarized rats: Shaping, and specificity to discriminative stimulus. *Journal of Comparative and Physiological Psychology, 63,* 12–19.

Morrow, G. R., Lindke, J., & Black, P. M. (1991). Anticipatory nausea development in cancer patients: Replication and extension of a learning model. *British Journal of Psychology, 82,* 61–72.

Mulhern, R. K., & Bearison, D. J. (1994). *Pediatric psychooncology: Psychological perspectives on children with cancer*. New York: Oxford University Press.

Nesse, R. M., Carli, T., Curtis, G. C., & Kleinman, P. D. (1980). Pretreatment nausea in cancer chemotherapy: A conditioned response? *Psychosomatic Medicine, 42*, 33–36.

Norcross, J., & Newman, C. F. (1992). Psychotherapy integration: Setting the context. In J. C. Norcross and M.R. Goldfried (Eds.), *Handbook of psychotherapy integration* (pp. 3–45). New York: Basic Books.

Novy, D. M., Nelson, D. V., Francis, D. J., & Turk, D. C. (1995). Perspectives of chronic pain: An evaluative comparison of restrictive and comprehensive models. *Psychological Bulletin, 118*, 238–247.

Omer, H., & Dar, R. (1992). Changing trends in three decades of psychotherapy research: The flight from theory into pragmatics. *Journal of Consulting and Clinical Psychology, 60*, 88–93.

Orleans, T. C., Kristeller, J. L., & Gritz, E. R. (1993). Helping hospitalized smokers quit: New directions for treatment and research. *Journal of Consulting and Clinical Psychology, 61*, 778–789.

Peterson, L., & Schick, B. (1993). Empirically derived injury prevention rules. *Journal of Applied Behavior Analysis, 26*, 451–460.

Rachlin, H. (1985). Pain and behavior. *Behavioral and Brain Sciences, 8*, 43–83.

Redd, W. H., (1995). Behavioral research in cancer as a model for health psychology. *Health Psychology, 14*, 99–100.

Rescorla, R. A. (1988). Pavlovian conditioning: It's not what you think it is. *American Psychologist, 43*, 149–160.

Roberts, A. H. (1994). "The powerful placebo" revisited: Implications for headache treatment and management. *Headache Quarterly, 5*, 208–213.

Roberts, M. C., McNeal, R. E., Randall, C. J., & Roberts, J. D. (1996). A necessary reemphasis on integrating explicative research with the pragmatics of pediatric psychology. *Journal of Pediatric Psychology, 21*, 107–114.

Romano, J. M., Turner, J. A., Friedman, L. S., Bulcroft, R. A., Jensen, M., Hops, H., & Wright, S. F. (1992). Sequential analysis of chronic pain behaviors and spouse responses. *Journal of Consulting and Clinical Psychology, 60*, 777–782.

Rudy, T. E., Turk, D. C., Kubinski, J. A., & Zaki, H. S. (1995). Differential treatment responses of TMD patients as a function of psychological characteristics. *Pain, 61*, 103–112.

Schwartz, G. E., & Weiss, S. M. (1977). What is behavioral medicine? *Psychosomatic Medicine, 39*, 377–381.

Skelly, J., & Flint, A. J. (1995). Urinary incontinence associated with dementia. *Journal of the American Geriatrics Society, 43*, 286–294.

Sobel, D. S. (1994). Mind matters, money matters: The cost-effectiveness of clinical behavioral medicine. In S. J. Blumenthal, K. Matthews, & S. M. Weiss. (Eds.), *New research frontiers in behavioral medicine: Proceedings of the National Conference* (pp. 25-36). Washington, DC: NIH.

Stevens, V. M., Hatcher, J. W., & Bruce, B. K. (1994). How compliant is compliant? Evaluating adherence with breast self-exam positions. *Journal of Behavioral Medicine, 17*, 523–534.

Sweet, J. J., Rozensky, R. H., & Tovian, S. M. (1991). *Handbook of clinical psychology in medical settings*. New York: Plenum.

Taylor, S. E. (1990). Health psychology. *American Psychologist, 45*, 40–50.

Turk, D. C., Meichenbaum, D., & Genest, M. (1983). *Pain and behavioral medicine: A cognitive-behavioral perspective*. New York: Guilford.

Turk, D. C., & Rudy, T. E. (1987). Towards a comprehensive assessment of chronic pain patients. *Behaviour Research and Therapy, 25*, 237–249.

U.S. Department of Health and Human Services. (1991). *Healthy People 2000: National health promotion and disease prevention objectives*. Washington, DC: U.S. Government Printing Office.

Vernon, D. T., & Bailey, W. C. (1974). The use of motion pictures in the psychological preparation of children for induction of anesthesia. *Anthesthesiology, 40*, 68–74.

Vernon, D. T., Schulman, J. L., & Foley, J. M. (1966). Changes in children's behavior after hospitalization. *American Journal of Diseases of Children, 111*, 581–593.

Viken, R. J., and McFall, R. M. (1994) Paradox lost: Implications of contemporary reinforcement theory for behavior therapy. *Current Directions in Psychological Science, 5*, 121–125.

Wright, L. (1967). The pediatric psychologist: A role model. *American Psychologist, 22*, 323-325.

Wright, L., & Friedman, A. G. (1992). Challenge of the Future: Psychologists in medical settings. In J. J.

Sweet, R. H. Rozensky & S. M. Tovian (Eds.), *Handbook of clinical psychology in medical settings* (pp. 603–614). New York: Plenum Press.

Wright, L., Nunnery, A., Eichel, B., & Scott, R. (1969). Application of conditioning principles to prob-lems of tracheostomy addiction in children. *Journal of Consulting and Clinical Psychology, 32,* 603–606.

Yates, A. J. (1958). The application of learning theory to the treatment of tics. *Journal of Abnormal Psychology and Social Psychology, 56,* 175–182.

13

FEMINISM AND BEHAVIOR ANALYSIS: A FRAMEWORK FOR WOMEN'S HEALTH RESEARCH AND PRACTICE

NANCY D. VOGELTANZ
Department of Psychology
University of North Dakota

SANDRA T. SIGMON
Department of Psychology
University of Maine

KRISTIN S. VICKERS
Department of Psychology
University of North Dakota

The Study of Women's Health: Development of a New Subdiscipline

In the past decade, the study of women's health has emerged as an integrative, multi-disciplinary field, blending biological, behavioral, and social-cultural perspectives on health issues and problems of women (Rodin & Salovey, 1989). The psychological study of women's health derives principles from health psychology and behavioral medicine, but also distinctly from feminist theory. Several factors necessitate the study of women's health as a separate subdiscipline. Most noticeably is that much of our knowledge about women's health has been generalized from studies of men's health. The male-dominated medical profession has long viewed women's health as differing from men's only with respect to their reproductive functioning (Harrison, 1992), when in fact women's health differs from men's in almost every major system of functioning, including cardiovascular, gastrointestinal, resistance to infection, musculoskeletal, urologic, and psychological (see Wallis, 1993). The failure to include females in both human and animal research studies, and the failure to study health factors that are of significant importance to women, necessitate immediate and concentrated research on women. Until recently, there was almost no understanding of heart disease and its risk factors in women because almost all major clinical trials excluded women (Gurwitz, Nananda, & Avorn, 1992), even though heart disease is a leading cause of death in women (Healy, 1991). Seventy percent of all psychoactive medications (e.g., antidepressants, antianxiety drugs) are prescribed to women, yet women have been excluded from the majority of clinical pharmacological research (Rodin & Ickovics, 1990). Nor is there adequate information about medical conditions that affect more women than men, including urinary incontinence, osteoporosis, and autoimmune diseases, such as systemic lupus erythematosus and rheumatoid arthritis (Chrisler & Parrett, 1995). Women currently comprise the group in which HIV/AIDS is most rapidly increasing, yet inadequate knowledge of HIV/AIDS progression in women causes health care workers to diagnosis AIDS in women an average of only fifteen weeks prior to death, compared to thirty months prior to death in men (Rosser, 1994). Additional barriers to understanding women's health have been the underrepresentation of women as physicians (Travis, 1988) and physicians' underdetection of problems in women that have been considered "male" problems (e.g., alcohol abuse, cardiac problems, and lung cancer; Council on Ethical and Judicial Affairs, American Medical Association, 1991; Vogeltanz & Wilsnack, 1997).

Fortunately, studies of women's health and women's health psychology are increasing, as evidenced by increasingly broad research areas and the creation of several journals and conferences dedicated to understanding gender differences in health and especially understanding women from their own perspectives (Stanton, 1995). Beginning in 1990, the National Institutes of Health (NIH) established the Office of Research on Women, and all funding through NIH now requires that women be included in clinical trials unless a compelling reason for their exclusion can be made. The largest clinical trial in U.S. history, the Women's Health Initiative, is currently investigating health processes in women, including heart disease, cancer, osteoporosis, and behavioral factors that may influence both risk factors for disease and treatment outcomes (Stanton, 1995).

Perhaps an even greater barrier to improving the health of women has been the reluctance to consider that the unique sociocultural contexts of women may dramatically affect their health and health care. In part one of this chapter, we argue that even as biomedical research of women's health problems increases, a more encompassing problem is the failure of the medical model to view health as a complex, multidimensional process that results from biology *and* the psychosocial environment. In presenting this argument, we will review current theoretical frameworks used in the study of women's health, including the importance of feminist theory, and propose a behavioral, contextual framework that should maximize accurate individual-level assessment and treatment approaches. At the group level of analysis, we will present a behavior-analytic strategy for understanding potential risk factors (as well as protective factors) that can inform prevention programs. In part two of the chapter, we will review the behavior therapy literature to provide information about effective treatments for three different problems experienced by women: dysmenorrhea (painful menstruation), eating disorders, and alcohol abuse. In keeping with the theme of this book, we will also provide a detailed example of how behavioral theory can be used to explain the etiology and inform treatment of hyperemesis gravidarum, a severe complication of pregnancy that involves severe nausea and vomiting.

Theoretical Considerations in Women's Health Research and Practice

Women's Health and the Biomedical Model

Although physicians may claim that medicine is scientific, practical, and eclectic, but not theoretical, it is almost totally based on a theory of biological primacy, that is, an individual's health status is the result of various genetic, biochemical, and physiological processes (Hamilton, 1993). The biomedical model emphasizes bottom-up research—inferring function from structure—which is not necessarily a good model for understanding the complexities of human molar behavior. In this view, behavioral processes are seen as mediators of biological processes and are of interest only for understanding the disease and/or improving the disease state. Behavioral processes, not just the endpoint of health problems, (i.e., disease), may be a more important area for health psychologists to study (Kaplan, 1990). Kaplan has argued that patients do not care about disease per se, but instead care about how disease will affect the quality and length of life. Although the fields of behavioral medicine and health psychology have made progress in moving health professionals' perspectives to a more behaviorally informed model, many behavioral intervention strategies are delivered without regard for the complex contextual structure in which the behavior was acquired and is being maintained (Epstein, 1992). The often atheoretical nature of behavioral medicine is discussed thoroughly in the behavioral medicine chapter (Friedman, Goldberg, & Okifuji) in this volume. Rather than repeat Friedman et al.'s concerns about the lack of behavioral theory in behavioral medicine, we will discuss how the field of women's health, in its quest for a new theoretical framework, provides a reinforcing environment for the inclusion of behavior theory in a women's health perspective.

Blending Feminist and Behavioral Perspectives in Women's Health

An important theoretical perspective in women's health is feminism. Feminist theory is dedicated to understanding the role of gender in our society, especially how gender is constructed and perpetuated by our society (Lott, 1990). As discussed above, feminists have shown that women's health and health care have been strongly influenced by socially constructed factors. More specific criticisms aimed at the medical community have been outlined by Travis (1988) as follows: (a) physician–patient relationships are basically sexist, resembling the subordinate status of women in the larger society; (b) the medical profession has contributed to the stereotyped, biased view of women's biology, thus contributing to the oppression of women; (c) the medical profession has discriminated against women physicians; and (d) the often inadequate health care of women and the failure to consider women's health as being influenced by the context of their lives has and may lead to disastrous consequences.

Analyzing the function of behavior, as it occurs in particular contexts, is the hallmark of radical behaviorism (Morris, 1988) and is consistent with the goals of feminist women's health approaches. Ruiz (1995) has discussed how radical behaviorism offers feminist scholarship an available theoretical view that will advance feminist epistemology, as well as other marginalized groups. Ruiz is correct when she asserts that radical behaviorism is often misunderstood by feminist scholars (indeed by many scholars), even though Skinner's world view is contextualistic—a world view that is consistent with feminist goals. Both radical behaviorists and feminists would agree that taking any behavior out of context (e.g., depression) and focusing solely on biological factors or thinking patterns is a disservice to women who experience depression in particular situations. Skinner's view also provides a theoretical rationale for how women and other groups may resist discriminatory practices and empower themselves. The radical behaviorist discusses how each person's acts operate on her environment and how then both the consequences of the act and the setting it occurs in strengthen or weaken the momentum of the acts. As Ruiz points out, our community often asks "How do you feel?" rather than "Why do you feel that way?" (p. 173).

Consistent with a feminist behavioral theory, research has shown that many differences between girls and boys (or women and men) are not due to biological sex, but rather to the antecedent and contextual factors that differentially promote sex-typed behaviors. The greater prevalence of certain disorders in women (e.g., depression, somatization disorders, eating disorders) are not solely the result of differences in biology or biologically predisposed tendencies, but are the result of psychosocial factors such as poverty, victimization, marital dissatisfaction, and biased interpretations by both women patients and their physicians (Hamilton, 1993). Researchers have suggested that the higher rate of childhood sexual abuse among girls may account for as much as one-third of the gender differences in rates of depression (Cutler & Nolen-Hoeksema, 1991). Other important aspects of women's lives such as ethnicity, economic status, and sexual orientation are equally important variables that must be considered before physical and psychological functioning can be understood. A feminist behavior-analytic approach is especially important in understanding the historical and current determinants of women's health problems when there is past or ongoing trauma or stigmatization, as found in women who have been sexually victimized. Follette (1994) has suggested that "a behavior analysis of the long-term correlates of sexual abuse is particularly appealing because it is inherently respectful of the client" (p. 256). In other words, the current problems that a woman may be experiencing are easily understood and predicted, given a particular behavioral repertoire in her history.

Not only does radical behaviorism assert that behavior be viewed in context, it also offers a technology for analyzing the function and value—the "good"—of socially constructed categories such as gender, class, age, and ethnicity. Although some scientists will argue that psychologists cannot determine what is "right" or "good" with respect to any set of behaviors, we argue that both feminist and Skinnerian goals insist the good of any practice can, and should be, analyzed to determine if the practice ultimately contributes to the maximal well-being of all individuals (Plaud & Vogeltanz, 1994; Vogeltanz & Plaud, 1992).

Behavior Analysis and Prevention Strategies in Women's Health

As discussed above, current biomedical theory and practice usually emphasizes understanding, assessing, and treating disease. Unfortunately, this approach tends to deemphasize the overarching importance of prevention and maintenance of health. For example, almost 80 percent of children in Third World countries receive immunizations compared to an immunization rate of only 57 percent in the United States (Morgan & Mutalik, 1992, as cited in Barroso, 1994). Access and affordability of quality health care is also quite limited for many persons in the United States. Almost thirty-eight million people in the United States have no type of health insurance; approximately 75 percent of the uninsured are under age thirty-five and are female (Short, 1990, as cited in Travis, Gressley, & Adams, 1995). Moreover, the costs of health care continue to grow, with current annual costs of around 800 billion dollars expected to rise to trillions of dollars by the turn of the century (Eastaugh, 1992). Prevention strategies are needed now, more than ever, and can be effective in increasing the health and well-being of all people, as well as curbing the seemingly insurmountable costs of health care. What behavior analysts have to offer from a prevention perspective is unique and soundly based on empirical findings with a guiding theoretical directive when difficulties are confronted. Behavioral analysis is a process, not just a collection of techniques, and represents more potential for advancement in the field as compared to a documented fait accompli. Despite the difficulties of imparting the "how to" of such a process, a few reminders of what constitutes a behavioral analysis may be in order before we discuss how taking a behavior-analytic approach would be helpful in the women's health field.

A behavioral analysis consists of identifying problem behaviors with their controlling variables, manipulating the environment in order to affect the target behaviors, and then to observe the outcome. In a true functional analysis, manipulation of environmental variables can be shown to directly affect the problem behaviors. More often than not, clinicians engage in a hypothetical behavioral analysis because of the difficulties in directly observing causal relations. Another important feature of behavioral analysis is that the process is ongoing, occurring throughout and linking together assessment, treatment, and outcome evaluation phases.

Several authors have addressed how the promise of behavior therapy has not been realized in the health prevention field (Samson-Fisher, Schofield, & Perkins, 1993; Wilson & Agras, 1992). As Samson-Fisher et al. have noted, an idiographic approach represents the hallmark of a behavior-analytic approach, but it is difficult to make rapid progress one client at a time. Yet there are ways that behavior analysts can shift focus from the individual to the larger population in order to address primary prevention issues. The first task would be to examine populations that are at risk for common antecedents and contingencies for engaging in less healthy behaviors or, similarly, to examine healthy populations to identify what are the controlling variables and immediate consequences that maintain more healthy behaviors. Too often researchers focus on psychopathological or disease risk factors at the expense of being able to learn more about adaptive behaviors (e.g., Follette, Bach, & Follette, 1993). Samson-Fisher et al. have suggested three areas that should enhance our understanding of risk and protective factors in health behavior. First is the development of more accurate measures of health behavior. The accuracy of self-report measures compared to direct observation continues to be an underinvestigated area. For example, asking women about the time of their last PAP smear and then corroborating the report may lead to more reliable reports (e.g., Bowman et al., 1991). Researchers can also investigate the variables that influence the accuracy of self-reports of health behaviors and the environmental conditions that could be manipulated to affect this behavior. This relates to the second suggestion of increasing descriptive research from a behavioral perspective (Samson-Fisher et al., 1993). Research should not only focus on identifying risk factors, but should also focus on the behavioral contingencies that influence the development of these risk factors. For example, if poor women are less likely to obtain regular PAP smears, it will be important to determine what types of controlling variables influence and maintain this behavior.

Third, Samson-Fisher et al. (1993) recommend the development and evaluation of intervention strategies aimed at changing contextual and behavioral factors that put individuals at risk for certain health problems. One important way of doing this is providing training for physicians, nurses, and other health-care providers. For example, physicians and nurses could ask women when their last PAP smear occurred, even when women present for unrelated health problems. Indeed, the fragmentation of women's medical care has been considered a significant problem for improving health and preventing health problems (Wallis, 1993). In addition, studies examining the effectiveness of primary prevention programs using modeling of positive health behaviors and providing positive reinforcement for engaging in more healthy behaviors should be undertaken at more global levels in the social community. At the level of secondary prevention, behavior analysts can also aid in the screening and detection of health problems. Identifying what variables contribute to better direct observation and what variables influence the utilization of initial and follow-up health-care services are poorly understand and are important areas for future research in women's health. At the level of tertiary prevention, women's health researchers can assess the controlling variables for treatment compliance and more effective treatment outcomes. Thus, behavior-analytic strategies could contribute greatly to a better understanding of why and how women engage in certain health-related behaviors.

Effective Behavioral Interventions for Women's Health Problems

Below we will review how behavior therapy has been successfully used in treating three very different women's health problems. First we will review the behavior therapy literature on treating dysmenorrhea, a condition involving painful menstruation that affects large numbers of women (National Institutes of Health, 1988). In further exploring reproductive health issues of women, we will present a literature-based analysis of hyperemesis gravidarum (severe nausea and vomiting in pregnancy) in which we propose that classical conditioning factors may explain the development and inform treatment of this condition. Next, we will present current treatment studies using behavioral (and cognitive-behavioral) interventions for the treatment of anorexia nervosa, bulimia nervosa, and obesity, all of which have wide-ranging and serious health consequences for women who develop these problems. Finally, we will review literature that suggests that behaviorally oriented interventions may be the treatment of choice for women's alcohol abuse and problem drinking.

Dysmenorrhea

Although there is great variability in the type and severity of menstrual symptoms reported, researchers have estimated that more than half of the female population report menstrual pain (NIH, 1988). Primary dysmenorrhea refers to symptoms associated with the menstrual cycle that are not attributable to organic pathology. Dysmenorrhea can be further divided into spasmodic (i.e., mainly physical symptoms associated with the onset of bleeding) and congestive (i.e., physical and mental symptoms associated with the premenstrual phase) types. In the following review of the behavior therapy literature on dysmenorrhea, the majority of treatment studies employing behavioral techniques have focused on pain and pain-related behaviors associated with spasmodic dysmenorrhea.

In 1968, Frank Mullen published a case study detailing the successful treatment of a woman with severe dysmenorrhea. Although the primary goal of this report was to document the effectiveness of behavior therapy techniques for "female troubles," it also provided the impetus for future research that would help minimize dynamic explanatory concepts in dysmenorrhea (e.g., the role of unconscious conflicts and the rejection of femininity). In this case, a woman reported severe disability from menstrual cramps, often remaining in bed when the cramps became severe and avoiding household tasks. In addition to the functional impact of dysmenorrhea upon her activity level, the client related anticipatory anxiety regarding her coming menses, as early as fourteen days before her cycle began. She also reported attacks of anxiety when she observed women in the final stages of pregnancy.

Mullen saw the client for sixteen sessions over a period of six months. First, the client was trained in the Jacobsonian progressive muscle-relaxation procedure. Second, two anxiety hierarchies were constructed. The first consisted of behavioral scenes that occurred prior to and during menses (e.g., "It is the morning of the day your period is to start. You observe blood on the sanitary napkin as you wear it"; Mullen, 1968, p. 373). In the second hierarchy, scenes relating to observing pregnant women were presented (e.g., "You see a large woman dressed in maternity clothes. The physician tells you that you are pregnant"; Mullen, 1968, p. 373). An additional component of treatment involved having the husband ignore any menstrual complaints and withhold any comments regarding menstrual behavior.

During the remaining sessions, the client relaxed and then was asked to imagine the dysmenorrhea and pregnancy scenes until she was able to imagine each scene without anxiety. As treatment progressed, she reported less and less menstrual pain. At the final session, the client reported that she had had two pain-free cycles and she was able to observe pregnant women without any anxiety attacks. At a six-month follow-up, treatment gains were maintained with the client reporting only one menstrual cycle with severe cramps.

Following the case study, Mullen (1971) conducted a group treatment study utilizing a desensitization procedure similar to his first and a nontreatment control condition. Subjects received individual treatment sessions consisting of a progressive muscle-relaxation procedure followed by individually constructed menstrual anxiety hierarchies. After six weekly sessions, subjects in the desensitization condition reported a significant decrease in dysmenorrhea symptoms compared to subjects in the control group.

Following Mullen's initial success in reducing menstrual pain with behavioral techniques, other researchers improved upon methodological and design issues to further explore the effectiveness of behavioral techniques in the treatment of dysmenorrhea symptoms. In treating seven female college students with dysmenorrhea, Tasto and Chesney (1974) obtained objective pre- and post- measures of menstrual symptoms. Instead of seeing each woman individually as in the Mullen studies, the students were seen in a group. Similarly, the students were trained in progressive muscle-relaxation procedures during the first two sessions with instructions to practice these procedures daily and monitor effectiveness. For the third session, students relaxed to a series of neutral scenes. In contrast to Mullen's hierarchy of scenes, Tasto and Chesney presented the women with common menstrual scenes that focused on pain reduction during the fourth and fifth sessions. The women were instructed to practice the relaxation procedures until the follow-up, two cycles later. The results indicated that the desensitization procedure produced significant reductions in dysmenorrhea symptoms from pretreatment to post-treatment and after follow-up. According to the authors, the content of the scenes was more important than the hierarchical presentation and that women with dysmenorrhea could be treated just as quickly and effectively in groups.

Because Tasto and Chesney (1974) found that some of the women suffered more from premenstrual symptoms, they conducted a subsequent study to investigate the effects of a desensitization procedure dividing subjects into spasmodic and congestive sufferers. In this study, Chesney and Tasto (1975) included a pseudotreatment and waiting-list control group to rule out the effects of therapist contact and the passage of time. Subjects (N = 69) received one of the three treatments over a five-week period. The desensitization group received progressive muscle-relaxation training and were presented with scenes in which women who had begun menstruating focused on reducing their pain. The results indicated that only the spasmodic sufferers receiving the desensitization procedure reported significant reductions in dysmenorrhea symptoms.

Improving on previous assessment methods, Cox and Meyer (1978) used multiple self-report and psychophysiological measures in a desensitization-based treatment for fourteen women with primary dysmenorrhea. Individual treatment sessions consisted of muscle relaxation, cued breathing, and exposure to hierarchical menstrual scenes over four sessions. Multimodal assessments continued throughout treatment until a six-month follow-up. At post-treatment and follow-up, subjects reported reduced use of medications, less resting time, fewer negative menstrual attitudes, and less dysmenorrhea symptoms.

Because desensitization-based procedures combined muscle-relaxation training with anxiety hierarchies, it was difficult to ascertain what were the effective components responsible for the reduction in reported dysmenorrhea symptoms. In an initial effort to address this issue, Amodei, Nelson, Jarrett, and Sigmon (1987) compared muscle-relaxation training, desensitization, and waiting-list control groups in women with dysmenorrhea. For women with spasmodic symptoms, both relaxation training and desensitization treatments effectively reduced resting time compared to the control condition. Similar to previous findings, no significant improvements were reported by women with congestive dysmenorrhea in any of the treatment groups. These results suggested that relaxation alone could be an effective treatment for spasmodic symptoms but still did not address how this procedure impacts reports of menstrual symptoms.

In an effort to address the functional impact of menstrual-related symptoms (e.g., reduced activity level, increased resting time, avoidance of tasks) in women with dysmenorrhea, Sigmon and Nelson (1988) investigated the effectiveness of an operant approach to pain management for dysmenorrhea. Borrowing heavily from Fordyce's operant approach to pain, the researchers developed an activity scheduling treatment that focused on teaching reinforcement principles, including teaching clients how to use rest and interactions with others as reinforcers following activity completion. A group receiving progressive muscle-relaxation treatment and a wait-list control group were used for comparison groups, and target-specific (e.g., levels of daily activity and pain reports) dependent measures were included. College women received six individual treatment sessions and were followed for two consecutive cycles. Results indicated that both active treatments resulted in significant increases in activity level and reductions in pain reports compared to the control condition.

Based on the treatment literature for dysmenorrhea, several general conclusions can be reached. Behavior therapy techniques have demonstrated effectiveness in reducing reports of menstrual distress and functional impairment in women suffering from spasmodic dysmenorrhea. In particular, desensitization-based procedures, relaxation procedures, and operant approaches to pain have been shown to be effective with community and college populations. We believe that future research should concentrate on further understanding the specific learning factors that underlie successful behavioral treatments.

Hyperemesis Gravidarum: The Role of Interoceptive Conditioning

Hyperemesis gravidarum (HG) is a condition in which severe nausea and intractable vomiting during pregnancy may result in dehydration, electrolyte imbalance, ketonuria, weight loss, and possibly more severe problems such as renal abnormality (Levine & Esser, 1988). Once organic causes have been ruled out (e.g., urinary tract infections, gastroenteritis, peptic ulcer, pancreatitis, early hepatitis), medical treatment may include intravenous hydration, antiemetic medication, and dietary management (Kucharczyk, 1991). Medical personnel have enlisted the help of mental health professionals in patient management. Important tasks for health psychologists are to assist physicians in treating HG and to explore and define psychological factors contributing to the maintenance of the disorder. For decades, psychodynamically trained professionals argued that nausea in pregnancy was symbolic of disgust, and vomiting was an attempt at symbolic abortion (Deutsch, 1945; Kestenberg, 1977; Menninger, 1943). Many current reports still postulate the role of unconscious desires and conflicts in the development of HG (e.g., Caruso, El-Mallakh, & Hale, 1990; El-Mallakh, Liebowitz, & Hale, 1990; Fitzgerald, 1984).

These theories have not been empirically supported, and although the causes of HG are not known, there is evidence to suggest that certain biochemical or hormonal influences of pregnancy may cause nausea and vomiting. Specifically, HG has been associated with increased concentrations of human chorionic gonadotropin (hCG) in urine and blood (Kauppila, Huhtaniemi, & Ylikorkala, 1979; Callahan, Desiderato, Heiden, & Pecsok, 1984), and increased hCG may lead to increased vomiting by stimulating the release of vasopressin (Robertson, 1987), which is known to be emetic at high doses (Kucharczyk, 1991). Increased levels of estradiol and sex hormone binding-globulin binding capacity (SHBG-BC) were also found in HG patients when compared to pregnant controls.

The successful treatment of HG using behavioral interventions, including stimulus control and relaxation (Callahan, Desiderato, Heiden, & Pecsok, 1984; Kanfer, 1975; Simone & Long, 1985), have alerted researchers to the possible role of learning factors in HG. After reviewing the behavioral treatment literature on HG, Callahan and Desiderato (1988) concluded that women experiencing "stressors" during pregnancy were more vulnerable to HG, speculating that vomiting may lead to escape of or avoidance from difficult situations. Although one study noted that biological responses are capable of being conditioned to environmental stimuli (Long, Simone, & Tucher, 1986) there have been no theoretical models presented that describe how HG may develop and maintain through the process of classical conditioning. Although operant factors may be an important etiological factor in HG, we believe that knowledge about the role of conditioning factors in the nausea and vomiting resulting from chemotherapy serves as a more informed theoretical model for the development of HG (see Friedman et al., this volume, for a review of anticipatory nausea and vomiting in chemotherapy). Below we present a model of HG based on biological and interoceptive conditioning factors.

HG can be considered functionally similar to "normal" morning sickness, but is quantitatively different from less severe nausea and vomiting. Nausea and vomiting during early pregnancy is common—50 to 90 percent of women experience nausea and 25 to 55 percent experience vomiting (Feldman, 1987). Diagnosis of HG is not based on a clearly defined set of criteria. Generally, the defining features are that severe nausea and vomiting occur in the absence of known organic causes and that the condition requires either outpatient or inpatient intervention. It is proposed that HG results from naturally occurring hormonal influences that cause nausea and vomiting and from interoceptive conditioning that occurs to certain tastes and smells. Furthermore, the amount of conditioning that occurs will be a function of the intensity/potency of the UCS (Domjan & Burkhard, 1986). In other words, as naturally occurring UCSs (hormonal levels) increase, interoceptive conditioning of certain tastes and smells will also increase. The following set of parameters are to be identified in the model:

1. The UCS is operationally defined as the internal set of biochemical/hormonal influences normally evident during pregnancy.
2. The UCR is operationally defined as the naturally occurring nausea/vomiting response that is elicited by the UCS (biochemical/hormonal influences).
3. The conditioned stimuli (CS complex) is operationally defined as a set of neutral, internal stimuli such as the taste and smell of distinctive or novel foods.

These tastes and smells paired with the UCS (biochemical/hormonal influences) will elicit nausea/vomiting, even when the hormonal influences are not active, for example, postmorning and after the first trimester of pregnancy, when hormonal levels decrease and cease to exert their emetic influence. Additionally, other neutral internal stimuli (e.g., sensation of a full stomach) may become conditioned to the first set of conditioned stimuli (taste of food), resulting in the elicitation of the CR (nausea/vomiting). This higher-order conditioning may account for a wide range of conditioned stimuli that cause nausea/vomiting in HG.

Taste and smell aversions during pregnancy.   Fairburn, Stein, and Jones (1992) found in a sample of primigravid women that 91 percent reported nausea and 52 percent reported vomiting during the first trimester of pregnancy. Strong aversions to specific foods were reported by 80 percent of the women. The most commonly reported aversions were to coffee and tea, followed by smell aversions to fried or fatty foods. The taste of highly spiced foods and the smell of cigarette smoke were also commonly reported as aversive. These authors stated that "an altered sense of smell appeared to underlie the majority of the aversions including the more unusual ones such as aversion to the smell of previously liked perfume or to household detergent" (p. 667). This study suggests that learned taste and smell aversions (i.e., interoceptive conditioning) may occur during pregnancy. The foods and smells that were considered aversive were distinctive in the following ways: (a) the taste aversions were more commonly to substances that contained either *potential toxins* (i.e., caffeine) or were highly spiced (i.e, distinctive), and (b) the most common smell aversions were to fried or fatty foods.

It can be speculated, following from the work of Seligman and Hager (1972), that through the process of evolution, certain hormones in pregnancy may serve to alter taste and smell so as to heighten the ability of the organism to avoid suspicious foods. Interoceptive conditioning will then occur to these distinctive or novel tastes and smells. Regarding food preferences, it can be speculated that previously liked foods that did not have highly distinctive smells or potential toxins were interoceptively conditioned due to some biologically prepared need (e.g, citrus fruits) and/or their familiar, that is, safe status. Although the primary conditioning process implicated in this model is interoceptive conditioning of certain foods and smells, other internal stimuli may become conditioned. For example, the sensation of a full stomach, queasiness, and a dry mouth may also become paired with the first CS (tastes and smells) or become directly paired with the UCS. Even exteroceptive stimuli, such as the sight of a frequently used vomit basin, may become a conditioned stimulus. Interestingly, Callahan and Desiderato (1988) reported on a case in which a women would orient her head over an emesis basin every time she felt nauseous, reliably resulting in a vomiting episode each time she did this. The authors did not, however, implicate the role of conditioning in the behavior.

Although the foregoing discussion proposes the mechanisms through which certain neutral foods and smells can lead to nausea and vomiting during pregnancy, it does not account for why only a small percentage of women develop HG. One possible contributing factor may be the potency of the UCS (hormonal influences). As the intensity, duration, and frequency of the UCS increases, the likelihood of conditioning increases, as well as the occurrence of higher order conditioning. A potent UCS (i.e., high hormonal levels) must be identified in HG patients if a biological/conditioning model is to be supported.

Hormonal and other risk factors in HG.   As part of the Collaborative Perinatal Project (Klebanoff, Koslowe, Kaslow, & Rhoads, 1985), factors associated with early pregnancy vomiting were studied in 9,098 first-trimester women. A subset of these women diagnosed with HG were compared with controls on levels of estrogen, hCG, and sex hormone binding-globulin binding capacity (SHBG-BC). It was found that all hormones were greater in the HG patients, but differences in hCG did not reach significance. In a Swedish study, nulliparity (first pregnancy), twinning, and younger maternal age were associated with HG in a sample of 3,038 women diagnosed with the condition (Kallen, 1987). Findings from both these studies indicated that HG patients are more likely to be primigravids, younger, heavier, nonsmokers, or experiencing a twin pregnancy. All of these factors have been associated with increased hormonal levels. In the case of nonsmokers, it has been proposed that smoking serves to decrease certain hormones (Depue, Bernstein, Ross, Judd, & Henderson, 1987), but we would suggest in the absence of confirmed biological data that is equally as likely that smokers may be less sensitive to smells and tastes, thus lowering their risks for developing learned aversions. Nonetheless, these findings support the idea that women diagnosed with HG have higher levels of specific pregnancy hormones, which suggests that the potential for conditioning may be increased. Not only should HG patients experience more naturally occurring nausea and vomiting, but they should also experience more conditioned nausea. Furthermore, as hormonal levels decrease after the first trimester, HG patients may continue to experience conditioned nausea. There was also evidence for increased vomiting in African-American women compared to white women, but the difference disappeared when geographical region was controlled for. The majority of African-American women in the study were from southern regions in U.S., and it could be speculated that these women came into contact with more fried and fatty foods than their northern counterparts. If regional diet was the predictive factor, this would lend support to the idea that learned aversions (i.e, conditioning processes) could be responsible for nausea and vomiting in these women.

As the foregoing discussion has suggested, the nausea and vomiting that occurs in HG is initiated by hormonal increases and is exacerbated and maintained by conditioned taste and smell aversions. Two further areas of psychological investigation provide support for this model. First, there is an absence of data to suggest that HG results from psychological conflict arising from an unplanned or undesired pregnancy, or the lack of a cohabitating partner (Klebanoff et al., 1985). There have been no studies to date that have attempted to reliably and validly measure levels of anxiety, depression, and/or somatic complaints in HG patients in comparison to control groups. This research will need to be conducted before any predictions can be made regarding the influence of these variables. Secondly, if HG is developed through the mechanisms outlined above, then behavioral interventions such as stimulus control, relaxation and dietary education should reduce or eliminate a significant portion of nausea and vomiting. As discussed, there have been published reports of the successful treatment of HG using these approaches. In the case of less-severe nausea and vomiting, it is assumed that extinction of the learned aversions, conditioned bodily sensations, and any extero-ceptively conditioned stimuli should occur after several presentations of conditioned stimuli in the absence of the UCS (hormonal influences). In more severe reactions, how-ever, direct behavioral intervention may be needed. The use of antiemetics is often help-ful for HG since these drugs alter the emetic influence of pregnancy hormones. However, this type of treatment may complicate fetal development if used extensively (Kallen, 1987), and should provide only short-term relief as the learned aversions and any conditioned body sensations persist. This may account for the commonly asserted claim by medical personnel that recurrent HG remains "a uniquely frustrating and poorly understood complication of early pregnancy" (p. 287; Godsey & Newman, 1991).

Behavioral Treatment of Eating Disorders and Obesity in Women

Eating disorders and disordered eating affects a large segment of the female population, and therefore constitute a major area of focus in the women's health field. Major health consequences may occur with disordered eating, including menstrual/reproductive, bone, gastrointestinal, cardiovascular, dental, and electrolyte/fluid imbalance problems (for review, see Mitchell, 1995). The complications of obesity are an increased risk for di-abetes, hypertension, cardiovascular disease, stroke, gallbladder disease, and some types of cancer (Pi-Sunyer, 1995, as cited in Pike & Striegel-Moore, 1997). Eating dis-orders are also commonly associated with depression, anxiety, obsessive-compulsive disorder, and substance abuse (Pike & Striegel-Moore). Additionally, women with eat-ing disorders appear to have significantly more relationship problems (Striegel-Moore, Silberstein, & Rodin, 1993). Behavioral methods used in treatment of anorexia nervosa, bulimia nervosa, and obesity have been the subject of considerable study over the past two decades. In the following section, we present an overview of behavioral theories and treatments for anorexia, bulimia, and obesity.

Bulimia nervosa.
Sociocultural emphasis on thinness is considered a primary factor in the development of eating disorders in women (Williamson, Barker, & Norris, 1993). By depicting women with thinner, more angular body shapes as the cultural ideal, the mass media are thought to have contributed to current contingencies that provide rein-forcement (beauty and success) for women's thinness. Women with eating disorders commonly report experiencing anxiety about weight gain, body image disturbances, and overconcern with body size (Williamson et al., 1993). In order to avoid weight gain, bulimic women and men impose high levels of dietary restraint that often result in binge eating or eating forbidden foods with concomitant anxiety. Purging then often fol-lows in an effort to reduce the anxiety associated with the binging and possible weight gain. Purging behavior is likely maintained through the negatively reinforcing conse-quences of reduction in anxiety. Because purging eliminates nutrients from the body and lowers metabolic rate, the probability of weight gain and the continuation of the binge-purge cycle is further strengthened (Williamson, Davis, Duchmann, McKenzie, & Watkins, 1990).

Several behavioral intervention strategies have been developed to treat bulimia nervosa (Smith, Marcus, & Eldredge, 1994; Williamson, Cubic, & Fuller, 1992). Currently, most treatment involves using a combination of various behavioral and cognitive-behavioral interventions. As reviewed below, these treatment packages have proven efficacy, and published manuals outlining cognitive-behavioral treatment protocols are available (Smith et al., 1994). Self-monitoring of binge eating and compensatory behaviors is often used throughout treatment, and antecedents to binge and purge behaviors are identified primarily through the patient's self-monitored records. Regular eating and exercise habits are developed. Behavioral contracts may also be used to elicit specific behaviors. Exposure and response prevention may be employed to prevent vomiting following binge-eating, and a systematic desensitization technique may be used to introduce foods that cause increasing levels of anxiety. Similarly, temptation exposure with response prevention involves exposure to the environmental stimuli that under most circumstances would cause an individual to binge, followed by the prevention of the opportunity to binge. Body-image therapy is frequently utilized to address and correct perceptual and attitudinal distortions related to body size. Interventions to reduce body-image concerns include relaxation training, systematic desensitization, and cognitive therapy. Cognitive restructuring involves training the patient to dispute faulty attitudes and beliefs about food, eating, dieting, and her body size with alternative, rational thoughts. Relapse prevention techniques may be taught, in which high-risk situations are identified by the bulimic individual and strategies to cope with these situations are generated.

Substantial research exists supporting the efficacy of behavioral treatment methods in reducing the binging and compensatory behaviors associated with bulimia nervosa (e.g., Kennedy, Katz, Neitzert, Ralevski, & Mendlowitz, 1995); however, current research suggests that cognitive-behavioral treatment of bulimia is superior to either cognitive or behavioral strategies used alone and should be used as the treatment of choice for bulimia (Smith et al., 1994; Williamson et al., 1992). For example, Fairburn (1994) found a simplified behavioral version of cognitive behavior therapy to be markedly less effective than a complete cognitive-behavior therapy in treating bulimia nervosa. In another study of bulimia, behavioral and cognitive-behavioral intervention groups reported less binging and purging than did the control group, but women in the cognitive-behavioral group showed the greatest improvement at follow-up (Thackwray, Smith, Bodfish, & Meyers, 1993).

Anorexia nervosa.   Increasing social pressure to be thin is again associated with the development of anorexia nervosa in women. Fear of weight gain has been suggested as the primary factor motivating anorexic individuals to employ starvation, excessive exercise, and purgative behaviors (Williamson et al., 1993). According to the Williamson et al. (1990) model of eating disorders, anorexia may be conceptualized as a weight phobia. As with bulimia nervosa, fear of weight gain, preoccupation with body size, and body-image disturbances are considered the underlying problems associated with this disorder. Anorexics severely restrict their diet. Starvation eventually suppresses the appetite, allowing greater control over food and avoidance of anxiety. Efficiently, the metabolic rate lowers with starvation, causing the anorexic individual to gain weight with fewer calories, subsequently reinforcing the fear of weight gain.

Several behavioral methods are commonly implemented in treatment of anorexia nervosa (Andersen, 1986; Williamson et al., 1992). Operant conditioning techniques such as positive reinforcement are used in the first stage of treatment for weight restoration. To correct women's unhealthy attitudes and misconceptions about their body's nutritional requirements, behavioral treatments often include meal planning. Cognitive restructuring is often used to dispute and correct the distorted beliefs about eating, weight, and body size that the patient holds by providing alternative and contradictory evidence for each such distortion. As women treated for anorexia nervosa increase their weight, body-image therapy is used to address body size concerns. Behavior-modification techniques are considered the core of nearly all programs of nutritional rehabilitation for women with anorexia nervosa (Andersen, 1986).

There are very few controlled treatment studies of anorexia nervosa because malnutrition and other medical concerns require immediate and effective interventions, eliminating wait-list or less effective control group strategies. Thus, despite the similarities of behavioral treatment methods used, anorexia nervosa has received less empirical attention in this area than bulimia nervosa. Operant conditioning methods have, however, been found to be very effective for nutritional rehabilitation (Andersen, 1986; Bemis, 1987). Using a brief form of outpatient psychotherapy compared to educational-behavior therapy in which subjects were taught methods such as self-monitoring, Treasure et al. (1995) found that both groups had a good or intermediate recovery in terms of nutritional outcome. Studies that have reported the efficacy of cognitive-behavioral treatment methods for anorexia nervosa often include other treatment methods such as family therapy, insight-oriented therapy, group therapy, and pharmacotherapy (Williamson et al., 1992). Consequentially, additional research is needed to control for the effects of any other methods accompanying behavioral techniques in package approaches for treating women with anorexia nervosa.

Obesity.   Obesity is commonly conceptualized as the result of consuming more energy than is expended (Williamson et al., 1992). Elaborating upon this energy balance model, Williamson et al. (1990) propose that excessive eating is maintained by short-term positive reinforcement, while avoidance of an active lifestyle is maintained by short-term negative consequences such as fatigue. This energy imbalance results in weight gain, which often leads to attempts at dieting. Immediate weight loss may be reinforcing, but over time dieting lowers the metabolic rate, which in turn increases the probability of further weight gain.

Basic behavioral methods designed to modify excessive eating and increase activity are frequently used in treatment of obesity (Agras, 1987; Martin & Pear, 1992; Williamson et al., 1992). Many behavioral techniques are used together in comprehensive behavioral treatment programs. Self-monitoring of eating, exercise, and behavioral changes are all used to aid the individual in acknowledging constructive and detrimental behaviors and in assessing behavioral repertoires. Stimulus control techniques regulate the antecedents of eating, and individuals are often instructed to eat each of their meals at a specific time and location. Direct modification of eating behavior is used to aid individuals in changing specific eating behaviors. Exercise programs are often employed to increase calories expended and improve metabolism, aiding individuals in achieving and maintaining an optimum weight. Behavioral contracts may be made with the client. Very low-calorie diets used in combination with other behavioral methods have been used for weight loss. Body-image therapy is used to help the obese person challenge negative stereotypes of obesity and modify intrusive thoughts of body dissatisfaction and overvalued beliefs about physical appearance. These behavior modification methods are frequently considered an established part of obesity treatment programs, and it has been argued that behavior modification is the preferred treatment for individuals with mild to moderate obesity (Jeffery et al., 1993).

Behavioral treatment methods for obesity have been found in numerous controlled studies to be more effective for weight loss than no treatment, placebo, or traditional diets (Williamson et al., 1992). Individual treatment components have also been evaluated, and some techniques appear to be more effective than others. Exercise has had continued empirical support as a behavioral method associated with weight loss and weight maintenance, and studies suggest that exercise programs that advocate exercise as an essential lifestyle modification are the most effective (Williamson et al., 1992). In a study comparing obese women with severe caloric restriction to moderate caloric restriction, Wadden, Foster, and Letizia (1994) found that women on a very low-calorie diet lost significantly more weight initially than those on a moderate diet, but regained a substantial amount of weight at follow-up. The difference between treatment groups at follow-up was insignificant, and the authors suggest that there is little benefit to severely restricting caloric intake. Jeffery et al. (1993) investigated behavioral interventions for weight loss in obese individuals, adding either food provision, monetary incentives, or both to a standard behavioral treatment for obesity that incorporated such methods as stimulus control, problem-solving, cognitive restructuring, and relapse prevention. No significant effects for monetary incentives were found, but food provision when added to a standard behavioral treatment for obesity significantly enhanced weight loss.

Agras et al. (1994) compared a weight-loss treatment using behavioral techniques such as self-monitoring, modification of eating behavior and exercise, and relapse prevention to a cognitive-behavioral treatment that included cognitive restructuring and focused attention on binge eating problems. These treatments were compared to desipramine treatment in an additive design. No differences among the three groups appeared at the end of treatment and at follow-up. In a study that compared a standard behavioral weight-loss treatment to a binge eating weight-loss treatment, obese women with severe binge eating lost more weight with binge eating treatment, while women with moderate binge eating lost more weight in a standard behavioral treatment (Porzelius, Houston, Smith, Arfken, & Fisher, 1995). Exposure-based methods led to significant improvement in obese women's self-reported body image. Methods used included asking the women to refrain from body checking and to engage in several previously avoided, anxiety-provoking behaviors, ranging from mild (e.g., wearing more form-fitting clothing to extremely difficult, e.g., wearing a swimsuit in public; Rosen, Orosan, & Reiter, 1995).

Overall, these recent studies suggest that behavioral treatment methods are integral to the treatment of obesity in women. Moreover, as discussed above, we believe that a feminist behavioral-analysis approach for treating eating disorders is inherently more respectful for women. By acknowledging to our clients the important role that socially constructed ideas about beauty and thinness play in disordered eating, women will be in a more informed position for resisting these beauty ideals and improving their treatment outcomes.

Behavioral Interventions for Women's Problem Drinking

Until very recently, almost all research on and treatment of alcohol abuse and dependence in women was based on findings from studies of men. Despite a persistent myth that alcohol abuse is a "male" disorder, approximately 10 to 15 percent of U.S. women report some type of drinking problem and heavy drinking in women is implicated in a wide range of women's physical and psychological problems (Vogeltanz & Wilsnack, 1997). Although there is evidence for genetic transmission of alcohol-use disorders in women (Heath, Slutske, & Madden, 1997), much of the variance in women's alcohol problems appears to be related to environmental factors. Several risk factors for women's problem drinking have been identified, including a history of sexual abuse (Wilsnack, Vogeltanz, Klassen, & Harris, 1997), adult violent victimization (Martin, 1992), sexual dysfunction (Wilsnack, 1984), depression (Hartka et al., 1991), and anxiety disorders (Kushner, Sher, & Beitman, 1990). All of these findings indicate the role of learning factors, particularly negative reinforcement (i.e., tension reduction and coping) in women's alcohol abuse. Importantly, women's alcohol- and drug-abuse problems appear related to the presence of a problem drinking or drug-abusing partner or spouse (Roberts & Leonard, 1997; Feucht, Stephens, & Roman, 1990). Treating alcohol abuse and dependence in both women and men should focus on identifying life stressors and conditions that maintain the cycle of abuse; however, the causes of women's problem drinking (and drug abuse) as well as women's responses to treatment may be very different from the currently established assessment and treatment practices that were formulated almost exclusively based on men's alcohol abuse.

In the past, there have been suggestions in the alcohol-treatment literature that women may be more difficult to treat and have worse treatment outcomes than men; currently there is evidence that women may have more treatment success than men (Vannicelli & Nash, 1984). There are, however, significant barriers that may reduce the likelihood that women will enter treatment or have successful outcomes, including a lack of child care during treatment, the fear of being considered an unfit mother, and the greater lack of support, relative to men in treatment, from friends, family, and spouses (Beckman & Amaro, 1986; Thom, 1987; Blume, 1997).

Even though there is no "best" treatment for all individuals with alcohol abuse and dependence, there is evidence that certain treatment approaches may be more effective with women. Jarvis (1992) used meta-analysis to measure sex differences in twenty treatment-outcome studies conducted between 1953 and 1991. The results showed that at six-month and twelve-month follow-up periods, women had better treatment outcomes than men. In the long-term follow-up period (more than twelve months), however, men appeared to have slightly better outcomes than women. Jarvis noted that the majority of studies that reported better long-term results for men were from inpatient programs that included milieu therapy, psychotherapy, and AA, with or without drug therapy. Conversely, most of the programs that reported better results for women used behavioral therapies. Similarly, in a bibliotherapy outcome study designed to reduce heavy drinking (Sanchez-Craig, Spivak, & Davila, 1991), clients were given either three sessions of advice on how to use a step-by-step manual for achieving abstinence or moderate drinking, three sessions of more detailed instructions about how to use the manual, or an indefinite number of therapist sessions in which application of the manual was the focus. Women were much more likely than men to achieve moderate drinking in both the advice and instructions conditions. Men, however, were more likely than women to achieve moderation under the therapist condition.

In contrast, the most comprehensive alcohol treatment outcome study to date (Project MATCH Research Group, 1997) found that both women and men were significantly improved at one-year posttreatment in response to three treatment modalities: cognitive-behavioral coping skills therapy, twelve-step facilitation, and motivational enhancement therapy, although it had been predicted that cognitive-behavioral treatment would be superior for women. It should be noted, however, that all three treatment approaches used in Project MATCH were conducted at the individual level, therapists were well-trained and continually monitored for treatment quality, and extensive follow-up sessions were conducted during the posttreatment year. This type of treatment approach may differ considerably from more common alcohol treatment approaches that are delivered in group settings, often mixed-sex groups. Because women often present for treatment with life circumstances requiring more specialized services, it seems likely that alcohol treatment programs that provide specialized services for women may increase treatment efficacy. Services such as child care, assessment and treatment for mood and anxiety disorders, and skills training for increasing social, parental, and marital/relationship functioning appear important for women, as well as assistance with practical issues such as employment, housing, and health care (Finkelstein, 1993a & b). As a result of increased awareness of women's specialized treatment needs, treatment facilities have begun to include more services for women. About 53 percent of public and private treatment facilities for drug and alcohol problems currently offer some type of women's services. Although the percentage of women-only substance-abuse programs made up only 6 percent of total substance-abuse treatment options in 1992, this percentage is up from 3 percent in 1982 (Schmidt & Weisner, 1995). These women-only units have tended to de-emphasize traditional, medically oriented, inpatient alcoholism treatments while focusing on a self-help, outpatient mode of treatment. Both empirical findings and practical considerations lead us to conclude that several behaviorally oriented therapies may be efficacious treatments for women.

Brief interventions.   Following the identification of women with alcohol problems in the community (e.g., in medical settings), it may be determined that the severity of problems does not warrant a referral to a specialized alcohol treatment program. Given the stigma attached to alcohol treatment for women (e.g., physicians may be reluctant to refer and some women will be reluctant to accept treatment), a brief intervention in the health care setting may be an effective intervention strategy (Babor, 1990). Research has found that brief interventions can be highly effective and economical (Holder, Longabaugh, Miller, & Rubonis, 1991; Institute of Medicine, 1990), and may consist of a single session conducted by an experienced nurse or other health professional or several outpatient sessions conducted in a mental health facility.

The overall goal of brief intervention is to convince the woman that reduction or elimination of alcohol use is necessary in order to reduce or prevent alcohol problems. This is usually achieved through (a) feedback about the woman's individual risks from drinking, (b) emphasizing the woman's responsibility in change, giving clear advice for change and a selection of options for achieving change, and (c) providing a high level of empathy and enthusiasm in order to increase self-efficacy and motivation for change in the woman (Miller, 1989; Miller & Rollnick, 1991). Research has shown that brief interventions are more effective than no interventions, often are equally effective as longer, more intensive treatment, and can enhance the overall effectiveness of any subsequent, longer-term treatment (Bien, Miller, & Tonigan, 1993).

Behavioral Self-Control Training (BSCT) and Guided Self-Change therapy (GSC). Behavioral and cognitive-behavioral treatments for alcohol problems are based on the theory that alcohol-use disorders are learned behaviors that can be changed with behavior modification techniques, such as skills training, marital/family therapy, relapse prevention skills, and a variety of strategies aimed at increasing self-efficacy, motivation for change, and adaptive social functioning. Another important characteristic of behavioral approaches is that clients are often allowed to choose their own goals for modifying their drinking problems (i.e., moderation or abstinence). For this reason, behavioral approaches are often called "controlled drinking" approaches, although abstinence goals are easily accommodated with this approach. One example of this type of approach is Behavioral Self-Control Training (BSCT), which involves setting limits on consumption, self-monitoring of drinking behavior, learning drink-refusal skills, learning which cues in the environment reliably predict drinking or the desire to drink, learning alternative methods of coping with stress, and setting up a reward system for achievement of goals (Hester & Miller, 1989).

Because women often report drinking in response to stress or negative affective states, this type of approach may be especially helpful. BSCT has been empirically evaluated more than any other alcohol intervention in the field, and its long-term efficacy and cost-effectiveness have been demonstrated (Holder et al., 1991). Combining BSCT with other behavioral skills training (e.g., assertiveness, parenting training, and marital-communications skills training) should enhance overall treatment retention and outcome.

Another similar alcohol program based on cognitive-behavioral principles is Guided Self-Change (GSC) therapy (Sobell, Sobell, & Gavin, 1995). Treatment usually consists of a detailed assessment followed by four structured treatment sessions. Clients select their own goals regarding their alcohol use and are given several readings and homework assignments to enhance overall treatment efficacy. Following the brief treatment, two aftercare phone calls are provided by the therapist at one and three months, and either treatment is concluded or the client may determine that additional sessions are needed. Results of a treatment outcome study of GSC therapy indicated that both men and women showed significant reductions in drinking one year following treatment.

Summary and Conclusions

In this chapter, we have advocated using a behavior-analytic framework for research and practice in women's health that is infused and informed by a feminist, women-centered philosophy. We believe that current research in women's health, like research and practice in behavioral medicine, lacks theoretical focus and a methodology that is sufficiently informed by environmental information. Although behavioral medicine may appear on the surface to be based on learning principles, much of the research is based on the medical model, and often behavioral interventions are used without regard to sound hypotheses about the causes of the maladaptive behavior. As an illustration of this problem, we discussed how behavioral interventions had been used successfully in treating hyperemesis gravidarum (HG) without any clear theoretical explanation about the causes of the condition. In describing how interoceptive conditioning may account for the symptoms and treatment success found in HG, we have attempted to provide a model that other researchers in this area can test for its reliability and validity. In our sections describing behavioral interventions for eating disorders, alcohol abuse, and dysmenorrhea, we illustrated how many of the advances in treating these conditions have been based on learning principles and the application of these principles in behavior therapy.

Unlike behavioral medicine, women's health is strongly influenced by a feminist epistemology, which we have argued is functionally similar to Skinner's radical behaviorism. This feminist behavior-analytic approach asserts that any unit or units of behavior may be understood only by viewing the behavior in the context in which it occurred. Because the context of women's lives may be very different from men's, or vary greatly depending on age, ethnicity, or sexual orientation, attempts to treat women's health problems as solely biological phenomenon are incomplete and potentially harmful.

There are many ways that a feminist, behavior-analytic approach could potentially advance our current understanding of women's health. At an individual analysis level, behavioral analysis provides a more contextual, therefore valid, view of the causes and factors maintaining any problem behavior of women, potentially increasing the effectiveness of assessment and treatment approaches. Of course, these assumptions await empirical scrutiny. As discussed above, the largest clinical health study in U.S. history will focus on understanding women's health problems, and will include the study of behavioral factors. We strongly suggest that as new studies such as this are designed, behavior analysts provide input about what they do best: providing answers about the function of any behavior through a careful analysis of controlling variables and consequences of the behavior—including the importance of how gender and socially constructed concepts impact what we know and believe about women.

References

Agras, W. S. (1987). *Eating disorders: Management of obesity, bulimia, and anorexia nervosa.* New York: Pergamon.

Agras, W. S., Telch, C. F., Arnow, B., Eldredge, K., Wilfley, D. E., Raeburn, S. D., Henderson, J., & Marnell, M. (1994). Weight loss, cognitive-behavioral, and desipramine treatments in binge eating disorder: An additive design. *Behavior Therapy, 25,* 225–238.

Amodei, N., Nelson, R. O., Jarrett, R. B., & Sigmon, S. T. (1987). Psychological treatments of dysmenorrhea: Differential treatment effectiveness for spasmodics and congestives. *Journal of Behavior Therapy and Experimental Psychiatry, 18,* 95–103.

Andersen, A. E. (1986). Inpatient and outpatient treatment of anorexia nervosa. In K. D. Brownell and J. P. Foreyt (Eds.), *Handbook of eating disorders: Physiology, psychology, and treatment of obesity, anorexia, and bulimia* (pp. 334–350). New York: Basic Books.

Babor, T. F. (1990). Brief intervention strategies for harmful drinkers: New directions for medical education. *Canadian Medical Association Journal, 143,* 1070–1076.

Barroso, C. (1994). Building a new specialization on women's health: An international perspective. In A. J. Dan (Ed.), *Reframing women's health: Multidisciplinary research and practice* (pp. 93–101). Thousand Oaks, CA: Sage.

Beckman, L. J., & Amaro, H. (1986). Personal and social difficulties faced by women and men entering alcoholism treatment. *Journal of Studies on Alcohol, 47,* 135–145.

Bemis, K. M. (1987). The present status of operant conditioning for treatment of anorexia nervosa. *Behavior Modification, 11,* 432–463.

Bien, T. H., Miller, W. R., & Tonigan, J. S. (1993). Brief interventions for alcohol problems: A review. *Addiction, 88,* 315–336.

Bowman, J. A., Redman, S., Dickinson, J. A., Gibberd, R., Samson-Fisher, R. W. (1991). The accuracy of *Pap* smear utilization self-report: A methodological consideration in cervical screening research. *Health Service Reserach, 26,* 97–107.

Blume, S. B. (1997). Women and alcohol: Issues in social policy. In R. W. Wilsnack & S. C. Wilsnack (Eds.), *Gender and alcohol: Individual and social perspectives* (pp. 462–489). New Brunswick, NJ: Rutgers University Center of Alcohol Studies.

Callahan, E. J., & Desiderato, L. (1988). Disorders in pregnancy. In E. A. Blechman & K. D. Brownell (Eds.), *Handbook of behavioral medicine for women* (pp. 103–115). New York: Pergamon.

Callahan, E., Desiderato, L., Heiden, L., & Pecsok, E. (1984). Prevention and intervention through obstetrics and gynecology. *Behavioral Medicine Update, 5,* 11–19.

Caruso, S., El-Mallakh, R., & Hale, M. (1990). Systems dynamics in hyperemesis gravidarum. *Family Systems Medicine, 8,* 91–95.

Chesney, M. A., & Tasto, D. L. (1975). The effectiveness of behavior modification with spasmodic and congestive dysmenorrhea. *Behaviour Research and Therapy, 13,* 245–253.

Chrisler, J. C., & Parrett, K. L. (1995). Women and autoimmune disorders. In A. L. Stanton & S. J. Gallant (Eds.), *The psychology of women's health: Progress and challenges in research and practice* (pp. 171–195). Washington, DC: American Psychological Association.

Council on Ethical and Judicial Affairs, American Medical Association (1991). Gender disparities in clinical decision making. *Journal of the American Medical Association, 266,* 559–562.

Cox, D. J., & Meyer, R. G. (1978). Behavioral treatment parameters with primary dysmenorrhea. *Journal of Behavioral Medicine, 1,* 297–310.

Cutler, S. E., & Nolen-Hoeksema, S. (1991). Accounting for sex differences in depression through female victimization: Childhood sexual abuse. *Sex Roles, 24,* 425–438.

Depue, R., Bernstein, L., Ross, R., Judd, H., & Henderson, B. (1987). Hyperemesis gravidarum in relation to estradiol levels, pregnancy outcome, and other maternal factors: A seroepidemiologic study. *American Journal of Obstetrics and Gynecology, 156,* 1137–1141.

Deutsch, H. (1945). *The psychology of women.* New York: Grune & Stratton.

Domjan, M., & Burkhard, B. (1986). *The principles of learning and behavior.* Monterey: Brooks/Cole.

Eastaugh, S. R. (1992). *Health economics: Efficiency, quality, and equity.* Westport, CT: Auburn House.

El-Mallakh, R., Liebowitz, N., & Hale, M. (1990). Hyperemesis gravidarum as conversion disorder. *Journal of Nervous and Mental Disease, 178,* 655–659.

Epstein, L. H. (1992). Role of behavior therapy in behavioral medicine. *Journal of Consulting and Clinical Psychology, 60,* 493–498.

Fairburn, C. G. (1994) Psychotherapy and bulimia nervosa: Longer-term effects of interpersonal psychotherapy, behavior therapy, and cognitive behavior therapy. *Journal of the American Medical Association, 271,* 106H.

Fairburn, C. G., Stein, L., & Jones, R. (1992). Eating habits and eating disorders during pregnancy. *Psychosomatic Medicine, 54,* 665–672.

Feldman, M. (1987). Nausea and vomiting. In M. Feldman and J. Fordtran (Eds.), *Gastrointestinal disease.* New York: McGraw-Hill.

Feucht, T., Stephens, R., & Roman, S. (1990). The sexual behavior of intravenous drug users: Assessing the risk of sexual transmission of HIV. *Journal of Drug Issues, 20,* 195–213.

Finkelstein, N. (1993a). The relational model. In D. Kronstadt, P. F. Green, & C. Marcus (Eds.), *Pregnancy and exposure to alcohol and other drug use* (pp. 126–163). Washington, DC: U.S. Department of Health and Human Services, Center for Substance Abuse Prevention.

Finkelstein, N. (1993b). Treatment programming for alcohol and drug-dependent pregnant women. *International Journal of the Addictions, 28,* 1275–1309.

Fitzgerald, C. (1984). Nausea and vomiting in pregnancy. *British Journal of Medical Psychology, 57,* 159–165.

Follette, V. M. (1994). Survivors of child sexual abuse: Treatment using a contextual analysis. In S. C. Hayes, N. S. Jacobson, V. M. Follette, & M. J. Dougher (Eds.), *Acceptance and change: Content and context in psychotherapy* (pp. 255–268). Reno: Context Press.

Follette, W. C., Bach, P. A., & Follette, V. M. (1993). A behavior-analytic view of psychological health. *The Behavior Analyst, 16,* 303–316.

Friedman, A. G., Goldberg, J. S., & Okifuji, A. (1997). Behavior theory in behavioral medicine. In J. J. Plaud & G. H. Eifert (Eds.), *From behavior theory to behavior therapy.* Boston: Allyn & Bacon.

Godsey, R., & Newman, R. (1991). Hyperemesis gravidarum: A comparison of single and multiple admissions. *Journal of Reproductive Medicine, 36,* 287–290.

Gurwitz, J. H., Nananda, F. C., & Avorn, J. (1992). The exclusion of the elderly and women from clinical trials in acute myocardial infarction. *Journal of the American Medical Association, 268,* 1417–1422.

Hamilton, J. A. (1993). Feminist theory and health psychology: Tools for an egalitarian, woman-centered approach to women's health. *Journal of Women's Health, 2,* 49–54.

Harrison, M. (1992). Women's health as a specialty: A deceptive solution. *Journal of Women's Health, 1,* 101–106.

Hartka, E., Johnstone, B. M., Leino, V., Motoyoshi, M., Temple, M., & Fillmore, K. M. (1991). A metaanalysis of depressive symptomatology and alcohol consumption over time. *British Journal of Addiction, 86,* 1283–1298.

Healy, B. (1991). Women's health, public welfare. *Journal of the American Medical Association, 264,* 566–568.

Heath, A. C., Slutske, W. S., & Madden, P. A. F. (1997). Gender differences in the genetic contribution to alcoholism risk and to alcohol consumption patterns. In R. W. Wilsnack & S. C. Wilsnack (Eds.), *Gender and alcohol: Individual and social perspectives* (pp. 114–149). New Brunswick, NJ: Rutgers University Center of Alcohol Studies.

Hester, R. K., & Miller, W. R. (1989). Self-control training. In R. K. Hester & W. R. Miller (Eds.), *Handbook of alcoholism treatment approaches: Effective alternatives* (pp. 141–149). Elmsford, NY: Pergamon.

Holder, H. D., Longabaugh, R., Miller, W. R., & Rubonis, A. V. (1991). The cost-effectiveness of treatment for alcohol problems: A first approximation. *Journal of Studies on Alcohol, 52,* 517–540.

Institute of Medicine (1990). *Broadening the base of treatment for alcohol problems.* Washington, DC: National Academy Press.

Jarvis, T. J. (1992). Implications of gender for alcohol treatment research: A quantitative and qualitative review. *British Journal of Addiction, 87,* 1249–1261.

Jeffery, R. W., Wing, R. R., Thorson, C., Burton, L. R., Raether, C., Harvey, J., & Mullen, M. (1993). Strengthening behavioral interventions for weight loss: A randomized trial of food provision and monetary incentives. *Journal of Consulting and Clinical Psychology, 61,* 1038–1045.

Kallen, B. (1987). Hyperemesis during pregnancy and delivery outcome: A registry study. *European Journal of Obstetrics, Gynecology and Reproductive Biology, 26,* 291–302.

Kanfer, F. (1975). Self management methods. In F. Kanfer and A. Goldstein (Eds.), *Helping people change: A textbook of methods.* New York: Pergamon.

Kaplan, R. M. (1990). Behavior as the central outcome in health care. *American Psychologist, 45,* 1211–1220.

Kauppila, A., Huhtaniemi, I., & Ylikorkala, O. (1979). Raised human chorionic gonadotrophin concentrations in hyperemesis gravidarum. *British Medical Journal, 1,* 1670.

Kennedy, S. H., Katz, R., Neitzert, C. S., Ralevski, E., & Mendlowitz, S. (1995). Exposure with response prevention treatment of anorexia nervosa-bulimic subtype and bulimia nervosa. *Behaviour Research and Therapy, 33,* 685–689.

Kestenberg, J. (1977). Regression and re-integration in pregnancy. In H. Blum (Ed.), *Female psychology.* New York: International Universities Press.

Klebanoff, M., Koslowe, P., Kaslow, R., & Rhoads, G. (1985). Epidemiology of vomiting in early pregnancy. *Obstetrics and Gynecology, 66,* 612–616.

Kucharczyk, J. (1991). Humoral factors in nausea and emesis. In J. Kucharczyk, D. Stewart, and A. Miller (Eds.), *Nausea and vomiting: Recent research and clinical advances.* Boca Raton: CRC Press.

Kushner, M. G., Sher, K. J., & Beitman, B. D. (1990). The relation between alcohol problems and the anxiety disorders. *American Journal of Psychiatry, 147,* 685–695.

Levine, M., & Esser, D. (1988). Total parenteral nutrition for the treatment of severe hyperemesis gravidarum: Maternal nutritional effects and fetal outcome. *Obstetrics and Gynecology, 72,* 102–107.

Long, M., Simone, S., & Tucher, J. (1986). Outpatient treatment of hyperemesis gravidarum with stimulus control and imagery procedures. *Journal of Behavioral Therapy & Experimental Psychiatry, 17,* 105–109.

Lott, B. (1990). Dual natures or learned behavior: The challenge to feminist psychology. In R. T. Har-Mustin & J. Marecek (Eds.), *Making a difference: Psychology and the construction of gender* (pp. 65–101). New Haven, CT: Yale University.

Martin, G., & Pear, J. (1992). *Behavior modification: What it is and how to do it* (4th ed.). Englewood Cliffs, NJ: Prentice-Hall.

Martin, S. E. (1992). The epidemiology of alcohol-related interpersonal violence. *Alcohol Health and Research World, 16,* 230–237.

Menninger, W. (1943). The emotional factors in pregnancy. *Menninger Clinic Bulletin, 7,* 15–24.

Miller, W. R. (1989). Increasing motivation for change. In R. K. Hester & W. R Miller (Eds.), *Handbook of alcoholism treatment approaches: Effective alternatives* (pp. 67–80). Elmsford, NY: Pergamon.

Miller, W. R., & Rollnick, S. (1991). *Motivational interviewing: Preparing people to change addictive behavior.* New York: Guilford.

Mitchell, J. E. (1995). Medical complications of bulimia nervosa. In K. D. Brownell & C. G. Fairburn (Eds.), *Eating disorders and obesity* (pp. 271–275). New York: Guilford.

Morgan, R., Jr., & Mutalik, G. (1992). *Bringing international health back home.* Paper presented at the 19th Annual Conference of the National Council for International Health, Washington, DC.

Morris, E. K. (1988). Contextualism: The worldview of behavior analysis. *Journal of Experimental Child Psychology, 46,* 289–323.

Mullen, F. (1968). The treatment of a case of dysmenorrhea by behavior therapy techniques. *Journal of Nervous and Mental Disease, 147,* 371–376.

Mullen, F. (1971). *Treatment of dysmenorrhea by professional and student behavior therapists.* Paper presented at the 5th Annual Meeting of the Association for the Advancement of Behavior Therapy, Washington, DC, September 1971.

National Institutes of Health. (1988). *Dysmenorrhea.* Bethesda, MD: Author.

Pi-Sunyer, F. X. (1995). Medical complications of obesity. In K. D. Brownell & C. G. Fairburn (Eds.), *Eating disorders and obesity* (pp. 401–405). New York: Guilford Press.

Pike, K. M., & Striegel-Moore, R. (In press). Disordered eating and eating disorders. In S. Gallant, G. Puryear Keita, & R. Royak-Schaler (Eds.), *Psychosocial and behavioral factors in women's health: A handbook for medical educators, practitioners, and psychologists.* Washington, DC: American Psychological Association.

Plaud, J. J., & Vogeltanz, N. D. (1994). Psychology and the naturalistic ethics of social policy. *American Psychologist, 49,* 967–968.

Porzelius, L, K., Houston, C., Smith, M., Arfken, C., & Fisher, E. (1995). Comparison of a standard behavioral weight loss treatment and a binge eating weight loss treatment. *Behavior Therapy, 26,* 119–134.

Roberts, L. J., & Leonard, K. E. (1997). Gender differences and similarities in the alcohol and marriage relationship. In R. W. Wilsnack & S. C. Wilsnack (Eds.), *Gender and alcohol: Individual and social perspectives* (pp. 289–311). New Brunswick, NJ: Rutgers University Center of Alcohol Studies.

Robertson, G. (1987). Physiology of ADH secretion. *Kidney International, 32,* 20.

Rodin, J., & Ickovics, J. R. (1990). Women's health: Review and research agenda as we approach the 21st century. *American Psychologist, 45,* 1018–1034.

Rodin, J., & Salovey, P. (1989). Health psychology. *Annual Review of Psychology, 40,* 533–579.

Rosen, J. C., Orosan, P., & Reiter, J. (1995). Cognitive behavior therapy for negative body image in obese women. *Behavior Therapy, 26,* 25–42.

Rosser, S. V. (1994). Gender bias in clinical research: The difference it makes. In A. J. Dan (Ed.), *Reframing women's health: Multidisciplinary research and practice* (pp. 253–265). Thousand Oaks, CA: Sage.

Ruiz, M. R. (1995). B. F. Skinner's radical behaviorism: Historical misconstructions and grounds for feminist reconstructions. *Psychology of Women's Quarterly, 19,* 161–179.

Samson-Fisher, R. W., Schofield, M. J., & Perkins, J. (1993). Behaviour therapy's role in preventing physical illness. *Behaviour Change, 10,* 25–31.

Sanchez-Craig, M., Spivak, K., & Davila, R. (1991). Superior outcome of females over males after brief treatment for the reduction of heavy drinking: Replication and report of therapist effects. *British Journal of Addictions, 86,* 867–876.

Schmidt, L., & Weisner, C. (1995). The emergence of problem-drinking women as a special population in need of treatment. In M. Galanter (Ed.), *Recent developments in alcoholism, Volume 12: Alcoholism and women* (pp. 309–334). New York: Plenum.

Seligman, M. E. P., & Hager, J. L. (Eds.). (1972). *Biological boundaries of learning.* New York: Meredith.

Short, P. (1990). *Estimates of the uninsured population, calendar year 1987.* National Medical Expenditure Survey Data Summary 2, Agency for Health Care Policy and Research (DHHS Pub. No. PHS 90-3469). Rockville, MD: Public Health Service.

Sigmon, S. T., & Nelson, R. O. (1988). The effectiveness of activity scheduling and relaxation training in the treatment of spasmodic dysmenorrhea. *Journal of Behavioral Medicine, 11,* 483–495.

Simone, S., & Long, M. (1985). Behavioral treatment of hyperemesis gravidarum. *The Behavior Therapist, 8,* 128–129.

Smith, D. E., Marcus, M. D., & Eldredge, K. L. (1994). Binge eating syndromes: A review of assessment and treatment with an emphasis on clinical application. *Behavior Therapy, 25,* 635–658.

Sobell, M. B., Sobell, L. C., & Gavin, D. R. (1995). Portraying alcohol treatment outcomes: Different yardsticks of success. *Behavior Therapy, 26,* 643–669.

Stanton, A. L. (1995). Psychology of women's health: Barriers and pathways to knowledge. In A. L. Stanton & S. J. Gallant (Eds.), *The psychology of women's health: Progress and challenges in research and practice* (pp. 3–21). Washington, DC: American Psychological Association.

Striegel-Moore, R. H., Silberstein, L. R., & Rodin, J. (1993). The social self in bulimia nervosa: Public self-consciousness, social anxiety, and perceived fraudulence. *Journal of Abnormal Psychology, 102,* 297–303.

Tasto, D. L., & Chesney, M. A. (1974). Muscle relaxation treatment for primary dysmenorrhea. *Behavior Therapy, 5,* 668–672.

Thackwray, D. E., Smith, M. C., Bodfish, J. W., & Meyers, A. W. (1993). A comparison of behavioral and cognitive-behavioral interventions for bulimia nervosa. *Journal of Consulting and Clinical Psychology, 61,* 639–645.

Thom, B. (1987). Sex differences in help-seeking for alcohol problems: II. Entry into treatment. *British Journal of Addiction, 82,* 989–997.

Travis, C. B. (1988). *Women and health psychology: Biomedical issues.* Hillsdale, NJ: Erlbaum.

Travis, C. B., Gressley, D. L., & Adams, P. L. (1995). Health care policy and practice for women's health. In A. L. Stanton & S. J. Gallant (Eds.), *The psychology of women's health: Progress and challenges in research and practice* (pp. 531–565). Washington, DC: American Psychological Association.

Treasure, J., Todd, G., Brolly, M., Tiller, J., Nehmed, A., & Denman, F. (1995). A pilot study of a randomized trial of cognitive analytical therapy vs educational behavioral therapy for adult anorexia nervosa. *Behaviour Research and Therapy, 33,* 363–367.

Vannicelli, M., & Nash, L. (1984). Effects of sex bias on women's studies on alcoholism. *Alcoholism: Clinical and Experimental Research, 8,* 3324–336.

Vogeltanz, N. D., & Plaud, J. J. (1992). On the goodness of Skinner's system of naturalistic ethics in solving basic value conflicts. *The Psychological Record, 42,* 457–468.

Vogeltanz, N. D., & Wilsnack, S. C. (1997). Alcohol problems in women: Risk factors, consequences, and treatment strategies. In S. Gallant, G. Puryear Keita, & R. Royak-Schaler (Eds.), *Health care for women: Psychological, social, and behavioral influences* (pp. 75–96). Washington, DC: American Psychological Association.

Wadden, T. A., Foster, G. D., & Letizia, K. A. (1994). One-year behavioral treatment of obesity: Comparison of moderate and severe caloric restriction and the effects of weight maintenance therapy. *Journal of Consulting and Clinical Psychology, 62,* 165–171.

Wallis, L. A. (1993). Why a curriculum on women's health? *Journal of Women's Health, 2,* 55–60.

Williamson, D. A., Barker, S. E., & Norris, L. E. (1993). Etiology and management of eating disorders. In P. B. Sutker & H. E. Adams (Eds.), *Comprehensive handbook of psychopathology* (2nd ed.) (pp. 505–561). New York: Plenum.

Williamson, D. A., Davis, C. J., Duchmann, E. G., McKenzie, S. J., & Watkins, P. C. (1990). *Assessment of eating disorders: Obesity, anorexia, and bulimia nervosa.* New York: Pergamon.

Williamson, D. A., Cubic, B. A., & Fuller, R. D. (1992). Eating disorders. In S. M. Turner, K. S. Calhoun, & H. E. Adams (Eds.), *Handbook of clinical behavioral therapy* (pp. 355–371). New York: Wiley.

Wilsnack, S. C. (1984). Drinking, sexuality, and sexual dysfunction in women. In S. C. Wilsnack & L. J. Beckman (Eds.), *Alcohol problems in women: Antecedents, consequences, and intervention* (pp. 189–227). New York: Guilford.

Wilsnack, S. C., Vogeltanz, N. D., Klassen, A., & Harris, T. R. (1997). Childhood sexual abuse and women's substance abuse: National survey findings. *Journal of Studies on Alcohol, 58,* 264–271.

Wilson, G. T., & Agras, W. S. (1992). The future of behavior therapy. *Psychotherapy, 29,* 39–43.

14

THE RELATION BETWEEN BEHAVIOR THEORY AND BEHAVIOR THERAPY: CHALLENGES AND PROMISES

SHAWN P. CAHILL
Department of Psychology
Binghamton University

MAUREEN H. CARRIGAN
Department of Psychology
Binghamton University

IAN M. EVANS
Department of Psychology
University of Waikato

The mere possibility of the present book is a tribute to the depth and endurance of the ties between the basic science of psychology and behavior therapy. The origin of that relationship was in the context of learning theory, a controversial alliance that has frequently been declared to be incompatible. Early in the courtship, Breger and McGaugh (1965) advised against it, claiming that learning theory—particularly S-R concepts—had no prospects. London (1972) thought it a trivial infatuation that would soon pass. Bandura (1974) recommended moving on to a new partner. Yet here the two are, still living together after all these years, even though the passion might have faded a little.

It is worth continuing to subject the relationship to critical examination. If behavior therapy is no more than the extension of learning principles, then the affiliation is sym-

Preparation of this chapter was made possible by the Graduate Research Initiative at Binghamton University, designed to support the development of clinical psychology as an applied science, and a research award from the School of Social Sciences, the University of Waikato. Order of authorship is alphabetical.

biotic indeed, and of great importance. But if behavior therapy has a firm, empirical, and self-supporting identity of its own, it needs little help from the basic science and, therefore, learning theory and behavior therapy—while remaining good friends—can contentedly go their separate ways. If, as we would argue, there is valuable interaction that lies somewhere between these two extremes, then it might be helpful to understand its nature better. The purpose of this chapter is to highlight some of the challenges and promises of the interaction and reveal some possible new fruits of the union. We attempt to do this by examining the current status of learning theory as well as trends within clinical psychology to acknowledge the importance of "common factors" in treatment effectiveness. We also propose a way in which these two considerations might be integrated. The chapter concludes with a discussion of the relevance of these issues to the training of the next generation of behavior therapists.

Models for Relating Theory to Practice

Past Approaches

It is worth looking back briefly at the primary ways in which behavior therapists have attempted to integrate behavior (learning) theory and behavior therapy, remembering that the models are not necessarily incompatible.

Direct Extensions of Laboratory Paradigms

Literal transposition occurred historically when an application of behavior therapy was the same as an animal study, except that it was a human patient who was the subject. The very early work in behavior modification had this quality: Skinner and Lindsley (e.g., Lindsley, 1956), among others, simply extended the operant paradigm to humans, complete with manipulanda, automatically delivered reinforcers, and artificial stimulus and schedule control of behavior.

Even today, operant procedures are sometimes transposed very literally into methods of change (for a critique, see Meyer & Evans, 1993). It is still possible, for example, to read guidelines for the "therapeutic" use of punishment to change behavior, in regard to timing and intensity of the aversive event that are based on the parameters of punishment that produce the most rapid response suppression in rats. Similarly, prescriptions for ensuring maintenance and generalization of behavior change are simply exact extensions of partial reinforcement and transfer of stimulus-control procedures. As clients are neither rats or cats or pigeons, nor do they have single conditioned responses in need of change, the lack of material on more complex learning, especially that mediated by language and other symbols, is a major detriment, Staats's (1963) work being the notable exception.

Shared Behavioral Metatheory and Empiricism

Although not all learning theory is behavioristic, it was the neobehaviorism of Hull, Guthrie, Tolman, and Skinner that actually produced behavior therapy, with the earlier influence of Pavlov, Thorndike, and Watson being of great importance. Behavior therapy was, therefore, by definition as well as predilection, *behavioristic*. The metatheoretical tenets of behaviorism provided a critical focus that clearly contrasted with psychoanalysis in its domination of the entire mental health field (e.g., Ullmann & Krasner, 1965). H. J. Eysenck's (1960) championing of behavior therapy was heavily influenced by this perspective.

Because learning theory has also been synonymous with rigorous experimental research, behavior therapy has been characterized by its empirical orientation. Many scholars were attracted to behavior therapy because of its tough-minded scientific foundations, instead of being behaviorists who appreciated its metatheory. As a consequence, they became much less insistent on theoretical purity and the links with learning research than had previous pioneers.

Retroactive Translations

A third type of relationship between learning theory and clinical application grew out of the work of the Yale social learning/Hullian group. The tendency was to accept the validity of some particular theory of psychopathology or therapeutic method (e.g., psychoanalysis), and then to try to account for it in learning terms. Thus, Mowrer and Miller had a large impact on behavior therapy by suggesting, for example, how defense mechanisms could be seen as avoidance behaviors, and understood in accordance with two-factor theory. This had the effect of giving behavior therapy permission to use and reinterpret a variety of traditional psychoanalytic observations. The trend continues to this day, with the work of Levis (e.g., 1991) and Stampfl (1991) being perhaps the most prominent examples.

Retroactive translations of psychodynamic theories or therapies into learning terminology have the possible benefit of incorporating clinical insights, important to the therapeutic enterprise (but historically underemphasized by behavior therapists), into a potentially unified framework. Also, by putting behavior therapists into contact with novel but relevant literatures, new theoretical predictions might emerge. A drawback of this approach is that knowledge bases would likely stagnate unless more prospective applications of learning theory evolved.

Prospective Translations

Systematic desensitization represents the classic behavior therapy that was derived prospectively from two learning research areas. These were the elimination of traumatic fear conditioning through exposure and Hullian extinction theory, although Wolpe's principle of reciprocal inhibition is actually closer to Guthrie's analysis of extinction than Hull's. In any event, the hierarchy was analogous to the need to move the organism closer and closer to the feared situation. The relaxation was analogous to the need to "inhibit" anxiety in some way, and it was more appropriate for human clients than feeding them. The imaginal scene presentation was a convenient way to present the relevant stimuli. Evans (1973a) proposed that in order to decide whether the clinical method was still true to the original experimental paradigm, the rules for these translations by analogy needed careful specification.

It is interesting to note how quickly, in fact, systematic desensitization was institutionalized as a technique, not as an analogy to a learning process. Leading behavior therapy researchers, following Paul (1966), argued that particular methods of treatment need to be developed, their boundaries specified, and their effectiveness for a given syndrome investigated. This emphasis on a procedure, rather than the variable and flexible application of a learning principle, continues to be criticized by a few in the current behavior therapy scene (e.g., Evans, 1993; Eifert, Evans, & McKendrick, 1990).

Another metatheoretical insight revealed by systematic desensitization comes from the fact that Wolpe, by translating animal learning principles into a human-appropriate context, relied heavily on cognitive events (words, images, and thoughts) as stimuli and responses. At no time was the therapy perceived by him to be a cognitive intervention. He is rightly somewhat perplexed that, as other therapists realized the need to consider words and thoughts as the phenomena of clinical concern, they felt they had to switch to cognitivist positions in which expectancies or beliefs are seen as the causal elements of change. Part of what we will try to do in this chapter is demonstrate that as learning theory has changed, it has embraced certain principles and constructs from information processing. Thus, the distinction in the basic science between conditioning and cognition has blurred. Meanwhile, since many behavior therapists have essentially denounced conditioning theories in favor of what they see as an alternative (cognitive theory), the task of sustaining behavior therapy within one paradigm has become difficult.

We believe that there is great potential for advancing the current state of behavior therapy through the use of prospective derivations of clinical techniques from learning theory. One major challenge to this approach lies in being able to bridge the gap between the relatively simple stimuli and responses usually used in the laboratory and the responses and functional controlling stimuli found in the natural environment, which are more difficult to specify. Theoretical as well as empirical advances are needed, especially in the area of defining rules or principles of translation, that will allow therapists to understand a client's problems according to principles of behavior and to develop intervention strategies that take advantage of naturally available resources or contingencies. Of course, the question remains as to whether application of *modern* learning theory will prove to be as fruitful to behavior therapy as was the case in the past. However, we strongly believe that an increased familiarity with modern learning theory is necessary before this question can be answered.

Contemporary Needs for Integrating Theory and Practice

Dealing with Cognition

Where are the new ideas for therapy actually coming from today? Is it the learning lab, as in the past, or are the therapies themselves evolving as new treatment studies emerge? Or are the new therapies really derived from new experimental principles—principles of *cognitive* change rather than learning/conditioning principles? Certainly much of current behavior therapy has shifted away from using behavioral learning theory as the basis on which to build clinical interventions. Beginning in the early to mid-1970s it became increasingly more common to use loosely defined cognitive constructs such as automatic thoughts (Beck, 1976), perception of self-efficacy (Bandura, 1977), or attributions of causality (Abramson, Seligman, & Teasdale, 1978) to understand behavior disorders and the process of behavior change. In part, this was due to the rejection of traditional S-R learning theory as inadequate (cf. Eifert, Forsyth, & Schauss, 1993).

Another reason for the theoretical shift in behavior therapy was the "cognitive revolution" that occurred in *experimental* psychology at about the same time. Unfortunately, the cognitive theories that were developed within behavior therapy had little to do with the developing cognitive science, beyond the adoption of cognitive-sounding jargon (MacLeod, 1993). A more promising approach is illustrated by recent researchers (e.g., M. W. Eysenck, 1993) using cognitive science preparations to identify information-processing anomalies associated with different disorders. At the present, this approach appears to hold promise for improving our understanding of processes involved in the etiology and maintainence of psychopathology. However, it has yet to lead to any substantial changes in treatment procedures.

Beyond Basic Empiricism

A second prominent trend in behavior therapy has been the development of empirically validated treatment packages. This "dust-bowl empiricism" approach is supported by research programs in which homogenous populations are defined, interventions are detailed in manuals, and specific outcome measures taken to validate the techniques. The goal of this strictly empirical approach is to produce formal treatment plans for specific diagnoses that can be easily disseminated for implementation by other clinicians. Along with this approach comes a trend toward official sanctioning of treatments, such as APA's Division 12 Task Force list of empirically validated treatments.

Although we are certainly not against building a research base to support the use of behavioral treatments, we believe that what is lacking in a purely empirical approach is theory (Evans, 1993, 1996). Unless a clinical decision-making tree can be so detailed as to include all possible person–situation–problem combinations, clinical judgment will always be required to determine which problems to target, what treatment methods to employ, the outcomes to be considered "positive," and when treatment is to be terminated. Additionally, since most treatment protocols include multiple components, how does one choose which components to use in order to maximize treatment effectiveness for a particular client? And, when two or more "empirically validated treatments" exist, as in the case of depression, on what basis do we decide between them?

Finally, in the face of meta-analytic research (e.g., Anderson & Lambert, 1995; Barker, Funk, & Houston, 1988; Landman & Dawes, 1982; Smith & Glass, 1977) suggesting that most therapies are effective, and given the lack of adequate comparative research that would provide empirical indicators as to which approach is best under what conditions, what are the factors that may be useful in helping the therapist in treatment planning? We believe that a theoretically driven, case-formulation approach would not only provide the guidance needed, but would open up new areas of research that would have much more clinical relevance (cf. Persons, 1991).

Unfortunately, many of the recent innovations in behavior-therapy techniques seem to have been developed in isolation with little or no connection to learning theory or other generic behavior change principles. A recent example is Shapiro's (1989) Eye Movement Desensitization and Reprocessing (EMDR) therapy. EMDR is a cognitive-behavioral treatment developed for the alleviation of symptoms related to traumatic memories (i.e., PTSD symptoms) and later applied to other anxiety disorders. Shapiro reports discovering EMDR accidentally one day when she noticed that engaging in eye movements while having disturbing thoughts diminished her anxiety. Thus, EMDR was not derived from any accepted theoretical framework. Additionally, the technique has been developed, marketed, researched, and applied without reference to any existing literature base. As we have pointed out elsewhere (Carrigan & Cahill, 1995), researchers of EMDR would benefit greatly from an increased understanding and integration of the vast literature on the treatment of anxiety disorders.

Levels of Analysis

Behavior therapists need a theoretical framework that is broad enough to encompass the diversity of clinical phenomena that present themselves in the clinic, while being specific enough to guide the clinical decision-making processes. However, the trend in many areas of *experimental* psychology has been toward a more and more molecular analysis of phenomena of interest. Although this is to be expected in basic science, extremely molecular theories that are not systematically connected to other bodies of information become difficult to use in guiding decisions at the more macro level of clinical intervention. On the other hand, a theory must also not be so broad or abstract that it becomes difficult to identify specific interventions to effect behavior change. For instance, some generalized clinical theories (such as psychoanalytic theory) manage to capture the richness of the clinical picture and provide fascinating explanations for the etiology of psychopathology, but they fail to provide adaquate guidance in the selection of specific interventions, for specific clients, under specific conditions.

As an alternative to either approach, we propose that theory construction be thought of as hierarchical (Staats, 1975, 1995; see also Eifert & Evans, 1990), in which there are several potential levels of analysis, each of which is to be connected with the levels lying both above and below it. Progress from this perspective occurs in two ways. The first is, of course, working within a specific level to increase the breadth of phenomena under analysis and depth of understanding. The second is to systematically build bridges between adjacent levels of analysis, so that knowledge at both higher and lower levels of analysis is made more available to those working at an intermediary level. For a clinical theory to be most useful, it needs to provide a framework that encompasses multiple levels of analysis in a meaningful way.

Why Learning Theory Fits the Bill

Shared Phenomena

We believe that contemporary learning theory can go a considerable way to meeting these needs for several reasons. First, broadly defined, the term *learning* is used to refer to any relatively permanent change in behavior that is the result of experience and that is not due to changes in motivation, sensory adaptation, or motor fatigue (Chance, 1979). Learning theory is therefore concerned with identifying the conditions under which learning occurs and the content of what is learned.

What is the relevance of this definition to behavior therapy? Consider the general goals and methods of behavior therapy. As behavior therapists, our goal is to promote relatively permanent changes in behavior—broadly defined to include overt skeletal responses, physiological reactions, and verbal statements in response to life circumstances—by arranging therapeutic experiences. The way in which these therapeutic experiences are provided, of course, can take many different forms. Behavior change can be promoted through didactic instruction, Socratic dialogue, reflection and interpretation, imaginal or direct exposure to emotional stimuli, imaginal or behavioral rehearsal of new skills, contingency contracting, participant modeling, and so forth. However, the *process* of behavior therapy is inherently a "learning experience" for the client. Therefore, the basic questions of learning theory ("What are the conditions of learning?" and "What is learned?") are as relevant to behavior therapists as they are to learning theorists.

Progress Has Been Made

Second, learning theory has advanced considerably since the beginnings of behavior therapy (see, for example, an earlier review of learning theory by Evans, 1976), although these changes have not been well appreciated in the clinical domain. Most of the objections to learning-theory analyses of human behavior problems continue to focus on the mythical monolith of "traditional learning-theory" (Rachman, 1977, 1991) while continuing to ignore the crucial point that contemporary learning theory is "not what you think it is" (Rescorla, 1988). Classical conditioning, for example, is still often thought of as simply the transfer of a discrete, reflexive unconditioned response (UR) to any new stimulus that is presented in temporal contiguity with the unconditioned stimulus. Similarly, instrumental conditioning is often characterized in terms of the automatic nature of reinforcement, such that any response followed by a reinforcer will be automatically strengthened. In response to these assumptions, critics of learning-theory analyses of human behavior argue that human behavior does not follow such simple laws and that numerous cognitive variables, such as "awareness" (Brewer, 1974), "attributions of causality" (Abramson, Seligman, & Teasdale, 1978), or "self-efficacy" (Bandura, 1977) intervene between the objective contingencies in the environment and the person's behavior.

However, as we hope to illustrate below, learning theory itself has gone far beyond the simple assumptions outlined above. Not only is most human behavior too complex to be explained by "traditional learning theory," so too are the phenomena of the basic learning laboratory. In order to evaluate the relevance of learning theory for an understanding of human behavior and the process of therapeutic intervention, we must consider not what learning theory was in the 1950s and 1960s, but what it is now (Dickinson, 1987).

Common Theoretical Problems

Third, researchers interested in animal learning processes, human learning and memory, and behavior therapists have all faced similar theoretical problems. It is not surprising, then, that some researchers in the field of animal learning have reached similar solutions to those reached by human memory theorists. For example, Spear (1978; Spear

& Riccio, 1994) has shown how a large body of both human and animal research on learning and forgetting can be integrated according to a memory-retrieval principle similar to Tulving's principle of encoding specificity (e.g., Tulving & Thomson, 1973). From this point of view, instrumental and classical conditioning are simply two additional paradigms from which to study the more general processes of memory formation and retrieval.

There is an advantage to this approach of looking for similarities, in that research conducted in very different content areas (such as basic animal conditioning, human memory, and treatment outcome) may be able to mutually inform one another. Being aware of similarities in problems as well as their solutions would help eliminate the frequent "reinventing of the wheel" that happens in psychology and help our science to develop in a more cumulative manner, rather than the current state of isolated islands of knowledge (Staats, 1983). One of the goals of this chapter is to illustrate how being familiar with several recent developments in basic learning theory may help to inform behavior therapy.

Reevaluating Conditioning Theory

What Are the Conditions of Learning?

Interestingly, some of the enigmas in early learning theories that were confronted in the behavior-therapy literature are similar to anomalies that appeared in the basic-learning literature. For example, Rachman (1977, 1991) cites as one of the challenges to the "classical theory" of phobia acquisition the finding that individuals may fail to display fear conditioning under known traumatic conditions, such as being in an air raid. Similarly, under the rubrics of stimulus selection, relative validity, and contingency learning, laboratory findings were appearing in which putative conditioned stimuli (CSs) were presented in temporal contiguity with an unconditioned stimulus (US), but did not appear to support a conditioned response (CR). Perhaps the most important of these phenomena has been that of *blocking* (Kamin, 1968).

A typical blocking experiment involves two phases, followed by a test for conditioned responding. The first phase consists of simple classical conditioning in which, say, a tone is paired with shock. In the second phase, the now-conditioned tone is presented in compound with a second stimulus, such as a light, and the compound is then paired with shock. The result of interest during the test is that, compared to a group of subjects that did not receive the initial conditioning with the tone, experimental subjects show little responding to the light. When this happens, the preconditioning with the tone is said to "block" conditioning to the light during the second phase. Conditioning failed to be observed under conditions in which contiguity theory predicted that conditioning should occur.

A related phenomena is that of *overshadowing* (Kamin, 1969), in which it has been found that simply conditioning a stimulus in compound with another stimulus results in less control of responding than occurs when only one of the elements serves as the CS. This phenomenon is especially strong when one element of the compound stimulus is more salient than the other. In contemporary learning-theory terms, the more salient stimulus "overshadows" the less salient stimulus. A final example of the failure of simple contiguity theory is the well known CS pre-exposure effect, or *latent inhibition* (Lubow, 1965). It has been well established that if a to-be-conditioned stimulus is first presented alone several times prior to beginning pairings with a US, the course of acquisition of the CR is retarded.

These findings indicate that despite being presented in contiguity with a US, some stimuli may come to elicit only a weak CR due to the presence of other stimuli during conditioning (overshadowing), an effect that is further weakened when the to-be-conditioned stimulus is accompanied by a previously conditioned stimulus (blocking), or through previous nonreinforced exposure of the CS (latent inhibition). Thus, similar to clinical findings that stimuli present during traumatic experiences may not always elicit a CR, contemporary findings in the field of learning indicate that simple contiguity is not enough to promote conditioned responding. It is curious then, that the two fields of basic learning and behavior therapy adopted radically different solutions to a similar problem. Whereas learning theorists attempted to better understand the circumstances that produce these apparent failures to learn and to devise a better theory of learning, behavior therapists began to abandon learning theory. Instead of attempting to find the characteristics of the conditioning situation that resulted in these failures (for example, the role of stimulus saliency in overshadowing), or developing a theory to account for when conditioning does and does not occur (for examples, see the suggestions of Mackintosh, 1975; Pearce & Hall, 1980; Rescorla & Wagner, 1972), behavior therapists attempted to understand these phenomena in terms of characteristics of the subjects. Thus, human conditioning might be thought to depend upon whether or not the person was "aware" of the CS–US contingency, whether or not the person "attributed" the presence of the US to the occurrence of the CS, or the degree to which the person "perceived" him or herself to be in danger.

Aside from the problem of circularity with many of these concepts (e.g., the attribution is the cause of behavior, while the behavior is the evidence of the attribution), there is a decided practical advantage to the learning theory approach. An understanding of the conditions that interfere with learning can help to provide suggestions for the prevention of unwanted conditioning. A recent example of this comes from the field of behavioral medicine (Okifuji & Friedman, 1992; see also the chapter in this volume by Friedman, Okifuji, & Goldberg). It has been observed that individuals undergoing chemotherapy for cancer often develop aversions to foods that have been consumed prior to a treatment session (Andrykowski, Redd, & Hatfield, 1985), an effect that is easily understood in terms of taste-aversion conditioning (Bernstein, 1991). As with other forms of classical conditioning, the expression of flavor aversions can be attenuated through blocking and overshadowing. For example, presenting a highly salient and novel gustatory stimulus in the interval between the putative CS (normal food) and US (chemotherapy) would be expected to result in the novel stimulus overshadowing the food, conditioning an aversion to the novel taste while preventing an aversion to normal foodstuffs. Just such an intervention, called a "scapegoat" procedure (Brodberg & Bernstein, 1987), has been shown to reduce conditioned food aversions in chemotherapy patients.

What Is Learned?

A second criticism of the classical theory of fear acquisition is the opposite of the preceding: fears often appear when, according to "classical learning theory," they should not (Rachman, 1977, 1991). Many individuals seeking treatment for phobias, for example, are not able to recall any relevant direct conditioning experiences to account for the phobia onset. Instead, evidence suggests that some phobic reactions are acquired through observation of the phobic reaction of another person. Still other phobias appear to be acquired through the transmission of verbal information. These additional "sources" of phobia acquisition have been interpreted to mean that they involve processes other than classical conditioning.

As with the conditioning failures discussed in the preceding section, "traditional learning theory" was also faced with a number of instances of learned responding when, according to a simple S-R theory, responding should not have been observed. Several of these phenomena were integral in the general shift from S-R theories of classical conditioning to an S-S theory. According to the S-S interpretation, conditioning operations result in the formation of an association between internal representations of the CS and US, rather than between the CS and the UR. One good example of learning where learning should not occur is the phenomenon of reinforcer revaluation. In this preparation, a CS–US association is first established in the normal fashion, and then the hedonic value of the US is changed in some fashion.

An especially nice example of US revaluation is provided by an elegantly designed within subject experiment by Holland (1989, cited in Holland, 1990). In the first phase of the experiment, two different tones were established as CS, each signaling a discriminably different flavored food pellet (wintergreen and peppermint). Following acquisition of the appetitive CR, the value of one of the pellets was changed from positive to negative through pairing the food with injections of lithium chloride (LiCl), a procedure which makes the animal ill. Upon recovery from the acute poisoning, subjects were then tested with both of the CS in the absence of any further US. The results of this experiment indicated a selective suppression of the appetitive CR to the tone whose food pellet had been devalued. Additionally, the reduced-appetitive CR was accompanied by an increase in facial displays associated with the rejection of ill-tasting food. Importantly, these changes in conditioned responding following the US revaluation procedure were not observed in response to the tone whose food pellet had not been paired with LiCl. This finding helps to rule out nonassociative alternative explanations.

These findings are difficult to reconcile with a simple S-R account of Pavlovian conditioning. If all that is established in the first phase of conditioning is an association between the tones and discrete motor responses, then changing the animals' response to the US should have no impact on their response to the CS. The standard interpretation of such results is that the first phase of the experiment results in the CS ability to conditionally activate an internal representation of the US. Then in the second phase, when the US is itself revalued through a conditioning procedure, the memory for the US is altered to reflect its new hedonic value. Therefore, it is the activation of this updated US representation that causes the aversive reaction to the CS during the test.

Although US revaluation procedures have been reported in the basic learning literature since the 1970s (Rescorla, 1973), behavior therapists have only recently begun to evaluate whether or not they may be of relevance to understanding clinical phenomena. Chief among the theorists discussing the relevance of reinforcer revaluation to behavior therapy has been Davey (1989, 1992). He suggests that many fearful reactions for which a primary conditioning event cannot be easily established may have come about through a process of reinforcer revaluation. For example, a child visits her grandparents' farm on several occasions where she is learning to ride a pony. One day while riding a horse at a circus, she falls off, is hurt and badly frightened. She now refuses to join the family in their next visit to Grandma and Grandpa's. Notice that the child's fear is not just of horses, but also of visiting the farm. Theoretically this would be due to the farm being associated with horses, such that when horses are revalued through the accident, so are other stimuli associated with horses. Davey, DeJong, and Tallis (1993) have published a number of case studies that appear to follow this general pattern.

In addition to the mechanism of reinforcer revaluation, it is possible to submit both of the alternative sources of phobia acquisition suggested by Rachman (1977, 1991) to an analysis in terms of Pavlovian conditioning. Vicarious learning of emotional reactions, for example, has been extensively investigated by Mineka and her associates (see Mineka, 1987, for a summary) using rhesus monkeys. Monkeys raised in the wild are quite understandably afraid of snakes. Monkeys raised in captivity, however, do not typically display fearful reactions to snakes, *unless* they have had the opportunity to observe a fellow monkey react fearfully to a snake. Monkeys' fear of snakes, therefore, clearly depends on learning. Investigation of this phenomenon indicates that the kind of learning involved follows the basic associative laws of classical conditioning. In this case, the functional US appears to be the model monkey's emotional reaction to the snake. Mineka and her associates found a correlation of .83 between the model monkey's reaction to the snake and the observer monkey's reaction to the model (the hypothesized unconditioned response). Additionally, positive correlations were obtained between the strength of the observer monkey's reaction during conditioning and several measures of fear during testing. Thus, US intensity affects observational conditioning in the same manner as it does in other forms of classical conditioning. Additional investigations of Pavlovian conditioning phenomena such as overshadowing (Cook & Mineka, 1987) and extinction (Mineka, Keir, & Price, 1980) have generally supported the conditioning hypothesis.

Similarly, Staats (1963, 1975) has long argued for a role of classical conditioning in the development of word meaning. According to his analysis, one important component of word meaning is the emotional response that is controlled by the word. Some words acquire their ability to elicit emotions through the process of primary classical conditioning, such as when a parent says the word *bad* immediately before spanking a child. Later, additional words acquire emotional meaning through second-order conditioning with previously conditioned words serving as the US. So, for example, providing the child with information that "Snakes are bad" actually constitutes a second-order conditioning trial. Such verbal interchanges between a parent and child, or between people in general, are a frequent occurrence. Therefore, it might be expected that verbal conditioning would permit a wide variety of stimuli to develop the ability to elicit negative (and positive) emotional reactions in the complete absence of any prior, direct experience. However, since second-order conditioning is generally weaker than primary conditioning, it might also be expected that verbally conditioned emotional reactions would not be especially intense (cf. Eifert, 1990, for a more detailed review of this field of study).

Compare this analysis with Rachman's (1977) descriptions of fear learning via the transmission of information: "Information-giving is an inherent part of child-rearing and is carried on by parents and peers in an almost unceasing fashion. . . . It is probable that informational and instructional processes provide the basis for most commonly encountered fears of everyday life. Fears acquired through informational channels are more likely to be mild than severe" (p. 384). Although the similarities between the two analyses are uncanny, there is one important difference. Rachman (1977) confesses that his view is not based on "any conventionally acceptable evidence" (p. 384), whereas Staats' position was developed in conjunction with an empirical research program.

Rather than studying fears, however, Staats studied appetitive verbal conditioning. For example, Staats and Hammond (1972) found that food words (e.g., bacon and pancakes) elicited a greater amount of salivation than did nonfood words such as square and edge. Additionally, they found that the food words elicited greater salivation in food-deprived individuals compared to nondeprived people. This study demonstrated that food words can be shown to be eliciters of a response. In the next study (Staats, Minke, Martin, & Higa, 1972), this fact was exploited to show that food words could serve as reinforcement in a Pavlovian second-order conditioning experiment. The pairing of food words with nonsense syllables resulted in greater transfer of salivation to the nonsense syllables in food-deprived individuals than in nondeprived ones. These data together are consistent with the interpretation that word meaning is in part the result of classical conditioning and that the transfer of verbal information may also involve such conditioning.

The Form of the CR

Additional evidence that illustrates conditioning does not result merely in the transfer of a simple reflex to the CS comes from reviewing some of the common preparations used to conduct learning research. First, although simple reflexive responses such as the eye blink are still used today, other research preparations focus on much larger and highly organized units of behavior. Second, the response that becomes conditioned to the CS may be topographically quite different from that directly elicited by the US (Evans, 1973b). Third, the exact nature of the observed CR may additionally depend upon the sensory qualities of the CS itself, such that one CS may support one response while a different CS supports another CR, despite using the same US. All three points may be illustrated by a single example.

Holland (1977) has developed a simple conditioning procedure in which rats are trained with two different-flavored food pellets, each of which is signaled by either a light or a tone. Three different response patterns may be observed in this preparation. In direct response to food presentations, a hungry rat typically approaches the food dispenser, handles and then consumes the pellet. Such consummatory behaviors are noticeably absent in response to the conditioned stimuli. When the CS is a light, the rat rears on back on its hind legs and looks about. The rat may also attempt to contact the CS, followed by passive waiting at the food dispenser. When the CS is a tone, however, the CR is a characteristic response of rapid head movements described as head jerking. Neither CR much resembles the observed UR, and the specific CR depends critically upon the nature of the CS.

Such results are difficult to explain in terms of a transfer-of-a-simple-reflex account of classical conditioning. Rather, something more general appears to be learned that permits the rat to, in some sense, anticipate the outcome. Taken in combination with the US revaluation effect, these data justify the characterization of the association underlying such behavior as serving the function of an "expectancy." As with the failures to learn discussed above, however, the shift from S-R to S-S theory by animal-learning theorists follows the pattern of modifying rather than abandoning conditioning theory. In fact, the S-S view of conditioning has brought many new phenomena under the purview of conditioning theory than would be the case if classical conditioning were defined in terms of the experimental operations rather than in terms of the nature of the responses and the processes involved. Perhaps the most clinically exciting example of this issue is the phenomenon of conditioned tolerance.

Conditioned Tolerance

It was Pavlov (1927) himself who first called attention to the fact that drug administrations are typically preceded by a pre-injection ritual which could be thought of as playing the role of a CS. Indeed, one of his students (Krylov, reported in Pavlov, 1927, pp. 35–37) reported that naturally occurring cues that had preceded injections of morphine, which elicits copious salivation, later were shown to acquire the ability to also elicit salivation. Much later, Wickler (1973) suggested that the experience of withdrawal may support conditioning to drug administration stimuli, based on the clinical observations that the sight of drug paraphernalia can produce drug cravings.

It may be argued that both Pavlov and Wickler missed what ultimately turned out to be a very exciting discovery because they were looking for conditioned responses that mimicked the unconditioned response. However, by focusing on the operations used to produce classical conditioning, rather than the nature of the response, Siegel (1975) made the observation that tolerance to the effects of a drug may be shown to be, in part, dependent upon the environment in which the drug is administered. Specifically, greater tolerance is displayed when the drug is administered in the presence of stimuli that were also present during previous drug administrations than when the context is shifted. Freed from the assumption that the CR must mirror the UR, this observation led Siegel to speculate that tolerance may result from classical conditioning in which the form of the CR compensates for the effect of the US. This analysis led to the testable (and largely verified) hypotheses that tolerance to drug effects should display numerous other effects of classical conditioning including extinction (Siegel, 1975), blocking (Dafters, Hetherington, & McCartney, 1983), overshadowing (Walter & Riccio, 1983), and latent inhibition (Siegel, 1977).

These findings have generated considerable interest in recent years, as they may help us to understand several of the facts of addictive disorders. For example, drug-addicted individuals report that the presence of drug-relevant cues can elicit feelings of withdrawal (Blakey & Baker, 1980), suggesting some degree of stimulus control over drug withdrawal. Additionally, some drug-overdose deaths occur with drug doses that had previously been tolerated (Government of Canada, 1973). These observations make good sense from Siegel's model. His model further suggests that drug urges can be extinguished, thus reducing the likelihood of relapse. Behavior therapists are currently testing whether or not cue-exposure treatments, based on the notion of extinguishing the situation-drug association, can promote better resistance to relapse (Niaura, Rohsenow, Binkoff, Monti, Pedraza, & Abrams, 1988). However, failure to be familiar with the subtleties of conditioning theory may result in the design of less than optimal tests of cue-exposure treatments. Just as behavior therapy has benefited from paying attention to the observation of drug-compensatory conditioning, behavior therapy would likely make further advances by incorporating conditioning theory in the development of maximally effective cue-exposure treatments.

New Learning during Extinction

There can be little doubt that exposure-based therapies for anxiety disorders represent one of the most important contributions of behavior therapy to the treatment of psychological problems. Although many early theorists conceptualized exposure-based therapies in basic learning-theory terms, such as Pavlovian extinction, it is currently more in vogue for behavior therapists to talk about exposure providing "corrective information" with a resulting increase in "emotional processing" (e.g., Foa & Kozak, 1986). It is not clear, however, whether such "nonconditioning" conceptions really differ from our contemporary understanding of extinction.

Most traditional conceptions of extinction have thought of it as a process that is the opposite of acquisition. For example, according to the influential Rescorla–Wagner model (1972), acquisition results in an increase in the strength of the CS–US association, and extinction results in the loss of that associative strength. Levis (1989) has similarly described extinction as an "unlearning" process. The clear implication of this position is that once extinction occurs, it should be permanent. Therefore, observations of the return of fear following successful treatment (Rachman, 1989), often under times of stress (Jacobs & Nadel, 1985), provide evidence against an unlearning interpretation of the fear-reduction process involved in therapeutic exposure to a fearful stimulus.

However, this should not be taken as evidence against an extinction interpretation of therapeutic exposure. Pavlov (1927) himself provided the initial evidence that the extinction process did not simply result in an erasure of the previously learned association. The observations of (a) the spontaneous recovery of an extinguished response after a retention interval, and (b) external disinhibition, the recovery of an extinguished response following presentation of a startle stimulus, prompted Pavlov to speculate that extinction produced new inhibitory learning that simply masked the excitatory association. A similar notion has recently been advanced by Bouton (1988; Bouton & Swartzentruber, 1991), consideration of which may prove enlightening to our understanding of exposure therapy.

Bouton's Theory

Bouton has spent much of his career trying to understand a single phenomenon (Bouton & Bolles, 1979). Rats conditioned to an external CS (e.g., a light or tone) in one context (e.g., a conditioning chamber with particular stimulus attributes such as size and odor) and then extinguished in the same context show little evidence of spontaneous recovery of the CR. However, when extinction is conducted in a discriminably different context, the CR will or will not be evidenced depending upon whether the test for the CR occurs in the initial acquisition context or the extinction context. He calls this effect the *renewal effect*, based on the observation of "renewal" of an extinguished response by returning the animal to the conditioning environment.

Bouton has proposed an explanation for this effect in terms of a general memory retrieval model (Bouton, 1993, 1994; see also Spear, 1978; Spear & Riccio, 1994). According to Bouton, the rats learn two competing associations. First, they learn that the CS will be followed by the US, and then they learn an inhibitory association that may be translated into the semantic equivalent of the "CS is not followed by the US." Both associations are maintained in memory, and what determines behavior is which of the two possible associations is retrieved. This, in turn, is determined by the presence of additional cues ("context" cues) that help discriminate between the two possible "meanings" of the CS. In other words, when the subject is tested in the conditioning context, the CS–US association is activated, which then promotes the conditioned response. When the subject is tested in the extinction context, however, both the excitatory and an inhibitory associations are activated, the net effect of which is to reduce or even eliminate the CR.

One variation of the renewal effect that may be of particular clinical relevance is what amounts to a case of state-dependent extinction. Bouton, Kenney, and Rosengard (1990) found that carrying out extinction of conditioned fear while the rats were under the influence of an acute dose of either of two commonly prescribed anxiolytics, librium and valium, resulted in a return of fear when subjects were later tested in a nondrug state. The interpretation of this finding offered by Bouton et al. (1990) is that the drug state served as the functional context for extinction, so when testing occurred in the nondrug state, only the excitatory fear association was activated.

Another potentially important class of internal stimuli that may serve to retrieve the acquisition memory following extinction are sensations associated with strong emotions elicited during initial learning. For example, an acute administration of the stress hormone adrenocorticotrophin (ACTH), which is released naturally during aversive learning experiences, renews the performance of a previously extinguished avoidance response (Richardson, Riccio, & Devine, 1984). Thus ACTH, and possibly other stress hormones, may serve as a context for aversive learning experiences. As such, their presence or absence may later serve to facilitate or inhibit retrieval of the relevant memories.

Implications

We concur with Bouton that such observations have relevance for understanding relapse following exposure treatments. First, the effect of nonreinforced exposure is the acquisition of a new association, but this new association inhibits, rather than eliminates or replaces, the learning that caused the problematic emotional/behavioral reaction. The underlying association is still present and may be reactivated at a later time.

Second, renewal of the problematic association is most likely to occur when the extinction context is different from the acquisition context. This may happen when treatment either occurs in the presence of unique cues, such as the therapist's office, or a physiological state induced by medications, or by the absence of important cues that occurred during the initial learning. One particular class of such stimuli are those internal cues associated with strong emotional reactions that occur naturally during traumatic experiences. Therapy under either of these conditions could theoretically "set up" a client to experience a relapse or renewal experience.

Ideally, treatment should be applied under conditions as similar to the initial learning conditions as possible, while ensuring that the US does not occur. However, it is often difficult to specify the exact acquisition conditions. In these circumstances, treatment should be conducted under conditions that are functionally as similar as possible to the context in which the person actually experiences the problematic reaction. As with ACTH renewed avoidance responding, the relevant cues may often be internal states, and the failure to elicit strong emotional reactions in therapy may contribute to less than optimally effective therapy. This mechanism may also account for the success of nonbehavioral therapies that, for different reasons, also emphasize the importance of evoking strong emotions in therapy.

When treatments cannot be conducted under such ideal conditions, two additional strategies are recommended. One is to conduct therapy under a variety of different conditions. A recent study with rats (Gunther, 1995, personal communication) found that extinguishing a conditioned fear in multiple contexts was effective in reducing renewal of the CR when subjects were returned to the conditioning context compared to subjects extinguished in only a single context. The other is to teach clients to use self-exposure as a form of relapse prevention. Specifically, therapists could provide clients with information about the possibility of the return of fear and about situations most likely to be associated with this. Clients would then be taught how to devise and implement a self-administered exposure-therapy plan after a renewal experience has occurred.

Finally, we emphasize that, although we have focused on exposure treatments for fear reduction, Bouton's model is based on the more general principle of encoding specificity. According to this simple but powerful principle, the likelihood of a response occurring is determined by the similarity between the prevailing stimulus conditions and those present during acquisition. This principle has garnered considerable support from studies of instrumental and classical conditioning as well as human memory research. It also has the virtue of emphasizing the role of the context or situation, something we can measure and potentially manipulate, rather than characteristics of the person. Further, this principle may help us understand another important contributor to effective therapy, the therapeutic relationship.

Integrating Learning Principles within the Therapeutic Context

In the preceding sections we have highlighted several changes in contemporary learning theory and suggested that there is still much of value there for behavior therapists.

This constitutes what we see as the "promise" for behavior therapy referenced in our title. But is an updated learning theory all that is needed? Our tentative answer is "No."

One of the greatest challenges we see comes from meta-analytic studies indicating the effectiveness of therapy *in general,* with little evidence for the superiority of any particular type of therapy (e.g., Anderson & Lambert, 1995; Landman & Dawes, 1982; Smith & Glass, 1977). Although our stance is not quite as strong as this, we do feel that the evidence is substantial enough that it would be remiss to continue to neglect the study of these factors in behavior therapy. For example, Barker, Funk, and Houston (1988) conducted a meta-analysis comparing cognitive-behavioral treatments to a variety of "nonspecific factors" control groups as well as to untreated controls. Compared to no treatment, the average effect sizes for the nonspecific and cognitive-behavioral treatments were .55 and 1.06 respectively. Thus, the difference in effect size between no treatment and nonspecific treatments is as large as that between nonspecific treatments and formal cognitive-behavioral interventions. We view such nonspecific treatment effects as substantial and worthy of systematic investigation—a view that has not been widely shared among behavior therapists.

An alternative view of the general effectiveness of widely varied treatments is that, rather than *nonspecific* variables, they reflect the operation of a class of *common factors* that are present to some extent in most forms of therapy. In this section, the common factor we choose to highlight is the therapeutic relationship, which is obviously a major component of any therapeutic intervention. More importantly, the quality of the relationship between client and therapist has been empirically demonstrated to be positively related to treatment outcome (see Garfield, 1995, and Wright & Davis, 1994, for fuller discussions of this issue). Simply obtaining empirical evidence for "common clinical wisdom" is a good start but not a sufficiently detailed map for developing optimal treatments. What remains is to integrate such findings with our knowledge of specific techniques within a unified theoretical framework.

An additional reason to highlight the therapeutic relationship is that many client problems are interpersonal in nature. Thus, we see the therapeutic relationship as presenting a unique opportunity in which to assess interpersonal difficulties and to intervene therapeutically. The therapeutic relationship may be, for many clients, an integral part of the necessary learning experience.

Behavior Therapy and the Therapist–Client Relationship

Historically, little attention was paid to the therapist–client relationship in the behavior-therapy literature. With the initial emphasis placed on the development of a technology of behavior change, research focused on isolating objective procedures to promote adaptive behavior. The role of the therapist during this early stage of behavior therapy was to design, implement, and evaluate the specific behavioral techniques that were thought to constitute the actual treatment. The founders of the behavior-therapy movement promoted the belief that the therapeutic relationship was generally not a necessary condition for behavior change (e.g., Eysenck, 1959; Wolpe & Lazarus, 1966). At most, the therapeutic relationship was viewed as providing a positive emotional experience, which would serve to inhibit anxiety and promote counterconditioning (Wolpe & Lazarus, 1966). To prove the effectiveness of the newly developed behavioral techniques, many studies were designed to illustrate the relative *unimportance* of the therapeutic relationship to behavior change (e.g., Lang, Melamed, & Hart, 1970). These views were perhaps necessary at the time to differentiate behavior therapy from more psychodynamic and humanistic therapies, which used such amorphous constructs as "warmth, empathy, and genuineness" to help the client achieve "self-actualization."

Although equating behavior therapy with learning-principle-*derived* techniques helped the field gain initial scientific respectability, it led to an emphasis on a relatively narrow range of targets for behavior change. For example, behavior therapists are quite effective at treating specific phobias, but simple specific phobics almost never come in for treatment. Real clients typically have multiple problems, many of which are interpersonal in nature. Another undesirable consequence of equating therapy with technique was the promulgation of sterile interventions that often did not generalize well to the natural environment. For example, elaborate token-economy systems required such precise control over an individual's environment that it was unrealistic to expect behavior changes maintained by such intricate engineering to transfer to alternate environments, or to be socially and ethically acceptable (cf. Leduc, Dumais, & Evans, 1990).

An advance in the conceptualization of the client–therapist relationship in behavior therapy came with the increasing influence of social learning theorists, such as Goldstein, Feldman, and Wilson. The role of the therapist was expanded by recognizing several sources of social influence that the therapist could use to effect change. Thus, the therapist could serve as a model or reinforcer of new behavior patterns. Goldstein (1975) suggested that relationship-enhancement techniques and principles of social influence could be used to strengthen the discriminative and reinforcing value of the therapist. A well-liked therapist, for example, should be more effective as a reinforcer and in persuading the client to try new behaviors. Feldman (1976) is notable for his application and integration of the social psychological theories of attitude formation and attitude change to understanding the therapeutic relationship. Wilson and Evans (1977) furthered the social influence position by providing an integration of several functions of the therapist as implementer of technique, social reinforcer, role model, and source of positive expectancies for change. Although this conceptualization represented an advance in the way behavior therapists thought about the therapeutic relationship, one of its limitations was that it still did not recognize the potential of the relationship to be a vehicle for behavior change per se. Furthermore, there has since been little systematic theoretical or empirical development of the social-influence positions.

More recently, the centrality of the therapeutic relationship as the context for learning has gained greater acceptance in the field of behavior therapy. Hayes (1987), Kanfer and Schefft (1988), Kohlenberg and Tsai (1991), and Linehan (1993) are examples of behavior therapists who have described the therapeutic relationship as providing an important context in which to intervene clinically. Similar develoments can be observed in Europe (cf. Schulte, 1996), and Emmelkamp (1986) even stated that "it is becoming increasingly clear that the quality of the therapeutic relationship may be influential in determining success or failure of behavioral therapies" (p. 432).

Relationships as Learning Experiences and Contexts

Our position is, essentially, that while the therapeutic relationship is necessary to enhance the effectiveness of specific techniques, it may also be a vehicle for change in and of itself. Thus, the relationship serves as the functional context for understanding and intervening in the client's problem areas. Similar to the models reviewed, we hypothesize that initially therapist warmth and empathy will reinforce the client's willingness to continue in therapy, a prerequisite for any successful outcome. Additionally, in the assessment phase, the development of a working alliance permits the evaluation of interpersonal attributes (skills and deficits) that may be relevant to the client's difficulties. As the relationship develops and therapy moves into a more active treatment phase, a good client–therapist relationship allows the therapist to become more effective as a reinforcing and directive stimulus, which would allow the therapist to be considerably more influential in encouraging the client to try out new forms of thought and action.

Somewhat paradoxically, however, an intense nonexploitive relationship with the therapist can be expected to also elicit the client's problematic behavior, because of the strong relationship cues. By responding in predetermined and atypical ways to the client's social and communicative behaviors, the therapist uses the relationship as a means to generate alternative behaviors, since the therapist will react to problematic behavior differently than other significant people in the client's life; these notions are similar to the interpersonal perspectives of Teyber (1992), Benjamin (1993), and Wachtel (1987). Intervening within the context of the therapeutic relationship is not qualitatively different from the choice of another form of intervention (role playing, imaginal rehearsal, etc.): the same theoretical framework can and should be used to conceptualize both types of intervention, relational or procedural.

It is important to emphasize, however, that the therapist's reactions are not simply role-plays with the client. Rather, the therapist is actively intervening in the actual client–therapist relationship. Why rehearse an imaginary event when the client can participate in an actual social interaction? When clients have interpersonal or relationship difficulties, these difficulties are likely to have a strong emotional component. Based on the principle of encoding specificity discussed previously, the more functionally similar two environments are, the more likely is newly acquired behavior to transfer to the new environment. In order to maximize the functional similarity between new learning in therapy and the client's natural environment, one would seek to equate the levels of affect involved. We hypothesize that intervening within the therapeutic relationship would be a way to provide a more similar learning context, because of the emotional connection between the client and therapist. Thus, when the therapist is able to use the therapeutic relationship as the vehicle for behavior change, rather than didactic instructions or role-plays, any behavior change would be more likely to generalize to the client's other relationships, and also be more resistant to extinction.

Finally, we certainly do not see the client–therapist relationship as the only or even a separate means of intervention. Techniques such as relaxation training, social-skills training, and exposure-based treatments will always be an important part of a behavior therapist's arsenal, but these techniques are conducted within the context of a human relationship. Moreover, the inclusion of relationship-based interventions would serve to increase the range of treatment options available to behavior therapists. Of course, as the number of treatment options increases so does the therapist's need for guidelines in choosing among them. Once again, we suggest that systematic theory building would be the most useful way to aid in the clinical decision-making process.

Implications for Training

The discussion thus far has significant implications for training behavior therapists. Until we have a clear idea of the essence of behavior therapy we cannot really specify the competencies that are needed by its future practitioners. In this section we suggest certain competence domains that arise from our analysis of the learning theory/behavior therapy relationship in its therapeutic context.

Behavioral World View

We suggest that behavior therapists maintain, or return to, a behavioral world view in which psychology is seen as the science of behavior. While the term *behaviorism* can encompass a wide range of specific positions (radical behaviorism, paradigmatic behaviorism, methodological behaviorism, etc.), there are a number of important familiar characteristics. One, of course, is a focus on behavior and its environmental determinants. We define the term *behavior* to include affect and cognition, and we view the use of properly defined intervening variables as both acceptable and useful. Furthermore, a behavioral world view would emphasize the importance of learning variables as causes of behavior, while recognizing they may not be the *only* ones.

Specific Knowledge of Current Learning Principles

We believe we have demonstrated that there are enough exciting and novel ideas within learning theory that have implications for clinical practice. Therefore, the traditional foundation of the behavior therapist's knowledge in modern learning theory needs to be sustained. This is not to say that there are not other areas of experimental psychology of importance—particularly in the development of models of psychopathology—but when it comes to designing behavior-change programs (therapy), it is the principles of learning that should take center stage.

One reason that learning theory has become limited in terms of its extension to the clinical arena is that there are many phenomena of importance to clinicians that have not been fully reduced to, or even reconciled with, principles of learning. Among the examples of such phenomena are developmental processes, social influence phenomena, and complex information processing such as reasoning, problem solving, and intelligence.

Valuing the Relationship

It seems clear from our analysis that the social context within which variables are arranged or planned to change behavior are of great importance. For some client problems the social context *is* the network of variables that will change behavior. A behavioral theory of social and intimate relationships would help behavior-therapy trainees understand the interrelationship between the design of the therapy (often a traditional technique) and the social influence context in which it is embedded by the successful therapist. There are few examples of this in the behavior-therapy literature, but the writings of Hayes (1987), Kanfer and Schefft (1988), and Kohlenberg and Tsai (1991) provide useful starting points.

Hierarchical Theory Construction

For many clinical areas, knowledge of such processes as developmental processes and complex information processing are also important. As systematic translation (deriving more complex phenomena from more simple elements, such as associations) is so intellectually demanding, the continuous derivation of complex phenomena from simple elements is, at times, simply not worth the effort. In this case, we believe it is necessary to "change set" and bring in a new group of more molar and directly applicable principles and explanations. For example, we might decide that the nature of the relationship a young child has with its primary caregiver has importance for his or her adjustment to social relationships as an adult. While it might be possible to account for this influence in terms of learning and conditioning history, it may be more convenient to use a concept such as attachment to understand the connection between the two phenomena. As attachment is a construct that historically derived from the psychoanalytic literature, behavior therapists (and behaviorally oriented students) might shy away from this concept as an explanation. This is the narrowness that has characterized behavior therapy when it seemed to judge acceptable versus unacceptable constructs in terms of social criteria, such as who invented them, what philosophical tradition did they emerge from, and so on.

Staats (1983; see also Eifert & Evans, 1990) has been a champion of the idea that this intellectual apartheid has been very damaging to our field and has prevented whole domains of knowledge from reaching the behavior therapist. We agree. Sound knowledge of learning principles should make one more rather than less tolerant of accepting the potential value and importance of other empirically derived knowledge areas. Once again, the extent to which a separate knowledge base is useful will depend on the degree to which there are intermediate blueprints that will help translate abstract knowledge into tangible therapy.

Many of us have struggled with feelings among students of behavior therapy that taking basic courses in learning theory is irrelevant. We believe that this misperception comes about because the students have no framework within which to make the extensions from basic principle to ecologically valid and meaningful practice. Learning principles cannot simply be applied directly to clinical problems; stages of translation are needed.

Nobody has yet come up with a good pedagogical strategy to assist this process. In our view, two things are needed. First, we need a conceptual framework for the translation process. We believe that the theoretical writings of Staats provide one such model, and that it would be a major assistance to students if they were to read and understand his arguments concerning the need for framework theories. At the very least this would prevent the naïveté we have seen in students who claim to be behavior therapists but do not see the relevance of learning principles.

Second, we need learning theorists themselves to assist in the translation process. It would be helpful if scientists in this area were better able to explain the bigger picture of their work and assist in defining the broader implications. Often, learning researchers simply do not know that there are applied implications of their work, or they are scornful of concepts such as relevance and application. If this continues it will be detrimental, because the audience for their work will shrink to just a few other researchers working in roughly the same area as themselves. Not all learning researchers are going to be able to recognize and understand the applied implications of their work, and some will make naive suggestions that reduce their credibility (for a nice exception to this generalization, see the work of Levey & Martin, 1987; Martin & Levey, 1987). This is why it is useful to have teams of researchers, some working at the basic level and some working at the applied extension level, who can collaborate.

Conclusions

There was a time, not that long ago, when a reasonably conscientious scholar could basically know all of behavior therapy. The reason for this was that behavior therapy was a unitary endeavor, driven by a limited number of principles and applied to behavior that was seen as lawful and thus similar—whether the behavior was described as autistic, depressed, obsessive, addictive, and so on. Today, this is no longer the case. Researchers in both pathology and treatment of clinical disorders divide according to the diagnostic category within which they work. This is revealed very nicely in the way the chapters of this book are organized. Distinctions of this kind are probably inevitable as knowledge expands and what were once mere topics for illustrating a principle of change have become research themes in their own right.

One of the inevitable implications of this is that there is a great deal of duplication and concepts that are highly similar to each other are discovered or reinvented in all the different subject literatures. Every now and then a fundamental principle breaks through, such that problems related to combat neurosis, rape, natural disaster, and childhood sexual abuse, all coming together under the rubric of trauma. That is because we have models of traumatic conditioning and exposure/flooding-based interventions that are essentially identical across these disparate topics. We see great value in such conceptual links that are derived from common basic principles.

We would contrast this kind of development with what is happening in the research programs that are trying to develop specific behavioral intervention protocols for specific categories of disorder. This dust-bowl empiricism has become extremely popular and in some ways is yielding fruit, given the large amount of research and positive attention the approach is generating. However, as we have argued throughout this chapter, we feel that this trend ultimately has negative implications for behavior therapy, which has lost ground theoretically as a result. If you are to be a clinical scientist, you need to do more than switch from therapy to research. In this chapter we have tried to expand on the kind of conceptual movement between principle and practice that is necessary to be a clinical scientist.

References

Abramson, L. Y., Seligman, M. E. P., & Teasdale, J. D. (1978). Learned helplessness in humans: Critique and reformulation. *Journal of Abnormal Psychology, 87*, 49–74.

Anderson, E. M., & Lambert, M. J. (1995). Short-term dynamically oriented psychotherapy: A review and meta-anaysis. *Clinical Psychology Review, 15*, 503–514.

Andrykowski, M. A., Redd, W. H., Hatfield, A. K. (1985). Development of anticipatory nausea: A prospective analysis. *Journal of Consulting and Clinical Psychology, 53*, 447–454.

Bandura, A. (1974). Behavior theory and the models of man. *American Psychologist, 29*, 859–869.

Bandura, A. (1977). Self-efficacy: Toward a unifying theory of behavior change. *Psychological Review, 84*, 191–215.

Barker, S. L., Funk, S. C., & Houston, B. K. (1988). Psychological treatment versus nonspecific factors: A meta-analysis of conditions that engender comparable expectations for improvement. *Clinical Psychology Review, 8*, 579–594.

Beck, A. T. (1976). *Cognitive therapy and the emotional disorders*. New York: Meridian.

Benjamin, L. S. (1993). *Interpersonal diagnosis and treatment of personality disorders*. New York: Guilford.

Bernstein, I. L. (1991). Aversion conditioning in response to cancer and cancer treatment. *Clincal Psychology Review, 11*, 185–191.

Blakey, R., & Baker, R. (1980). An exposure approach to alcohol abuse. *Behaviour Research and Therapy, 18*, 319–325.

Bouton, M. E. (1988). Context and ambiguity in the extinction emotional learning: Implications for exposure therapy. *Behaviour Research and Therapy, 26*, 137–149.

Bouton, M. E. (1993). Context, time, and memory retrieval in the interference paradigms of Pavlovian learning. *Psychological Bulletin, 114*, 80–99.

Bouton, M. E. (1994). Conditioning, remembering, and forgetting. *Journal of Experimental Psychology: Animal Behavior Processes, 20*, 219–231.

Bouton, M. E., & Bolles, R. C. (1979). Contextual control of the extinction of conditioned fear. *Learning and Motivation, 10*, 445–466.

Bouton, M. E., Kenney, F. A., & Rosengard, C. (1990). State dependent fear extinction with two benzodiazepine tranquilizers. *Behavioral Neuroscience, 104*, 44–55.

Bouton, M. E., & Swartzentruber, D. (1991). Sources of relapse after extinction in Pavlovian and instrumental learning. *Clinical Psychology Review, 11*, 123–140.

Breger, L., & McGaugh, J. L. (1965). Critique and reformulation of "learning theory" approaches to psychotherapy and neurosis. *Psychological Bulletin, 63*, 338–358.

Brewer, W. F. (1974). There is no convincing evidence for operant or classical conditioning in adult humans. In W. B. Weimer & D. S. Palermo (Eds.), *Cognition and the symbolic processes* (pp. 1–42). Hillsdale, NJ: Erlbaum.

Brodberg, D. J., & Bernstein, I. L. (1987). Candy as a scapegoat in the prevention of food aversions in children receiving chemotherapy. *Cancer, 60*, 2344–2347.

Carrigan, M. H., & Cahill, S. P. (1995). The relevance of the anxiety literature to research on EMDR. *Journal of Behavior Therapy and Experimental Psychiatry, 26*, 365–366.

Chance, P. (1979). *Learning and behavior*. Belmont, CA: Wadsworth.

Cook, M., & Mineka, S. (1987). Second-order conditioning and overshadowing in the observational conditioning of fear in monkeys. *Behaviour Research and Therapy, 25*, 349–364.

Dafters, R., Hetherington, M., & McCartney, H. (1983). Blocking and sensory preconditioning effects in morphine analgesic tolerance: Support for a Pavlovian conditioning model of drug tolerance. *Quarterly Journal of Experimental Psychology, 35B*, 1–11.

Davey, G. C. L. (1989). UCS revaluation and conditioning models of acquired fears. *Behaviour Research and Therapy, 27*, 521–528.

Davey, G. C. L. (1992). Classical conditioning and the acquisition of human fears and phobias: A review and synthesis of the literature. *Advances in Behaviour Research and Therapy, 14*, 29–66.

Davey, G. C. L., DeJong, P. J., & Tallis, F. (1993). UCS inflation in the aetiology of a variety of anxiety disorders: Some case histories. *Behaviour Research and Therapy, 31*, 495–468.

Dickinson, A. (1987). Animal conditioning and learning theory. In H. J. Eysenck & I. Marin (Eds.), *The-*

oretical foundations of behavior therapy (pp. 57–79). New York: Plenum.

Eifert, G. H. (1990). The acquisition and cognitive-behavioral therapy of phobic anxiety. In G. H. Eifert & I. M. Evans (Eds.), *Unifying behavior therapy: Contributions of paradigmatic behaviorism* (pp. 173–200). New York: Springer.

Eifert, G. H., & Evans, I. M. (Eds.). (1990). *Unifying behavior therapy: Contributions of paradigmatic behaviorism*. New York: Springer.

Eifert, G. H., Evans, I. M., & McKendrick, V. (1990). Matching treatments to client problems not diagnostic labels: A case for paradigmatic behavior therapy. *Journal of Behavior Therapy and Experimental Psychiatry, 21,* 163–172.

Eifert, G. H., Forsyth, J. P., & Schauss, S. L. (1993). Unifying the field: Developing an integrative paradigm in behavior therapy. *Journal of Behavior Therapy and Experimental Psychiatry, 24,* 107–118.

Emmelkamp, P. M. G. (1986). Behavior therapy with adults. In S. L. Garfield & A. E. Bergin (Eds.), *Handbook of psychotherapy and behavior change* (pp. 385–442). New York: Wiley.

Evans, I. M. (1973a). The logical requirements for explanations of systematic desensitization. *Behavior Therapy, 4,* 506–514.

Evans, I. M. (1973b). An unusual phenomenon in classical eyelid conditioning: The double conditioned response. *South African Journal of Psychology, 3,* 83–89.

Evans, I. M. (1976). Classical conditioning. In N. Feldman & A. Broadhurst (Eds.), *Theoretical and experimental bases of the behaviour therapies* (pp. 73–112). New York: Wiley.

Evans, I. M. (1993). A constructional perspective on target behavior selection: Can state of the art behavioral assessment survive empiricism? In A. M. Nezu (Chair), *State of the art conceptual models of target behavior selection in behavior therapy.* Symposium conducted at the Annual Meeting of the Association for Advancement of Behavior Therapy, Atlanta, GA.

Evans, I. M. (1996). Individualizing therapy, customizing clinical science. *Journal of Behavior Therapy and Experimental Psychiatry, 27,* 99–105.

Eysenck, H. J. (1959). Learning theory and behaviour therapy. *Journal of Mental Science, 105,* 61–75.

Eysenck, H. J. (1960). *Behaviour therapy and the neuroses.* Oxford: Pergamon.

Eysenck, M. W. (1993). *Anxiety: The cognitive perspective.* Hillsdale, NJ: Erlbaum.

Feldman, M. P. (1976). Social psychology and the behaviour therapies. In M. P. Feldman & A. Broadhurst (Eds.), *Theoretical and experimental bases of the behaviour therapies* (pp. 227–268). New York: Wiley.

Foa, E. B., & Kozak, M. J. (1986). Emotional processing of fear: Exposure to corrective information. *Psychological Bulletin, 99,* 20–31.

Garfield, S. L. (1995). *Psychotherapy: An electic-integrative approach* (2nd ed.). New York: Wiley.

Goldstein, A. P. (1975). Relationship enhancement methods. In F. H. Kanfer & A. P. Goldstein (Eds.), *Helping people change: A textbook of methods.* New York: Wiley.

Government of Canada. (1973). *Final report of the commission of inquiry into the nonmedical use of drugs.* Ottawa: Information Canada.

Hayes, S. C. (1987). A contextual approach to therapeutic change. In N. Jacobson (Ed.), *Psychotherapists in clinical practice: Cognitive and behavioral perspectives* (pp. 327–387). New York: Guilford.

Holland, P. C. (1977). Conditioned stimulus as a determinant of the form of the Pavlovian conditioned response. *Journal of Experimental Psychology: Animal Behavior Processes, 3,* 77–104.

Holland, P. C. (1990). Forms of memory in Pavlovian conditioning. In J. L. McGaugh, N. M. Weinberger, & G. Lynch (Eds.), *Brain organization and memory: Cells, systems, and circuits* (pp. 78–105). New York: Oxford Press.

Jacobs, W. J., & Nadel, L. (1985). Stress-induced recovery of fears and phobias. *Psychological Review, 92,* 512–531.

Kamin, L. J. (1968). "Attention-like" processes in classical conditioning. In M. R. Jones (Ed.), *Miami Symposium on the prediction of of behavior: Aversive stimulation* (pp. 9–33). Miami: University of Miami Press.

Kamin, L. J. (1969). Predictability, surprise, attention, and conditioning. In B. A. Campbell & R. M. Church (Eds.), *Punishment and aversive behavior* (pp. 279–296). New York: Appleton-Century-Crofts.

Kanfer, F. H., & Schefft, B. K. (1988). *Guiding the process of therapeutic change.* Champaign, IL: Research Press.

Kohlenberg, R. J., & Tsai, M. (1991). *Functional analytic psychotherapy: Creating intense and curative therapeutic relationships.* New York: Plenum.

Landman, J. T., & Dawes, R. M. (1982). Psychotherapy outcome: Smith and Glass' conclusions stand up under scrutiny. *American Psychologist, 37,* 504–516.

Lang, P. J., Melamed, B. G., & Hart, J. (1970). A psychophysiological analysis of fear modification using an automated desensitization procedure. *Journal of Abnormal Psychology, 76,* 220–234.

Leduc, A., Dumais, A., & Evans, I. M. (1990). Social behaviorism, rehabilitation, and ethics: Applications for people with severe disabilities. In G. H. Eifert & I. M. Evans (Eds.), *Unifying behavior therapy: Contributions of paradigmatic behaviorism* (pp. 268–289). New York: Springer.

Levey, A. B., & Martin, I. (1987). Evaluative conditioning: A case for hedonic transfer. In H. J. Eysenck & I. Marin (Eds.), *Theoretical foundations of behavior therapy* (pp. 113–131). New York: Plenum.

Levis, D. J. (1989). The case for a return to a two-factor theory of avoidance: The failure of non-fear interpretations. In S. B. Klein & R. R. Mowrer (Eds.), *Contemporary learning theories: Pavlovian conditioning and the status of traditional learning theory* (pp. 227–277). Hillsdale, NJ: Erlbaum.

Levis, D. J. (1991). A clinician's plea for a return to the development of nonhuman models of psychopathology: New clinical observations in need of laboratory study. In M. R. Denny (Ed.), *Fear, avoidance, and phobias: A fundamental analysis* (pp. 395–427). Hillsdale, NJ: Erlbaum.

Lindsley, O. R. (1956). Operant conditioning methods applied to research in chronic schizophrenia. *Psychiatric Research Reports, 5,* 118–139.

Linehan, M. M. (1993). *Cognitive-behavioral therapy for Borderline Personality Disorder.* New York: Guilford.

London, P. (1972). The end of ideology in behavior modification. *American Psychologist, 27,* 913–920.

Lubow, R. E. (1965). Latent inhibition: Effects of frequency of nonreinforced preexposure of the CS. *Journal of Comparative and Physiological Psychology, 60,* 454–459.

Mackintosh, N. J. (1975). A theory of attention: Variations in the associability of stimuli with reinforcement. *Psychological Review, 82,* 276–298.

MacLeod, C. (1993). Cognition in clinical psychology: Measures, methods or models? *Behavior Change, 10,* 169–195.

Martin, I., & Levey, A. B. (1987). Knowledge, action, and control. In H. J. Eysenck & I. Marin (Eds.), *Theoretical foundations of behavior therapy* (pp. 133–151). New York: Plenum.

Meyer, L. H., & Evans, I. M. (1993). Science and practice in behavioral intervention: Meaningful outcomes, research validity, and usable knowledge. *Journal of the Association for Persons with Severe Handicaps, 18,* 224–234.

Mineka, S. (1987). A primate model of phobic fears. In H. J. Eysenck & I. Marin (Eds.), *Theoretical foundations of behavior therapy* (pp. 81–111). New York: Plenum.

Mineka, S., Keir, & Price, V. (1980). Fear of snakes in wild- and lab-reared rhesus monkeys. *Animal Learning and Behavior, 8,* 653–663.

Niaura, R., Rohsenow, D. J., Binkoff, J. A., Monti, P. M., Pedraza, M., & Abrams, D. B. (1988). Relevance of cue reactivity to understanding alcohol and smoking relapse. *Journal of Abnormal Psychology, 97,* 133–152.

Okifuji, A., & Friedman, A. G. (1992). Experimentally induced taste aversions in humans: Effects of overshadowing on acquisition. *Behaviour Research and Therapy, 30,* 23–37.

Paul, G. L. (1966). *Insight vs. desensitization in psychotherapy.* Stanford, CA: Stanford University Press.

Pavlov, I. P. (1927). *Conditioned reflexes.* Oxford: Oxford University Press.

Pearce, J. M., & Hall, G. (1980). A model of Pavlovian learning: Variations in the effectiveness in conditioned but not unconditioned stimuli. *Psychological Review, 87,* 532–552.

Persons, J. B. (1991). Psychotherapy outcome studies do not accurately represent current models of psychopathology. *American Psychologist, 46,* 99–106.

Rachman, S. (1977). The conditioning theory of fear-acquisition: A critical examination. *Behaviour Research and Therapy, 15,* 375–387.

Rachman, S. (1989). The return of fear. *Clinical Psychology Review, 9,* 142–157.

Rachman, S. (1991). Neo-conditioning and the classical theory of fear acquisition. *Clinical Psychology Review, 11,* 155–173.

Rescorla, R. A. (1973). Effect of US habituation following conditioning. *Journal of Comparative and Physiological Psychology, 82,* 137–143.

Rescorla, R. A. (1988). Pavlovian conditioning: Its not what you think it is. *American Psychologist, 43,* 151–160.

Rescorla, R. A., & Wagner, A. R. (1972). A theory of Pavlovian conditioning: Variations in the effectiveness of reinforcement and nonreinforcement. In A. H. Black & W. F. Prokasy (Eds.), *Classical conditioning II: Current research and theory* (pp. 64–99). New York: Appleton-Century-Crofts.

Richardson, R., Riccio, D. C., Devine, L. (1984). ACTH-induced recovery of extinguished avoidance responding. *Physiological Psychology, 12*, 184–192.

Schulte, D. (1996). Tailor-made and standardized therapy: Complementary tasks in contemporary behavior therapy. *Journal of Behavior Therapy and Experimental Psychiatry, 27*.

Shapiro, F. (1989). Efficacy of the eye movement desensitization procedure in the treatment of traumatic memories. *Journal of Traumatic Stress, 2*, 199–223.

Siegel, S. (1975). Evidence from rats that morphine tolerance is a learned response. *Journal of Comparative and Physiological Psychology, 89*, 498–506.

Siegel, S. (1977). Morphine tolerance acquisition as an associative process. *Journal of Experimental Psychology: Animal Behavior Processes, 3*, 1–13.

Smith, M. L., & Glass, G. V. (1977). Meta-analysis of psychotherapy outcome studies. *American Psychologist, 32*, 752–760.

Spear, N. E. (1978). *The processing of memories: Forgetting and retention.* Hillsdale, NJ: Erlbaum.

Spear, N. E., & Riccio, D. C. (1994). *Memory: Phenomena and principles.* Boston: Allyn & Bacon.

Staats, A. W. (1963). (With contributions by C. K. Staats). *Complex human behavior.* New York: Holt, Rinehart, & Winston.

Staats, A. W. (1975). *Social Behaviorism.* Homewood, IL: Dorsey.

Staats, A. W. (1983). *Psychology's crisis of disunity: Philosophy and method for a unified science.* New York: Praeger.

Staats, A. W. (1995). Paradigmatic behaviorism and paradigmatic behavior therapy. In W. O'Donohue & L. Krasner (Eds.), *Theories of behavior therapy.* (pp. 659–693). Washington, D. C.: American Psychological Association.

Staats, A. W., & Hammond, O. R. (1972). Natural words as physiological conditioned stimuli: Food-word-elicited salivation and deprivation effects. *Journal of Experimental Psychology, 96*, 206–208.

Staats, A. W., Minke, K. A., Martin, C. H., & Higa, W. R. (1972). Deprivation-satiation and strength of attitude conditioning: A test of attitude-reinforcer-discriminative theory. *Journal of Personality and Social Psychology, 24*, 178–185.

Stampfl, T. G. (1991). Analysis of aversive events in human psychopathology: Fear and avoidance. In M. R. Denny (Ed.), *Fear, avoidance, and phobias: A fundamental analysis* (pp. 363–393). Hillsdale, NJ: Erlbaum.

Teyber, E. (1992). *Interpersonal process in psychotherapy: A guide for clinical training* (2nd ed.). Pacific Grove, CA: Brooks/Cole.

Tulving, E., & Thomson, D. M. (1973). Encoding specificity and retrieval processes in episodic memory. *Psychological Review, 80*, 352–373.

Ullmann, L. P., & Krasner, L. (1965). *Case studies in behavior modification.* New York: Holt, Rinehart, & Winston.

Wachtel, P. L. (1987). *Action and insight.* New York: Guilford.

Walter, T. A., & Riccio, D. C. (1983). Overshadowing effects in the stimulus control of morphine analgesic tolerance. *Behavioral Neuroscience, 97*, 658–662.

Weinberger, J. (1995). Common factors aren't so common: The common factors dilemma. *Clinical Psychology: Science and Practice, 2*, 45–69.

Wickler, A. (1973). Conditioning of successive adaptive response to the initial effects of drugs. *Conditioned Reflex, 8*, 193–210.

Wilson, G. T., & Evans, I. M. (1977). The therapist-client relationship in behavior therapy. In A. S. Gurman & A. M. Razin (Eds.), *Effective psychotherapy: A handbook of research* (pp. 544–565). New York: Pergamon.

Wright, J. H., & Davis, D. (1994). The therapeutic relationship in cognitive-behavioral therapy: Patient perceptions and therapist responses. *Cognitive and Behavioral Practice, 1*, 25–45.

Wolpe, J., & Lazarus, A. A. (1966). *Behavior therapy techniques.* New York: Pergamon.

15

THE ROLE OF THEORY IN BEHAVIOR THERAPY: CONCEPTUAL AND PRACTICAL CONCLUSIONS

JOSEPH J. PLAUD
Department of Psychology
Judge Rotenberg Educational Center

GEORG H. EIFERT
Department of Psychology
West Virginia University

JOSEPH WOLPE
Graduate School of Education and Psychology
Pepperdine University

The Importance of Being Theoretical, Revisited

The present volume has focused on the importance of being theoretical when conceptualizing and applying the principles of behavior therapy. In the foreword, Franks cautions that even seasoned practitioners disregard the importance of a theoretical framework for advancing the aims and the practice of behavior therapy. Franks concludes that behavior therapists pay much attention to technique-oriented manuals but devote much less time and effort to conceptual innovations that may translate into innovative clinical interventions. In addition, the lack of conditioning based theoretical grounding of behavior therapy has contributed to the infusion of cognitively based procedures into behavior therapy (Wolpe, 1989). According to Plaud and Vogeltanz (1997), the relevance of behavior theory to behavior therapy can be observed in two major ways: (1) many of the advances and current trends in behavior therapy have been and continue to be solidly connected to basic experimental research in behavior analysis; and (2) advances in behavior analysis, including new theoretical models and their applied derivatives, are increasing our understanding and modification of psychological problems.

Given the importance of behavior theory to behavior therapy, it is problematic to observe that some behavior therapists appear uninterested in the link between basic research and behavior theory to behavior therapy. This lack of attention may account, in part, for the infiltration that Wolpe argues has contributed to the present day confusion about the conceptual base of behavior therapy. If complex human behavior can be accounted for, understood, predicted, and explained by direct applications of modern learning theory, should we not question our present reliance on cognitivism as a unifying principle?

Cognitive or mentalistic constructs such as self-efficacy, bias, attitudes, beliefs, and self-esteem are used to categorize *behaviors* that fall within each categorical domain, and in some instances cognitivists have shown significant correlations between constructs and actual behavioral events (cf. Bandura, 1995). Ascribing causation or otherwise giving mentalistic constructs antecedent status in psychopathology undermines a complete understanding of the behavioral contingencies and other environmental factors that precede the design and implementation of effective interventions (Plaud & Vogeltanz, 1997). As Biglan and Hayes (1996) point out, cognitive constructs may accurately describe relations between intraorganismic variables (e.g., attitudes and depression), but such constructs do not permit an understanding of how the environment affects organismic events.

According to Eifert and Plaud (Chapter 1), mainstream behavior therapy appears to have lost its link with basic research and behavior theory. In the place of theory, behavior therapists appear to have adopted nonspecific notions about the so-called cognitive control of emotions and behavior, and now clearly identify themselves as cognitive-behavior therapists. We conclude that such pseudo-integration is the result of divisive debates and confusion about the conceptual basis of behavior therapy. These changes have also contributed to confusion regarding the creation and adherence to a cognitive-behavioral dichotomy. As Houts and Krasner (Chapter 2) emphasize, however, the field of behavior therapy did not start out that way. At its inception, behavior therapists were *united* by a shared endorsement of certain philosophical assumptions and principles dedicated to building a science of behavior that would ultimately lead to better interventions to reduce psychological suffering. So, where have we gone wrong?

Contributions of the Present Volume

The present volume of behavior theory and therapy is dedicated to the proposition that the theoretical foundations of behavior-therapy are not only alive and well, but crucial to the continued development of the most effective behavioral assessment and behavior-therapy techniques. As the chapters of this volume illustrate firsthand, these techniques are based on a continually evolving theoretical base that arises from conceptual advances and empirical research. Our book shows that advances and refinements in behavior theory have significant relevance for the practice of behavior therapy, despite arguments that downplay the role of behavior theory in the development and advancement of behavior therapy (e.g., Marks, 1981).

The Importance of Behavior Theory for the Development of Behavior Therapy

Rather than replacing behaviorism with some type of cognitivism, Eifert and Plaud (Chapter 1) argued that behavior therapists need a type of behaviorist theory that is clinically relevant by focusing on human functioning. Eifert and Plaud also advocate that behavior therapists need to re-establish the link between basic behavioral theory and research and behavioral therapy. This volume represents a contemporary survey of this link. At the same time, we must avoid a pseudo-integration of cognitive and behavioral theories that has led to problems in the appropriate integration of many advances attained in basis behavior analysis.

The central goal of this volume is to delineate the relation between behavioral principles and their application in the practice of behavior therapy. In line with the model of behavioral integration offered by Hayes (1987), the Mutual Interest Model, behavioral theoreticians, experimental psychologists, and behavior therapists can productively work together with the main goal of integrating experimental and clinical phenomena in areas of mutual interest. The chapters of this book provide evidence that behavior therapy does indeed rely to a significant extent on contemporary behavior theory, not only to achieve scientific status but also in the continued development of the major assessment and treatment regimens associated with contemporary behavior therapy.

Behavior Pathology and Behavior Therapy

The infusion of cognitive theories and therapies has had a profound influence on behavior therapy in the past few decades. By focusing on thinking and language, and their presumed relation, in a manner that is potentially useful for clinicians, one could argue that cognitive theory has identified an important problem and deficit of early behavior theory. Although early behavior therapists *used* language and imagery (e.g., in systematic desensitization; Wolpe, 1958), one could argue that behavior therapy did not pay sufficient attention to behavioral accounts of private events that already existed in the 1950s and 1960s (e.g., Skinner, 1957; Staats, 1963). Moreover, basic behavioral accounts of private events were not systematically extended to account for abnormal behavior and its treatment (Evans, Eifert, & Corrigan, 1990). We question the argument, however, raised by proponents of cognitive approaches (e.g., Bandura, 1995) that current behavior theory is unable to account for the role of language and emotional behavior. Introducing cognitive theory to account for language and emotional behavior was one solution; developing behavior theory to account for language–emotion relations is our solution. In various chapters of this volume (e.g., Chapters 3 and 4), we have therefore included a detailed presentation of paradigmatic behaviorism and contextualist radical behavioral approaches to demonstrate that not only can behavioral accounts deal with private events, but they can do so in a manner that is consistent with basic behavior theory and principles of language conditioning and verbal or rule-governed behavior. Moreover, these developments have led to new and promising interventions that are only beginning to be explored (e.g., Hayes & Wilson, 1994; Kohlenberg & Tsai, 1991).

Forsyth and Eifert (Chapter 3) provide a comprehensive behavioral model to study the nature of anxiety-related phenomena and how they can be addressed in behavior therapy. They point out that maladaptive anxiety is not some *thing* that exists awaiting our discovery, but rather anxiety is a set of behaviors that people engage in to avoid unpleasant experiences. Proceeding from an analysis of the theoretical foundations of understanding anxiety and fear, Forsyth and Eifert examine the important learning processes that account for fear acquisition by focusing on the critical role of unconditioned responses (UCR). Indeed, the core concern that brings many clients into therapy is not a fear of environmental stimuli, but a fear of unpleasant aversive bodily responses (UCR or CR). Forsyth and Eifert provide both clinical and new experimental evidence that the critical event is the occurrence of false alarms that evoke a complete UCR. These false alarms are the principle traumatic event *and* are what is being conditioned in fear acquisition. Importantly, false alarms can be associated with both environmental (external) as well as internal (bodily) events. Forsyth and Eifert also address the related question of how people learn to be anxious and afraid as a function of conditioning processes. They provide a detailed analysis of two behavioral approaches (paradigmatic behaviorism and contextualist behaviorism) that specifically and extensively deal with language and thinking (private behavior), and how they are functionally related to the behavior we refer to as anxiety. The exciting avenues of exploration and clinical implications of their theoretical journey provide ample evidence that theoretical advances and new developments in behavior theory are central to the identification and implementation of appropriate behavior therapy techniques.

Eifert, Beach, and Wilson (Chapter 4) continue the theoretical exploration and exposition in relation to mood disorders. They present an integrative, interactional, multivariate framework theory of depression that is derived from principles and concepts of paradigmatic behaviorism (Staats, 1972, 1996). The model relates inherited and acquired biological vulnerabilities with early and current learning processes that include both basic conditioning processes and higher-order learning involving language and thinking. This model is a heuristic framework that could serve as a paradigm (hence the term *paradigmatic*) to guide the actions of both researchers and clinicians in dealing with the problems of depressed individuals.

Salzinger (Chapter 5) demonstrates the importance of behavior theory for behavioral-management techniques for schizophrenia. Although schizophrenia is an area of psychopathology that has traditionally received much attention from proponents of a medical model of behavioral disorders, behavior theory has significantly aided the formulation of behavior-therapy principles in several areas. Behavior theory, for example, has led to a completely empirical approach of simply applying the techniques of conditioning to arbitrary behaviors of schizophrenic patients to determine the nature of the contingencies acting on them. This approach has also resulted in the application of behavioral interventions to change particular response classes relevant for schizophrenic behavior as well as to an investigation of which conditioning events might simulate schizophrenic behavior.

Salzinger's chapter focuses on the behavioral aspects of schizophrenia. This behavioral focus is not to imply that biological processes are unimportant in developing behavior-therapy techniques or that they are incompatible with behavior theory. In fact, as outlined by Lejuez, Schaal, and O'Donnell in Chapter 6, physiology plays an important role in the development and maintenance of substance use and abuse. The authors' main point is that substance use and abuse is subject to the same conditioning principles as is any other behavior. What makes substance use unique, however, is that environmental contingencies make up only half the story; internal stimuli (e.g., the "high" experienced after smoking marijuana) also enter into contingencies, particularly in the development of substance use. Using basic research as their guide, the authors explain that the development and maintenance of substance use and abuse result from a constant interplay between classical and operant conditioning processes. Initial substance use arises because the substance is an unconditioned reinforcer. Susequent use, and eventual abuse, occurs because it prevents or eliminates withdrawal symptoms. This is where physiology is important: the body's functioning actually changes because of the individual's overt behavior. Thus, to maintain that altered state, an individual must engage in substance use more frequently. In addition to these internal contingencies, the authors also emphasize the importance of environmental contingencies in the maintenance of substance use. Specifically, they explain that because the effects of substance use are powerful reinforcers, the reinforcing value of other activities is diminished. As a result, the individual is faced with a choice situation in which he or she chooses the more reinforcing option: substance use. After establishing the link between basic psychopharmacological research with animals and substance use with humans, the authors describe how several effective behavior therapy techniques use the findings from the laboratory to modify substance abuse. Basically, these techniques are designed to reduce the reinforcing value of drugs by making the entire drug-taking episode including ingestion aversive, and by making other, nondrug activities including abstinence more reinforcing. Throughout this section, the authors offer suggestions for preventing relapse, and conclude by urging behavior therapists to seriously consider what we know from basic research when designing and implementing substance-abuse treatments.

The rich theoretical foundations of behavior therapy approaches for sexual dysfunctions and sexual disorders are illustrated by Gaither, Rosenkranz, and Plaud (Chapter 7) and Plaud and Holm (Chapter 8). Models of sexual behavior derived from behavioral theorizing in classical (respondent) conditioning, operant conditioning, and habituation are discussed by the authors as the basis for most of the intervention strategies employed to change sexual behavior. Scotti, Mullen, and Hawkins (Chapter 9) and Albano and Morris (Chapter 10) accomplish the same analysis of the relation of theory to behavioral-intervention techniques with children. Scotti, Mullen, and Hawkins note that the practice of behavior analysis and therapy is closely associated with the treatment of excess behaviors of children and persons with developmental disabilities. Indeed, these authors point out that behavioral principles were first applied to issues involving children when behavior analysis was moving from the operant laboratory to the clinical setting, emphasizing that the behavior-analytic framework is the central theoretical focus in this area.

Albano and Morris further examine the relation of behavior theory to behavior therapy in clinical behavior therapy with children, concluding that the treatment of children and adolescents remains a fertile area for bridging the gap between theory and therapy, with behavioral models at the forefront of continuing advances in the treatment of children with anxiety and depression. It is worth noting that adult interventions have not simply been transferred to children. Instead, efforts have been made to understand the mechanisms of action exerting influence over the etiology and maintenance of these behavioral disorders such that developmentally appropriate treatments can be devised and applied. As behavior therapists, we have a strong tradition of empirical validation through rigorous experimentation of our models of behavior and intervention. Albano and Morris indicate that our task with regard to childhood anxiety and depression is to further our understanding of the risk and protective factors operating in the etiology and maintenance of these disorders. We must also increase our focus on developing and validating effective treatment protocols that are grounded in behavioral theory.

Plaud, Mosley, and Moberg (Chapter 11) highlight the central importance of operant behavior principles and the integration of biological and behavioral factors in conceptualizing and understanding dementing processes such as Alzheimer's disease. Friedman, Goldberg, and Okifuji (Chapter 12) continue to trace the development and roles of theory in behavior therapy. They argue that behavioral medicine has served as a prototype for the successful integration of research, theory, and clinical practice. Friedman, Goldberg, and Okifuji point out that historically, behavioral medicine has been closely tied to behavior theory. Learning theory served as the foundation for the development of assessment techniques and intervention strategies geared towards improving health and psychological well-being, even though the gap between behavioral science and the field of behavioral medicine has widened in recent years.

Friedman and colleagues also describe how recent changes in the health care system and medical service delivery have impacted behavior therapists working in medical settings. We share the authors' continued optimism about the future of behavior therapy in medical settings. The increased pressure to demonstrate the efficacy of psychological interventions has been advantageous to behavior therapists. After all, the results of large-scale clinical trials show that behavioral therapies continue to top the list of empirically supported treatments for a large number of psychological disorders (Chambless et al., 1996; Ollendick, 1995; Sanderson & Woody, 1995). A threat, however, is that forces from inside the medical setting and community may encourage behavior therapists to adopt an atheoretical, pragmatic approach toward treatment and focus exclusively on physiological indices as the outcome of importance. As a consequence, the increased focus on advances in treatment techniques has not been accompanied by advances in behavioral models for understanding the relation between physical and behavioral health. Many of these concerns, however, are not specific to medical settings or behavioral medicine but apply to the field in general.

The importance of theoretical issues in behavior therapy continues to be discussed in the analysis of women's health issues in Chapter 13 by Vogeltanz, Sigmon, and Vickers. During the past several years, the study of women's health has emerged as an integrative, multidisciplinary field that blends biological, behavioral, and social-cultural perspectives on health issues and problems of women. Cahill, Carrigan, and Evans (Chapter 14) reinforce the main theme of this volume by pointing out that this book is a tribute to the depth and endurance of the ties between the basic science of psychology and behavior therapy. One of their most enduring points in this final examination of theoretical factors in behavior therapy is the conclusion that behavior therapists need a theoretical framework broad enough to encompass the diversity of clinical phenomena that present themselves in the clinic, but also specific enough to guide clinical decision-making processes. The present volume has attempted to provide an in-depth analysis of that very framework and to make a contribution to closing the gap between basic theory and practice.

Current Threats to Theory–Practice Relation

Throughout this volume, and contrary to popular belief, we have pointed out how the infusion of cognitive theories and procedures into behavior therapy has weakened the field by misrepresenting or ignoring the relevance of behavior theory for behavior therapy. In this section, our goal is to discuss two additional current trends that *could* pose a threat to advancing the relation between behavioral theory and the practice of behavior therapy. Both of these trends are related to a focus on disorder-based models and treatments and the challenge that comes from the increasing development and use of standardized treatment protocols for disorders recognized by the DSM-IV. Finally, we address the problem of how we can bridge the ever-widening gap between behavior theory and practice.

Manualized Behavior Therapy

Cost-cutting pressures and health care policy changes demand that psychological services follow guidelines for relatively brief treatments that have an empirical basis for outcome (Barlow, 1996). Behavior therapy has always been committed to empirical scrutiny, time-efficient treatment strategies, and a focus on concrete and quantifiable behavior change (Eysenck, 1987). Thus, our field is well-equipped to meet these new challenges. The development of manual-based behavioral treatments seems to be a natural extension of this commitment. Treatment manuals specify empirically tested techniques for a variety of psychological problems, provide concise guidelines for delivering operationalized techniques, and encourage assessment of treatment effects in clinical practice. Manualized therapy protocols also offer structured devices for training purposes and are conducive to research investigations and third-party evaluation (Barlow, 1996; Chambless, 1996; Wilson, 1997). As a result, treatment manuals have been described as an important breakthrough in the development, evaluation, and dissemination of empirically validated therapies (Wilson, 1996).

Yet the use of manuals seems contradictory to the original model of behavior therapy according to which (a) practice involves the application of validated principles of behavior rather than the application of fixed strategies, and (b) successful behavioral interventions must be based on an idiographic functional-problem analysis and tailored to each individual patient (Kanfer & Saslow, 1969; Schulte, 1992; Wolpe, 1977, 1989).

Although empirical data favoring the use of manualized treatments are encouraging (Barlow, 1996), there remains some concern about the uncritical and rigid use of standardized treatment manuals in the absence of individual case formulations guided by conceptual models and behavior theory. Manual-based treatment has been accused of emphasizing technique at the expense of individualized problem analysis and treatment. A review of studies addressing the issue (Eifert et al., 1997), however, revealed that tailoring treatment to target an individual's particular problem beyond the level of clinical diagnosis does not seem to improve overall treatment outcome for certain well-circumscribed problems such as phobic anxiety, panic disorder, obsessive-compulsive disorder, and depression. Some multiple-behavior and other problems not adequately covered by DSM diagnoses, however, will continue to require individualized functional analysis and treatment.

Individualizing treatment and manual use, however, are not necessarily incompatible. Eifert et al. (1997) have proposed the use of manuals in a flexible and theory-driven fashion guided by empirically tested clinical decision rules. In fact, an increasing number of protocols propose implementing manuals in a flexible way (cf. Wilson, 1997). Although overreliance on manualized treatments *may* impede the adaptive use of alternative therapeutic procedures for unresponsive patients, nobody supporting the use of manuals advocates such rigidity. There appears to be agreement that manuals must be flexible enough to allow the therapist to deviate from the protocol when events arise that interfere with the implementation of manualized behavior therapy (Chambless, 1996; Garfield, 1996). Other studies report that structured protocols clearly keep therapists on track and focused on behavior change (e.g., Hickling & Blanchard, 1997).

Finally, results of manualized outcome studies have contributed to challenging the "dodo-bird verdict," which suggests that all psychological interventions are equally effective, substantiating the efficacy of behavior therapy to health care providers, HMOs, and the public at large (Barlow, 1994; Giles, 1993). In view of increasing managed care and policy pressures to promote pharmacological treatments, these results are important to prevent the elimination of behavioral interventions from our health care delivery and reimbursement system. As Barlow (1996, p. 237) put it, "it is time to let the public know of our success."

The challenge of modifying empirically established manualized behavioral treatments for use with individual patients will be a top priority in our field (Wilson, 1997). We should meet this challenge with careful empirical examination as well as by drawing on the principles of psychology in general, and behavior theory in particular. After all, unlike most other forms of psychotherapy that have developed in relative separation from empirical psychology, part of the remarkable success and proliferation of behavior therapy is due to its unique and close relation to the science of behavior.

Disorder-Specific Models and Behavior Therapy

Although the DSM-IV classificatory system is a useful heuristic for describing and distinguishing behavioral problems at a phenomenological level, many behavior therapists and clinical behavior analysts are concerned about the current nosological diagnostic system (Hayes, Wilson, Gifford, Follete, & Strosahl, 1996). Foremost, this system classifies disorders and anxiety subtypes based on symptoms defined topographically and structurally rather than functionally. In other words, the system tells us little about what behavioral processes account for the development and maintenance of behavioral problems. Indeed, references to causes of disorders are deliberately omitted from DSM-IV. The problem that ensues for the design of behavioral interventions has been described in vivid terms by Wolpe (1989, p. 7): "While response similarity in maladaptive habits provides a convenient basis for placing [persons] in diagnostic pigeonholes (e.g., anorexia, claustrophobia, or stuttering), common pigeonholes do not necessarily imply common treatment, because the stimulus antecedents vary."

One solution for this problem is to design individualized interventions for each patient based on an idiographic analysis of the patient's problem. This approach, however, is time-consuming, and may be unnecessary for a number of common problems that are topographically as well as functionally similar (cf. Eifert et al., 1997). An alternative approach to treatment design is to use disorder-specific behavioral models that employ knowledge from basic theory and psychopathology studies. In contrast to universally valid psychological theories (e.g., learning theory), the validity of a particular model is limited to patients with that particular diagnosis (Schulte, 1996). These disorder-specific models include statements about which dysfunctional behaviors are typical for a disorder, which factors tend to maintain these behaviors, which variables treatment should target, and which methods are available and likely to obtain the best results (cf. Barlow, 1988; Eifert, 1992; Heiby & Staats, 1990; see also Chapter 4, this volume).

In the future, we are likely to see more disorder-specific behavioral models and treatment manuals. As a result, the process of developing hypotheses for a single case will become more structured and less susceptible to a therapist's personal preferences, thereby improving the validity, utility, objectivity, and reliability of problem analysis. This more standardized way of making treatment decisions is one of the most important contributions of clinical research to clinical practice (Schulte, 1992). Indeed, the therapist can apply effective treatment methods according to prescribed method rules that are increasingly being formulated and validated by empirical research (Hickling & Blanchard, 1997; Wilson, 1997). It should be emphasized, however, that therapists still need to adapt these rules to the specific personal and environmental circumstances of their individual patient. This adaptation process, in conjunction with promoting the therapist–client relationship and client treatment motivation, may indeed constitute the art of behavior therapy (Chambless, 1996; Schulte, 1996).

Lack of Bridges Linking Theory and Practice

As indicated throughout this volume, behavior therapy's origins were closely tied to the application of laboratory-derived principles for understanding behavior. The nature of the relation between theory and therapy, or between scientific underpinnings and application, was never closely examined because there was no adequate framework for conceptualizing the relation. The application of theoretical principles, however, requires a dictionary of translation rules in order to ascertain whether the clinical procedure really resembles the circumstances and conditions under which the original principles hold (cf. Evans, 1973, 1985). In the absence of translation guidelines, moving from research to practice has often been quite literal. An example is the literal translation of operant principles into the implementation of token economies. Other literal translations in behavior therapy are some of the aversive-conditioning procedures used to change excessive drinking or sexual preferences. It is interesting to note, but hardly surprising, that many of the techniques based on literal translation have been shown to be of limited effectiveness and have subsequently been abandoned (cf. Evans, Eifert, & Corrigan, 1990). Behavior-therapy researchers will need to pay more attention to the manner in which scientific knowledge is translated into something that can be used or applied by the practitioner. As learning theory has only ever provided analogies for the design of treatment (Evans, 1973), in clinical work the basic principles from theory must be translated into a secondary set of principles from which treatment may be derived. The process by which a clinician can make transformations from theory to practice most effectively is an important, complex, and poorly understood process and, therefore, a topic worthy of more detailed study (cf. Evans, 1985; Schulte, 1996).

From our experience in training clinicians within a scientist–practitioner model, we doubt whether behaviorally oriented clinicians will be that much different or end up being more avid readers of the basic research literature than practitioners trained in a different mode (Evans & Hubbard, 1988). This is because the theory rarely evolves in a mode that influences practice until there has been much greater interaction between the two. Moreover, the lack of influence of research on practice is as much the fault of practitioners who may be uninterested in theory and scientific research, as it is the fault of academic researchers who do not spend sufficient time and effort on organizing, relating, and integrating their research findings to *make* them relevant for practitioners. In order to bridge the gap between theory and practice, Kanfer (1990) makes the interesting suggestion of training some psychologists as "translators" who would devote systematic attention to research and dissemination of practical implications and methods derived from various domains of psychology. In addition, they could formulate professional problems in basic science language and collaborate with or act as scientists whose expertise encompasses the domain in which these researchable questions are phrased. Apart from narrowing the gap between theory and practice, Kanfer's recommendations could be beneficial in that their implementation would contribute to the development of translation rules and skills. As it now stands, such translation rules and skills are scant and their absence contributes to the growing gap between behavior theory and practice.

Conclusion

The many important and diverse areas of the behavioral foundations of behavior therapy techniques discussed in this volume showcase how behavioral theories, broadly defined, have contributed to the many advances in basic behavioral science, which ultimately lead to new and innovative behavior-therapy strategies. The strength of behavior therapy, however, has not come from its techniques (other schools of therapy also have some effective techniques), nor can behavior therapy be defined or distinguished from other schools of therapy primarily by its methods of practice (Evans et al., 1990).

Behavior therapy's strengths are its roots in and relation to behavior theory. Reinforcement schedules, aversive control, stimulus control, behavioral momentum, rule-governed behavior, stimulus equivalence, and paradigmatic behaviorism represent a cross section of cutting-edge analytical areas that can add significantly to clinical behavior therapy.

Research questions posed in contemporary behavior therapy seem to be derived more from other research within behavior therapy than from extensions of the basic science (Evans, 1996). By analyzing the nature of current behavior theory and pointing out areas of extension, we hope to demonstrate that there is a need for continued examination of the manner in which basic concepts can be translated into clinical practice. Both basic and applied behavioral psychology will benefit from further exploration, elaboration, and application of the principles of the experimental analysis of behavior. Even though it has been argued that behavior therapists are not knowledgeable about advances in behavior analysis, it should be clear by now that there are many good reasons for behavior therapists to be interested in and active explorers of the theoretical foundations of behavior therapy. Further, behavior therapists are in the unique position of being on the front lines of employing behavior-analytic techniques in the service of adaptive behavior change. Despite a number of ideological, professional, and political challenges, the future of the discipline looks bright for both basic and applied behavioral research as we continue on the journey from behavior theory to behavior therapy.

References

Bandura, A. (1995). Comments about the crusade against the causal efficacy of human thought. *Journal of Behavior Therapy and Experimental Psychiatry, 26*, 179–190.

Barlow, D. H. (1988). *Anxiety and its disorders*. New York: Guilford.

Barlow, D. H. (1994). Psychological interventions in the era of managed care. *Clinical Psychology: Science and Practice, 1*, 109–122.

Barlow, D. H. (1996). The effectiveness of psychotherapy: Science and policy. *Clinical Psychology: Science and Practice, 3*, 236–240.

Biglan, A., & Hayes, S. C. (1996). Should the behavioral sciences become more pragmatic? The case for functional contextualism in research on human behavior. *Applied and Preventive Psychology, 5*, 47–57.

Chambless, D. L. (1996). In defense of dissemination of empirically supported psychological interventions. *Clinical Psychology: Science and Practice, 3*, 230–235.

Chambless, D. L., Sanderson, W. C., Shoham, V., Bennett-Johnson, S., Pope, K. S., Crits-Christoph, P.,

Baker, M., Johnson, B., Woody, S. R., Sue, S., Beutler, L., Williams, D. A., McCurry, S. (1996). An update on empirically validated therapies. *The Clinical Psychologist, 49*, 5–18.

Eifert, G. H. (1992). Cardiophobia: A paradigmatic behavioral model of heart-focused anxiety and nonanginal chest pain. *Behaviour Research and Therapy, 30*, 329–345.

Eifert, G. H., Schulte, D., Zvolensky, M. J., Lejuez, C. W., & Lau, A. W. (1997). Manualizing behavior therapy: Merits and challenges. *Behavior Therapy, 28*, 499–509.

Evans, I. M. (1973). The logical requirements for explanations of systematic desensitization. *Behavior Therapy, 4*, 506–514.

Evans, I. M. (1985). Building systems models as a strategy for target behavior selection in clinical assessment. *Behavioral Assessment, 7*, 21–32.

Evans, I. M., Eifert, G. H., & Corrigan, S. A. (1990). A critical appraisal of paradigmatic behaviorism's contribution to behavior therapy. In G. H. Eifert & I. M. Evans (Eds.), *Unifying behavior therapy: Con-*

tributions of paradigmatic behaviorism* (pp. 293–317). New York: Springer.

Evans, I. M. (1996). Individualizing therapy, customizing clinical science. *Journal of Behavior Therapy and Experimental Psychiatry, 27,* 99–105.

Evans, I. M., & Hubbard, B. A. (1988). The clinical psychology training program at SUNY–Binghamton: Behavioral training and the new Boulder model. *The Behavior Therapist, 11,* 231–234.

Eysenck, H. J. (1987). Behavior therapy. In H. J. Eysenck & I. Martin (Eds.), *Theoretical foundations of behavior therapy* (pp. 3–34). New York: Plenum.

Garfield, S. L. (1996). Some problems associated with "validated" forms of psychotherapy. *Clinical Psychology: Science and Practice, 3,* 218–229.

Giles, T. R. (Ed.). (1993). *Handbook of effective psychotherapy.* New York: Plenum.

Hayes, S. C. (1987). The relation between "applied" and "basic" psychology. *Behavior Analysis, 22,* 91–100.

Hayes, S. C., & Wilson, K. G. (1994). Acceptance and commitment therapy: Altering the verbal support for experiential avoidance. *The Behavior Analyst, 17,* 289–303.

Hayes, S. C., Wilson, K. G., Gifford, E. V., Follete, V., & Strosahl, K. (1996). Experiential avoidance and behavioral disorders: A functional dimensional approach to diagnosis and treatment. *Journal of Consulting and Clinical Psychology, 64,* 1–16.

Heiby, E. M., & Staats, A. W. (1990). Depression: Classification, explanation, and treatment. In G. H. Eifert & I. M. Evans (Eds.), *Unifying behavior therapy: Contributions of paradigmatic behaviorism* (pp. 220–246). New York: Springer.

Hickling, E. J., & Blanchard, E. B. (1997). The private practice psychologist and manual-based treatments: A case study in the treatment of posttraumatic stress disorder secondary to motor vehicle accidents. *Behaviour Research and Therapy, 35,* 191–203.

Kanfer, F. H. (1990). The scientist–practitioner connection: A bridge in need of constant attention. *Professional Psychology: Research and Practice, 21,* 264–270.

Kohlenberg, B. S., & Tsai, M. (1991). *Functional analytic psychotherapy.* New York: Plenum.

Marks, I. (1981). Behavioral concepts in the treatment of neuroses. *Behavioural Psychotherapy, 9,* 137–154.

Ollendick, T. H. (1995). AABT and empirically validated treatments. *The Behavior Therapist, 18,* 81–82.

Plaud, J. J., & Vogeltanz, N. D. (1997). Back to the future: The continued relevance of behavior theory to modern behavior therapy. *Behavior Therapy, 28,* 75–86.

Sanderson, W. C., & Woody, S. (1995). *Manuals for empirically validated treatments: A project of the Task Force on Psychological Procedures.* Washington, DC: Division of Clinical Psychology, American Psychological Association.

Schulte, D. (1992). Criteria of treatment selection in behaviour therapy. *European Journal of Psychological Assessment, 3,* 157–162.

Schulte, D. (1996). Tailor-made and standardized therapy: Complementary tasks in behavior therapy. A contrarian view. *Journal of Behavior Therapy and Experimental Psychiatry, 27,* 119–126.

Skinner, B. F. (1938). *The behavior of organisms.* New York: Appleton-Century-Crofts.

Skinner, B. F. (1957). *Verbal behavior.* New York: Appleton-Century-Crofts.

Staats, A. W. (1963). *Complex human behavior.* (With contributions by C. K. Staats). New York: Holt, Rinehart, & Winston.

Staats, A. W. (1972). Language behavior therapy: A derivative of social behaviorism. *Behavior Therapy, 3,* 165–192.

Staats, A. W. (1996). *Behavior and personality.* New York: Springer.

Wilson, G. T. (1996). Manual-based treatments: The clinical application of research findings. *Behaviour Research and Therapy, 34,* 295–315.

Wilson, G. T. (1997). Treatment manuals in clinical practice. *Behaviour Research and Therapy, 35,* 205–210.

Wolpe, J. (1958). *Psychotherapy by reciprocal inhibition.* Palo Alto, CA: Stanford University Press.

Wolpe, J. (1977). Inadequate behavior analysis: The Achilles heel of outcome research in behavior therapy. *Journal of Behavior Therapy and Experimental Psychiatry, 8,* 1–3.

Wolpe, J. (1989). The derailment of behavior therapy: A tale of conceptual misdirection. *Journal of Behavior Therapy and Experimental Psychiatry, 20,* 3–15.

INDEX